1988-89
HOCKEY
Scouting Report

1988-89
HOCKEY
Scouting Report

Michael A. Berger
John Davidson
Jiggs McDonald

Summerhill Press
Toronto

© 1988 Michael A. Berger

Published by Summerhill Press Ltd.
52 Shaftesbury Avenue
Toronto, Ontario M4T 1A2

Cover photography: Bruce Bennett
Cover design: Rob McPhail

Printed and bound in the United States.

Canadian Cataloguing in Publication Data

The National Library of Canada has catalogued this annual as follows:

Berger, Michael, 1960-
  Hockey scouting report

1986/1987-
Annual.
ISBN 0-929197-56-6 (1988/1989)

1. Hockey — Scouting — Periodicals.   2. Hockey
players — Periodicals.   3. National Hockey
League — Periodicals.   I. Davidson, John, 1953-
II. McDonald, Jiggs.   III. Title.

GV847.8.N3B4   796.96'26   C88-039002-6

DEDICATION

To Stu, for putting me in the center of the action.

ACKNOWLEDGEMENTS

After three years, something in this book should come easy. Luckily, it's always easy to thank those who've been kind enough to help.

Thanks:

To Barry Watkins, public relations assistant of the New York Rangers, for once again providing the player photos used in this book. And thanks also to the rest of the Ranger P.R. staff — Art Friedman, Ginger Killian, Matt Loughran and P.R. Director John Halligan — for their constant help throughout the book's research.

To Greg Bouris and Dave Freed, Directors of Public Relations for the New York Islanders and New Jersey Devils respectively, for their aid throughout the season.

To the NHL coaches, general managers, chief scouts, scouts and players — you know who you are — who took us into their confidence and helped us compile these reports. And thanks to the NHL personnel who ask for copies — so they can see what the competition is saying.

To the NHL writers and broadcasters who use this book as a reference work.

To Steve Levy, a close friend whose simple question — "Why don't you include seasonal penalty minutes for goalies?" — led to that simple addition, an addition that prompted thoughts for further changes that will show up in future editions.

To Eric Berger, for his invaluable help in the preparation of this manuscript.

And finally to my publishers, Jim Williamson and Gordon Montador at Summerhill Press, for their continued belief in this project.

Ladies and gentlemen, take a bow. And put the first one on my tab.

Mike Berger NYC July 1988

Contents

The Authors

Michael A. Berger

The editor of GOAL Magazine, the NHL's official program, Mike has frequently written about hockey in international publications like Sport Magazine and The Hockey News. Mike, a member of the Professional Hockey Writers Association, is single and lives in Brooklyn.

John Davidson

The NHL's best color commentator is entering his third season as the analyst for the New York Rangers on Madison Square Garden Network. He also appears frequently on Canada's Global Television Network. John and his family live in Armonk, N.Y., during the season and spend their summers visiting family in western Canada.

Jiggs McDonald

A founder of the NHL Broadcaster's Association, Jiggs has been broadcasting hockey since 1967. He has been the play-by-play voice of the New York Islanders since 1980, and was introduced to national audiences in February 1988 as part of the ABC Network's Calgary Olympic Games announcing crew. He makes his home year-round in Dix Hills, N.Y., with his wife and two daughters.

Introduction

This is a heavy book. And that's no surprise, because there are a lot of people in it.

We're not just talking about the 400-plus NHL players about whom you'll read. We're talking about the people who talked to us about those 400-plus NHLers: NHL general managers, coaches, scouts and players.

And of course, we're talking about the 1988-89 Hockey Scouting Report, the only book that looks at National Hockey League players the way professionals themselves do:

Through consideration of a player's talents and abilities. Between these covers you get scouting reports presented in the same way hockey coaches, general managers, players and scouts all over the world present their views to their colleagues.

And you don't get a lot of extraneous stuff. No pie charts or bar graphs or theories or formulas. Ever see a pie chart backcheck? If you have, you know why there aren't any pie charts in the NHL.

You get all this with no-holds-barred — that's why our top-level sources have to stay anonymous. If a player backchecks like that pie chart, you'll read it here. The truth, the whole truth and nothing but the truth.

And we can swear to that because of the thousands of hours we've spent researching during hundreds of games. We can swear to that because of the input we've gotten from NHL executives who share their expertise with us, and then read Hockey Scouting Report to see what the *other* big-wigs are saying.

And we can swear to that because we analyze players the way the pros do.

Each player's game is broken down into three parts, categories which consolidate the factors used by the pros to evaluate talent at all hockey levels. We discuss a player's skating, stickhandling, scoring, passing, play-making, checking and defensive abilities in The Finesse Game. How he uses his body, whether he takes advantage of his size and strength, his balance, his ability — and willingness — to play physically and to fight in The Physical Game. How he relates to his teammates, whether he's frequently injured, if he works hard to improve his game and if he's dedicated to his profession in The Intangibles.

And we've of course retained the scoring graphic that accompanies every player and indicates his best scoring area (or weakness, for goaltenders).

We'll even tell you the things we got wrong last year — but first you have to read about the things we got right.

Because we've expanded our coverage of players we've eliminated our Team Scouting Report graphics, but kept the Team Scouting Report itself. In those reports you'll read about line combinations and specialty team strategy.

Sometimes blank spaces have been left in either the Line Combination or Defense Pairing section of the team reports. Two examples would be different left wings rotating onto different lines, or a defenseman whose partner has retired. On certain teams, where change is more constant than stability, the headings *Line Combinations* and *Defense Pairings* might give way to the simpler *Forwards* and *Defensemen*.

In at least one case we've deliberately included a now-retired player in a power play explanation. Why? To show you how the play worked last year and to tell you that it'll have to change this year.

As the season progresses, some of this team information will no doubt be rendered inaccurate because of trades or injuries. We debated including the strategies for just those reasons, but we decided that some information — even if ocassionally inaccurate — made people think and was better than no information at all.

In short, we're once again bringing the game to you. You'll decide if what we have to say is valuable or worthwhile, and you couldn't do that if we didn't give you the goods in the first place.

We hope you enjoy the fruits of our labors.

We Told You So

This is our chance to be self-congratulatory — and self-defeating. We don't undertake this book to make predictions, but we get a lot of satisfaction in knowing we gave you solid information. And we know we made mistakes, but we admit those freely. We think that recognizing our errors adds to our credibility.

Among other things, readers of this book last year learned months ahead of time:

That Ron Hextall would score goals in the NHL. That Paul Coffey's relationship with Glen Sather was in bad shape. That Jan Erixon was a great defensive forward (he was a Selke Trophy finalist). That Phil Housley would no longer be switched between center and defense, and would remain a defenseman. That Risto Siltanen's NHL career was over. That Dave Semenko was on his way out of Hartford. That Bernie Federko, 83 points away and coming off a 72-point season, would score his 1,000th point as a Blue.

That Murray Bannerman was history in Chicago. Ditto Craig Billington in New Jersey, Pat Riggin in Pittsburgh, Paul MacLean in Winnipeg, Steve Dykstra in Buffalo, Geoff Courtnall in Boston, Doug Wickenheiser in St. Louis and Ed Hospodar in Philadelphia.

That Michel Petit had a lot of offensive skill (he had a career year in 1987-88). That Rick Tocchet could play hockey and not just fight (he had a career year in 1987-88). That Craig Simpson could score more than 35 goals by driving to the net. That Bob Probert would score 30 goals (all right, sue us for one goal), and we questioned whether he could indeed bring his drinking under control.

That Gary Suter would return to his Rookie of the Year form. That Perry Berezan's health was questionable. Ditto Paul Reinhart. That Stephane Richer could be a superior offensive player and that his third year would tell the tale. That the Canadiens don't play as well without Chris Nilan in the lineup (think they could have used him against Boston?)

That the Penguins would break in Steve Guenette and Gilles Meloche's role would become questionable. That Brad McCrimmon was a valuable member of the Flyers. That Randy Cunneyworth (career year in 87-88) would develop as a player. That playing in Quebec would pose problems for Alan Haworth (that's why he's in Switzerland this season). That Gary Leeman would improve (career year in 87-88). That Reggie Lemelin was a money goalie and could get hot for long stretches.

That an attitude adjustment would mean a career year for Mike Bullard. That it was time for Kjell Dahlin to put up or shut up (he shut up). That Steve Tambellini was a marginal NHL player (he was released by Vancouver). That Mark Reeds was eminently replaceable in St. Louis.

Of course we also said:

That Pat Verbeek's 36-goal season of 1986-87 was a mistake (and that's why he scored 46 goals in 87-88). That Tom Fergus would finish with 30 goals (we meant to say 19). That Steve Yzerman "was not a scorer, if you could call 30-40 goals not scoring," (Yeesh!). That Bill Ranford was the goalie of the future for the Brui—-um, Oilers (yeak, that's the ticket). That Lanny McDonald was still an effective offensive player and that Hakan Loob didn't have enough talent or drive to be a star (ooooh, we *hate* it when that happens). That Duane Sutter had to be one of the Islanders' nine forwards. That Claude Lemieux won't back down from anyone.

That Charlie Huddy's career appeared headed toward its end. That Steve Smith might be better off someplace other than Edmonton. That Esa Tikkanen was the long-awaited left wing for Wayne Gretzky and Jari Kurri. That Ron Francis would score 30-35 goals (not 25 — but we did say he was inconsistent from year to year and he was: 93 points in 86-87, 75 points last season).

What's ahead for this season? We're not going to tell you here. You're going to have to see the games — and read the book.

Team Reports

BOSTON BRUINS

LINE COMBINATIONS
BOB JOYCE-CRAIG JANNEY-CAM NEELY
RANDY BURRIDGE-STEVE KASPER-LYNDON
BYERS
RICK MIDDLETON-KEN LINSEMAN-KEITH
CROWDER

DEFENSE PAIRINGS
GORD KLUZAK-RAY BOURQUE
GLEN WESLEY-MICHAEL THELVEN
ALLEN PEDERSEN-

GOALTENDERS
REGGIE LEMELIN
ANDY MOOG

OTHER PLAYERS
REED LARSON — Defenseman
NEVIN MARKWART — Left wing
TOM MCCARTHY —Center
JAY MILLER — Right wing
WILLI PLETT — Right wing
BOB SWEENEY — Center

POWER PLAY

FIRST UNIT:
BOB JOYCE-CRAIG JANNEY-CAM NEELY
RAY BOURQUE-REED LARSON

JOYCE and NEELY are posted at the bottom of their respective faceoff circles while JANNEY controls behind the net. He feeds BOURQUE and LARSON, and the forwards crash the net for rebounds. Feeding the puck inside to JOYCE and NEELY is a second alternative.

CROWDER and LINSEMAN will combine on a second power play unit, and KLUZAK will join BOURQUE on the point, BOURQUE plays as much of the two minutes as possible.

Last season the Boston power play was POOR, scoring just 74 goals in 446 opportunities (17.2 percent, 19th overall).

PENALTY KILLING

FIRST UNIT:
RICK MIDDLETON-STEVE KASPER
GORD KLUZAK-RAY BOURQUE

SECOND UNIT:
RANDY BURRIDGE-BOB SWEENEY
ALLEN PEDERSEN-RAY BOURQUE

Both units play a box defense and both force the puck in the corners and less so at the points. They are calmly aggressive and not often out of position, but they'll go for the shorthanded goal when possible.

Last season Boston's penalty killing was EXCELLENT, allowing just 70 goals in 425 shorthanded situations (83.5 percent, fourth overall).

CRUCIAL FACEOFFS

Mostly KASPER, but LINSEMAN will also take his share.

RAY BOURQUE

Yrs. of NHL service: 9
Born: Montreal, Quebec, Canada; December 28, 1960
Position: Defenseman
Height: 5-11
Weight: 197
Uniform no.: 77
Shoots: left

Career statistics:

GP	G	A	TP	PIM
658	193	501	694	526

1987-88 statistics:

GP	G	A	TP	+/−	PIM	PP	SH	GW	GT	S	PCT
78	17	64	81	34	72	7	1	5	0	344	4.9

LAST SEASON

Bourque led the Bruins in scoring for the third time. He also finished first on the club in assists and shots on goal, and he finished third in League defensive scoring (second in assists). His plus/minus mark was the team's second best.

THE FINESSE GAME

What makes Ray Bourque a superior hockey player is his skating. Bourque is one of the two or three best in the League — one of the best in the world — and, because of his excellent change of pace and lateral movement just might be the League's best overall.

He has great fluidity *and* power on his skates, possessing explosive acceleration and the balance and foot speed to change direction — any direction — within one step. Bourque makes his skating an even more devastating weapon by excellently changing his pace to avoid predictability and to adapt to any situation. He is an excellent rushing defenseman, but Ray tempers that habit by showing excellent discretion in his runs up-ice.

If his skating is skill Number 1, Ray's shot is skill Number 1A. Bourque is dangerous anywhere he has the puck and he can put the puck anywhere he wants (oblique shooting angles don't mean anything to him). His shot is strong from any distance and lands in the net as if fired from a gun. He has an excellent selection of shots, from a howitzer slap shot to a laser-like wrist shot, and any of his shots can beat any goaltender in the world. He switches to the right side on the power play and loves to sneak toward the net to fire an almost unstoppable wrist shot.

Vision and anticipation are skills Number 1B. He sees everything on the ice, the offensive rush as it moves away from him and the defensive rush as it moves toward him. These skills combine with his excellent hand skills and allow him to get the puck to his teammates better than nine times out of ten.

THE PHYSICAL GAME

As if his superior finesse skills weren't enough, Bourque is also a fine physical player. He's tremendously strong in the upper body (hence the powerful shot), thick in the chest and shoulders. He combines that upper body strength with his exceptional balance to become practically invincible in confrontations in the corners.

Ray also puts his size and strength to work in clearing the front of the net, though that job more than usually falls to his defense partner so Bourque can start the play up-ice.

THE INTANGIBLES

Two-time Norris Trophy winner as the defense who "demonstrates throughout the season the greatest all-round ability in the position." That's all there is to say, because there ain't nobody who plays the total game better than Ray Bourque.

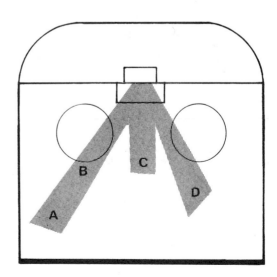

LYNDON BYERS

Yrs. of NHL service: 2
Born: Nipawin, Sask., Canada; February 29, 1964
Position: Right wing
Height: 6-1
Weight: 190
Uniform no.: 33
Shoots: right

Career statistics:

GP	G	A	TP	PIM
119	17	31	48	371

1987-88 statistics:

GP	G	A	TP	+/−	PIM	PP	SH	GW	GT	S	PCT
53	10	14	24	10	236	0	0	2	0	69	14.5

LAST SEASON

Byers was sidelined throughout the season with knee, shoulder and hand injuries, but his games played total was still a career high. Ditto all point totals and his PIM mark, which was the club's second highest.

THE FINESSE GAME

Byers is a good skater, not blessed with a lot of speed, but good in balance and strength. He can read a play fairly well and is also relatively tireless, both merits in checking and good reasons why he was assigned a checking role.

Lyndon has some talents in the passing and scoring areas. He's not a bad puck handler, though he won't make anyone forget Denis Savard, but he can find open teammates and get the puck to them. His play reading ability helps him to recognize the opportunities his checking creates, but his hands aren't good enough to fool NHL goaltending — not yet, anyway. He'll have to score from near the net on rebounds and broken plays.

THE PHYSICAL GAME

Byers plays the game physically, and that is his primary asset. He uses his size well in checking, and can put his strength to use along the boards and in the corners in order to gain control of the puck, not that he will accomplish much after he does so.

He is a willing and able fighter, regardless of the competition. In short, he is a scrapper — the typical Boston Bruin.

THE INTANGIBLES

Injury and durability remain the biggest question regarding Byers. His physical ability is very strong and we haven't seen the best of Byers finesse skills, but until he shows he should be more than a third or fourth line checker he'll have to be considered a role player. As such, he's in a vulnerable position for replacement.

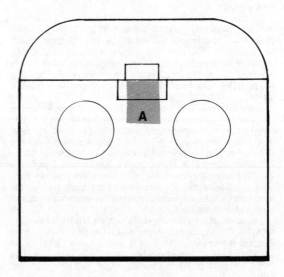

RANDY BURRIDGE

Yrs. of NHL service: 2
Born: Fort Erie, Ontario, Canada; January 7, 1966
Position: Left wing
Height: 5-9
Weight: 180
Uniform no.: 12
Shoots: left

Career statistics:

GP	G	A	TP	PIM
154	45	57	102	149

1987-88 statistics:

GP	G	A	TP	+/-	PIM	PP	SH	GW	GT	S	PCT
79	27	28	55	0	105	5	3	3	1	159	17.0

LAST SEASON

Randy finished fifth on the club in scoring with career highs in all point categories. He was third in goal scoring and fifth in shots on goal.

THE FINESSE GAME

Burridge is a good skater, equipped with agility and quickness and good balance. He has good mobility and lateral movement because of his balance and foot speed, and he can beat people to loose pucks. Randy also has good acceleration, but over the long haul his speed is not exceptional.

Randy has good hockey sense and he puts that sense to work both offensively and defensively. He can be a good checker because of his play reading abilty and anticipation, and he can close the holes because of his quickness. Those same mental capabilities allow him to hit the openings himself, and his quickness makes him dangerous when there are loose pucks around the net.

He's currently more of an opportunist in goal scoring than an artist, meaning that his shot is good enough around the net but won't fool NHL goaltending from a distance.

Burridge handles the puck fairly well when he's moving, and he keeps his head up in order to take advantage of his teammates.

THE PHYSICAL GAME

Burridge's nickname is "Stump," and it refers to his size. He's got good strength for his size, but he's not going to outmuscle many people in traffic situations. Not that he's afraid of the high population areas around the corners and the front of the net, but Randy knows that his best and most effective work is done outside the scrums.

Still, he's a willing physical player and he'll take his licks when he has to make a play.

THE INTANGIBLES

Burridge seems to have stuck with the Bruins for good this time after two previous attempts. While he had good success last season, bear in mind that his center (Steve Kasper) had a career year and that Burridge scored just 12 of his 29 goals in the season's second half — and just 10 of those came at even strength.

We said in the first edition of this book three years ago that

Burridge had great skills and desire. He proved that to a degree last season. Now let's see him do it consistently.

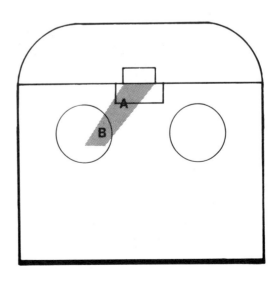

KEITH CROWDER

Yrs. of NHL service: 8
Born: Windsor, Ontario, Canada; January 6, 1959
Position: Right wing
Height: 6-0
Weight: 190
Uniform no.: 18
Shoots: right

Career statistics:

GP	G	A	TP	PIM
538	204	240	444	1,114

1987-88 statistics:

GP	G	A	TP	+/-	PIM	PP	SH	GW	GT	S	PCT
68	17	26	43	14	173	6	0	3	0	123	13.8

LAST SEASON

Shoulder and hand injuries limited Crowder's playing time, and his point totals reflect that. His goal and point totals were the lowest of any full season he's played, and his assist total was second lowest. His plus/minus rating was the team's sixth highest, his PIM total fourth highest.

THE FINESSE GAME

Crowder's finesse game perfectly lays the ground work for his physical play. His very powerful skating stride combines with his overall strength and great balance on his skates to serve Keith well in the corners and the front of the net.

He is not an open-ice stickhandler and won't usually carry the puck, but he moves the puck well to his teammates after digging it out of the corners.

Another reason he moves the puck well is because he has his head up at all times instead of moving or passing with his head down. Because he's always aware of where he is in regard to the opposition, Crowder's passes are delivered accurately and without interception.

Using his teammates is the great strength of Crowder's game, and that is what makes his physical play so effective. He's unselfish, but when he gets within 15 feet of the net his eyes light up and he just barges through.

He'll get many of his goals on second effort, shooting from the bottom of the faceoff circle and chasing the puck, but he also likes to work his way around the back of the net and tuck the puck in.

THE PHYSICAL GAME

Crowder is probably the prototypical Boston Bruin. He's a scrapper in the corners and he hits everything in an opposing uniform. Don't read fighter into Keith's physical play, because he doesn't throw his fists around unless provoked. Rather, he sacrifices his body shift after shift.

He is fearless in the corners and works them excellently, making him a grinder with a goal scorer's touch. Again, it is his strength and willingness to take physical abuse that makes Crowder successful when he charges the net and, because of his strength, his shot is a powerful one.

Keith plays the same way at both ends of the ice and will rub out the opposiiton in the defensive zone as well as the offensive zone. He maximizes his talent.

THE INTANGIBLES

Doggedly working at both ends of the ice regardless of score or opponent, Crowder is probably the Bruins' hardest worker and definitely one of the club's leaders.

His physical style takes a toll on him in terms of injuries, and the durability question is one that must be addressed. But figure Crowder to play as long as he can lace up skates, and figure him to keep on inspiring the club through his effort and work ethic.

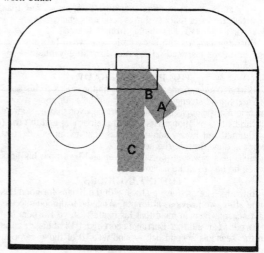

CRAIG JANNEY

Yrs. of NHL service: 1
Born: Hartford, Conn., USA; September 26, 1968
Position: Center
Height: 6-0
Weight: 175
Uniform no.: 23
Shoots: left

Career statisics:

GP	G	A	TP	+/−	PIM	PP	SH	GW	GT	S	PCT
15	7	9	16	6	0	1	0	1	0	29	24.1

LAST SEASON

Janney joined the Bruins immediately following the Olympic Games. He was their first round pick in 1986.

THE FINESSE GAME

Janney is a superb finesse player, with potential to excel in all finesse categories.

He is already an excellent skater, and that means he has all the attributes excellence encompasses—speed, agility, quickness, balance and acceleration. His foot speed is excellent, so his acceleration is explosive and his speed of the rink-length/breakaway variety. He adds balance to foot speed to become extremely agile, able to change directions and speeds with a step or two — or to stop and start on a dime. Janney also moderates all of his speed, making it that much more effective.

Good as his skating skill is, it may be secondary in quality to Janney's playmaking ability. He has tremendous hockey sense in all that the term implies: anticipation, understanding, play reading. He sees the play open up before him and — like only the game's best players — has a knack for being one or two plays ahead of the game.

Craig complements that mental capacity with extraordinary hand skills. His hands are super-soft, meaning he can feather passes or rifle them as the situation demands. He passes equally well to both the forehand and backhand sides, and he leads his teammates well. When he chooses to handle the puck and take advantage of an opportunity himself (which is not often enough), Janney's stickhandling ability combines with his skating to become very good.

His hockey sense gets him near the net in scoring situations, and his hand skills allow him to score in tight and in traffic. He'll get most of his goals in tight, because when he's farther out he looks to pass. His shot isn't bad, but right now it's not at the level of his other skills.

He plays positionally up and down the ice and Craig will conscientiously cover his check.

THE PHYSICAL GAME

The best way to describe Janney now — in terms of physical ability — is to say that he's similar to Calgary's Joe Nieuwendyk. Janney is tall but whippet-thin, so he doesn't have a lot of strength or bulk to bring to his physical game.

But that's not to say that Craig won't play physically. Again, like Nieuwendyk, Janney goes to the traffic areas and let's his finesse skills do the work. He's unafraid of traffic and unintimidated around the opposition goal.

He has a good reach and he uses it well when checking to break up passes or poke pucks away from the opposition.

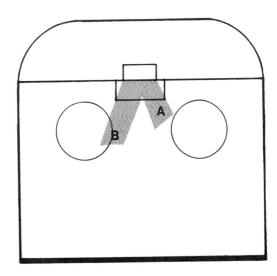

THE INTANGIBLES

If it sounds like we're high on this kid, then you're right — we are. Janney has a long way to go in his NHL career, but study of him now combined with some projection says that we could be looking at a player with almost limitless potential.

Right now, he'll have to prove his worth over the long haul and succeed in the NHL grind. He needs to be a little more selfish to make his playmaking more effective, and he'll need to fight off a lot of checking because — unlike other rookies — Janney isn't coming into the League unnoticed.

In his favor is his attitude. He's a worker who's determined to succeed, one with heart and character. That — along with all his skill — bodes well for his future.

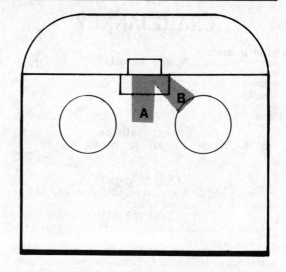

BOB JOYCE

Yrs. of NHL service: 1
Born: St. John, N.B., Canada; July 11, 1966
Position: Left wing/center
Height: 6-1
Weight: 190
Uniform no.: 27
Shoots: left

Career statisics:

GP	G	A	TP	+/−	PIM	PP	SH	GW	GT	S	PCT
15	7	5	12	4	10	2	0	0	0	30	23.3

LAST SEASON

Joyce joined the Bruins after the Winter Olympics. He was a fourth round pick in the 1984 Entry Draft.

THE FINESSE GAME

Joyce is a strong skater equipped with powerful strides, good balance and speed. His acceleration skill is good and should get better, and his balance gives him a degree of agility and mobility that's unexpected in a player with his size and bulk. That said, he's not an elegant skater but more of a straight-ahead one, and that fits his style.

Joyce plays his wing without much flair, but he also has fine anticipation skills and hockey sense to apply to his game. That means he knows how to get into position to score, and scoring is something Bob Joyce does very well.

Bob has an excellent shot from within 20-feet or so, very quickly released and accurate. Combined with his ability to get open, that makes him a very dangerous player indeed.

But Joyce's scoring skill goes beyond that quick release. He has extremely good hands and can operate with the puck in traffic very well, so even when he's checked he's going to get that shot off. Joyce's good hands also mean that he converts pucks around the net with ease; all he needs is the slightest opening to slip the puck through.

He's a scorer first, but Joyce can use his teammates well when passing from the corners. It's just that he expects a return pass as he gets to the net.

He needs work defensively in his transition game, and he has to learn to get back down the ice with the same speed he raced up.

THE PHYSICAL GAME

Joyce has good size and he's willing to use it in the high traffic areas. He's not yet a thumper, but he'll get up against the boards and bump around and he certainly has the skill to make a play coming out of the corner.

His balance and strength also come into play when he goes to the net, as they allow him to remain vertical and in position.

THE INTANGIBLES

Like teammate Craig Janney, Joyce has a fine future ahead of him. His style of play is quieter that Janney's, a lot less flashy, but we have a feeling the long-term results of Joyce's style are going to be anything but quiet.

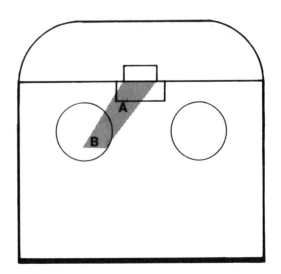

STEVE KASPER

Yrs. of NHL service: 7
Born: Montreal, Quebec, Canada; September 28, 1961
Position: Center
Height: 5-8
Weight: 159
Uniform no.: 11
Shoots: left

Career statistics:

GP	G	A	TP	PIM
515	125	204	329	401

1987-88 statistics:

GP	G	A	TP	+/-	PIM	PP	SH	GW	GT	S	PCT
79	26	44	70	-1	35	9	3	5	0	166	15.7

LAST SEASON

All point totals were career highs for Kasper, who finished third on the team in scoring. He was second on the club in power play goals and tied for first in shorthanded scores. He finished fourth on the team in shots on goal.

THE FINESSE GAME

Kasper's skills are of the quiet variety, in that nothing he does leaps out at you on first notice. He's a fine skater with average speed and quickness, but his biggest skating strength is his stamina; he can just go and go and go. That's important for him in his role as a checking forward.

The skills in Kasper's game that do demand attention are his ice vision and anticipation, both of which are excellent. He uses them in checking to keep himself between the man and the puck, and at breaking up forming plays, two reasons he is an excellent penalty killer. Kasper always knows where he is on the ice in relation to his man, the puck and the net.

Offensively, Steve can put that vision and sense to work with his teammates. He is a good stickhandler and controls the puck well, moving the puck smoothly to his wingers and the point men.

Even with last year's offensive success — and including his previous 20-goal seasons — Kasper is a little difficult to figure as a scorer. He doesn't seem to take full advantage of the opportunities he gets, primarily because he is so pre-occupied with his defense. He has a good, hard wrist shot from the slot (last year we said that he didn't shoot enough — just 110 SOG) and his increased scoring total is partly attributed to his shooting more. He also has an NHL-caliber slap shot.

Kasper is also a very strong faceoff man and he's one of the guys the opposition is most likely to see on the ice for those crucial draws in the Bruins' zone late in the game.

THE PHYSICAL GAME

Pure effort and conditioning are the keys to Kasper's game, the physical reasons he is able to work so efficiently so often against the League's top stars.

He certainly doesn't have great size but that's okay, because Kasper plays the game with his head more than his body. He can hit but is not punishing when he does so, and rare are the times that he hits anyway.

He does have good strength that he puts to use when he takes his man out of the play, holding him for that extra second necessary to disrupt the offense's rhythm.

Kasper has the stamina and the conditioning to double-shift if need be, and trying to run him ragged won't work.

THE INTANGIBLES

Even after a 70-point season, Kasper's great value to the Bruins is the scoring he prevents. He truly enjoys playing defensively and checking the opposition's stars and he takes great pride in doing so. Kasper continued to do his superb job at checking the opposition's offensive threats, while putting up the best numbers of his career.

And don't be fooled by that minus1. For the job Kasper does against the Gretzkys, Savards and Lemieuxs of the NHL, to be *only* minus1 is to really be *at least* plus20.

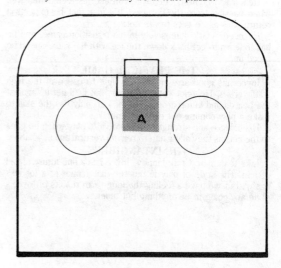

GORD KLUZAK

Yrs. of NHL service: 4
Born: Climax, Sask., Canada; March 4, 1964
Position: Defenseman
Height: 6-3
Weight: 214
Uniform no.: 6
Shoots: left

Career statistics:

GP	G	A	TP	PIM
286	25	95	120	530

1987-88 statistics:

GP	G	A	TP	+/-	PIM	PP	SH	GW	GT	S	PCT
66	6	31	37	18	135	0	1	0	0	168	3.6

LAST SEASON

Kluzak made a successful comeback from major knee surgery, even though his games played total was a career low. A subsequent knee injury sidelined him for 13 games. He matched his career high for assists. He led all Bruins defensemen in PIM.

THE FINESSE GAME

Time away from the game compounded by injury has retarded Kluzak's finesse development. While he has a long and strong stride, Gord lacks true speed and quickness in his pace. His balance and agility are average, and he gains ground up-ice (or close the gaps defensively) more by size and length of stride than by any other means.

He's aided by playing in Boston Garden (an arena to which, more than any other venue, a team can be tailored — sort of like turf teams in baseball), but on larger ice surfaces speedy forwards can take advantage of his lack of foot speed and faulty pivots. In those arenas he has to temper his offensive impulses in order to play better defense, because he'll have difficulty regaining his defensive position after loitering in the opposition zone.

He has a tendency to wander in the defensive zone (and leave openings for the opposition), so his positional play and concentration on the man should be improved. He likes to pinch in and challenge in the offensive zone.

Kluzak is a good passer, not the least of which is because he can see over almost everyone else. He reads plays fairly well but could move the puck a liitle quicker from his own zone. He has fairly good hands and puts them to use well in the offensive zone, containing the point and finding the open man. He'll see some power play time because of that. He will occasionally carry the puck from the zone, but he prefers to pass it.

He has a hard shot from the blue line, but needs to improve his accuracy.

THE PHYSICAL GAME

Gord uses his size to good end as a hard and heavy hitter. He'd improve as a bodychecker with some more balance, and he can occasionally be pushed off the puck by smaller foes because of his high center of gravity. He uses his reach fairly

well and is almost impossible to get away from in Boston Garden because of the small ice surface and Kluzak's huge wingspan. He is less effective on ice that is of regulation size.

THE INTANGIBLES

Kluzak benefitted this past season by being paired with Ray Bourque. That pairing allowed Gord to mkae his offensive forays, knowing that Bouque could always cover for him. It's debatable whether Kluzak would have played as aggressively in the offensive zone with another partner.

Now that he's returned, Kluzak still needs to have an injury-free year. And he still needs to show why — other than his great size — he was a number one draft choice.

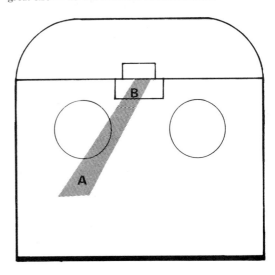

REED LARSON

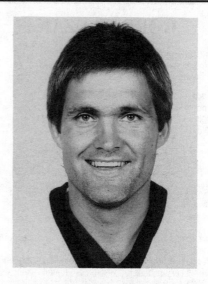

Yrs. of NHL service: 12
Born: Minneapolis, Minn., USA; July 30, 1956
Position: Defenseman
Height: 6-0
Weight: 195
Uniform no.: 28
Shoots: right

Career statistics:

GP	G	A	TP	PIM
849	213	434	647	1,323

1987-88 statistics:

GP	G	A	TP	+/-	PIM	PP	SH	GW	GT	S	PCT
62	10	24	34	3	93	5	1	1	0	151	6.6

LAST SEASON

Shoulder and preseason bicep woes forced Larson to play his fewest games per season ever, excepting his break-in year. All point totals were career lows, but he finished second among defensemen in goals. His plus/minus rating was the worst among defensive regulars.

THE FINESSE GAME

Time and injury have taken their toll on Larson's finesse skills. He's still a good skater, and Larson's never really had a change of pace or outstanding agility. He retains some of his rink-length speed, and that speed allows him to join the play as a fourth attacker. Reed will also start the occasional rush himself, but he doesn't do that as frequently as he once did.

Reed is still a good puckhandler, and he uses his hand skills more than his skating when he rushes the puck or contains the point. He's very good at taking the puck off the boards in one motion, ready to shoot the puck or pass it to an open teammate. He can handle the puck well defensively too, but his concentration does fail at times and he forces plays where none exist. That creates turnovers.

Larson sees the offensive zone well and can use his teammates effectively, but he's always thought shoot first and pass second. And why not, because he still has a tremendous shot from the point. That shot either scores or leaves rebounds, and Larson will get his assists when a teammate converts his shot.

The shot is an awesome weapon and it is one that has knocked goaltenders unconscious and out of games. Reed's slapshot will either blow right by the goaltender or take him into the net and lately he has developed a half wrist shot-half slap that is very difficult to read, but just as fast and just as powerful.

Larson likes to deliver the shots from the right point, but he'll cheat into the deep slot if he can.

THE PHYSICAL GAME

Larson has never been a thumper along the boards, in that he doesn't make the big check with a lot of flash and dash. He's generally — but quietly — effective along the boards and in front of the net, and just a little mean with his stick. He uses his size well to keep his defensive area clear, and his strength is the reason why his shot is so powerful.

THE INTANGIBLES

Larson is a good team man coming to the end of his career. He fills a role for the Bruins now, especially with what will be the almost certain emergence of Glen Wesley's offensive talent.

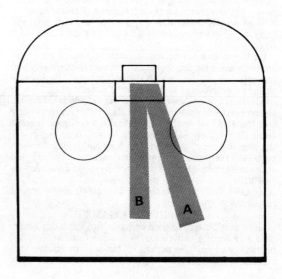

REGGIE LEMELIN

Yrs. of NHL service: 9
Born: Sherbrooke, Quebec, Canada; November 19, 1954
Position: Goaltender
Height: 5-11
Weight: 160
Uniform no.: 1
Catches: left

Career statistics:

GP	MINS	G	SO	AVG	A	PIM
373	20,526	1,220	9	3.56	14	55

1987-88 statisics:

GP	MINS	AVG	W	L	T	SO	GA	SA	SAPCT	PIM
49	2,828	2.93	24	17	6	3	138	1,244	.889	2

LAST SEASON

Lemelin was signed as a free agent by the Boston Bruins prior to last season. Minutes played total was third highest of his career, and his goals-against-average was his best ever (fourth best in the League last year). He finished sixth in the League in shutouts, and his three shutouts was a career high for a season. He missed two games with a finger injury.

THE PHYSICAL GAME

Where previously he had been a standup goaltender almost to a fault, Lemelin introduced a greater reflex element to his game last year (credit his new, lightweight pads for Reggie's newfound mobility). He still plays his angles very well, squaring himself to the puck excellently and controlling his rebounds well.

He's a good skater and moves well from post to post and in and out of the net. He doesn't waste much energy chasing the puck so he won't handle it much. Instead, he'll just cut it off behind the net and leave it for the defense. He communicates well with his defense.

Because Reggie has good balance he is quick to regain his stance once he leaves it. He'll regain his positioning for the next save, or regain his feet after flopping to the ice (though he went to the ice in scarmbles far more last year than ever before). He has good hands (better on the glove side) and sees the puck well.

His feet remain his consistent weakness, in that he is vulnerable after he opens up and has his feet moving. But Reggie countered his foot speed problem with the new pads, and has improved that part of his game.

THE MENTAL GAME

Reggie's concentration and anticipation are excellent. He reads the play in front of him very well and maintains his concentration after bad goals; he'll fight you for every goal you score.

He's unemotional on the ice and easily puts bad games behind him. He can come into a game cold and immediately charge up his concentration, and he most definitely has big save capability.

THE INTANGIBLES

We told you last year that Lemelin was a money goaltender and that he could get hot for long stretches of time. The effect of his new pads on his performance shouldn't be underestimated, because they refreshed both Lemelin's game and his attitude. Remember, he'd been dumped by the Flames and, to complete the irony, former Flames coach Bob Johnson hadn't wanted Lemelin to wear his new pads. Johnson didn't like them.

In this case, and for another few years we suspect, Reggie got the last laugh.

KEN LINSEMAN

Yrs. of NHL service: 10
Born: Kingston, Ontario, Canada; August 11, 1958
Position: Center
Height: 5-11
Weight: 175
Uniform no.: 13
Shoots: left

Career statistics:

GP	G	A	TP	PIM
663	211	452	663	1,369

1987-88 statistics:

GP	G	A	TP	+/−	PIM	PP	SH	GW	GT	S	PCT
77	29	45	74	36	167	7	0	5	0	150	19.3

LAST SEASON

Linseman's best as a Bruin in many ways. Games played total was highest in six years, goal total second highest of his career and PIM total highest in five seasons. He finished second on the club in scoring, goals, assists and shooting percentage and first in plus/minus. He missed three late season games with an ankle injury.

THE FINESSE GAME

Skating is the best of Linseman's considerable finesse abilities, and he is one of the NHL's best skaters. His skating skill is excellent. Though not the fastest skater end-to-end in the League, Linseman wouldn't be far behind the winner. His lateral movement, agility and change of directions skills — all keyed by his outstanding one-step quickness — are excellent. He has very few peers in movement (turns, reversals, stops and starts) within one or two strides, and that shiftiness is what makes him so effective.

Linseman is an above average stickhandler and playmaker. He performs excellently with the puck at top speed. Linseman has excellent vision of the ice and good anticipation, able to lead a teammate into a hole that has just opened. His own skating and puckhandling allow him to exploit those openings himself and he should be more selfish in taking advantage of openings, instead of looking to make plays.

His goal scoring comes from anticipation and quickness, not from great shot selection. Linseman usually gets his goals from in close — deflections and the like — and he could increase that total if he would take advantage of the opportunities he creates and shoot more.

Linseman is an excellent checker and defensive player as well, pursuing the puck relentlessly in all three zones. He is one of the NHL's best faceoff men and will take many of the important defensive zone faceoffs late in the game.

THE PHYSICAL GAME

Despite his lack of size, Linseman has always been a physical player. He is unafraid to hit in the corners and it is his willingness to put his stick into people — along with his non-stop yapping — that has gained him his nickname as the Rat. He is mean and does whatever's necessary to stop an opponent. That often means an extra elbow or a high stick.

He augments his good board and corners work with his fine hand skills, though Linseman uses his hands well in another way. He's one of the League's best holder and that's another of his tactics that drives the opposition to distraction. He has strong hands and wrists and that's why he's effective on faceoffs.

For all the disturbing he does, however, Linseman won't fight his own battles. That's what Jay Miller is for.

THE INTANGIBLES

Linseman finished his fine year by leading the Bruins in playoff scoring. If he can keep away from the injuries that have dogged his career (though he pretty much escaped the injury jinx last year), Linseman should continue to perform well for the Bruins.

He's a tremendous competitor, has an excellent attitude toward the game and is a good team leader and hard worker who will do anything to win.

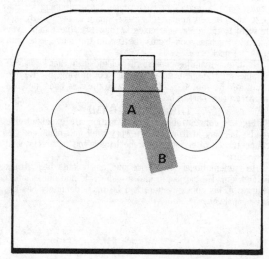

NEVIN MARKWART

Yrs. of NHL service: 5
Born: Toronto, Ontario, Canada; December 9, 1964
Position: Left wing
Height: 5-11
Weight: 175
Uniform no.: 17
Shoots: left

Career statistics:

GP	G	A	TP	PIM
250	32	56	88	674

1987-88 statistics:

GP	G	A	TP	+/−	PIM	PP	SH	GW	GT	S	PCT
25	1	12	13	4	85	0	0	0	0	24	4.2

LAST SEASON

Shoulder and groin injuries conspired to limit Markwart to his career low in games played.

THE FINESSE GAME

Even after five NHL seasons, Markwart still looks, plays and skates like a kamikaze pilot. Often, he seems to have less control of his skates than he should and, as he bounces from opponent to opponent, looks like a spinning top.

His balance has improved slightly and he's coming away from most collisions more vertical that previously, but Markwart's 'wildness' on his skates still costs him.

He accelerates well but is not a shifty skater, and he still lacks a change of pace that would make his good speed better.

Markwart is an average stickhandler and, because he lacks the knowledge of what precisely to do with the puck after he has it, he doesn't see his options or use them well. He must think about improving his offensive game a little more. Again, a slower pace would help, because he can't apply his modest offensive skills at high speed.

He is not a goal scorer. He does deliver his shot low and hard, but has neither the instincts to get into scoring position nor the power to blow the puck past NHL goaltending.

THE PHYSICAL GAME

Pound for pound, Markwart is as tough as anyone in the League. He is a great hitter, so when he hits you, you know it. Markwart initiates almost every physical encounter and his hitting will often separate the opposition from the puck.

Patient opponents can take advantage of Markwart, however, by taking his hits and then working the puck, as he will more than likely be unable to make a play following a hit.

Markwart is also a fighter and will take on any and all comers, readily and willingly, reagrdless of size or reputation.

THE INTANGIBLES

Almost nothing has changed in this report from year to year. What we must include now is the question of Markwart's durability. His physical style is admirable, but it clearly inhibits Nevin's playing time. Without that physical play Markwart wouldn't get playing time, but with that physical play Markwart still isn't getting playing time.

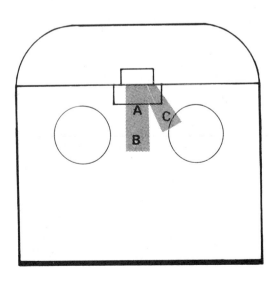

TOM MCCARTHY

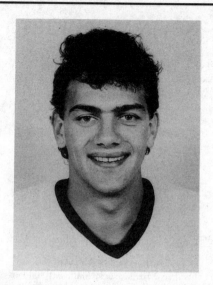

Yrs. of NHL service: 9
Born: Toronto, Ontario, Canada; July 31, 1960
Position: Center
Height: 6-2
Weight: 200
Uniform no.: 19
Shoots: left

Career statistics:

GP	G	A	TP	PIM
460	178	221	399	330

1987-88 statistics:

GP	G	A	TP	+/−	PIM	PP	SH	GW	GT	S	PCT
6	2	5	7	3	6	1	0	0	0	10	20.0

LAST SEASON

Knee injury sidelined McCarthy for almost the entire season. He returned to see action late in the year and during the playoffs. All totals were career lows.

THE FINESSE GAME

Make no mistake, McCarthy is a tremendously skilled finesse player. He is a good skater with both one-step quickness and long haul speed — to a degree. He is agile, has good lateral movement and excellent balance.

Tom's other skills make his skating better than it would otherwise be. His anticipation, puck handling, shooting and goal scoring abilities are all excellent.

McCarthy has tremendous hockey sense and knows where his teammates are and will be, *and* he knows where the openings will be for himself. He controls the puck excellently and can keep it away from most any defender long enough to make not only a good play but the right play.

He passes the puck equally well on his forehand and backhand, and shoots the puck equally well too. McCarthy has a quick, hard shot that he releases immediately, and he can also score with the slapshot. He is dangerous anywhere in the offensive zone because of his passing and shooting skills.

He operates equally well in open ice or in traffic.

THE PHYSICAL GAME

McCarthy is big and strong and he can work the boards as a wing, or fight through checkers as a center. His strong hands and wrists are big assets for him, as is his excellent reach. Add all that together, and McCarthy becomes deadly in close.

He's not a banger, but he will accept hits to make his plays.

THE INTANGIBLES

Because of McCarthy's absence last season, we've made few changes in this report. Years from now, McCarthy may be remembered less for his NHL career than for the fact that — thanks once again to his incessant injuries — his absence on the roster was filled by kids with names like Bob Sweeney and Craig Janney.

Talent-wise there are few better. Desire-wise there are few worse. Unless he's moved back to the wing, we wish Tom a lot of luck in getting his roster spot back.

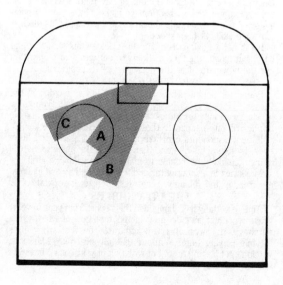

RICK MIDDLETON

Yrs. of NHL service: 14
Born: Toronto, Ontario, Canada; December 4, 1953
Position: Right wing
Height: 5-11
Weight: 170
Uniform no.: 16
Shoots: right

Career statistics:

GP	G	A	TP	PIM
1,005	448	540	988	157

1987-88 statistics:

GP	G	A	TP	+/−	PIM	PP	SH	GW	GT	S	PCT
59	13	19	32	3	11	2	3	1	0	79	16.5

LAST SEASON

Middleton missed eight games with a pulled hamstring, nine games with a rib injury. Games played total was the third lowest of his career, goal and point totals were career lows, assist total second lowest of his career. He finished tied for first in team shorthanded goals.

THE FINESSE GAME

The two skills that gave birth to Middleton's nickname — "Nifty" — are almost gone, and suddenly Rick Middleton is very old. Part one was his skating. He's noticeably slower and has lost much of his once-deceptive skating speed. Part two was his mesmerizing puckhandling, but that is also on the wane.

He retains good vision and anticipation, but is unable to make his body operate as agilely as his mind. He is a stalwart penalty killer and a still-underrated defensive performer. He checks well and is a short-handed goal threat on the penalty killing unit.

One reason Middleton's not the scorer he once was is his shot. He now takes a big windup on his slap shot, allowing the goaltender to react and set his position. He still shoots carefully — only when an opportunity presents itself will he let the puck go — and still chooses to rely on his hand skills to get him to the net.

But since his hand skills have diminished so has his offense.

THE PHYSICAL GAME

Middleton has never been a physical player, and he's one of the few exceptions to the rule about a physical game improving a finesse game. He's always accepted whatever abuse was necessary to make his plays. He will hit on occasion, but he's always succeeded in the corners and against the boards by using his stickhandling wizardry.

THE INTANGIBLES

Middleton's age plus the emergence of youth may make Nifty an endangered species this year. He's been reduced to role playing and his retirement may be imminent.

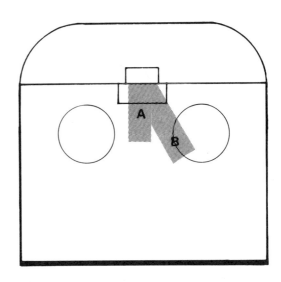

JAY MILLER

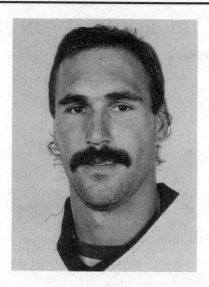

Yrs. of NHL service: 3
Born: Wellesley, Mass., USA; July 16, 1960
Position: Left wing
Height: 6-2
Weight: 205
Uniform no.: 29
Shoots: right

Career statistics:

GP	G	A	TP	PIM
179	11	16	27	690

1987-88 statistics:

GP	G	A	TP	+/−	PIM	PP	SH	GW	GT	S	PCT
78	7	12	19	-5	304	0	0	1	0	44	15.9

LAST SEASON

Games played total, all point totals and PIM mark were all career highs. His minus5 rating was the team's second worst among regulars, worst among players with at least 66 games played. He finished sixth in the League in PIM.

THE FINESSE GAME

Miller is an average skater, with no real speed or quickness. He does have good balance, and he puts that balance to work in his physical game. It allows him to generally remain vertical after collisions, and it certainly allows him to plant himself when fighting.

He demonstrates no real ability in handling the puck, whether by carrying it or passing it to teammates, and rarely — if ever — shoots when he is in position to do so. If he's going to make a play, Miller needs plenty of time and space.

Jay will occasionally find himself on a checking line and that's because he has improved his view and understanding of the game around him, a natural consequence of NHL experience. Miller is unable, however, to put that increased understanding to work offensively and probably never will.

Miller rarely, if ever, scores and as such must be in close proximity of the net to take advantage of whatever he can.

THE PHYSICAL GAME

With no pun intended, this is where Miller makes his impact. He makes fairly good use of his body when checking, and his excellent strength and size means he can hurt the opposition when checking — if he can catch them.

More consistent hitting, combined with skating instruction to further improve his balance after he hits, would gain Miller more ice time. If he could catch those enemy skaters, Miller would be more valuable, to say nothing of less one-dimensional.

Miller is also an enforcer, plain and simple with no disguise. When the going gets rough, he is used on search and destroy missions against the other team's tough guys. Miller's willingness is an asset for him and the team, because it keeps players like Cam Neely on the ice and out of the penalty box.

Jay's size, strength and balance make him a good fighter, one of the NHL best and most feared. It is also that combination of physical skills that gains him some room in which to operate on the ice.

THE INTANGIBLES

Miller is a typical Bruin. His robust style (not dirty, because he doesn't use his stick and he doesn't bully smaller players) is Bruins at its best, and the hometown boy is a crowd favorite because of it.

That said, his role will continue to be as a role player, unless he can improve his skills enough to merit a regular shift. Otherwise he'll remain an enforcer and a fourth line player.

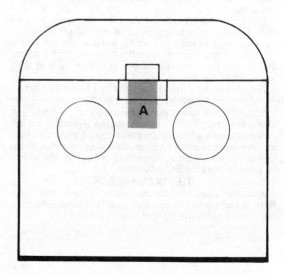

ANDY MOOG

Yrs. of NHL service: 7
Born: Penticton, B.C., Canada; February 18, 1960
Position: Goaltender
Height: 5-8
Weight: 165
Uniform no.: 35
Catches: left

Career statistics:

GP	MINS	G	SO	AVG	A	PIM
241	13,261	794	5	3.59	11	46

1987-88 statisics:

GP	MINS	AVG	W	L	T	SO	GA	SA	SAPCT	PIM
6	360	2.83	4	2	0	1	17	181	.906	0

LAST SEASON

Moog sat out Edmonton's training camp, refused to report to the Oilers and joined the Canadian Olympic team instead, and was then traded to the Bruins. Games played total was the lowest of his career.

THE PHYSICAL GAME

Quickness is the name of Moog's game, and it is a game he plays very well. He plays on the balls of his feet and is an excellent reflex goaltender, a kick save goalie. In previous years Andy was very scrambly because of his reflexes, but is much more in control now.

His game is also based on playing his angles properly, especially because he is small and smart shooters will just put the puck over his shoulders if he hasn't cut the angle correctly. When he is on, Moog will be perched at the top of the goal crease. When he is having a bad night, however, he will be deep in his net.

He has a good glove and is sharp with his stick and sees the puck very well, making him effective on screen shots, despite the inequalities in height between him and the League's forwards.

Moog skates very well and can move the puck but that is not his game and he prefers to leave it for his defense. He is occasionally sloppy in closing his legs but that is a mental error and not a physical one, because Andy has very fast feet.

He regains his stance very quickly and is very balanced, always in position to make the second save.

THE MENTAL GAME

Moog has good concentration, though he does suffer those little lapses in meaningless games when the result has already been decided. In other words, he raises his concentration depending on the importance of the contest.

He is mentally tough and will recover from bad goals or games and he has good anticipation of the plays, able to understand what the offense is doing and moving accordingly — for example — to cut off a goal mouth pass.

Moog can also come in cold and perform well, and he does have the ability to make big saves.

THE INTANGIBLES

Without the corps of superstars that surrounded him, Moog will be asked to do more in Boston than he's ever been asked to do before. He'll also have to sit — at least in the season's beginning — behind Reggie Lemelin. We saw last year that Moog wasn't content to be a backup, and now we'll have to see how he adapts to a new team but the same backup situation.

CAM NEELY

Yrs. of NHL service: 5
Born: Comox, B.C., Canada; June 6, 1965
Position: Right wing
Height: 6-1
Weight: 205
Uniform no.: 8
Shoots: right

Career statistics:

GP	G	A	TP	PIM
345	129	116	245	638

1987-88 statistics:

GP	G	A	TP	+/−	PIM	PP	SH	GW	GT	S	PCT
69	42	27	69	30	175	11	0	3	0	207	20.3

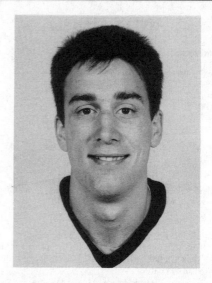

LAST SEASON

Neely finished fourth on the club in scoring, but first in goals, power play goals and shooting percentage. He was second in SOG (first among forwards), third in plus/minus and PIM. He missed four games with a knee injury, and missed two contests with a nose injury.

THE FINESSE GAME

Though not usually thought of in a finesse way, Cam Neely is a very good finesse player. He's an excellent skater with a strong stride and exceptional balance. His stride adds strength and power to his physical game (important for driving home checks) and his balance allows him to stay upright and in the play after collisions.

Neely also has some rink length speed and more than a little agility for operating in close quarters, but he is basically a power skater rather than a fancy one.

He carries the puck fairly well when skating — long a weakness — and he's also learned to keep his head up to make plays. He's not exceptionally gifted in terms on anticipation, so he'll have to look over the ice after gaining the puck in the corner instead of knowing where to make the play.

His skill at taking the puck off the boards and moving with it remains only average, but that doesn't mean he can't make a play coming out of the corner; Cam just needs space and time.

Much of that hand skill in playmaking along the boards is academic, because Neely is a scorer and shooter. If he gains the puck he's going to wheel right to the net and bull his way through for a shot. He controls the puck better in traffic than previously, and he puts a hard shot on net. Neely usually aims low and for the five-hole, and he has improved the release of his shot to make it quicker and more accurate.

THE PHYSICAL GAME

Neely is a titan in the physical game, fearless and ferocious. He is very physical and he puts his size and strength to work exceedingly well in the cramped confines of the Garden. He can muscle anyone off the puck in the corners and is almost impossible to knock down himself (courtesy of his balance).

Neely hits punishingly hard in the corners and the open ice and he is afraid of no one. He may take his lumps, but he'll give out a few too, as he is a good fighter.

The physical game does have its side effects in game-missing injury.

THE INTANGIBLES

Neely is a tremendous worker and has great character and heart. By and large, he does everything well. Neely just goes and goes and doesn't know the meaning of the word quit, and would be an asset to any team. He is still young and still learning (and his teaming with Craig Janney and Bob Joyce as a line during last spring's playoffs had many NHL observers saying they were already the best threesome in hockey).

His future is brilliant.

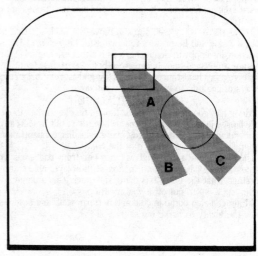

ALLEN PEDERSEN

Yrs. of NHL service: 2
Born: Edmonton, Alberta, Canada; January 13, 1965
Position: Defenseman
Height: 6-3
Weight: 210
Uniform no.: 41
Shoots: left

Career statistics:

GP	G	A	TP	PIM
157	1	17	18	161

1987-88 statistics:

GP	G	A	TP	+/−	PIM	PP	SH	GW	GT	S	PCT
78	0	6	6	6	90	0	0	0	0	43	0.0

LAST SEASON

Pedersen faltered slightly offensively, down from 1g-11a in 1986-87. He was the only regular among Bruin blueliners to not score a goal last year.

THE FINESSE GAME

Though he's not yet above the level of a fifth or sixth defenseman, Pedersen has shown improvement in his skating and understanding of the NHL play. He doesn't have rink-length speed, but Allen's foot speed has improved so his quickness and pivots are better.

He's also shown much better comprehension of his defensive angles and play reading ability. Pedersen recognizes the play coming toward him fairly well and now forces the play wide of the net with good consistency.

Pedersen handles the puck fairly well, so he's smart enough *and* talented enough to make the correct pass from his own end quickly. He still makes the first play he sees, instead of examining his options, but he's making the safe play most of the time. Additional experience and confidence should teach him to scan the ice.

He will not carry the puck from the zone, will not join the attack and he almost has to be dragged into the attacking zone. Obviously, his tentativeness was born from worrying primarily about his defense, but he's also missing openings that could be converted to additional offensive pressure.

He'll shoot the puck from the point with a no-better-than-average slap shot, and he certainly won't take any chances at pinching in.

THE PHYSICAL GAME

Pedersen gets the most from his good size, using it to his advantage along the boards and in front of the net as a stay at home defenseman. He has the strength to win those battles and he plays physically but smartly, not taking penalties that could cost his team. He's toned down his cross-ice wanderings for the big hit that just took him out of position.

Allen is willing to sacrifice his body as a good shot blocker and, though he is physical, Pedersen is not a fighter.

THE INTANGIBLES

Defensemen take longer to mature into their positions than other skaters, but Pedersen seems well on his way toward that maturity. If he is, he can be an important part of Boston's success because the Bruins don't have a strictly defensive force in front of their net.

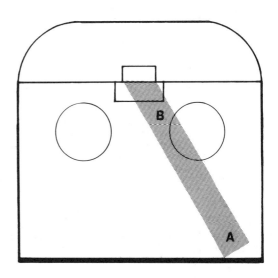

WILLI PLETT

Yrs. of NHL service: 12
Born: Paraguay, South America;
June 7, 1955 Position:
Right wing Height:
6-3 Weight:
205 Uniform no.:
25 Shoots:
right

Career statistics:

GP	G	A	TP	PIM
834	222	215	437	2,572

1987-88 statistics:

GP	G	A	TP	+/−	PIM	PP	SH	GW	GT	S	PCT
65	2	3	5	-10	170	1	0	0	0	29	6.9

LAST SEASON

Plett was claimed fom the New York Rangers during the waiver draft. All point totals were career lows, and PIM total was lowest in three seasons (he finished fifth on the team in PIM). His plus/miuns was the team's worst.

THE FINESSE GAME

Plett is a good skater, surprisingly so for a man his size. He has good balance and that makes him somewhat agile, but he's not very quick. Like most big forwards, Plett has some difficulty with his turns.

He handles the puck fairly well in front of him, but that's because the opposition gives him plenty of room. He thinks of using his teammates, but his hands are too tough — and he's missing the anticipation necessary to be a playmaker.

Plett doesn't have much of a shot, so he'll get most of his goals from deflections and the like. He'll need plenty of time and space even to put home a rebound.

He's no better than adequate defensively, worse if he's matched against a speedy forward. He wanders from his position and creates openings that way, and he doesn't come back as deep as he should.

THE PHYSICAL GAME

Obviously, this is the strength of Plett's game. He uses his body very effectively, when he catches someone. He doesn't hit as often as he used to, but he still has the strength to be a punishing hitter.

His superior upper body strength means he can out-muscle the opposition along the boards, but he has no idea what to do with the puck after gaining it. His balance and strength make him almost impossible to move when he plants himself in front of the enemy goal.

Willi used to be a good fighter, but he doesn't have the heart for it any more.

THE INTANGIBLES

Plett's value comes in the open space his presence creates for his teammates. He's also fairly effective as a deterrent, but his NHL time is almost up. After all, what do you do with a fighter who doesn't want to fight?

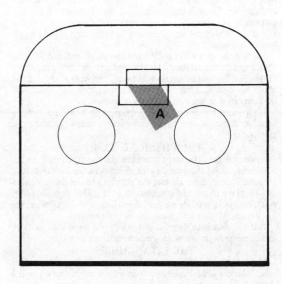

BOB SWEENEY

Yrs. of NHL service: 2
Born: Concord, Mass., USA; January 25, 1964
Position: Center
Height: 6-3
Weight: 210
Uniform no.: 42
Shoots: left

Career statistics:

GP	G	A	TP	PIM
94	24	27	51	94

1987-88 statistics:

GP	G	A	TP	+/−	PIM	PP	SH	GW	GT	S	PCT
80	22	23	45	11	73	6	0	7	0	118	18.6

LAST SEASON

Sweeney was the only member of the Bruins to play all 80 games. He led the club in game winners and was third in shooting percentage. He finished sixth in rookie scoring, second in rookie game winners.

THE FINESSE GAME

Puckhandling is currently the best of Sweeney's finesse skills, and more for physical reasons than finesse ones. He has outstanding reach and sensitive hands. Combined, Bob controls the puck well while skating and in traffic. He likes to carry the puck over the blue line to set up the offense, and Sweeney's hands are good enough that he can lead his teammates with passes.

He prefers, however, to put his puckhandling skill to work one-on-one and will drive the net if he can. His stickhandling and reach help him keep the puck from the defenders as he heads goalward.

Bob amplifies his hand skill with anticipation and vision. He reads the play fairly well in both directions. A year's experience has helped Sweeney recognize and improve his transition game. He's a conscientious backchecker and will fall back to directly in front of his goaltender.

His skating is a little awkward and slow at the NHL level, so increased foot speed would be beneficial. Bob has a degree of agility, but so far he plays almost solely as a straight-ahead player when he is checked; he won't try any fancy evasive maneuvers.

Sweeney has a decent shot, and he showed he can get it away quickly enough that — again, with experience — it might be something to contend with on the NHL level.

THE PHYSICAL GAME

Sweeney improved his physical games last year, using his body solidly if unspectacularly to thwart the opposition. He has excellent size but is not a hitter, so don't expect to see people flying into the cheap seats.

We've already discussed his reach, but Sweeney also uses his body well to protect the puck from the opposition while he's carrying it.

THE INTANGIBLES

One reason Tom McCarthy couldn't get back into the lineup after recovering from injury was Sweeney's play. The rookie started the season like a house afire (nine goals in the first 20 games), but then he slowed down (13 goals by midseason, just nine in the last half).

Part of that can be attributed to Sweeney playing a full NHL schedule for the first time, but Sweeney must also develop his conditioning and stamina for the NHL game.

He still has plenty of potential to improve, but only time will tell to what degree.

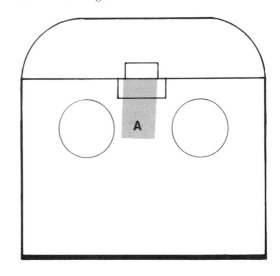

MICHAEL THELVEN

Yrs. of NHL service: 3
Born: Stockholm, Sweden; January 7, 1961
Position: Defenseman
Height: 5-11
Weight: 180
Uniform no.: 22
Shoots: left

Career statistics:

GP	G	A	TP	PIM
161	17	60	77	123

1987-88 statistics:

GP	G	A	TP	+/−	PIM	PP	SH	GW	GT	S	PCT
67	6	25	31	12	57	1	0	1	0	106	5.7

LAST SEASON

Thelven missed six games with groin injury, but still recorded career highs in games played assists and points. He had the fewest PIM of any Bruins defensive regular.

THE FINESSE GAME

Thelven has the European skills of skating and puck handling, both reflected in his offensive bent. He is not a speedster, but he does recognize openings on the ice and he can get to them.

His puck handling ability shows itself in traffic, where Thelven maneuvers well. He can grab the puck and carry it from the defensive zone to relieve offensive pressure, and Thelven likes to carry the puck and become a fourth attacker when he can.

He'll cut to the slot after dropping a pass back to the point and he looks for the pass when he gains the slot, but the majority of Thelven's goals will come from the point.

THE PHYSICAL GAME

Thelven likes contact only when he can initiate it. He is not an aggressive individual and won't really take the hits to make his plays. When forechecked heavily during the Prince of Wales Conference Final, Thelven threw a lot of snow instead of going into the corners for the puck.

Basically, he's a holder and a pusher, not a banger. He covers the man in front by blocking the passing lanes, but is not particularly effective along the boards.

THE INTANGIBLES

Durability is a major question for Thelven, as he was knocked out of the Stanley Cup Finals with yet another injury. He must learn to be more aggressive (you're more likely to be hurt catching checks than you are throwing them), and he must find a way to stay out of the hospital.

GLEN WESLEY

Yrs. of NHL service: 1
Born: Red Deer, Alta., Canada; October 2, 1968
Position: Defenseman
Height: 6-1
Weight: 190
Uniform no.: 26
Shoots: left

Career statisics:

GP	G	A	TP	+/–	PIM	PP	SH	GW	GT	S	PCT
79	7	30	37	21	69	1	2	0	0	158	4.4

LAST SEASON

Wesley was the Bruins first round Entry Draft choice in June of 1987. He finished second on the club in defensive scoring, was fifth overall in assists, sixth in shots on goal. His plus/minus rating was the team's fourth highest, second among defensemen. He finished fifth among rookies in assists and SOG total, fourth in shorthanded goals and first in rookie plus/minus.

THE FINESSE GAME

Wesley is a big package of finesse skills. He's a good skater with the potential to be excellent at the NHL level. Glen has a lot of power in his stride and that contributes to his speed, but he also has good foot speed and balance for agility and quickness. He can change direction well and has good acceleration (again, the power) and his skating backward is as good as it is forward.

He has excellent hockey sense, and that sense includes anticipation and vision. He sees the ice very well (both in the rush toward him and the rush away), and he understands a play's implications. Wesley knows how to recognize the openings and he can take advantage of them himself or help a teammate to do so.

Glen speed and quickness will get him to those openings, but he also passes extremely well and will lead a teammate into the clear with an accurate pass that will be as strong as the situation demands. If he chooses to attack himself, Wesley's hand skills will certainly back him up. He controls and carries the puck excellently, and his skating makes his puck-handling that much more effective, because Glen can move with the puck at any speed.

All of this means he's a solid scoring threat at the offensive blue line — and that's just by passing. Wesley also has excellent shot selection, and he delivers both his slap and wrist shots quickly and accurately.

All of these abilities are also evident in Wesley's defensive play. He reads the rush toward him well and has the skating tools to cut it off or angle it wide.

THE PHYSICAL GAME

Wesley plays a fairly physical game, but he's not a juggernaut. He takes the body well along the boards or in front of the net, but he's not yet a punishing hitter.

He does well with his size and strength and makes the attempt to apply them at all times. His skating and anticipation also make him a good checker in the open ice, as he closes opening with his body.

THE INTANGIBLES

Wesley plays a fairly complete NHL game, and he was just a rookie. He has tremendous potential — particularly on the offensive side — but he showed good jugdment last year by keeping that offense in check to concentrate on defense. He'll be more of a freewheeler this season.

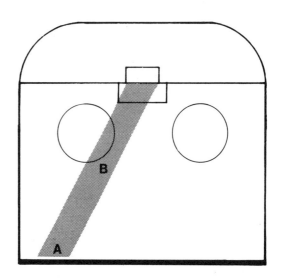

BUFFALO
SABRES

LINE COMBINATIONS
MIKE DONNELLY-PIERRE TURGEON-RAY
SHEPPARD
DAVE ANDREYCHUK-CHRISTIAN RUUTTU-MIKE
FOLIGNO
-DOUG SMITH-SCOTT ARNIEL

DEFENSE PAIRINGS
MIKE RAMSEY-PHIL HOUSLEY
JOE REEKIE-CAL JOHANSSON
LINDY RUFF-UWE KRUPP

GOALTENDERS
TOM BARRASSO
JACQUES CLOUTIER

OTHER PLAYERS
MARK NAPIER — Right wing
KEN PRIESTLAY — Center
JOHN TUCKER — Center
ADAM CREIGHTON — Center

POWER PLAY

FIRST UNIT:
MIKE FOLIGNO-CHRISTIAN RUUTU-DAVE
ANDREYCHUK
PHIL HOUSLEY-CALLE JOHANSSON

FOLIGNO stands in front to occupy a defenseman and screen the goaltender, while ANDREYCHUK works the right wing corner and RUUTU the left side. RUUTU will work a give and go with HOUSLEY, cutting to the bottom of the left faceoff circle for a shot, and ANDREYCHUK

will do the same thing with JOHANSSON on the right side, though ANDREYCHUK will also crash the net for a rebound on someone else's shot. RUUTU will not charge net; he stays outside of pileup for loose pucks.

TUCKER, when healthy, will work this unit, which is Buffalo's primary power play squad. RAMSEY will also see power play time. The second unit will feature TURGEON running the play and SHEPPARD parked in front. When healthy, CREIGHTON also sees power play time.

Last season, Buffalo's power play was POOR, scoring 80 goals in 464 man advantage opportunities (17.2 percent, 18th overall).

PENALTY KILLING

FIRST UNIT:
SCOTT ARNIEL-MARK NAPIER
MIKE RAMSEY-JOE REEKIE

ARNIEL and NAPIER use their speed to pressure puck in defensive zone, with pursuit fairly deep to net. Defensemen do not pressure as much, protecting the front of the net instead.

RAMSEY plays almost all of penalty killing time, while some combination involving RUUTU and HOUSLEY makes up the second unit. These two are both aggressive on the puck.

Last season, Buffalo's penalty killing was FAIR, allowing 96 goals in 439 times short-handed (78.1 percent, 15th overall).

CRUCIAL FACEOFFS

When healthy, TUCKER will take most of these. Otherwise the Sabres don't have a superior faceoff winner.

DAVE ANDREYCHUK

Yrs. of NHL service: 6
Born: Hamilton, Ontario, Canada; September 29, 1963
Position: Center
Height: 6-3
Weight: 219
Uniform no.: 25
Shoots: right

Career statistics:

GP	G	A	TP	PIM
422	174	242	416	331

1987-88 statistics:

GP	G	A	TP	+/−	PIM	PP	SH	GW	GT	S	PCT
80	30	48	78	1	112	15	0	5	0	253	11.9

LAST SEASON

Andreychuk played all 80 games for the second time in his career and second time in three seasons. He led the club in scoring, assists, power play goals (tied with Ray Sheppard) and shots on goal. He was the only Sabre to play all 80 games. His plus/minus was third best among the club's regulars, second best among forwards.

THE FINESSE GAME

Luckily for Andreychuk, skating is the least important factor in his finesse game. He has little foot speed or quickness above the NHL average and probably less agility. He gets past the opposition because of his long stride, but don't mistake length for speed.

But Dave makes excellent use of the skating assets he does have, which are excellent balance and great strength on his feet. He goes to the net now more than ever before, and his strength and balance combine with his bulk to make him difficult — if not impossible — to budge from the crease. While his shot is good enough for him to score from anywhere, Andreychuk prefers an inside position near the net.

Andreychuk has a good, hard shot that is fairly accurate (how could he miss from two feet away?) and he makes great use of it by shooting more than anyone on the team. He particularly likes to use the backhand shot.

But though shooting frequently, Andreychuk still looks to use his teammates as best as he can. He is a good stickhandler and has excellent anticipation, making him a good passer. He sees openings for his teammates and gets the puck to them well. Of course, that anticipation helps him in his scoring too.

He is a good defensive player and pays attention to that aspect of the game, backchecking deeply in his own zone.

THE PHYSICAL GAME

Andreychuk won't clobber people, that's not his style. What he does is delicately place his bulk where it will do him the most good, and that's usually just in front of the opposing goaltender. His great size and strength have the added benefit of drawing penalties, because he's practically impossible to move legally.

His great strength comes to the fore not in the form of bashing people but in hand and arm strength. Andreychuk will get the puck away while people are draped all over him.

Andreychuk also puts his big wingspan to use around the net, first to gather in pucks (good hand and wrist strength helps here) and then to muscle a shot away despite checking.

Dave will use his size while checking and will rub out the opposition along the boards, but he won't knock anyone into the cheap seats.

THE INTANGIBLES

Andreychuk, Mike Foligno and Tom Barrasso were the three players responsible for turning around the fortunes of the team. Dave has become a big game player (six points in six playoff games, by the way) and he wants that responsibility. That's a sign of maturity.

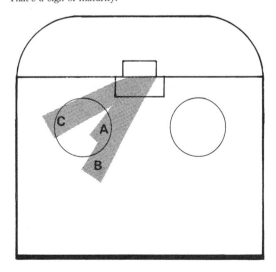

SCOTT ARNIEL

Yrs. of NHL service: 7
Born: Kingston, Ontario, Canada; September 19, 1960
Position: Right wing/left wing
Height: 6-1
Weight: 190
Uniform no.: 9
Shoots: left

Career statistics:

GP	G	A	TP	PIM
467	103	132	235	369

1987-88 statistics:

GP	G	A	TP	+/−	PIM	PP	SH	GW	GT	S	PCT
73	17	23	40	8	61	0	3	2	0	111	15.3

LAST SEASON

His plus/minus total was the team's second best, highest among forwards. He led the club in shorthanded goals and missed five games with an abdominal injury.

THE FINESSE GAME

What you see with Arniel is what you're going to get — maybe less. He's not an outstanding skater but does have speed and balance to offer. He doesn't put his skating to great use offensively, but it combines with his fair degree of understanding and anticipation to make him a very good penalty killer or checker.

That anticipation doesn't translate into offensive success because he doesn't have the hands to be a playmaker. He doesn't use his teammates well and isn't a scorer. He'll pick up 15-20 goals a year by crashing the net for rebounds, and by converting a handful of shorthanded opportunities.

He plays his position fairly well defensively and is not a liability in that regard.

THE PHYSICAL GAME

Arniel is inconsistent in the use of his size, and that's bad because he has the frame to play a physical game. Some nights he'll hit, others he'll push and shove. Some nights he won't go into the high density areas, others he does nothing except get trapped along the boards.

He has decent strength, but could certainly benefit from an upper body workout. Scott has not shown that he can effectively and consistently win the battles along the boards.

Yet when he plays a physical game, Arniel gets his best results, probably because he is more aware of what is going on around him as he hits and grinds away and attempts to avoid checks so he can make his plays.

In other words, when he keeps his head up, he can make plays. He will also sacrifice his body to block shots.

THE INTANGIBLES

He is a very hard worker and a very coachable player, but he is not a great player. Smartly, the Buffalo coaching staff used Arniel for what he could give the team and didn't set expectations he can't meet.

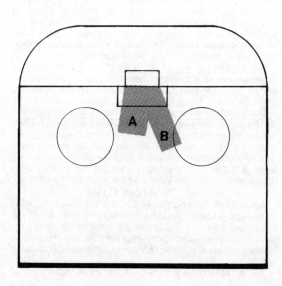

TOM BARRASSO

Yrs. of NHL service: 5
Born: Boston, Mass., USA; March 31, 1965
Position: Goaltender
Height: 6-3
Weight: 206
Uniform no.: 30
Catches: right

Career statistics:

GP	MINS	G	SO	AVG	A	PIM
256	14,918	800	13	3.21	14	161

1987-88 statisics:

GP	MINS	AVG	W	L	T	SO	GA	SA	SAPCT	PIM
54	3,133	3.31	25	18	8	2	173	1,658	.896	50

LAST SEASON

Barrasso finished fifth in the NHL in wins and third in save percentage. He finished eighth in games played and second among goalies for PIM. Games played total tied the second highest of his career, and his goals-against-average was the second best of his career. He missed a week of action during December with a hip injury.

THE PHYSICAL GAME

Barrasso is an excellent skater for a goaltender. He moves in and out of his net well and is very quick to recover his stance after leaving his feet. Because he is so fast, Barrasso is not as vulnerable to low shots as many taller goaltenders are.

Oddly, Barrasso plays more of a little man's game (in that he plays by reflex) than he does a big man's (which is to to stand up and challenge the shooter). He is challenging shooters and using every bit of his size to obstruct the goal. Tom also uses his size excellently when he butterflies to the ice, covering a lot of net with his long legs.

He handles the puck pretty well and will come out of his net to play it to a teammate, but Barrasso is weak in controlling rebounds. He is very prone to rebounds on saves that are off his stick and upper body, and has yet to learn what to do with the puck after making a pad save. He must either cover the rebounds off his pads or kick them to the corners.

Barrasso is betrayed by his inconsistent angle game when he loses his position on the ice and doesn't mark his short post. This makes him susceptible to shots on the short side, especially shots low to the ice. Greater confidence in his angle game would help Barrasso here.

THE MENTAL GAME

Because the new Sabre management told Barrasso he was their number one goaltender, Tom was more mentally prepared to play this season than previously. That helped his consistency from game to game, and within games themselves.

Barrasso has good concentration and anticipates well too. He'll fight you after a bad goal and, since Barrasso is confident in his abilities, so he's able to bounce back after a bad outing as well.

THE INTANGIBLES

We've taken runs at Barrasso because of his lack of maturity and his me-first attitude, so let us tell you a story now.

On Dec. 23, 1987, with Barrasso 3-7-4 on the season and the Sabres in fifth place and out of the playoff picture, Barrasso delivered a 5-2 win against Detroit in the Joe Louis Arena. The win is not the point. What is the point is that Tom, after a closed-door meeting that day with GM Gerry Meehan, said to himself, "It's time to put up or shut up."

And more important than that, this kid who had always had problems with his teammates came to the aid of teammate Kevin Maguire while he was fighting Detroit's Bob Probert. Even took a Probert punch in the head. And boy, did Barrasso send a message to his team with that effort.

That win started him on a 22-11-4 streak that led the Sabres to the playoffs for the first time in three seasons. Barrasso, Mike Foligno and Dave Andreychuk are the three responsible for turning Buffalo's season around, and in Tom's case new-found maturity was the reason.

He's more consistent now and he responds to the responsibility of being the number one goalie. He's improved his all-around effort and works harder in practice now too.

Quite a change. And while he's got five years of NHL experience. Barrasso is still only 23 years old. The Sabres wanted some consistency and leadership from him, and he delivered in a big way.

Now we just want to see him do it again.

JACQUES CLOUTIER

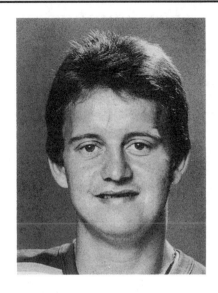

Yrs. of NHL service: 4
Born: Noranda, Quebec, Canada; January 3, 1960
Position: Goaltender
Height: 5-7
Weight: 169
Uniform no.: 1
Catches: left

Career statistics:

GP	MINS	G	SO	AVG	A	PIM
108	5,656	351	1	3.73	5	23

1987-88 statisics:

GP	MINS	AVG	W	L	T	SO	GA	SA	SAPCT	PIM
20	851	4.72	4	8	2	0	67	450	.850	11

LAST SEASON

Games played total was lowest in three seasons. Among NHL goaltenders who played at least 10 games, Cloutier's goals-against-average was the NHL's worst.

THE PHYSICAL GAME

Cloutier is a little guy and as such must be able to play his angles very well or else the league's better shooters will put the puck over his shoulder before he can blink. He is at his best when he stays on his feet.

But that doesn't mean he does that often. He scrambles, he flops, he's very helter-skelter. To play angles and challenge the shooters requires confidence, something that is not always in long supply for Cloutier.

He handles the puck fairly well and will come out of his net to stop the puck from rolling around the boards. He is not a terrific skater, moving in and out of his net a little sluggishly, and that leaves him susceptible on rebound shots and two-on-ones where he must regain his position quickly. His balance problems are another reason why he's always flopping around.

Cloutier has difficulty with shots low to the glove and short sides, both classic indications of failure to cut down the angle properly.

He is also very quick with his hands and feet, so he is successful in scrambles around the net.

THE MENTAL GAME

Cloutier folds his tent if reached early and a bad goal destroys his confidence. He doesn't carry bad games with him, but — because he is Tom Barrasso's backup and will not play many games in succession — Jacques will be rusty in his next start and the process is likely to start all over again.

THE INTANGIBLES

Cloutier is a tremendously hard worker in practice, always giving his best effort. He's a very quick goaltender but he can't sustain his performances because he's just not good enough at the NHL level.

ADAM CREIGHTON

Yrs. of NHL service: 3
Born: Burlington, Ontario, Canada; June 2, 1965
Position: Center
Height: 6-5
Weight: 216
Uniform no.: 38
Shoots: left

Career statistics:

GP	G	A	TP	PIM
149	33	50	83	152

1987-88 statistics:

GP	G	A	TP	+/−	PIM	PP	SH	GW	GT	S	PCT
36	10	17	27	7	87	4	0	1	0	61	16.4

LAST SEASON

Creighton missed 15 games with a shoulder injury and then the rest of the season with a knee injury. Games played total was still the second highest of his career.

THE FINESSE GAME

Skating is Creighton's weakness as a finesse player, and it might be his Waterloo following his knee injury. While he has agility and balance that's almost remarkable for a guy with his size and weight, Adam is handicapped by his lack of speed and quickness. He gets where he's going because of a long stride, but don't confuse the way he covers ground with speed. He's a decent skater at best.

Where he shows best is in his hand skills. Creighton handles the puck well in traffic and at his feet, and that's where his agility helps him; no one expects such shiftiness from a bigger man. He controls the puck well when he skates and makes his moves.

His anticipation and sense reveal the exploitable openings, but Adam's lack of speed leaves him hamstrung because he can't get to those holes or those loose pucks. He'll score his 20-25 goals a year from within 10 feet of the net, for while he has good hands for puck control his shot is not at the NHL level in terms of speed or release.

He tries to take advantage of his teammates, but that's difficult when he can't keep away from the opposition. His lack of speed makes Creighton no better than average defensively.

THE PHYSICAL GAME

Don't be deceived by his great size; Creighton is not a power forward. He is big and gangly, and would do well to beef himself up, because he is easily removed from the puck despite his balance; he's simply out-muscled. He also has no desire to impose himself physically on the opposition.

He has a good reach and he puts it to work well in snaring loose pucks along the boards or in traffic, but all told Creighton must be said to play smaller than his size — about two feet shorter.

THE INTANGIBLES

Two big ones. First, there's that knee injury and the subsequent rehabilitation. Let's see how that injury hurts Creighton's game. Second, every team in the League is interested in trading for him. The Sabres would love to have him in the lineup so he could develop, but he's not going to move beyond third-line — John Tucker and Christian Ruuttu are ahead of him.

Ted Sator has always seen something about Creighton he likes, and even went so far to push Phil Esposito to acquire him while Sator was with the Rangers. Still, if Creighton has a fairly good camp and good start to the season, don't be surprised if he finishes the year with another team.

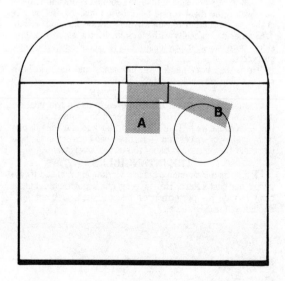

MIKE DONNELLY

Yrs. of NHL service: 1
Born: Detroit, Mich., USA; Ocotber 10, 1963
Position: Left wing
Height: 5-11
Weight: 185
Uniform no.: 16
Shoots: left

Career statistics:

GP	G	A	TP	PIM
62	9	11	20	52

1987-88 statistics:

GP	G	A	TP	+/−	PIM	PP	SH	GW	GT	S	PCT
57	8	10	18	-6	52	0	0	0	0	99	8.1

LAST SEASON

Donnelly was traded to Buffalo by the Rangers in exchange for Paul Cyr.

THE FINESSE GAME

Donnelly has good raw skills. He has tremendous speed and quickness and those traits get him to the puck before most of the other players on ice. It creates scoring opportunities for him, and Buffalo needs that scoring on left wing.

His hand skills are not as developed as his foot skills, and he has to work on finishing plays in the offensive zone. He plays fairly well defensively because he gets to those loose pucks and gets them out of the zone.

Mike looks to use his teammates when he can, but right now he concentrates on rocketing down the wing.

THE PHYSICAL GAME

He doesn't have good strength or size, so Donnelly will be over-matched along the boards and in traffic. He would benefit from better upper body strength.

THE INTANGIBLES

Mike is a good honest player, very coachable and with excellent work habits. He suffers because of his emotionalism, in that he takes bad games with him to the next game. Consistent efforts are important so he doesn't give his emotions the chance to kick in. The Sabre coaching staff will work with him to correct his faults and Donnelly is eager to learn.

Whether he can become a consistent NHLer is yet to be seen.

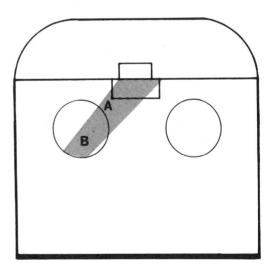

MIKE FOLIGNO

Yrs. of NHL service: 10
Born: Sudbury, Ontario, Canada; January 29, 1959
Position: Right wing
Height: 6-2
Weight: 195
Uniform no.: 17
Shoots: right

Career statistics:

GP	G	A	TP	PIM
683	278	295	573	1,500

1987-88 statistics:

GP	G	A	TP	+/−	PIM	PP	SH	GW	GT	S	PCT
74	29	28	57	-11	220	10	0	7	1	159	18.2

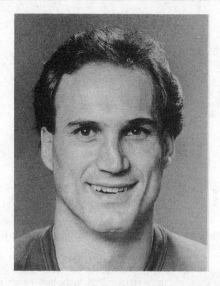

LAST SEASON

Games played total was lowest in five seasons, goal and point totals lowest in three seasons and assist mark lowest in four seasons. PIM total was a career high (it led the club) and Foligno led the club in game winners. His PPG total was the team's third best, his plus/minus total the second worst — worst among forwards. He missed five games with a back injury.

THE FINESSE GAME

Mike's skating style suits his straight ahead style of play. He's a hard skater, very strong and sturdy on his skates and with good acceleration up-ice. There isn't a lot of weaving or swirling in this body because Foligno's sturdinees and balance don't translate into agility. But since he's a power forward, that all right.

His anticipation and hockey sense are very good, and he uses those traits to set up his vicious wrist shot: strong, heavy and *very* accurate. Foligno can put the puck wherever he likes whenever he likes. He undercuts the effectiveness of his shot by not shooting enough.

Foligno is an excellent checker, determined and successful (so forget that plus/minus), and he is aided in that by his skating and anticipation; Foligno sees the play well defensively.

The same holds true offensively, but Foligno is a little tough with the puck and sometimes too strong with his passes. He does have the stick skills to defend the puck well when he has it and can carry it at top speed for big slap shot off the wing.

THE PHYSICAL GAME

The physical game is very much Foligno's game. He is a very aggressive forward and is extremely effective against the boards, using his bigger frame to hit hard and to jar the puck loose. What makes the hitting more effective is that Foligno also positions his body so that he can make a play after a hit, rather than just smashing an opponent.

He backs down from nothing and is an excellent fighter. His upper body strength, especially in his hands, wrists and forearms, power his shot and it is that strength that makes him so effective along the boards.

THE INTANGIBLES

Foligno, Andreychuk and Barrasso were the three players who turned the club around last year, and Foligno did it because of his work ethic. He is in tremendous physical shape for an older player and always comes to camp ready to play.

His attitude and work habits make him a team leader.

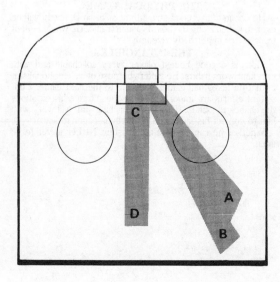

PHIL HOUSLEY

Yrs. of NHL service: 6
Born: St. Paul, Minn., USA; March 9, 1964
Position: Defenseman
Height: 5-11
Weight: 180
Uniform no.: 6
Shoots: left

Career statistics:

GP	G	A	TP	PIM
456	131	276	407	307

1987-88 statistics:

GP	G	A	TP	+/−	PIM	PP	SH	GW	GT	S	PCT
74	29	37	66	-17	96	6	0	1	1	231	12.6

LAST SEASON

Games played total was second lowest of his career, lowest in three seasons. Goal total was second highest of career, assist total a career low and point total tied career low. He led Sabre defensemen in scoring (sixth overall in NHL) and led the League's defenders in goals. He finished third in team scoring and second in shots on goal. His plus/minus rating was the club's worst. He missed five games with a back injury.

THE FINESSE GAME

There are world class players — the Gretzkys, Lemieuxs and Krutovs — and there are players just below that plateau. Phil Housley is on that second level, and we mean that as a compliment about his excellent skills.

He is an excellent skater, fluid in his stride and with great agility. He has tremendous acceleration, superb balance and quickness and excellent lateral movement.

Housley can handle the puck well and his rushing up-ice to relieve pressure on the forwards is a given. He does a good job of carrying the puck at full speed but he still shows a weakness in his mental playmaking skills. He goes 1-on-1 against the opposition's defense a lot, and that's more because he hasn't projected his next play than because of selfishness.

He's very smart about using his speed to drive the defensemen off the blue line, and Housley is a much better playmaker with the play in front of him — as on the power play — than to his side or behind him.

Housley does well on the power play unit, where he can put his speed and puckhandling ability to use, and he can score. He has a good wrist shot that he likes to deliver from the high slot and he can slap the puck well (quick, not heavy) from the point.

He forces many plays at the Buffalo blue line, and he can do that because he closes the gap on the puck carrier excellently. He has developed a better understanding of his defensive angles, and when he fails to play positionally his skating will bail him out.

That said, he still needs help defensively — as his plus/minus will attest.

THE PHYSICAL GAME

Housley has improved the tenor of his physical game over the course of the last two seasons and, while he won't bash anyone, Phil is more than dependable in front of his own net. He plays a much more determined physical game and takes body strongly in front of his net. He's shown a developing mean streak too.

The combination of strength and finesse is a potent one, for when Housley takes an opponent off the puck in the corner he not only turns the play around but makes the transition an instantaneous one.

THE INTANGIBLES

Housley's season last year began with great expectations, as he notched the 10 fastest goals ever by an NHL defensemen (10 in the first 15 games). Perhaps signing a new contract in August of 1987 had something to do with that.

But again, consistency is the problem here. Thirteen goals in the first 20 games, three in the next 17, nine in the next 19 and just four in the last 18 games — and of those four just three at even strength.

We repeat what we said last year. Though he is a player of fine talent, his inability to consistently harness that talent makes him an underachiever.

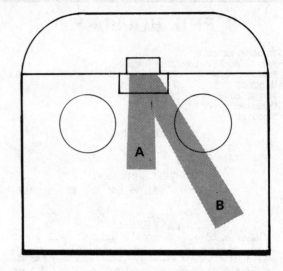

CALLE JOHANSSON

Yrs. of NHL service: 1
Born: Goteborg, Sweden; February 14, 1967
Position: Defenseman
Height: 5-11
Weight: 198
Uniform no.: 3

Career statisics:

GP	G	A	TP	+/−	PIM	PP	SH	GW	GT	S	PCT
71	4	38	42	12	37	2	0	0	0	93	4.3

LAST SEASON

Johansson's NHL premier. He led the club in plus/minus, finished 10th in scoring among league rookies (second in assists). He finished third on the squad in assists.

THE FINESSE GAME

Johansson's poise is the best of his finesse skills. Thrust into the lineup because of injuries among the defensive corps, Johansson showed good patience and decision making in the defensive zone.

He's strong and quick, which is a not-always-usual combination. He has good speed and quickness on his feet, and that speed allows him to get the puck and look over his options before making a play.

Calle passes very well, and he does so because of his good hands and ice vision. He shoots well from the point, but not as frequently as he should. He contains the offensive play well and is especially effective on the power play, where he easily finds the open man and gets the puck to him.

His defensive game is marked by the same smarts. Johansson closes the gap well on the puck carrier and turns the play up-ice well.

THE PHYSICAL GAME

Calle has good strength and he uses that strength well defensively. He's good in the corners and takes the body well when he can. He covers the front of the net fairly well.

THE INTANGIBLES

Johansson showed well in his rookie year, and he has the potential to improve his game and become an above-average NHL player. He was used in all situations last year, and that indicates the Sabres' confidence in him.

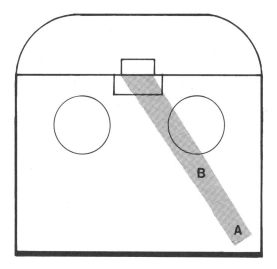

UWE KRUPP

Yrs. of NHL service: 2
Born: Cologne, West Germany; June 24, 1965
Position: Defenseman
Height: 6-6
Weight: 230
Uniform no.: 40
Shoots: right

Career statistics:

GP	G	A	TP	PIM
101	3	13	16	174

1987-88 statistics:

GP	G	A	TP	+/−	PIM	PP	SH	GW	GT	S	PCT
75	2	9	11	-1	151	0	0	0	0	84	2.4

LAST SEASON

Krupp's first full NHL season. He was the team's lowest scoring regular. His PIM total was second highest among defensemen.

THE FINESSE GAME

Krupp is a very skilled player with good NHL potential. He skates and handles the puck well, though he's not a rushing defenseman. He makes fairly good decisions with the puck in his own zone and plays a fairly steady defensive game by playing positionally.

All of his skills are good but would benefit from improvement in quickness, as the NHL game is generally too fast paced for Krupp. Still, he is catching up to major league speed.

THE PHYSICAL GAME

Krupp is not a basher, though he's not afraid to be involved physically. His size and bulk immediately brings board-breaking checks to mind, but that's not his game. He is very similar in style to Philadelphia's under-rated Kjell Samuelsson, in that they both play efficiently and unspectacularly. Krupp takes the body well and then moves the puck up-ice.

THE INTANGIBLES

Experience is the biggest intangible in Krupp's case but, like other Sabre youngsters who have benefitted from the club's decision to go with youth, he's sure to get that experience in the seasons to come.

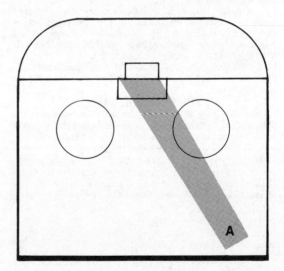

MARK NAPIER

Yrs. of NHL service: 10
Born: Toronto, Ontario, Canada; January 28, **1957** Position:
Right wing Height:
5-10 Weight:
185 Uniform no.:
65 Shoots:
left

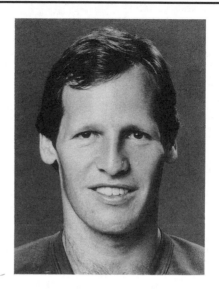

Career statistics:

GP	G	A	TP	PIM
701	224	289	513	124

1987-88 statistics:

GP	G	A	TP	+/−	PIM	PP	SH	GW	GT	S	PCT
47	10	8	18	-3	8	0	1	2	0	81	12.3

LAST SEASON
Games played total and all point marks were career lows.

THE FINESSE GAME
Mark is near the end of the road, but his great speed keeps him around for spot duty on the specialty teams. He remains an excellent skater, equipped with a good burst of speed, excellent acceleration ability and good agility. He'll turn the juice up now and again, dip his shoulder and cut past the opposition. His good balance is why he moves well laterally.

His puck handling ability is another reason why he'll see power play or penalty killing duty. Mark handles the puck well at all speeds, and his deking and diving serve to keep the passing lanes open on the power play or to kill time when penalty killing.

Though he still shoots and holds the puck well, Napier is nowhere near his 40-goal seasons. He doesn't waste his opportunities and puts a hard and accurate shot on net. He will score most of his goals from wihin the slot area.

Napier's speed lets him hold his own defensively. He comes back with his check and plays a good positional game.

THE PHYSICAL GAME
During the days of his goal scoring, Napier's hand and his wrist strength powered his shot and keyed his finesse game. It allowed him to reach into the pileups from the outside and come away with the puck. No more. The opposition is too big and too strong.

Mark will play a physical game when he can, but his best work has always been in open ice. Since he's used for his speed, it's unlikely he'll be found along the boards with any regularity.

THE INTANGIBLES
He's got an excellent work ethic, but that can't keep him from aging. He'll probably be unprotected in the Waiver Draft.

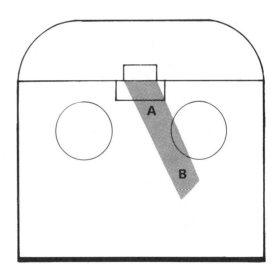

KEN PRIESTLAY

Yrs. of NHL service: 2
Born: Vancouver, B.C., Canada; August 24, 1967
Position: Center
Height: 5-10
Weight: 175
Uniform no.: 12
Shoots: left

Career statistics:

GP	G	A	TP	PIM
67	16	18	34	43

1987-88 statistics:

GP	G	A	TP	+/-	PIM	PP	SH	GW	GT	S	PCT
33	5	12	17	-4	35	1	1	0	0	63	7.9

LAST SEASON

Games played and goal totals fell in second season, while assist total rose and point total stayed the same. He split time between Buffalo and the American Hockey League.

THE FINESSE GAME

Speed and quickness are the hallmarks of Priestlay's skating game. Priestlay has excellent speed over the long-haul and one-step quickness that's just as good. Ken is also an agile player and can jump into the openings he finds.

He has good hockey sense and is good at finding the holes and understanding what's going on around him. He needs more time to develop his other skills so he cannot take as great an advantage of those openings as he'd like in terms of playmaking, passing and so on.

He does not have an NHL shot, mostly because he cannot control the puck as well as he'd like at the NHL speed. Any goals he'll get at this point will come from close to the net.

Priestlay is fairly conscientious defensively, playing his position well. He's also able to use his speed to bail him out if he does make a defensive mistake.

THE PHYSICAL GAME

Priestlay has never been a particularly physical player, but he is willing to take his knocks if need be. He doesn't have great NHL size, and so he will be forced off the puck if caught along the boards. He would do well to increase his upper body strength for those battles in the trenches.

THE INTANGIBLES

Priestlay was forced into the lineup because of injuries to Tucker and Creigton, and he's clearly not ready to contribute full-time in the NHL. The coaching staff likes him, and he'll be given ample opportunity to prove himself.

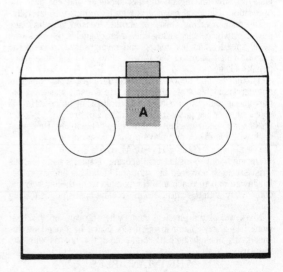

MIKE RAMSEY

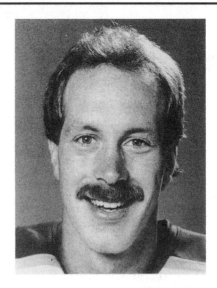

Yrs. of NHL service: 8
Born: Minneapolis, Minn., USA; December 3, 1960
Position: Defenseman
Height: 6-3
Weight: 185
Uniform no.: 5
Shoots: left

Career statistics:

GP	G	A	TP	PIM
612	56	185	241	660

1987-88 statistics:

GP	G	A	TP	+/−	PIM	PP	SH	GW	GT	S	PCT
63	5	16	21	6	77	1	0	0	0	94	5.3

LAST SEASON

Games played total was a full season career low (groin injury, three games with a concussion and an eight-game suspension for high sticking). All point totals were second lowest of his career, lowest in seven seasons. His plus/minus total was second best among defensemen.

THE FINESSE GAME

Great instincts and just plain brains are the keys to Ramsey's game, and they are the reasons why he's a perennial All Star candidate. He very rarely makes a bad decision in the defensive end of the ice because he reads the play — whether defensively as it moves toward him or offensively as it moves away — so well. Those instincts are doubly important in Buffalo, where Ramsey has less time than usual to make decisions because of the smaller rink.

His anticipation and sense tell him what to do after he has the puck or after he has made a takeout. Ramsey is not a one-play defenseman; he's right back into the action following anything he does. He is an excellent positional player who understands his defensive angles and plays them almost to perfection.

His smarts allow Ramsey to make the most of his unexceptional skating skills. Don't get us wrong — Ramsey is not a bad skater by any means. Rather, his consistent defensive play and positioning strength always puts him in the right place at the right time, and that asset is frequently attributed to skating.

In Ramsey's case, he is able to skate forward or backward equally well and he is strong on his turns. Mike passes the puck from his zone very well, but he can carry the puck to take pressure off his forwards. He'll never overhandle the puck.

Ramsey is not considered an offensive force and will score 7-10 goals a year on a good low shot (with more than a little power) from the right point.

THE PHYSICAL GAME

Mike is a physical player and he is very tough in front of his own net. He'll take most anyone off the puck along the boards and is always in position to make a play after he has gained the puck.

He is also a good open-ice checker. Ramsey keeps you honest; you don't make any plays with your head down when he's around. Mike is also willing to sacrifice his body to block shots, and is one of the league's best in that category.

That penchant for shot blocking is indirectly his only weakness, for he takes himself out of the play by going down to block the puck. His physical play has been amplified by his ability to stay generally healthy.

THE INTANGIBLES

He's smart, he works hard, he plays in pain. While his numbers don't equal Phil Housley's, Mike Ramsey is still Buffalo's best defenseman.

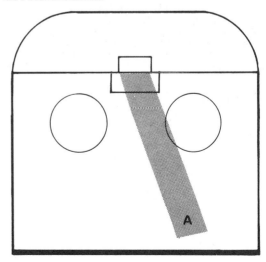

JOE REEKIE

Yrs. of NHL service: 2
Born: Petawawa, Ontario, Canada; February 22, 1965
Position: Defenseman
Height: 6-3
Weight: 215
Uniform no.: 27
Shoots: left

Career statistics:

GP	G	A	TP	PIM
89	2	12	14	164

1987-88 statistics:

GP	G	A	TP	+/–	PIM	PP	SH	GW	GT	S	PCT
30	1	4	5	-3	68	0	0	0	0	23	4.3

LAST SEASON

Suffered a separated shopulder during training camp and missed four games, then suffered a knee injury November 15 and didn't return until February 14.

THE FINESSE GAME

Joe is an average skater, possessing good balance and foot speed as well as a small snap of speed over the long haul. He also has a long stride, so he covers ground quickly. Still, his skating is just average at the NHL level and it must be improved for him to improve as a player.

Because of his less-than-exceptional skating Reekie has had to learn to play defense positionally, and he's learned well. He ably forces the play wide of the net, and also reads the play at the blue line and thwarts it there.

Joe shows good poise when handling the puck in the defensive zone, making the quick and correct pass to get the puck out of danger. Because he's concerned with his defensive responsibilities he is not a threat at the offensive blue line.

THE PHYSICAL GAME

Reekie is a tremendous body checker. He has good strength and he uses it well along the boards or in front of the net to out-muscle the opposition and force them off the puck.

Joe uses his size to force the play wide of the net and is difficult to get around. He also uses his reach effectively in pokechecking at the blue line.

THE INTANGIBLES

A full season's worth of play is what Reekie needs, and what the Sabres need from him. He's shown well in his infrequent stints, and he has the potential to be a solid NHL defenseman.

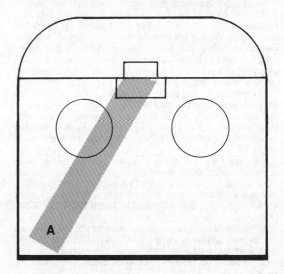

LINDY RUFF

Yrs. of NHL service: 9
Born: Warburg, Alta., Canada; February 17, 1960
Position: Left wing
Height: 6-2
Weight: 196
Uniform no.: 22
Shoots: left

Career statistics:

GP	G	A	TP	PIM
545	96	172	268	1,040

1987-88 statistics:

GP	G	A	TP	+/−	PIM	PP	SH	GW	GT	S	PCT
77	2	23	25	-9	179	0	0	0	0	106	1.9

LAST SEASON

Games played total was second highest of his career, highest in six seasons. Goal total was a career low while assist total was four-season high. PIM total was secnd highest of career, highest in six seasons. He finished second on the club in PIM.

THE FINESSE GAME

As a finesse player, Ruff isn't. He's never been better than average as a skater, and nine tough seasons and their attendant injuries have slowed Ruff down. He just cruises up and down the ice.

Ruff isn't a good puckhandler but that's all right, because he doesn't know what to do with the puck anyway. He has little vision of the ice or his teammates, and less anticipation for possible plays. If he wins the puck during a foray into the corner, the best Ruff will do with it is the blind pass to the slot.

His shot is consistent with his other finesse skills, and he's unlikely to score from any place other than the edge of the goal crease by shovelling home rebounds and other garbage.

Lindy is a conscientious back checker, very concerned with his defensive play and disciplined enough to stay on his wing and not create any openings by leaving the zone too soon. He is aided in his defensive play by his experience as a defenseman and understands what angles are all about so as to keep his man from the puck.

THE PHYSICAL GAME

Ruff is.

He's big and strong and uses that strength to bang around in the corners and jar the puck loose from opposing defensemen. He doesn't have the skills to make a play out of the corner, so his physical game is one-dimensional in that regard.

Ruff also uses his strength to wreak havoc in front of the opposition goal, daring a defenseman to move him from the crease. He is aggressive and will take pokes at people when he has to stand up for the team. Lindy also applies himself physically in the defensive zone, where he will rub out an opposing winger along the boards.

His injury record is a direct result of his play, rather than an indication of any fragility on his part. Ruff counters the injury problem by staying in great condition.

THE INTANGIBLES

Ruff is a great team player, and he knows when it's necessary to assume leadership in the lockerroom or on the ice so as to produce the best effect for the club.

Ruff also helps himself stay around through his versatility, his ability to play either forward or defense as required. Hard work is all he knows.

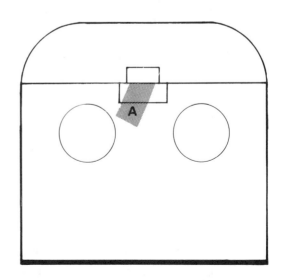

CHRISTIAN RUUTTU

Yrs. of NHL service: 2
Born: Lappeenranta, Finland; February 20, 1964
Position: Center
Height: 5-11
Weight: 180
Uniform no.: 21
Shoots: left

Career statistics:

GP	G	A	TP	PIM
149	48	88	136	147

1987-88 statistics:

GP	G	A	TP	+/-	PIM	PP	SH	GW	GT	S	PCT
73	26	45	71	-3	85	8	1	4	0	185	14.1

LAST SEASON

Games played total fell from rookie season (he missed seven games with a knee injury) but all point totals rose. He finished second on the club in scoring and assists. He finished third in plus/minus among fulltime forwards, fourth among all regulars.

THE FINESSE GAME

Ruutu is well on his way toward an outstanding NHL career, and his excellent skating ability is the reason why. He has excellent speed, quickness and acceleration, plus a change of pace to make those assets all the more valuable. He drives the defensemen off the blue line with that speed. His gear shift and excellent balance give him excellent agility and lateral movement, and he uses those skills to great effect on his inside (rather than outside speed) work.

What makes his speed even more impressive is his ability to generate the play in his own zone and move up-ice with the puck. There aren't many centers who have to be checked in their own zones, but Ruutu's speed makes that imperative.

Ruutu's stick skills match his skating skills and that means he can carry the puck *and* make his plays at top speed, always an asset. He sees the ice well and makes excellent use of his teammates, making his plays with his head up in order to take advantage of the open man.

Excellent hockey sense and anticipation go along with that vision, so Christian can create an opening for himself (using his quickness and vision), or make an opening for a teammate with a pass. He is a very creative offensive player and that makes itself apparent on the power play, where Ruutu makes good use of the extra open ice.

He drives a quick and accurate wrist/snap shot at the goalie and, because he rarely shoots from outside the slot area, his shots are usually high percentage plays.

He uses his speed and sense to play a very good defensive game.

THE PHYSICAL GAME

Like Tomas Samdstrom, Ulf Samuelsson and Esa Tikkanen, Ruutu's physical play irritates the opposition. For a guy without great size Ruutu is pretty tough, and he's unafraid of the corners or physical play. He hits when he can and his physical willingness amplifies his finesse game.

His excellent balance comes into play in the physical game, keeping him upright and in the play after collisions. The strength of Christian's game is obviously in the finesse quarter, but his finesse game is aided by his willingness to play physically and to sacrifice his body when necessary.

THE INTANGIBLES

Ruutu's second year success, and improvement on his first year's numbers, speaks volumes. The second year, when a player no longer sneaks up on the opposition, is always a difficult season, but Christian practically breezed through it.

He's much more confident and comfortable with the NHL pace, and his mental toughness — that ability to stay prepared to play while adapting to the schedule, and injury, and the pace and so on — is superb.

The best is still to come with this young man. He's a solid all-around player, and further experience will only make his good points better.

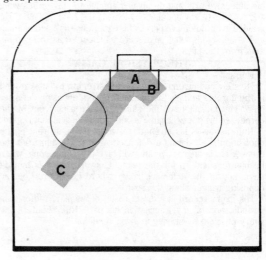

RAY SHEPPARD

Yrs. of NHL service: 1
Born: Pembroke, Ontario, Canada; May 27, 1966
Position: Right wing
Height: 6-1
Weight: 206
Uniform no.: 23
Shoots: right

Career statisics:

GP	G	A	TP	+/−	PIM	PP	SH	GW	GT	S	PCT
74	38	27	65	-6	14	15	0	5	2	173	22.0

LAST SEASON

Sheppard finished second in League-wide scoring among rookies. He was second in goals, power play goals and first goals, third in game winners, shots on goal and shooting percentage. He led in game-tying goals. He finished fourth on the club in scoring, but first in goals. He tied for the team lead in power play goals and he led the Sabres in game-tying scores and shooting percentage.

THE FINESSE GAME

Sheppard is a natural goal scorer. He has a nose for the net that's very reminiscent of Phil Esposito at his best. Espo could be looking in the stands and score — he just *knew* where the opening was — and Sheppard is the same way.

Ray shares another of Espo's traits, good hands. Sheppard has tremendously soft hands and he can finesse three inches of puck into two inches of space. His release of the puck is exceptional, very quick. He shoots off the pass very well and is a natural slot scorer. And like Espo, Sheppard gets many shots away during the game.

His skating is very questionable, but his shot and goal scoring ability are good enough to cover for him until his skating improves (which it will do almost by default as he continues playing in the NHL).

His playmaking and defensive skills are adequate and could stand improvement.

THE PHYSICAL GAME

Sheppard has good size but he uses it passively, making himself a target for the defense while in front of the net. He should begin muscling some of those defensemen, bumping them a little bit so as to earn some more space.

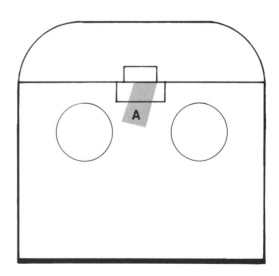

THE INTANGIBLES

Sheppard gave the first indications he could score in the NHL during the American Hockey League playoffs two seasons ago, when he scored 12 goals in 15 games.

Scoring will be tougher for Sheppard this time around, as the goaltenders will be more aware of his ability and will anticipate his shots. He's also going to see much tighter checking this season than he did last year.

DOUG SMITH

Yrs. of NHL service: 7
Born: Ottawa, Ontario, Canada; May 17, 1963
Position: Center
Height: 5-11
Weight: 185
Uniform no.: 15
Shoots: right

Career statistics:

GP	G	A	TP	PIM
466	107	128	235	514

1987-88 statistics:

GP	G	A	TP	+/−	PIM	PP	SH	GW	GT	S	PCT
70	9	19	28	-10	117	1	0	0	0	136	6.6

LAST SEASON

Goal total was a career low. He finished sixth on the club in SOG, and his PIM total was a career high.

THE FINESSE GAME

If speed was skating then Smith would be an excellent skater. He is very fast on his feet — and that includes both rink-length speed and one-step quickness — but he's consistent in his inconsistency. He has yet to learn that he must use his speed all the time in order to be effective, for that is his best weapon.

He is not as agile as he could be, and Smith has worked with a figure skater to learn how to cut to the net without sacrificing any of his speed.

Doug's hand and mental skills don't come up to the ability he has in his feet. He does handle the puck well when he carries it, but he really has no aim in mind when he's racing up-ice — except to beat the defense to the other end of the rink. Ilis hands are good enough for him to move the puck well to his teammates, but that's only if he sees them.

Because there isn't a lot of anticipation or hockey sense behind his plays, Doug tends to make a play and then have no idea what to do. He is not particularly good at spotting the openings on the ice and consequently is not a big goal scorer.

Smith will score from the slot or the hashmarks of the faceoff circles, but he doesn't have the power to rocket the puck past a goaltender.

THE PHYSICAL GAME

Without bowling anyone over, Smith will play an aggressive style. Doug will take a hit to make a play or vice versa, but is more effective in open ice.

He's shown tendency toward injury in his career, and it's ironic that he will have to battle back from an off-season injury just to be prepared for possible in-season injuries.

THE INTANGIBLES

While he works hard at improving his game (the figure skating bit is a good example of that), Smith is only slightly above being a role player. He suffered a shoulder injury (and subsequently underwent surgery) during the summer, and he'll have to rehabilitate — and prove — himself this fall.

But even if he comes back healthy his position with the team is a tenuous one. His ice-time shrank as last season went on, and Smith played just one playoff game while rookie Pierre Turgeon awakened. There's a good chance that Smith will be somewhere other than Buffalo this winter.

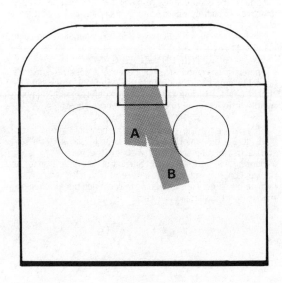

JOHN TUCKER

Yrs. of NHL service: 5
Born: Windsor, Ontario, Canada; September 29, 1964
Position: Center
Height: 6-0
Weight: 193
Uniform no.: 7
Shoots: right

Career statistics:

GP	G	A	TP	PIM
259	101	118	219	105

1987-88 statistics:

GP	G	A	TP	+/-	PIM	PP	SH	GW	GT	S	PCT
45	19	19	38	4	20	6	0	0	1	93	20.4

LAST SEASON

Games played total was a full season career low (he missed 15 games with a knee injury and then a month-and-a-half with a shoulder separation). Point total was also a full season career low.

THE FINESSE GAME

There are some players who don't seem to be much to write home about — until you see them regularly. Because his finesse skills are of the quiet variety, John Tucker is unfortunately lumped into this category. But his talent should really be labeled first class, special delivery.

What Tucker has — and why it is so difficult to see — is outstanding anticipation. He sees the openings excellently and he combines his anticipation and excellent vision with his superior hand skills to exploit those openings in a number of ways.

John makes great passes to both sides, on target and easy to handle. While he can always find the open man, he also has the capability to lead his teammates into the openings.

When he chooses to exploit the openings himself, Tucker applies excellent puckhandling in conjunction with his excellent one-step quickness, an outstanding burst in any direction. He is not fast in the long haul, but since he gets what amounts to a head start in his race up-ice, Tucker doesn't need all out speed. With that ability, Tucker is able to slide away from checks and slip away from his man quickly to get clear.

He uses that troika of skills (hands, feet and brains) to great effect around the opposition net, and Tucker needs only the slightest opening to finesse the puck home. He also has the strength to score from farther out.

Those skills also make him a regular on both specialty teams.

THE PHYSICAL GAME

Tucker wouldn't be called a physical player, in that he doesn't impose himself on the opposition. Don't think he's intimidated though, because that's not the case. Tucker willingly goes to the traffic areas and takes whatever abuse is necessary for him to make his plays.

THE INTANGIBLES

It is quite within Tucker's character as a player to score four goals in a game, as he did last spring against the Bruins in the Adams Division semifinals. He is a hard working center and a full season would go a long way toward dispelling the cloud of anonymity he works under.

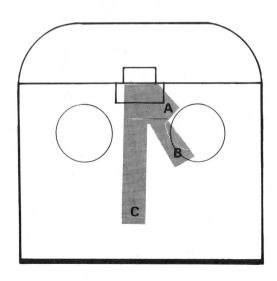

PIERRE TURGEON

Yrs. of NHL service: 1
Born: Rouyn, Quebec, Canada; August 29, 1969
Position: Center
Height: 6-1
Weight: 200
Uniform no.: 77
Shoots: left

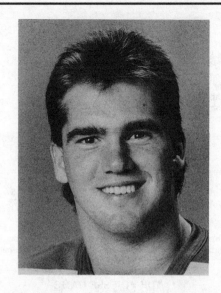

Career statisics:

GP	G	A	TP	+/−	PIM	PP	SH	GW	GT	S	PCT
76	14	28	42	-8	34	8	0	3	0	101	13.9

LAST SEASON

Turgeon was Buffalo's first pick in the 1987 Entry Draft. He finished ninth in rookie scoring.

THE FINESSE GAME

Turgeon is not a flashy or fancy finesse player. He does have great speed and acceleration because of his very strong stride, but the strength of his game is in his stickhandling and anticipation skills — the playmaking game.

He has great ice vision and hockey sense, and he uses those abilities to put him in the clear for shots himself or to lead teammates to the openings with excellent passes. Pierre easily finds the open man and passes to him well.

Turgeon shoots the puck very well and he has excellent shot selection to choose from. He uses his sense to get into scoring position, and all his skills improve in the open ice of the power play.

THE PHYSICAL GAME

Opponents have to respect Turgeon's size, and he has good strength to match it. He's not a banger or a power forward, but he goes to the traffic areas to score. He takes checks to make his plays and he uses his body very well to protect the puck.

Pierre controls the puck well with his feet, and his good hand and arm strength make him a good faceoff man.

THE INTANGIBLES

The Sabres have smartly done everything in their power to keep the pressure off Turgeon. They know how young he is and they don't want him burdened with extra pressure.

He showed relatively well during the season, but shone in the playoffs when he finished second on the team in scoring. Buffalo has to be encouraged by that.

It is still way too early to declare what kind of player Turgeon will be, and this season will go a long way toward determining that fact, but he's given good indications of his talent and ability to play in difficult situations.

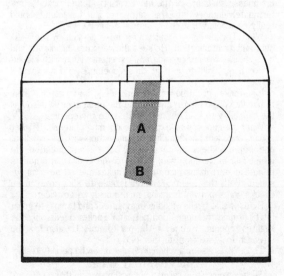

CALGARY FLAMES

LINE COMBINATIONS
COLIN PATTERSON-JOE NIEUWENDYK-HAKAN LOOB
JIM PEPLINSKI-MIKE BULLARD-JOE MULLEN
TIM HUNTER-JOEL OTTO

DEFENSE PAIRINGS
GARY SUTER-BRAD MCCRIMMON
BRIAN GLYNN-DANA MURZYN
-AL MACINNIS

GOALTENDERS
MIKE VERNON
RICK WAMSLEY

OTHER PLAYERS
PERRY BEREZAN — Center
CRAIG COXE — Left wing
LANNY MCDONALD — Right wing
RIC NATTRESS — Defenseman
ROB RAMAGE — Defenseman
PAUL REINHART — Defenseman
GARY ROBERTS — Left wing
JOHN TONELLI — Left wing

POWER PLAY

FIRST UNIT:
HAKAN LOOB-JOE NIEUWENDYK-MIKE BULLARD
GARY SUTER-AL MACINNIS

SECOND UNIT:
TIM HUNTER-JOEL OTTO-JOE MULLEN

On the first unit NIEUWENDYK goes to the front of the net and LOOB and BULLARD assume identical positions in the left and right faceoff circles respectively. Those two play catch with SUTER and MACINNIS at the points until the pointmen can get clear for a shot. LOOB and BULLARD then crash the net.

OTTO takes NIEUWENDYK's place in unit two, with MULLEN and HUNTER filling in for LOOB and BULLARD. SUTER and MACINNIS play the entire two minutes, but GLYNN and RAMAGE will also see some time.

Last season the Calgary power play was EXCELLENT, collecting 109 goals in 383 extra man situations (28.5 percent, first overall).

PENALTY KILLING

FIRST UNIT:
JOE NIEUWENDYK-HAKAN LOOB
GARY SUTER-BRAD MCCRIMMON

The Flames primary penalty killing unit is very aggressive, with all but MCCRIMMON pressuring the puck at the points and in deep. NIEUWENDYK and LOOB go for shorthanded goals and SUTER will move up to support a forecheck by his forwards. MCCRIMMON is the safety valve, but he will join the play if possession is gained in the offensive zone.

When healthy, BEREZAN is also a penalty killing regular. Otherwise, a number of players rotate through the penalty killing chores.

Last season Calgary's penalty killing was GOOD, allowing just 94 goals in 480 shorthanded situations (80.4 percent, ninth overall).

CRUCIAL FACEOFFS

JOEL OTTO is the guy for these while protecting the lead and in the defensive zone, while NIEUWENDYK and BULLARD will take offensive zone draws.

PERRY BEREZAN

Yrs. of NHL service: 3
Born: Edmonton, Alta., Canada; December 5, 1964
Position: Center
Height: 6-2
Weight: 190
Uniform no.: 21
Shoots: right

Career statistics:

GP	G	A	TP	PIM
117	27	38	65	133

1987-88 statistics:

GP	G	A	TP	+/−	PIM	PP	SH	GW	GT	S	PCT
29	7	12	19	11	66	0	2	1	0	69	10.1

LAST SEASON

Games played total was second lowest of his career, courtesy of a recurring groin injury. He also missed time with a hand injury. PIM total was a career high.

THE FINESSE GAME

When he is healthy, Berezan is an excellent skater. He has great speed, agility and quickness and is also a strong, tireless skater. He combines that skating skill with superb puck smarts and anticipation and vision to be an excellent penalty killer and checker.

He reads the play very well and can use that ability as a play maker, where he can also put his good hands to work. He would be more of a playmaker than a scorer, because Perry's shot is not outstanding. He does have a touch around the net and the strength to score from a little farther away, but Perry's goals will usually be few and far between.

THE PHYSICAL GAME

Berezan has good size and he can take the rough going in the corners, along the boards or in front of the net. He'll initiate contact in those areas and is unafraid to work in those high-traffic areas.

Perry needs to improve his upper body strength in order to be more effective in those traffic situations, but any improvement will be fruitless unless Berezan can become less injury prone.

He is constantly out of action because of his injuries, injuries that he gets simply from running into people.

THE INTANGIBLES

We told you last year that Berezan's health is the biggest question in his career. Since he's entering the option year of his contract, it would behoove him to have a healthy season. Otherwise, despite his great potential Perry may be sent packing.

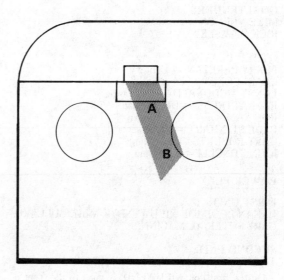

MIKE BULLARD

Yrs. of NHL service: 8
Born: Ottawa, Ontario, Canada; March 10, 1961
Position: Center
Height: 5-10
Weight: 183
Uniform no.: 25
Shoots: left

Career statistics:

GP	G	A	TP	PIM
518	261	256	517	490

1987-88 statistics:

GP	G	A	TP	+/−	PIM	PP	SH	GW	GT	S	PCT
79	48	55	103	25	68	21	0	3	2	230	20.9

LAST SEASON

Games played total was career high, as were assist and point totals. Goal total was second highest of career, and Bullard finished second on the club in scoring (second in power play goals, third in goals, fourth in assists). His SOG total was the team's second highest, first among forwards, and his shooting percentage was the team's third best. He finished as the NHL's 11th best scorer. He missed one game with a leg injury.

THE FINESSE GAME

Speed and acceleration mark Bullard's game, and they power him as a finesse player. He'll beat many opponents with his speed to the outside, and his balance helps him make his cuts around those defenders. Bullard is a very agile player, possessing great foot speed and lateral movement. That's where he benefits from his balance.

Mike's hockey sense and scorer's anticipation complement his fine skating skill. His vision and sense show him the openings and his speed gets him to them. These skills make him a natural for specialty teams play, but they are far from the only skills Bullard has.

Bullard is also a good passer, a skill he's made better use of in Calgary (because he has more skilled teammates) than he did in Pittsburgh — where he often had to work on his own. Mike applies his sense and sensitive hands to his passing, leading teammates with accuracy and good timing. His puck-handling is good, certainly good enough to keep up with his skating, but his goal scoring ability — his ability to get into scoring position — is excellent.

Mike shoots off the pass very well, especially on his off wing. Both his slap shot and wrist shot are effective weapons.

Defensively, Bullard has learned to play positional hockey and will stay with his check into the Calgary zone.

THE PHYSICAL GAME

He is not a physical guy himself, but Bullard will take his punishment to make his plays. He has good strength and uses it shrug off defenders along the boards, and he also uses his body very well to shield the puck. Mike is also taking the body more — at both ends — than he has previously, but he is not a crushing hitter.

THE INTANGIBLES

We told you last year that Bullard, because of his improved attitude toward a team game, would have a career year in 1987-88. The maturity he demonstrated by becoming a team player is the reason why. He's got the capabilities to hit the 100-point plateau again. But, since Calgary as a team had a career year, some fall-off is not only expected but unavoidable.

In his favor, Bullard scored at a fairly consistent rate last year (26g-53 points in first 43 games, 48-103 total), but almost 50 percent of his goals came on the power play; a better balance between ESG and PPG is needed.

And again, like many of the Flames, Bullard four games, one assist) needs to redeem himself following last spring's playoff humiliation suffered at the hands of the Oilers (four games, one assist).

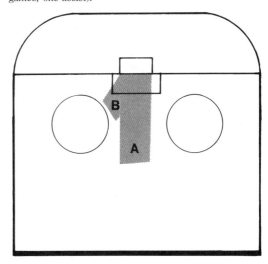

CRAIG COXE

Yrs. of NHL service: 3
Born: Chula Vista, Calif., USA; January 21, 1964
Position: Center
Height: 6-4
Weight: 185
Uniform no.: 18
Shoots: left

Career statistics:

GP	G	A	TP	PIM
152	11	20	31	474

1987-88 statistics:

GP	G	A	TP	+/−	PIM	PP	SH	GW	GT	S	PCT
71	7	15	22	2	218	1	0	1	0	48	14.6

LAST SEASON

Coxe was acquired from Vancouver late in the year in exchange for Brian Bradley. All of his totals were career highs. He finished fourth on the club in PIM.

THE FINESSE GAME

Coxe is a good skater, strong on his skates and with a lot of balance. That serves him well in his physical game.

He isn't an offensive threat because he neither sees the ice very well nor has the hand skills to exploit the openings he stumbles into. He doesn't handle the puck well when carrying it and doesn't move it to his teammates well either. Any goals he gets will have to come from loose pucks in front of the net and with plenty of time and an open net in front of him.

He plays fairly well defensively because he plays conscientiously and is aware of his check. His positional play is flawed, however, and he has a tendency to wander.

THE PHYSICAL GAME

Coxe is very aggressive and very strong, and he uses his strength and size to create havoc around the opposition net and to pound opposition troublemakers.

He is a good hitter and does so at every opportunity. Because of his strength he can neutralize the defenseman in front of the enemy net. He has good balance and comes out of most collisions vertical and ready to belt someone again.

He is also a good and willing fighter, and is aided by his good reach in winning more than his share of scraps.

THE INTANGIBLES

Coxe has tremendous heart and is a solid team man, fighting the battles that have to be fought. Coxe also works very hard at improving his skills so as to shed the goon label his play carries.

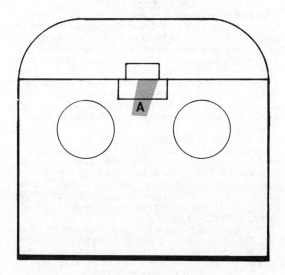

BRIAN GLYNN

Yrs. of NHL service: 1
Born: Iserlohn, West Germany; November 23, 1967
Position: Defenseman
Height: 6-4
Weight: 225
Uniform no.: 32
Shoots: left

Career statisics:

GP	G	A	TP	+/−	PIM	PP	SH	GW	GT	S	PCT
67	5	14	19	-2	87	4	0	1	0	84	6.0

LAST SEASON

Brian's first in the NHL. He had the lowest plus/minus rating of any Calgary defender except Rob Ramage (who was a plus-16 in his 12 games with the Flames).

THE FINESSE GAME

For a guy with his size, Glynn is a good skater. He has some speed but it's mostly his long stride that will carry him past the opposition. He has a fairly good degree of agility and can move to contain the opposition — or the opposing blue line — fairly well, but he's no Nureyev.

Glynn plays his position with fairly good judgment, but he does have the tendency to stickhandle into traffic after gaining the puck at the opposing blue line. That leads to turnovers and Brian is not yet quick enough to get completely back into the play as it heads up-ice.

He moves the puck from his zone fairly well and sees the ice well enough to make the simple play, but he is not yet at the NHL level in terms of consistent puck movement. He could also be more consistent in his positional play with his zone. While Glynn will most usually send the play wide of the net, he tends to get hypnotized by the puck and loses the man he's supposed to be checking. That flaw should be corrected with experience.

Any goals Brian is going to score will come on his low and hard slap shot from the point.

THE PHYSICAL GAME

Brian has excellent size and strength and he uses both efficiently. He likes to hit and will go to the corner with anyone, and Brian can also control the front of the net well. When we use the word efficiently we mean that he doesn't take penalties for his physical play, and that he gets the big hit if he can but doesn't usually run around looking for it.

He also uses his size and reach well at the point, where he keeps the puck alive.

THE INTANGIBLES

All in all, Glynn had a respectable first year. He has some things to learn and improve upon, and his great size and strength makes what should be a short wait worthwhile.

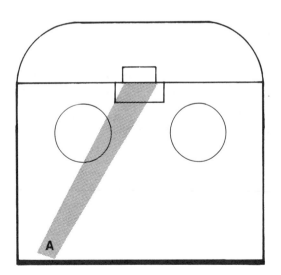

TIM HUNTER

Yrs. of NHL service: 6
Born: Calgary, Alta., Canada; September 10, 1960
Position: Right wing
Height: 6-2
Weight: 202
Uniform no.: 19
Shoots: right

Career statistics:

GP	G	A	TP	PIM
339	38	42	80	1,441

1987-88 statistics:

GP	G	A	TP	+/−	PIM	PP	SH	GW	GT	S	PCT
68	8	5	13	-8	337	0	0	0	0	60	13.3

LAST SEASON

Games played total was third highest in career, goal total tied for second highest. He led the club in PIM (third overall in the League) and once again had the team's worst plus/minus mark.

THE FINESSE GAME

Hunter is an average skater at best, with no real speed or agility in his stride. He does have good balance and strength on his skates and that serves him in his physical game. He has a slow driving stride that carries him from one end of the rink to the other.

Otherwise, Hunter is not gifted offensively. He does not have good hands with which to move or carry the puck, nor does he see the ice well. He is not a goal scorer, but maybe the pucks will bounce off him enough for 10 goals a year.

THE PHYSICAL GAME

Hunter is a one-man hammer-show, and his success is in his physical game. He is big, tough and strong, willing not only to mix it up but to provoke the battles. Hunter is also tough when he stations himself in front of the opposition net, where his strength and size make him a practically immovable object.

Because of his size and strength, Hunter is very difficult to out-muscle along the boards, but he will wander out of position because he's looking to belt someone. Hunter is also mean with his stick, and will use it with abandon. After all, something has to provoke his fights.

THE INTANGIBLES

Hunter has a small and defined role with the Flames that he fills exceedingly well. He is one of the NHL's best conditioned athletes and also one of its most under-rated, because he can also play steady defense if he's needed to fill the position.

He too is entering his option year, but his is not the kind of talent to be influenced by contract negotiations.

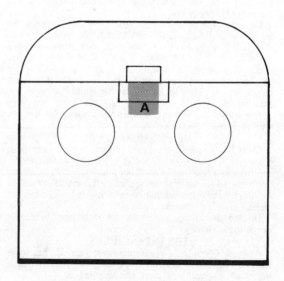

HAKAN LOOB

Yrs. of NHL service: 5
Born: Karlstad, Sweden; July 3, 1960
Position: Right wing
Height: 5-9
Weight: 180
Uniform no.: 12
Shoots: right

Career statistics:

GP	G	A	TP	PIM
371	166	178	344	145

1987-88 statistics:

GP	G	A	TP	+/−	PIM	PP	SH	GW	GT	S	PCT
80	50	56	106	41	47	9	8	4	1	198	25.3

LAST SEASON

Loob played a full NHL season for the first time in his career. All of his point totals were career highs, and he finished ninth in League scoring. He was second League-wide in shorthanded tallies, third overall in plus/minus and fourth in shooting percentage. He led the Flames in scoring, was second in goals and third in assists (first among forwards in the last category). He also led the club in shorthanded goals and shooting percentage.

THE FINESSE GAME

Loob is an excellent skater and it is his quickness on his feet that is his strength. He has the speed to pull away from a defender, and he has the agility to beat the defender to either the inside or outside. That agility comes from his excellent balance, and the balance combines with his foot speed to make him extremely shifty.

That balance also makes Loob very sturdy on his skates and difficult to dislodge from the puck, and he puts that balance to best use in his play around the net and in other high-traffic areas. Crashing the net was an aspect of his game that had been missing for the last several seasons, but Loob re-introduced it last year to great result.

Loob's hockey sense and anticipation also serve him in scoring, as they get him to the openings where the puck wil appear. Those mental faculties complement his passing game, which is also good. Loob uses his teammates very well, and he makes sure to take good advantage of Calgary's super-talented point men. His vision and skating make him a natural for both specialty teams.

His good hands enable him to score from in tight. His wrist shot is quickly released and very accurate. He'll score from the mid-ranges as well, but has neither the strength nor the desire to score from farther out. He's going to make a play — either by skating with the puck or passing it — to get closer to the net. He handles the puck very well when skating.

THE PHYSICAL GAME

Loob can take the rough going but he is not primarily a physical player. His success comes by dancing around outside the pack and picking up loose pucks that come his way. He will occasionally initiate some contact — and certainly goes to the traffic areas — but he isn't a power forward in the way that another player his size — Pat Verbeek, for example — might be.

THE INTANGIBLES

We were wrong last year when he said that, "Loob just may not have enough talent and/or drive to be a star." His season this year argues against that opinion.

But we're still not 100 percent convinced about Loob's ability to consistently reach this plateau. Hell, we're not convinced he can consistently reach the 70-point level, let alone 100. And we remember such great scorers of yesteryear like Wayne Babych, Dennis Maruk and Bob Carpenter. So we're asking Loob to prove us wrong — again.

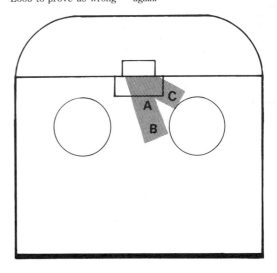

AL MACINNIS

Yrs. of NHL service: 5
Born: Inverness, N.S., Canada; July 11, 1963
Position: Defenseman
Height: 6-2
Weight: 195
Uniform no.: 2
Shoots: right

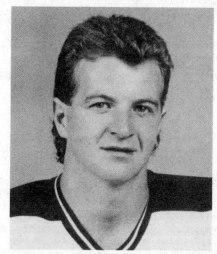

Career statistics:

GP	G	A	TP	PIM
370	82	260	342	413

1987-88 statistics:

GP	G	A	TP	+/−	PIM	PP	SH	GW	GT	S	PCT
80	25	58	83	13	114	7	2	2	0	245	10.2

LAST SEASON

MacInnis played 80 games for the first time in his career and was rewarded with career highs in all point categories. He finished second in scoring among the League's defensemen, and second on the Flames as well (beind teammate Gary suter both times). He led Flames defenders in goals, power play goals and shots on goal (leading the club in the last category). His PIM total was also a career high.

THE FINESSE GAME

MacInnis' skating has long been the weakest of his skills, but Al has worked to improve his foot speed and that improvement has made him a more balanced and mobile defender. He moves into openings offensively — and closes gaps defensively — better than anytime in his NHL career. The agility has also made him a better player in close quarters, so he no longer needs as much empty ice as previously to maneuver his body.

Al sees the ice well (his size helps there), has good anticipation and is able to lead teammates into the open with his passes. He doesn't generally rush the puck, but chooses instead to move up with the attack to become a fourth attacker in the enemy zone. He makes good passing decisions in the defensive zone, and his hand skills combine with his improved foot speed to make his transition game excellent.

His claim to fame has always been his slap shot — labelled the hardest in hockey — and it is the kind of slap shot that goaltenders fear, for it will either blow right past them or hurt them as they stop it. Al knows a good thing when he sees it, and he puts his shot to use many times during a game by shooting as often as possible. If he finishes a game with 4-5 official SOG, you know he shot the puck 10-12 times.

MacInnis uses his slap shot to great effect on the power play, unloading from the blue line and collecting assists as teammates bang home an uncontrolled rebound. That "rebound efficiency" is the major difference in style between MacInnis and teammate Gary Suter.

THE PHYSICAL GAME

The root of MacInnis' blistering slap shot is his tremendous upper body stength. MacInnis also makes use of that strength by being fairly strong at clearing the slot and at holding the opposition away from the play, but that is more the role of his defense partner. MacInnis can take hits in the corners and still make his plays, and improved balance (he has a high center of gravity) helps him remain vertical. He too has suffered the ravages of NHL life, and also plays with braces on his knees.

Because he skates in an upright position, and because he keeps his hands high together on the end of the stick, MacInnis has a good reach advantage that he puts to use to pokecheck and deflect pucks.

THE INTANGIBLES

A key to MacInnis' development and confidence is the fact that he no longer practices what he is good at — his shot — and now concentrates on what he truly needs to improve. For a guy who was originally a very shy, very insecure player and person, that's a pretty important step. He is a dedicated athlete and will continue to make those improvements.

But like many of his teammates he too needs to address his failures in the Edmonton series last spring. MacInnis scored just one goal in four games, and he'll need to redeem himself this May.

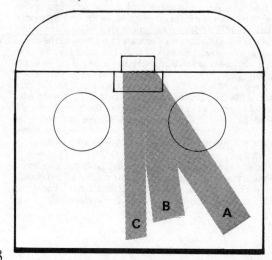

JAMIE MACOUN

Yrs. of NHL service: 5
Born: Newmarket, Ontario, Canada; August 17, 1961
Position: Defenseman
Height: 6-2
Weight: 200
Uniform no.: 34
Shoots: left

Career statistics:

GP	G	A	TP	PIM
320	37	111	148	381

1987-88 statistics:

GP	G	A	TP	+/−	PIM	PP	SH	GW	GT	S	PCT
79	7	33	40	33	111	1	0	0	0	137	5.1

LAST SEASON

Macoun spent last season recovering from a summer of 1987 car accident, hence his 1986-87 statistics. His report is included here unchanged, should he return to the Flames lineup this fall.

THE FINESSE GAME

Macoun is a tremendously skilled skater, both forward and back, but the best of his skating qualities is speed. He is very fast breaking from a standstill and he'll use his speed to join the attack and to penetrate all the way to the opposition's net. He also uses one-step quickness to get to loose pucks. His ability to move around, however, leaves him with a tendency to wander. He is a free-spirit on the ice.

He doesn't like to handle the puck when he's moving that quickly, but Jamie is an above average passer. When he handles the puck, Macoun moves it quickly and smartly up-ice, and can hit the open man in the offensive zone, or will shoot a low slap shot from the point.

Macoun sees the ice well and anticipates well too, and he puts those talents to use on the penalty killing unit. Defensively, he plays his position well, using his defensive angles to force the opposition wide of the net.

THE PHYSICAL GAME

Macoun is a tough and aggressive defenseman. He hits well and often and has good strength to put into those hits, so when he hits it hurts. He clears the front of the net well and can out-muscle forwards along the boards and take them off the puck.

Macoun makes good use of size by shielding the puck well with his body, by using his reach to pokecheck or deflect pucks efficiently and by holding the opposition out of the play when necessary. He can also be mean with his stick.

He has excellent eye/hand coordination and will occasionally be used for faceoffs.

THE INTANGIBLES

Jamie is a great athlete and is one of those players who loves to play the game. Though often overlooked because of his non-spectacular style, Macoun has nonetheless been an important player for the Flames, and just how important will be determined this year, as Calgary must do without his services for quite some time — and maybe permanently — because of the injuries he suffered in an off-season car accident.

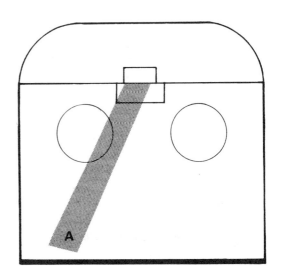

BRAD MCCRIMMON

Yrs. of NHL service: 9
Born: Dodsland, Sask., Canada; March 29, 1959
Position: Defenseman
Height: 5-11
Weight: 195
Uniform no.: 4
Shoots: left

Career statistics:

GP	G	A	TP	PIM
675	59	224	283	778

1987-88 statistics:

GP	G	A	TP	+/−	PIM	PP	SH	GW	GT	S	PCT
80	7	35	42	48	98	1	3	2	0	102	6.9

LAST SEASON

McCrimmon led the NHL in plus/minus. He played all 80 games for the second time in his career.

THE FINESSE GAME

Powerful skating and defensive smarts make Brad one of the NHL's finest defensive defensemen. He's got a very strong stride and he uses it to close the gaps between himself and the opposition. He doesn't have a lot of rink-length speed, but in the confines of the defensive zone McCrimmon moves well. He's not a very agile skater, and his pivots and turns are not exceptional, but Brad counters that flaw with superior positioning.

He has excellent understanding of his defensive angles and almost always succeeds in forcing the play wide of the net. His positioning is also good in the offensive zone, where Brad knows when to challenge and when to fall back.

He's not much of a weapon in the offensive zone. He makes the simple play in his end and can rush the puck if necessary. he'll find the open forward when he's stationed at the offensive blue line.

THE PHYSICAL GAME

McCrimmon is good at keeping the front of the net clear and he does it physically and meanly. He's strong in the upper body and he'll muscle the opposition off the puck either in front of the net or along the boards.

His short reach betrays him when larger forwards are camped in the crease, but Brad makes them pay for every shot they get off.

THE INTANGIBLES

We told you last year how valuable McCrimmon was to the Flyers, and Philadelphia spent all season whining about how much his steadying influence was missed.

He's 50 percent responsible for the super season Gary Suter had, for once the two were paired Suter's offense just took off. McCrimmon is a quiet player who lets his actions speak for him, and because he's quietly effective he's often been unappreciated.

But he's certainly not unappreciated by the Flyers, by Suter or by the Flames.

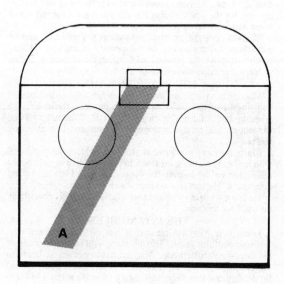

LANNY MCDONALD

Yrs. of NHL service: 15
Born: Hanna, Alta., Canada; February 16, 1953
Position: Right wing
Height: 6-0
Weight: 185
Uniform no.: 9
Shoots: right

Career statistics:

GP	G	A	TP	PIM
1,060	489	499	988	873

1987-88 statistics:

GP	G	A	TP	+/−	PIM	PP	SH	GW	GT	S	PCT
60	10	13	23	2	57	0	0	2	0	79	12.7

LAST SEASON

Games played total was third lowest of his career, as he was spotted in and out of the lineup. Goal and point totals were career lows.

THE FINESSE GAME

Once a blazing skater and shooter, age and wear have taken their physical tolls on McDonald. He is less than a shadow of his former finesse self.

His explosive speed is almost all gone, and McDonald has never been exceptionally agile. He has always preferred to drive to the net from around the outside of the defense, but he won't beat many NHL defensemen any more. He retains the balance he's always had, in that he still uses that attribute in his physical game.

McDonald's howitzer slapshot is no longer as effective as it had been, in part because he can't get into the open ice to use it. His release with it is also slower now, so goaltenders have time to set for it. He still has his anticipation and hockey sense, but his body can't follow his brain's orders quickly enough for him to consistently get into scoring position.

His passing and playmaking skills have also suffered because of his decreased skating quickness. Again, the brain far out-races the body's ability to perform.

THE PHYSICAL GAME

There's no doubt that McDonald's career-long willingness and ability to play a physical game are big reasons for his decline, notably in his gimpy knees. He's always been a very tough hockey player, grinding it out and banging along the boards at both ends of the ice, and he still makes good hits in the corners — when he can catch anybody.

His balance and strength on his feet have always served him in this regard, and they continue to do so now. McDonald will take the abuse when he goes to the front of the net and will certainly give it back. He is also unafraid to throw his fists.

THE INTANGIBLES

Unfortunately, McDonald has stayed in hockey too long. There was much talk of him retiring in the middle of last season, but Lanny felt he still had things to contribute. Obviously, he still feels the same way. He's always been a char- acter individual, and he deserved a better ending than the casual phaseout his diminishing skills have caused.

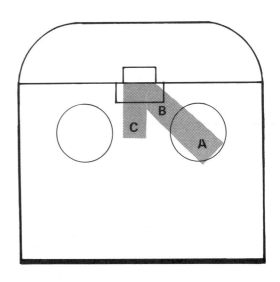

JOE MULLEN

Yrs. of NHL service: 7
Born: New York City, N.Y., USA; February 26, 1957
Position: Right wing
Height: 5-9
Weight: 180
Uniform no.: 7
Shoots: right

Career statistics:

GP	G	A	TP	PIM
489	254	290	544	100

1987-88 statistics:

GP	G	A	TP	+/−	PIM	PP	SH	GW	GT	S	PCT
80	40	44	84	28	30	12	0	5	0	205	19.5

LAST SEASON

Mullen played a complete season for the second time in his career and first time with Calgary. Assist total tied for second highest in his career. His plus/minus mark was second highest among the club's forwards, third best overall. PIM total was a career high. He finished second on the team in game winners, fourth in goals and shooting percentage, fifth in SOG.

THE FINESSE GAME

Mullen's incredible balance keys all his skating skills. Because he is usually operating in traffic, Mullen is often forced off-balance by opposition checkers. But he is able to maintain control of both his hands and his feet to score, and most of his goals will come from those off-balance shots.

He is also a powerful skater, as demonstrated by his outstanding acceleration ability. He uses that explosive start to break into the clear, and he also has tremendous one-step quickness which he uses to dart into openings after loose pucks. He moderates his speed excellently, never allowing the opposition to predict what he will do.

Once in those narrow openings (where he often needs to shift his weight and twist his body — and where his balance allows him to do so), Mullen puts his great hands to work. Mullen's shot is keyed by his quick wrists and release. He is good at one-timing his shots and can score from anywhere in the zone. He is very dangerous when he has the puck, but more so around the slot or just inside the faceoff circle. His shot selection is excellent forehand or back hand, wrist, slap or snap.

His goal scorer's anticipation and great hockey sense also make him a good playmaker, and Mullen is a selfish player. He looks to use his teammates and makes the better play at all times. If that means a good pass to a teammate in better position, then that's the play Mullen makes. His hand skills also allow him to carry the puck well, and they combine with his skating skills to make Mullen very shifty.

THE PHYSICAL GAME

Though his size says otherwise, Mullen is a supertough player. That doesn't mean he's punching people out; rather, it means he takes all the abuse handed to him in order to make his plays. He's completely unafraid of traffic, and Mullen will do his own mucking in the corners. He consistently hits on his own (though sometimes — against the League's bigger players — the effect is negligible), and Joe is obviously talented enough to make play from the corner after gaining the puck.

His balance aids him tremendously in his physical game, as it makes him difficult to dislodge from the puck. Mullen knows the benefits a finesse game can gain from a physical style, and he converts those benefits into points.

THE INTANGIBLES

He's been overlooked and underrated for most of his career, and the career years attained by other teammates last year forced Mullen farther into the background. But Joe couldn't care less. He's a superb team man and a character individual. He works hard on the ice and plays in pain.

Whether he will continue to be in the background this year depends largely on the production of Joe Nieuwendyk, Hakan Loob and Mike Bullard. With Bullard and Nieuwendyk scoring 52 power play goals between them (almost 50 percent of Calgary's 109 PPG), Mullen's importance to the power play was lessened.

And, not to place all the blame on him, but Mullen had no goals and just three assists as the Flames were swept by the Oilers in the Smythe Division Playoff Finals. That non-performance is a question begging an answer.

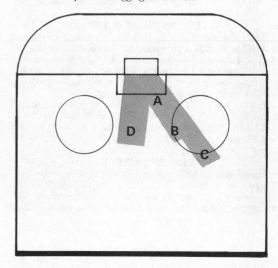

DANA MURZYN

Yrs. of NHL service: 3
Born: Regina, Sask., Canada; December 9, 1968
Position: Defenseman
Height: 6-2
Weight: 200
Uniform no.: 5
Shoots: left

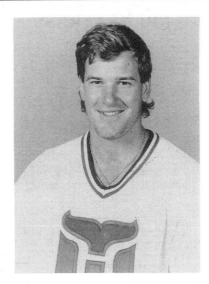

Career statistics:

GP	G	A	TP	PIM
226	19	60	79	359

1987-88 statistics:

GP	G	A	TP	+/−	PIM	PP	SH	GW	GT	S	PCT
74	7	11	18	1	139	1	0	1	0	107	6.5

LAST SEASON

Murzyn (along with Shane Churla) was acquired at mid-year in exchange for Neil Sheehy and Carey Wilson. Games played total matched career low, and assist and point totals were career lows. PIM total was a career high mark. He was Calgary's lowest scoring defenseman.

THE FINESSE GAME

Though he is a good skater forward and back, Murzyn still lacks that extra little bit of agility that would make him a consistent and solid defender in his own zone. He's weak turning to his left, and his lack of foot speed doesn't help when he makes his turns late (because he's watching the puck instead of the man. He has good balance and strength on his skates, so he'll hold his own during goal mouth collisions. He doesn't have a lot of rink-length speed, but his long stride covers a lot of ground so he isn't frequently left in the dust.

Dana handles the puck well and likes to carry it to center ice. He's improved his understanding of the pace of the NHL game and so he makes his passes quickly and efficiently when he chooses not to carry the puck.

He's shown little potential for scoring at the NHL level, though he has improved his playreading ability and will consistently get the puck to the open man. Murzyn shoots well from the point, either a slap shot or a wrist shot, and both are low, hard and accurate.

Murzyn plays well positionally and uses his defensive angles well, but his lack of foot speed forces him to concede the blue line too quickly.

THE PHYSICAL GAME

Murzyn has great size and he likes to play a physical game. He can hold the man out along the boards and he can clear the crease as well. Murzyn is very strong and uses his strength to his advantage.

He will sacrifice his body to block shots, and he has a good reach that he puts to use by pokechecking effectively. He is aggressive, hitting hard and often, but he's not a big fighter.

THE INTANGIBLES

We say again that Dana can play the game at a level above average, and he has shown good development in his three NHL seasons. But that improvement in foot must be forthcoming in order for his total game to improve.

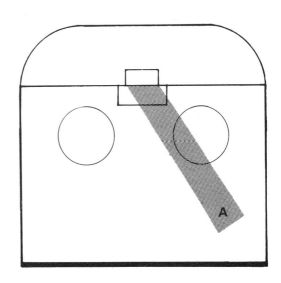

RIC NATTRESS

Yrs. of NHL service: 6
Born: Hamilton, Ontario, Canada; May 25, 1962
Position: Defenseman
Height: 6-2
Weight: 208
Uniform no.: 6
Shoots: right

Career statistics:

GP	G	A	TP	PIM
293	13	71	84	149

1987-88 statistics:

GP	G	A	TP	+/−	PIM	PP	SH	GW	GT	S	PCT
63	2	13	15	14	37	0	0	0	0	48	4.2

LAST SEASON

Games played total was lowest in three seasons (he was sidelined by a late season shoulder injury). He was the Flames lowest scoring defenseman.

THE FINESSE GAME

Nattress improved his skating last season, so he's now a more smooth skater than before, but he remains less than fluid skating backward. His pivots from back to front as an opponent passes him are still weak, but his improved back-skating has help Nattress avoid these pivots by forcing the play wide more consistently. Still, he is far from a sure thing.

Ric does not handle the puck well and is subject to giveaways if pressured. He doesn't clear the zone well at all, either by skating the puck or moving it to a forward, so he's going to have to be paired with a more skilled partner.

He's playing his defensive angles better, but Nattress still has a tendency to wander from his position. That creates breakdowns all through the defensive zone and creates openings for the opposition.

He is not a goal scorer and any goals he gets will come on shots from the point.

THE PHYSICAL GAME

Nattress is big and strong but he doesn't play the body well or consistently. He is a pusher and a shover and not a hitter and he fails to use his size to out-muscle the opposition either in the corners or the front of the net.

He does not take the opposition out of the play, let alone hold them out when necessary, and Nattress is likely to give the puck up when hit because he doesn't use his body well to shield the puck.

THE INTANGIBLES

As a fifth or sixth defenseman, Nattress isn't too out of place. But he's neither an exceptionally hard worker nor a consistent player, and the development of players like Bryan Glynn and Kevan Guy, as well as the possible return of Jamie Macoun, may make Nattress the odd man out.

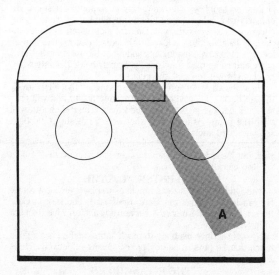

JOE NIEUWENDYK

Yrs. of NHL service: 1
Born: Oshawa, Ontario, Canada; September 10, 1966
Position: Center
Height: 6-1
Weight: 175
Uniform no.: 25
Shoots: left

Career statistics:

GP	G	A	TP	PIM
84	56	42	98	23

1987-88 statistics:

GP	G	A	TP	+/−	PIM	PP	SH	GW	GT	S	PCT
75	51	41	92	20	23	31	3	8	0	212	24.1

LAST SEASON

Nieuwendyk finished fifth overall in goal scoring in the NHL (first on Calgary). He led the NHL in power play goals and was tied for third League-wide in game winners. He led all rookies in all point categories, shots, power play goals and game winners. He was second among rookies in shorthanded goals, shooting percentage and plus/minus. He finished third in team scoring, first in game winners and shooting percentage and fourth in SOG. He missed two games with a concussion.

THE FINESSE GAME

Nieuwendyk is a tremendously talented finesse player, and unlike many tremendously talented finesse players his skating isn't the best of his skills. The best thing that has been said about Joe's skating is that it's awkward, and it is. He has a kind of bowlegged stance that belies his agility and, speed and balance. He doesn't have tremendous speed, but Nieuwendyk can accelerate past the opposition. He has excellent balance and foot speed and is very agile, and those skills come into play in his play around the net.

Nieuwendyk's primary skills are great hockey sense and excellent hands. He gets into position to score excellently — courtesy of his sense of the game and excellent vision — and then he lets his hands and balance go to work. Joe's hands are very sensitive for puck work, and he can make any move with the puck in traffic and still control the puck. His balance allows him to extend himself for seemingly unreachable pucks — or to squeeze into seemingly unenterable spaces — and it also allows him to get off his shots while being checked.

He makes great plays along the boards and out of the corners because of his hand skills, and Nieuwendyk passes fairly well too. He'll find the open man — again, vision and anticipation — and he'll lead that teammate to an opening.

Joe has an excellent selection of shots, though he's most likely to score from somewhere in close proximity to the net. He loves to shoot and will do so from all angles. He's a natural on the specialty team units because of his ability to exploit openings and create scoring situations.

THE PHYSICAL GAME

Nieuwendyk plays an extremely physical game. That doesn't mean he's a power forward because he's not; no opponent will hesitate to go into the corner with him for fear of being crushed.

What Joe's physical game entails is doing his own dirty work. He works the corners in both zones and charges the net with impunity. He's completely unintimidated by the rough going and he can't be brutalized.

And most important, his physical game makes his finesse game that much more effective. He can certainly make a play coming out of the corner, and his great balance makes him almost impossible to knock down.

THE INTANGIBLES

The most important thing to remember about Nieuwendyk's success is that he's already playing the style of game that will insure his success. He's already taking the checking and the beatings and succeeding on the ice. That bodes well for him.

While he certainly has 50-goal talent, a natural dropoff in production could be expected this year. However, Nieuwendyk now knows how to better pace himself for the NHL season, so his erratic scoring (32 goals in the first 40 games, just eight goals in his last 16) should even out. Also of concern would be his scoring distribution: Just 17 of his 51 goals came at even strength.

But these things don't merit much concern. Nieuwendyk is a player of great potential, and last season's Rookie of the Year is also a tireless worker. Though he may not score 91 points again this year — and he's just as likely to score 100 or more — he'll continue to develop into a game breaker for Calgary. And by the way, he led the Flames in goal scoring versus the Oilers in last spring's playoffs — two goals in four games. Not bad for a rookie.

JOEL OTTO

Yrs. of NHL service: 3
Born: St. Cloud, Minn., USA; October 29, 1961
Position: Center
Height: 6-4
Weight: 220
Uniform no.: 29
Shoots: right

Career statistics:

GP	G	A	TP	PIM
226	61	112	173	597

1987-88 statistics:

GP	G	A	TP	+/−	PIM	PP	SH	GW	GT	S	PCT
62	13	39	52	16	194	4	1	4	0	105	12.4

LAST SEASON

Games played and goal totals were career lows, while assist total was a career high. A strained knee sidelined him early in the season. He finished fifth on the club in PIM.

THE FINESSE GAME

Otto is a power forward, designed for checking and strength rather than speed. He is a strong skater but doesn't have a lot of speed. He moves up and down the ice with a long stride that will either get him away from the opposition offensively or near the opposition defensively.

He sees the ice and anticipates the play well, and combines those attributes to be a fine defensive center. Because of those assets, Otto also gets many offensive opportunities, but he fails to convert them because he doesn't shoot enough. He over-passes the puck and must take better advantage of the chances he creates.

He will score from in close by picking up rebounds or deflections, but his shot is the weakest of his finesse skills.

THE PHYSICAL GAME

Otto is strong and tough. He takes the body very well in all three zones and is very effective in the corners and along the boards. Joel has the strength to hit punishingly and to move the opposition off the puck, as well as the talent to make plays after the puck is loose.

Otto is very strong on his skates and stands in front of the opposition net and gives the defense all kinds of trouble. Once Otto has stationed himself, he's very difficult to uproot and that's something he does on the power play to great result.

Because he plays an oustandingly physical game, Otto will tire over the course of a season. Therefore, on nights when there is no big, strong center to neutralize, Otto will coast.

THE INTANGIBLES

Otto is a dedicated athlete and a tireless worker, a workaholic really. He skates all through the summer to stay in shape, yet is a notoriously slow starter in terms of scoring; he needs 20 games to get acclimated offensively.

His main responsibility is to neutralize Edmonton's Mark Messier, but Otto does a good job against the League's other centers as well. Quiet off the ice, he is an on-ice leader.

He enters his third full season this year, and it's time to see whether Joel can raise the level of his play — particularly offensively.

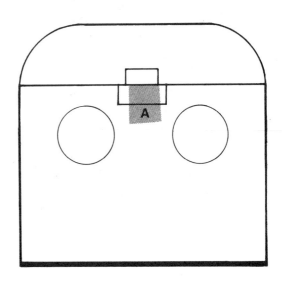

COLIN PATTERSON

Yrs. of NHL service: 5
Born: Rexdale, Ontario, Canada; May 11, 1960
Position: Right wing
Height: 6-2
Weight: 195
Uniform no.: 11
Shoots: left

Career statistics:

GP	G	A	TP	PIM
281	69	72	141	111

1987-88 statistics:

GP	G	A	TP	+/−	PIM	PP	SH	GW	GT	S	PCT
39	7	11	18	7	28	0	0	0	0	37	18.9

LAST SEASON

Patterson missed 21 games with hamstring pull and 12 games with an ankle injury. Games played total was the lowest of his career, with correspondingly low point totals. His PIM total was second highest of his career.

THE FINESSE GAME

Speed is the hallmark of Patterson's skating skill, and he uses that speed in conjunction with his hockey smarts to be a good defensive forward. He has good hockey sense and anticipation and Colin sees the ice well and can read the plays. Because of those factors, Patterson gets many offensive opportunities, so it would be in character for him to notch 20-25 goals a season.

What will prevent him from getting those goals is his shot, which is not at the level of the two aforementioned skills. Patterson has decent hands and his wrist shot is fairly accurate, but he must be in tight to the net to score because of his merely-average release and shot strength.

He is skilled enough to move the puck fairly well (again, credit his vision and sense), but Patterson will always primarily be a defensive forward.

THE PHYSICAL GAME

Though not overwhelmingly strong, Patterson has the strength to be good checker, a role that he fills well. He is a kamikaze with his body, willing to sacrifice it when necessary, and as such he is frequently banged up.

THE INTANGIBLES

Like bookend teammate Perry Berezan, Patterson spends much of his season pulling himself together after injury. For a 28-year-old role player a healthy season is a must. For after all, if you have to replace a role player with another role player, how valuable could the first one have been in the first place?

In Colin's favor is his attitude. Like most of the Flames, Patterson is a character individual. He's a very hard worker and a very dedicated athlete. In the lockerroom he's the kind of guy to crack jokes and keep the team loose, and on the ice he gives 100 percent of himself and is very coachable.

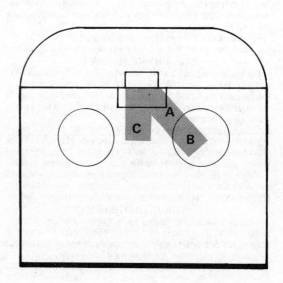

JIM PEPLINSKI

Yrs. of NHL service: 8
Born: Renfrew, Ontario, Canada; October 24, 1960
Position: Left wing/center
Height: 6-2
Weight: 201
Uniform no.: 24
Shoots: right

Career statistics:

GP	G	A	TP	PIM
620	147	237	384	1,211

1987-88 statistics:

GP	G	A	TP	+/−	PIM	PP	SH	GW	GT	S	PCT
75	20	31	51	20	234	0	2	4	0	128	15.6

LAST SEASON

Games played total continues pattern of Peplinski's attendance he follows each 80-game season with a year in the mid-70s. He finished third on the club in PIM.

THE FINESSE GAME

Peplinski is surprisingly fast for a big guy. He's got a lot of speed (courtesy of his powerful skating stride), and he's fast enough to beat defenders to the outside and then swoop inside toward the goal. He also has good acceleration ability, again courtesy of his strength and stride. He has good balance on his skates, as well as good strength, and those factors are important because of his physical style. Jim doesn't, however, have great agility.

His speed presents him with scoring opportunities, and his strength takes him to the front of the net, but he does not have outstanding offensive or finishing skills. He'll score in the 20-goal range by sweeping home rebounds and other junk, but don't expect him to turn the goaltender inside out. He enjoys playing the left wing because he is a right-handed shot.

Peplinski's not much of a fancy playmaker, because he lacks great hands and great anticipation, Instead, he'll get his assists because the opposition leaves him a lot of room to operate in, and Peplinski needs that time and space to make his plays. He does get a fairly good read of the ice and combines that with good positional play to be a good checker and defensive player.

THE PHYSICAL GAME

Physical is the name of Peplinski's game. He is tough and strong and hits hard along the boards and in the corners. Peplinski can't do much after he makes the hits, but he is strong enough to out-muscle the opposition along the boards.

Jim is very hard to knock off his skates because of his balance and strength and that means he can recover from collisions and be in position to make some kind of play. That steadiness on his skates also serves him when he plugs the front of the opposition net and has to withstand the defense's abuse.

He can fight, and he's pretty good at it.

THE INTANGIBLES

Peplinski is a leader for Calgary, a good team man and a rah-rah type of guy who will do whatever he can to help the team. He's versatile and can play all three forward positions, giving the Flames some flexibility with their lineup. He adds a spark with his enthusiasm and attitude.

In many ways he is a role player with great size. For the record, he's entering his option season. Since he's a consistent player the contract pressure should have no effect on his play.

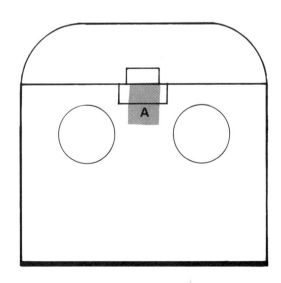

ROB RAMAGE

Yrs. of NHL service: 9
Born: Byron, Ontario, Canada; January 11, 1959
Position: Defenseman
Height: 6-2
Weight: 210
Uniform no.: 55
Shoots: right

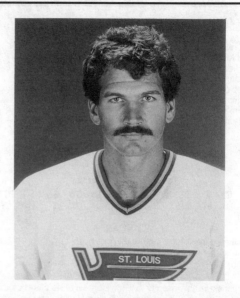

Career statistics:

GP	G	A	TP	PIM
687	109	326	435	1,464

1987-88 statistics:

GP	G	A	TP	+/−	PIM	PP	SH	GW	GT	S	PCT
79	9	40	49	-4	164	6	0	0	0	215	4.2

LAST SEASON

Ramage was traded to the Flames along with Rick Wamsley in exchange for Brett Hull and Steve Bozek. Games played total was highest in three years and, while Ramage finished as one of just three minus players, he was plus-16 in his 12 games with Calgary.

THE FINESSE GAME

For a defenseman, Ramage skates as well as a forward. He moves well backward and forward and is fairly agile on his skates for a man with his size. He has good foot speed and lateral movement.

He will grab the puck and rush with it, alleviating pressure on the forwards, but Ramage is also sound defensively and is an anchor for the Flames.

Ramage reads rushes well and is sound coming back into his own end, playing good positional hockey and not wandering from his check. When he gains the puck Ramage's transition game is sound, and he moves the puck well to the forwards.

Rob moves up into the play well, though with Calgary's array of talent from the blue line he doesn't need to challenge much. He does become a fourth attacker, and Ramage passes the puck very well in the offensive zone because of his vision. He has good anticipation for the openings and will get the puck to his teammates in those openings. He has a good shot from the point and will sneak to the slot if he can.

THE PHYSICAL GAME

Ramage is one of the NHL's strongest players, and he plays a bruising style of defense. He hits when he can along the boards and eliminates the man well. He is very tough in front of the net and only the NHL's strongest forwards will win a 1-on-1 battle with Ramage in front of his net.

His sturdiness on his skates makes him tough to knock off the puck along the boards or in the corners.

THE INTANGIBLES

Ramage is a steady, dependable above-average defenseman. He's not Ray Bourque — and the Flames don't need that kind of offensive skill — but Ramage is no journeyman either. He is the kind of defensive anchor the Flames need to counter their offensive style along the backline, and Ramage's maturity and work ethic are positive influences for a team's younger players.

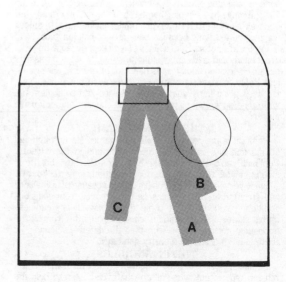

PAUL REINHART

Yrs. of NHL service: 9
Born: Kitchener, Ontario, Canada; January 8, 1960
Position: Defenseman
Height: 5-11
Weight: 205
Uniform no.: 23
Shoots: left

Career statistics:

GP	G	A	TP	PIM
517	109	336	445	203

1987-88 statistics:

GP	G	A	TP	+/−	PIM	PP	SH	GW	GT	S	PCT
14	0	4	4	0	10	0	0	0	0	22	0.0

LAST SEASON

Reinhart's back injury felled him again, limiting to a career low in games played and all point categories.

THE FINESSE GAME

Though almost an old man in terms of years of service, Reinhart shows no signs of wear in his finesse skills. He remains an excellent skater, both forward and backward, with exceptional balance and the resulting agility. He has a low center of gravity and is very strong in the thighs, so he is very difficult to take off the puck. He is not a flowing or graceful skater, but he gets the job done.

Reinhart will use his skating skill to carry the puck from the Flames' zone, relieving pressure on the forwards, though he can also move the puck excellently up-ice. He likes to carry the puck up on the power play and he is a mainstay on that Flames' specialty team.

Paul is able to use his excellent anticipation and uncanny vision to great at even strength as well. He finds the open man excellently and passes very well, either through traffic or into an opening to lead a teammate. Reinhart controls the point well, able to keep the puck in the zone and heading toward a teammate.

When he elects to shoot rather than pass, Reinhart has a strong, low slap shot from the point, but he will move to the deep slot if he can.

He uses his skating and vision to play his position well defensively. Reinhart is rarely beaten one-on-one because he is good at forcing the opposition wide of the net.

THE PHYSICAL GAME

His skating strength is undoubtedly the biggest physical plus Reinhart has. He can play a physical style, though his best game is clearly in the open ice. He can turn a play up-ice after either making a hit or being hit because his strength on his skates means he is balanced and almost always vertical.

Paul is, however, generally weak in his coverage in front of his own net. While he has the size and strength to be effective in front of the opposition's net, Reinhart is less than consistently effective in front of his own goaltender.

THE INTANGIBLES

We told you last year that Reinhart's health must always be raised as question to his further playing, and he once again fell prey to his back injury. He returned to play eight of Calgary's nine playoff games, and was the club's fourth leading scorer. What he can do when healthy has been well-documented. But how much longer can he survive in the League flitting in and out of the lineup? And how much longer will Calgary put up with it?

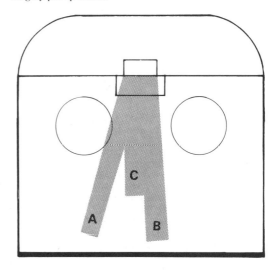

GARY ROBERTS

Yrs. of NHL service: 1
Born: North York, Ontario, Canada; May 23, 1966
Position: Center/left wing
Height: 6-1
Weight: 190
Uniform no.: 10
Shoots: left

Career statistics:

GP	G	A	TP	PIM
106	18	25	43	367

1987-88 statistics:

GP	G	A	TP	+/−	PIM	PP	SH	GW	GT	S	PCT
74	13	15	28	24	282	0	0	1	0	118	11.0

LAST SEASON

Roberts first full year with Calgary, so all numbers are career highs. He finished second on the club in PIM and had the sixth best plus/minus rating.

THE FINESSE GAME

Roberts is a good skater in all facets of that skill, except for agility. He has good speed and acceleration capability and he's fairly well balanced on his feet. He's not exceptionally quick and could improve his foot speed. Improved foot speed would also help his lateral movement by combining with his balance.

He showed flashes last season of being able to make plays at the NHL level, and he seems to have a good understanding of the NHL play, but right now he doesn't move the puck quickly enough to be consistently effective. Since he's often playing in the traffic areas Roberts isn't going to get a lot of time, so his playreading capability will have to improve.

His hand skills are developable and Roberts can get the puck to an open man now, but he needs time and space to do so. He also could improve the release of his shot and the frequency with which he shoots. Right now his goals will have to come from near the net.

He plays the wing position very well and is always cognizant of where he is and where his check is in relation to the puck and the net.

THE PHYSICAL GAME

Roberts has good size and he is certainly willing to use it — just look at his PIM total for proof. He checks and uses his body well along the boards, and he's aided in his confrontations there by his good balance.

His physical play is one-dimensional right now, in that he's not going to make many plays coming out of the corner. That ability to move the puck would make his physical play more valuable.

THE INTANGIBLES

Roberts played part of the year with Joe Nieuwendyk and Hakan Loob, and his role on that line was pretty clear — bang a few bodies, spring loose a few pucks, make a few passes to the artists. Playing with talented players like the above duo

will help Roberts improve his skills, and he can contribute physically while doing that improving.

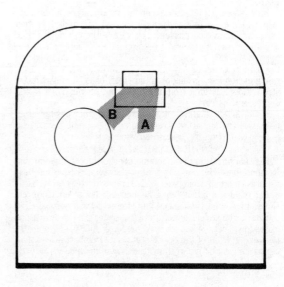

GARY SUTER

Yrs. of NHL service: 3
Born: Madison, Wisc., USA; June 24, 1964
Position: Defenseman
Height: 6-0
Weight: 190
Uniform no.: 20
Shoots: left

Career statistics:

GP	G	A	TP	PIM
223	48	159	207	335

1987-88 statistics:

GP	G	A	TP	+/−	PIM	PP	SH	GW	GT	S	PCT
75	21	70	91	39	124	6	1	3	0	204	10.3

LAST SEASON

Games played total was second highest of Suter's career, but point totals were all career highs. He was the NHL's top scoring defenseman (first in assists, third in goals), and he led the club in assists. He finished third on the club in plus/minus, sixth in SOG (an astounding *third* among defensemen).

THE FINESSE GAME

There are very few players in the NHL — and still fewer defenders — with the skating skills Suter possesses. He is an excellent skater, superior in all skating categories—speed, quickness, agility, balance and power. His one-step quickness and balance are the two best of those assets, and they make Suter almost unsurpassed in terms of agility and lateral movement. He changes speeds and directions within a stride.

He also has good rink-length speed, though he isn't the fastest overall player in the League, and he can out-distance most opponents as he moves up-ice. He skates just as well backward as he does forward, and his mobility and speed allow him to force plays wide of the net and instantaneously begin the transition game with a loose puck.

He carries the puck excellently from the Flames' zone and he does it well at all speeds. He is not a rink-length rusher, however, and will look to make a pass in center or immediately after he crosses the opposing blue line. He finds the open man excellently in all situations, and he can get a pass aywhere because of his excellent hands. He'll lead his teammates into the clear, or he can take advantage of the openings himself because of his speed.

Gary has a very hard shot from the point, low and accurate, and he will cheat into the zone a few strides if the opportunity exists. The important thing to note in light of his SOG total is that, as one of the lower among Flames defensemen, Suter must be making plays for his 70 assists and not just collecting points from deflections and rebounds.

THE PHYSICAL GAME

Suter is a powerful player, strong in the upper body and shoulders, and that strength powers his slapshot and allows him to keep the front of his net clean, though that is more often his partner's responsibility. His leg strength obviously powers his skating.

He can withstand hits and still make his plays, or he can muscle the opposition off the puck. Suter also does a good job of shielding the puck with his body when he is in the corners.

THE INTANGIBLES

We told you last season that Gary Suter would return to his higher level, though in the early going of this past year things looked bleak. So bleak, that the super-talented defender was being played on left wing. But, after being paired with rock-solid Brad McCrimmon, Suter just went wild.

He had just one goal and nine points in his first 16 games last year, then followed with 82 points in his last 59 games. So much for the regular season blues.

But, like many of his teammates, Suter went south in the playoff series against the Oilers. After picking up one goal and nine points in five games versus Los Angeles, Suter added but a single assist in the four games against the Oilers.

So now, while Suter must prove that his regular season success wasn't a fluke (and we don't think it was) he must also redeem himself for his poor playoff performance.

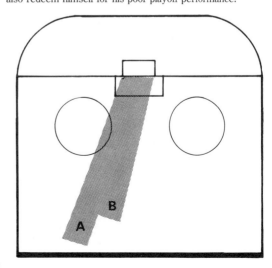

JOHN TONELLI

Yrs. of NHL service: 10
Born: Hamilton, Ontario, Canada; March 23, 1957
Position: Left wing
Height: 6-1
Weight: 190
Uniform no.: 27
Shoots: left

Career statistics:

GP	G	A	TP	PIM
755	246	414	660	639

1987-88 statistics:

GP	G	A	TP	+/−	PIM	PP	SH	GW	GT	S	PCT
74	17	41	58	10	84	6	0	1	0	128	13.3

LAST SEASON

Goal total matched second lowest of career. PIM total was highest in three seasons.

THE FINESSE GAME

Once a good skater with a lot of power, Tonelli's skills are now on the downslide. He doesn't have the acceleration he once did and for a straight-ahead player who had little agility loss of speed and power is the worst loss that could be suffered. He retains a kind of laziness he's long had, in that he won't backcheck as well as he should, sort of coasting back to save his energy for another offensive rush.

He holds the puck too long while looking to make his plays, and John will circle away from the play instead of facing it. He'll leave good ice to go to bad ice, and when he does that in his own end, defensive breakdowns occur.

Tonelli also goes to bad ice in the offensive zone, often at an angle as wide from the net as possible. He is frequently off balance when he shoots because of his proclivity toward working in traffic, and his best weapon remains the big slap shot from the left wing. But since John has difficulty getting down the wing and into the clear now (decreased speed), and since he's always at wide angles, he's not going to score very often.

THE PHYSICAL GAME

John has always had a reputation for physical play, charging the corners with reckless abandon. He does less of that now, and a lot more leg grinding to look busy. He's always been mean with his stick, but has never fought after provoking an incident.

THE INTANGIBLES

Tonelli's future with the club remains unclear, as the Flames vacillated between giving Tonelli a new contract (he's in his option year) or just signing him to a termination deal. Whether Tonelli can stem his declining play is a big question, but not as big as the one the Flames have to answer regarding his future with them.

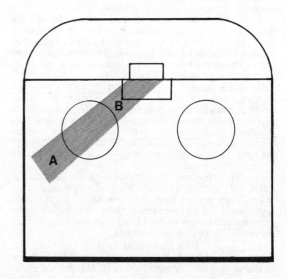

MIKE VERNON

Yrs. of NHL service: 3
Born: Calgary, Alta., Canada; February 24, 1963
Position: Goaltender
Height: 5-7
Weight: 150
Uniform no.: 30
Catches: left

Career statistics:

GP	MINS	G	SO	AVG	A	PIM
139	7,554	455	3	3.61	10	65

1987-88 statisics:

GP	MINS	AVG	W	L	T	SO	GA	SA	SAPCT	PIM
64	3,565	3.53	39	16	7	1	210	1,708	.887	47

LAST SEASON

Games played total was a career high. He finished second in the League in wins and games played. He finished fourth among goaltenders in shots faced and third in PIM.

THE PHYSICAL GAME

Despite what his size indicates, Vernon is a standup goaltender. While many smaller goaltenders fall into the acrobatic, flopping category, Vernon uses his excellent balance to retain his stance and stay on his feet. He has excellent lateral movement, so bang-bang passing plays won't often find him out of position. Vernon is excellent at going from side to side and post to post.

He will go to his knees when the play gets in close and that's the time to beat him, because Mike won't make the mistakes that result in long shot goals. However, he regains his feet very quickly so those openings won't be open for long. He clears rebounds effectively — especially of his stick side.

Though he is a good skater, Vernon is not big on coming out of his net to handle the puck; he does communicate well with his defense. And, while he employs that solid standup style, Vernon also has outstanding reflexes.

Vernon is very quick with his hands and feet, but is slow to get his legs closed and he'll give up a lot of goals through the five-hole. But Mike knows that and will not, therefore, open up his stance. One consequence of his not opening up, and of his playing his angles a little too deeply in the net, is that he'll give up a few goals low and away.

THE MENTAL GAME

Vernon is very tough mentally, able to rebound after a bad goal or a bad game and continue without effect. He has great poise and will fight you for every goal. He has the ability to make the big save too. His concentration is good and so is his anticipation, with most of the goals he allows coming from physical, rather than, mental miscues.

His concentration is pretty good from game to game too, though it does have a tendency to wane. That's an area where Vernon could be more consistent.

THE INTANGIBLES

While Vernon is clearly the Flames' number one goaltender, the arrival in Calgary of Rick Wamsley as a dependable backup may mean that Mike won't carry the burden — in terms of playing time — as he has the last two years. Still, any hope Calgary has of advancing to the Stanley Cup rests squarely on Vernon's shoulders.

RICK WAMSLEY

Yrs. of NHL service: 8
Born: Simcoe, Ontario, Canada; May 25, 1959
Position: Goaltender
Height: 5-11
Weight: 185
Uniform no.: 31
Catches: left

Career statistics:

GP	MINS	G	SO	AVG	A	PIM
287	16,512	924	8	3.35	7	38

1987-88 statisics:

GP	MINS	AVG	W	L	T	SO	GA	SA	SAPCT	PIM
33	1,891	3.42	14	16	1	2	108	958	.887	14

LAST SEASON

Wamsley was traded mid-season (along with Rob Ramage) to the Flames from St. Louis for Brett Hull and Steve Bozek. Games played total was career low since breaking into the NHL fulltime (five GP in 1980-81). Last season was also Wamsley's first sub-.500 year. He suffered a late season groin injury.

THE PHYSICAL GAME

Wamsley is a standup goaltender almost to a fault. He rarely leaves his feet and uses his good size to his advantage by doing so.

Rick is an average skater and he won't often stray from his net, but when he does he will cut the puck off for his defensemen and handle the puck outside the net. He moves in and out of his net well, but is not particularly smooth in his backskating.

Because his feet are constantly in motion forward and back Wamsley is susceptible to shots along the ice — you can't kick your feet sideways when they're going forward and back. Rick has decent balance on his feet but will spend more time on the ice recovering from a save than he should as he scrambles back to his feet. In general, once his feet get moving he's a dead duck.

Wamsley handles his rebounds well and directs them away from traffic for the most part. His hands are not especially fast so Rick benefits from cutting down the angles so the puck just hits him. He sees the puck fairly well and has good anticipation.

THE MENTAL GAME

Wamsley is a fairly consistent goaltender mentally, neither getting too high after a win nor too low after a loss. He approaches each game prepared to do his job and is mostly unaffected by a bad performance the night before or a bad goal at any time.

His concentration is good, but it does tend to wander when he has nothing to do for stretches of time, and he looks unsteady on shots following that "empty" period.

THE INTANGIBLES

Wamsley is not on the level of the NHL's better goaltenders. He just does his job with a fair degree of success. He has

never been a backup, as he's split time fairly evenly in Montreal and St. Louis, so being a caddy is new to him. And that's what he'll be in Calgary, so we'll have to see how he reacts to his second citizen status.

CHICAGO
BLACKHAWKS

LINE COMBINATIONS
DAN VINCELETTE-BRIAN NOONAN-WAYNE
PRESLEY
DUANE SUTTER-DENIS SAVARD-DIRK GRAHAM
EVERETT SANIPASS-TROY MURRAY-RICK VAIVE

DEFENSE PAIRINGS
GARY NYLUND-BEHN WILSON
TRENT YAWNEY-KEITH BROWN
DAVE MANSON-BOB MURRAY

GOALTENDERS
DARREN PANG
BOB MASON

OTHER PLAYERS
MARC BERGEVIN — Defenseman
STEVE LUDZIK —Center
BOB MCGILL — Defenseman
MIKE STAPLETON — Center
STEVE THOMAS — Left wing
DOUG WILSON — Defenseman

POWER PLAY

FIRST UNIT:
STEVE LARMER-DENIS SAVARD-RICK VAIVE
TRENT YAWNEY-BOB MURRAY

SECOND UNIT:
DIRK GRAHAM-TROY MURRAY-WAYNE PRESLEY
BEHN WILSON-KEITH BROWN

On the first unit SAVARD controls from behind the net, VAIVE is at the left circle and LARMER at the base of the right circle. Perimeter passing from SAVARD, VAIVE and YAWNEY tries to loosen box for give-and-go between YAWNEY and VAIVE, or to free LARMER for quick shot in front. Other option is for YAWNEY to skate in and shoot, with forwards going for rebounds.

On the second unit MURRAY controls from the left faceoff circle, working the give and go with B.WILSON or feeding the points for shots with GRAHAM plugging the net. The forwards crash the net for rebounds.

When healthy, both DOUG WILSON and THOMAS will be regulars.

Last season the Chicago power play was EXCELLENT, scoring 98 goals in 426 opportunities (23.0 percent, third overall).

PENALTY KILLING

FIRST UNIT:
TROY MURRAY-STEVE LARMER
TRENT YAWNEY-BOB MURRAY

All four members pressure the puck from the box defense. Other forwards are SAVARD and LUDZIK, other defense are BROWN and B.WILSON. NYLUND will also get a fairly regular turn, and MCGILL will occasionaly see time too. DOUG WILSON would be a regular when healthy.

Last season the Hawk penalty killing was GOOD, allowing 96 goals in 484 shorthanded situations (80.2 percent, 10th overall). The Hawks finished fifth in SHGs for.

CRUCIAL FACEOFFS
TROY MURRAY.

MARK BERGEVIN

Yrs. of NHL service: 4
Born: Montreal, Quebec, Canada; August 11, 1965
Position: Defenseman
Height: 6-0
Weight: 185
Uniform no.: 2
Shoots: left

Career statistics:

GP	G	A	TP	PIM
255	12	29	41	265

1987-88 statistics:

GP	G	A	TP	+/−	PIM	PP	SH	GW	GT	S	PCT
58	1	6	7	-19	85	0	0	0	0	51	2.0

LAST SEASON

Bergevin was spotted in and out of the lineup for the fourth season, including a stint in the minors. Games played total was a career low, and he was the lowest scoring regular on the squad.

THE FINESSE GAME

Marc is a good skater for his size, with good foot speed, agility and great balance, and he uses that skill in his work in the defensive zone. He could be better at forcing the play wide because he still reacts to the puck and not the player, and that means he begins his turns late and is chasing the opposing forward rather than containing him.

Bergevin is hesitant to use his skating ability in an attacking manner, and he prefers to tend to the defensive zone first. He can read the breakout fairly well and get the puck to the forwards, but he's not necessarily going to make the best play. He doesn't follow the play up-ice and is rarely involved in play from the blue line. Bergevin likes to shoot from the point, taking at most one or two steps in before releasing an average slapshot.

THE PHYSICAL GAME

Since his role is that of the takeout defenseman and not the breakout defenseman, Bergevin should be using his size better than he is currently. He's nowhere near physical enough in his takeouts, and he doesn't apply himself consistently either.

His balance allows him to hit very well in open ice — when he feels like — because his balance allows him to plant himself to his best advantage and then to recover and return quickly to the play.

THE INTANGIBLES

The way he played last year, Bergevin was neither fish nor fowl. He didn't show outstanding offensive skills, but he didn't show outstanding physical skills either.

He's still a youngster with untapped potential in terms of strength and physical play, but if he continues to play this season as he did last season he'll find himself on the bench again.

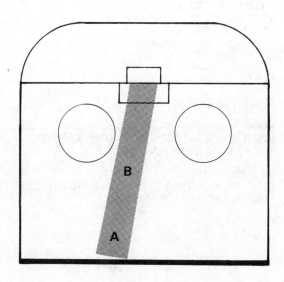

KEITH BROWN

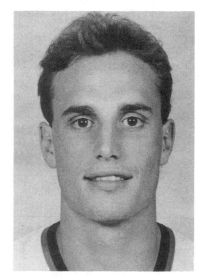

Yrs. of NHL service: 9
Born: Corner Brook, Nfld., Canada; May 6, 1960
Position: Defenseman
Height: 6-1
Weight: 192
Uniform no.: 4
Shoots: right

Career statistics:

GP	G	A	TP	PIM
536	47	204	251	520

1987-88 statistics:

GP	G	A	TP	+/–	PIM	PP	SH	GW	GT	S	PCT
24	3	6	9	5	45	0	0	1	0	39	7.7

LAST SEASON

Games played total was a career low; he missed 55 games with a knee injury. Assist and point totals were career lows, goal total was third lowest of career. It marked the eighth time in nine years that Brown failed to play a full season.

THE FINESSE GAME

Brown is a very gifted skater, and that skill is clearly the best of his finesse abilities. He has balance and foot speed, excellent power and agility. He's quick, he's fast, he's agile and he's all of these things forward, backward and sideways.

What he is not is smart. Keith doesn't have good vision on the ice, and he isn't heavy in the anticipation department either. He has little understanding of the play at the NHL level, despite nine years of experience, and can do little more offensively than run with the puck into the opposing corner and then wonder what play to make, or hit the open man — and only occasionally on the latter skill.

He'd be greatly aided if he kept his head up all the time, but after nine seasons what do you think the chances of change are? He has obvious mechanical skills, but Brown just doesn't have good instincts. The application of those skills is what's lacking in his play.

Defensively, Brown reads the rush no better than fairly. He plays the point on the power play with an above average shot and likes to use his speed as a fourth attacker, going all the way to the right faceoff spot if the opening exists.

THE PHYSICAL GAME

Hours in the weight room have made Brown the strongest of the Hawk defensemen. He uses that strength to play a fairly tough game but could be more consistent in using that strength. He could take on almost anyone in the NHL along the boards or corners and be expected to win, yet Brown doesn't use his strength to follow through on his takeouts.

Part of this problem may be his skating stance. Keith is stiff-legged and as such his balance is high, so he can be tipped off the puck by better balanced, but not necessarily stronger, opponents.

THE INTANGIBLES

The Hawks need a decent season health-wise from Brown to help stabilize the club, but they probably won't get it. As we said, he's very strong but always seems to be coming back and coming back and coming back from injury. It's hard to play well when you're constantly regaining the conditioning you've lost, and that's a big problem for Keith.

Add an attitude that allows for coasting and what you've got is a follower more than a leader, and a classic underachiever. What you've got is Keith Brown.

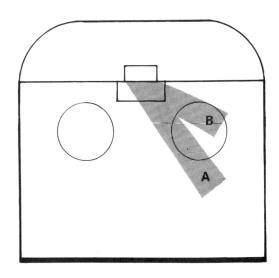

MIKE EAGLES

Yrs. of NHL service: 2
Born: Sussex, N.B., Canada; March 7, 1963
Position: Center
Height: 5-10
Weight: 180
Uniform no.: 11
Shoots: left

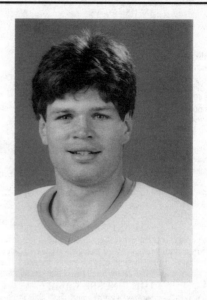

Career statistics:

GP	G	A	TP	PIM
224	34	41	75	180

1987-88 statistics:

GP	G	A	TP	+/−	PIM	PP	SH	GW	GT	S	PCT
76	10	10	20	-18	74	1	2	2	0	89	11.2

LAST SEASON

Games played was a career high, but all point totals were career lows. PIM total was a career high. His plus/minus was the team's fourth worst and he tied for the club lead in short-handed goals.

THE FINESSE GAME

Eagles is a good skater at the NHL level, but none of his skating skills are exceptional. He has a strong stride and can muster some speed because of it, and that skill makes him a good checking forward (forget the plus/minus; when he's not on the checking line he's often with the Stastnys to play defense for them).

Mike has never been much of a scorer because of his less-than-exceptional hand skills, but his constant hustle will get him into scoring position. He's smart enough to go to the net for rebounds and deflections and that's how he'll get his goals. He has a fairly good view of the ice from a defensive standpoint, but he can't make use of the vision offensively; he doesn't have the anticipation to see the openings or know when to break for them.

He will willingly use his teammates but his bad hands derail his intentions. He's not a good passer in terms of accuracy or sensitivity, and he certainly can't thread a needle with a puck. He'll need time and space for any play he's going to make.

THE PHYSICAL GAME

Eagles is neither an overwhelmingly physical nor exceptionally aggressive player, but he willingly gets involved along the boards and in traffic. He has improved his strength to add some zest to his body checking, and that improved strength helps him retain the puck when checked himself.

THE INTANGIBLES

Eagles is a role player with some versatility: he can play the left side or center. He can lift his game to better numbers but the strength of his game will always be as a dependable — but not exceptional — checker, and that lack of standout ability in any department leaves him prey for replacement by a player who's better able to contribute in the offensive end.

DIRK GRAHAM

Yrs. of NHL service: 4
Born: Regina, Sask., Canada; July 29, 1959
Position: Right wing
Height: 5-11
Weight: 190
Uniform no.: 33
Shoots: right

Career statistics:

GP	G	A	TP	PIM
268	84	98	182	323

1987-88 statistics:

GP	G	A	TP	+/−	PIM	PP	SH	GW	GT	S	PCT
70	24	24	48	-7	71	10	1	2	0	173	13.9

LAST SEASON

Games played total was a full season career low, as were assist and point totals. He finished fifth in Hawk scoring and, though he concluded the season as a minus-player, Graham was plus 4 in 42 Hawk games. He was traded to Chicago by Minnesota in exchange for Curt Fraser.

THE FINESSE GAME

Graham is an average skater, not equipped with a lot of speed but strong and sturdy on his skates and tireless as well, making him well suited for his checking role. He is not very agile on his skates, but he has sufficient foot speed to get a jump on an opposing defenseman controlling the point in the Hawks' zone. Dirk would be best described — at least skating-wise — as a power forward.

He combines skating with good anticipation and vision. Dirk reads the play well and is able to spot the opening and jump into it even though he is not tremendously quick. That quickness makes him particularly effective killing penalties, because his persistent skating efforts result in turnovers that he can convert into shorthanded goals.

Dirk has some talent with his hands and can use his teammates, able to get a pass to them with good touch. He can fake and deke, and likes especially to go to his right. He has shown a degree of goal scoring talent at the NHL level, but is not a natural goal scorer; the puck doesn't follow him around, he has to go get it.

THE PHYSICAL GAME

Graham is very tough, under-rated tough. He stands up for his teammates and is a mucker and a grinder. Dirk plays a very physical style, using his body well along the boards to take the opposition off the puck. He can take care of himself when the going gets rough and is a fairly good fighter.

He is difficult to take off the puck because of his sturdiness on his skates, one reason why he can work the boards well. Because he goes into traffic to get the puck and to score, Graham gets punished a lot.

THE INTANGIBLES

Graham works so hard that his spirit becomes infectious. He garners tremendous respect from teammate and foe alike because of his work habits, and those work habits are the embodiment of his character. He developed his skills in three minor leagues before making the jump to the NHL, and he deserves a ton of credit for his accomplishments.

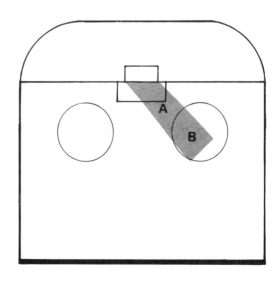

STEVE LARMER

Yrs. of NHL service: 6
Born: Peterborough, Ontario, Canada; June 16, 1961
Position: Right wing
Height: 5-10
Weight: 185
Uniform no.: 28
Shoots: left

Career statistics:

GP	G	A	TP	PIM
487	224	277	501	189

1987-88 statistics:

GP	G	A	TP	+/-	PIM	PP	SH	GW	GT	S	PCT
80	41	48	89	-5	42	21	7	0	0	245	16.7

LAST SEASON

Larmer played all 80 games for the sixth consecutive season. Goal total was highest in three seasons, assist and point totals second highest of career. He finished second on the team in assists and points, third in goals, first in power play goals and shorthanded goals (tied with Denis Savard in SHG total) and second in shots on goal. His shooting percentage and plus minus totals were second best among regulars.

THE FINESSE GAME

Smarts, instincts, anticipation — all the mental abilities for goal scoring that can't be taught — are the highlights of Larmer's game. It's a game that's easily explained: Larmer gets into position to shoot the puck before the puck gets to him. His tremendous sense of the game puts him in a prime scoring area, and when the puck gets to him his excellent shot does the rest.

Larmer's quick and soft hands would allow him to handle the puck well, but because Denis Savard is his center, Larmer doesn't have to. When he does have the puck he passes extremely well, using his sense to find the openings. He obviously accepts a pass excellently, and he prefers to shoot from the base of the right faceoff circle, but will move to the goal-crease if opportunity demands.

His skating is nothing to write home about, and it is his skating that keeps him hidden from the general public. Because he doesn't have blazing speed or exceptional agility — and because his center does — Larmer can get lost in the shuffle. Which is precisely what happens until he pops up in the middle of nowhere to score.

He doesn't have a lot of speed or quickness, but Steve does have great strength and balance on his skates; he has to, because he's always operating in the traffic areas near the net.

And his skating is good enough, combined with his brains, to make him a very solid defensive performer.

THE PHYSICAL GAME

Steve is not a physical player in terms of imposing himself on the opposition. He doesn't bang in the corners and he doesn't fight, but he's alway working in traffic (which makes his consecutive game streak that much more admirable). He willingly takes his punishment when he flits around the net.

THE INTANGIBLES

Larmer is the kind of player that even NHL coaches don't know how good he is — until they see him day in and day out. He'd carried a reputation for not being in good condition and he worked especially hard prior to last season's training camp to discard that label.

Certainly it worked, because he had 13 goals and 24 points in his first 20 games. He slipped in the second quarter (just four more goals by game 42), but he closed well — scoring 15 goals in his last 19 games.

What is more important in those numbers is the fact that he had just 13 even strength goals all year (21 PPG and seven SHG). While we know how valuable he can be in specialty team situations because of his brains and scoring touch, 13 ESGs is an awful total (a guy who scores 13 ESGs is a guy who can be ignored in even-strength situations). That total must be improved.

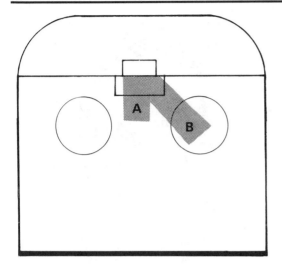

STEVE LUDZIK

Yrs. of NHL service: 6
Born: Toronto, Ontario, Canada; April 3, 1962
Position: Center
Height: 5-11
Weight: 186
Uniform no.: 29
Shoots: left

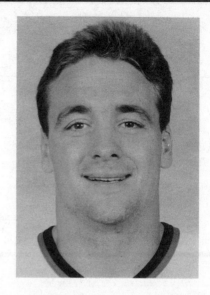

Career statistics:

GP	G	A	TP	PIM
407	45	92	137	319

1987-88 statistics:

GP	G	A	TP	+/-	PIM	PP	SH	GW	GT	S	PCT
73	6	15	21	-14	40	1	0	1	0	55	10.9

LAST SEASON

Games played total was highest in three seasons, ditto point total. His PIM total was lowest among full time players.

THE FINESSE GAME

Ludzik is a defensive forward, a role player so tightly type-cast that in many games the only ice time he sees is during penalty killing. He works well on this unit because of his skating (his good quickness helps him to pressure the points while killing penalties) and his hands are good enough for him to control the puck well while skating to kill time.

He has fairly good defensive anticipation, but his sense of the game and read of the ice doesn't extend to the offensive game.

THE PHYSICAL GAME

Ludzik is an aggressive player, bringing good strength and willingness to hit to bear for Chicago. He's not the biggest guy in the world, but Steve will definitely take his lumps while cruising up and down the wing.

That willingness goes a long way toward explaining his tendency toward injury, because Ludzik's body takes a pounding.

THE INTANGIBLES

Ludzik's lack of offensive smarts restricts him to fourth line, role-playing status. He can be valuable in that role, but he is also eminently replaceable.

DAVE MANSON

Yrs. of NHL service: 2
Born: Prince Albert, Sask., Canada; January 27, 1967
Position: Defenseman
Height: 6-2
Weight: 190
Uniform no.: 3
Shoots: left

Career statistics:

GP	G	A	TP	PIM
117	2	14	16	331

1987-88 statistics:

GP	G	A	TP	+/−	PIM	PP	SH	GW	GT	S	PCT
54	1	6	7	-12	185	0	0	0	0	47	2.1

LAST SEASON

Second season games played, assist and point totals were career lows, while PIM was career high (and was team's third highest total).

THE FINESSE GAME

Manson's skating is better than would be expected for a defenseman who concentrates on the physical game. He has good balance and a touch of speed in his skating, but most impressive is his turning ability. Not that his turns are awesome, but the agility he shows is surprising for a predominantly physical player. Dave moves fairly well in traffic.

Balance plays a big part in Manson's game as well, because it is his balance that makes him so effective as a hitter. He remains vertical after collisions, and that means he is able to re-join the play immediately.

What he doesn't do well is handle the puck. Dave is willing to try containing the offensive blue line but his hands betray him. He doesn't carry the puck well when he skates, and he'll try to find his man for a breakout pass but won't always be successful. That's why he's going to be taking guys to the boards and covering the front of the net, and not starting the offensive play.

When he shoots (which is obviously a rare occurrence — Manson won't often follow the play up-ice) he lets go a hard slap shot from the middle of the blue line, as he tries to get a better angle.

THE PHYSICAL GAME

Manson is a tough, tough kid. He enjoys playing the physical game and is a punishing hitter, using his size and strength to advantage in the corners and the front of the net.

He's also one of those guys who doesn't have to be told what his job is. No coach has to tap him on the shoulder and say, "You see that guy on the other team? He's running our guys; why don't you do something about it?" Manson sees what has to be done on the ice, and then he goes and does it.

His physical play remains one-dimensional because he is not yet able to follow up a hit that yields the puck with a good play.

Manson also sacrifices his body to block shots.

THE INTANGIBLES

Mike Keenan should love this guy. If Manson is paired properly, if he teams with a guy who can take care of the finesse part of the game, then he could become a real stabilizing force for Chicago. Dave does have the tendency to put pressure on himself, but his confidence should grow as his NHL experience deepens.

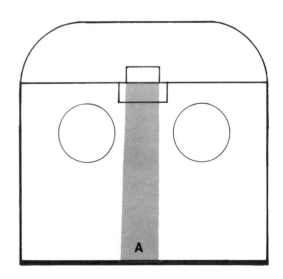

BOB MCGILL

Yrs. of NHL service: 7
Born: Edmonton, Alta., Canada; April 27, 1962
Position: Defenseman
Height: 6-1
Weight: 190
Uniform no.: 25
Shoots: right

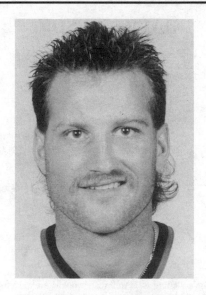

Career statistics:

GP	G	A	TP	PIM
365	7	32	39	1,085

1987-88 statistics:

GP	G	A	TP	+/-	PIM	PP	SH	GW	GT	S	PCT
67	4	7	11	-19	131	0	0	1	0	56	7.1

LAST SEASON

Games played total was the second highest of his career, while all point totals were career highs.

THE FINESSE GAME

McGill is not blessed with a plethora of finesse skills. He doesn't skate very well, he doesn't handle the puck very well and he doesn't see the ice very well, though he has improved on all three of those skills since his NHL debut in 1981.

He has learned to play his defensive position a little better, but still is confused in his own end of the ice. He is not an offensive threat because his slap shot is soft, belying his size and strength.

THE PHYSICAL GAME

McGill is a very physical player and will hit hard and often when he can. He doesn't always catch the fleeter of the League's forwards, but if he does they're destined for a ride to the boards.

He can clear the front of the net or take the opposition off the puck along the boards, but McGill doesn't know what to do with the puck once he gains it.

He must play tough to play at all. He benefits from playing in Chicago Stadium because of the smaller ice surface, which makes his skating better and his hitting more insistent.

THE INTANGIBLES

McGill is a one-dimensional and very marginal NHLer. He survives as an enforcer, a player to take the physical heat off his teammates so they can stay on the ice and out of the penalty box.

He'll get starts against rivals like Detroit and Minnesota, in order to neutralize Joey Kocur and Basil McRae (respectively), but don't expect to see McGill on the ice in the last minute of a close game.

Bob does work hard at improving but it's his physical play that will keep him in the League — because he's just brutal on the blue line.

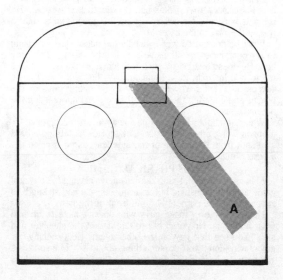

BOB MURRAY

Yrs. of NHL service: 13
Born: Kingston, Ontario, Canada; November 26, 1954
Position: Defenseman
Height: 5-10
Weight: 185
Uniform no.: 6
Shoots: right

Career statistics:

GP	G	A	TP	PIM
944	125	359	484	799

1987-88 statistics:

GP	G	A	TP	+/-	PIM	PP	SH	GW	GT	S	PCT
62	6	20	26	-7	44	1	0	0	1	97	6.2

LAST SEASON

Games played total was the second lowest of his career and lowest in six seasons. Point total was lowest in 11 seasons, assist total lowest in six seasons. PIM total was lowest in 10 seasons. Murray finished with the best plus/minus and lowest PIM total among regular defensemen.

THE FINESSE GAME

Solid, dependable, consistent and unknown: that's Bob Murray. He doesn't do anything fancy, he just gets the puck and moves it out of the Hawks zone quickly, efficiently and correctly. Murray plays his defensive angles as if he were writing a textbook, and he has to do that because of his size. He reads the offensive rush and anticipates its ramifications very well. He's an above average defenseman, so forget that plus/minus rating.

Bob remains an outstanding skater, but he doesn't have the quickness he once had, so he doesn't rush the puck as he used to — at least not when partner Doug Wilson is healthy. When Wilson is out, Murray opens up his offense to compensate. His offensive instincts are very good and that's why he's a fixture on the power play.

He sees the lay well in both zones and gets the puck to his teammates in the openings. He'll pinch in prudently at the blue line and he uses a good slap shot from the point as a scoring weapon.

THE PHYSICAL GAME

Murray is a direct contradiction to Darwinian principle of only the strong surviving. Rather, he embodies the theory regarding the inheritance of acquired characteristics: He learned how to be smart, how to play the body when the situation is in his favor, how to make the most of what he has.

He can't make the play in the corner on strength alone if he runs into a strong, hard-working forward. Vision and ability to move the puck quickly to teammates once it's won are Murray's assets here.

Because of his strength (or lack thereof) the opposition would like to get Murray isolated in front of the net, where he'll be unable to hold off big forwards. Murray counters that by holding and interfering smartly.

THE INTANGIBLES

He could have become the Hawks' best defender with Wilson out, but that would be a lot to ask of Murray physically after a decade-plus in the NHL. He's the kind of guy any of the young Hawk defenders should be learning from.

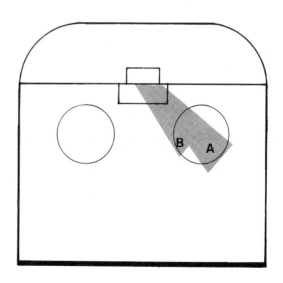

TROY MURRAY

Yrs. of NHL service: 6
Born: Winnipeg, Manitoba, Canada; July 31, 1962
Position: Center
Height: 6-1
Weight: 195
Uniform no.: 19
Shoots: right

Career statistics:

GP	G	A	TP	PIM
432	144	196	340	403

1987-88 statistics:

GP	G	A	TP	+/−	PIM	PP	SH	GW	GT	S	PCT
79	22	36	58	-17	96	3	2	2	1	148	14.9

LAST SEASON

Games played total was second highest of his career, but all point totals were lowest in three seasons. PIM total was a career high. He finished fourth in team scoring, third in assists. His plus/minus rating was third worst among forwards.

THE FINESSE GAME

Troy's skating is what powers his excellent defensive game, a game to which the plus/minus rating cannot be applied. Murray is very assertive on the puck, always driving toward it and is excellent at going into traffic and coming out with the puck. He succeeds because of the strength he has on his skates and because of his exceptional balance. He is very difficult to knock down, and that strength meshes perfectly with his robust style of play.

He doesn't usually take offensive advantage of his skating by carrying the puck, preferring to dump it in far too frequently. This despite the fact that he could barrel over the defense, or even use his agility to make a move or two.

Murray is in the wrist and snapshot range and is very dangerous if he can penetrate the area inside the faceoff circles, where he will unleash a quick and accurate shot. Twenty-five goals is in his character; 45 goals is a freak of nature.

Anticipation is the second asset that makes Murray's game go, and he applies it offensively and defensively. Troy can use his teammates well because his vision and anticipation reveal their moves to him, as well as revealing the openings. Defensively, he sees those openings and can thus thwart the opposing center in his attempts to exploit them.

THE PHYSICAL GAME

Murray's strength makes him very good without the puck, because that strength makes him difficult to get away from. Troy puts that strength — along with a healthy mean streak — to good use. He just hits non-stop, and his persistent physicalness wears down the opposition. It makes him an excellent forechecker because he really bruises the opposing defensemen.

Murray is successful in his drive toward the puck because he has great hand and wrist strength. That means he can take the puck away without having to use the strength of his whole body; very convenient in traffic when he can only get his hands near the puck.

That strength also makes him a good faceoff man, but he's slipped a little in that category and could improve.

THE INTANGIBLES

Many expect Murray to repeat his 45-goal season and are disappointed when he does not. While he can and will score goals, Murray's responsibility is to prevent goals. Anything he does in addition to that is gravy.

Troy's on-ice demeanor and off-ice attitude should stand him in good stead with new coach Mike Keenan, who will probably use Murray the same way he used Dave Poulin while in Philadelphia.

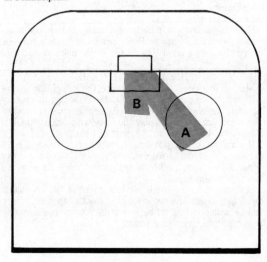

BRIAN NOONAN

Yrs. of NHL service: 1
Born: Boston, Mass., USA; May 29, 1965
Position: Center
Height: 6-1
Weight: 180
Uniform no.: 10
Shoots: right

Career statisics:

GP	G	A	TP	+/−	PIM	PP	SH	GW	GT	S	PCT
77	10	20	30	-27	44	3	0	2	0	87	11.5

LAST SEASON

Noonan's first in the NHL. He was a ninth round pick in 1983 and his plus/minus was the team's worst.

THE FINESSE GAME

Noonan showed good stick skills and puck sense for a rookie. He has good anticipation and vision and seems to see the ice well, and to his benefit he uses those assets both offensively and defensively (he wasn't as bad as that plus/minus indicates).

He is also poised and very patient with the puck, the kind of player that waits for the goaltender to commit himself on a play near the net instead of just slamming the puck into the goalie's pads.

Brian has soft hands, so he carries and passes the puck well. His hand skills mesh with his mental faculties to make him an effective power play performer.

THE PHYSICAL GAME

Noonan isn't a huge physical specimen but he gets his nose dirty. He works in the pits around the net and isn't afraid to get his nose dirty. He's not a big banger but he'll take his knocks, and his strength on his skates and balance help to mkae him effective in traffic.

THE INTANGIBLES

A good training camp put Noonan into the NHL, and he showed fairly well for himself. The Hawks could use another competent center behind Denis Savard and Troy Murray, especially they have three scoring right wings (Vaive, Presley and Larmer) with another — Ulf Sandstrom — possibly on the way.

He has the potential to improve, but must now impress Mike Keenan of that.

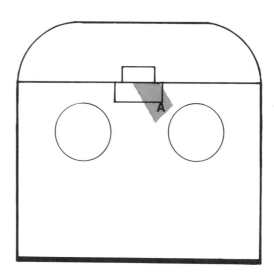

GARY NYLUND

Yrs. of NHL service: 6
Born: Surrey, B.C., Canada; October 23, 1963
Position: Defenseman
Height: 6-3
Weight: 210
Uniform no.: 22
Shoots: left

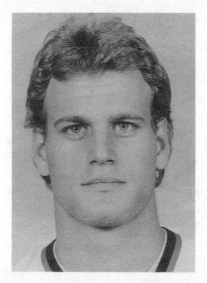

Career statistics:

GP	G	A	TP	PIM
374	18	85	103	796

1987-88 statistics:

GP	G	A	TP	+/-	PIM	PP	SH	GW	GT	S	PCT
76	4	15	19	-9	208	0	0	0	0	92	4.3

LAST SEASON

Games played total was lowest in three seasons, assist total lowest full season mark. He led the club in PIM.

THE FINESSE GAME

Nylund is a stay-at-home defenseman whose skills match his game. He has good balance for a big man but his foot speed is a little slow. Nylund plays his defensive angles fairly well, but his lack of foot speed makes him susceptible in his turns. Improved quickness would also make him more mobile and more able to get to loose pucks. But we're not saying Nylund is immobile, just that he could be more mobile.

He has great strength on his skates and is very difficult to knock off the puck. Nylund generally handles the puck well and he will most usually make the quick, correct pass to his forwards. He is not an exceptional stickhandler when carrying the puck, however, so his only play is going to be straight ahead.

He shoots from the point but could shoot more frequently, and Gary does have the potential to be effective at the offensive blue line because he does see the ice well. He can find open teammates and get the puck to them, but Nylund's depth of understanding is not such that he will see openings and exploit them.

Defensively he has a tendency toward the giveaway if he is pressured while going back for the puck. Once he's turned and has the play in front of him he's fairly poised and patient, but he's not guaranteed to clear the zone.

THE PHYSICAL GAME

Gary is a very physical player and he works hard at improving his already excellent strength. He is always in the weight room and the results can be seen on the ice, but sometimes they can be seen too frequently.

Nylund is often too aggressive, and that hurts the team. He's so determined to belt someone that he runs around and gets out of position, and that meandering opens up a lot of holes in the Hawk defense. He takes himself out of the play when his emotions get the better of him, and his over-aggressiveness makes him prone to stupid penalties.

He enjoys hitting and really punishes the opposition along the boards or in front of the net. He sacrifices his body to block shots and, though he is not a fighter per se, Nylund is tough and more than willing to mix it up.

THE INTANGIBLES

First impression says he's got to tone down his act, but then we remember Mike Keenan's the coach now and we know what he likes. Still, Nylund has got to exercise some kind of control over his temper.

And as for us saying he can become effective at the offensive blue line, effective is a relative term. Gary's not going to turn into Doug Wilson, but could contribute offensively. That would serve to make him more valuable, but he's got to stay out of the penalty box to do so.

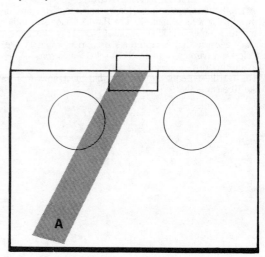

DARREN PANG

Yrs. of NHL service: 1
Born: Medford, Ontario, Canada; February 17, 1964
Position: Goaltender
Height: 5-5
Weight: 155
Uniform no.: 40
Catches: left

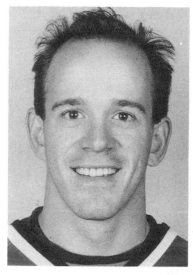

Career statistics:

GP	MINS	G	SO	AVG	A	PIM
468	2,608	167	0	3.84	6	2

1987-88 statisics:

GP	MINS	AVG	W	L	T	SO	GA	SA	SAPCT	PIM
45	2,548	3.84	17	23	1	0	163	1,501	.891	

LAST SEASON

Pang's rookie season. He played more games than any other rookie goaltender. He tied for third place with Ron Hextall for most assists by a goaltender.

THE PHYSICAL GAME

Darren Pang plays goal the way kids play "Chicken." He dares you to score. Pang squeezes every bit of his size he can get from his midget-wrestler-sized body, and he does that by standing up in the net and challenging the shooters — most of the time.

Then there are the times Darren hangs back in his net and says "I dare you." He doesn't challenge as well as he could on screen shots, and he'll hang back in the goal when his concentration flags. But that only lets him use his considerable reflexes. He has a tremendous, just tremendous glove hand: it is super-fast and could become the best in the League if he sticks around. His feet are just as fast and Pang uses them well.

He has good balance and moves well from post to post, just as he moves well in and out of the net. Pang's balance also helps him regain his stance and his feet after going to the ice. He skates well and uses that skill when retrieving loose pucks for his defense. Darren will move the puck to his defense, but he can't handle the puck backhanded; he has to reverse his hands on the stick.

Darren uses his stick to clear rebounds well except for shots between his pads — the five-hole. He doesn't control those rebounds well and they come squirting back toward the opposition.

Because of his size, most opponents tend to go high on him, and that's where his challenging style helps. He has special pads for his shoulders because of all the shots that hit him there. Darren also gets hit in the head a lot, but remains unafraid.

THE MENTAL GAME

Pang has an attitude that is almost unmatched in the NHL. Nothing, absolutely nothing, bothers him. He's funny, talkative, bouncy, has fun and is just happy to be in the NHL. He'll give up four goals in the first period and come back for the second as if nothing has happened. Bad goals don't get to him,

bad games don't get to him — his poise is just incredible. The only comparison in terms of nervelessness would have to be Grant Fuhr, but Fuhr is less outgoing than Pang.

In terms of concentration, Pang is fairly solid. He maintains it well from game to game and within the contest (he doesn't have too many chances to lapse: the Hawks allowed more shots on goal last year than any other team).

He also showed, as the Hawks gasped and limped their way into the playoffs and then lost to St. Louis, that he has big save capability.

THE INTANGIBLES

The fans love him, the media loves him, his teammates love him. Now he has to prove he wasn't a one-hit wonder and that he can sustain his position as the club's number one goalie.

WAYNE PRESLEY

Yrs. of NHL service: 3
Born: Dearborn, Mich., USA; March 23, 1965
Position: Right wing
Height: 5-11
Weight: 175
Uniform no.: 17
Shoots: right

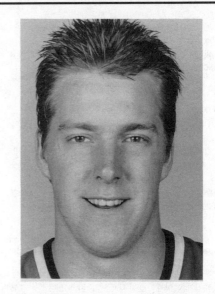

Career statistics:

GP	G	A	TP	PIM
163	51	48	99	204

1987-88 statistics:

GP	G	A	TP	+/−	PIM	PP	SH	GW	GT	S	PCT
42	12	10	22	-13	52	4	0	1	1	89	13.5

LAST SEASON

Presley missed several months with a knee injury. His point totals were the second best of his career.

THE FINESSE GAME

Presley skates well, though not with outstanding speed or agility. He uses his teammates well and he carries the puck well and he can do all these things because he is intelligent on the ice, because he's developing patience and because he has good instincts.

He's becoming very creative without the puck, looking for openings and opportunities, and he's learned to do this without sacrificing his defensive game. Where previously he failed to apply himself defensively the way he does offensively, Wayne has worked at improving his positional play; now the Hawks don't have to worry about him in the defensive zone.

When he gets the opening, Presley likes to gun his shot from the top of the right faceoff circle.

THE PHYSICAL GAME

Presley is willing to take hits if necessary, or to make a hit for the play. He stepped up his physical involvement last year, but is not so much a physically dominant player as he could be a finesse one. Still, his willingness is important.

THE INTANGIBLES

Wayne was showing signs of goal-scoring consistency last season when he went down with the knee injury that made last year a throwaway year in terms of development.

Now that he's covered the defensive end the Hawks want to see some more offense from the guy who scored 139 points one year in junior. Presley has it to give, and this — his third season — would generally be the time to look for it.

Unless he succeeds, he will be pressed for ice time and for a center, as Presley has Rick Vaive and Steve Larmer ahead of him, and centers Troy Murray and Denis Savard doing the honors for Presley's competition.

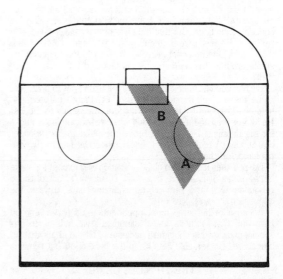

EVERETT SANIPASS

Yrs. of NHL service: 1
Born: Big Cove, N.B., Canada; February 13, 1968
Position: Left wing
Height: 6-1
Weight: 192
Uniform no.: 7
Shoots: left

Career statistics:

GP	G	A	TP	PIM
649	15	24	128	

1987-88 statistics:

GP	G	A	TP	+/-	PIM	PP	SH	GW	GT	S	PCT
57	8	12	20	-9	126	0	0	0	0	55	14.5

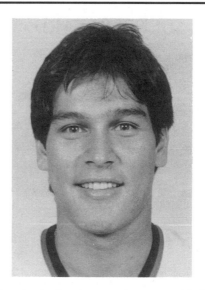

LAST SEASON
First full NHL season. Sanipass was Chicago's first round pick in 1986. He missed five games with a back injury, five games with a broken nose and was also sidelined with rib and hand injuries. His PIM total was highest among forwards.

THE FINESSE GAME
Sanipass's skating is not yet at the level needed to be successful in the NHL, but injuries may make him seem worse than he is. He has a strong stride that keeps him driving through checks, but has not shown NHL speed, quickness or agility.

He has demonstrated good poise and patience on the ice, demonstrated by his smarts in protecting the puck while he prepares to be checked. He's going to be checked a lot because he works in the traffic areas, and that's where his strength afoot and balance help him.

Everett is also smart enough to get into position to score. Though he doesn't yet have the foot speed to consistently do this at the NHL level, he does understand the game well enough to go to the scoring areas when he can. Sanipass also uses his smarts to move the puck alertly, and his vision tells him where to send it. Again, the speed of the game is still too quick for him, but the seeds are there.

He has a very good slap shot from the wing, but he also uses his wrist/snap shot well. It too must be improved speed-wise in terms of release.

THE PHYSICAL GAME
Sanipass has good size which he uses willingly and well. He protects the puck well with his body while in traffic, and he uses his feet well while controlling the puck along the boards.

He takes a check to make his play, but he also uses his body against the opposition aggressively to get the puck from the enemy.

THE INTANGIBLES
While the Hawks need scoring from the left side, Sanipass isn't going to be the one to give it to them — not yet anyway. He is reminiscent of Al Secord in style (though far less aggressive) and he'll get his goals through physical play. Which is okay, if Steve Thomas comes through as a port-side scorer. In which case Everett would make a good complement to him.

Sanipass is a hard worker, a good team man with plenty of character and desire to succeed.

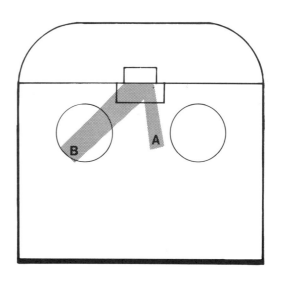

DENIS SAVARD

Yrs. of NHL service: 8
Born: Pointe Gatineau, Quebec, Canada; February 4, 1961
Position: Center
Height: 5-10
Weight: 170
Uniform no.: 18
Shoots: right

Career statistics:

GP	G	A	TP	PIM
618	301	550	851	669

1987-88 statistics:

GP	G	A	TP	+/-	PIM	PP	SH	GW	GT	S	PCT
80	44	87	131	4	95	14	7	6	1	270	16.3

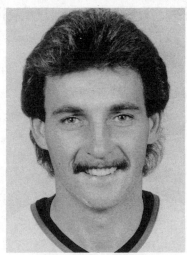

LAST SEASON

Savard played all 80 games for the third time in his career and second time in three seasons. Goal total was second highest of his career and assist total tied career high. Together they formed his best statistical season. He finished third overall in League scoring and assists and fifth in shorthanded goals. He led the Hawks in scoring for the seventh consecutive season, topping the club in goals, assists, points, shorthanded goals (tied with Steve Larmer), shots on goal, plus/minus and game winners (tied with Rick Vaive).

THE FINESSE GAME

Savard is a tremendous package of finesse skills, and his skating is the best of those skills. From a complete standstill, Denis is one of the quickest — if not the quickest player in the League. He has almost incomparable one-step acceleration. He has a low center of gravity and skates very low to the ice, darting from place to place like a bug on linoleum. Savard's incredible balance and foot speed allow him to execute rapid directional changes in any plane — forward, backward or laterally. He uses that one-step quickness to keep the passing lanes open, especially on the power play.

Denis is one of the NHL's best playmakers, and his combination of soft hands and amazing ice vision and anticipation are the reasons why. Savard can get a pass anywhere at any time so a teammate can take advantage of an opening, or he can maneuver through traffic at will. Those high skill levels make him one of the best one-on-one players in the League, a talent he sometimes uses excessively.

Savard is almost as good a scorer as he is a playmaker, and can score from anywhere within the offensive zone because of his excellent wrist shot (accurate, quickly released, heavy). He'll also finesse the puck home from in tight — just leave him half an inch and he can score.

THE PHYSICAL GAME

Savard likes to stay out of the fray in front of the opposition net because of his size, but his small stature does him no harm because he is quick and difficult to hit. He is not, by any means, a physical player, but he will use his stick on occasion. He is also not big on playing in pain.

THE INTANGIBLES

Last year we asked how Savard would get along with his new coach. Turns out he liked Bob Murdoch just fine. Now we wonder how he'll get along with Mike Keenan, who's big on two-way play but has never had a superstar center before.

Though Denis is searching for consistency in his game, his scoring last year shows he's not quite found it. Twenty five of his goals and 79 of his assists came in the first 42 games: that left 19 goals and 52 points for the last 38 games. That's not even distribution.

He had just seven goals in his last 19 games, just five at even strength.

But this is quibbling. Without Savard, the Hawks wouldn't be anywhere. They withstood — barely — the loss of Doug Wilson. They could never withstand the loss of Savard, and that's a true measure of his value.

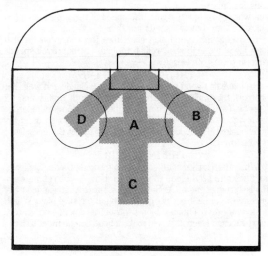

MIKE STAPLETON

Yrs. of NHL service: 2
Born: Sarnia, Ontario, Canada; May 5, 1966
Position: Center
Height: 5-10
Weight: 183
Uniform no.: 12
Shoots: right

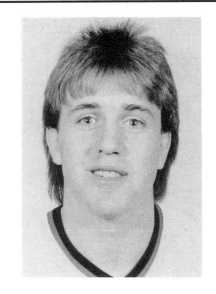

Career statistics:

GP	G	A	TP	PIM
92	5	15	20	65

1987-88 statistics:

GP	G	A	TP	+/−	PIM	PP	SH	GW	GT	S	PCT
53	2	9	11	-10	59	0	0	1	0	50	4.0

LAST SEASON

Mike, son of former Chicago great Pat Stapleton, made his NHL debut last year, although he was recalled (but did not see action) for the 1985-86 playoffs.

THE FINESSE GAME

Mike is an average finesse player at the NHL level, without one particular element of his game that is exceptional. He has good balance and agility on his feet, and he also has some power in his stride for acceleration, but all of these aspects of his skating could be improved at the NHL level. He also needs to improve his foot speed so as to help develop his lateral mobility.

Stapleton has, at various times, demonstrated puckhandling ability complemented by hockey sense to equal play making ability, but he's been unable to harness those talents consistently.

On the whole, he does not yet function well at the NHL level in terms of his finesse skills, but has shown the potential to develop nicely. Currently, his blend of skating ability and hockey sense make him a good penalty killer.

THE PHYSICAL GAME

Stapleton does not have the size to play an outstanding physical game and he hasn't shown outstanding finesse play, so he's going to have trouble succeeding against larger opponents. He's willing to take the body, but he must increase his strength because he is easily pushed off the puck easily.

THE INTANGIBLES

A hard worker and a great kid, Stapleton may just not have the talent to be a consistent NHLer. He has the ability to sit for 15 minutes and then go great guns off the bench, but he's going to make mistakes that his hard work can't cover up.

Right now he's beyond role player. He's a fringe NHLer who must prove he belongs in the League for 80 games.

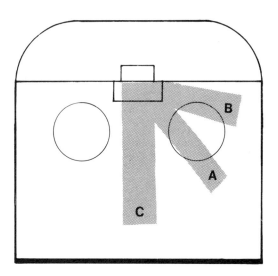

DUANE SUTTER

Yrs. of NHL service: 9
Born: Viking, Alberta, Canada; March 16, 1960
Position: Right wing
Height: 6-1
Weight: 185
Uniform no.: 16
Shoots: right

Career statistics:

GP	G	A	TP	PIM
584	128	180	308	961

1987-88 statistics:

GP	G	A	TP	+/-	PIM	PP	SH	GW	GT	S	PCT
37	7	9	16	2	70	3	0	0	0	74	9.5

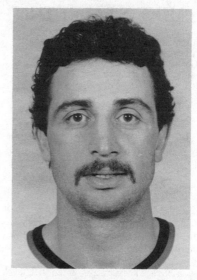

LAST SEASON

Games played total was the second lowest of his career, lowest in seven seasons (he missed 30 games with a knee injury). Goal and assist total matched career lows, and point total was a career low.

THE FINESSE GAME

Finesse is the one word never used to describe a Sutter and Duane is a good example of a reason why. He's not an artist with the puck, but he's not a butcher either, but he lacks consistency in his playmaking — not through lack of trying, but through lack of understanding his own limits. He'll come down the ice and occasionally take himself out of the play by going to his backhand and the bad ice.

Duane is a determined skater, and he does boast a bit of quickness in his feet, though he is not very agile. He brings a lot of strength to bear through his stride as he traverses the wing, which is important for his physical game.

He can carry the puck well enough and he's able to play both wings. When he's hot, Sutter is better on the left side, but he'll always make prettier plays — and be more effective — on the right side because his stick is open to the center of the ice and he's on his forehand.

But when you need a goal in the last minute of a tight game, he's not the guy you put out, because he's not a pure goal scorer.

THE PHYSICAL GAME

Duane is a very strong player and he plies his strength to good effect in hockey's trenches. He hits and hits and never stops going because his strong stride carries him through checking. He works 100 percent of the time and he's good in the corners because he works so hard and is fearless. He will throw his body to make plays, or take hits as well.

His corner work ties up defensemen to allow openings for the pure goal scorers and he might be on the ice in a crucial situation for just that purpose because Duane is a disturber.

Because he is unafraid to take the punishment and stickwork that accompanies a position in the crease, Duane is tough in front of the net and will do most of his scoring from within 15 feet.

THE INTANGIBLES

Chicago absolutely needs Duane Sutter. The Hawks are a team trying to get over the hump of mediocrity and they need the leadership and extra push Duane can give them. He stands up for the team and they need that badly.

He's a character individual and plays in pain, and he doesn't have to score 30 or 40 goals to be a valuable hockey player. His problem is his health: Will he be physically able to play the way he has to?

And don't you think Mike Keenan is going to love having the prototypical Sutter in his lineup?

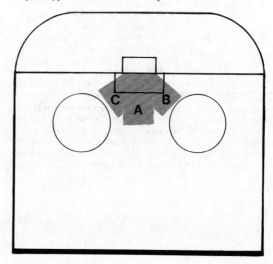

STEVE THOMAS

Yrs. of NHL service: 3
Born: Stockport, England; July 15, 1963
Position: Left wing
Height: 5-10
Weight: 185
Uniform no.: 32
Shoots: left

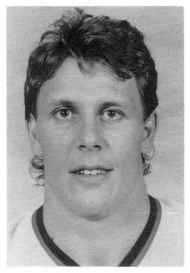

Career statistics:

GP	G	A	TP	PIM
191	69	78	147	192

1987-88 statistics:

GP	G	A	TP	+/−	PIM	PP	SH	GW	GT	S	PCT
30	13	13	26	1	40	5	0	3	1	69	18.8

LAST SEASON

Games played total was full season career low. Stomach/groin and shoulder injuries kept him sidelined for much of the season.

THE FINESSE GAME

Thomas is a very good skater with excellent speed. He's also sturdy on his skates and has good balance, attributes that aid him in his physical game. He has good lateral movement and can change direction quickly, though he is not especially quick. He likes to gain the blue line, pull up short, and then shoot.

Steve has a tremendous shot, which is fortuitous since he's a goal scorer. He knows where the net is and he dents it frequently with his big slap shot from the wing, and he can beat any goaltender with it. But effective as it is, it could be more so. Thomas' shot is not very accurate, with maybe only three or four of 10 attempts on net. The slap shot is not his only weapon, as he uses a good snap shot too.

For as often as he shoots, Thomas doesn't pull the trigger fast enough. Improvement in accuracy and release would bolster Thomas' scoring marks. He succeeds because of good anticipation, concentration on the puck and sense of where he is in relation to the goal, his teammates and the opposition. He uses that anticipation to elude checking and get into position to score.

Thomas also uses that sense for passing. He has nice hands and can pass well, but remember, he's s scorer so he looks to the net first.

THE PHYSICAL GAME

Thomas is a mucker and a grinder. He works the corners well and is fearless, banging bodies with any of the opposition. He has good upper body strength and can get the puck free, while his balance and sturdiness on skates keep him vertical to make his plays.

THE INTANGIBLES

Last year was a wash because of injury, a problem that will creep into this season because of the shoulder surgery Thomas underwent in the off-season. He must show rehabilitation from that.

He will be counted on greatly by the Hawks, because they could use his scoring from the left side. He's even lucked out center-wise, because Denis Savard, Troy Murray and Brian Noonan are all right-handed shots, which means Thomas will be on their forehands as a left wing.

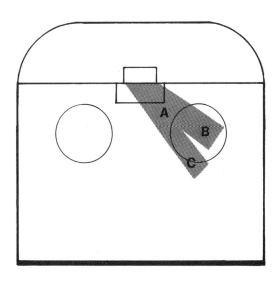

RICK VAIVE

Yrs. of NHL service: 9
Born: Ottawa, Ontario, Canada; May 14, 1959
Position: Right wing
Height: 6-1
Weight: 190
Uniform no.: 27
Shoots: right

Career statistics:

GP	G	A	TP	PIM
657	355	272	627	1,159

1987-88 statistics:

GP	G	A	TP	+/−	PIM	PP	SH	GW	GT	S	PCT
76	43	26	69	-20	108	19	0	6	0	229	18.8

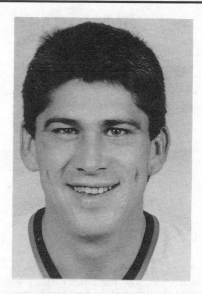

LAST SEASON

Vaive finished third in scoring, second in goals. He was also second in power play goals, tied for the team lead with Denis Savard in game winners, finished third in shots on goal and first in shooting percentage. Games played total was highest in four seasons, ditto goal and point totals.

THE FINESSE GAME

Strength is Vaive's hallmark as a player, so much so that perhaps he should be called a power forward (more later). His excellent skating is powered —if you'll pardon the pun — by his strength on his feet and his ability to drive through checks, and that strength also gives him good acceleration ability and rink-length speed. He'll pull away from checking within several strides.

His skating is so good that the opposition is often forced to resort to penalties to slow him. But Vaive helps the referee make that call by executing some of the League's best dives. His favorite tactic when being closely checked is to grab the opponent's stick — on the ref's blind side, naturally — to make it look like he's being hooked, and then fling himself to the ice and flop like a fish out of water.

Excellent anticipation and instincts around the net serves as the complements to his physical finesse skills, because he knows where to be to score. His skating gets him to that opening but so does his stickhandling, which helps him get tight to the net.

He has a good wrist shot and an excellent slap shot, and Vaive is a threat to score from anywhere inside the offensive zone because his strength drives the puck through the traffic and to the net. All his finesse talents manifest themselves especially well on the power play. He's a goal scorer and he'll look to the net before he looks to his teammates.

His defense is no more than perfunctory.

THE PHYSICAL GAME

As would be expected, strength is the basis of Vaive's physical game. He is a very physical hockey player, excellent along the boards or in the corners at muscling the opposition off the puck with strong hits and good upper body strength.

Vaive hits hard and those hits jar the puck free, and he has the talent to make plays after he gains the puck. He is very difficult to control in front of the net because of his strength and will find a way to get his hand and arms free for a shot on goal.

He obviously accepts hits, because Vaive's entire game is based on playing in traffic. He gets hammered every shift because he's always going to the front of the net.

THE INTANGIBLES

Rick benefited from a more pressure-free environment in Chicago than the one he labored under in Toronto. Of concern would be the inequity between his power play and even strength goal scoring, with almost half of his goals coming with the man-advantage.

His season-long consistency is also questionable because Vaive had 29 of his 43 goals by his 39th game, leaving just 14 goals (and only seven of those at even strength) for his last 37 games.

But he's still a tremendous goal scorer, and he deserves respect for the punishment he's taken to score those goals.

He has yet, by the way, to play a full NHL season — a result of his physical style, no doubt.

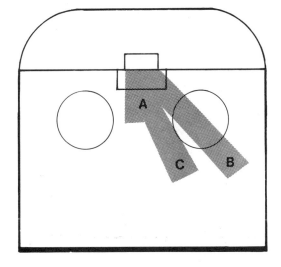

DAN VINCELETTE

Yrs. of NHL service: 1
Born: Verdun, Quebec, Canada; August 1, 1967
Position: Left wing
Height: 6-1
Weight: 202
Uniform no.: 11
Shoots: left

Career statisics:

GP	G	A	TP	+/−	PIM	PP	SH	GW	GT	S	PCT
69	6	11	17	-15	109	2	0	0	0	67	9.0

LAST SEASON

Vincelette's first NHL season after three 1987 playoff games. He was a fourth round draft choice in 1985. He missed three games with a shoulder injury. His PIM total was second highest among forwards.

THE FINESSE GAME

Let's put it this way: It means something when you come out of the Quebec Major Junior Hockey League with a reputation as a grinder. Shall we say that most of Vincelette's best assets are not rooted in the finesse game?

If not for his skating we would say *all* his best assets are not rooted in the finesse game. Vincelette is a strong skater with a powerful stride, and that stride aids him tremendously in his checking game and his mucking in the corners. He doesn't yet have NHL speed or agility, but if he improves his foot speed he could develop the quickness and mobility necessary to be a very good skater.

And who knows? Maybe then he'd be better able to make a play. Right now, Dan has to play a very simple finesse game because he can't see enough of the ice or move the puck well enough in the time alloted him by his skating. The extent of his play is going to be the almost-blind centering pass from the corner.

He has a hard slap shot but won't fool anyone with it consistently, so his scoring right now will have to come from close to the net.

THE PHYSICAL GAME

Vincelette has good size and strength and he uses them to his advantage in his grinding game along the boards. His strength carries him through his checks and his balance keeps him upright and in the play after collisions.

Dan makes his physical play more effective by making sure he completes his checks. He doesn't just bump into the opposition, he hits them. He's an aggressive winger and enjoys playing that game, and that game could be even more effective if he improved his foot speed. Then he could close gaps better and depart from the corner quicker.

THE INTANGIBLES

Vincelette currently benefits by Chicago's dearth of talent along left wing. Notice we didn't say lack of depth, for Chicago adheres to Branch Rickey's philosophy: "From quantity, quality."

The Hawks have the quantity (Everett Sanipass, Vincelette, Steve Thomas, Graham [who can play left or right wing], Behn Wilson [who got shifted from defense], Steve Larmer and

Duane Sutter [converted from right wing]) but have yet to find the quality, so Vincelette can make his mark here with his physical play — which is a characteristic coach Mike Keenan loves.

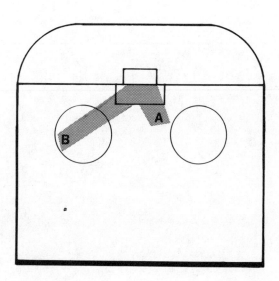

BEHN WILSON

Yrs. of NHL service: 9
Born: Toronto, Ontario, Canada; December 19, 1958
Position: Defenseman
Height: 6-3
Weight: 210
Uniform no.: 23
Shoots: left

Career statistics:

GP	G	A	TP	PIM
601	98	261	359	1,480

1987-88 statistics:

GP	G	A	TP	+/−	PIM	PP	SH	GW	GT	S	PCT
58	6	23	29	-19	166	3	0	0	0	103	5.8

LAST SEASON

Wilson missed all of 1986-87 with a back injury, then missed four games last season with a groin injury and two more with a hamstring pull. He was also shuttled in and out of the lineup.

THE FINESSE GAME

Wilson has above average finesse skills, something a little surprising for such a big man. He is a good skater with a long, strong stride and he can carry the puck well or move it as the opportunity allows.

He has above average intelligence but just doesn't think clearly on the ice, negating his fine skills. Because he hurries his plays without taking that extra second to analyze a situation, Wilson frequently will give the puck up on bad passes, both in the offensive and defensive zones, again rendering useless the skills he does possess.

Wilson takes a low, accurate slap shot from the point and will sneak into the high slot for a good wrister if given the opening.

But when he is on his game, Wilson can be a very dangerous weapon for the Hawks.

THE PHYSICAL GAME

Wilson can be a brutally punishing hitter, smashing forwards with abandon (not to mention his stick, which once gained him a League suspension), yet in the same shift he'll allow a 5-8, 170-pound forward to stand unmolested in front of the Chicago net.

He is not at all aggressive about tying men up or getting in their way, almost as if he says "if I can't really let them have it, why bother?" He has outstanding strength that is underutilized, and thus his physical game must be rated as no more than average, even though he has above average skills.

When Wilson does become aggressive he invariably takes cheap shots at smaller, less physical players — thus adding to his reputation as a thug — but he is also backs up his actions with his fists.

THE INTANGIBLES

When his feet move, Wilson is an asset for Chicago. When his feet don't move he's a liability, and his feet didn't move a lot last year. He's the kind of player Mike Keenan would like,

but Behn's less than consistent output will not endear him to his new coach.

Because he has the skills but doesn't use them, Wilson is one of the League's top five underachievers.

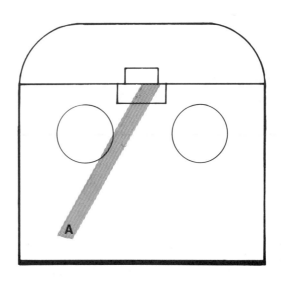

DOUG WILSON

Yrs. of NHL service: 11
Born: Ottawa, Ontario, Canada; July 5, 1957
Position: Defenseman
Height: 6-1
Weight: 187
Uniform no.: 24
Shoots: left

Career statistics:

GP	G	A	TP	PIM
751	176	428	604	625

1987-88 statistics:

GP	G	A	TP	+/−	PIM	PP	SH	GW	GT	S	PCT
27	8	24	32	-17	28	6	1	1	1	87	9.2

LAST SEASON

Recurring shoulder woes and subsequent surgery sidelined Wilson for the season in December. He still finished as the Hawks' number one defensive scorer in all point categories, including PPGs. Games played total was the lowest of his career, point totals lowest in nine seasons.

THE FINESSE GAME

Wilson is an exceptional finesse player with few peers in the NHL, and this despite 11 seasons and countless injuries. His superb skating is probably the primary reason, for all physical skills branch off from there. He's got speed, quickness, agility, superb lateral movement — unmatched by all but the best NHLers — and a change of pace that makes his skating twice as effective.

The ice opens up to him because of his superb play reading ability, and Doug will either find the openings for himself and his teammates or make the openings himself. He has an understanding of both the offensive and defensive plays that is truly world class. His vision meshes with his excellent hand skills to allow him to use his teammates excellently. He can get a pass anywhere, or he can lead a teammate into the clear just as easily. Doug also carries the puck very well and he moves excellently up-ice with it at all speeds.

Defensively, he contains the left point better than almost anyone in the League, and is superb at controlling the puck, taking a step and getting a good shot on net. He uses his oustanding quickness and agility to close the passing lanes and force the play to the puck carrier. If he can intercept a pass, he'll easily turn the play back up-ice.

Wilson's slap shot is well known for its quickness and strength. It's the kind of shot that drives goalies backward — if they see it at all — and it is delivered low to the ice and always on net. Doug charges the slot whenever possible (since his skating will get him back defensively), and his only flaw is that he doesn't shoot to score enough.

He is the Hawks' offensive general whenever he's on the ice, and he's a power play and penalty killing regular.

THE PHYSICAL GAME

What makes Wilson's finesse play so outstanding is his physical game. No thunderous hitting, just solid bodychecking, solid takeouts along the boards and frustrated forwards in front of the net. He stands the man up well and follows through on his checks so that give-and-gos are impossible.

Wilson can also take a forward out of the play and then carry the puck up-ice or pass it for the breakout — again, speed and skills. He succeeds in those confrontations because of his strength and balance.

THE INTANGIBLES

The number one question will be Wilson's health. He must demonstrate that the surgically repaired shoulder can stand NHL wear and tear. Wilson is confident it will.

Doug is the one player the Hawks can't afford to lose, because their defense is by and large clueless without him. His absence has a domino effect on the defense: Partner Bob Murray can no longer concentrate solely on defense any more; players have to be shifted around as the Hawks attempt to fill the offensive void; roles have to be changed because of all the shifting, and so on.

And about that offense: Wilson had six PPGs, the rest of the corps had nine *combined*. Unbelievable. Defense is Chicago's weakest position to begin with, and Wilson's world class skill and intelligence is needed back desperately.

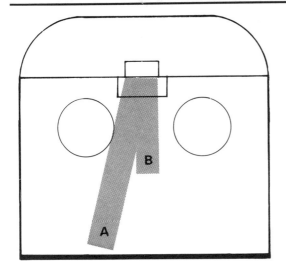

TRENT YAWNEY

Yrs. of NHL service: 1
Born: Hudson Bay, Sask., Canada; September 29, 1965
Position: Defenseman
Height: 6-3
Weight: 185
Uniform no.: 8
Shoots: left

Career statisics:

GP	G	A	TP	+/−	PIM	PP	SH	GW	GT	S	PCT
15	2	8	10	1	15	2	0	0	0	26	7.7

LAST SEASON

Yawney debuted with the Hawks following the Winter Olympic Games. He was a first round choice in the 1984 Entry Draft.

THE FINESSE GAME

Trent is a very talented finesse player. He's a good skater in terms of balance but he could improve for the NHL by bettering his overall quickness. That would bring him to the NHL pace and would also rectify his trouble turning, especially to his left. Currently he has to hold far too often to thwart the opponent's progress as the opposing winger darts past Yawney on the outside.

Make no mistake, Yawney is a good defensive player — he'd have to be to play for Dave King in the Canadian Olympic program. He understands how to force the play wide of the net and how to anticipate the offensive rush. Now Trent just has to pull himself to the NHL tempo.

Yawney also has to improve the speed of his puck movement. He's very smart and has great sense for the game but his hands don't react at NHL speed. That results in missed passes and possible turnovers. But these are not negatives: rather they are to be expected from a player with just 15 games of NHL experience. Yawney will learn and improve.

He has excellent vision as well as anticipation and Trent moves to the openings himself when he can, otherwise he'll attempt to lead a teammate into the clear. Because of his innate vision and hand skills he'll be a specialty teams regular. Yawney takes the puck off the boards very well.

He's got a good shot from the blue line and Trent will definitely cheat into the zone for shots if he can. He controls the point well and will pinch in to contain the play.

THE PHYSICAL GAME

He has good size and reach, which he uses effectively when snaring loose pucks or deflecting shots with his stick. Trent is also unafraid to play the man by taking the body, and he does so effectively and efficiently. He is not a thunderous hitter, so he won't knock anyone senseless, but that's okay because Trent's finesse skills make his physical play more effective.

He could use some greater upper body strength for his duels with opposing forwards camped in the crease.

THE INTANGIBLES

From the minute he joined the Hawks last spring, Yawney was their best defenseman. He has tremendous character and

drive — anyone who plays 58 games against the Soviets in three years and isn't demoralized by it *has* to have strong character — and will no doubt make the improvements that will make him a superior NHLer.

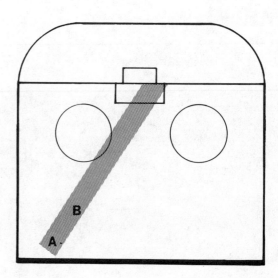

DETROIT RED WINGS

LINE COMBINATIONS
GERARD GALLANT-STEVE YZERMAN-BOB
PROBERT
JOE MURPHY-SHAWN BURR-TIM HIGGINS
PETR KLIMA-ADAM OATES-JOE KOCUR

DEFENSE PAIRINGS
LEE NORWOOD-GILBERT DELORME
STEVE CHIASSON-DOUG HALWARD
JEFF SHARPLES-MIKE O'CONNELL

GOALTENDERS
GREG STEFAN
GLEN HANLON

OTHER PLAYERS
DAVE BARR — Right wing
JOHN CHABOT — Center
MIROSLAV FRYCER — Right wing
PAUL MACLEAN — Right wing
JIM NILL — Right wing
RICK ZOMBO — Defenseman

POWER PLAY

FIRST UNIT:
GERARD GALLANT-STEVE YZERMAN-BOB
PROBERT
JEFF SHARPLES-MIKE O'CONNELL

SECOND UNIT:
PETR KLIMA-ADAM OATES-JOE KOCUR
LEE NORWOOD-DOUG HALWARD

On the first unit, PROBERT posts up in front of the net for rebounds, YZERMAN controls behind the cage and GALLLANT is posted at the right faceoff circle. YZERMAN will feed to SHARPLES and O'CONNELL at the point to move the box around, and the defense will play catch for the same effect before shooting.

On the second unit, KOCUR (and sometimes DAVE BARR), plugs the net, while OATES runs the power play from the left wing circle. NORWOOD and HALWARD will sub for the original defense pair for a short time, and they'll try to free KLIMA on a give and go in the left circle. Otherwise, rebounds are the key again.

Last season, the Detroit power play was FAIR, scoring 72 goals in 383 opportunities (18.8 percent, 13th overall).

PENALTY KILLING

FIRST UNIT:
SHAWN BURR-STEVE YZERMAN
DOUG HALWARD-RICK ZOMBO

SECOND UNIT:
JOHN CHABOT-JIM NILL
DOUG HALWARD-MIKE O'CONNELL

Both units play a standard box defense, with the first forward pairing the more aggressive of the two duos. They'll pressure the puck up high and try to spring for offense and the shorthanded goal (the Wings were second in SHGs last season).

Last season the Detroit penalty killing was EXCELLENT, allowing just 73 goals in 453 shorthanded situations (83.9 percent, second overall).

CRUCIAL FACEOFFS

SHAWN BURR will take all of these.

DAVE BARR

Yrs. of NHL service: 5
Born: Edmonton, Alta., Canada; November 30, 1960
Position: Center/right wing
Height: 6-1
Weight: 185
Uniform no.: 22
Shoots: right

Career statistics:

GP	G	A	TP	PIM
286	59	100	159	237

1987-88 statistics:

GP	G	A	TP	+/−	PIM	PP	SH	GW	GT	S	PCT
51	14	26	40	20	58	3	1	0	0	64	21.9

LAST SEASON

Barr was twice struck with injury last year, missing 17 games with a separated shoulder and 11 games with a broken foot. He had the team's fifth highest plus/minus rating, the second highest shooting percentage.

THE FINESSE GAME

Barr is an average skater in terms of speed and agility. He can get from Point A to Point B fairly well, but will never overwhelm anyone with his foot speed. Also, he is not overly agile on his skates. He does skate well enough, though, to more than fill his role as a checker. He gets up his lane on desire and work, rather than talent.

Dave is a good checker because he is determined and persistent, and Barr is also good defensively, attentive to his responsibilities. He has good hockey sense and is smart with the puck, knowing when to get rid of it and when to hound it.

Barr will score a few goals, picking them up from the area directly around the crease, and he gets those goals through his persistence and forechecking. He shot is no better than average, and he doesn't handle the puck particularly well, so don't expect any rink-length rushes or dynamic passing plays.

THE PHYSICAL GAME

Barr is a big, strong winger and he'll go into the corners and work effectively along the boards. He can hit and jar the opposition off the puck, and he accepts hits in order to make his plays.

THE INTANGIBLES

The quintessential role player. Coach Jacques Demers had Barr in St. Louis, and he realized the value Dave could be to a team in terms of versatility up front and attitude on the ice. Barr is a hard worker, nothing glamorous, and his presence adds depth to the Wings.

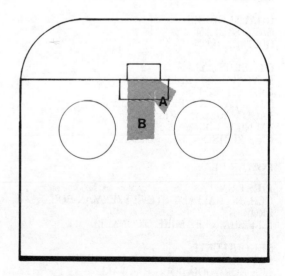

SHAWN BURR

Yrs. of NHL service: 1
Born: Sarnia, Ontario, Canada; July 1, 1966
Position: Center
Height: 6-1
Weight: 180
Uniform no.: 11
Shoots: left

Career statistics:

GP	G	A	TP	PIM
94	23	25	48	113

1987-88 statistics:

GP	G	A	TP	+/−	PIM	PP	SH	GW	GT	S	PCT
80	22	25	47	2	107	1	2	1	0	153	14.4

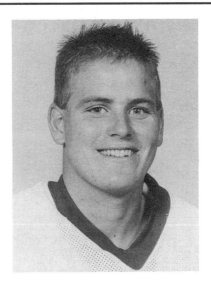

LAST SEASON

All point totals were down from Burr's freshman year (when he went 22-25-47).

THE FINESSE GAME

Burr is a strong skater and almost tireless, and he has shown improvement in his stride, foot speed and acceleration. His strength and improved stride have combined to give him some breakaway speed, and his foot speed has made him a more mobile player. He has excellent balance and that powers his outstanding physical game.

While his hand skills are still no better than average at the NHL level, Burr's shot and puckhandling abilities are good and show potential for improvement. Confidence is a big key here, as he hesitates to try offense (for fear of shirking his defensive responsibilities) and then his offensive skills suffer because they don't get enough work. Burr must strike a balance between the two.

What can make him an excellent playmaker is his excellent hockey sense and vision, which he currently uses to star as a defensive forward and penalty killer. He reads the play extremely well and his skating gets him there. He checks primarily by keeping himself between the opposing player and the puck (but he's also a physical checker).

His goal scoring is an offshoot of his checking, because Burr's anticipation also makes him an excellent forechecker. He'll turn over a lot of pucks because of that, and he does have the hand skills to turn those pucks into goals. Increased confidence will make him a better goal scorer.

THE PHYSICAL GAME

Burr has good size and he uses it well. He's a tough kid and likes to hit, and his persistent checking and banging will wear down many an opponent. His balance helps him here, keeping him vertical after collisions so that he can continue the play. Additionally, he can also make a play after freeing the puck, and that's always a plus.

Shawn's hand and wrist strength make him a good faceoff man, probably the team's best. Burr will also improve in the physical aspect of the game as he continues to mature.

THE INTANGIBLES

Currently, Burr is a solid two-way player, a complete player, and he works very hard to stay that way. His youth means he'll give the Wings a lot of good years, and if he should find the scoring touch that made him so effective in junior he'll help give the Wings one of the best one-two center combinations in the League.

This, his third year in the NHL, is a must year for Shawn. If he's going to step forward, now's the time for him to show he's ready.

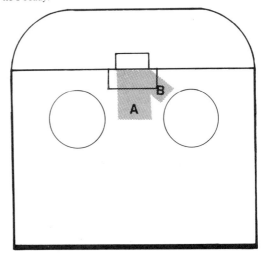

JOHN CHABOT

Yrs. of NHL service: 5
Born: Summerside, P.E.I., Canada; May 18, 1962
Position: Center
Height: 6-2
Weight: 190
Uniform no.: 16
Shoots: left

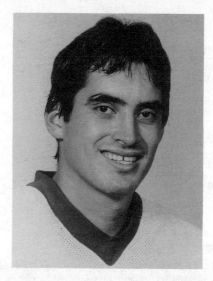

Career statistics:

GP	G	A	TP	PIM
360	68	173	241	51

1987-88 statistics:

GP	G	A	TP	+/-	PIM	PP	SH	GW	GT	S	PCT
78	13	44	57	12	10	0	2	0	0	83	15.7

LAST SEASON

For the fifth straight year —his entire career —Chabot failed to play an entire season. Still, his games played total was a career high, as was his point total. His PIM total was the lowest on the club, lowest in fact for any regular in the League last year. He was second on the club in assists.

THE FINESSE GAME

John has above average finesse skills. He is a very good skater with a fluid style. He's not terribly fast, but he happens to materialize wherever the puck is. He has excellent balance and his lateral movement is superb. He's shifty on his skates and has good foot speed, so Chabot is a very agile player.

He is an excellent playmaker and puckhandler, putting his long reach to work very effectively. That reach also helps him carry the puck, especially in traffic.

John's anticipation and hockey sense meld superbly with his skating to make him an excellent defensive forward. They also power his offensive game, showing him the openings. Chabot takes advantage of those chances by leading his teammates into the clear with good passes.

If Chabot could improve his shot by getting it away more quickly he'd be a better scorer, because his abilities give him plenty of scoring opportunities.

THE PHYSICAL GAME

Chabot is not physically tough at all. He does not hit, preferring to poke check the puck away from the opposition (there's that reach again) so he can remain free to skate with it. He does his defensive work by staying between the puck and his check, rather than by wearing his check down with hits.

In turn, he is difficult to hit because he is willowy on his skates, bending and swaying away from contact in order to keep working on the puck. Chabot is not unlike Wayne Gretzky in that regard.

THE INTANGIBLES

After two years of just checking work in Pittsburgh, Chabot showed once again that he is a talented playmaker. He gave further proof during the playoffs when, as the team's number one center, he set a team record for assists with 15. This improved offense didn't come at the expense of his defense, and that makes Chabot doubly valuable.

Like the other team members involved in the curfew-breaking incident from last spring's Campbell Conference final, Chabot has much to answer for.

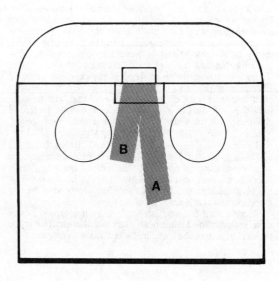

STEVE CHIASSON

Yrs. of NHL service: 2
Born: Barrie, Ontario, Canada; April 14, 1967
Position: Defenseman
Height: 6-0
Weight: 202
Uniform no.: 3
Shoots: left

Career statistics:

GP	G	A	TP	PIM
74	3	13	17	63

1987-88 statistics:

GP	G	A	TP	+/-	PIM	PP	SH	GW	GT	S	PCT
29	2	9	11	15	57	0	0	0	0	45	4.4

LAST SEASON

Hip and recurring shoulder injuries, plus demotions, all served to limit Chiasson's time. Though he played less games in his sophomore season than in his rookie year, Chiasson posted career highs in all point categories.

THE FINESSE GAME

Chiasson showed some improvement last season in his skating skills, which we categorized as "plodding, un-agile, un-quick, un-many things." He has some foot speed that can be applied to his tasks now, but Steve has a ways to go before he's solidly at the NHL level. He makes up for that below-average skating skill with good positional play.

Steve forces the play wide by playing his defensive angles well. He stays in position, doesn't wander around the ice and doesn't try to do things that are beyond his abilities. Chiasson moves the puck well to the forwards and is unlikely to carry it from the zone.

Chiasson has developable offensive talents, but for the time being he will take no chances at the offensive blue line. He does shoot well (quick, low and hard) from the point, so any goals Steve gets will come from there.

THE PHYSICAL GAME

Steve is a rugged kid and he likes to hit. He'll go to the corners with anyone and can handle himself well there. He has the strength to battle in front of the net with most of the League's bigger players and he'll be successful in most physical contests.

His one mistake is in trying to be too tough, because that extra elbow or punch in the face costs him in penalties.

THE INTANGIBLES

Chiasson is a defensive throwback, in that he concentrates primarily on being a defensive defenseman, and he has the potential to be a very good stay-at-home defender. If he is successful in improving his skating, he'll become that player.

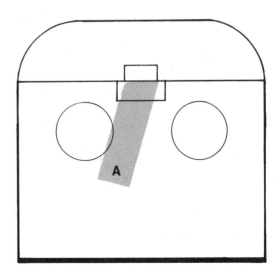

GILBERT DELORME

Yrs. of NHL service: 7
Born: Boucherville, Quebec, Canada; November 25, 1962
Position: Defenseman
Height: 6-1
Weight: 205
Uniform no.: 29
Shoots: right

Career statistics:

GP	G	A	TP	PIM
445	27	82	109	425

1987-88 statistics:

GP	G	A	TP	+/−	PIM	PP	SH	GW	GT	S	PCT
55	2	8	10	9	81	0	0	0	0	46	4.3

LAST SEASON

Delorme missed five games with a shoulder injury, four games with an ankle problem. His games played total was the third lowest of his career, his point total the lowest.

THE FINESSE GAME

Strength, balance and agility are the assets in Delorme's skating. He doesn't have rink-length speed, but Gil has good quickness and mobility. He moves well laterally, and keeps good pace with the incoming opposing forward. His lateral movement also makes him difficult to beat one-on-one.

He's conservative in his defense, playing positionally in all three zones. He uses his defensive angles effectively, doesn't wander all over the ice and doesn't take chances he knows he won't recover from. Simply, Gilbert plays smart defense.

That intelligence is tranferred to his puckhandling, as Delorme moves the puck quickly to the open man without trying to be fancy. He is not apt to carry the puck from the zone, but Delorme does handle it fairly well when skating.

Delorme is not a goal scorer and he seldom seizes an offensive opportunity. He can contain the point and find the open man from there, but he is not going to pinch often or charge deeply into the zone. He has an average shot from the blue line.

THE PHYSICAL GAME

The physical game is to Delorme's liking, and he puts his good size and strength to work well in that setting. He is a hard hitter and can flatten many forwards if he hits them squarely, displaying good strength and balance in his less-than-giant sized body.

He is strong along the boards and will force forwards off the puck or tie them up — doing both effectively — but the larger forwards do give him trouble both there and in front of the net.

THE INTANGIBLES

Delorme is enthusiastic and has a super attitude, but his durability and tendency toward injury raise many questions about his season-long effectiveness.

He may find his already limited ice time cut further as the Wings try to integrate some younger players along the blue line.

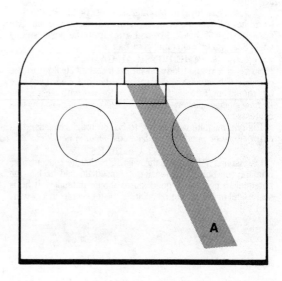

GERARD GALLANT

Yrs. of NHL service: 4
Born: Summerside, P.E.I., Canada; September 2, 1963
Position: Left wing
Height: 5-11
Weight: 185
Uniform no.: 17
Shoots: left

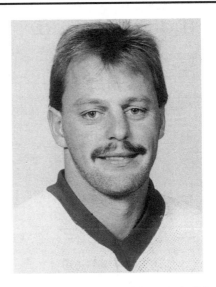

Career statistics:

GP	G	A	TP	PIM
237	98	104	202	630

1987-88 statistics:

GP	G	A	TP	+/–	PIM	PP	SH	GW	GT	S	PCT
73	34	39	73	24	242	10	0	3	1	197	17.3

LAST SEASON

Shoulder and knee injuries limited Gallant's time, but he still recorded career highs in assists, points and penalty minutes. He finished second on the team in scoring, plus/minus, power play goals and shots on goal. He was third in PIM and goal scoring.

THE FINESSE GAME

Though his finesse game is often overshadowed by his physical game, Gallant does have skills he brings to bear well. He is not an exceptional skater in terms of the more "graceful" skills of speed and agility, but he's very strong on his skates. That strength complements his good balance and makes his physical game more effective by allowing him to remain vertical after checks. Gerard gets where he wants to go by skating over — instead of around — people.

He's got an above average view of the ice, and that vision helps him offensively and defensively. He can get the puck to an opening for a teammate, and Gallant can also close down openings while checking. He plays a solid defensive game and will be on ice in the last minute of a game to either score that tying goal or to prevent it.

His vision and sense doesn't translate into his goal scoring. Gallant's success comes from freeing the puck along the boards and not creating artistic puckhandling plays. If he wrestles the puck free he's going to pass it. If he's going to score it will be from near the net.

Gallant has an excellent shot but doesn't use it enough for the openings his strength creates. His best way of scoring goals is to plant himself in front of the net and work from there. But since linemate Bob Probert is often in the slot, Gerard can also take advantage of his heavy wrist shot from farther out.

Occasionally he will attempt to be an artist, and that leads to his overhandling the puck. He loses offensive opportunities then, because Gallant is almost always in traffic and is skilled — but not that skilled — in controlling the puck in a crowd.

THE PHYSICAL GAME

Like the League's other power forwards, Gallant thrives on a physical game. He loves to hit and that keys his game, as he wins the battles along the boards to free the puck. He is also successful in scoring because of his strength. Gallant will take the hits in front and in the corners in order to make his plays, and he *will* make those plays.

He has excellent upper body strength, and will fight off the opposing checker to make his plays or take a shot. He is also a willing and able fighter.

THE INTANGIBLES

Gallant has an excellent attitude, is very coachable and approaches each game and practice with an excellent work ethic; that makes him a leader for the Wings. His willingness to succeed in physical confrontations and his ability to score make him the type of player any team would want.

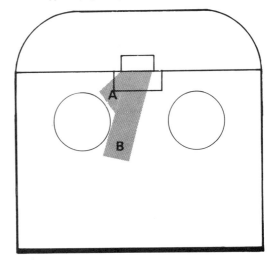

DOUG HALWARD

Yrs. of NHL service: 13
Born: Toronto, Ontario, Canada; November 1, 1955
Position: Defenseman
Height: 6-1
Weight: 198
Uniform no.: 7
Shoots: left

Career statistics:

GP	G	A	TP	PIM
611	69	216	285	713

1987-88 statistics:

GP	G	A	TP	+/−	PIM	PP	SH	GW	GT	S	PCT
70	5	21	26	6	130	3	0	1	0	88	5.7

LAST SEASON

Bronchitis sidelined Halward for three games, but he still played more games than any other Detroit defenseman.

THE FINESSE GAME

Halward is a good skater, balanced and strong on his skates but not particularly fast. He is difficult to take off the puck because of his balance and that same trait allows him to handle the puck in traffic.

Halward can carry the puck from the zone but is more likely to move it quickly and effectively to the forwards. He has poise and confidence and doesn't often make a bad play, taking the extra second necessary to make a safe pass.

Halward sees the ice well, both offensively and defensively, and can get the puck to his teammates in the opposing zone. He will control the point and charge the net himself, and he will force the play wide of the net in the defensive end. His vision and hand skills make him a regular on both specialty teams.

However, because Doug has the tendency to play the puck instead of the body, he can be beaten one-on-one. That forces him to take penalties.

THE PHYSICAL GAME

Halward is not a physical player per se, in that he doesn't bash everything he sees. He can hit but is most effective when playing smartly.

Doug is effective along the boards in the pushing and shoving and he can come up with the puck. He is steady in front of his own net and can tie up the opposition forward stationed there. He can also hold the opposition out of the play when necessary.

Halward is not a fighter, but will have the odd scrap when he has to and won't back down from anyone.

THE INTANGIBLES

Halward is with the Wings to fill a role until one of the younger defenders is ready for a full-time job. He is a pressure performer and can play best when it counts.

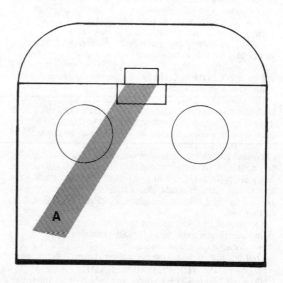

122

GLEN HANLON

Yrs. of NHL service: 10
Born: Brandon, Man., Canada; February 20, 1957
Position: Goaltender
Height: 6-0
Weight: 175
Uniform no.: 1
Catches: right

Career statistics:

GP	MINS	G	SO	AVG	A	PIM
374	20,793	1,237	11	3.56	7	197

1987-88 statisics:

GP	MINS	AVG	W	L	T	SO	GA	SA	SAPCT	PIM
47	2,623	3.23	22	17	5	4	141	1,292	.891	30

LAST SEASON

Hanlon led the League in shutouts, and his shutout total was a career high. Minutes played total was the third highest of his career, and win total was second highest of his career. Last season was only his second winning season. He missed three games with a finger injury.

THE PHYSICAL GAME

Hanlon has graduated from being a reflex goaltender to a standup one, and that's a big reason for his success the last two seasons. He uses his body to block the puck, positioning himself well in the net and squaring himself to the puck. When he does this, he's successful.

Once he gets his feet moving is another story. He doesn't have good balance and once he opens up he's going to be on the ice. Glen will lose his balance once he moves his feet, so he often seems unready for the second save, but his innate quickness allows him to somehow recover and get his body in front of that shot. All of this could be avoided he challenged a little more, as Hanlon is square to the puck from deep in his net instead of farther out.

He'll leave the net to handle the puck and moves it fairly well to his defensemen. He clears rebounds fairly well, but he still has the annoying habit of turning his back to the play when he skates back to his net after challenging a shooter. So he loses sight of the play in front of him and can get caught out of position.

He is weak on his glove side on any shot below the waist, but is good above it. He flops immediately on screen shots, but doesn't butterfly his pads, and that makes it difficult for him to move around once he is on the ice.

THE MENTAL GAME

Glen does well at maintaining his concentration within a game, but he could still improve between games. His concentration flags slightly if he's alternating games with a partner, just as it tends to droop in a contest following a big game. He's shown that in the playoffs he has his concentration down, so he can be more consistent during the regular season too.

He has always had the ability to make the big save. Glen has always been a tough competitor and because of that used to punish himself mentally when he allowed a goal. But he's become looser in attitude, so that the goals — good or bad — no longer distract him from doing his job.

THE INTANGIBLES

Funny, upbeat and positive, Glen Hanlon is a super team guy. His teammates enjoy being around him because of his attitude, and it is his attitude and mental outlook that has made him successful in Detroit.

TIM HIGGINS

Yrs. of NHL service: 10
Born: Ottawa, Ontario, Canada; February 7, 1958
Position: Right wing
Height: 6-1
Weight: 185
Uniform no.: 20
Shoots: right

Career statistics:

GP	G	A	TP	PIM
664	149	189	338	657

1987-88 statistics:

GP	G	A	TP	+/−	PIM	PP	SH	GW	GT	S	PCT
62	12	13	25	5	94	0	1	1	0	63	19.0

LAST SEASON

Games played total was second lowest of Higgins' career since he became an NHL regular. Point total was lowest in five years.

THE FINESSE GAME

Higgins is a strong skater with a powerful stride and that stride gives him very good speed. He translates that speed and almost tireless skating ability into superb checking and defensive work, and that's how he makes his best contributions to the Wings.

On the offensive end, Tim gets his chances because his speed and checking create loose pucks. His problem in those situations is that he has hands of stone. He has a good shot and can get it off quickly, but because Tim can't handle the puck well in the high traffic area of the slot, the most he'll score in a year is 20 goals. But because of his attitude, his physical play and his defensive prowess, any goals he scores are a bonus.

Higgins hesitates when handling the puck and that flaw — along with his tough hands — means he doesn't use his teammates particularly well.

He also brings pretty good hockey sense to his game, and that greatly complements his checking ability.

THE PHYSICAL GAME

Higgins is a bull in a china shop. He's not afraid to be aggressive along the boards or in the corners, and he uses his size and strength well in those areas. His hitting also serves to wear down the opposition over the course of the game, taking the enemy out of the contest.

THE INTANGIBLES

Higgins is a great team man, a tremendous leader off the ice for the Wings through his attitude. An example of that was his accompanying Bob Probert to an Alcoholics Anonymous meeting in New York, and becoming Probert's roommate and guardian on the road.

He is otherwise a role player, and teams with Joe Murphy and Shawn Burr to form a pretty good checking line.

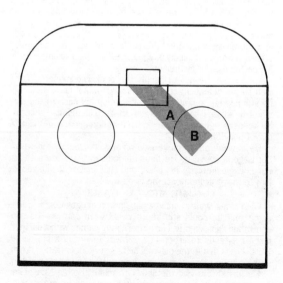

PETR KLIMA

Yrs. of NHL service: 3
Born: Chaomutov, Czechoslovakia; December 23, 1964
Position: Left wing
Height: 6-0
Weight: 190
Uniform no.: 85
Shoots: left

Career statistics:

GP	G	A	TP	PIM
229	99	72	171	104

1987-88 statistics:

GP	G	A	TP	+/−	PIM	PP	SH	GW	GT	S	PCT
78	37	25	62	4	46	6	5	5	0	174	21.3

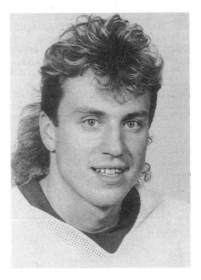

LAST SEASON

Games played and all point totals were career highs. He finished second on the club in goals, third in scoring. He was second in shorthanded goals and game winners, third in shots on goal. His shooting percentage was second highest among regulars. His plus/minus was the lowest of any Detroit regular.

THE FINESSE GAME

Though tremendously skilled, even frighteningly so, Klima's parts are better than the whole. He is an excellent skater and has great ability in all skating assets—quickness, speed, balance, power and agility. He will out-race most any checker, or cut inside most any defenseman. His agility and lateral movement allow him to stop on a dime and to move from side to side with great ease. He also has tremendous one-step quickness for snaring pucks or hitting the slightest opening, and his explosive acceleration will put him in the clear within two strides.

Petr can work magic with the puck when he carries it or when he is standing still, and Klima has the hands to work with the puck in tight situations. He's moving the puck much better now than ever before, but Klima remains a one-on-one player. Learning to move the puck and then gun for the openings (to work the give and go) would make him just devastating.

His shot selection is excellent, and his slap shot from the wing will beat any goaltender in the League. It is not an accurate one, however; Klima will shoot 10-15 times a game and have just 2-3 shots on goal. He must make goaltenders work to stop his shot.

His abilities to anticipate and get into position to score are very high. He has excellent hockey sense in the offensive zone, and he uses his finesse skills to drive for the openings. Because of these skills, Klima is also an asset on the power play.

His Waterloo has always been his defense, but Klima showed a grasp of the defensive game last year that had been missing to date. He was playing better positionally in his own zone, and picking up a winger coming out of the offensive end. On most nights, that is.

He must also find more consistency in his scoring. He had 25 of his 37 goals by his 41st game, just 12 goals in his last 39.

THE PHYSICAL GAME

An improved physical willingness was evident in Klima's game last year, both offensively and defensively. While he is still an open ice player, Klima was working closer to the boards and the front of the net. There is still room for improvement in that area, as Klima still prefers the outside of the scrum.

His application of a physical game to his defensive effort was more pronounced. Klima was consistently getting in the opposition's way along the boards, even tossing the occasional check here and there. Klima improved his defensive game to such a degree that by season's end he was hitting even Mark Messier behind the Wings' net.

Now that's improvement.

THE INTANGIBLES

All this begs the question of Klima's emotional maturity. He could take a lesson in physical play from Steve Yzerman, who added a physical game and became a 100-point scorer. Only problem is, Klima alienates himself from the team by being intensely jealous of Yzerman and the attention he receives.

So Klima did something about that attention by leading the Red Wings in playoff scoring, until he was sidelined by a broken thumb (another questionHow will that thumb heal?).

And then Klima got involved in drinking and breaking curfew during the Campbell Conference Final. And then we learned that he had been previously arrested for drunk driving. And now we know he has an alcohol problem.

Just as it seemed Klima was getting his act together and playing with the commitment and dedication coach Jacques Demers demands, the bottom falls out. Petr is more talented than 95 percent of the players in the NHL, and he has all the capability to do in Detroit what Stephane Richer has done in Montreal. But Klima must want to do this yet, as we've seen, his desire is the biggest question of all.

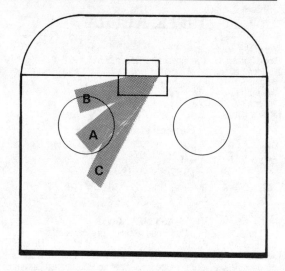

JOE KOCUR

Yrs. of NHL service: 3
Born: Calgary, Alta., Canada; December 21, 1964
Position: Right wing
Height: 6-0
Weight: 195
Uniform no.: 26
Shoots: right

Career statistics:

GP	G	A	TP	PIM
217	26	22	48	980

1987-88 statistics:

GP	G	A	TP	+/−	PIM	PP	SH	GW	GT	S	PCT
64	7	7	14	-11	263	0	0	1	0	41	17.1

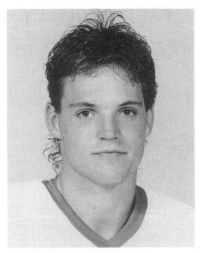

LAST SEASON

Goal and point totals were career lows, as was PIM total. He finished second on the club in PIM, the first time in three years he didn't lead the Wings in that category. He was sidelined early in the season with a bruised sternum.

THE FINESSE GAME

Impossible as it may be to believe, Kocur has finesse skills. Disguised by all his brawling is the fact that he's a very good skater, in terms of balance and speed. When he hits he remains vertical, and it is that balance after all that gives him solid footing for fighting. He can also move at a pretty good clip (and that helps him in checking), though not as well as the League's fastest skaters. Joe is not, however, an exceptionally agile skater and he does need some room for turns.

His great flaw in skating — and one big reason why he keeps getting minus ratings — is that he doesn't keep his feet moving. While many of his penalty minutes are of the confrontational kind, Kocur also gets his share of interference penalties, accumulated because his checks skate by him and he has to hook or hold them. For that reason, he'd have to be termed lazy.

Joey can also handle the puck at a fair speed, and he's not afraid of carrying it across the blue line and toward the defense. He sees passing openings and he can get the puck there. He also has a great shot which he doesn't use enough. He doesn't drive for openings and doesn't think offensively. He can take and give a pass, and he will look to make plays, but he could improve all aspects of his play without the puck.

THE PHYSICAL GAME

Kocur isn't a bad bodychecker, though he does have some difficulty tracking down his prey along the boards because they have greater agility than he. He hits hard and he hits to hurt people.

As for fighting, he is absolutely frightening. The punching power he generates is visible halfway up into the stands, and it's no wonder the guy has literal knockout power in his hands. Joey revels in that reputation, and if credit can be given for such a thing it would be that he does his damage with his fists and not his stick.

Kocur hurts people when he hits them and he is fearless. He'll take however many shots he has to in order to get in one or two punches, but Joey's not a beast when he fights.

That is, if he really stings a guy and knocks him silly, Kocur won't keep hitting him. Once Joey has made his point — so to speak — he'll just lower the guy to the ice and leave him alone.

He is also, by the way, in phenomenal physical shape.

THE INTANGIBLES

His on-ice presence is invaluable, but it is Kocur's off-ice attitude that troubles the Wings. He began last season by cursing out assistant coach Don MacAdam in training camp, continued in the preseason by not working on the ice and closed the year by getting caught breaking curfew.

Invaluable though his presence is, Kocur isn't in the untouchable category. His attitude will need some adjustment in order for him to stay in Detroit long-term.

For this year, he must demonstrate recovery from his playoff injured shoulder.

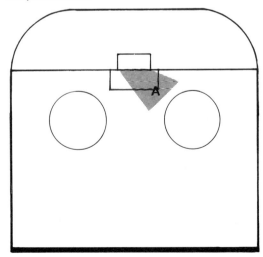

PAUL MACLEAN

Yrs. of NHL service: 7
Born: Grostenquin, France; March 9, 1958
Position: Right wing
Height: 6-0
Weight: 205
Uniform no.:
Shoots: right

Career statistics:

GP	G	A	TP	PIM
528	248	270	518	726

1987-88 statistics:

GP	G	A	TP	+/−	PIM	PP	SH	GW	GT	S	PCT
77	40	39	79	-16	76	22	0	2	1	176	22.7

LAST SEASON

MacLean was acquired by the Wings in the off-season in exchange for Brent Ashton. MacLean finished second on the Jets in scoring and goals, first in power play goals and fifth in assists. His games played total was highest in three seasons, as were his goal and point totals.

THE FINESSE GAME

MacLean is a good skater, very well balanced and strong on his skates and that's surprising, because he's very upright in his stance and would seem to be vulnerable to any shove. He is not a speed demon but has foot speed that is surprising for a bigger man, and that relative agility makes him successful in traffic.

Paul has excellent hands and can make feather light passes or pull the puck out of traffic. MacLean is excellent at making plays from along the boards, taking the puck off the boards in one motion and sending it speeding on its way, or carrying the puck through the traffic areas while retaining control.

Because of his control skills — and also because he sees the play very well and has excellent anticipation — Paul can be said to use his teammates very well. He's also smart in that he doesn't overhandle the puck while looking for a fancy play. Paul just gets the job done.

He has a terrific shot from in close, very powerful because of his wrists and hands, and he can also blow the puck past a goaltender from a distance.

He plays sound positional hockey and backchecks well, despite the plus/minus numbers.

THE PHYSICAL GAME

MacLean plays a very physical game. He's a superior mucker and grinder, digging the puck out of the corner and then charging the net for a return pass.

His size and strength work in tandem to make MacLean difficult to control in front of the net or to out-muscle along the boards. He hits hard and well and is an aggressive though clean hockey player.

THE INTANGIBLES

We told you last year that MacLean would get moved from Winnipeg because of the contract fuss he got into with Jets general manager John Ferguson. MacLean's style is such that he can succeed anywhere, though he will obviously have to get acclimated to his new surroundings. He is a key step in the Wings' attempt to shore up their right side.

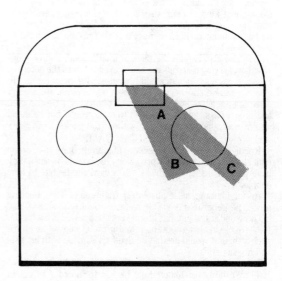

JOE MURPHY

Yrs. of NHL service: 1
Born: London, Ontario, Canada; October 16, 1967
Position: Left wing/center
Height: 6-1
Weight: 190
Uniform no.: 10
Shoots: left

Career statistics:

GP	G	A	TP	PIM
55	10	10	20	39

1987-88 statistics:

GP	G	A	TP	+/−	PIM	PP	SH	GW	GT	S	PCT
50	10	9	19	-4	37	1	0	2	0	82	12.2

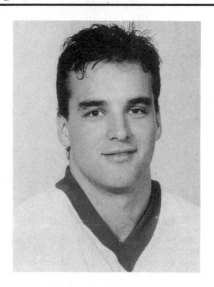

LAST SEASON

Murphy broke into the big leagues, sidelined though he was by ankle injury and spotted in and out of the lineup. His plus/minus mark was the team's third worst.

THE FINESSE GAME

Murphy is a good skater with foot speed, acceleration ability and balance. The three combine to make him fairly agile, but he could improve on all three at the NHL level (right now, only his acceleration stands out).

He handles the puck with average skill at the NHL level, more because the play is still a little too quick for him than because he doesn't have the hand skills. He can stickhandle and control the puck in traffic, and that's because Murphy has sensitive hands for puck work.

His hockey sense and passing skills can combine to make him a good playmaker, but again he's not yet reacting with NHL speed, so his passes will hit skates and the opposition instead of finding their intended targets. Still, he can pass well to both sides.

His sense and vision also help him get into position to score, but he has yet to show that he reads the ice fully or that his anticipation is above the ordinary. He plays with his head up, and that always helps all phases of the game.

Murphy has a good slapshot, heavy and quick, and he can deliver it from a distance. Right now, because of his checkiong role, most of his goals will come from loose pucks forced free near the net. That's okay, because Murphy's wrist shot is also good (well released and accurate) and he can shoot of the stickhandle too.

He's playing fairly sound defense, but he needs to concentrate on staying with his man all the way back to the Wing net.

THE PHYSICAL GAME

Murphy has good size and strength, and he's putting it to use by going into the corners and by banging along the boards. He bodychecks well and his balance helps him stay involved in the play by keeping him vertical after collisions.

THE INTANGIBLES

There's nothing more questionable — and questioned — than a first round draft choice. Unless it's a first round draft choice with a bad reputation.

While he has long way to go, Murphy seems to have found the right road. He's working hard at improving and his desire to excel is coming to the forefront. He can expect to see more ice time as the year goes by (though he already teams well with Tim Higgins and Shawn Burr on a checking line), and if he continues to progress the Wings can expect to see more improvement.

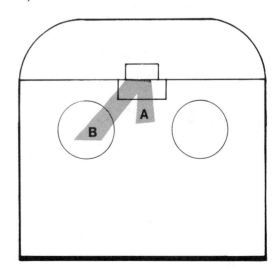

JIM NILL

Yrs. of NHL service: 8
Born: Hanna, Alta., Canada; April 11, 1958
Position: Right wing
Height: 6-0
Weight: 185
Uniform no.: 8
Shoots: right

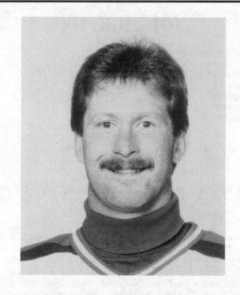

Career statistics:

GP	G	A	TP	PIM
438	50	78	128	753

1987-88 statistics:

GP	G	A	TP	+/-	PIM	PP	SH	GW	GT	S	PCT
60	3	12	15	-5	99	0	0	0	0	38	7.9

LAST SEASON

Was acquired by Detroit in exchange for Mark Kumpel. Missed four games with a groin injury. Point total was highest in three seasons, as was assist mark. Though he finished the season as a minus player, Nill was plus-2 in Detroit.

THE FINESSE GAME

Nill is an average skater. He's not equipped with much speed or agility, nor is he exceptionally quick either in terms of acceleration or changing direction. He's an up-and-down winger without much imagination.

He's a good checker and plays his position well and that reflects in his defensive game as well. He patrols his wing in the offensive zone and doesn't wander, and he picks up his man and comes back deeply wth him on the backcheck.

Jim has good anticipation and vision skills, abilities that make him good as a checking forward but, since he doesn't handle the puck or skate all that well, those mental qualities don't translate into offensive production.

THE PHYSICAL GAME

Despite his physical misfortunes, Nill remains a physical hockey player. He takes the body fairly well, getting in the way of his check and holding him out of the play. He has good strength and size and both serve him when he works along the boards, allowing him to out-muscle the opposition.

That ability is somewhat minimized because Nill doesn't have the skills to take full advantage of the pucks he wins in those battles. He does play the same way all the time and is consistent in the use of his body home or away, winning or losing.

THE INTANGIBLES

Nill is a dedicated player and a hard worker, a character player and an individual who'll play when hurt. In short, a Jacques Demers player. He's a role player in Detroit, but his dependability guarantees him ice time.

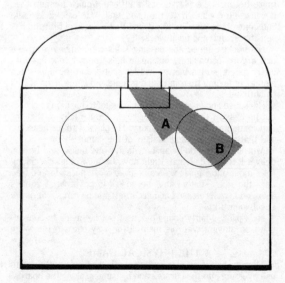

130

LEE NORWOOD

Yrs. of NHL service: 5
Born: Oakland, Calif, USA; February 2, 1960
Position: Defenseman
Height: 6-1
Weight: 198
Uniform no.: 23
Shoots: left

Career statistics:

GP	G	A	TP	PIM
226	28	79	107	578

1987-88 statistics:

GP	G	A	TP	+/−	PIM	PP	SH	GW	GT	S	PCT
51	9	22	31	4	131	3	0	2	0	106	8.5

LAST SEASON

Goal and point totals were career highs despite missing weeks with groin and knee injuries. Norwood led the defense in PIM, finishing fourth in the team in that category. Games played total was lowest in three seasons (since becoming an NHL regular).

THE FINESSE GAME

The finesse game is not Norwood's forte. He is no better than average as a skater, with little speed and mobility, but he maximizes this talent by playing within his limits. He plays defense positionally, using his defensive angles to force the play wide of the net.

Though he recorded career highs in assists and points, Norwood is not an offensive threat. Rather, when he's playing at his best, he moves the puck quickly and smartly to the forwards and gets his points on their offensive forays.

He sees the ice fairly well and makes those good passes, but he will not rush the puck himself or become a true fourth attacker. He'll follow the play up-ice only if there's no risk involved.

Once in the offensive zone, Norwood demonstrates a good shot from the point, and he'll sneak between the circles for a shot if the opening presents itself.

He will occasionally be hypnotized by the puck and lose his man, but Norwood is generally Detroit's steadiest defender.

THE PHYSICAL GAME

Norwood is a fearless player, very rugged and completely without regard for his body. He blocks shots, he mixes it up in front of the net, he muscles with forwards against the boards. He enjoys the physical game and makes the most of his size.

THE INTANGIBLES

Norwood has grown into a large role in Detroit, that of being the number one defensive defenseman. He'll see a lot of ice time in that role, and will most likely be paired with one of the younger players the Wings will try to break in this year.

A hard worker and a coachable athlete, Norwood is a character player for the Wings.

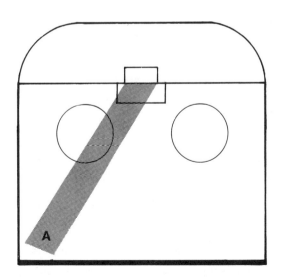

ADAM OATES

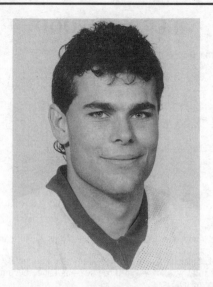

Yrs. of NHL service: 3
Born: Weston, Ontario, Canada; August 27, 1962
Position: Center
Height: 5-11
Weight: 190
Uniform no.: 21
Shoots: right

Career statistics:

GP	G	A	TP	PIM
177	38	83	121	51

1987-88 statistics:

GP	G	A	TP	+/−	PIM	PP	SH	GW	GT	S	PCT
63	14	40	52	16	20	3	0	3	0	111	12.6

LAST SEASON

A two-game hip injury and 15-game groin injury limited Oates' time, but he still recorded career high assist and point marks. He finished third on the team in assists.

THE FINESSE GAME

Oates is loaded with finesse potential, primary of which are his good hands. He handles the puck very well when he carries it and he passes it extremely well to both his forehand and backhand sides. He takes the puck off the boards in one move and gets it to a teammate with a pinpoint pass.

Complementing his hand skills are his anticipation and vision skills. Adam sees the ice well and recognizes the plays, and he can get the puck to his teammates either when they are in the clear or by leading them to the openings. He still has difficulty getting his hands to move as fast as his brain, so he is not yet adept at playmaking at NHL speed but has the potential to improve.

Finally, his hand speed makes him one of the Wings' best faceoff men.

His skating is merely average at the NHL level, as he is neither exceptionally agile nor exceptionally strong. Oates is not blessed with great quickness either. Improved skating would give Oates more time to use his good hand skills.

His anticipation and hands give him some scoring ability, but he does not shoot the puck enough and is not quick enough to get to loose pucks around the net.

THE PHYSICAL GAME

Though not a banger, Oates uses his decent size fairly well along the boards by taking the body. He's never going to knock anyone into the cheap seats. He's begun to accept more of a hitting game — though he's still primarily an open ice player — and is making more plays in traffic.

THE INTANGIBLES

Oates has potential to improve, and this season — his third in the NHL — will be a crucial one for him. At 26 years old he doesn't have much time left, especially with three centers in front of him (Yzerman, Chabot and Burr) and at least one (Adam Graves) behind him.

In Oates' favor are his attitude and work ethic. His good

showing in last season's playoffs (where he finished second in team scoring) should help his confidence for this season.

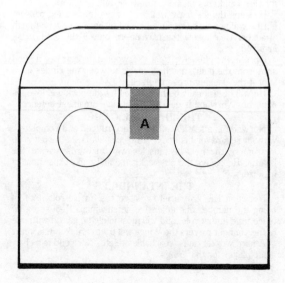

MIKE O'CONNELL

Yrs. of NHL service: 10
Born: Chicago, Ill., USA; November 25, 1955
Position: Defenseman
Height: 5-11
Weight: 176
Uniform no.: 2
Shoots: right

Career statistics:

GP	G	A	TP	PIM
728	100	305	405	542

1987-88 statistics:

GP	G	A	TP	+/−	PIM	PP	SH	GW	GT	S	PCT
48	6	13	19	24	38	0	0	0	1	68	8.8

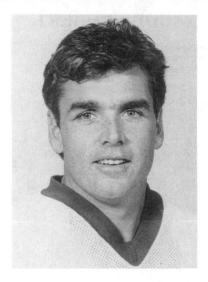

LAST SEASON

O'Connell missed 18 games with finger surgery. Games played total was career low, as were assist and point totals. His plus/minus rating was tied for second highest on the club.

THE FINESSE GAME

Pending the development of Jeff Sharples, O'Connell is Detroit's best puckhandling defenseman. That's not surprising, because puckhandling is O'Connell's best finesse skill. Because of his soft hands, O'Connell makes excellent passes to his teammates. O'Connell will rush the puck as likely as not, with his hand and skating skills carrying past defenders. He's particularly valuable in moving the puck from the Wings zone, but Mike can also create offense from the opposing blue line.

His ice vision complements his hand skills, so O'Connell can see the openings and make the correct play smoothly and efficiently. He'll follow the play up-ice and join in the attack in the offensive zone, controlling the point with his hands and getting the puck to the open man because of his hands and vision. He's unafraid to pinch in to pressure the opposition.

He contributes from the blue line with a very accurate shot that is tailor-made for deflections. He'll sneak to the top of the faceoff circle if he can for his shot, knowing that his skating and anticipation will get him back into defensive position.

Though not as gifted a skater now as he was earlier in his career, Mike counters the opposition with his brains by anticipating and reading the play well. Still, he does retain enough quickness to intercept a pass and start the play up-ice. Mike is a good positional defenseman, playing his defensive angles very well in order to compensate for his lack of size. Between his ability to play those angles and his strong skating, O'Connell is not often beaten one-on-one.

THE PHYSICAL GAME

Because of his size or lack thereof, O'Connell must play a smart physical game. He can't go running at people because he isn't going to be effective that way. But Mike takes the body along the boards well, understanding that sometimes the best check is just getting in someone's way.

Because he does have strength he can tie up wingers in the corners or the front of the net, but he'll be overpowered by the League's bigger forwards. He's willing to hit, but he'll never plant anyone into the cheap seats.

THE INTANGIBLES

O'Connell contributes to the Wings in more ways than just on the ice. He's a very upbeat guy and possesses a great work ethic despite his NHL years. He's coachable and a leader on the ice. While it's possible he'll see his ice time cut as the Wings attempt to get some youth into their blue line corps, O'Connell is the perfect type of player to teach youngsters the NHL game.

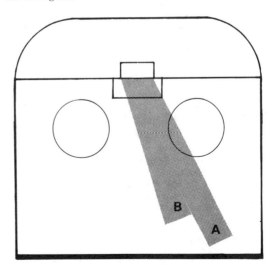

BOB PROBERT

Yrs. of NHL service: 3
Born: Windsor, Ontario, Canada; June 5, 1965
Position: Right wing
Height: 6-3
Weight: 215
Uniform no.: 24
Shoots: left

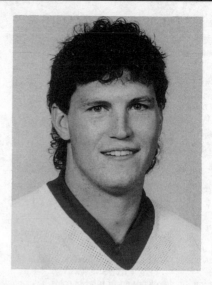

Career statistics:

GP	G	A	TP	PIM
181	50	57	107	805

1987-88 statistics:

GP	G	A	TP	+/−	PIM	PP	SH	GW	GT	S	PCT
74	29	33	62	16	398	15	0	5	1	126	23.0

LAST SEASON

Games played, all point totals and PIM were all career high marks. He led the League in PIM, and the team in power play goals and shooting percentage (his second consecutive year leading the team in the last category). Game misconduct suspensions account for his six-game absence.

THE FINESSE GAME

While he may produce offensively like a fine finesse player, Probert is not necessarily a well-rounded finesse player. His skating is average at best, lacking agility and foot speed. He does have great balance, and that balance is the key to Probert's physical game, as it allows him to remain upright after hitting an opposing player. Bob is facilitated in his skating by the fact that no one comes near him, and by his long stride which pulls him away from the opposition. Just don't confuse that with speed.

His great finesse strength is in his hand skill, which is very good. Probert carries the puck well while skating and has the talent to handle the puck in traffic and tight to the net. While he's again aided by the fact that no one wants to challenge him, Probert can make plays on his own because of his hands. He can certainly make a play coming out of the corner with the puck, and he has enough talent to get the puck over sticks or through traffic to his teammates. He's dangerous enough with the puck to draw penalties.

He doesn't have a lot of anticipation or hockey sense in the offensive zone, and if in doubt he'll just throw the puck behind the net.

He doesn't have an outstanding shot (his slap shot is easily blocked because it takes him so long to release it) in terms of blazing speed or power, but Probert gets his wrist shot off very quickly from in front of the net: He's a power play regular there, and his hand skills are good enough for him to finesse the puck into a small opening.

Because of desire rather than anticipation or skating talent, Probert is good defensively. He stays with his check up and down the ice, and is fairly disciplined in terms of positional play, not wandering from his lane.

THE PHYSICAL GAME

Probert is one of several players in the vanguard of the power forward movement. Next to his hand skills, power is the greatest component in his game. He hits people hard and he hurts them when he checks them. He has tremendous strength, and he couples that with great reach to be more effective in traffic.

His hands will beat the opposition two ways, through goals and fights. He is one of the League's toughest players — maybe the toughest — and he is the NHL's best fighter. Unlike teammate Joe Kocur, who remains relatively calm during a fight, Probert loses control.

That threat of physical punishment is why he's avoided on the ice, and why players from all teams allow him to camp in front of the net. Better, they think, to leave the big guy alone than to wake him up.

They're right.

THE INTANGIBLES

There are many questions for Probert to answer, his drinking problem not the least of them. After a year in which he was named to the All-Star game, where he supplanted Gordie Howe as the Wings' most productive playoff player, where he scored 29 goals and proved himself a legitimate NHL player — after all of these things that should have shown Probert what his hockey life could be, he succumbed once again to his alcoholism problem.

Reality says the Wings won't abandon him, if only for selfish reasons: you can't find players with his size and scoring ability. But the truth is that both general manager Jimmy Devellano and coach Jacques Demers also care about Probert personally. So once again the Wings will try to get him into a therapy program he will accept.

Part of Probert's emotional or image problem also manifests itself in his work ethic off the ice. He doesn't have one. He does no conditioning work in the off-season, and little during the season. He is unmotivated in that respect. He must also become a more consistent scorer at even strength. Over half of his goals (15 of 29) came on the power play, and 19 of his 29 came in his first 38 games.

There are those who say he succeeded only because he was paired with Steve Yzerman, but it's no accident that Yzerman had his best year when teamed with Probert. We told you Bob can score 30 goals and be a player in this League. We also told you he must answer the most important question: Can Bob Probert control his drinking problem and remain in the NHL?

Time is on his side. After all, he's still only 23 years old. We hope he can take control of his life.

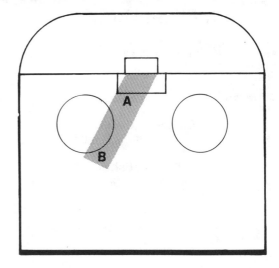

JEFF SHARPLES

Yrs. of NHL service: 1
Born: Terrace, B.C., Canada; July 28, 1967
Position: Defenseman
Height: 6-0
Weight: 187
Uniform no.: 34
Shoots: left

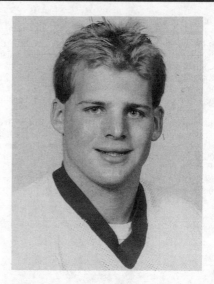

Career statistics:

GP	G	A	TP	PIM
59	10	26	36	44

1987-88 statistics:

GP	G	A	TP	+/−	PIM	PP	SH	GW	GT	S	PCT
56	10	25	35	13	42	2	0	0	0	94	10.6

LAST SEASON

Sharples' first "full" NHL season. He finished second in defensive scoring.

THE FINESSE GAME

Sharples is a solid package of finesse skills, and that package begins with his skating and puckhandling. Jeff is a good skater with a lot of power in his long stride. He doesn't have great speed, but his stride helps him cover a lot of ice in a hurry.

He makes that skating more effective by carrying the puck well. He likes to rush with it and create offense in the opposing zone, and Sharples will also join the play as a fourth attacker after making a breakout pass. He handles the puck well at all speeds, and he can pass it and receive a pass at top speed too. He passes well to both sides.

Jeff's good hockey sense helps him as a playmaker, and he'll make the correct pass most of the time. His vision helps him see the openings and his hands help him lead his teammates into position with good passes. His abilities make him a natural for the power play. Sharples has a hard and accurate shot from the blue line, and he'll sneak to the top of the faceoff circle if he can.

He uses his skating ability to get back into defensive position, and Sharples likes to try to force the play at his own blue line. He plays a fairly good positional defensive game from his blue line in, and he's certainly mobile enough to force most players wide of the net.

THE PHYSICAL GAME

Sharples is not a physical player per se, but he does use his body to trap the play along the boards and in the corners. He won't knock anyone through the glass with his hitting, but Jeff takes the body fairly well and has good strength in front of the net.

He's willing to sacrifice his body by blocking shots, and that speaks well for his attitude.

THE INTANGIBLES

Sharples is one of the youngsters the Red Wings will have to find room for on the blue line. He can be an above average offensive defenseman (without sacrificing defense) and that is the one component the Wings are sorely missing.

He has plenty of potential and should only get better with time. If, that is, coach Jacques Demers — who prefers veterans — squeezes him into the lineup.

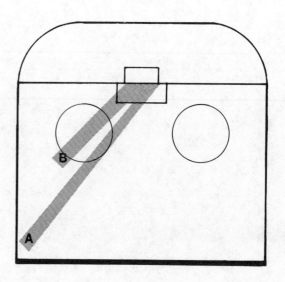

GREG STEFAN

Yrs. of NHL service: 6
Born: Brantford, Ontario, Canada; February 11, 1961
Position: Goaltender
Height: 6-0
Weight: 178
Uniform no.: 30
Catches: left

Career statistics:

GP	MINS	G	SO	AVG	A	PIM
246	13,475	877	5	3.90	12	165

1987-88 statisics:

GP	MINS	AVG	W	L	T	SO	GA	SA	SAPCT	PIM
33	1,854	3.11	17	9	5	1	96	923	.896	36

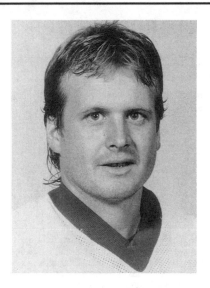

LAST SEASON
Games played total was a career low (Stefan missed 26 games with a leg injury). Goals-against-average was career best, fifth best in the NHL.

THE PHYSICAL GAME
Reflexes are the hallmark of Stefan's game, and he showcases them excellently. Greg is very fast with his hands and feet and he uses that quickness to his best ability in goalmouth scrambles and on deflections, whipping an arm or leg into the path of a seemingly inevitable goal. The team picks up on that flashiness and gets charged by it. He'll usually get a piece of any shot, even if the puck gets by him for a goal. That's his quickness at work.

He's a good skater with exceptional balance, and that allows him to regain his stance very quickly after making a save or flopping to the ice. That balance also allows him to lunge in one direction to get a piece of the puck, even after leaning the other way. He frequently goes to the ice, and one reason is because he doesn't cut his angles as well as he should. Greg will make phantom saves because he isn't squared with the puck, so after kicking out a leg he has to regain his stance.

Stefan sees the puck well and tracks the play alertly. He will not generally leave his net to handle the puck, and is content to allow it to skitter behind the goal instead of stopping it for his defense.

THE MENTAL GAME
Stefan is mentally tough, able to come back from bad goals or games. His concentration is pretty good, though it has historically been affected by interference by the opposition. His concentration between performances, however, still tends to waiver and that makes him inconsistent from night to night.

But when he is on he's super.

THE INTANGIBLES
Competition makes Stefan go, whether it's interal or external. A goaltending partner who can be a number one goalie makes Greg work harder. A pressure situation such as the playoffs makes Greg work harder. His competitiveness makes him a leader for the Wings.

Given the fact that when he's consistent he's one of the NHL's best goaltenders, and given the fact that Greg is 27 years old with six NHL seasons behind him, it's time for him to show he can play consistently at a high level and time to stop flirting with success.

DARREN VEITCH

Yrs. of NHL service: 8
Born: Saskatoon, Sask., Canada; April 24, 1960
Position: Defenseman
Height: 5-11
Weight: 188
Uniform no.:
Shoots: right

Career statistics:

GP	G	A	TP	PIM
472	45	201	246	280

1987-88 statistics:

GP	G	A	TP	+/−	PIM	PP	SH	GW	GT	S	PCT
63	7	33	40	10	45	4	0	1	0	156	4.5

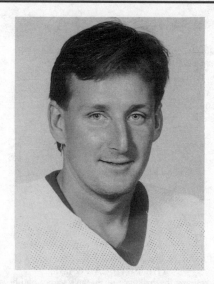

LAST SEASON

Veitch led all Detroit defenders in points and assists, despite missing two games with a thigh injury and 12 games with an ankle injury. He also led all Wings defenders in power play goals and shots on goal and was fifth overall in the latter category. Games played total was lowest in three seasons, while assists total was third highest of his career.

THE FINESSE GAME

Veitch is no better than a good skater, and that's because of his bad knees; he wears braces on both of them. He's a little suspect in his backskating and turns but is equipped with some acceleration speed. Improved judgement and decreased expectations have made Veitch a more effective skater, because he now knows when to rush with the puck and when to stay back.

Darren is finally seeing the ice well from his own end, making good plays to the breaking forwards by passing the puck quickly and safely. That vision is extended to the offensive zone, where Veitch is making excellent plays and supporting the power play.

He's able to spot the openings for the forwards, and Darren is getting the puck to them. He also has a great shot from the blue line, and will sneak to the top of the circle if he can.

Defensively, Veitch plays positionally and can force wingers wide by playing his defensive angles. He's also improved to the point where he can make good transitional plays when he gains the puck. He prefers to move the puck from the zone, but can skate it if necessary.

THE PHYSICAL GAME

Veitch is not overly physical, but he has begun to apply himself in his defensive end. He's taking the body with more authority than ever before, but he won't ever be confused with a Harold Snepsts or Scott Stevens.

THE INTANGIBLES

Several things mitigated against Veitch while he was in Detroit. First, the club wanted to get some of its younger defenders into the lineup on a regular basis. Second, the arrival of Jeff Sharples (and with Yves Racine on the way) meant that Darren's role could best be filled by a younger player.

Third and most important, Veitch was one of the Gang of

Six caught in an Edmonton bar past curfew during last season's Campbell Conference finals. That was the last straw, and it made him expendable.

He must bring his new-found steadiness to Toronto, a team desperately in need of stability.

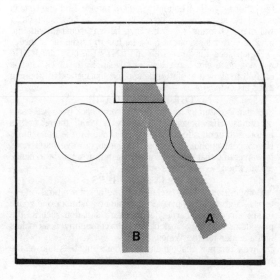

STEVE YZERMAN

Yrs. of NHL service: 5
Born: Cranbrook, B.C., Canada; May 9, 1965
Position: Center
Height: 5-11
Weight: 175
Uniform no.: 19
Shoots: right

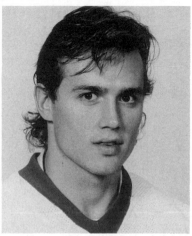

Career statistics:

GP	G	A	TP	PIM
355	164	246	410	194

1987-88 statistics:

GP	G	A	TP	+/−	PIM	PP	SH	GW	GT	S	PCT
64	50	52	102	30	44	10	6	6	0	242	20.7

LAST SEASON

Yzerman led the Wings in all point totals, despite playing his second fewest games (knee injury and surgery). He led the club in plus/minus, shorthanded goals, game winners and shots on goal. He was third in shooting percentage and finished 12th overall in League scoring. Goal and point totals were career highs.

THE FINESSE GAME

Yzerman is a superior player, one of the top five in the NHL in terms of skills and their applications. He skates excellently, explosive in his acceleration and fast over the long haul, and exceptionally agile on his feet. Superior balance and quickness make him very tricky on his skates, and he's almost impossible to run down because of his ability to change directions and speeds within a stride.

Steve complements that shiftiness with excellent puck handling skills. Yzerman uses his teammates excellently because he has tremendous anticipation and vision. He sees the opening before anyone and can lead his teammates there with a soft pass or can thread the puck through a maze of legs. He is an excellent play-making center, a quarterback on ice because he's that dominating a player. Defenders *must* play the body with Yzerman, because he'll turn them inside out if they don't.

Yzerman can score as well as he sets up a teammate. His quick wrist shot is excellently released, and he'll score from varying depths around the slot, both because of his shot and because he has the hands to work in traffic. He needs only the slightest opening to slide the puck home, and he'll put a lot of shots on goal. Though he has previously excelled more at playmaking, Steve showed last year that a little selfishness can go a long way — and his assist total was still higher than his goal total.

His defense is exemplary, and Yzerman doesn't sacrifice any of his defense for offense — or vice versa.

THE PHYSICAL GAME

Yzerman is the League's best example of how a finesse game can benefit from a physical style. While he won't knock anyone unconscious with his hits, Yzerman applies himself in all areas of the ice. He's fearless about going to the corners and the front of the net, and he'll fight to protect himself too.

He uses his body well in all three zones, initiating contact in all areas. The result is he gets more respect on the ice, and more open space in which to work his finesse magic.

THE INTANGIBLES

For four months last season, it was Yzerman — and not Mario Lemieux — touted as the successor to Wayne Gretzky as the NHL's most valuable player. Yzerman is the Wings leader, and they need him for any hope of winning the Stanley Cup. He doesn't have to score 100 points to be the Wings' most important player.

The only question that could have possibly applied to one of the NHL's top five players was his recovery from knee surgery. Yzerman answered that question (as well as demonstrated how determined and full of character he is) by playing in the Campbell Conference Final versus the Edmonton Oilers.

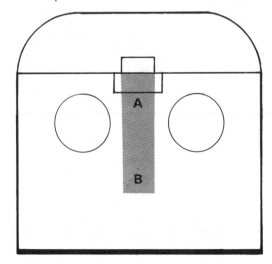

RICK ZOMBO

Yrs. of NHL service: 2
Born: Des Plaines, Illinois, USA; May 8, 1963
Position: Defenseman
Height: 6-1
Weight: 195
Uniform no.: 4
Shoots: right

Career statistics:

GP	G	A	TP	PIM
121	4	19	23	171

1987-88 statistics:

GP	G	A	TP	+/−	PIM	PP	SH	GW	GT	S	PCT
62	3	14	17	24	96	0	0	2	0	48	6.3

LAST SEASON

Zombo set career marks in games played and all point total categories, despite being sidelined with a shoulder injury. His plus/miuns rating was tied for the team's second best.

THE FINESSE GAME

A year's experience has sharpened Zombo's skating skills, so he is no longer a below average skater. Still, he's not exceptional either. He has developed some foot speed and the mobility that foot speed infers, so he's more agile in the defensive zone. His lateral movement has also improved, so he's moving better across the net toward the incoming forward.

Zombo makes good plays from his own end. He handles the puck well in his defensive zone and is patient in his passing, making sure to execute the right play. He understands his defensive angles and plays them well, so he is sound positionally.

His play reading ability aids him in gaining the correct position, and it's that same trait that helps him make good breakout plays.

Because of his conservative style, Zombo will attempt to make almost no contribution at the offensive blue line in terms of containing the point. If he does gain the line Rick can get the puck to his teammates because of his play reading ability. He has a low, hard shot from the point.

THE PHYSICAL GAME

Zombo likes to play a physical game and will use his body well in the defensive zone. He handles the front of the net fairly well and has good strength, and his play against the boards has improved because of his improved balance. Zombo can hold his own now in terms of getting checked and maintaining his position, rather than being knocked off the puck as he was previously.

THE INTANGIBLES

Zombo has taken a solid role with Detroit, because his developable skills have done just that. He showed well during the Wings playoff run by leading the club in plus/minus, and he can still improve as an NHL player. In his favor is coach Jacques Demers penchant for older, more experienced players. Working against him will be Detroit's attempts to bring some younger blood into the lineup.

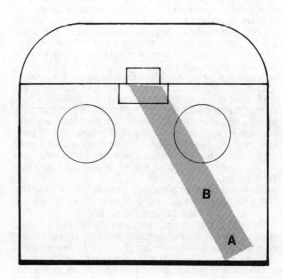

EDMONTON OILERS

LINE COMBINATIONS
GEOFF COURTNALL-WAYNE GRETZKY-JARI KURRI
CRAIG SIMPSON-MARK MESSIER-GLENN ANDERSON
ESA TIKKANEN-KEITH ACTON-MARTY MCSORLEY

DEFENSE PAIRINGS
CHARLIE HUDDY-JEFF BEUKEBOOM
STEVE SMITH-CRAIG MUNI
KEVIN LOWE-

GOALTENDERS
GRANT FUHR
BILL RANFORD

OTHER PLAYERS
RANDY GREGG — Defenseman
MIKE KRUSHELNYSKI — Left wing
CRAIG MACTAVISH — Center
KEVIN MCCLELLAND — Center

POWER PLAY

FIRST UNIT:
CRAIG SIMPSON-WAYNE GRETZKY-GLENN ANDERSON
CHARLIE HUDDY-STEVE SMITH

SECOND UNIT:
GEOFF COURTNALL-WAYNE GRETZKY-JARI KURRI

On the first unit, SIMPSON posts up in front of the net, GRETZKY controls the left wing boards and behind the net, and ANDERSON takes the right wing side. GRETZKY distributes the puck, looking for ANDERSON on a one-touch pass in the right faceoff circle or feeding the points for shots. The forwards will converge on the net for rebounds.

COURTNALL takes SIMPSON's place on the second unit, KURRI subs for ANDERSON on the right side. MARK MESSIER will occasionally see time on the point, or he will substitute for GRETZKY. KEVIN LOWE and JEFF BEUKEBOOM also see time, but HUDDY and SMITH are the main pair.

Last season the Oiler power play was GOOD, scoring 88 goals in 402 opportunities (21.9 percent, seventh overall).

PENALTY KILLING

FIRST UNIT:
CRAIG MACTAVISH-MARK MESSIER
STEVE SMITH-CHARLIE HUDDY

All of Edmonton's penalty killers pressure the puck, with the forwards especially aggressive toward the points. They'll jump the puck carrier when they can, and they also look to create an offensive play in the opposition zone — the Oilers were third overall last season in shorthanded goals scored. Many Oilers see penalty killing time, with GRETZKY, ANDERSON and TIKKANEN the other forwards, LOWE and MUNI the other defensemen.

Last season Edmonton's penalty killing was GOOD, allowing just 86 goals in 447 shorthanded situations (80.8 percent, seventh overall).

CRUCIAL FACEOFFS

MESSIER's the man, but MACTAVISH and KRUSHELNYSKI are also good.

KEITH ACTON

Yrs. of NHL service: 9
Born: Newmarket, Ontario, Canada; April 15, 1958
Position: Center
Height: 5-10
Weight: 167
Uniform no.: 23
Shoots: left

Career statistics:

GP	G	A	TP	PIM
607	168	264	432	630

1987-88 statistics:

GP	G	A	TP	+/−	PIM	PP	SH	GW	GT	S	PCT
72	11	17	28	-19	95	1	1	1	0	75	14.7

LAST SEASON

Acton was acquired late in the season from Minnesota in exchange for Moe Mantha. Games played total was lowest in seven seasons, since rookie season of 61 games. Point totals were career lows. His plus/minus mark was Edmonton's worst.

THE FINESSE GAME

Acton skates well, applying some good foot speed and agility, strength and acceleration in his role as a checking forward. He combines those assets effectively with good anticipation and hockey sense. He likes to use his speed to jump into openings and he loves to dive to draw a call from the referee.

Those finesse skills make him persistent in his pursuit of the puck and also make him effective on the specialty team units, particularly the penalty killing squad where he is a definite threat for a shorthanded goal.

Acton has a good feel for the play and its implications and he sees the ice well, allowing him to close the openings the opposition was planning to exploit. He is conscientious defensively, more so than his plus/minus would indicate. He checks and works hard at both ends of the ice.

Keith has good hands and he controls the puck well and is able to use his teammates well because of his hand skills and anticipation. He is fairly creative away from the puck when he is on offense, but lacks the dynamic shot that would make him an offensive force. He must be within medium range of the net to score.

THE PHYSICAL GAME

Acton plays a physical game and is aggressive, certainly more so than his size would indicate. He will hit and bump and take the rough going up and down the ice. He is also very liberal in the use of his stick, and that use (constantly jabbing the opposition in the back of the knee, for example) works for him as a checker by distracting the opposition.

He will not, however, extend his physical play toward fighting, which is the common result of his own belligerence. Once he's instigated a commotion, Acton retires to the outer edges of the fray.

THE INTANGIBLES

Acton is a hard worker and an honest hockey player. He is feisty and also yaps incessantly to drive the other team to distraction. He is well-liked by his teammates and is a leader through his work ethic.

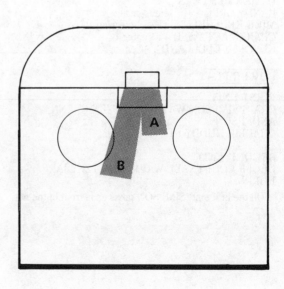

GLENN ANDERSON

Yrs. of NHL service: 8
Born: Vancouver, B.C., Canada; October 2, 1960
Position: Right wing
Height: 5-11
Weight: 175
Uniform no.: 9
Shoots: left

Career statistics:

GP	G	A	TP	PIM
602	339	366	705	512

1987-88 statistics:

GP	G	A	TP	+/−	PIM	PP	SH	GW	GT	S	PCT
80	38	50	88	5	58	16	1	3	0	255	14.9

LAST SEASON

Anderson played all 80 games for the second consecutive season and fifth time in his eight-year career. He finished fifth on the club in scoring (fourth in goals, fifth in assists), second in power play goals and first in shots on goal. His plus/minus mark was fourth worst on the club.

THE FINESSE GAME

Anderson is a world-class player, and he earns that ranking because he does more things faster than anyone else in the League — except Mark Messier. Glenn is an excellent skater in all aspects of that skill. He has unbelievable tremendous speed and he moderates it well, but he doesn't have to because no one can catch him.

His speed is amplified by great balance on his feet, and that balance makes the opposition suffer the brunt of the physical punishment when Andersdon gets hit, rather than the other way around. He's quick and agile and almost unstoppable once he gets going.

On top of that, unlike most other players who have to slow down their feet so their hands can catch up, Anderson work excellently at full throttle — though he handles the puck well at all speeds.

His physical finesse skills are complemented by his good vision and anticipation, so Anderson is able to make good use of his teammates. He is very creative in the offensive zone and not at all predictable (except that he likes to go to the net from the right side), and that makes him even harder to defend against.

Anderson tortures opposing goalies by scoring from anywhere in the offensive zone with excellent wrist and slap shots. He is at his most dangerous from around the net, where he can put his soft hands and lightning-quick release to work. He makes the most of his opportunities by shooting accurately and making the goaltender work.

Oh yes, he's also solid defensively, playing his check well into the defensive zone.

THE PHYSICAL GAME

Anderson plays with reckless disregared for his own safety. He is a kamikaze on the ice, fearlessly running into anything he can. He definitely initiates a good deal of contact and is unafraid of the hitting that accompanies his work in the corners. He'll also get his stick into people, as Winnipeg's Steve Rooney found out in last spring's playoffs.

The reverse is that Glenn is diffcult to hit because he is so fast, and his balance keeps him vertical and ready to work after a check.

THE INTANGIBLES

Glenn lacks the concentration skills to apply himself night in and night out, but when the playoffs come he can't be stopped. After nine years Anderson knows what's important and what isn't, so the days of his 50-goal seasons may be past as he saves himself for springtime. Yet that doesn't mean he can't score 50 goals if he wants to.

And wanting to is the key to Anderson. As long as he wants to in April and May, he'll get along just fine.

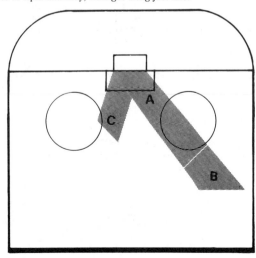

JEFF BEUKEBOOM

Yrs. of NHL service: 2
Born: Ajax, Ontario, Canada; March 28, 1965
Position: Defenseman
Height: 6-4
Weight: 210
Uniform no.: 6
Shoots: right

Career statistics:

GP	G	A	TP	PIM
117	8	28	36	325

1987-88 statistics:

GP	G	A	TP	+/−	PIM	PP	SH	GW	GT	S	PCT
73	5	20	25	27	201	1	0	1	0	76	6.6

LAST SEASON

Games played, all point totals and PIM mark were all career highs. Beukeboom finished fourth on the team in plus/minus and PIM.

THE FINESSE GAME

Beukeboom has made improvements in his NHL game, most notably in his skating and play reading ability. He is a smoother skater now than he was a year ago, improving his speed, quickness and agility both forward and back.

Jeff has also improved his understanding of the NHL play, including reading the play and reacting to it more quickly. He is recognizing the rush toward him earlier and combines that with his better skating to more consistently force the play wide and close the gap on the puck carrier.

He can make the plays to the forwards and has improved in this aspect of his game (better skating equals more time to look and make a play), but right now is content to be the takeout defenseman, rather than the breakout defender.

THE PHYSICAL GAME

Jeff is big and likes to hit, to he can certainly be said to get the most from his size. He is an aggressive player in front of the net and in the corners — sometimes a little too aggressive as his PIM total indicates — and he punsihes people when he hits them.

Again, his improved finesse skills — notably his skating — help him to be a better physical player. Since he moves his feet better, Jeff is better able to get to the opposition and use his strength.

THE INTANGIBLES

Beukeboom is another of the young Oiler defensemen who was not supposed to stand up to this spring's playoff grind, but Jeff fared very well for himself. He is an intelligent player and an earnest young man, one who works hard at developing his skills. His improvement should continue.

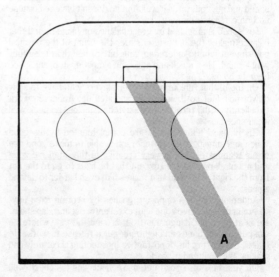

GEOFF COURTNALL

Yrs. of NHL service: 4
Born: Victoria, B.C., Canada; August 18, 1962
Position: Left wing
Height: 6-0
Weight: 185
Uniform no.: 15
Shoots: left

Career statistics:

GP	G	A	TP	PIM
271	82	85	167	383

1987-88 statistics:

GP	G	A	TP	+/−	PIM	PP	SH	GW	GT	S	PCT
74	36	30	66	25	123	8	0	5	0	252	14.3

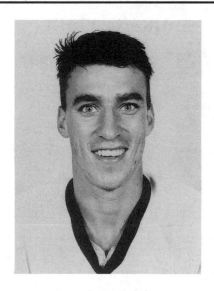

LAST SEASON

Courtnall was acquired (along with Bill Ranford) from Boston late in the year in exchange for Andy Moog. Games played total, all point totals and PIM mark were all career highs. He finished second on the Oilers in shots on goal.

THE FINESSE GAME

Courtnall is an excellent skater, strong on his feet and with good acceleration and that's been both his strength and his weakness. In previous seasons his other skills couldn't keep up with his speed; while his feet were of NHL caliber his hands and smarts were not.

Geoff changed all that last year as he moderated his speed for the first time in his NHL career, throwing something other than full throttle at the defense. The result was, Courtnall kept the play in front of him instead of out-racing it. Because of that his vision improved and he began making plays to his teammates.

His hands also improved, because suddenly they didn't have to keep up with his feet. That meant that he could get off more and better shots, and that's no small reason for his increased scoring production. His shot is very good, hard and very quick to the net.

His play improved defensively too, as Courtnall got a better look at the opposition attack and then used his speed to break it up.

THE PHYSICAL GAME

Courtnall's other great asset is his physical game. He is in great shape and has strength to match his conditioning, and Courtnall hits hard when he checks — his leg power gives his checks extra oomph.

He eagerly hits in the corner and doesn't back down from a challenge. He also takes hits to make plays.

THE INTANGIBLES

Courtnall had 22 of his 36 goals by the 40-game mark last season, and that means he scored only 14 goals in the last 34 games. Consistency has never been his hallmark, and the feeling is Harry Sinden felt he'd gotten all he was going to get out of Geoff (we told you last year his time in Boston was coming to an end) and thus dumped him.

Courtnall needs to disprove that theory, but the numbers are not in his favor: zero goals and three points in 19 playoff games with the Oilers. Certainly his speed fits their style, but in many ways this season is the most important of Courtnall's NHL life.

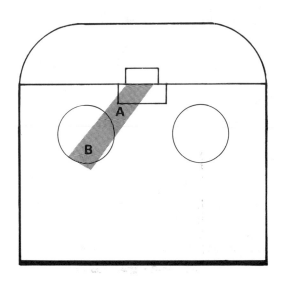

GRANT FUHR

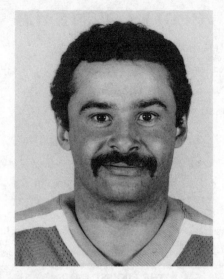

Yrs. of NHL service: 7
Born: Spruce Grove, Alta., Canada; September 28, 1962
Position: Goaltender
Height: 5-10
Weight: 185
Uniform no.: 31
Catches: right

Career statistics:

GP	MINS	G	SO	AVG	A	PIM
330	18,710	1,148	6	3.68	35	46

1987-88 statisics:

GP	MINS	AVG	W	L	T	SO	GA	SA	SAPCT	PIM
75	4,304	3.43	40	24	9	4	246	2,066	.881	16

LAST SEASON

Fuhr led the NHL in games and minutes played, both career highs, and also led the NHL in shots faced and goals allowed (Grant allowed more goals personally than the Montreal Canadiens — the NHL's best defensive team — allowed as a team). He finished first in the NHL in wins and third in shutouts.

THE PHYSICAL GAME

Grant's goaltending game combines his outstanding reflexes with his outstanding demeanor. His hand foot speed is the best in the National Hockey League, and he makes those skills better by playing a challenging, angle cutting style. He stays square with the puck very well, but when he has to move he does so with great ease. Between his angle play and his reflexes, it's rare that a first shot — or even a deflection — will get by him.

His excellent skating skill is at the root of his success, for he is tremendously balanced on his skates and regains his feet (after going to the ice) or his stance (after movement) almost instantaneously. If there is a weakness at all, it would be between his pads — but good luck trying to score there (his foot and leg speed will close the five-hole very quickly). Grant's balance also gives him the NHL's best lateral movement. He moves in and out of the net and around the defensive zone excellently.

Fuhr handles the puck better than almost any other goaltender and often starts plays up ice by sending the puck to the forwards. Grant handles his stick well and has the fastest glove hand — just pure radar — in the world.

THE MENTAL GAME

Grant is almost robotic in his approach to each game. Pressure means nothing to him. Stanley Cup games, Canada Cup games, mid-December Norris Division games — they're all the same to Fuhr, and he doesn't get nervous for any of them.

Since he has no nerves bad goals don't bother him. Ditto bad performances — which are few and far between anyway; Fuhr just shrugs them all off. Because of that (and because he makes his physical skills work in conjunction with his mental ones) he is the supreme money goaltender.

His concentration is excellent and he maintains it throughout any type of game, knowing that because of the Oilers' brand of hockey he may see little action or too much.

THE INTANGIBLES

Finally Fuhr was officially recognized as the NHL's best goaltender, winning the Vezina Trophy and being named a First Team All-Star for the first time in his career. He's even begun to get recognition for his role in the Oilers' success, as his MVP nomination shows.

Not that Grant cares. He just wants to play and have fun. But enroute to that goal he's also made himself the world's best goaltender.

RANDY GREGG

Yrs. of NHL service: 6
Born: Edmonton, Alta., Canada; February 19, 1956
Position: Defenseman
Height: 6-4
Weight: 215
Uniform no.: 21
Shoots: left

Career statistics:

GP	G	A	TP	PIM
348	33	113	146	239

1987-88 statistics:

GP	G	A	TP	+/−	PIM	PP	SH	GW	GT	S	PCT
15	1	2	3	4	8	0	0	0	0	20	4.2

LAST SEASON
Gregg rejoined the Oilers after the Calgary Winter Olympics.

THE FINESSE GAME
Gregg is a good skater but not an overwhelmingly fast one. He is solid both forward and backward, good on his turns and he plays a good positional game.

He is a defensive style defenseman, moving the puck quickly for the forwards to carry up-ice. Though he will make a foray or two, rushing the puck is not Gregg's strong point.

Randy reads the rush very well and channels it wide of the net effectively. He rarely makes a defensive mistake and that's important for a scoring team like the Oilers.

Gregg will join the play up-ice and he will control the point well, but rarely pinches in. He has an average shot from the point but will find the open man for a pass.

THE PHYSICAL GAME
Gregg hits and plays a steadily unspectacular physical game. He is strong and clears the front of the net or holds the opposition out of the play well.

He puts his reach to work deflecting passes and pokechecking the puck, and he will also sacrifice his body to block shots.

THE INTANGIBLES
The good doctor is a hard worker and a character player. He's one of the best of the NHL's solid, stay-at-home defensemen.

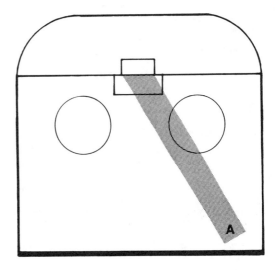

WAYNE GRETZKY

Yrs. of NHL service: 10
Born: Brantford, Ontario, Canada; January 26, 1961
Position: Center
Height: 6-0
Weight: 170
Uniform no.: 99
Shoots: left

Career statistics:

GP	G	A	TP	PIM
696	583	1,086	1,669	323

1987-88 statistics:

GP	G	A	TP	+/-	PIM	PP	SH	GW	GT	S	PCT
64	40	109	149	39	24	9	5	3	0	211	19.0

LAST SEASON

Gretzky finished second in NHL scoring for the first time in eight years. He led the League in assists and was fifth overall in plus/minus (second among forwards). He led Edmonton in scoring and shorthanded goals, was third on the club in goals and shots on goal and second in plus/minus (best among forwards). Goal total was the lowest of his career, point total the second lowest (and lowest in eight seasons). He missed 13 games with a knee injury and three more with an eye injury.

THE FINESSE GAME

OVERALL SKATING ABILITY: Excellent.

Speed: Good, but not outstanding from point to point.

Agility and lateral movement: Excellent, the League's best lateral movement.

Balance: Excellent. It keys his League-leading lateral movement and mobility:

Quickness: Good, not exceptional.

ANTICIPATION AND HOCKEY SENSE: Excellent, the world's best.

In the way a chessmaster reads two and three moves ahead, Wayne examines the ice and the options, factoring in his teammate's possible plays and the opposition's possible reponses. He then acts on those possible resolutions of every play.

His good skating speed and quickness are powered by his understanding of the game to get Gretzky to the soon-to-be loose pucks. In essence, his brain out-races his opponent's feet.

STICK SKILLS: Excellent, the League's best — maybe the world's.

Passing and playmaking ability: Excellent, the League's best passer. But what else would you expect from a player who has hands so feather-soft he's *never* — by all claim — broken a stick while in the NHL. Wayne has the ability to put a pass on a teammate's stick anywhere at anytime, regardless of circumstance. If the puck has to get through a crowd, over some sticks, around a corner and into the lockerroom, Wayne has the hands to make that pass.

Those passing skills are amplified by his understanding and anticipation. Gretzky does more than just see the opening and lead his teammates to them; he creates the openings by hypnotizing defenders with the puck. Even after 10 years, defensemen still fall for his tricks and chase him all over the ice, leaving openings for his teammates.

Puckhandling: Excellent, no worse than second best in the NHL. Skating, sensitive hands and hockey sense combine to make Wayne's puckhandling as tantalizing as a cobra hypnotizing its prey. That's why the defense keeps falling for it.

Shooting: Excellent, the League's best. There may be more dynamic shots, harder ones, faster ones. But for making one shot in the most important circumstance, there's no one better. Who else could have scored the shorthanded goal Gretzky scored against the Flames during last spring's playoffs — left handed shot against the left wing boards, heading toward the net with an ever-tightening angle and only the far, fadeaway top corner open?

No one.

Gretzky exploits the top of the net better than any NHLer, but Wayne can put the puck anywhere he wants from anywhere he wants. He will make the puck rise or sink depending upon how he releases it from his stick blade. He'll score even if the opening doesn't exist; more than once he has banked the puck off a goaltender for a goal — including from behind the net.

Breakaway skills: Good. He thinks too much about his options rather than just reacting to openings. He must shoot more on those occasions.

DEFENSIVE PLAY: Excellent. The great myth of the Great One's performances is that he doesn't play defense and never has. Wrong. Critics are confusing physical play with defense. He is always around the puck in all three zones, and his presence on the ice immediately forces the opposition to think defensively. What better defense is there?

THE PHYSICAL GAME

The physical game is not Greztky's game, and there's no need for it to be. In fact, he'd most likely be ineffective if he did play physically because he lacks the innate strength necessary.

That is not to say that Wayne won't play physically or is afraid of hits. He plays in the high traffic areas all the time, but he uses his balance and anticipation to avoid the hits that would do the damage. If someone does get a piece of him, Wayne is able to lean away from the hit to avoid much of its impact; again, balance.

THE INTANGIBLES

Always there has been talk of how Gretzky makes average players better, like the left wings he's teamed with throughout his career who have their best ever seasons on Wayne's port side and then never repeat that success with other centers.

But the Great One also makes the great ones better. Gretzky keyed Mario Lemieux's incredible season in several ways: he led Lemieux to the phenomenal success the Penguin superstar had in the Canada Cup, and it was from that Canada Cup experience that Lemieux went on to his best ever season.

The irony of course is that Mario's superb season served to put a statistical end to Gretzky's seven-year dominance of the scoreboard and eight-year hold on the NHL's MVP trophy.

And the critics came out again, the ones who nine years ago said 'Prove it,' to Wayne's talent. Then after two or three seasons that showed his undeniable greatness the critics said 'He's nothing until he wins a Stanley Cup.' Then after two Cups and failure to win a third consecutive the critics said, 'Great player, but no staying power.' And last season, with Mario's growing success the critics wasted no time in saying to Wayne, 'Thanks for your time, it's been nice having you. Here's your hat; what's your hurry?

The truth is, as his playoff showing last spring reinforced, Gretzky is the world's greatest player. And something tells us that his determination to be the best will carry him back to the top of the charts this season.

Don't bet against him.

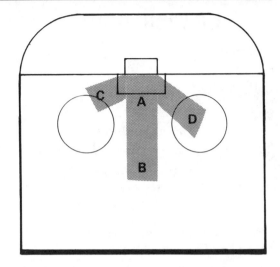

CHARLIE HUDDY

Yrs. of NHL service: 7
Born: Oshawa, Ontario, Canada; June 2, 1959
Position: Defenseman
Height: 6-0
Weight: 200
Uniform no.: 22
Shoots: left

Career statistics:

GP	G	A	TP	PIM
495	64	209	273	360

1987-88 statistics:

GP	G	A	TP	+/−	PIM	PP	SH	GW	GT	S	PCT
77	13	28	41	23	71	2	0	2	1	163	8.0

LAST SEASON

Games played total was highest in three seasons. Goal total was the second highest of his career (best in five seasons), while assist total was lowest of any full season. He led the team's defensemen in goals and shots on goal, and his plus/minus was the corps' second-worst.

THE FINESSE GAME

Huddy is a good skater, carrying neither a particular strength nor particular weakness in that skill. He lacks the tremendous speed and agility of some of his teammates, but he gets where he's going. He skates well both forward and backward and is smooth in his pivots.

Charlie's hockey sense is his one outstanding skill. He reads plays very well, breaks up rushes excellently by forcing the opposition wide of the net and he can step into an offensive rush up-ice if need be, moving the puck quickly and smoothly. That play reading ability makes him one of the best pinching defensemen in the League.

Huddy combines his ice vision with his hand skills to move the puck to the open man well in both zones. He controls the point well because he is a good stickhandler, much better than he is given credit for.

When shooting, Charlie delivers a hard slap shot from the point, one that is accurate and low, good for tip-ins and deflections.

THE PHYSICAL GAME

Huddy bangs along the boards and in front of the net and, though he isn't the strongest guy in the league, can handle most any opposing forward in the slot.

He can outmuscle the opposition along the boards and after doing so can make a play quickly because he is balanced on his skates and in position. He will sacrifice his body by blocking shots.

THE INTANGIBLES

We were wrong last year when we said that Huddy's Oiler career was approaching its end, and we have Paul Coffey to thank for that. With Coffey out of Edmonton, Huddy got a chance to open up his offense and pick up some of the attacking slack left by Coffey's absence.

Charlie is a steady and unspectacular performer, but he is

one reason why Edmonton is such a great team; they take advantage of what each member has to offer. What Huddy offered was his goal-scoring ability. It's not in Coffey's class, but it fit in well with Edmonton's new look.

And it should continue to do so, even if much-heralded defenseman Chris Joseph makes the jump to the Oilers this season.

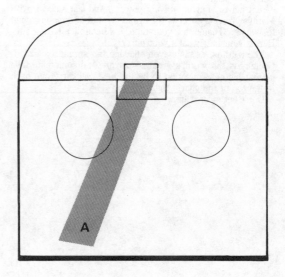

MIKE KRUSHELNYSKI

Yrs. of NHL service: 7
Born: Montreal, Quebec, Canada; April 27, 1960
Position: Left wing/center
Height: 6-2
Weight: 200
Uniform no.: 26
Shoots: left

Career statistics:

GP	G	A	TP	PIM
452	146	196	342	313

1987-88 statistics:

GP	G	A	TP	+/−	PIM	PP	SH	GW	GT	S	PCT
76	20	27	47	26	64	4	0	0	0	124	16.1

LAST SEASON

Goal total was highest in three seasons. He finished fifth on the club in plus/minus, second among forwards. He missed two games with a back injury.

THE FINESSE GAME

Skating is the best of Krushelnyski's skills, one where he ranks as excellent. Mike has a long stride and covers a lot of ground with it, though he doesn't have exceptional speed. He accelerates very well and he puts that asset to work as he bursts down the wing. He is also very balanced on his feet and that makes him very agile; he can take a hit and maintain his composure to make a play. Mike doesn't get the most he can from his skating though, and he can be downright lazy in the offensive zone in terms of forechecking.

Mike's good hands mean good puck control skills. He is an excellent faceoff man and stickhandler and can dance the puck past a defenseman because of his skills and reach (here too his balance helps, giving him the ability to sway out of reach). His good vision and anticipation help him to find the open man and to therefore pass well.

Mike is an accurate shooter, possessing a hard and accurate wrist shot that he releases quickly and that forces the goaltender to make saves. He is an opportunist and will swoop to the net to pick up a loose puck in an attempt to shovel it home.

THE PHYSICAL GAME

The physical game has never been Krushelnyski's cup of tea, and he prefers to stay out of the high traffic areas in the corners and in front of the net. He will make his plays while being hit (an indication of good concentration) but Krushelnyski doesn't enjoy the physical part of the game.

He uses his reach very well in snaring pucks and he has good strength in his wrists and arms and that's what powers his shot.

THE INTANGIBLES

Skills he's got, desire he don't got. Mike plays without spark or emotion, just sort of cruising up and down the ice. That makes him an underachiever. Unfortunate, because he definitely has the skills to be an above-average player.

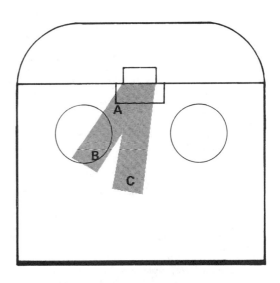

JARI KURRI

Yrs. of NHL service: 8
Born: Helsinki, Finland; May 18, 1960
Position: Right wing
Height: 6-0
Weight: 190
Uniform no.: 17
Shoots: right

Career statistics:

GP	G	A	TP	PIM
600	397	451	848	231

1987-88 statistics:

GP	G	A	TP	+/−	PIM	PP	SH	GW	GT	S	PCT
80	43	53	96	25	30	10	3	5	1	207	20.8

LAST SEASON

Kurri played all 80 games for just the second time in his career and first time in the last five seasons. He finished third on the club in scoring with his lowest goal, assist and point totals in six seasons (second in goals, third in assists). He was fourth on the club in power play goals and shots on goal, first in shooting percentage. He was sixth in plus/minus ranking, and tied for second in shorthanded goals.

THE FINESSE GAME

Kurri's shot is the best of his excellent finesse skills. He needs just the slightest opening and his accurate, hard wrist shot is en route to the goal. He releases his shot very quickly, one reason he's so successful scoring goals, and he also has tremendous ability in one-timing the puck.

Jari complements that ability — in fact, makes that ability what it is — by using his great instincts and anticipation to get into position to score. Kurri may be the NHL's most creative player without the puck, using the ice well to create openings by moving from lane to lane.

His outstanding skating skill is what moves him from lane to lane. He has excellent speed and agility, and he uses his speed and acceleration ability to rocket past the defense and snare passes and loose pucks. Jari also has outstanding one-step quickness that translates into excellent lateral movement and direction changing ability.

When he chooses to carry the puck into the offensive zone, he likes to skate parallel to the blue line from the left wing to the right wing boards, and then jet around the defense. He has excellent hands to control the puck (he takes a pass in stride better than most other NHLers) and is a good passer and stickhandler. He is dangerous around the net because his balance and superior hand skills allow him to control the puck in traffic.

Kurri uses his skills to be an exceptional specialty teams player. He uses his one-step quickness to dart into the holes on the power play, meeting the pass and one-timing the puck into the net. On the penalty killing unit he uses his breakaway speed and anticipation to score short-handed.

He is also a fine positional player defensively, and uses his skills to make the transition from offense to defense.

THE PHYSICAL GAME

Unlike teammates Glenn Anderson and Mark Messier, Kurri is not reckless in his physical play — but that doesn't mean he's any less effective. He isn't a physical player per se, in that he doesn't smash the opposition into the boards, but Kurri takes the body well by getting in his man's way. He is strong enough to hold the opposition out of the play when necessary. That ability is one big reason why Kurri succeeds defensively; he's always in the opposition's way.

Kurri is fearless, unafraid to go into the corners after the puck if need be and he can certainly take any abuse aimed his way. All of his physical play is made possible by his superior balance, the trait that keeps him vertical in almost every situation.

THE INTANGIBLES

Kurri is another of the Oilers — a la Glenn Anderson — who subscribed last season to the attitude of pacing oneself throughout the season. And he was no doubt affected by the absence of his center — Wayne Gretzky — for 16 games. After all, would Kurri have scored seven more goals in 16 games to hit the 50-goal mark?

Some quick numbers juggling (goals-to-games-played ratio: 1.51 per) suggests he would have finished with 53 goals. But that number crunching just begs the question of Kurri's intensity.

He wasn't anywhere near as dynamic in the offensive last season as he had been in the four seasons prior to 1987-88, and that's because Kurri didn't want to be. Last year's long season could be one reason: Canada Cup, plus regular season plus playoffs makes a compelling case for relaxing.

But Mark Messier didn't relax. Gretzky didn't relax. And Kurri shouldn't have either. In that light, and without taking anything away from Kurri's world class skill, he has something to prove this season.

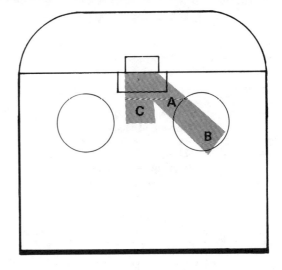

KEVIN LOWE

Yrs. of NHL service: 9
Born: Lachute, Quebec, Canada; April 15, 1959
Position: Defenseman
Height: 6-2
Weight: 195
Uniform no.: 4
Shoots: left

Career statistics:

GP	G	A	TP	PIM
684	54	231	285	706

1987-88 statistics:

GP	G	A	TP	+/-	PIM	PP	SH	GW	GT	S	PCT
70	9	15	24	18	89	2	1	2	0	82	11.0

LAST SEASON

Games played total was second lowest of Lowe's career, lowest in eight seasons; he missed 10 games with a broken wrist. Goal total ties his second best career mark and was his best total in six seasons. His plus/minus rating was lowest among regular Oiler defensemen.

THE FINESSE GAME

Lowe is an oustanding example of the whole being greater than the sum of the parts, and the reasons for that are his hockey sense and vision; they are excellent. Kevin's understanding of the defensive play is superior, as good as the best defensive defenseman on any day. He reads the rush toward him with great anticipation and even as he makes his move to force the opposition wide of the net Lowe knows what he's going to do after he gains the puck.

He is the kind of defenseman that opposing forwards avoid. Not because of fear, but because they know he can counter whatever they have planned. Kevin's anticipation and vision work on the second half of the defensive play, when he relieves the enemy of the puck and starts the play up ice.

He not only sees the openings but sees the best play presented and Lowe will make that best play eight-to-nine times out of 10. He moves the puck quickly and crisply to the forwards, knowing that the opposition can't skate with the Oilers. He has good hand skills and demonstrates them on the breakouts and at the opposing blue line (when he follows the play up ice), but he won't make too many fancy passes. Kevin will let the forwards do the fancy stuff while he controls the point and hits the open man.

He's a good skater forward and backward, not very fast but strong and balanced for work in traffic. Lowe can skate the puck if necessary, but he isn't a puck carrying defender. Nor is he an offensive threat at the NHL level, so the handful of goals he scores each year will come from the point.

THE PHYSICAL GAME

Kevin's intelligent game extends to his physical play, and here too the whole is greater than the sum of the parts. While he has good size and strength, Lowe plays stronger than he is and he does that by playing intelligently. Instead of pounding the opponent from the moment he sets foot in front of the crease, Lowe waits for the correct moment to start pounding. By doing so he stays physical and avoids penalties.

Kevin is very good in his crease coverage and just as good in the corners, where he again hits intelligently and with purpose instead of just claiming victims. He can jar the puck free with a check and is always in position to make a play afterward because of his good balance: He is rarely knocked down.

Kevin is also the best at two of the NHL's dying arts: open ice body checking and shot blocking. He is absolutely fearless in sacrficing his body but, though he has shown good durability over the course of his career, his propensity for sacrifice has begun to manifest itself in injury.

He also has a good reach and he uses it pokecheck or deflect pucks efficiently.

THE INTANGIBLES

Despite four Stanley Cup championships, despite being the number one defender on hockey's number one team, Kevin Lowe remains under-appreciated. His intelligence in never extending his game beyond its limitations has made him a superstar defenseman, and it also — through example — makes youngsters like Craig Muni better players.

We told you last year that he is a character individual and plays in pain, and Lowe demonstrated that during the Cup playoffs when he played despite a broken wrist and three broken ribs. He leads by example of his hard work and is a fine, fine player.

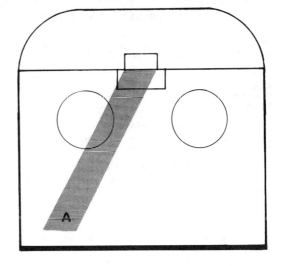

CRAIG MACTAVISH

Yrs. of NHL service: 7
Born: London, Ontario, Canada; August 15, 1958
Position: Center
Height: 6-0
Weight: 190
Uniform no.: 14
Shoots: left

Career statistics:

GP	G	A	TP	PIM
450	102	126	228	246

1987-88 statistics:

GP	G	A	TP	+/−	PIM	PP	SH	GW	GT	S	PCT
80	15	17	32	-3	47	0	3	5	0	90	16.3

LAST SEASON

Games played total was the highest of MacTavish's career, the first time he's played all 80 games. All point totals were lowest in last four seasons. His minus-3 was the team's second worst.

THE FINESSE GAME

MacTavish has become a good skater with a lot of strength in his stride. He is neither exceptionally fast nor outstandingly quick, but he pursues the puck well at a steady pace. He has good balance — which helps his physical game — and he uses his skating skills to be a good two-way player who's able to contribute at both ends of the ice. Craig can move the puck fairly well within his class of player, and he can get it to his teammates effectively. He also demonstrated a scoring touch around the net.

Craig's anticipation, hockey sense and ice vision are his primary tools as a defensive center. He recognizes where the openings will be and uses his strong skating to thwart the opposition's intentions.

THE PHYSICAL GAME

MacTavish complements his checking by body checking. He initiates contact along the boards and in open ice, and he also absorbs his share of abuse when camped out in front of the opposition's net. He applies himself along the boards and can muscle the opposition off the puck. He's still not a belter, more of a pusher and shover, but he's become increasingly effective in the traffic areas.

One reason for that is his improved balance, for it is that skill that adds to his leg strength and helps keep him vertical in contact situations.

He is strong on faceoffs because of his eye/hand coordination.

THE INTANGIBLES

MacTavish is a dedicated athlete, and he works hard at his game. He is one of those unglamourous role players, the kind that any team must have to be successful.

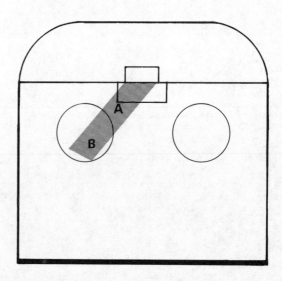

KEVIN MCCLELLAND

Yrs. of NHL service: 6
Born: Oshawa, Ontario, Canada; July 4, 1962
Position: Center
Height: 6-2
Weight: 200
Uniform no.: 24
Shoots: right

Career statistics:

GP	G	A	TP	PIM
411	57	91	148	1,263

1987-88 statistics:

GP	G	A	TP	+/–	PIM	PP	SH	GW	GT	S	PCT
74	10	6	16	1	281	0	0	0	0	61	16.4

LAST SEASON

Games played total was second highest of McClelland's career. Goal total was lowest in three seasons. PIM total was a career high, second highest on the team and first among forwards. McClelland was Edmonton's lowest scoring regular. He missed three games with a knee injury.

THE FINESSE GAME

There isn't much about Kevin's play to which the word finesse could be applied. He is a good skater in a strength way. No curves and swirls for McClelland: he's all straightaway and power. He has a burst of speed keyed by his powerful stride, but he won't out-race anyone over the length of the ice. His skating means he can be — and is — a good checker. He pursues the puck relentlessly.

Kevin succeeds in his checking by playing positionally and remaining with his check up and down the ice. He comes back deeply into the Oiler zone on defense.

McClelland sees his defensive plays well and uses his anticipation in league with his skating to shut down the opposition, but he doesn't translate those skills into offensive contributions. He needs time and space to get the puck to the open man, and he rarely takes advantage of an opportunity by shooting the puck himself. Kevin doesn't have a great shot, so he'll have to do his scoring from within close proximity of the net.

THE PHYSICAL GAME

Tough physical play is McClelland's type of play. He loves to hit and play rough all over the ice, and his excellent upper body strength and leg power make him very effective along the boards. His balance enters into play here, keeping him upright and driving after collisions.

He fears nothing and no one, and Kevin is only too willing to back up his play with his fists.

He sacrifices his body to block shots, a rare trait among forwards, and stands up for his teammates in any situation.

THE INTANGIBLES

McClelland works hard and has tons of heart and enthusiasm and is a very important part of the Oilers. He's the type of player who will do anything to win, and his ability and willingness to play a tough physical game has allowed Mark Messier to open up his offense.

Kevin's is the type of yeoman effort in the trenches crucial to any team's success.

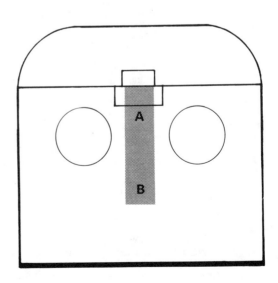

MARTY MCSORLEY

Yrs. of NHL service: 5
Born: Hamilton, Ontario, Canada; May 18, 1963
Position: Defenseman/right wing
Height: 6-1
Weight: 210
Uniform no.: 33
Shoots: right

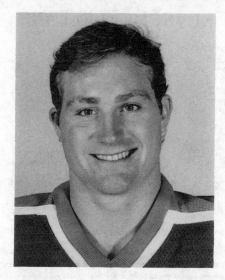

Career statistics:

GP	G	A	TP	PIM
247	24	40	64	886

1987-88 statistics:

GP	G	A	TP	+/−	PIM	PP	SH	GW	GT	S	PCT
60	9	17	26	23	223	0	0	1	0	66	13.6

LAST SEASON

Games played total was the second highest of McSorley's career, highest since his rookie year in 1983-84. Assist and point totals were career highs, and he finished third on the squad in PIM. He missed 15 games with a knee injury.

THE FINESSE GAME

McSorley is an average skater at the NHL level, making do more with his power and strength than with any speed, quickness or agility. Like teammate Craig MacTavish, McSorley has improved his skating by association: playing and practicing with and against the world's best players naturally makes Marty a better skater.

That improved — but less than exceptional — skating ability came into play late last season and through the playoffs when McSorley was shifted back to defense. He acquitted himself well, more through discipline and intelligence than skill, never forcing plays and never trying to go beyond his modest limits.

Marty doesn't handle the puck all that well, and he counters that weakness by not handling the puck except when necessary. When moving the puck from the defensive end, rare was the time that he took more than three strides with it.

As a forward he reads the offensive play fairly well, though he is not heavy in the anticipation department. He holds his position fairly well in the offensive zone, but he does have a tendency to wander because he goes on search and destroy missions. It is that penchant for wandering that was tempered when he resumed his defensive duties.

THE PHYSICAL GAME

McSorley hits at every opportunity and does so punishingly. He has good strength and will win the battles in the corners and the boards, as well as the front of both nets.

McSorley is a fighter and sees more than his share of action. He is one of those players with a Jekyll-and-Hyde personality, and he can 'click out' (as the vernacular goes) on the ice and go crazy. His spearing of Mike Bullard during last spring's playoffs is a good example.

THE INTANGIBLES

The key to McSorley's character is that, despite the fact he is just legitimately happy to be in the NHL, he works constantly at improving his skills. He is one of the NHL's legitimate heavyweights in terms of toughness, and that role is one he willingly accepts with the Oilers.

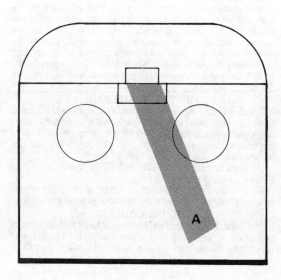

MARK MESSIER

Yrs. of NHL service: 9
Born: Edmonton, Alta., Canada; January 18, 1961
Position: Center
Height: 6-1
Weight: 205
Uniform no.: 11
Shoots: left

Career statistics:

GP	G	A	TP	PIM
647	302	445	747	879

1987-88 statistics:

GP	G	A	TP	+/−	PIM	PP	SH	GW	GT	S	PCT
77	37	74	111	21	103	12	3	7	2	182	20.3

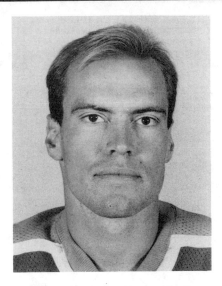

LAST SEASON

Messier finished second in team scoring, seventh overall in the League, with a career high in points scored — his second consecutive career-best season. He finished fifth in the NHL in assists (second on the club) with a career high total. He finished sixth in PIM among forwards, third in power play goals and shooting percentage, second in game winners and fifth in shots on goal. His goal total tied his third best total ever. He missed two games with a hip injury.

THE FINESSE GAME

Another of the Oilers' world-class players, Messier is blessed in both the finesse and physical games.

Mark is an excellent skater in all categories of that skill. He has blazing speed and he controls that speed with clock-like precision. He has excellent — really, superior — agility and lateral movement, the ability to change direction and speed within a stride. Messier has excellent balance on his skates and the balance is the key to his other foot skills. All of this is the more remarkable because of his size and strength, and because the stereotype says he shouldn't be able to play this way.

Ironically, Messier can't use his incredible speed all the time because most of his teammates can't keep up with him. Still, along with Glenn Anderson — but in more consistent fashion — Messier does more things faster than anyone else in the League.

Messier makes his speed more effective by being an excellent stickhandler who not only carries the puck well at all speeds but can pass it accurately at any speed too; Mark can get the puck to a teammate anywhere. His superior anticipation, hockey sense and ice vision mesh perfectly with his physical finesse skills to power both his offensive and defensive game.

Messier has the team's best wrist shot and he uses that almost exclusively when scoring, particularly because he can deliver that shot while in motion. Mark is another player who can score from anywhere, but the majority of his goals will come from the high traffic area in front of he net.

His skills seem to have been created specifically for specialty team situations. He is a shorthanded scoring threat and his presence on the power play — either working the corners or the front of the net, or keeping the passing lanes open with his one-step quickness — has greatly helped make the Oilers' power play a potent weapon.

Defensively he is unparalleled, simply skating over the opposing center almost without exception. He backchecks excellently and is aided by his play reading ability and hockey sense.

THE PHYSICAL GAME

Messier plays an excellent physical game, courtesy of his size and incredible strength. He will out-muscle anyone anywhere, hit often and punishingly (thanks to leg and upper body strength) and hurt the people he hits. Mark will fight and he has a nasty temper — which helps make him mean with his stick — but he has learned to not over-react and thus land in the penalty box.

His hand and wrist strength, combined with his quickness and eye/hand coordination, make him one of the best faceoff men in hockey.

THE INTANGIBLES

If we wanted to complain, we could tell you that Messier was less consistent than he could have been in his scoring last year. He had 14 goals in the first 20 games for a 56-goal pace. He had 25 goals by midseason, and added just 12 more in the second half — and just 10 of those 12 came at even-strength. Or we *could* complain about the reverse, how he scored just two PPG in the last 40 games.

We *could* complain, but we won't. Because that would raise a smokescreen of questions where none should exist.

His leadership ability is well-documented, as is his hunger for success and his hatred of losing. There is nothing Mark Messier cannot do when he puts his mind to it, and his mind is still on winning Stanley Cups.

It is that physical skill in combination with his mental toughness that serves to make Mark the best all-around player in the world.

CRAIG MUNI

Yrs. of NHL service: 2
Born: Toronto, Ontario, Canada; July 19, 1962
Position: Defenseman
Height: 6-2
Weight: 201
Uniform no.: 28
Shoots: left

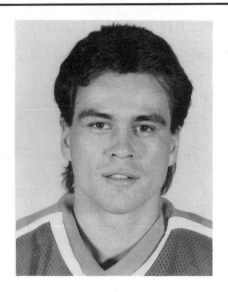

Career statistics:

GP	G	A	TP	PIM
167	11	39	50	168

1987-88 statistics:

GP	G	A	TP	+/-	PIM	PP	SH	GW	GT	S	PCT
72	4	15	19	32	77	0	1	0	0	56	7.1

LAST SEASON

Muni's plus/minus was the team's third best. His point totals fell from his first year totals.

THE FINESSE GAME

We might be beating a dead horse here but, like teammates Marty McSorley and Craig MacTavish, Muni's skating has improved through association. The opportunity to practice with the world's best players has made Muni a better player. While still far from exceptional as a skater, Muni has developed some speed and quickness in his stride. He can do some forcing on his own now, acting on the opposing forward rather than reacting to what that forward does.

Craig still plays a conservative and positional game, and he's a smart player so he won't over-extend himself. That smartness extends to his play selection and Muni will make good plays quickly. He knows to move the puck with his head up, so he sees his options and his best opportunities.

Offensively he is not a threat, as he will fall back from the blue line if remotely challeneged. But when given the time, Muni can find the open man in the offensive zone. His shot is no better than average, and he'll do his scoring from the point.

THE PHYSICAL GAME

Muni is a strong and physical player. He takes men out of the play in front of the net and along the boards with great efficiency. He has gone a long way toward playing a controlled (as in non-wandering) physical game, and he has also made improvement in his takeouts by not letting the opposition back into the play too quickly.

THE INTANGIBLES

His improvement from 1986-87 to last season was tremendous, and Muni can still develop as a player. He benefits greatly by being partnered with Steve Smith, as that allows Craig to play with one of the NHL's better defensemen. His improvement should continue.

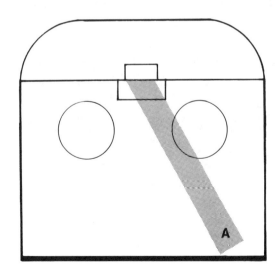

BILL RANFORD

Yrs. of NHL service: 2
Born: Brandon, Man., Canada; December 14, 1966
Position: Goaltender
Height: 5-11
Weight: 165
Uniform no.: 30
Catches: left

Career statistics:

GP	MINS	G	SO	AVG	A	PIM
51	2,799	1503	3.21	3	8	

1987-88 statisics:

GP	MINS	AVG	W	L	T	SO	GA	SA	SAPCT	PIM
6	325	2.95	3	0	2	0	16	159	.899	0

LAST SEASON

Ranford was acquired by Edmonton (along with Geoff Court-nall) from Boston in exchange for Andy Moog. All games played were with Edmonton.

THE PHYSICAL GAME

Ranford is a standup goaltender, coming out of his net to challenge the shooters because he is a strong skater. When he is on Ranford plays his angles very well, but he does have the disturbing tendency of losing his net at times.

He has very quick reflexes and moves well across the crease but he has not yet learned to control a rebound after a save, so the second save is a problem for him. He gets by because of the speed of his hands and feet, but he must learn to position himself properly for rebound shots, rather than just surviving on reflex.

He is suspect on the ice low to the stick side, and he is also weak high to the glove, indicating inconsistent angle play.

THE MENTAL GAME

Ranford's confidence keeps him in a game regardless of the score, but his concentration takes him out. That's the explanation for sub-par angle play.

He can read the play and see it develop, and he anticipates well, but Ranford doesn't always see the puck as well as he should. He allows the opposition to screen him and otherwise block his vision. He must learn to prevent those screens by either physical (slashing) or mental (disciplining himself to move to the top of a screen) means.

THE INTANGIBLES

Ranford showed with the Bruins that he had the capability of playing at a high level in the NHL. In Edmonton, where he'll be Grant Fuhr's caddy, Bill will get the chance to develop without pressure.

CRAIG SIMPSON

Yrs. of NHL service: 3
Born: London, Ontario, Canada; February 15, 1967
Position: Center/left wing
Height: 6-2
Weight: 195
Uniform no.: 18
Shoots: right

Career statistics:

GP	G	A	TP	PIM
228	93	76	169	183

1987-88 statistics:

GP	G	A	TP	+/−	PIM	PP	SH	GW	GT	S	PCT
80	56	34	90	20	77	22	0	8	0	177	31.6

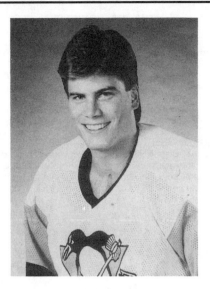

LAST SEASON

Simpson was acquired by Edmonton (along with Moe Mantha, Chris Joseph and Dave Hannan) from the Pittsburgh Penguins in exchange for Paul Coffey, Dave Hunter and Wayne Van Dorp last December. Games played, all point totals and PIM mark were all career highs. He finished 19th in NHL scoring, second in goals, seventh in power play goals, fifth in game winners and first in the NHL in shooting percentage. He finished fourth on the Oilers in scoring, first in goals, power play goals and game winners.

THE FINESSE GAME

Simpson is very talented in the finesse areas of the game, but his skating is the least of his talents. While his skating skill has improved — and we're not saying he's a bad skater, just that his skating doesn't match his other skills — he could still do better in terms of NHL foot speed, quickness and agility. What Craig's skating does have is a lot of power, and that strength gives him good acceleration ability. His balance is the most important part of his skating, because it keys his ability to work in traffic.

Craig's excellent balance makes him very strong on his skates, almost impossible to knock down. Because of that he has great goal-scoring success from the area near the net, both with his own shot and on deflections and tip-ins. His success in the slot makes him a natural for power play work and could only be improved by better foot speed, because quicker feet and the attendant agility would get him to loose pucks ahead of the opposition.

His stick skills are very good and Craig is an excellent passer and puckhandler, putting his reach to work for him in the rink's congested areas. His shot is also very good, both forehand and backhand, and one reason he's found success in the slot is because of the quickness of his release.

Simpson's anticipation and vision have grown with his skills, and he is very good at getting into position to score. As good as his finesse skills are and will be, smarts are definitely the keys to his game. His vision is excellent and he tries to make the most of his teammates. He's begun to find the openings for his teammates and himself, and he's getting to the openings and shooting the puck with great result.

His defensive play, the one true weak link in his game, has also improved. Craig plays a conscientious defensive game and he does so positionally. He makes a good — not great — transition from offense to defense (again, lack of foot speed hurts — especially since Craig is so deep in the offensive zone) and stays with his check deep into the Oilers zone.

THE PHYSICAL GAME

Craig's physical ability and potential is very high. Only 21 years old he's already very strong and he combines his strength with his puckhandling to drive to the net. He uses his reach very well in keeping the puck from the opposition, or to snare loose pucks, and he uses his body well to protect the puck when he carries it.

Simpson will only become stronger as his body matures, yet even now he is unafraid of traffic or the fearsome areas in front of the net and in the corners. Most important is the fact that Craig not only takes hits to make plays, but he takes hits and makes successful plays.

He is currently more of a reactive than active physical player and he could initiate more of the contact along the boards, but that will come with time.

THE INTANGIBLES

Simpson is a hard worker and a very determined player, and his improvement will undoubtly continue (aided and abetted by the world's best players). His playmaking role moved to the rear after he was traded to the Oilers, mostly because he couldn't keep up with linemates Mark Messier and Glenn Anderson. Instead, Craig got out of their way by going to the front of the net and reaped the benefits.

Is he, as his goal total asserts, the NHL's second best goal scorer? No, he is not. He may never score 50 goals again, though with his shot and penchant for abuse further 50-goals seasons aren't being ruled out.

What he is, is a solid player with exceptional all-around talent playing with teammates whose talent is superior to his own. He will continue to benefit from both his and his teammate's abilities and he will continue to improve, much to the regret of the rest of the NHL.

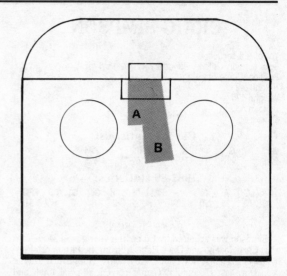

STEVE SMITH

Yrs. of NHL service: 3
Born: Glasgow, Scotland; April 30, 1963
Position: Defenseman
Height: 6-4
Weight: 210
Uniform no.: 5
Shoots: right

Career statistics:

GP	G	A	TP	PIM
198	23	78	101	619

1987-88 statistics:

GP	G	A	TP	+/-	PIM	PP	SH	GW	GT	S	PCT
79	12	43	55	40	286	5	0	1	0	116	10.3

LAST SEASON

Games played, all point totals and PIM mark were all career highs. He led the Oiler defensemen in points, power play goals and assists, and his plus/minus mark was the team's best (fourth best in the NHL). His PIM total led the team, and he was the NHL's second most penalized defender (Gord Donnelly).

THE FINESSE GAME

Smith is a good skater and rapidly improving into a very good one at the NHL level. He carries his size and bulk excellently both forward and backward and he has improved his foot speed to become fairly quick for a big man. He has good agility and balance as well, and he uses his skating skills well at both blue lines.

Steve reads the rush well and anticipates the opposition's plays fairly well, and is always in good position to break up the rush. By playing positionally Smith can use his improved foot speed to close the gap on the puck carrier and take him off the puck before starting the play up-ice. He plays his angles well to force those forwards wide of the net.

Steve can carry the puck from the zone, but is more likely to move it well to forward and then join the play as it heads up ice. His play reading ability extends to the offensive zone (and has been improved by his improved skating) and Steve will not only find the open forward but will find an opening and lead a forward to it with a good pass.

His hand skills have developed along with his foot skills and Smith contains the play very well at the offensive blue line, so much so that he will get good power play time. He has a good slap shot, nothing exceptional, and Smith wil shoot from the point or the middle of the blue line.

THE PHYSICAL GAME

Steve is an excellent and aggressive physical player, and the improved meanness he's developed (something we told you he needed last year — just check out his PIM) is one big reason why. Another is his improved skating. Now that he can track down the opposition, Smith can put his excellent size and strength to work against them.

He's very strong in front of his net and can succeed against almost all NHL forwards, including those of the power variety. He's just as sure to win the battles in the corners, and his ability to make plays coming out of the corner magnifies his already superb physical play.

His size makes him very difficult to get around at the blue line and Smith will sacrifice his body to block shots.

THE INTANGIBLES

We told you last year that Smith has been called a young Larry Robinson, and that the potential for excellence existed in his play. Then he went out and led the Oilers' defensemen in scoring in both the regular season and the playoffs.

Like Charlie Huddy, Smith also benefitted from the trade of Paul Coffey to Pittsburgh, in that Coffey's absence allowed Smith to come forward and grow as a player.

Smith remains a player of great potential and is already a defensive force. Should his improvement continue, it's not hard to envision him as the NHL's best defenseman.

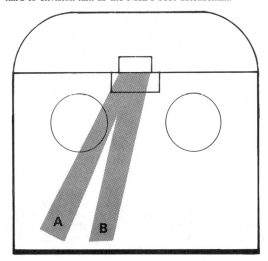

ESA TIKKANEN

Yrs. of NHL service: 3
Born: Helsinki, Finland; January 25, 1965
Position: Left wing
Height: 5-11
Weight: 185
Uniform no.: 10
Shoots: left

Career statistics:

GP	G	A	TP	PIM
191	64	101	165	301

1987-88 statistics:

GP	G	A	TP	+/-	PIM	PP	SH	GW	GT	S	PCT
80	23	51	74	21	153	6	1	2	0	142	16.2

LAST SEASON

Tikkanen played 80 games for the first time in his career. Assist total was a career high, as was PIM mark (third highest among forwards). He finished sixth in team scoring.

THE FINESSE GAME

Tikkanen has excellent finesse skills which he has not yet brought to bear consistently. He is an excellent skater with great speed, acceleration, quickness, balance and agility, yet was not aggressive enough in using these skills last season. He didn't break for the holes, he didn't force defensive mistakes with his speed. Instead of rocketing past the defense — which is then forced to hook and hold him to stop him — Tikkanen often pulled up short. That's bad, because his balance and agility allows him to retain his body position (and thus control of the puck) as he's being fouled.

Esa is a smart player and when he's playing well he uses his smarts in several ways: to moderate his speed to make it more effective and to read the ice and get to the openings. He uses his play reading ability both offensively and defensively, and he is very good at turning the play around by intercepting a pass or closing a hole.

Tikkanen's hand skills make him extremely effective in traffic and along the boards and in tight circumstances around the net; his smarts amplify the ability of his hand skills by putting him in places where his hands can go to work.

He has an excellent shot that makes him dangerous from the top of the circle and in; it is quickly released and strong to the net, but Tikkanen didn't use it as often as he should have last season. After hitting a lot of posts in his first few games, Esa lost confidence in his shot — and his offensive game — and that's why he became tentative.

He is an excellent player defensively, playing his position and checking well in all three zones.

THE PHYSICAL GAME

Tikkanen's physical play works against the European stereotypes. He is a very tough player and loves hitting and working in the trenches. He plays bigger than his size and is fearless in the corners, and that style had made him an excellent counterpart for the styles of Wayne Gretzky and Jari Kurri.

Esa's excellent balance aids him in his physical play by allowing him to remain vertical after he initiates a hit, and he more than has the skills to make the play coming out of the corner.

THE INTANGIBLES

Tikkanen is a major-league disturber. He chirps non-stop at the opposition, and elbows and slashes — all regardless of who the opponent is. He's a flamboyant player and he plays with emotion and spark that enlivens the Oilers.

For a player with his finesse potential he struggled offensively last season (his disappointing performance had to have irritated more than one hockey pool player), and so with Tikkanen his third full season — this year — becomes a very important one.

We're not arguing that he can't play or that he hurts the Oilers. What we're saying is that while his performance would be good for another player, it shouldn't be good enough for Tikkanen.

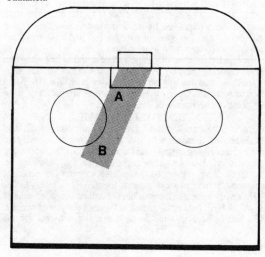

HARTFORD
WHALERS

LINE COMBINATIONS
DAVE TIPPETT-CAREY WILSON-DEAN EVASON
SYLVAIN TURGEON-RAY FERRARO-PAUL
MACDERMID
LINDSAY CARSON-RON FRANCIS-KEVIN DINEEN

DEFENSE PAIRINGS
RANDY LADOCEUR-SYLVAIN COTE
NEIL SHEEHY-ULF SAMUELSSON
JOEL QUENNEVILLE-DAVE BABYCH

GOALTENDERS
MIKE LIUT
RICHARD BRODEUR

OTHER PLAYERS
JOHN ANDERSON — Left Wing
STEWART GAVIN — Left Wing
SCOT KLEINENDORST — Defenseman
TORRIE ROBERTSON — Left Wing

POWER PLAY

FIRST UNIT:
KEVIN DINEEN-RON FRANCIS-SYLVAIN TURGEON
DAVE BABYCH-ULF SAMUELSSON

The Whalers like to isolate FRANCIS in front of a goaltender off a SAMUELSSON pass if possible, but a TURGEON shot from the faceoff circle is option 1A. WILSON will substitute for TURGEON and control play from the right wing boards on the second unit and SAMUELSSON will play as much of the two minutes as possible.

Last season the Hartford power play was POOR, scoring just 84 goals in 477 man advantage opportunities (17.6 percent, 17th overall).

PENALTY KILLING

FIRST UNIT:
DAVE TIPPETT-CAREY WILSON
JOEL QUENNEVILLE-ULF SAMUELSSON

All of Hartford's forwards are very aggressive toward the points, jumping the puck carriers as soon as they enter the zone. The penalty killers are not as aggressive offensively as they are defensively. GAVIN will see a lot of PK time too.

Last season Hartford's penalty killing was EXCELLENT, allowing just 67 goals in 426 shorthanded situations (84.3 percent, first overall).

CRUCIAL FACEOFFS

WILSON will get most of these, especially in the defensive zone.

JOHN ANDERSON

Yrs. of NHL service: 11
Born: Toronto, Ontario, Canada; March 28, 1957
Position: Left wing
Height: 5-11
Weight: 180
Uniform no.: 20
Shoots: left

Career statistics:

GP	G	A	TP	PIM
752	266	325	591	235

1987-88 statistics:

GP	G	A	TP	+/-	PIM	PP	SH	GW	GT	S	PCT
63	17	32	49	-5	20	9	0	3	0	149	11.4

LAST SEASON

Games played total was the lowest full season mark of his career, goal total tied for second lowest of career (lowest in seven seasons — as was his point total). His PIM total was lowest among "fulltime" Whaler forwards. He missed the last 16 games of the season and all of the playoffs with a shoulder injury.

THE FINESSE GAME

All of a sudden, John Anderson got very old very fast. Where previously there was speed and agility, last season there was a slower stride and a little less vigor in the swoops behind the defense. The foot speed was slower and the lateral movement was almost invisible.

Anderson still showed signs of his playmaking skill, using his good hands and ice vision to find his teammates, but the goal scoring anticipation that got him in position to score was missing in action. And since he has always been a shooter and a scorer instead of a playmaker, the resulting drop in his goal production was precipitous.

Another reason for that drop — interlocked with his not getting into position — was Anderson's low shot total, even given his games missed. John has the power to rip a slapper past the goaltender from the top of the faceoff circle, but he also has the hands to tuck the puck into the net from close quarters. He has a quick wrist shot that is particularly effective from the bottom of the faceoff circle. Yet Anderson undercut the effectiveness of his shot by not shooting anywhere near enough.

In previous seasons he'd been a power play mainstay, but not last year. And his positional and defensive play, never much to begin with, were also affected by his decreased foot speed.

THE PHYSICAL GAME

Anderson is not a big player but he will hit, and he works the corners without fear. He will take the tough stuff in front of the net, but has always been more effective in the open ice on the outside of the skirmishes, where he heretofore had put his foot speed to work.

THE INTANGIBLES

One good reason for Anderson's backslide may be the growing proclivity of linemate Kevin Dineen to work 1-on-1 versus the defense. Dineen's selfish play *may* serve to explain Anderson's goal slump and bad shot total — can't shoot when you don't have the puck, and there's no reason to get into scoring position if you won't get the puck — but it doesn't explain the lack of spark in Anderson's skating and overall game.

For John Anderson this season is tremendously important. At 31 years old, he must prove his ability to function as an NHL goal scorer.

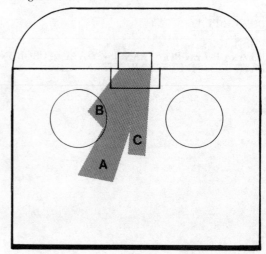

DAVE BABYCH

Yrs. of NHL service: 8
Born: Edmonton, Alta., Canada; May 23, 1961
Position: Defenseman
Height: 6-2
Weight: 215
Uniform no.: 44
Shoots: left

Career statistics:

GP	G	A	TP	PIM
589	105	360	465	528

1987-88 statistics:

GP	G	A	TP	+/-	PIM	PP	SH	GW	GT	S	PCT
71	14	36	50	-25	54	10	0	2	1	233	6.0

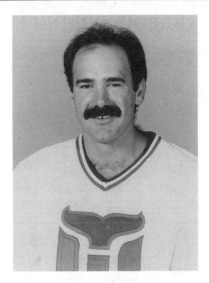

LAST SEASON

Babych led the Whaler defensemen in scoring and was third overall on the club in assists. He finished second on the club in shots on goal (first among defensemen) and his plus/minus was the team's second worst (worst among defensemen). He was sidelined by a recurring knee injury.

THE FINESSE GAME

Babych has long had good skating skills, but time and injury are beginning to take their toll. Dave still has good speed as he carries the puck up-ice, but the rust is starting to show in his quickness, foot speed and turns. He's a little slower getting back to the defensive zone after challenging in the offensive zone than in previous years, and he's a little slower making his turns toward the opposition in the defensive zone.

Still, Babych does rush the puck well most of the time, and he uses the speed he does have to create plays in the offensive zone. That skill is particularly valuable on the power play where Dave is the general of Hartford's offense. He combines his skating with good puckhandling skills and is especially effective in traffic.

Dave uses his teammates very well because of his good vision and anticipation. He sees the openings as they develop and skims an accurate and soft pass to a teammate. Babych likes to shoot the puck at any opportunity and he'll blast away from the point or move to the faceoff circle if he can.

Those vision skills don't necessarily translate to Babych's defensive game, especially in his lack of patience. He'll make poor passes because he does not examine his options before passing, and that leads to turnovers.

THE PHYSICAL GAME

Babych is primarily a finesse player with size. He is inconsistent is his attempts at clearing the front of the net and he allows his checks to sneak back into the play, so he could improve his takeouts. On the whole, he plays a no better than fair physical contest though he has the tools to play a good one.

He is good along the boards, where he can take the puck in one motion and start a play while being harassed.

THE INTANGIBLES

Babych has always been a pretty much one-dimensional player, but now even that dimension is slipping away from him as he ages. Injuries and durability are also questions, as is his awful showing at even strength last season: 37 of his 50 points came on the power play. That makes his plus/minus rating even worse.

The Whalers weren't especially pleased with his performance last season, so he might not be long for the Insurance City.

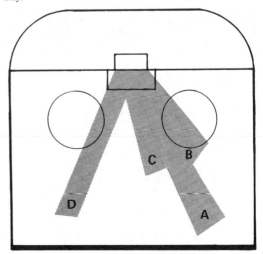

RICHARD BRODEUR

Yrs. of NHL service: 8
Born: Longueuil, Quebec, Canada; September 15, 1952
Position: Goaltender
Height: 5-7
Weight: 185
Uniform no.: 31
Catches: left

Career statistics:

GP	MINS	G	SO	AVG	A	PIM
385	21,965	1,410	6	3.85	8	26

1987-88 statisics:

GP	MINS	AVG	W	L	T	SO	GA	SA	SAPCT	PIM
17	1,010	3.80	9	8	2	0	64	489	.876	

LAST SEASON

Games played total was a full season career low (demoted to American Hockey League). He was traded to Hartford by Vancouver at the trading deadline in exchange for Steve Weeks. Brodeur's record in Hartford was 4-2-0 with a 2.65 GAA.

THE PHYSICAL GAME

Brodeur does everything well and he does nothing well. In other words, while he has no standout features to his goaltending he is adept at all facets.

He's an excellent reflex goaltender who also does a fine job of playing the angles to cut down the shooter's chances. Richard skates well, moving in and out of the net and around the crease with authority, but he does not usually roam from the net to handle the puck, preferring to leave it for his defensemen. He holds his posts well in action around the goal.

He is a little scrambly balance-wise, and that's one reason he looks so acrobatic. That small lack of balance is why he's sometimes slow to regain his feet after going to the ice.

Brodeur is quick with his hands and feet and is also very flexible, able to get at that difficult shot with the toe of his skate or the tip of his glove even when seeming to move in the opposite direction.

He has a good glove hand and is fairly strong on his left side, but he has a tendency to be weak below the waist on his stick side. Richard also indicates a susceptibility up high, as evidenced by the times he gets hit in the head.

Usually, though, he sees the puck very well, making him strong on screen shots, and his quickness will get him to pucks that are deflected or otherwise re-directed.

THE MENTAL GAME

Brodeur's experience playing with Vancouver has made him very tough mentally. Richard has the ability to make the big save and can maintain his concentration through most circumstances.

He is very rarely rattled by bad goals or games, able to bear down immediately and worry about the next goal rather than the last one. He has good anticipation skills and they readily complement his quickness, making him difficult to beat from in close.

He'll get caught off-guard in his concentration every once in a while, but that is definitely the exception and not the rule.

THE INTANGIBLES

Brodeur has faced a lot of shots in his life, but his sterling performance against the Canadiens in the Adams Division semifinals show he's ready, willing and able to face a lot more.

He might find himself jockeying for a job this year, but if Hartford had another goaltender ready for the NHL they wouldn't have had to trade for Brodeur. Richard should do well playing for a team that — finally — plays defense in front of him.

LINDSAY CARSON

Yrs. of NHL service: 7
Born: North Battleford, Sask., Canada; November 21, 1960
Position: Left wing
Height: 6-1
Weight: 200
Uniform no.: 28
Shoots: left

Career statistics:

GP	G	A	TP	PIM
373	66	80	146	525

1987-88 statistics:

GP	G	A	TP	+/−	PIM	PP	SH	GW	GT	S	PCT
63	7	11	18	-4	67	1	1	1	0	39	9.6

LAST SEASON

All point totals were full season career lows (he missed three games with a knee injury). Carson was acquired by Hartford in late January in exchange for Paul Lawless. Though he finished as a minus player, Carson was even with the Whalers.

THE FINESSE GAME

Carson is an excellent skater but he is lazy, and he doesn't use his good speed to drive the defensemen deep frequently enough. He likes to make his plays at the blue line, so when he reaches it he stops skating. That's a bad flaw for someone with speed.

He is a good stickhandler and can control the puck fairly well, but he has very little idea of what to do with it once he has it. Lindsay has a hard shot, but has no control over it. He does not see the ice well and thus cannot use his teammates well.

Carson is average as a defensive player, not driving back with his check and a little lazy in staying with his check once he returns to the defensive zone.

THE PHYSICAL GAME

Carson is one of those guys who gets tough when he has a tough team behind him, otherwise he's not much of a physical player. He doesn't have a good deal of strength and is therefore ineffective along the boards; a defenseman with average strength can take him off the puck and hold him out of the play fairly easily.

He doesn't hit consistently and when he does it is usually someone smaller and meeker than himself. Even his reach, something that he needs little effort to use, is not consistently evident.

Carson doesn't apply all he has to the physical game.

THE INTANGIBLES

Carson is a fourth line player, good for putting out on the ice when someone else needs a rest. He is no more than an average player at this point and he just doesn't seem to have the desire necessary to sustain an NHL career.

He is the kind of player who gives nothing much to the team, either offensively or defensively.

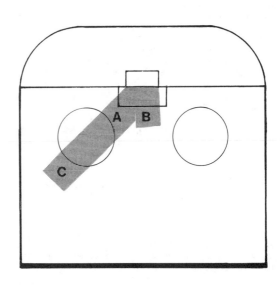

SYLVAIN COTE

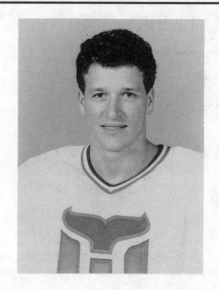

Yrs. of NHL service: 3
Born: Quebec City, Quebec, Canada; January 19, 1966
Position: Defenseman
Height: 5-11
Weight: 185
Uniform no.: 21
Shoots: right

Career statistics:

GP	G	A	TP	PIM
203	12	38	50	67

1987-88 statistics:

GP	G	A	TP	+/−	PIM	PP	SH	GW	GT	S	PCT
67	7	21	28	-8	30	0	1	0	0	142	4.9

LAST SEASON

Cote matched his career high for games played and set career highs in all point categories. His PIM total was the lowest among defensive regulars.

THE FINESSE GAME

Cote has a number of finesse skills that he can bring to bear at the NHL level. Skating is his best skill, as Cote uses his speed and quickness very effectively as the play moves up ice. His quickness and agility insure that he won't often be beaten 1-on-1, and Sylvain uses his skating prowess instead of solid positional play to play defense. His speed counters any positional mistakes he makes.

Cote has improved his ability to handle the puck at the NHL level, mostly because he's grown acclimatized to the NHL's pace. He's making decisions faster and that helps his play-making ability, especially at the opposing blue line. He handles the puck well when he carries it from the Whaler zone, which he does frequently, but he is also taking advantage of his greater understanding of NHL speed to move the puck to the forwards for breakout passes with greater efficiency.

He anticipates both the offensive and defensive play well, and Cote is taking chances at both ends now knowing that his skating can help him recover. He charges the net in the offensive zone now and will score some of his goals from there, but most will come from the point.

THE PHYSICAL GAME

Cote plays an unspectacular physical game, and his finesse and offensive background are evident in his checking. While he makes attempts at tying up the opposition along the board it's obvious that Sylvain grew up as a rushing defenseman and not a physical one.

He has average strength and is more of a pusher and shover than a hitter, but he's not averse to a physical contest.

THE INTANGIBLES

Cote's development is progressing nicely in the offensive end of the game. In order to be a more rounded player he should develop some strength that he could apply to his physical game. Greater use of defensive angles would also make him more efficient.

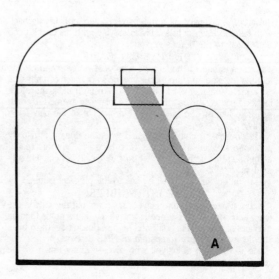

KEVIN DINEEN

Yrs. of NHL service: 4
Born: Quebec City, Quebec, Canada; October 28, 1963
Position: Right wing
Height: 5-10
Weight: 180
Uniform no.: 11
Shoots: right

Career statistics:

GP	G	A	TP	PIM
266	123	115	238	573

1987-88 statistics:

GP	G	A	TP	+/−	PIM	PP	SH	GW	GT	S	PCT
74	25	25	50	-14	219	5	0	4	1	223	11.2

LAST SEASON

Goal total tied career low and was lowest in three seasons. Assist and point totals were also lowest in three seasons. PIM total was career high, second highest on the club. He finished third in team scoring and shots on goal, and his plus/minus rating was the team's third worst. He missed four games with a shoulder injury.

THE FINESSE GAME

Kevin's excellent skating skills are the keys to both his finesse and physical games. Dineen has a strong stride that gives him good acceleration (and drives him through checks), and that power also gives him rink-length speed. He combines his speed with quickness and agility that allow him to move better laterally than would be expected for a physical player. His excellent balance makes him effective physically, as he retains his upright stance despite his many collisions.

Making Dineen's skating even more effective are his hand skills. He passes and carries the puck well at full speed, but he makes better plays when he is skating slower. He has excellent anticipation and can either break for the holes or lead a teammate with a perfect pass.

But here's the rub. Last season Dineen began to believe himself an artist and not a plumber, a change no doubt related to his 40 goals in 1986-87. Where previously he made the pass when necessary, Dineen now goes 1-on-1 versus the defense all the time. He wants to make the fancy plays between the blue lines and he can't, because while his skills are exemplary they aren't exemplary enough to make him an artist.

He has good scoring instincts but has always gotten into position to score by doing the dirty work along the boards and the front of the net. Now he likes to take the fancy top-shelf shot that usually ends up in the ninth row. What he has in his hands is strength, not great finesse, and he's not going to be successful finessing the puck.

His defensive play reflects the change. Where Dineen used to come back deeply and start a rush by taking the puck off the boards and sending it to a breaking teammate — now he wants to be the breaking teammate.

THE PHYSICAL GAME

Dineen is a tough and fearless player, but he is also over-aggressive. While his physical ability is very high (and made better by his ability to make a play coming out of the corner) Kevin has regressed in his attempts to stay out of the penalty box.

An example: Whaler management wanted him to cut down his penalty minutes (which he didn't) — especially versus Quebec. The result? Last season Dineen had zero goals versus Quebec in the season series, and 45 minutes in penalties.

THE INTANGIBLES

Once the paramount team player, Dineen has become spoiled by his success: the 40 goals, the selections to the Rendez-Vous '87, All-Star game and Canada Cup squads. He displays great immaturity in his play now, particularly regarding the Quebec penalty business when you realize the Nords and the Whalers spent last season dueling for the division's final playoff berth.

The Whalers' stumbling and Dineen's change are not co-incidental; that's how important Dineen is to Hartford's success. He must change his attitude if Hartford is to re-establish itself as a rising — and not falling — team.

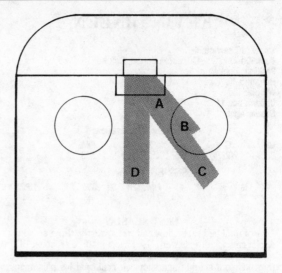

DEAN EVASON

Yrs. of NHL service: 3
Born: Flin Flon, Man., Canada; August 22, 1964
Position: Center
Height: 5-10
Weight: 180
Uniform no.: 12
Shoots: left

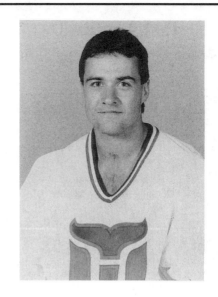

Career statistics:

GP	G	A	TP	PIM
231	55	87	142	253

1987-88 statistics:

GP	G	A	TP	+/−	PIM	PP	SH	GW	GT	S	PCT
77	10	18	28	-29	117	6	0	0	0	126	7.9

LAST SEASON

All point totals were full season career lows. His plus/minus rating was the team's worst.

THE FINESSE GAME

Evason is a fairly gifted finesse player — but not for the National Hockey League. He's a good skater in terms of speed and he combines that skating with a degree of ice vision and anticipation.

While Evason can utilize that vision to make some plays (his hands aren't bad), and while he controls the puck well enough to take advantage of the openings his skating can create, today's NHL players make him look like a midget among redwoods. He's just not talented enough to consistently get into the clear to use his skills. Note exhibit A: A whopping 10 goals, of which just four came at even strength — or, when the ice was full of players.

His skating and anticipation make him valuable as a penalty killer because he has better room in which to operate, and he is also fairly successful on the power play because of the open ice.

Dean has a little bit of a scoring touch and can score from the bottom of the faceoff circle with a quick wrist shot or from the top of the circle with a snap shot.

THE PHYSICAL GAME

Like another prodigy from the Western Hockey League (Ray Ferraro) Evason is just not big enough to consistently succeed at the NHL level, and his skills aren't good enough to make up for that fact.

Dean isn't afraid of physical play but so what? He's not going to be effective in traffic anyway because of his lack of size, and his hand and foot skills aren't good enough for him to negotiate his way among the giants he has to face.

THE INTANGIBLES

Evason is another of the over-rated parts that make up the interchangeable cast of characters general manager Emile Francis has assembled for the Whalers. He is a quality player in terms of heart and character, but it's doubtful that his skills are going to develop further.

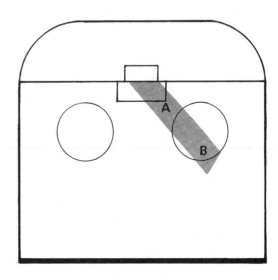

RAY FERRARO

Yrs. of NHL service: 4
Born: Trail, B.C., Canada; August 23, 1964
Position: Center
Height: 5-10
Weight: 185
Uniform no.: 26
Shoots: left

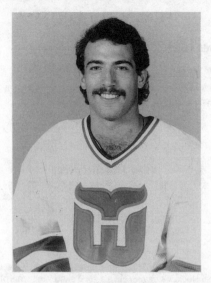

Career statistics:

GP	G	A	TP	PIM
268	89	125	214	222

1987-88 statistics:

GP	G	A	TP	+/−	PIM	PP	SH	GW	GT	S	PCT
68	21	29	50	1	83	6	0	2	0	105	20.0

LAST SEASON

In his third full NHL season Ferraro's point totals fell for the second year in a row. All point totals were full season career lows, while PIM total was a career high. His plus/minus was the team's fourth highest. He finished second on the club in shooting percentage.

THE FINESSE GAME

Ferraro is an excellent skater in all categories of that skill. He's blessed with terrific speed and agility. He gets to the openings — or to create them — by using his one-step quickness and change-of-direction ability, excellent acceleration and balance. All those skills are magnified on the power play, where Ferraro is a regular.

His hand skills are not quite at the level of his foot skills, but he makes his playmaking work by using his head. He's patient in his playmaking and looks the ice over for the best option, and Ray helps himself by being able to make his plays while moving (though he can't make those plays at his top speed).

As a goal scorer he is opportunistic, using the quickness of his shot and the quickness of his feet to get to rebounds and other pucks around the goal. He shows good anticipation offensively and knows how to get into goal scoring position.

That anticipation and skating are not applied as intensely to his defense, where Ferraro is no better than fair.

THE PHYSICAL GAME

Now that his speed is familiar to most of the NHL, Ray's size is beginning to mitigate against him. Since he is going to score his goals from traffic areas he should be able to function in those areas — and Ray is more than willing — but he can be just physically overwhelmed by bigger players.

He's also going to have trouble getting to those loose pucks because of his size and lack of reach, especially since the opposition knows how quick he is and that they have to guard against that quickness.

In his favor is the fact that he's not intimidated by play along the boards, nor afraid of the rough stuff in front of the net. His hand and wrist strength helps him pull the puck out of traffic and power his shot past the goaltender.

THE INTANGIBLES

Speed and a shot, that about sums up Ferraro's game. While he works fairly hard each night to put those assets to work, it seems clear that Ferraro's talents — or maybe more precisely the Whalers' hopes for those talents — have been exaggerated.

As with many NHLers, the third full season (which will be this season) should tell us about Ray Ferraro.

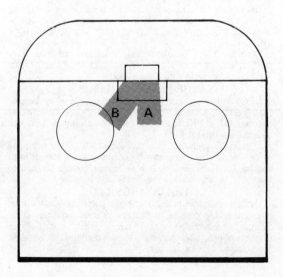

RON FRANCIS

Yrs. of NHL service: 7
Born: Sault Ste. Marie, Ontario, Canada; March 1, 1963
Position: Center
Height: 6-2
Weight: 200
Uniform no.: 10
Shoots: left

Career statistics:

GP	G	A	TP	PIM
498	182	385	567	380

1987-88 statistics:

GP	G	A	TP	+/−	PIM	PP	SH	GW	GT	S	PCT
80	25	50	75	-8	89	11	1	3	0	172	14.5

LAST SEASON

Francis played 80 games for just the second time in his career, and the second time in the last four years. He led the club in scoring and assists and was second in power play goals. His assist total was a full season career low.

THE FINESSE GAME

Francis is a very good skater in a non-spectacular way. He has excellent balance for a man his size and he combines those assets with his deceptive foot speed and loping stride to gain superior lateral movement and agility. We say unspectacular because he won't make moves like Denis Savard. His style is a smooth one, à la Jean Ratelle for instance.

Ron's foot speed will surprise unwitting defensemen and, though he doesn't have outstanding one-step quickness his ability to lean away from checks combines with his long stride to make him difficult to catch. He also functions well in traffic because of his balance.

Those physical skills mesh with his hockey sense (he knows where he is in relation to his teammates, the puck, the net and the opposition at all times) and his soft hands to make Francis a good playmaker. He can thread the needle through traffic or throw the puck into the open for a teammate to snare.

Francis is a better playmaker than scorer (largely because he's unselfish), but he will generally provide numbers in the 30-goal range. He operates best from the slot, about 15 feet out, but can blast a slap shot past the goaltender from farther away.

Francis is a fairly complete player, coming back to his zone to aid in the breakouts instead of hanging at the red line looking for breakaway passes.

THE PHYSICAL GAME

If he used his size the way he uses his finesse skills, Francis could be a consistent 100-point scorer. Instead he garners the left-handed compliment of being a finesse player with size. Ron plays a physical game only when confronted — literally — by the opposition.

Ron has good upper body strength and can combine that strength with his superior balance to muscle the opposition off the puck, but he rarely finds himself in the traffic areas.

Instead he waits outside the scrums to snare loose pucks with his good reach.

He does not shy away from contact but initiates very little on his own. He clearly prefers the open ice.

THE INTANGIBLES

Point distribution should concern both Francis and the Whalers, because his is not good. He had 24 power play assists and 11 power play goals, which means that 35 of his 75 points — almost 50 percent — came on the power play.

That makes Francis a less-than-awesome even strength player and shows that, while Ron is a strong two-way center, he's clearly not in the class of the NHL's best centers: the Yzermans, Gretzkys, Savards and Hawerchuks. He's a level below the best and his own inconsistency is what puts him there. We told you last year about that consistency and Francis' performance bore that out: 93 points in 1986-87, just 75 last year.

He is an unselfish player who puts the team first, and he has learned to do the character things like play through pain, but the bad news is that he and his team seemed to have levelled off. That might make those 90-point seasons — both past and future — memories and dreams.

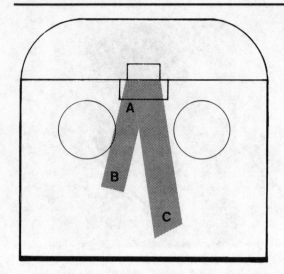

STEWART GAVIN

Yrs. of NHL service: 7
Born: Ottawa, Ontario, Canada; March 15, 1960
Position: Left wing
Height: 6-0
Weight: 185
Uniform no.: 7
Shoots: left

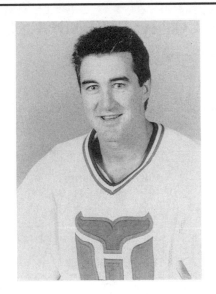

Career statistics:

GP	G	A	TP	PIM
479	91	109	200	352

1987-88 statistics:

GP	G	A	TP	+/−	PIM	PP	SH	GW	GT	S	PCT
56	11	10	21	-17	59	2	3	1	1	125	8.8

LAST SEASON

Games played total was lowest in six seasons (ankle injury sidelined him for 22 games). Goal total was lowest in four seasons, assist and point totals lowest in five seasons. He led Hartford in shorthanded goals and his plus/minus was the team's third worst, second among forwards.

THE FINESSE GAME

Gavin is an excellent skater, possessing superior speed and acceleration abilities. He's a good two-way winger because of that skill and is better defensively and while checking than he is as an offensive player. He reads the defensive play very well and uses his speed to counter it, and his anticipation toward offense is good enough for him to score more than a handful of goals. When he doesn't score, chances are Gavin's forechecking has provided an opportunity for a teammate.

Stewart handles the puck fairly well as he rushes up-ice and he uses good vision to help him make good passes to his teammates. He'll score by driving for the openings (remember his speed) and does his best work from near the net by pouncing on loose pucks. He also has a big slap shot off the wing and will use it often.

He is a very sound positional player, always aware of where he is on the ice, especially in the defensive zone. He comes back very deeply with his check and is tenacious when assigned a particular winger to watch.

His skills also combine to make him a very good penalty killer.

THE PHYSICAL GAME

Because he has good strength and balance, Gavin is very effective at rubbing his man out along the boards. His speed helps him in his physical game by getting him to the opposition for a check, and Gavin's physical game is an underrated part of his entire performance.

THE INTANGIBLES

Gavin is a very hard worker and he goes all out on the ice, but he is often just lumped into the rest of Hartford's crew of semi-anonymous forwards. Gavin, Evason, Ferraro — they all look alike. But they're not, and Stew's ability to function at the NHL level — both offensively and defensively, physically and finesse-wise — is what separates Gavin from the others.

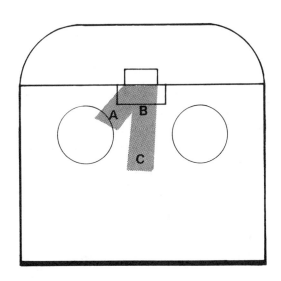

SCOT KLEINENDORST

Yrs. of NHL service: 5
Born: Grand Rapids, Minn., USA; January 16, 1960
Position: Defenseman
Height: 6-3
Weight: 215
Uniform no.: 18
Shoots: left

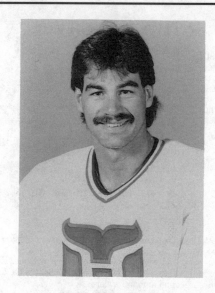

Career statistics:

GP	G	A	TP	PIM
239	11	41	52	390

1987-88 statistics:

GP	G	A	TP	+/−	PIM	PP	SH	GW	GT	S	PCT
44	3	6	9	-5	86	0	0	0	0	44	6.8

LAST SEASON

Games played total was second highest of his career. He missed 21 games because of a shoulder injury.

THE FINESSE GAME

Scot is no better than fair as a finesse player at the NHL level, and it is his modest — rather than exceptional — talent that keeps him on the borderline between regular duty and the bench. He is no better than average as a skater, blessed with neither an abundance of speed nor agility.

He does not handle the puck very well, so Scot rarely will rush from the defensive zone, but he does make the smart plays to the breaking forwards. Kleinendorst will rarely follow the play up ice and will almost never become a fourth attacker, so any points he does get will have to come from either blue line goals or breakout passes turned into assists. His role is that of the safety valve, protecting against a breaking opposition forward.

He plays his defense positionally, and uses his defensive angles to keep the play wide of the net. Though he does not have great foot speed, this solid positional play makes him difficult — not impossible, just difficult — to beat one-on-one. Good play reading helps him here.

THE PHYSICAL GAME

Kleinendorst has good size and he uses it effectively in the defensive zone. He takes the man out well from the front of the net, and he will also wipe out the opposition along the boards. Though he can deliver a jarring check, Scot is not primarily a thunderous hitter.

Scot also has a good reach, and he uses it well when poke-checking. He will also fight, but not well enough to gain fulltime NHL status.

THE INTANGIBLES

Scot has a super attitude and wants to do anything he can to help the team (one reason he fights so frequently). He works very hard at improving his skills and because of that work has matured into a steady defenseman and a solid player.

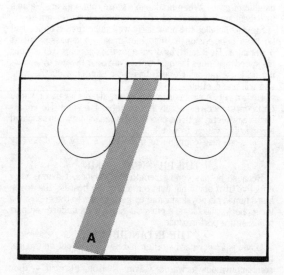

RANDY LADOCEUR

Yrs. of NHL service: 6
Born: Brockville, Ontario, Canada; June 30, 1960
Position: Defenseman
Height: 6-2
Weight: 220
Uniform no.: 29
Shoots: left

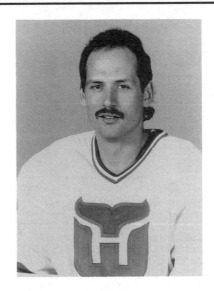

Career statistics:

GP	G	A	TP	PIM
394	17	77	94	590

1987-88 statistics:

GP	G	A	TP	+/-	PIM	PP	SH	GW	GT	S	PCT
68	1	7	8	7	91	0	0	1	0	42	2.4

LAST SEASON

Games played total was a full season career low, as were all point totals. His plus/minus was the team's second best, and he was Hartford's lowest scoring regular.

THE FINESSE GAME

There's not much here in terms of finesse skills, but Ladoceur smartly stays within his modest limits. He skates just well enough to keep up with the NHL play, though his agility in turning and pivoting is weak and could be improved.

Randy doesn't anticipate exceptionally well, so he finds himself reacting instead of acting defensively. He plays his position well, keeping himself in the correct areas to force the opposition wide of the net; that's what we mean by not overstepping his limits. Ladoceur knows he needs a certain amount of time and space to make his defensive plays and he makes sure to get that space.

He does very little handling of the puck, leaving that for the backchecking forward or his defensive partner. He will not carry the puck from the defensive zone and doesn't see the openings on the ice well. He will follow the play up-ice and will shoot from the point, so any goals he gets will come from those shots.

THE PHYSICAL GAME

Size and strength — and the willingness to use them — are the elements Randy brings successfully to his game. He's a big guy and doesn't hesitate to throw his weight around. He uses his size fairly well in front of the net but could benefit from greater strength in his upper body, as well as better balance in his legs.

Because he is somewhat lacking in the latter two categories, Randy can be knocked off the puck. Still, he plays the body willingly and can generally tie up opposing wingers when necessary.

THE INTANGIBLES

Ladoceur is a competent but no better than average NHL player. He helps give Hartford depth on the blue line but he'll never be more than a fifth defenseman.

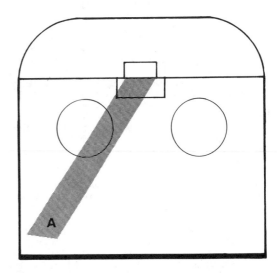

MIKE LIUT

Yrs. of NHL service: 9
Born: Weston, Ontario, Canada; January 7, 1956
Position: Goaltender
Height: 6-2
Weight: 195
Uniform no.: 1
Catches: left

Career statistics:

GP	MINS	G	SO	AVG	A	PIM
535	31,026	1,801	19	3.48	11	20

1987-88 statistics:

GP	MINS	AVG	W	L	T	SO	GA	SA	SAPCT	PIM
60	3,532	3.18	25	28	5	2	187	1,620	.884	4

LAST SEASON

Games played total was highest in five seasons, but goals-against-average tied career low. He finished sixth in the NHL in wins and was fourth in games played.

THE PHYSICAL GAME

Skating is the key to Liut's ongoing success as a goaltender. Mike moves in and out of his net very well. He has good balance on his skates and rapidly regains his stance when he leaves his feet so as to be in position to make a second save if a rebound is given.

Mike will frequently skate out to snare the puck and is smart about his ventures from the net, so he rarely gets caught. He handles the puck very well and will pass it to a defenseman or forward quickly for a breakout. He is also very good at poke checking the puck away from incoming forwards.

His style is a standup, challenging one and he plays the angles very well. Because he cheats to the glove side Liut is weak on the short stick side and — like most big men — can fall prey to shots low to the ice, most noticeably on the stick side again and also between the legs, as he is a little slow snapping his pads closed.

Liut generally handles his rebounds, sticking them to a corner or covering them if necessary to keep them from the opposition. He has a good glove hand and will catch anything he can, but is less sure on his stick side, where pucks bounce off his blocker and into the air like jump balls in basketball. He also leaves the puck at his feet after left pad saves on shots from the right point.

Liut is a big man and when he butterflies on the ice he takes up a lot of net, and that's an intimidating factor when a shooter looks up. However, he goes down too early on screen shots, leaving himself vulnerable on subsequent shots. He is standing up more on play around the net.

THE MENTAL GAME

Liut enters games ready to play in terms of concentration, but will blow his cool if scored on early. He has a tendency to follow that early goal by allowing goals in bunches, so often a 4-1 game turns into a 5-5 tie. He pulls himself together though, and demonstrates mental toughness.

He anticipates the play very well, is very intelligent and can come back from a bad performance.

THE INTANGIBLES

There are those who call Mike Liut the Tony Esposito of the 80s — as in he can't win the big game. His critics cite the 1981 Canada Cup loss to the Soviet Union, Hartford's Game 7 overtime loss to the Canadiens in 1986, the six-game upset loss to the Rangers in April 1981 after the St. Louis Blues finished second in the League in points, the 1987 loss to the Nordiques in the first round.

Whether or not there is substance to the claim that Liut plays well enough to lose, he opened his own can of worms by bailing out of last spring's division semifinal against the Canadiens because of a sprained shoulder.

In any case, chances are good the Whalers wouldn't even get their playoff opportunities if not for Liut's heroics over the course of the season. For that reason alone, he just might be the Whalers' most valuable player.

PAUL MACDERMID

Yrs. of NHL service: 4
Born: Chesley, Ontario, Canada; April 14, 1963
Position: Right wing
Height: 6-1
Weight: 205
Uniform no.: 23
Shoots: right

Career statistics:

GP	G	A	TP	PIM
270	45	43	88	534

1987-88 statistics:

GP	G	A	TP	+/−	PIM	PP	SH	GW	GT	S	PCT
80	20	14	34	2	139	4	0	2	0	96	20.8

LAST SEASON

MacDermid played 80 games for the first time. All point totals were career highs, and his PIM total was a career low. His plus/minus was the team's third best, best among forwards.

THE FINESSE GAME

Balance is the key to MacDermid's skating game, and in turn the key to his physical game. Because he is a physical forward, MacDermid must have the balance to remain upright after collisions so that he is ready to continue his game.

MacDermid has that balance and so he remains vertical after hits instead of horizontal. Paul is average in the other aspects of his skating game. He has fairly good speed and agility (which is how he gets to the opposition in order to hit them) and he uses those assets as a good forechecker, but they play second fiddle to his balance and strength.

He sees the ice and reads the play with average ability, about the level with which he scores goals. MacDermid will collect most of his goals on muscle work around the crease, but he certainly has the power to score from farther out and can let a shot go from the far end of the faceoff circle for a goal every once in a while.

He'll see power play time in front of the net because of his size and strength.

THE PHYSICAL GAME

As mentioned, physical play is the best element in Paul's game. He hits hard and often, and those hits will cough up the puck and hand it to the Whalers. He'll go after the opposition's defensemen (the ones that like to wheel and carry the puck) and crack them as soon as he can within a contest to get them off their games and worried about him.

He can level most players if he hits them squarely and he has a pretty good penchant for doing that. Paul goes in the corners and bangs around and he is very successful there, often forcing the puck free.

THE INTANGIBLES

The successful checking troika of Dave Tippett, Doug Jarvis and Paul MacDermid was broken up last season, but MacDermid's is the kind of game that can help any forward combination. He is a very hard worker and his scoring success last season made his already valuable physical play even more important to the Whalers, because guys who can hit *and* score are tough to find.

MacDermid, however, doesn't have a history of being a scorer, so last year's relative success may have been a one-time thing.

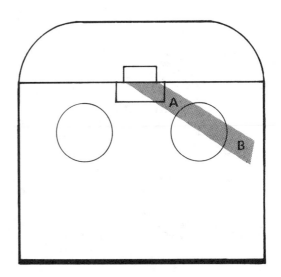

JOEL QUENNEVILLE

Yrs. of NHL service: 10
Born: Windsor, Ontario, Canada; September 15, 1958
Position: Defenseman
Height: 6-1
Weight: 200
Uniform no.: 3
Shoots: left

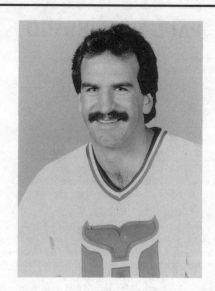

Career statistics:

GP	G	A	TP	PIM
681	48	125	173	639

1987-88 statistics:

GP	G	A	TP	+/−	PIM	PP	SH	GW	GT	S	PCT
77	1	8	9	-13	44	0	0	0	0	42	2.4

LAST SEASON

Games played total was highest in three seasons, but goal and point totals were career lows. His plus/minus was the defense's second worst.

THE FINESSE GAME

Because he lacks outstanding skating ability, Quenneville must play a defensive game based on smarts and not skills. He plays a conservative and unspectacular defensive game, simply forcing the play to the outside and moving the puck to the forwards.

Because he sees the ice well, Joel is good at getting the puck out of the Whaler end. He moves it quickly up-ice (rare are the times you'll see him take more than three strides with it) and he will not carry the puck from the zone. He makes the easy play up the boards instead of the risky cross-ice pass. That's smart.

Though he is not an offensive defenseman, Quenneville will be on ice in the last minute of play with a faceoff in the opposition end because the Whalers want his smarts at the point.

Smarts means Quenneville makes the right play. Containing the point is something Joel does well when he moves up-ice with the play, and he will not get trapped in a position where he cannot recover defensively.

Quenneville shoots from the point with a low slap shot, not overly powerful, and he'll slide to the middle of the blue line for the same shot.

THE PHYSICAL GAME

Quenneville is not a very physical player. He doesn't hit very often and just pushes and shoves in the corners. He succeeds in front of the net by doing a lot of clutching and grabbing, and he's good at it because he has the upper body strength to hold opponents out of the play. He is also good at shielding the puck with his body along the boards to kill time or get a faceoff, but he doesn't otherwise sacrifice his body (he doesn't block shots).

THE INTANGIBLES

Dependability is the value Joel brings to Hartford, and because he plays intelligently he has become a solid defensive defenseman.

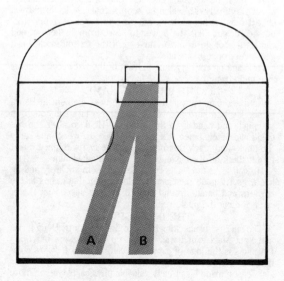

TORRIE ROBERTSON

Yrs. of NHL service: 6
Born: Victoria, B.C., Canada; August 1, 1959
Position: Left wing
Height: 5-11
Weight: 200
Uniform no.: 32
Shoots: left

Career statistics:

GP	G	A	TP	PIM
361	44	88	132	1,492

1987-88 statistics:

GP	G	A	TP	+/−	PIM	PP	SH	GW	GT	S	PCT
63	2	8	10	0	293	0	0	1	0	46	4.3

LAST SEASON

Robertson returned from a year-old broken ankle, missing the season's first 16 games while recuperating. He led the club in PIM and his plus/minus was the club's fifth best.

THE FINESSE GAME

Torrie is not a good skater. He mucks along his wing with neither speed nor agility and with no idea where he is going and what he's going to do when he gets there — except bash the nearest opponent as soon as possible.

He'll get a lot of room to operate but he won't do anything with that room because he doesn't have the stick skills or vision necessary to do anything but make the most rudimentary NHL play. If given enough time and space he'll eventually find an open teammate and get the puck to him. Robertson will score a literal handul of goals during a year, but he exists otherwise in a finesse vacuum.

THE PHYSICAL GAME

Should he actually catch anyone during his seek-and-destroy missions, Robertson will jar the puck loose with a good hit. He likes to check and will attempt to connect every time he's on the ice.

But Robertson is mainly a fighter and a rough guy. Hartford starts him in the intra-divisional games against the Bostons and Montreals to set a tone and keep the opposition wary all night. He keeps you honest and you don't make too many plays around Robertson with your head down.

THE INTANGIBLES

Someone has to fight the Millers and the Kordics and the Donnellys, and that's what Robertson does. He is an enforcer and nothing else.

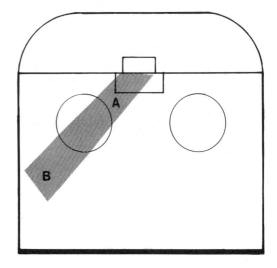

ULF SAMUELSSON

Yrs. of NHL service: 4
Born: Fagursta, Sweden; March 26, 1964
Position: Defenseman
Height: 6-1
Weight: 195
Uniform no.: 5
Shoots: left

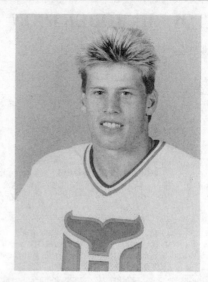

Career statistics:

GP	G	A	TP	PIM
275	17	90	107	576

1987-88 statistics:

GP	G	A	TP	+/-	PIM	PP	SH	GW	GT	S	PCT
76	8	34	42	-9	159	3	0	0	0	156	5.1

LAST SEASON

Games played total was lowest in three seasons, but all point totals were career highs. He finished second in scoring, shots on goal and penalty minutes among Hartford defenders.

THE FINESSE GAME

Samuelsson has some excellent finesse skills, skills that he has worked hard to bring to the NHL level. His skating has improved tremendously from his earliest NHL days, as he now demonstrates agility, quickness and speed. He has very good foot speed and is very agile in his turns and pivots, and that increased foot speed allows him to close the gap between himself and the puck carrier with great efficiency.

Ulf now performs all three stages of the defensive play (force the play wide, close the gap, turn the play up ice) very well. He's also much better at getting to and distributing loose pucks, showing consistent good judgement in patience and play selection. Another big reason for his improvement is his improvement in keeping his head up.

The improved skating and vision combine to give Samuelsson not only the confidence but the ability to successfully carry the puck from the defensive zone. He is very effective at containing the point once he moves into the offensive zone. Samuelsson pinches in smartly and effectively, and his skating allows him to drive to the net to snare a pass. Still, most of his goals will come from the blue line.

He has one trick he likes to use defensively when trailing a breaking forward and that is laying his stick on the ice as he heads back, to force that forward to make a better pass to his teammate than just a slider along the ice.

THE PHYSICAL GAME

Samuelsson has excellent physical abilities and he uses them to the utmost as a very physical defenseman. Ulf loves to bodycheck any opponent he can, and he puts some zest in his checking through the extracurricular meanness he adds via elbows and stick. He is very strong in front of his net and in the corners, making the opposition pay the price for venturing into Whaler territory.

There are times when he is too aggressive, more determined to rub his opponent's face into the boards than he is to

take advantage of a loose puck, but his improved skills have begun to allow him to do both.

He is also fearless and is a shot-blocker supreme.

THE INTANGIBLES

Samuelsson is one of just two or three players on the Whalers who could be classified as world class, and probably the only one of those players whose name wouldn't elicit an argument.

He is one of the NHL's best defensemen — easily Hartford's best — and his willingness to sacrifice his body in the trenches night after night, to constantly irritate the opposition through his yapping and his play and to accept the resulting abuse, speaks volumes of his dedication and character.

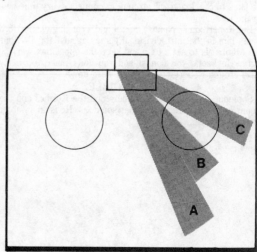

DAVE TIPPETT

Yrs. of NHL service: 4
Born: Moosomin, Sask., Canada; August 25, 1961
Position: Left wing/center
Height: 5-10
Weight: 175
Uniform no.: 15
Shoots: left

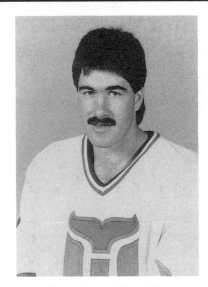

Career statistics:

GP	G	A	TP	PIM
337	50	77	127	104

1987-88 statistics:

GP	G	A	TP	+/−	PIM	PP	SH	GW	GT	S	PCT
80	16	21	37	-4	30	1	2	2	0	126	12.7

LAST SEASON

Tippett played 80 games for the fourth straight season, recording career marks in goals and points.

THE FINESSE GAME

Tippett is a great example of the whole being greater than the sum of the parts. He's not blessed with an abundance of talent, but Dave certainly gets the most from what he has. While not overly fast on his feet, Tippett has a strong and steady pace that gets him where he's going.

He has excellent anticipation and hockey sense and he combines those skills with his less-than-exceptional skating ability to become one of the NHL's top 10 defensive forwards. Dave sees the ice very well and he uses his vision and anticipation to stay with his check excellently. He is also an excellent penalty killer.

He doesn't translate that hockey sense into offensive production because his stick skills aren't good enough, but Tippett raises himself out of the third-line checker class and into premier defensive forward class by making some contributions in the opposing zone. In other words, if he scored just three goals a year he'd be a good checker, but 40 points from a defensive forward makes that forward's defensive work even more valuable.

Tippett is not very gifted in the stick skills department, so he'll have to make his plays on smarts and anticipation and not fancy skating or passing. He moves the puck well to his teammates because of his vision and he'll have to get his own goals from around the crease on rebounds and junk shots.

THE PHYSICAL GAME

Tippett doesn't succeed in his job by wearing down the opposition. He's neither big nor overly physical with the strength he does command, but he is strong enough to hold his check out of the play when necessary.

He is also smart when he does check, hitting and bumping cleanly so as not to hurt the club via penalties.

THE INTANGIBLES

Determination and tremendous work ethic help Tippett squeeze every bit of value from otherwise modest skills. The result is one of the NHL's premier role players. In fact, he has been Hartford's best defensive player for at least two seasons — including 1986-87 when he was overshadowed by the iron man accomplishments of Doug Jarvis.

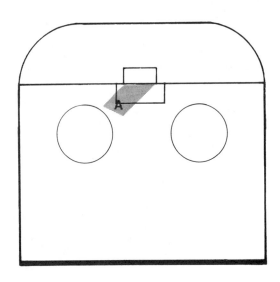

SYLVAIN TURGEON

Yrs. of NHL service: 5
Born: Noranda, Quebec, Canada; January 17, 1965
Position: Left wing
Height: 6-0
Weight: 190
Uniform no.: 16
Shoots: left

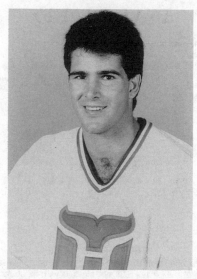

Career statistics:

GP	G	A	TP	PIM
328	162	136	298	326

1987-88 statistics:

GP	G	A	TP	+/-	PIM	PP	SH	GW	GT	S	PCT
71	23	26	49	-5	71	13	0	3	0	247	9.3

LAST SEASON

Turgeon led the Whalers in power play goals and shots on goal. He missed six games with an ankle injury.

THE FINESSE GAME

Turgeon is the kind of player that gets coaches fired and gives general managers ulcers: tremendous talent matched only by his lack of intensity.

Sylvain is an excellent skater with all the requisite components: excellent speed and acceleration, one-step quickness, balance and agility. His agility allows him to move laterally as well as he does forward, making moves with the puck that look like he's pulling it around on a string. He is not very creative, however, and that means he doesn't cut to the holes with his skating. Instead, he's going to decide on a play and make it, and that means a lot of 1-on-1 work versus the defense.

He is a goal scorer first and foremost and he thinks that way, looking to the net before looking to his teammates. He can make some good plays to his teammates but he's overrated as a passer — again because he lacks a feeling for creativity, for anticipating the openings and then leading his teammates to those openings. Turgeon doesn't do those things.

His quick release means that he can score from anywhere within the offensive zone, but because he doesn't get to those openings, because he is a skate-and-shoot scorer without the ability to get into position to score (because he lacks anticipation and vision skills), Turgeon won't score from anywhere.

He has the power to blast the puck past a goaltender from farther out (with his favorite spot the top of the faceoff circle), but Sylvain also likes to dip behind the defense and go one-on-one with the goalie, fake him to the ice, and deposit the puck in the far corner.

THE PHYSICAL GAME

Turgeon doesn't get involved in the physical part of the game and he doesn't want to get involved either. He'll make a show of bumping along the boards — and he can take the puck off the boards very quickly and make a play with it — but you're never going to find him at the bottom of a pileup in the corner.

THE INTANGIBLES

So what's the "But . . . ?" How does Turegon give GMs ulcers? Lack of motivation, just a complete lack of motivation. He brings no intensity to the rink, no desire to excel and probably no confidence. He has taken a lot of abuse from his teammates about his injuries and what they feel are just excuses on his part to pull the 'chute and bail out of games. There may be some truth to their suspicions, since Sylvain won't play hurt.

He's not a bad kid — and remember he's still only 23 years old — and he doesn't have a bad reputation off-ice regarding drinking or running around. Sylvain just sits home and plays his guitar, and wants to do little else.

The bottom line is, he's now Larry Pleau's problem. Will Pleau succeed in re-energizing Turgeon? There's no way to tell. In the meantime he remains a frustrating and underachieving player.

But Turgeon does force us to think about Hartford's draft success under Emile Francis. The Whalers made Turgeon their first choice in 1983's Entry Draft, but they could have had Steve Yzerman, Pat LaFontaine, Cam Neely, Claude Lemieux or Peter Zezel — just to name a few. Now, a lot of clubs could have selected those players and didn't, so Hartford's dismissal of those other guys isn't necessarily a fair criticism.

But consider this: Other than Turgeon, the Whalers have just one Francis draft choice among the regulars — Sylvain Cote. Six first-round draft picks — 52 players drafted from 1983 to 1987 — and only two players on the Hartford roster. And a third — Dana Murzyn — traded away.

Maybe Hartford's new ownership should find out just what Francis' plan is to build the Whalers.

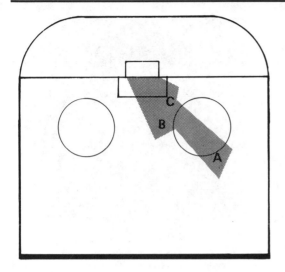

CAREY WILSON

Yrs. of NHL service: 4
Born: Winnipeg, Man., Canada; May 19, 1962
Position: Center
Height: 6-2
Weight: 205
Uniform no.: 33
Shoots: right

Career statistics:

GP	G	A	TP	PIM
315	102	160	262	135

1987-88 statistics:

GP	G	A	TP	+/−	PIM	PP	SH	GW	GT	S	PCT
70	27	41	68	-3	40	10	1	9	0	138	19.6

LAST SEASON

Wilson was traded to Hartford (along with Neil Sheehy and Lane MacDonald) in exchange for Dana Murzyn and Shane Churla early in January. He scored 38 points (18g-20a) in 36 games with the Whalers. He finished second on the club in scoring but first in goals and game winners (he was second in the NHL in GWGs). Games played total was a full season career low, but all point totals were the second highest of his career. He missed six games with a knee injury.

THE FINESSE GAME

Wilson is loaded with upper level finesse skills. To begin with, he is an excellent skater with speed, quickness and agility. He can move laterally or change directions at will.

He has exceptional hands and hockey sense and he can be an excellent playmaker because of those skills. He has the ability to give the soft pass and knows where to send that pass, leading his teammates to the opening if he doesn't take advantage of them himself. Wilson also likes to carry the puck (especially across the opposing blue line) and beat people 1-on-1 (he is an excellent 1-on-1 player), so he won't always make those passes.

Wilson has good sense around the net and is dangerous if left unguarded. He has an accurate and quick wrist shot that is effective both in close and from a distance.

He combines all his skills to be an excellent defensive player as well, and he's also a very smart one — as his PIM total indicates. He does the defensive job without taking penalties.

THE PHYSICAL GAME

Carey is not a physical hockey player in terms of bashing people into the boards, but he has outstanding physical skills. He has terrific eye/hand coordination (which makes him an excellent faceoff man) and his balance makes him a superior player in traffic — both along the boards and when checked in front of the net. He'll maintain his puck control through most all physical situations.

That balance also serves Wilson when he initiates the checking game. He is very strong and will out-muscle many opponents (but don't expect him to smack anyone into the middle of next week because he won't) along the boards, and stay vertical and ready to make plays after those collisions.

He is a remarkably conditioned athlete (a more-than-just-sometime triathlete, as a matter of fact) and works very hard at staying in shape year round.

THE INTANGIBLES

The key to Carey Wilson, from a team point of view, is to take him at face value. While he is tremendously talented, Carey just doesn't have the concentration skills necessary to apply his skills night after night. A very intelligent person, he simply gets bored with the game.

Bob Johnson and the Flames smartly accepted that and found ways of maximizing Wilson's performance. As long as Hartford management doesn't try pushing Wilson in a direction he doesn't want to go, as long as they don't ride herd on him to be an offensive savior, the player and the team should get along just fine.

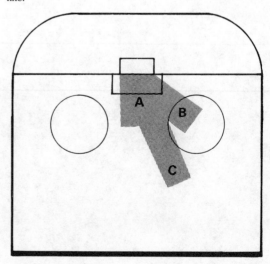

LOS ANGELES KINGS

LINE COMBINATIONS
PAUL FENTON-BERNIE NICHOLLS-JIM FOX
LUC ROBITAILLE-JIMMY CARSON-DAVE TAYLOR
PHIL SYKES-MIKE ALLISON-RON DUGUAY

DEFENSE PAIRINGS
KEN HAMMOND-DEAN KENNEDY
JAY WELLS-STEVE DUCHESNE

GOALTENDERS
ROLLIE MELANSON
GLEN HEALY

OTHER PLAYERS
BOB CARPENTER — Center
TOM LAIDLAW — Defense
LARRY PLAYFAIR — Defense

POWER PLAY

FIRST UNIT:
JIMMY CARSON-LUC ROBITAILLE-DAVE TAYLOR
STEVE DUCHESNE-BERNIE NICHOLLS

SECOND UNIT:
PAUL FENTON-BOB CARPENTER-JIM FOX

On the first unit, TAYLOR plugs the net, CARSON is at the left faceoff circle and ROBITAILLE at the right circle (on their off-wings to improve shooting angles) and DUCHESNE and NICHOLLS are on the points. The puck is worked around the outside to loosen up the defense in attempts to free CARSON or ROBITAILLE. Both DUCHESNE and NICHOLLS will shoot if box stays strong. TAYLOR gets rebounds/deflections.

On the second unit the Kings play a 1-3-1 with FENTON in front of the net (he's the "1"), CARPENTER at the right circle and FOX at the left (off wings again) and a defenseman between the two (this trio is the "3") and NICHOLLS at the point.

Last season the Kings power play was GOOD, scoring 103 goals in 474 opportunities (21.7 percent, ninth overall).

PENALTY KILLING

FIRST UNIT:
BERNIE NICHOLLS-DAVE TAYLOR
JAY WELLS-TOM LAIDLAW

The Kings forwards are generally aggressive in their defense, while the defense generally sits back. DUCHESNE will taje a turn on the PK unit and he pressures the puck. Other forwards will be SYKES, DUGUAY and ALLISON, all of whom look to jump the puck carrier as he enters the Kings zone.

Last season the Kings penalty killing was POOR, allowing 96 goals in 425 shorthanded situations (77.4 percent, 17th overall).

CRUCIAL FACEOFFS

ALLISON is very good, as is DUGUAY. NICHOLLS is a third option.

MIKE ALLISON

Yrs. of NHL service: 8
Born: Ft. Francis, Ontario, Canada; March 28, 1961
Position: Center
Height: 6-0
Weight: 202
Uniform no.: 10
Shoots: right

Career statistics:

GP	G	A	TP	PIM
389	86	133	219	430

1987-88 statistics:

GP	G	A	TP	+/−	PIM	PP	SH	GW	GT	S	PCT
52	16	15	31	3	67	5	1	2	0	61	26.2

LAST SEASON

Allison was traded from Toronto to Los Angeles in exchange for Sean McKenna. He missed four games with a groin injury. Goal and point totals were second highest of his career. His shooting percentage was the highest among all players who appeared with the Kings last season.

THE FINESSE GAME

Allison is a below average skater because he has too wide a stride, not much speed and even less agility. In fact, the knee and leg injuries that have hobbled him throughout his career are directly attributable to his stride.

Because it's so wide and his feet are so far apart, his weight is really planted when his feet are on the ice. When he gets hit, he is unable to shift his weight or dance away from the check, and so all the force is absorbed by one knee or the other.

Aside from skating, Mike has a good view of the ice and is a very good forechecker because of that. He pursues the puck well and gets good angles on the puck carrier to force him into a corner and into a poor play. He is also a very good penalty killer for the same 'angle' reasons.

He is not outstanding as an offensive player but for a checking center he gets good point production. He sees the game and makes the play necessary to score.

THE PHYSICAL GAME

Despite his injuries, Allison willingly plays a physical game. He is a grinder and a mucker, persistent in his pursuit of the puck. He works the boards and the back of the net well, taking the body to free the puck.

He wins all faceoffs very well, especially the crucial ones.

THE INTANGIBLES

We say "Despite the injuries . . . " but Allison is always going to be hurt. He's going to miss 10 games here, three games there.

On and off the ice, Mike is an excellent team man. What he lacks in skill he makes up for in desire and heart, so Mike brings an excellent attitude and work ethic to the Kings.

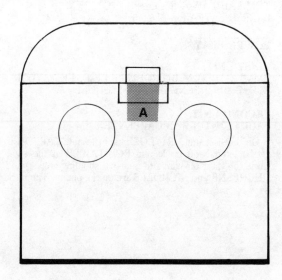

BOBBY CARPENTER

Yrs. of NHL service: 7
Born: Beverly, Mass., USA; July 13, 1963
Position: Center
Height: 6-0
Weight: 190
Uniform no.: 11
Shoots: left

Career statistics:

GP	G	A	TP	PIM
531	200	234	434	507

1987-88 statistics:

GP	G	A	TP	+/−	PIM	PP	SH	GW	GT	S	PCT
71	19	33	52	-21	84	10	0	2	0	176	10.8

LAST SEASON

Games played total was second highest of his career, though he missed eight games with a shoulder injury. His plus/minus was the team's third worst, and he finished third in power play goals.

THE FINESSE GAME

Carpenter is an excellent skater, with superb strength and balance. He is almost impossible to push off the puck and can carry it very well in traffic, and, because of his balance, you'll almost never see him thrown to the ice. He has great speed with and without the puck, is an agile skater and has good lateral movement for change of direction and has good quickness.

Bob anticipates and passes the puck well because of his good hands that are soft with the puck. He has a terrific slap shot and an accurate wrist shot, and is a good faceoff man because of his eye/hand coordination and speed. Those attributes combine with his hands to make him effective at handling the puck in traffic.

THE PHYSICAL GAME

The key to Carpenter's success is his physical game, but he's not consistently successful because he's not consistently physical. When he is up for the game and ready to battle for the puck, then he is a top player. When he's not mentally ready to play, his physical play and agggressiveness are questionable.

When he plays physically you know it, because he can be a punishing hitter. He'll take the pounding in front of the enemy net and dish it out the same way. He's strong in the upper body, especially in the arms and wrists, and can pull the puck out of a tangle because of that.

THE INTANGIBLES

Carpenter didn't show any of his negative attitude in Los Angeles in terms of non-coachability. The coaching staff never had a problem with Bob, other than the fact that — like every player — some nights he just wasn't there.

Carpenter responds to negative reinforcement. He's the kind of guy who, when blasted by the coach that morning, goes on to have a great game that night.

Los Angeles is looking for a solid two-way game and 60-70 points from him. When he plays the way he can, he can provide those points and that two-way game. He just has to want to.

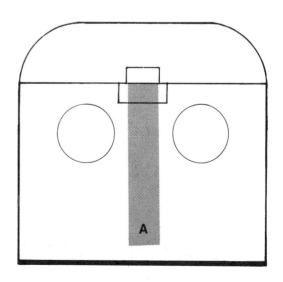

JIMMY CARSON

Yrs. of NHL service: 2
Born: Southfield, Michigan, USA; July 20, 1968
Position: Center
Height: 6-0
Weight: 185
Uniform no.: 17
Shoots: right

Career statistics:

GP	G	A	TP	PIM
160	92	94	186	67

1987-88 statistics:

GP	G	A	TP	+/−	PIM	PP	SH	GW	GT	S	PCT
80	55	52	107	-19	45	22	0	7	2	264	20.8

LAST SEASON

Finished eighth in overall League scoring, third in goals, sixth in power play goals. Finished second on the club in scoring, first in goals, power play goals, game winning goals, game tying goals and shots on goal. He was second in shooting percentage. His plus/minus was the team's fourth worst, third among forwards.

THE FINESSE GAME

Where the other half of the California Kids Connection — Luc Robitaille — has good to very good skills in most finesse categories, all of Carson's skills are excellent.

Carson has excellent quickness, the kind that allows him to stop and start in one direction or another within a step. He is not overly fast, but he has excellent acceleration, so he will pull away from the opposition. He has a smooth stride and is well balanced and agile in all three directions: forward, back and sideways.

Good as his skating is, Jimmy's hand skills are better. He regularly makes thread-the-needle passes and he has very soft hands that control the puck well. Combined with his ice vision and anticipation, the skills make him an excellent playmaker. He anticipates very well offensively, particularly in making the transition from offense to defense.

His shot selection is also excelllent and is already among the League's best, both slap shot and wrist shot. He shoots often and accurately and makes the goalie stop him, rather than firing shots wide of the net.

THE PHYSICAL GAME

Again, like Robitaille, Carson has good size and uses his body very well offensively. He protects the puck with his body very well and will certainly get stronger as he matures.

And like Robitaille his physicl play doesn't extend to the defensive zone. Carson is very casual in his defensive aggressiveness, often getting out-fought and out-positioned because he's not as intense as he should be.

He also needs greater strength on faceoffs, particularly in the defensive zone — where he frequently loses more than he wins. When he loses those faceoffs he's beaten to the net by the opposing center.

THE INTANGIBLES

The most important one is that Carson wants out of Los Angeles. He wants to be in a hockey environment, which L.A. clearly is not. How this will affect his steadily improving play (including defensively) remains to be seen but his loss would be a huge one for Los Angeles, because he will become one of the top five centers in the NHL.

As with Robitaille, the third year is less important for Carson as a test of NHL worthiness than it is a test of consistency. He has set high levels of performance for himself and must live up to that promise.

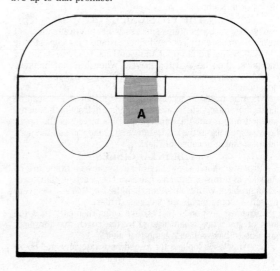

STEVE DUCHESNE

Yrs. of NHL service: 2
Born: Sept-Iles, Quebec, Canada; June 30, 1965
Position: Defenseman
Height: 5-11
Weight: 195
Uniform no.: 28
Shoots: left

Career statistics:

GP	G	A	TP	PIM
146	29	64	93	183

1987-88 statistics:

GP	G	A	TP	+/−	PIM	PP	SH	GW	GT	S	PCT
71	16	39	55	0	109	5	0	4	1	190	8.4

LAST SEASON

Point totals were all career highs. Duchesne led the Kings' defense in scoring, power play goals, game winners (third on the team), shots on goal (fourth on the team) and games played. His plus/minus was the defense's second best. He missed nine games with a knee sprain.

THE FINESSE GAME

Steve is an excellent offensive defenseman and is the most skilled of all the Kings' defensemen in his ability to handle the puck. He's a good skater with very good speed and he handles the puck well at that tempo when rushing it, which is often. He sees the ice and finds the open man very well, whether making a breakout pass from behind his own net or a break-away pass from the red line.

Duchesne joins the attack very well and he demonstrates that ability well on the power play. His skating also shines on the power play, allowing him to jump into holes and contain the point well or charge the slot for a shot. He has a good slap shot from the point, but when he comes off the point he goes high glove with his wrist shot all the time. He knows when to shoot to score and when to shoot for rebounds and deflections.

He plays defense smartly and ably combines his speed in checking with positional play. His ability to force the play and then make a play up-ice with a loose puck is an important one for the Kings.

THE PHYSICAL GAME

Duchesne is not an overwhelmingly physical player and will often be out-positioned and out-fought in his defensive coverage in front of the net and in the corners.

His physical game is generally weak, but he is aware of that and is working to improve it. He need not become a thunderous hitter, but he must be more of a sure thing when protecting his goalie.

THE INTANGIBLES

Duchesne is a hard worker and the Kings need his offensive style to succeed. All he has to do is improve his defensive play to become valuable at both ends of the ice.

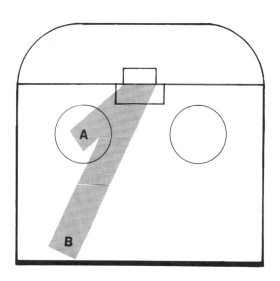

RON DUGUAY

Yrs. of NHL service: 11
Born: Sudbury, Ontario, Canada; July 6, 1957
Position: Right wing/center
Height: 6-2
Weight: 197
Uniform no.: 44
Shoots: right

Career statistics:

GP	G	A	TP	PIM
794	267	329	596	514

1987-88 statistics:

GP	G	A	TP	+/-	PIM	PP	SH	GW	GT	S	PCT
63	6	10	16	-14	40	0	2	1	0	80	7.5

LAST SEASON

Duguay was traded to Los Angeles by the Rangers in exchange for Mark Hardy late in the season. He finished second on the club in shorthanded goals, but both were scored in New York. He was sidelined throughout the season with a recurring back injury. Games played total was the second lowest of his career, point totals were all career lows.

THE FINESSE GAME

Duguay is a good skater, strong on his skates and fast for a big man. His quick foot, speed and choppy stride give him excellent acceleration and long-range speed, and he is also fairly agile on his skates.

He can handle the puck as he carries it up-ice, but no more than serviceable. His puck handling skills do not match his speed, and he is better at giving the passes than receiving him because of that.

Duguay sees the ice fairly well and looks to use his teammates, but he is not blessed with an abundance of anticipation. He does not always recognize the openings on the ice, though his speed (and strength) can get him there.

Because of his skating, Duguay will be used as a checker and as a penalty killer.

He will also get power play time by standing in front of the net and he'll convert rebounds for goals. Still, he doesn't have the hands to operate in close (which is why he misses many of the breakaways his speed affords him), so he'll need a fairly open opportunity.

Duguay likes to fire a big slapshot from the right circle, but — because he is not very accurate with it — it is more bark than bite.

THE PHYSICAL GAME

Duguay is a big, strong forward and he can use his size and strength very effectively in close quarters to bounce the opposition off the puck. His use of his size is very inconsistent though, and he must hit more often (rather than just pushing around) to be effective.

He can be a tough hockey player, willing to pay the price, and that can make him valuable, especially as he can be tough without hurting his team through penalties.

Duguay can and will fight when provoked, and he is not an easy target. His upper body strength and overall balance make him a good faceoff man.

THE INTANGIBLES

Duguay gives the Kings a dependable presence down the middle, a fairly strong center who can work to counter some of the Smythe Division's bigger centers and scorers. He will be an effective player as long as the Kings don't expect too much from him offensively.

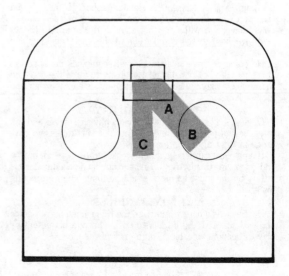

PAUL FENTON

Yrs. of NHL service: 2
Born: Springfield, Mass., USA; December 22, 1959
Position: Left wing
Height: 5-11
Weight: 180
Uniform no.: 8
Shoots: left

Career statistics:

GP	G	A	TP	PIM
113	27	28	55	58

1987-88 statistics:

GP	G	A	TP	+/−	PIM	PP	SH	GW	GT	S	PCT
71	20	23	43	-14	46	8	1	1	0	166	12.0

LAST SEASON

Games played and all point totals, as well as PIM mark, were career highs. He was traded from the Rangers to Los Angeles early in the season.

THE FINESSE GAME

Fenton is a quick skater and he uses that ability well as a two-way forward. He sees the offensive game well and positions himself to produce offense, and his hands are good enough around the net for him to convert on those chances.

He forechecks very well and pursues the puck as well as any of the other King forwards. He's very aggressive at getting to the puck but is not as strong when he is on it as you'd like.

Paul recognizes the hole when they develop and he explodes to them well enough to get a lot of chances and breakaways.

THE PHYSICAL GAME

The physical game presents drawbacks for Fenton. He can be taken off the puck by the opposition. Though his speed gets him to the corners he doesn't have the ability to get the puck out of the corner and to the front of the net.

He doesn't have a great deal of strength and toughness, and games that feature those traits render him ineffective.

THE INTANGIBLES

Fenton is a work horse, and his seemingly poor defensive play (as indicated by his plus/minus) comes because he cannot physically contain the opposition. His lack of toughness will always counter-balance his offensive contributions.

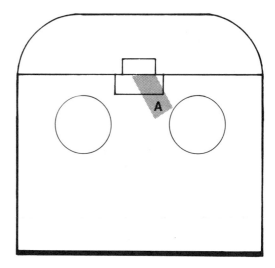

JIM FOX

Yrs. of NHL service: 8
Born: Coniston, Ontario, Canada; May 18, 1960
Position: Right wing
Height: 5-8
Weight: 183
Uniform no.: 19
Shoots: right

Career statistics:

GP	G	A	TP	PIM
567	185	291	477	143

1987-88 statistics:

GP	G	A	TP	+/−	PIM	PP	SH	GW	GT	S	PCT
68	16	35	51	-7	18	2	0	1	0	120	13.3

LAST SEASON

Games played total was second lowest of Fox's career, as was goal total. He finished fourth in plus/minus among regulars and his PIM total was the lowest accumulated by a regular. He was sidelined late in the season with a knee injury.

THE FINESSE GAME

The hallmarks of Fox's game are quickness and smarts. In a race around the rink many players would beat Jimmy to the finish line. But set Points A and B 30 feet apart and few players — none of them Kings — would beat him to the finish. His low center of gravity gives him excellent balance, so he can remain upright after taking hits and is very difficult to remove from the puck.

His quickness gets him to many loose pucks, and that's where his smarts come in. Jim is very smart and he sees the game especially well offensively. That ability (along with his selflessness) combines with his hand skill to make him a very good playmaker — regardless of the numbers. He'll get the pass to a teammate through traffic or lead him into the openings.

Jim handles the puck well himself, if a little predicatably (he screeches to a halt just after he crosses the offensive blue line so the defense races past him). He is one player who definitely *could* make a play to save his life. His hand and vision skills make him a power play regular, and he'd be a regular on that unit with any NHL team.

He has an accurate wrist shot, one released very quickly, and will beat goalies from in close. He can, on occasion, surprise them with longer drives as well, but Fox is more adept in tight.

THE PHYSICAL GAME

Fox takes his licks offensively, but he is not a tough or aggressive player. He goes to the traffic areas and willingly takes a pounding, but he initiates almost no contact. That's bad when he loses the puck.

His defense suffers too, for while he knows his defensive role Jim is not physical enough and not ready to be physical enough to complete his defensive assignment.

THE INTANGIBLES

He's not as tough, but Fox is probably as innately talented as Philadelphia's Brian Propp. Fox is an excellent competitor and a top team guy but his game is in a state of limbo right now, and he's not accomplishing the things he could. Now he has to rehabilitate a damaged knee.

A change of scenery might be best for all concerned.

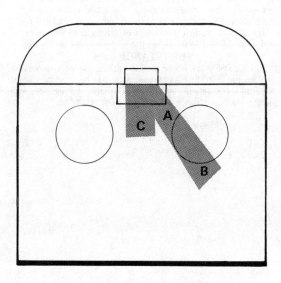

KEN HAMMOND

Yrs. of NHL service: 1
Born: Toronto, Ontario, Canada; August 23, 1963
Position: Defenseman
Height: 6-1
Weight: 190
Uniform no.: 2
Shoots: left

Career statistics:

GP	G	A	TP	PIM
56	7	11	18	80

1987-88 statistics:

GP	G	A	TP	+/−	PIM	PP	SH	GW	GT	S	PCT
46	7	9	16	-1	69	1	0	1	0	52	13.5

LAST SEASON

First "full" NHL season after three previous stints. An ankle injury sidelined him during March. He was second on the defense in goals.

THE FINESSE GAME

Hammond is a good skater and improving. His confidence grew tremendously as the season progressed and his skating did the same. He's not yet exceptional at the NHL level in agility or quickness, but Hammond moves well across the ice as well as up and down.

He can handle the puck but won't usually do so because his style is that of the stay-at-home defender. He can contribute offensively (as his goal total suggests) with a good shot from the blue line.

He plays well positionally on the rush toward him, but he has a tendency to give position in the corners or the front of the net. That too is improving.

THE PHYSICAL GAME

Hammond is not very big but he plays physically in the defensive zone. He has been out-fought in the corners and front of the net, but greater NHL experience should remedy these flaws.

THE INTANGIBLES

Hammond showed well during his short tenure with the Kings last season. His growing confidence helped him improve his total game, and that improvement should continue.

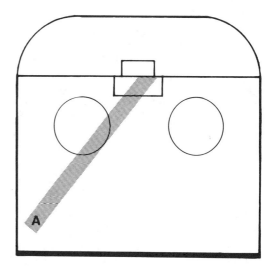

GLEN HEALY

Yrs. of NHL service: 1
Born: Pickering, Ontario, Canada; August 23, 1962
Position: Goaltender
Height: 5-10
Weight: 185
Uniform no.: 33
Catches: left

Career statistics:

GP	MINS	G	SO	AVG	A	PIM
35	1,920	141	1	4.40	2	6

1987-88 statisics:

GP	MINS	AVG	W	L	T	SO	GA	SA	SAPCT	PIM
34	1,869	4.33	12	18	1	1	135	1,005	.865	6

LAST SEASON

Healy made his full time NHL debut after one 1985-86 contest. He was a free agent signee in 1985, previously playing with Western Michigan University. He finished third in the NHL in games played by a rookie goalie.

THE PHYSICAL GAME

Healy is unorthodox to say the least. He relies a great deal on his cat-like reflexes and can be spectacularly acrobatic, but that means he can also look good and accomplish nothing.

Healy has a lot of trouble getting back into position after one of his flops around the ice. He doesn't have great balance — which is one reason he's always falling down — but Glen's biggest problem is that he loses his net. Since he's not an angle goaltender to begin with, the results can be disastrous.

He is weak on direct rush attacks (forwards breaking down the wing for example) because of his poor angle play, and so he allows goals to the corners to very average shooters.

Healy moves side to side fairly well, but when the puck goes behind the net and he has to move across the crease Glen has the habit of turning his back to the ice. In other words, he faces the puck and the back boards as he skates back to his net and doesn't see what's going on — a forward breaking to accept that pass from behind the goal — in front of the goal.

He has very fast hands and feet and will get to a puck if it's gettable. Because of his bad positioning in the goal he'll make a lot of phantom saves on pucks that are going wide.

THE MENTAL GAME

Healy is a very tough competitor and the kind of guy who will fight through adversity. Bad games don't weigh on him and he comes back strongly the next night. The same doesn't necessarily hold true within a game, but that's another problem.

Glen is a streaky goalie, the kind who can get hot for a few games, but can get cold too. When he's hot he'll win the game regardless of how many shots he faces; when he's cold he'll lose the game regardless of how few shots he faces. And when he's cold he's got to get the hook.

His concentration and preparation are good in all these instances; it is the result that is flawed.

THE INTANGIBLES

Healy bore the brunt of the Los Angeles playoff burden, but should the Kings decide to use him as their number one goaltender they're in for a lot of exciting games. Increased NHL experience could help Healy stabilize his game, but he's already 26 years old. True, goalies mature as players at an older age, but 26 is not young.

DEAN KENNEDY

Yrs. of NHL service: 5
Born: Redvers, Sask., Canada; January 18, 1963
Position: Defenseman
Height: 6-2
Weight: 198
Uniform no.: 6
Shoots: right

Career statistics:

GP	G	A	TP	PIM
294	10	52	62	528

1987-88 statistics:

GP	G	A	TP	+/–	PIM	PP	SH	GW	GT	S	PCT
58	1	11	12	-22	158	0	0	0	0	40	2.5

LAST SEASON

Games played total was lowest in three seasons, while PIM total was a career high (fourth highest on the club). His minus 22 was the club's second worst, worst among defensemen. He missed 18 games with a finger injury and was also sidelined by a late season hip injury.

THE FINESSE GAME

There isn't much of one, and for Kennedy to be successful there shouldn't be. He is no better than average as a skater and his agility is very questionable. Dean is very prone to forwards faking one way and heading the other because of his poor lateral movement, and when that happens he has no choice but to take penalties to stop the opposition.

He also has questionable balance and is susceptible to "blue dart syndrome," the NHL lingo for a guy who will — for no reason whatsoever but *always* in a crucial situation — fall down.

He doesn't see the game clearly, so his play has to be the simple, up-the-boards-and-out pass; Kennedy should not be passing the puck up the center of the ice. Bearing all this in mind, remember that his plus/minus is not completely unjustified.

Kennedy follows the play up-ice and tries to control play from the point, but his role is to be the safety valve — the one man back when necessary. Indicative of that role is the fact that he rarely shoots the puck. When he does, he fires a slap shot from the point that is no better than average in strength, speed or accuracy.

THE PHYSICAL GAME

Kennedy is a very physical hockey player. He's a good body checker and he makes the opposition pay for shots on goal or chances at the King net, and Dean has to play that way to succeed.

He hits at the blue line when he can, hoping to thwart the rush in that way. He ties up the opposition in front of the Kings' net and Kennedy will outmuscle many players because of good upper body strength.

THE INTANGIBLES

When he plays alertly and aggressively and makes the simple plays Kennedy can succeed in the NHL. When he does not play that way he is a very marginal NHLer.

Dean is the team's strongest player in the weight room and he works hard to stay in condition, doing some form of exercise each day. He is very well conditioned, and this effort speaks well of his dedication.

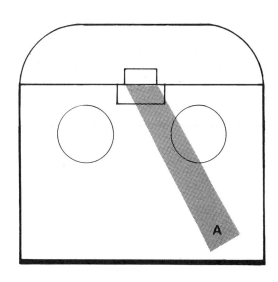

TOM LAIDLAW

Yrs. of NHL service: 8
Born: Brampton, Ontario, Canada; April 15, 1958
Position: Defenseman
Height: 6-2
Weight: 215
Uniform no.: 3
Shoots: left

Career statistics:

GP	G	A	TP	PIM
578	21	114	135	612

1987-88 statistics:

GP	G	A	TP	+/-	PIM	PP	SH	GW	GT	S	PCT
57	1	12	13	3	47	0	0	0	0	30	3.3

LAST SEASON

Games played total was a career low (he missed eight games with a knee injury, nine games with a leg injury).

THE FINESSE GAME

Laidlaw is a very smart defensemen, certainly the best defensive defenseman the Kings have. Though he is not a good skater he is the best one-on-one defenseman on the team, and Tom succeeds by playing within his limitations. What makes him valuable is his knowledge of positional play and his ability to combine that with good play reading ability.

Tom doesn't carry the puck very well, so he makes sure he hardly has to carry the puck at all by making quick and simple passes to his forwards. He will shoot from the point and has developed a tendency to sneak in a stride or two for a wrist shot, but he takes so long to deliver the shot that — considering the results — the effort seems hardly worth while.

THE PHYSICAL GAME

Laidlaw is very strong physically, and he uses that strength to win the one-on-one battles in the corners and the front of the net very often. He is an aggressive hitter, but not necessarily a punishing one. He uses his body well to clog up the middle of the ice or to block shots and he will take on anyone in the slot.

THE INTANGIBLES

Nine times out of 10, Laidlaw will make the correct defensive; on a team like Los Angeles that's no mean feat. He is unspectacular but highly effective at his job.

Tom is a very positive person, a top team player and great on the ice and in the dressing room.

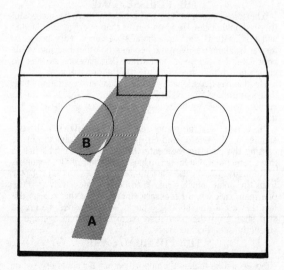

ROLAND MELANSON

Yrs. of NHL service: 8
Born: Moncton, N.B., Canada; June 28, 1960
Position: Goaltender
Height: 5-10
Weight: 180
Uniform no.: 31
Catches: left

Career statistics:

GP	MINS	G	SO	AVG	A	PIM
277	15,762	952	4	3.62	12	105

1987-88 statisics:

GP	MINS	AVG	W	L	T	SO	GA	SA	SAPCT	PIM
47	2,676	4.37	17	20	7	2	195	1,399	.860	16

LAST SEASON

Games played total was a career high, minutes played second highest of career. Win total was the lowest of his career, but shutout total was a career high. He, Glen Healy and Bob Janecyk (for five games) suffered as Los Angeles allowed more goals than any other team in the League.

THE PHYSICAL GAME

Rollie is a very fluid goaltender with great reflexes and good skills. He positions himself in the net very well and he challenges shooters very well, and he can do that because he is a good skater. He moves well from post to post and he moves well coming from the net to get out and get position. He cuts his angles well and is a pretty safe bet to make the first save.

On a team like Los Angeles, where opposition wingers are less likely to be prevented from cutting to the net, Melanson gets across the crease for a second save. His excellent balance helps here, but because he's set to move laterally (and has his feet apart), he'll give up goals between his legs.

His balance allows him to be very quick with his feet, and also to regain his stance after a save or after flopping to the ice. Rollie is not very mobile when he leaves his feet, as he has a tendency to sit down rather than kneel, and he can't move while on his behind.

He catches and handles the puck extremely well and is very good with his stick from his waist down. Melanson is weak above the waist on his stick side. He roams from his net to cut off pucks and pass them to teammates. Rollie also takes swipes at forwards in his crease.

THE MENTAL GAME

Rollie is not as strong mentally as he could be, because he gets down on himself and then has difficulty getting back to the top of his game. He's up-and-down in his concentration and always anticipates well, except in deking situations — where he makes the first move and gets burned.

He can make the big save and Melanson can certainly rebound from the bad goals or games, but he must be mentally prepared to play each and every game. Otherwise, a bad goal ruins him for the night and the vicious circle regarding his confidence starts again.

He performs better as the number one goaltender and likes the responsibility. The club's confidence feeds his own, and he knows that if he makes a mistake he'll be right back in there the next day.

THE INTANGIBLES

An offshoot of Melanson's confidence problem is his atitude toward his team. Nothing is ever Rollie's fault: there's always an alibi or finger pointing at teammates. His attitude and confidence have prevented him from repeating his success from one season to the next, but he's certainly underrated as an NHL goaltender.

BERNIE NICHOLLS

Yrs. of NHL service: 7
Born: Haliburton, Ontario, Canada; June 24, 1961
Position: Center
Height: 6-0
Weight: 185
Uniform no.: 9
Shoots: right

Career statistics:

GP	G	A	TP	PIM
476	230	303	533	603

1987-88 statistics:

GP	G	A	TP	+/−	PIM	PP	SH	GW	GT	S	PCT
65	32	46	78	2	114	8	7	1	1	236	13.6

LAST SEASON

Games played total was lowest since rookie season and snapped Nicholls' record of three seasons of perfect attendance (he suffered a broken finger early in the season). All point totals were four-season lows. Nicholls finished third on the club in scoring, first in shorthanded goals and second in shots on goal.

THE FINESSE GAME

Nicholls is the antithesis of the theory that says to succeed in the NHL you must be a great skater. A touch of quickness and good balance are highlights of Nicholls' skating, which could best be described as "getting the job done." Because of this lack of skating skill Bernie is not a good forechecker; he doesn't pursue the puck well.

What he does do is read the offensive zone very well to pick off that errant pass or that puck around the boards. Once he has the puck he's extremely strong on it; don't pull the stick lifting trick on Nicholls, because it won't work.

Bernie has all the skills to be an excellent one-on-one player, and his favorite offensive play when carrying the puck is to fake his slap shot (a shot the defense *must* respect) and then deke to his forehand. He also has excellent scoring ability and finds the goalie's holes with his excellent, accurate slap shot. He is an excellent one-touch shooter.

He has great hands and can slip the puck through the smallest opening to a teammate (his play reading helps here) and he demonstrates those abilities in specialty team situations.

He'll play the point on the power play to maximize his vision and hands, and his anticipation and quickness makes him a penalty killer par excellence.

Bernie can play sound defense when he puts his mind to it, but he's put himself into a scoring role and pays most attention to that phase of the game.

THE PHYSICAL GAME

As mentioned, Nicholls is very strong in the puck. He has big, strong hands and they power his wrist shot and help him win faceoffs. He's the team's best athlete and his wiry strength complements his size. He will play a physical game and initiate checks, and he will also accept them to make his plays. He needs that first hit of a game to wake him up or else he will sleepwalk.

THE INTANGIBLES

Nicholls is very casual in manner, very laidback (all right, California mellow), but don't let that demeanor fool you: inside he is a competitor who lives for pressure situations. He loves big games, the playoffs — any crucial situation.

He has great aerobic capacity and likes to play 25 minutes a game, which is a lot for a forward; he'll go out every other shift. That effort and attitude is what you'd expect from a team's top player, and that's what Bernie Nicholls is — the Kings' top player.

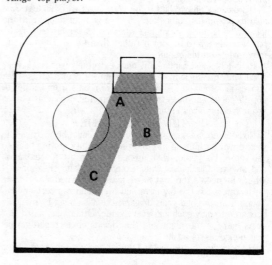

LARRY PLAYFAIR

Yrs. of NHL service: 10
Born: Fort St. James, B.C., Canada; June 23, 1958
Position: Defenseman
Height: 6-4
Weight: 200
Uniform no.: 23
Shoots: left

Career statistics:

GP	G	A	TP	PIM
636	26	87	113	1,684

1987-88 statistics:

GP	G	A	TP	+/−	PIM	PP	SH	GW	GT	S	PCT
54	0	7	7	-13	197	0	0	0	0	20	0.0

LAST SEASON

Games played total was second lowest of career; he missed two months recovering from knee surgery performed early in 1987. He led the club in PIM.

THE FINESSE GAME

Finesse has never been Playfair's game and most of his skills reflect that, but he does have a couple of finesse assets. He is not a good skater and has trouble with any kind of speed attack because of his lack of mobility. Playfair has a great deal of trouble stopping and starting, which means he won't be able to make the evasive maneuvers necessary to lose a forechecker when he goes back for the puck.

A defenseman without speed needs positional smarts, something Playfair does not have a great deal of. He is just average at playing his defensive angles, relying more on his imposing size to prevent the opposition from setting up camp in the Kings' zone than he does correct defensive positioning.

Larry does have some offensive ability that has been overshadowed by his physical play. While he won't join the rush as a fourth attacker, he can make a fairly positive offensive move at the blue line and he is an exceptionally good passer.

He can play a role on left wing as well as defense, functioning as the forward staying back to cover defensively or down low to plug the net. He'll get a goal or two a year from the front of the net, and another couple from the point.

THE PHYSICAL GAME

Playfair is a big tough guy, strong in his own end of the ice when he can catch the opposition. He is tough in the corners and in front of the net because of his good strength and he likes to hit — a lot. He is a punishing hitter and can also muscle the puck away from the opposition.

But he suffers from over-aggressiveness, charging at people, elbowing, obviously rubbing his gloves in their faces. Then the referee has no choice but to send him to the box.

He can contribute in a limited defensive role if he curbs his temper and he will sacrifice his body to block a shot or two. He is also an accomplished fighter.

THE INTANGIBLES

The skating flaws we mention are not flaws that have appeared following his knee surgery; Playfair's always had these problems. He's a quality team individual, a very positive guy and hard worker — all things for which he deserves credit. He is just very limited on the ice.

LUC ROBITAILLE

Yrs. of NHL service: 2
Born: Montreal, Quebec, Canada; February 17, 1966
Position: Left wing
Height: 6-0
Weight: 178
Uniform no.: 20
Shoots: left

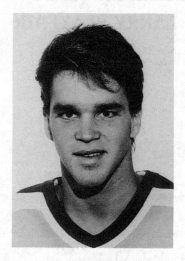

Career statistics:

GP	G	A	TP	PIM
159	98	97	195	100

1987-88 statistics:

GP	G	A	TP	+/−	PIM	PP	SH	GW	GT	S	PCT
80	53	58	111	-9	82	17	0	6	1	220	24.1

LAST SEASON

Robitaille finished fifth in League-wide scoring, fourth in goal scoring. He led the Kings in points, assists, and shooting percentage (first among the regulars in the last category). He was second in power play goals and game winners, and third in shots on goal. He played 80 games for the first time in his two-year career.

THE FINESSE GAME

Superior stick skills and excellent offensive anticipation are the keys to Robitaille's game.

From 15-feet and in he is as talented any of the NHL's most talented players. He knows where the puck is going to go and he gets to it to make a play. He is very strong on the puck and is not easily stripped of it; as with teammate Bernie Nicholls, the stick lifting trick won't work on Luc.

He has great hands in front of the net and a very quick stick, and his touch is demonstrated by his ability to score up high and between the goaltender's legs while in close. To score in front takes a bang-bang play, and for Robitaille to place his shots so well is a good barometer of his scoring skill.

He carries the puck well at most speeds and can make his plays with it, and his deking and faking ability make him a good — not great — one-on-one player. He is a very creative player away from the puck. He combines his sense and hand skills with good ice vision to make or receive his passes well. Luc's a given on the power play.

His skating isn't bad, but he needs to improve his starts. He's very slow getting started and the quickness in his stride is improvable. In order for him to improve as a player, that quickness must improve.

His defensive positioning is awful, particularly in his own zone. Robitaille chases the puck all over the defensive zone and that wandering leaves openings for the opposition.

THE PHYSICAL GAME

He is not an aggressive forward in terms of bashing bodies, but Luc is unafraid of the physical game and he will play it; his scoring from the high-density area in front of the net is proof of that. He knows that he earns respect with physical play so he willingly takes and gives his hits. He has good balance on his feet and works well in traffic because of that.

Where he is not aggressive is when he's forced to the boards by the defense. While he has the strength to shrug off the defense while making plays in front, Robitaille doesn't keep his feet moving or his legs pumping along the boards. He's satisfied to say, "Okay, I'm checked. Play's over."

Luc is also bad physically along the boards in his own zone. He doesn't handle the puck well there to make the play from the zone or to freeze the puck, and he'll lose those board battles frequently.

Robitaille also loses his temper with close checking and will take a lot of retaliatory penalties.

THE INTANGIBLES

Robitaille had an extremely slow start last season, scoring just seven goals in his first 20 games. He warmed up as the season progressed (24 goals in 44 games) but clearly came on in his last 36 games by scoring 29 goals. Consistency as the season wears on is important, and that speaks well for Luc's efforts.

The third year often forms the biggest test for a player who's had first year success. Usually that first year success is tempered by a good but not great second season, making the third season a signpost for the player's career. But Robitaille thwarted that theory by having a better second year than he did a first.

What this superstar must do now is continue working on the fine-tuning his game needs: better skating quickness and improved phsyical play defensively.

He is an extremely hard worker with tons of desire and dedication. We think he'll do the things necessary for his improvement as a player, even if it means he doesn't score 50 goals and 100 points (a letdown, by the way, wouldn't be surprising because of the League's familiarity with him).

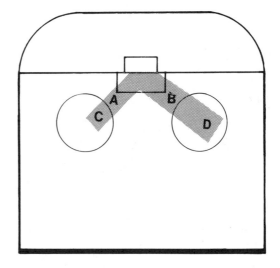

PHIL SYKES

Yrs. of NHL service: 4
Born: Dawson Creek, B.C., Canada; May 18, 1959
Position: Left wing
Height: 6-0
Weight: 175
Uniform no.: 7
Shoots: left

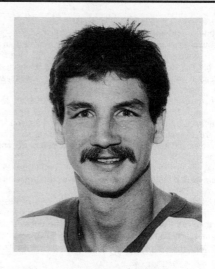

Career statistics:

GP	G	A	TP	PIM
263	54	66	120	354

1987-88 statistics:

GP	G	A	TP	+/−	PIM	PP	SH	GW	GT	S	PCT
40	9	12	21	5	82	3	1	0	0	61	14.8

LAST SEASON

Games played total was a full season career low (he missed 11 games with a groin injury).

THE FINESSE GAME

Though known more for his determination and persistence, Sykes has some skills that can be brought to bear in his game. Two stand out: his great skating skill and speed, and his excellent read of the defensive play.

Those two assets combine to make him a super penalty killer and an excellent checker. Toss in his desire and it's easy to see how he can succeed in the NHL.

He has great hands for handling and shooting the puck, but he just can't cash in on the chances that his skating provides him. Phil will have to be close to the net to score, but Sykes' anticipation and sense serve him well here by getting him into scoring position. Considering his defensive contributions, any scoring he does is a bonus.

Defensively he is very good, playing his position well and sticking with his man through all three zones. His vision and anticipation combine with his skating to allow him to pressure the puck carrier and score the short-handed goal.

THE PHYSICAL GAME

His size works against him in his checking role, but that doesn't stop Sykes from challenging bigger players. Sykes will muck along the boards and is fairly successful there, taking his hits to make his plays and delivering some as well. He is good at protecting the puck with his body and is also good at playing it with his feet.

THE INTANGIBLES

Sykes is a great competitor, a heart and soul player who will do anything to win. That's how he survives in the NHL. He's willing to pay any price for the team and that attitude meshes with his skills to make him an excellent role player.

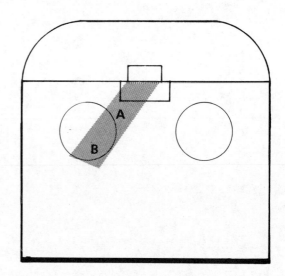

DAVE TAYLOR

Yrs. of NHL service: 10
Born: Levack, Ontario, Canada; December 4, 1955
Position: Right wing
Height: 6-0
Weight: 190
Uniform no.: 18
Shoots: right

Career statistics:

GP	G	A	TP	PIM
752	347	514	861	1,125

1987-88 statistics:

GP	G	A	TP	+/−	PIM	PP	SH	GW	GT	S	PCT
68	26	41	67	-4	129	9	0	2	1	149	17.4

LAST SEASON

Taylor missed 10 games with a groin injury; he has never played a full NHL season. He finished fourth in team scoring and power play goals and fifth in PIM total (first among forwards).

THE FINESSE GAME

Taylor is a case of the whole being greater than the parts. In a way, he is an excellent skater, very strong on his skates and very difficult to knock down because of his balance. For a player with his size and strength, Taylor has decent speed and agility. He can change direction quickly and that's what makes him so effective in traffic. He also uses his skating to be an excellent forechecker, and he uses his strength to drive to the net.

Taylor fights off checks tremendously and still maintains his concentration for playmaking. Because he can make a top play coming out of the corner, Taylor might be the best corner and boards guy in the NHL. His great hands and anticipation help him slip a pass through a maze of players, or lead a teammate to an opening.

He doesn't have a great shot and never has. All of his goals are hard earned and he's a top power play specialist in front of the net, very opportunistic and quick to pounce on any loose pucks.

He positions himself well defensively and is a smart defensive player, but Dave often sacrifices himself so much along the offensive boards that he can't be used defensively.

THE PHYSICAL GAME

Taylor is a very strong physical player. He can drag people all over the ice to make a play, and he has great toughness and ability to withstand checks. He hits hard and initiates contact along the boards whenever possible. He is not intimidated and will hit anyone in the league, regardless of size or reputation.

THE INTANGIBLES

Health is always a question mark with Taylor, but at least his injuries are a direct result of his style of play; that makes his absences more palatable. He has often been called an overachiever, but he deserves to be called one helluva hockey player.

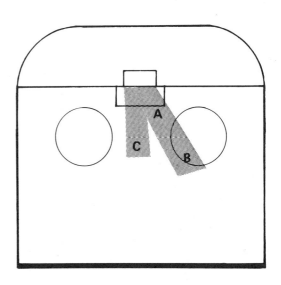

JAY WELLS

Yrs. of NHL service: 9
Born: Paris, Ontario, Canada; May 18, 1959
Position: Defenseman
Height: 6-1
Weight: 210
Uniform no.: 24
Shoots: left

Career statistics:

GP	G	A	TP	PIM
604	34	143	177	1,446

1987-88 statistics:

GP	G	A	TP	+/−	PIM	PP	SH	GW	GT	S	PCT
58	2	23	25	-3	159	1	0	0	0	76	2.6

LAST SEASON

Games played total was lowest since rookie year (he missed 18 games with a groin injury). Point total was lowest in three seasons but was still third highest of career. PIM total was team's third highest.

THE FINESSE GAME

Jay is another of those player for whom simple play is not only better, it's best. He grades out to average in all of his finesse abilities but Wells isn't a bad skater. He can contribute some speed and has some agility, and he can combine that agility with a degree of puckhandling talent so as to play more than just a defensive game.

But Wells runs into problems when he believes his skills to be better than they are. When he gets the puck it should be moved off his stick, preferably up the boards. Jay has a tendency — because he is a capable puckhandler — to force himself into situations where the puck gets pokechecked or stickchecked away while he was trying a one-on-one deke at his own blue line. More often than not the result of that poor play is a cheap goal against.

Wells reads the rush toward him well and is very difficult to beat one-on-one because of both his size and his positional play. He will follow the rush up-ice but doesn't jump into the play often, preferring to throw the puck around at the point to pinching into the zone. Once the puck is turned over, Wells is the first man back.

THE PHYSICAL GAME

Wells is unquestionably the Kings' strongest on-ice player. He is very tough and very underrated in his toughness because he hasn't had to show it off for several seasons.

He is one of the best in the league at clearing the opposition from the front of the net. And Wells doesn't care who's planted there, he'll take them on. He hits often and hard and is an excellent — and punishing — body checker. Wells will jar the puck loose with his hits and he's mean enough to add a little something extra if he can.

Wells will also sacrifice his body to block some shots and he can, by the way, throw 'em pretty good too.

THE INTANGIBLES

He is the defenseman other teams always ask for in trade talks. His reputation has brought him that extra yard of room so he can function, but he's not always consistent in his output. Wells has to be constantly reminded to keep the play simple, to move the puck quickly and to take the body consistently.

When he does those things he's a force defensively. When he doesn't do them he's a very average defenseman.

He enters this season in an interesting contract scenario. Wells will either be playing out his option or playing on the first year of a new pact. Either way, his play merits watching to see how he'll be affected.

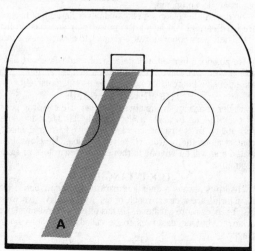

MINNESOTA NORTH STARS

LINE COMBINATIONS
SCOTT BJUGSTAD-NEAL BROTEN-BRIAN
BELLOWS
BRIAN MACLELLAN-DAVE GAGNER-DINO
CICCARELLI
BASIL MCRAE-BOB BROOKE-BRIAN LAWTON

DEFENSE PAIRINGS
CURT GILES-BOB ROUSE
FRANTISEK MUSIL-GORD DINEEN

GOALTENDERS
DON BEAUPRE
KARI TAKKO

OTHER PLAYERS
DAVID ARCHIBALD — Center
CURT FRASER — Left wing
MARC HABSCHEID — Center
MARK HARDY — Defenseman
CRAIG HARTSBURG — Defenseman
MOE MANTHA — Defenseman
DENNIS MARUK — Center
TERRY RUSKOWSKI —Left wing

POWER PLAY

FIRST UNIT:
BRIAN MACLELLAN-BRIAN BELLOWS-DINO
CICCARELLI
CURT GILES-MOE MANTHA

CICCARELLI darts in and out from the right faceoff circle, BELLOWS controls play behind the goal and MACLELLAN plugs the net. Puck works around the perimeter to loosen the defense for a CICCARELLI shot as he cuts to the net. Point shots are the second option with the forwards crashing the net.

When not injured, HARTSBURG and BROTEN are guaranteed power play performers.

Last season the Minnesota power play was FAIR, scoring 81 goals in 450 attempts (18 percent, 15th overall).

PENALTY KILLING

FIRST UNIT:
BRIAN LAWTON-BRIAN BELLOWS
GORD DINEEN-FRANTISEK MUSIL

The North Stars play a very scrambly box defense, and the results show. Again, barring injury, BROTEN and HARTSBURG are regulars here.

Last season Minnesota's penalty killing was POOR, allowing 108 goals in 436 shorthanded situations (75.2 percent, 21st overall).

CRUCIAL FACEOFFS

BROOKE will see most of these.

DAVID ARCHIBALD

Yrs. of NHL service: 1
Born: Vancouver, B.C., Canada; April 14, 1969
Position: Center
Height: 6-1
Weight: 193
Uniform no.: 37
Shoots: left

Career statisics:

GP	G	A	TP	+/–	PIM	PP	SH	GW	GT	S	PCT
78	13	20	33	-17	26	3	0	2	0	96	13.5

LAST SEASON

Archibald's first in the NHL. He was Minnesota's first round pick in the 1987 Entry Draft. He was third on the team in games played, second among forwards.

THE FINESSE GAME

Archibald is a finesse player with a great deal of potential. He skates very well, using his excellent balance and agility to be successful in traffic situations. He doesn't have great speed or quickness (though his long stride helps him out-distance the opposition), but he varies the pace of the speed he does own.

Dave has good hands and he passes the puck well, but what he does best is carry it through the neutral zone. A lot of players can't do that successfully (all of the best ones do — Gretzky, Messier, Richer and Smith, for example) and that skill reflects Archibald's desire. He wants the puck and he wants to make plays with it.

His anticipation and hockey sense are good and will get better. He finds openings and exploits them with his passing, but he also exploits them with his 1-on-1 skills (again, especially in the neutral zone). He controls the puck very well when carrying it, but he's smart enough to give it up to a teammate in better position.

He shows a good selection of shooting skills for the NHL level, but his shot will need to improve in terms of release in order for Dave to consistently beat NHL goaltending.

As his skills develop he'll become a regular on both specialty team units (and he's already seen power play time). He's also shown attentiveness to his defensive game that is masked by his poor plus/minus rating.

THE PHYSICAL GAME

Archibald has fair size and plenty of time to develop strength. He's not known as a physical player in terms of initiation, but he will go to the traffic areas and will take hits to make his plays. His balance helps him here, as it allows him to maintain his body positioning and thus maintain control of the puck.

THE INTANGIBLES

He's played with older players from the time he was 14 years old, when he played major junior hockey. Dave feels that the game has gotten bigger and he recognizes that he needs to as well, so he's working on that part of his game. He has good work habits and desire to succeed.

The biggest thing for his development now is stability in the organization. He needs a coach — and not a rotating set of coaches — to teach him and work with him. Only in that way can Archibald reach his high potential.

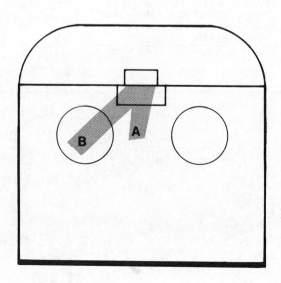

DON BEAUPRE

Yrs. of NHL service: 7
Born: Kitchener, Ontario, Canada; September 19, 1961
Position: Goaltender
Height: 5-8
Weight: 155
Uniform no.: 33
Catches: left

Career statistics:

GP	MINS	G	SO	AVG	A	PIM
315	17,774	1,108	3	3.74	3	128

1987-88 statisics:

GP	MINS	AVG	W	L	T	SO	GA	SA	SAPCT	PIM
43	2,288	4.44	10	22	3	0	161	1,257	.872	8

LAST SEASON

Games played total was third highest of career and lowest total in three seasons. He missed nine games with a groin injury. Goals-against-average was a career high. Beaupre didn't record a shutout for the first time in three seasons.

THE PHYSICAL GAME

The hallmarks of Beaupre's game are his hand and foot speed and his tremendous balance. He plays his angles fairly well, but lives and dies by his reflexes.

His exceptional balance makes him a fine skater and allows him to move in and out of the net very well. His balance comes to the forefront of his game by allowing him to regain his stance (or get back on his feet after flopping) very quickly after a save, and then get into position to stop the next shot.

Don's hands are also very quick. He has an excellent glove hand and is also strong high on his stick side, an area many goaltenders find hardest to defend. He is so successful with his hands and feet because he sees the puck well and is able to track its flight toward the goal.

He would profit by playing a better angle game and would reduce at least one area of weakness — low stick side on the short side — by doing so.

Beaupre is aggressive in his crease, becoming physically involved in keeping it clear, whether that means pushing or slashing an opposing player.

THE MENTAL GAME

Beaupre is going to give up that one bad goal per game. That's just the way he is. True, it's difficult for a goalie to be consistent when the team in front of him is anything but, but Don has a great deal of difficulty maintaining his concentration within a game and from contest to contest. He's very streaky; he can get hot but he won't stay hot and will in fact go through many cold outings.

Don does not get over bad goals or games, and he stays rattled for a period of time after the event; he'll give up goals in bunches. Those performances prompt criticism of his work and that just makes the problem worse, because Beaupre is very sensitive to criticism and is unnerved by it.

He needs a pat on the back and not a kick in the ass in order to succeed.

THE INTANGIBLES

He's a good guy and well liked by his teammates but consistency is going to remain Beaupre's problem. If he's lucky the new North Stars management will make some concessions to his sensitivity, and that could lead to Beaupre consistently harnessing the flashes of high-level talent that occasionally show up in his performances.

BRIAN BELLOWS

Yrs. of NHL service: 6
Born: St. Catharines, Ontario, Canada; September 1, 1964
Position: Right wing
Height: 6-0
Weight: 195
Uniform no.: 23
Shoots: right

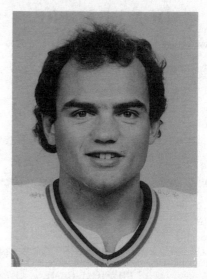

Career statistics:

GP	G	A	TP	PIM
453	199	224	423	326

1987-88 statistics:

GP	G	A	TP	+/-	PIM	PP	SH	GW	GT	S	PCT
77	40	41	81	-8	81	21	1	4	0	283	14.1

LAST SEASON

All point totals were second highest of his career and highest in four seasons. His PIM total was a career high. He finished second on the club in scoring, but led the Stars in power play goals and shots on goal, and was tied for the team lead in game winners (Brian MacLellan). His plus/minus mark was second best among full time forwards. He missed three games with a rib injury.

THE FINESSE GAME

Bellows combines tremendous scoring ability with excellent physical ability as one of the NHL's best — if unsung — power forwards. His skating ability is the weakest of his finesse skills in terms of fanciness — the exceptional quickness and agility of a Savard, for example — but his stride is very strong and his balance is exceptional.

That strength and balance makes him almost unbeatable along the boards, his stride driving him through checks and his balance keeping him upright to continue making plays. He doesn't have a lot of agility or rink-length speed but his strong stride gets him where he's going.

Bellows has very good hand skills and makes good plays out of the corner, making accurate passes through a maze of legs or leading a teammate into the clear. He is not, however, an exceptional puck carrier because of his straight ahead style and lack of agility. His excellent hockey sense and vision help him in his playmaking.

His touch around the net is very good. Brian can get a shot off quickly from the traffic areas in front of the net, and he also has the wrist and hand strength to power the puck past the goaltender from slightly farther out. He shoots a lot and will chase the rebounds.

Bellows is conscientious defensively, playing his position well at both ends of the rink.

THE PHYSICAL GAME

Brian is a very strong player in both open ice and along the boards. His leg strength has already been discussed, and is the main component of his physical success, but he is also very strong in the upper body. That strength helps him out-muscle the opposition along the boards and get his shot off in traffic.

Bellows is a mucker and a grinder and likes to initiate the hitting. He is, however, not a heavyweight and you won't find him in any battles with the Proberts and the Neelys. And interestingly, unlike other power forwards his size — like Gerard Gallant or Rick Tocchet — fighting is not a part of Bellows' game.

THE INTANGIBLES

The media out of the midwest is one reason why more people don't know how good a player Bellows is. He's tougher than Gallant and a better scorer than Tocchet, yet is virtually unmentioned when discussion rages about the League's best power forwards.

As with other North Star players Bellows struggled with the burden of leadership that was thrust upon him prematurely. But he's matured as a player, playing in pain now for example, and is a valuable member of the North Stars.

However, he was unhappy with the Stars' situation last season and even talked of signing with another club (he was a free agent with compensation but re-signed with Minnesota) or playing in Europe. Bellows freely admitted that former Stars coach Herb Brooks was the best coach he ever had, and now Brooks is gone and Bellows will have to start anew with another coach.

His goal distribution needs correction. Bellows had 29 of his 40 goals by his 43rd game of the year. That means he scored just 11 goals in his final 34 games — and just eight of those came at even strength.

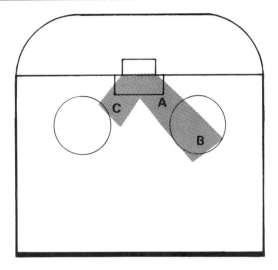

SCOTT BJUGSTAD

Yrs. of NHL service: 4
Born: St. Paul, Minn., USA; June 2, 1981
Position: Left wing/center
Height: 6-1
Weight: 185
Uniform no.: 14
Shoots: left

Career statistics:

GP	G	A	TP	PIM
229	68	58	126	116

1987-88 statistics:

GP	G	A	TP	+/−	PIM	PP	SH	GW	GT	S	PCT
33	10	12	22	2	15	3	0	3	1	72	13.9

LAST SEASON

Games played total was a full season career low for Bjugstad, who missed four games with a shoulder injury and 20 games with a knee injury before subsequent knee surgery sidelined him for the season. Point totals were the second best of his career.

THE FINESSE GAME

Other than his shot, which is a superior finesse skill, Bjugstad has little to offer in the finesse game. He has a tremendous shot: hard, accurate and frequent. Scott shoots often and makes the most of his opportunities, forcing the goaltenders to make saves instead of firing wide of the net. Good hands and wrists power that shot and make it fairly difficult to handle. It does take him some time to get it off, and one reason why he's not as successful as his shot might indicate is because he doesn't skate well enough to get that time.

Bjugstad has a small degree of speed up and down his wing but he's neither quick nor agile and those flaws result in two further problems. Scott cannot get to the openings when they are presented — and thus cannot use his shot — nor can he keep up with his check defensively. Consequently, he is often out of the play at both ends of the ice.

Scott could compensate for his less than exceptional skating skill if he had better anticipation and hockey sense, but he doesn't have the mental capability that would put him in position to score.

The quality of Scott's shot is an offshoot of his hand skill. He can pass the puck but needs time and space, but he's a scorer by nature and will look to the net before he looks to his teammates.

THE PHYSICAL GAME

Bjugstad is very strong and can play a terrific board game, but he doesn't always apply himself and his goal scoring is why. He wants to make that fancy play off the boards for the shot so his mucking and grinding goes — if you'll forgive the pun — by the boards.

He tries to do the fancy stuff of reaching into the pile-up from the outside when he should be freeing the puck from the inside. His strength will help him in retrieving pucks from goalmouth scrambles, and it is also his strength that powers his shot.

THE INTANGIBLES

The saying is that those who ignore history are condemned to repeat it — and boy would Bjugstad like to subscribe to that theory. But the problem is, both he and North Stars management remember that 43-goal season, and now both parties want Scott to repeat that success.

Ignorance really would be bliss in this case because Bjugstad has no confidence in his abilities right now; the mental part of the game — that confidence — is what Herb Brooks worked on with Scott last season.

But those 43 goals were a freak of nature. Bjugstad is a 25-goal scorer at the NHL level, and that's only if he can stay healthy. And his health — not whether he can repeat that single-season goal scoring success — is the primary question regarding Bjugstad right now.

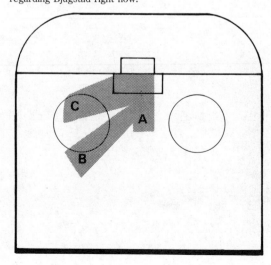

BOB BROOKE

Yrs. of NHL service: 4
Born: Melrose, Mass., USA; December 18, 1960
Position: Center/right wing
Height: 6-2
Weight: 205
Uniform no.: 13
Shoots: right

Career statistics:

GP	G	A	TP	PIM
317	50	74	124	400

1987-88 statistics:

GP	G	A	TP	+/−	PIM	PP	SH	GW	GT	S	PCT
77	5	20	25	-6	108	1	1	1	0	127	3.9

LAST SEASON

Games played total was lowest in three seasons, goal total was a full season career low. His plus/minus rating was the best among Star forwards who played at least 50 games. He missed two games with a back injury.

THE FINESSE GAME

Brooke's physical finesse skills are excellent — from the hips down. He's an excellent skater with strength, speed, and balance. His long, strong stride powers his acceleration and speed and helps Bob play the game at very high speeds. He doesn't have quickness or agility to match his speed, and his style is to rocket tirelessly down the ice. He makes his skating even more effective by always keeping his feet in motion, so he's ready to change with the flow of the puck.

Bob has excellent vision and hockey sense, reading the offensive and defensive plays well because he has intelligence and good hockey sense. His checking and anticipation will give him many scoring opportunities — and here comes the but — but they will fall by the wayside because Brooke has terrible hands.

His hands betray him when giving or accepting passes, and when he is carrying the puck. Skating and anticipation skills get Brooke into position to score, but his cement hands can't fire the puck fast enough. He will net his goals from being opportunistic around the net.

His defensive play is excellent, regardless of his plus/minus rating. Brooke is always aware of his check and plays his position deep into the defensive zone.

THE PHYSICAL GAME

Brooke has excellent size and strength and he uses both to his advantage at all times. He is aggressive and hits well at both ends of the ice, and those hits will dislodge people from the puck. He works the boards and corners and is strong enough to come away with the puck. The balance that marks Brooke's skating serves him well in his physical game, as he is able to remain upright after collisions.

He has excellent eye/hand coordination, so he'll get loose pucks and win faceoffs. He is a fantastically conditioned athlete and that conditioning makes itself evident in his seemingly effortless skating shift after shift.

THE INTANGIBLES

Brooke is a very honest player, a worker with a great team attitude. His versatility is such that he can play anywhere, but that doesn't mean he's going to play well everywhere. Bob's like one of those neighborhood fixit men, the kind that can change the oil in your car, paint your kitchen and fix the television — but won't be the best mechanic, painter or repairman.

But that versatility is valuable and teams need that kind of player. He's not a star, but if he ever got a chance to play a strictly defensive role — to be able to use his strength against other centers — then he might become a defensive star.

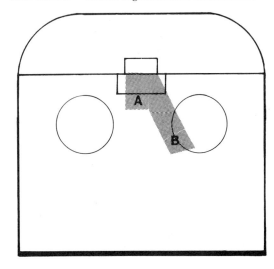

NEAL BROTEN

Yrs. of NHL service: 7
Born: Roseau, Minn., USA; November 29, 1959
Position: Center
Height: 5-9
Weight: 170
Uniform no.: 7
Shoots: left

Career statistics:

GP	G	A	TP	PIM
491	175	344	519	270

1987-88 statistics:

GP	G	A	TP	+/−	PIM	PP	SH	GW	GT	S	PCT
54	9	30	39	-23	32	4	1	0	1	121	7.4

LAST SEASON

Games played total was the second lowest full season total of his career, with all point totals career lows. Recurring shoulder problems and the resulting surgery sidelined him for the season in February. He still finished as Minnesota's fifth best scorer and had the Stars fourth best assist total.

THE FINESSE GAME

You name it in the finesse game, Broten can do it. Playmaking is primary among Neal's superior finesse skills, and he uses excellent mental skills (vision, anticipation and hockey sense) in combination with superb physical skills (passing, skating and puckhandling) to make those plays. He sees the ice very well and his anticipation tells him where the openings will be and where his teammates will be, thus laying the groundwork for his hand skills.

Broten can lead his teammates to the openings with soft passes, but he can also get the puck through traffic to an open teammate. He creates openings by carrying the puck very well; because the defense has to respect his puckhandling and his skating they back up to their own goal and create those openings. Those openings are the ones Neal fills with passes for his teammates.

Broten's foot skills are just as advanced as his hand skills, so each makes the other better. He is an excellent skater, very shifty on the ice and very quick, using his agility and speed to get him into the open. Broten has excellent acceleration and lateral movement, and all he needs to put his skills to work is one step.

His skills combine to make him a natural specialty teams player, and the Stars will sometimes take advantage of his playmaking skill by putting him on the point during the power play. He is also a good faceoff man because of his eye/hand coordination.

His shot doesn't match the capabilities of his passes, but Broten's sense and anticipation supply him with more than enough ability to score from around the net, sometimes further out on the power play. He should shoot more and be more selfish with the puck, but Neal takes greater pleasure in making plays than he does in scoring.

He is good without the puck defensively as well, and he makes the transition from offense to defense quickly and efficiently. He is a conscientious defensive player.

THE PHYSICAL GAME

What Broten doesn't have is strength, but his game doesn't need strength or physical play. He can take the puck away from anyone along the boards by virtue of his stick skills and — though he'll take whatever pounding the opposition is giving out — Broten is difficult to hit because of his skating skills.

There is a negative to his willingness to take that abuse. By season's end, after seven months of absorbing hits — often twice as many as his teammates because he double shifts so frequently — Broten is severely worn down. Thus his effectiveness is lessened.

THE INTANGIBLES

Every team, except perhaps the Flames, Oilers and Canadiens, has just one or two players who control that team's destiny. If those one or two players are injured or otherwise lost for the season, that team's season is down the tubes.

Neal Broten and Craig Hartsburg are those players for Minnesota. Both went down for the count last season, and so did the Stars. His health is obviously the biggest intangible regarding Broten's season and career. Neal is a player much like Detroit's Steve Yzerman — though less aggressive physically — but Minnesota isn't good enough as a team to succeed with Broten out the way Detroit succeeded when Yzerman went down with a knee injury.

Broten's the best center the North Stars have ever had, and they need him for any possible future success.

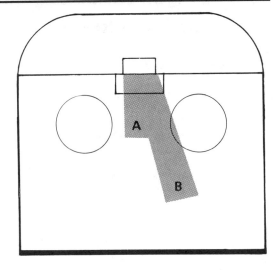

DINO CICCARELLI

Yrs. of NHL service: 8
Born: Sarnia, Ontario, Canada; February 8, 1960
Position: Right wing
Height: 5-10
Weight: 180
Uniform no.: 20
Shoots: right

Career statistics:

GP	G	A	TP	PIM
537	300	292	592	584

1987-88 statistics:

GP	G	A	TP	+/−	PIM	PP	SH	GW	GT	S	PCT
67	41	45	86	-29	79	13	1	2	0	262	15.6

LAST SEASON

Games played was the second lowest full season mark in his career. Goal total was lowest in three seasons but he led the club in points, goals, assists and shooting percentage. He was second in power play goals and shots on goal. His plus/minus total was the team's fourth worst, second worst among forwards.

THE FINESSE GAME

Ciccarelli was created to score goals, and his skating, anticipation and shot are how he does just that.

He's an excellent skater with terrific speed and agility, excellent balance and lateral movement. These skills get him into the open to use his shot, or they allow him to operate in traffic — which is key, because Dino certainly goes where the going gets tough. His balance keeps him in possession of the puck and allows him to get his shot away from all body angles and while being punished by the opposition.

His quickness and agility let him snare those loose pucks around the net and his speed carries him past the defense for a shot on goal. Dino makes his skating more effective by taking dives, getting calls that later serve to intimidate the opposition into not touching him — for fear of another penalty.

He has a goal scorer's anticipation, reading the ice and finding the openings; he's excellent at stepping in front of a defender to cut it off along the boards. Ciccarelli takes the pass very well once in the clear and delivers the puck to the net with a quick, hard wrist shot. He also has an excellent slap shot that will blow by goaltenders. He shoots often and well, and he can put the puck anywhere he wants. He has very good hands and can pass the puck, but Ciccarelli is a scorer first and a passer second.

The power play was made for Dino because he takes full advantage of the added ice. With his one-step quickness, Dino is very difficult to contain, getting to that crossing puck and one-timing it home. He works especially well from the left side.

His defensive game, oft-maligned by critics, has improved steadily over the course of his career so that Dino is no longer a liability when he is on the ice. He plays his position well and doesn't wander in the defensive zone.

THE PHYSICAL GAME

Ciccarelli is successful because he goes to the areas where he knows he's going to get beat up. And then he scores. He has great physical courage in that regard and in that respect is very similar to Calgary's Joe Mullen. This is where his balance serves him best.

Dino definitely initiates contact and likes to dish out the bodywork that creates more space for him in which to work. He has good strength and can apply it along the boards to muscle the opposition off the puck, but he is most effective in the open ice.

THE INTANGIBLES

Several questions, which are related in a way. First, at 180 pounds and playing in No-Man's Land each night, how much more abuse can Ciccarelli take? There are some fighters on the North Stars, but no one who's going to freeze the opposition with fear and keep the enemy from assaulting Ciccarelli.

That's where Link Gaetz comes. Link as in "Missing Link," in a number of ways. Selected by Minnesota in June's Entry Draft, Gaetz was the toughest player available in last year's draft and he'll be along in Minneapolis before long to administer some fistic justice.

The subject of the abuse Ciccarelli's taken is also related to Gaetz, because last year Dino took the law into his own hands versus Toronto's Luke Richardson and was suspended for it. Dino'd just had all he could stand of the hacking and slashing he's had to put up with.

That emotional outburst was just one of several odd incidents in which Ciccarelli was involved last year. It seems obvious that Ciccarelli is bothered by something, and clearing that something up will be high on new general manager Jack Ferreira's list of priorities.

And all of this is related because you can't last in the NHL if you're not thinking right. And Dino Ciccarelli clearly wasn't thinking right in 1987-88.

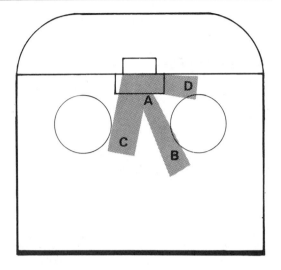

GORD DINEEN

Yrs. of NHL service: 5
Born: Toronto, Ontario, Canada; September 21, 1962
Position: Defenseman
Height: 5-11
Weight: 180
Uniform no.: 28
Shoots: right

Career statistics:

GP	G	A	TP	PIM
291	12	54	66	399

1987-88 statistics:

GP	G	A	TP	+/−	PIM	PP	SH	GW	GT	S	PCT
70	5	13	18	4	83	1	0	0	0	56	8.9

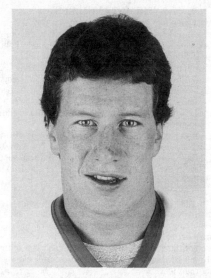

LAST SEASON

Dineen was acquired late in the season from the Islanders in exchange for Chris Pryor. Games played total was second highest of his career, with all point totals career highs. He led the team in plus/minus.

THE FINESSE GAME

Dineen has finally developed his skating to the NHL level, but it is still the weakest of his skills. He moves forward and backward as well as a defenseman should be expected to, and he turns well, but he lacks acceleration. His improved skating allows him to forecheck and backcheck well, and he pinches in at the blue line with increasing frequency.

Dineen has a good shot from the right point — low and hard for deflections and tip-ins — but he must improve his release in terms of quickness. Gordie must also pick up his head when he shoots, as he often has his shot blocked by an unseen (by him) defender. He must shoot more frequently.

He has good hands and his passing is above average. His pass is accurate because of good ice vision, and Gordie can take advantage of his teammates that way. He handles the puck pretty well in his own end but has difficulty carrying it through traffic. Because he does have some modest talent with the puck, he will sometimes be used as a second unit defenseman on the power play.

THE PHYSICAL GAME

Dineen takes people off the puck with fairly good consistency, and he completes his checks along the boards to eliminate the opposition from the play.

Gord has good strength and makes good use of it in front of the net, where he is also mean.

THE INTANGIBLES

Confidence remains the biggest factor in Dineen's play. He plays with a lot of fire and with tremendous intensity, but he wants to play so badly that sometimes that hurts him, because he tries to do too much and gets into trouble.

All his finesse skills are based on his having good confidence, for when he doesn't he makes bad decisions and mistakes. His ice time tripled when he got to Minnesota and he played good hockey because of his confidence and the feeling he had of contributing.

He has a great work ethic and plays in pain, and his attitude will be good for the club. Gord is driven by the knowledge that he has to work in each practice and every game to be successful at the NHL level.

Given all of that, there's still a good chance he won't be protected in the waiver draft.

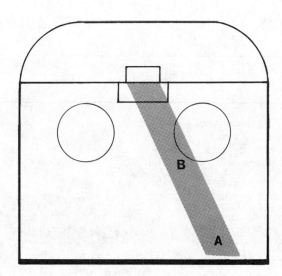

CURT FRASER

Yrs. of NHL service: 11
Born: Cincinnati, Ohio, USA; January 12, 1958
Position: Left wing
Height: 6-0
Weight: 190
Uniform no.: 18
Shoots: left

Career statistics:

GP	G	A	TP	PIM
661	187	235	422	1,208

1987-88 statistics:

GP	G	A	TP	+/−	PIM	PP	SH	GW	GT	S	PCT
37	5	7	12	-20	77	1	0	1	0	72	6.9

LAST SEASON

Games played total was second lowest of his career and lowest in four seasons. Point total was a career low and goal total matched career low. He was acquired from Chicago in exchange for Dirk Graham. A mononucleosis-like disease suffered in January sidelined him for the season.

THE FINESSE GAME

Balance is the key to Fraser's skating game — and thus his entire game. His great balance (and no small level of agility) allows Fraser to play the hitting game he relishes.

Fraser drives to the spots he has to be in to make the plays. He is also excellent in traffic because of superior upper body strength and he will drive to the net for the puck.

Fraser loves to work the corners and does so with success because of the good balance he has on his skates. His defensive coverages are good and his shot is a little above average because he gets it away quickly. He scores through hard work and determination, not artistry.

THE PHYSICAL GAME

Regardless of who he skates with, Fraser's incessant physical play opens up the ice.

The good balance Curt has on his skates serves him well in the corners and along the boards, and so does the willingness to hit or be hit in order to make a play. He uses his body at both ends of the rink and will plow into anything and throw his body at everything.

Fraser's strength and persistent hitting makes his checking especially telling on opposing forwards.

THE INTANGIBLES

This report has remained virtually unchanged, given the unsure status of Fraser's health. There can be no question of his tremendous skill level and determination (or of his teammates' respect for him), just as there can be no question that his health is the biggest thing standing in the way of his continuing his NHL career. Whether he ever returns to the NHL on a consistent basis because of his proclivity toward injury is questionable.

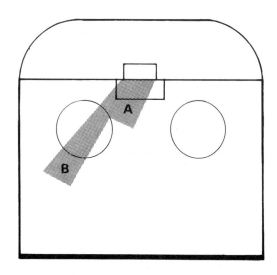

DAVE GAGNER

Yrs. of NHL service: 2
Born: Chatham, Ontario, Canada; December 11, 1964
Position: Center
Height: 5-10
Weight: 180
Uniform no.: 15
Shoots: left

Career statistics:

GP	G	A	TP	PIM
131	19	27	46	102

1987-88 statistics:

GP	G	A	TP	+/-	PIM	PP	SH	GW	GT	S	PCT
51	8	11	19	-14	55	0	2	0	0	87	9.2

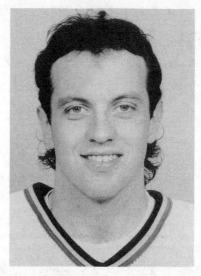

LAST SEASON

Gagner was acquired from the Rangers during the preseason. Games played, all point totals and PIM mark were all career highs. He tied for the team lead in shorthanded goals.

THE FINESSE GAME

Gagner is on the smallish side and quick with the puck. Dave doesn't have long-haul but does have one-step, darting quickness. He can move the puck pretty well and has good passing ability and vision.

He complements those physical skills with his mental ones. He's smart and that's one reason he succeeds as a checker and penalty killer, because he understands the play and anticipates it well.

Dave will have to be an opportunistic scorer at the NHL level, scooping up loose pucks that his quickness gets him to. His shot isn't bad, but it's not going to consistently beat NHL goaltending.

THE PHYSICAL GAME

Gagner is an aggressive player but he doesn't have good size. That hurts him because he plays big. With NHL players getting huger and huger, Dave's size mitigates against him because he'll get overpowered through no fault of his own.

And since he plays in the traffic areas, Gagner just keeps putting himself in the middle of all those redwoods. But he is willing to hit and does so at every opportunity, and he'll muscle against anyone.

THE INTANGIBLES

Was it Captain Ahab in *Moby Dick* who explained obsession by saying, "That which I will, I do. That which I do, I become"? That statement would perfectly describe Dave Gagner.

There may not be a harder worker in the NHL. He just never stops trying his butt off. If wishing could make it so, Gagner would be an NHL regular. He took a big step toward that last season under Herb Brooks, performing simple defensive functions for the North Stars but taking a regular turn.

He can contribute to a club through his attitude and his on-ice smarts, as long as the management doesn't over-project his on-ice results. Working against him is Minnesota's depth at center: a healthy Neal Broten and young Dave Archibald make Gagner third-line to begin with, and we haven't factored

in 1988 first pick Mike Modano, nor the possible return of Dennis Maruk, nor all-around player Bob Brooke.

But we like Gagner's attitude and hope he can play regularly for some NHL club.

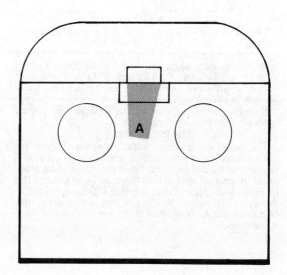

CURT GILES

Yrs. of NHL service: 9
Born: The Pas, Manitoba, Canada; Nov. 30, 1958
Position: Defense
Height: 5-8
Weight: 180
Uniform no.: 2
Shoots: left

Career statistics:

GP	G	A	TP	PIM
614	32	162	194	512

1987-88 statistics:

GP	G	A	TP	+/−	PIM	PP	SH	GW	GT	S	PCT
72	1	12	13	-33	76	0	0	0	0	72	1.4

LAST SEASON

Giles was traded from the Rangers to Minnesota for future considerations early in the season. Point total was a career low.

THE FINESSE GAME

Giles is equipped with more and better finesse skills than he gives himself credit for. He's a good skater, both forward and back, and his turns are strong both to the inside and the outside. He's got good vision on the ice and can rush the puck.

Curt will read the rush coming at him well, and he will turn the puck up to his forwards quickly. He'll join the play up-ice and will move into the offensive zone, but Giles is too quick to abandon his point position and fall back to defense.

Defensively, he plays his angles well and is not often beaten one-on-one. Because of his positional play, he's very good at breaking up two-on-ones and three-on-twos.

He has an average slap shot from the point and should shoot more, and he can see the play from the point and get the puck to his teammates. Because of that, he'll get some power play time.

THE PHYSICAL GAME

Giles is an excellent body checker and he plays with no fear. He hits as if he were a foot taller and 50 pounds heavier, and he'll hit anyone. He plays the body very well along the boards, and isn't prone to penalties in doing so.

He has the strength to muscle the opposition off the puck, and the skills to make a play afterward. Giles will sacrifice his body to block shots, and his willingness to play a physical game that belies his size is one reason why he has never played a complete season.

THE INTANGIBLES

Don't take this the wrong way, but if you have to use Giles a lot during the season, particularly on penalty killing, it's going to hurt you. He may be willing to tackle any individual, but his physical stature is a negative against the League's increasingly large forwards.

Curt is a very smart player and gets away with all the hooking and holding he has to use as an equalizer. He's a great person in the lockerroom, on the bus and on the ice and his upbeat personality is infectious. He is a true professional in every sense of the word.

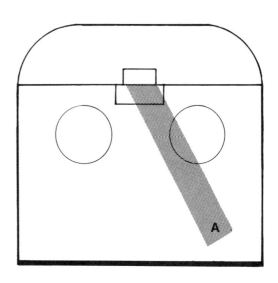

MARC HABSCHEID

Yrs. of NHL service: 3
Born: Swift Current, Sask., Canada; March 1, 1963
Position: Center
Height: 5-10
Weight: 170
Uniform no.: 10
Shoots: right

Career statistics:

GP	G	A	TP	PIM
111	18	30	48	34

1987-88 statistics:

GP	G	A	TP	+/−	PIM	PP	SH	GW	GT	S	PCT
16	4	11	15	-4	6	3	0	0	0	44	9.1

LAST SEASON

He rejoined the Stars after the Winter Olympic Games. His career game total is spread over parts of three seasons.

THE FINESSE GAME

Speed and quickness are the hallmarks of Habscheid's game. He's an excellent skater and he complements that skating skill with excellent puckhandling abilities.

His anticipation and smarts are such that he can play in all situations and he has improved his previously woeful defensive play (thanks to his work with Dave King and the Canadian Olympic team).

He's an opportunistic player who will get his goals by using his quickness around the opposition net.

THE PHYSICAL GAME

Habscheid fits in perfectly with the rest of Minnesota's munchkin forward crew. He's a good little player but his lack of size might catch up with him over a full season. He gets his nose dirty but is clearly a better finesse player than he is a physical one.

THE INTANGIBLES

Marc joined the North Stars after the Olympics and gave them a real spark, probably good enough to insure that he gets a long look for a roster spot this season. His improved defensive play just might be the factor that keeps him in the NHL after six previous attempts, but his size is going to be a problem.

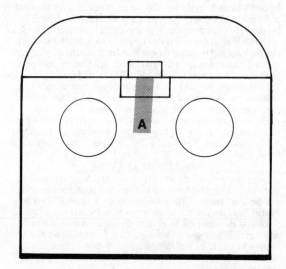

MARK HARDY

Yrs. of NHL service: 8
Born: Semaden, Switzerland; February 1, 1959
Position: Defenseman
Height: 5-11
Weight: 190
Uniform no.: 14
Shoots: left

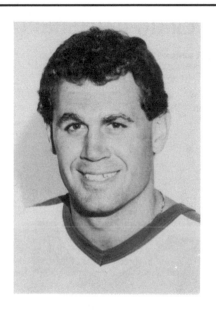

Career statistics:

GP	G	A	TP	PIM
608	55	246	301	858

1987-88 statistics:

GP	G	A	TP	+/−	PIM	PP	SH	GW	GT	S	PCT
80	8	24	32	-32	130	4	1	1	0	134	6.0

LAST SEASON

Traded to the Rangers in February in exchange for Ron Duguay. Was the only Ranger to play all 80 games, and did so for the first time in his career. His 130 PIM ranked third among regulars, and his point total was his highest in three seasons.

THE FINESSE GAME

Hardy is a strong skater, well balanced on his skates and equipped with a good burst of speed up ice. He is fairly agile while carrying the puck and is able to rush the puck from the defensive zone to relieve forechecking pressure.

Hardy sees the ice well and makes good use of his teammates. He makes for a good point man on the power play because of his puckhandling ability, anticipation and shot. He contains the point well and knows when to pinch in and when to fall back. His shot is low and hard from the blue line and is excellent for tip-ins or deflections. Smartly, Hardy shoots often.

Except for the occasional rush he's a fairly conservative defenseman and takes few chances with the puck. He forces the play wide of the net by using his defensive angles, and he is adept at moving the puck quickly from his own end. He is poised with the puck and will generally make the right play.

THE PHYSICAL GAME

Hardy plays a physical game when he can and will dish out checks whenever possible. He has good strength along the boards, but on occasion is guilty of not completely taking the opposing winger out of the play.

He's effective in front of the net, tying up the opposition, but his game is more in hitting and gaining the puck and then starting a play.

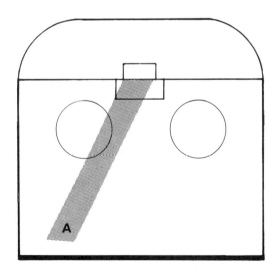

THE INTANGIBLES

The only flaw in Hardy's game is an occasional lapse. Steady though he is, he is also prone to a bad game once every seven or eight when his concentration takes a flyer. But he is a stabilizing force in the defensive zone (especially on the penalty killing unit).

CRAIG HARTSBURG

Yrs. of NHL service: 9
Born: Stratford, Ontario, Canada; June 29, 1959
Position: Defenseman
Height: 6-1
Weight: 195
Uniform no.: 4
Shoots: left

Career statistics:

GP	G	A	TP	PIM
540	94	301	395	770

1987-88 statistics:

GP	G	A	TP	+/−	PIM	PP	SH	GW	GT	S	PCT
27	3	16	19	-2	29	2	0	1	0	83	3.6

LAST SEASON

Games played total was second lowest of his career, lowest in four seasons. Goal total was a career low, assist and point totals were lowest in three seasons. PIM total was a career low. He finished second in scoring among North Star defenders. His season was a mess of injuries: groin injuries, hernia operations, shoulder injuries.

THE FINESSE GAME

Hartsburg is a good skater, extremely mobile and agile. He is one of the few North Star defensemen able to lug the puck out of the zone and up-ice, relieving pressure on the forwards.

He has good speed and agility and carries the puck very well up-ice. Craig has excellent vision and anticipation and is able to get the puck moving quickly to open men. He does have a tendency, however, to start the offensive play too quickly, so he still needs to be paired with a defensive defenseman.

Craig controls the point very well in the offensive zone, shooting low and hard to the net — a shot that allows for rebounds or tip-ins — and passing the puck well. He pinches smartly and doesn't often make mistakes. He has excellent eye/hand coordination and reflexes, and those qualities help him when reading the play and looking for his forwards.

He is very sound defensively, playing his defensive angles well and reading the rush well back into his own zone. Hartsburg has the ability to break up the play and turn it up-ice immediately.

THE PHYSICAL GAME

Not known as a physical hockey player, Hartsburg nevertheless is solid in the physical game. He uses his size to clear the front of the net well and Hartsburg is also strong enough to take the opposition wide and then out of the play.

He is not primarily a hitter, but will belt a few bodies every once in a while. Craig is strong enough to muscle anyone off the puck along the boards and he is always in position to make a play afterward.

THE INTANGIBLES

This report is basically unchanged and that's because everything in it is contingent on Hartsburg's healthy return to the NHL. He and Neal Broten are the two players Minnesota can least afford to lose, yet the Stars lost both last season. That's why the team went nowhere.

Hartsburg is Minnesota's real leader, its only stand up and take charge player. He is a tremendous team player who cares deeply about the team's success, but he's had enough of Minnesota's lack of stability and has asked to be traded.

Persuading Hartsburg to stay will be high on GM Jack Ferreira's list of priorities. But Craig's health is the real question. He is a defenseman in the Kevin Lowe mold — not great, but real good with tons of heart — but his health can never be any better than questionable.

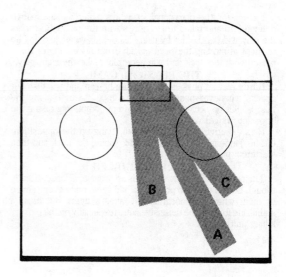

BRIAN LAWTON

Yrs. of NHL service: 5
Born: New Brunswick, N.J., USA:
June 29, 1965 Position:
Center Height:
6-0 Weight:
188 Uniform no.:
8 Shoots:
left

Career statistics:

GP	G	A	TP	PIM
303	71	91	162	250

1987-88 statistics:

GP	G	A	TP	+/−	PIM	PP	SH	GW	GT	S	PCT
74	17	24	41	-10	71	7	0	1	0	155	11.0

LAST SEASON

Games played total was a career high, but goal total was lowest in three seasons. He finished fourth in team scoring, third in power play goals. He missed two games with a rib injury and was sidelined early in the season with a broken thumb.

THE FINESSE GAME

The strengths that Lawton has are best applied to a finesse game. He is no better than average as a skater, and particularly lacks strength and balance on his feet — that's why he'd do better as a center, playing in the middle of the ice, than as a wing along the boards. He will get from Point A to Point B fairly effectively, and he uses his anticipation and vision to be a good checker.

While he has shown an increased ability to make plays, playmaking at the NHL level remains largely out of Lawton's reach for two reasons. One, he doesn't have great hands and tends to rush his passes to his teammates. Two, his hands and his brain don't function at NHL speed for offense. By the time Brian sees an opening, it's closed.

Lawton will do something with his opportunities but he won't finesse any plays, and his goal scoring is no exception. Because he releases his shot quickly Lawton has a degree of goal scoring talent, but neither his skating nor his anticipation will get him to the openings so he'll have to get his goals from close to the net by taking advantage of loose pucks.

Defensively Lawton is fairly sound, learning to play good positional hockey back into his own zone. He does anticipate well enough to be a good forechecker.

THE PHYSICAL GAME

He's gotten bigger but Lawton's size and the attendant strength remains only fair; that's another reason to take him off the boards and put him at center. Because he can't be successful here, Lawton is not much interested in the physical game. He's also very susceptible to an opposing player just lifting his stick and taking the puck.

THE INTANGIBLES

The chances of Lawton being moved to center, where he'd have a good chance to succeed as a checking player (which is more in line with his talents) are remote. There are at least three centers ahead of him (Neal Broten, Bob Brooke and Dave Archibald) and maybe a fourth if Mike Modano makes the club; that depth is one good reason *not* to put Brian in the middle.

But he cannot be consistently successful along the boards and will continue to hover near mediocrity if he stays as a wing. He has suffered from over-expectations and pressure since he was drafted by the Stars, but with Lawton you just have to take what you get.

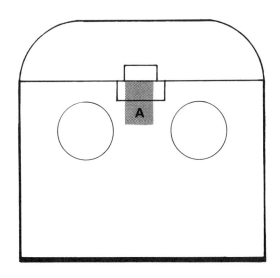

BRIAN MACLELLAN

Yrs. of NHL service: 4
Born: Guelph, Ontario, Canada; October 27, 1958
Position: Left wing
Height: 6-3
Weight: 212
Uniform no.: 27
Shoots: left

Career statistics:

GP	G	A	TP	PIM
389	120	178	298	314

1987-88 statistics:

GP	G	A	TP	+/-	PIM	PP	SH	GW	GT	S	PCT
75	16	32	48	-44	74	7	0	4	2	194	8.2

LAST SEASON

Games played total was lowest in four seasons (he missed one game with a virus). Goal total matched full season career low but he finished third on the Stars in scoring, tied for third in power play goals and tied for first in game winners. He finished fourth on the squad in SOG total, third among forwards. His plus/minus was the NHL's worst.

THE FINESSE GAME

MacLellan has one excellent and some very average finesse skills, all punctuated with a big IF — which will be explained later. He doesn't have great skating skill in terms of speed or agility, but he does have great strength and balance in his stride.

He is a straight ahead player and his puckhandling reflects that. He does not carry the puck well around the opposition, doesn't even carry it well as he heads up-ice unchecked. Nor does he have outstanding passing ability. Brian doesn't have good anticipation or hockey sense and therefore doesn't use his teammates well.

What he does have is an excellent shot. MacLellan releases his shot very quickly, and both his slap shot and wrist shot are heavy and accurate. His shots will carry into the net unless the goaltender is firmly in front of them.

Defensively he's a disaster, and his skating is why. Factor in laziness and the result is, while he is in his lane, MacLellan is usually far behind his check.

THE PHYSICAL GAME

This guy looks like Arnold Schwarzenegger. MacLellan has outstanding size and strength and uses neither of those skills regularly. To say he is inconsistent in the use of his size is an understatement. He is willing to be acted upon — to take hits and knocks and so on — but will not initiate anything that would put his strength and size advantage to use.

He will score from in front of the net with defensemen draped all over him, and that's a testament to MacLellan's strength, but he won't put that strength to consistent use in his battles along the boards or in front of the net — again preferring to be acted upon rather than acting.

He is not a fighter, though he can fight when he feels compelled, but MacLellan's size forces him into the role of policeman, a role he does not particularly relish.

THE INTANGIBLES

Herb Brooks tried everything with this guy to get him going. He put him on the point on the power play, he put him on defense in penalty killing. First line. Fourth line. Everything, and nothing happened.

MacLellan has much better skills than his numbers indicate, but the bottom line with him is that if you expect anything above these numbers you're just fooling yourself. When he gets fired up he's a great player, but Brian gets fired up as often as Halley's Comet comes along.

Because of that lack of intensity, MacLellan is no better than a third line left wing.

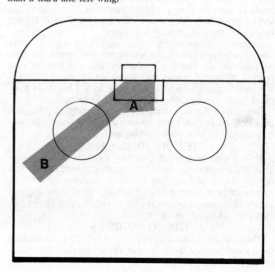

230

MOE MANTHA

Yrs. of NHL service: 7
Born: Lakewood, Ohio, USA; January 21, 1961
Position: Defenseman
Height: 6-2
Weight: 205
Uniform no.: 21
Shoots: right

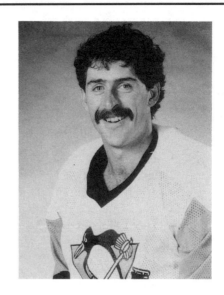

Career statistics:

GP	G	A	TP	PIM
463	66	230	296	389

1987-88 statistics:

GP	G	A	TP	+/−	PIM	PP	SH	GW	GT	S	PCT
76	1	27	38	-1	53	3	0	1	3	223	4.9

LAST SEASON

Mantha was traded twice, first from Pittsburgh to Edmonton as part of the Paul Coffey deal and then from Edmonton to Minnesota in exchange for Keith Acton. Games played total was the second highest of his career, but point total tied for second lowest. He led all North Star defensemen in scoring and his SOG total was the team's third highest. He missed a game with a knee injury.

THE FINESSE GAME

The Stars acquired Mantha after Craig Hartsburg went down with injury, and they wanted Mantha because of his offensive skills. He clears the zone and creates the attack because he's a skater with good speed, and his puckhandling is above average. If he cannot skate with the puck Mantha can move it up ice well because he is a good passer.

Mantha is a scorer and his particular area of importance is on the power play, where he reads the play extremely well and finds the open man or takes off on his own through an opening to score.

Moe likes to shoot from the slot and he has a good shot from there, and he also drifts along the boards to the outer edge of the faceoff circle. He shoots often.

His defense is nothing to write home about. He tries his butt off defensively but just makes bad decisions: blind passes, hurried passes, delayed passes.

THE PHYSICAL GAME

Moe is not as physical a player as he should be and that's one reason for his defensive mistakes: if he was more involved and accepted hits he wouldn't make those hurried passes.

He's not strong in front of the net, and he'll allow the opposition to camp in front of the net.

THE INTANGIBLES

Mantha's intensity and willingness to apply himself night after night have always been questionable. Another question has to do with the reappearance of Hartsburg, for if he's healthy the Stars have no reason to keep Mantha around.

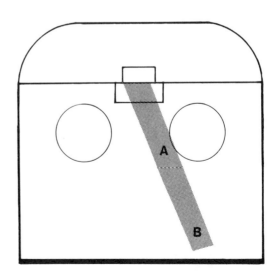

DENNIS MARUK

Yrs. of NHL service: 13
Born: Toronto, Ontario, Canada; November 17 1955
Position: Center
Height: 5-8
Weight: 170
Uniform no.: 9
Shoots: left

Career statistics:

GP	G	A	TP	PIM
882	356	521	877	757

1987-88 statistics:

GP	G	A	TP	+/−	PIM	PP	SH	GW	GT	S	PCT
22	7	4	11	1	15	2	0	0	1	45	15.6

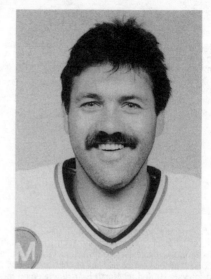

LAST SEASON

Games played total and all point marks were career lows. Foot and knee surgery sidelined him throughout the season.

THE FINESSE GAME

Though he has certainly lost a step or two, Maruk is still a good skater. He remains quick and agile, and he has a good change of pace. Dennis has good balance on his skates and is agile, able to make quick changes in direction. Dennis used to be a darter and an opportunist, but some of his quickness is gone.

He has a pretty good view of the ice and the implications of a play, but Maruk has never reached the highs envisioned for him by North Star management (though he does get into position to make plays). Instead, he has shown that he can use that vision and hockey sense very effectively as a two-way center.

Maruk has good puck handling skills and he carries the puck well. He can get the puck to his teammates but is not an exceptional passer. Maruk's strength has traditionally been shot, a quickly released wrist shot from the slot or side of the net. He constantly drives the net and is very opportunistic, and Dennis can get away with that because he has the hands to operate from in close. If he can, he likes to launch backhand shots from the bottoms of the circles.

He has become an effective checker and defensive player, and will stay on the puck and come back deep in his own zone to check.

THE PHYSICAL GAME

Maruk is a tough little guy, unafraid to move into the heavy traffic areas. He operates well there, though his game is in the open ice, but Maruk has the arm and hand strength to handle the puck in traffic or along the boards.

He has a little bit of a temper too and every once in a while will get fed up with the abuse he takes and will fight back. He uses his body well in checking and is one of the few guys in the League who will run a goalie when he is out of the net. Maruk certainly plays bigger than he is.

THE INTANGIBLES

Because of Maruk's injuries — the biggest question regarding his career — this report remains virtually unchanged from last year. He likes Minneapolis and wants to retire here, and had originally intended to do so after last season. The injuries have forced him to rethink that decision, and he's a 50-50 bet to play this season.

Maruk plays the game with a high level of intensity, and any player with that attitude will be welcomed by the Stars.

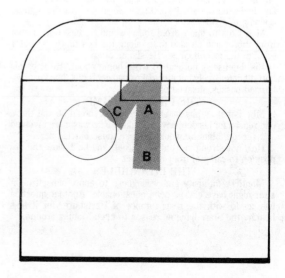

BASIL MCRAE

Yrs. of NHL service: 4
Born: Beaverton, Ontario, Canada; January 5, 1961
Position: Left wing
Height: 6-2
Weight: 205
Uniform no.: 17
Shoots: left

Career statistics:

GP	G	A	TP	PIM
199	21	22	43	872

1987-88 statistics:

GP	G	A	TP	+/−	PIM	PP	SH	GW	GT	S	PCT
80	5	11	16	-28	378	0	0	0	0	107	4.7

LAST SEASON

Games played total was a career high. He led the North Stars in PIM, finishing second in the NHL in that department (the total was a career high). His plus/minus was the club's fifth worst.

THE FINESSE GAME

Though immediately dismissed as without finesse skills, McRae does have some skills to bring to the game. He's a straight ahead player, so his turns and agility are weak, but he does have the balance and strength a physical game demands.

Basil can carry the puck (though he won't do anything fancy) and he accepts passes well as he goes up and down his wing, but he'll need time and space to make his plays. He lacks patience in his puckhandling and becomes nervous offensively, looking to get rid of the puck as soon as he can. He also has very strong defensive instincts (though the practice of those instincts is often flawed because of his lack of skills), and that's another reason for his impatience in the offensive zone; Basil wants to fall back to defense.

He doesn't have a great shot, so Basil will have to be in close proximity of the net to score.

THE PHYSICAL GAME

Minnesota acquired McRae for two reason. First, to show the rest of the club how to play with spirit and dedication and second, to counter as best as possible Detroit's combination of Bob Probert and Joe Kocur — in themselves two of the NHL's toughest players.

McRae knows his role and responds willingly to it, and there's no attempt to disguise his presence. If you're Tim Hunter or Chris Nilan, you know you're going to fight McRae. He's not big, but he has to go into the heavyweight class because he fights heavyweights all the time. But just because people know they're going to fight him doesn't mean they're afraid of him, and the League's heavyweights aren't. Hence the possible presence of Link Gaetz.

Aside from fighting Basil plays a physical game whenever possible. He has good strength along the boards and he can hurt people when he hits them. His leg strength and skating balance serve him here by keeping him vertical after collisions.

THE INTANGIBLES

McRae can play the game (he had good success for the Nordiques in the 1987 playoffs) and he is always working hard to improve his limited skills. Is he an enforcer/policeman/goon? Yes. Is he a great team player with an excellent attitude, a relentless competitor? Yes. Does Minnesota need everyone it can get who has that desire?

Yes.

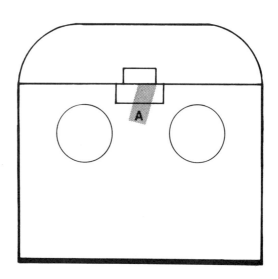

FRANTISEK MUSIL

Yrs. of NHL service: 2
Born: Pardubice, Czechoslovakia; December 17, 1964
Position: Defenseman
Height: 6-3
Weight: 205
Uniform no.: 6
Shoots: left

Career statistics:

GP	G	A	TP	PIM
152	11	17	28	361

1987-88 statistics:

GP	G	A	TP	+/−	PIM	PP	SH	GW	GT	S	PCT
80	9	8	17	-2	213	1	1	0	1	78	11.5

LAST SEASON

Musil was the only North Star defenseman to play all 80 games. He set career marks in all point categories. His PIM total was the team's third highest, tops among defensemen.

THE FINESSE GAME

Musil is a skilled finesse player and his abilities continue to grow at the NHL level. He reads plays better, he skates better, he moves the puck better and all because of NHL experience.

Musil's skating and hand skills let him carry the puck efficiently and create offense from the opposition's blue line. His play reading ability and anticipation tell him when to pinch in and when to fall back, and he's making good decisions more and more often.

He moves the puck quickly from his own end and follows the play up-ice intelligently. He forces the play wide defensively and already keeps the play to the outside fairly consistently.

His offense has improved and he has a good shot that could be put to better use with more use.

THE PHYSICAL GAME

The key to all of this improvement is Musil acclimatization to the physical pace of the NHL game. In Europe, on the big ice surfaces, moving the puck is like a walk in the park: get the puck, pass the puck, take a shot, get the puck and so on. In the NHL, you're going to get hit after you make that pass.

Where once Musil found that hitting wearing and taxing, now he's grown accustomed to the pace, knows what to expect and what to do to avoid those hits — that's why his passes have become quicker, for example. His size and strength naturally help handle the front of the net; his meanness helps too.

THE INTANGIBLES

Musil can be a tremendous player, but his growth is going to be limited by the development of the North Stars; as the team gets better, he'll get better. He works hard and has the skills to raise the level of his game.

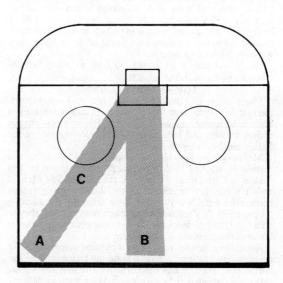

BOB ROUSE

Yrs. of NHL service: 4
Born: Surrey, B.C., Canada; June 18, 1964
Position: Defenseman
Height: 6-1
Weight: 210
Uniform no.: 3
Shoots: right

Career statistics:

GP	G	A	TP	PIM
285	5	45	50	611

1987-88 statistics:

GP	G	A	TP	+/−	PIM	PP	SH	GW	GT	S	PCT
74	0	12	12	-30	168	0	0	0	0	62	0.0

LAST SEASON

Games played total was second highest of his career; ditto assists total. He was Minnesota's lowest scoring regular and he finished fourth on the club in PIM, second among defensemen. He missed five games with a hip injury. His plus/minus rating was the club's third worst.

THE FINESSE GAME

Rouse's finesse game lags behind his physical one, and is one that must be improved if he intends to improve as an NHLer. He's not better than average as a skater (both forward and backward) and his agility is weak. His foot speed is substandard, and because of that so is his turning and pivoting ability (balance is also a factor here).

Because of his skating Rouse is no threat to carry the puck, and he will do so only on the rarest of occasions — and then never carrying it over the opposition's blue line. If he gets that far, Bob will dump the puck into the corner. His play is to move it up to the forwards to get it out of the zone.

His lack of foot speed leaves him susceptible to forechecking and he'll turn the puck over because of that. If he can turn back up-ice with the puck he'll usually move the puck efficiently. He reads the play defensively, as he sees and understands the rush coming at him well and he steers the opposition to the boards smartly.

As could be expected, Rouse rarely joins the play in the offensive zone; his responsibility is that of the fallback defenseman. It is when he plays outside his skills that Rouse gets into trouble, and those occasions are when his performances are inconsistent and downright poor.

Rouse has an average shot from the point and he doesn't shoot frequently. Any goals he gets will come from there and they will be few and far between.

THE PHYSICAL GAME

Like the little girl with the curl, when Rouse is good he's very good but when he's bad he's rotten. He can be one mean and miserable son of a gun, but he doesn't get the most out of his physical skills — doesn't even come close.

Why? Because he's very inconsistent in the use of his size. He's big and strong and when he plays that way his value to the team rises. He can clear the front of the net very well because of his strength and meanness. He hits well and hard — rather than just pushing and shoving along the boards — and can muscle the opposition off the puck.

He is a very tough player and plays that way. Sometimes.

THE INTANGIBLES

Rouse has got to play with more fire in his game, and that is tough for him because he's a low-key guy. And when he plays low-key his value to the team plummets. He is a hard worker and should improve with continued experience.

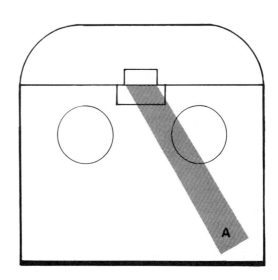

TERRY RUSKOWSKI

Yrs. of NHL service: 10
Born: Prince Albert, Sask., Canada; December 31, 1954
Position: Center
Height: 5-10
Weight: 178
Uniform no.: 8
Shoots: left

Career statistics:

GP	G	A	TP	PIM
626	112	312	424	1,354

1987-88 statistics:

GP	G	A	TP	+/−	PIM	PP	SH	GW	GT	S	PCT
47	5	12	17	-15	76	2	0	0	0	33	15.2

LAST SEASON

Ruskowski was signed as a free agent last July. Games played total was a career low (including five years in the WHA). He missed 23 games with back and knee injuries. All point totals were career lows.

THE FINESSE GAME

Most of Terry's finesse skills are average at best, but he can apply them in above average ways. For example, his passing is aided by his above average hockey sense, so he uses his teammates well. Ruskowski's skating is average (and falling because of age and injury) but his puck sense puts him in good position to score or to defend. Knowledge of the game, combined with anticipation and vision (he reads the play well), make Ruskowski an over-achiever, finesse-wise.

His goal scoring ability is not great and he'll have to get a lot of goals from 10 feet and in, getting the loose puck left from rebounds. Defensively, Ruskowski is very good, playing a consistent checking game and coming back deeply into his own zone.

THE PHYSICAL GAME

The physical game is where Ruskowski shines. He is aggressive and fearless, going to the corners and the front of the net exceptionally well and he initiates the contact there. He gets things done because he is willing to take his lumps to make a play.

Because he seems small, Ruskowski's size might appear detrimental to his play, but that is not the case. He is physically and mentally tough, as his penalty minute totals will attest, and his toughness and hockey sense allow him to make the right plays.

THE INTANGIBLES

There's a lot of mileage on that body and time is running out. In fact, don't be surprised if he's left unprotected and unclaimed in the waiver draft.

He has a great mind for the game and may become a coach when he retires. If Terry continues to play it won't be every game. He'll play here and there to add a little fire, because he's one of the best leaders both on and off the ice in the NHL. He is respected by both the team and its coaches because of his work ethic, hustle and desire.

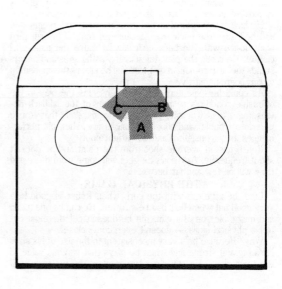

KARI TAKKO

Yrs. of NHL service: 2
Born: Kaupunki, Finland; June 23, 1962
Position: Goaltender
Height: 6-2
Weight: 182
Uniform no.: 1
Catches: left

Career statistics:

GP	MINS	G	SO	AVG	A	PIM
76	4,054	265	1	3.92	0	22

1987-88 statisics:

GP	MINS	AVG	W	L	T	SO	GA	SA	SAPCT	PIM
37	1,919	4.47	8	19	6	1	143	1,070	.866	8

LAST SEASON

Games and minutes played fell in Takko's second season, while goals-against and average rose.

THE PHYSICAL GAME

Takko is a standup goaltender who plays his angles well. He is not an outstanding skater, but he will come out of the net to challenge the shooter and to handle the puck. He moves well from post to post and likes to use his quick feet in the butterfly style. He goes to the butterfly on screen shots and is fairly agile, but his balance must be improved for the NHL level.

His balance is only fair and because of that he has some difficulty regaining his stance after opening up or after going to the ice.

Kari will handle the puck out of the net and he also uses his stick to pokecheck very well. He does not, however, handle his rebounds well, and that's where his agility comes into play. Takko will most usually be back in position for the second save, and will — at the very least — get some part of himself or his equipment in the way of that second attempt.

THE MENTAL GAME

Takko has good anticipation of the play. He tracks the puck well and combines his vision and anticipation with his good speed to get in the way of the shot.

He concentrates fairly well throughout a game and from contest to contest.

THE INTANGIBLES

Greater balance will be the key to Takko's NHL success. If he can gain it he will improve and succeed. But he also needs a better team to play in back of, because it's difficult for a goaltender to improve when his team does not.

MONTREAL CANADIENS

LINE COMBINATIONS
BOB GAINEY-GUY CARBONNEAU-JOHN KORDIC
SERGIO MOMESSO-BRIAN SKRUDLAND-CLAUDE
LEMIEUX
MATS NASLUND-STEPHANE RICHER-SHAYNE
CORSON

DEFENSE PAIRINGS
RICK GREEN-MIKE LALOR
PETR SVOBODA-LARRY ROBINSON
CRAIG LUDWIG-CHRIS CHELIOS

GOALTENDERS
PATRICK ROY
BRIAN HAYWARD

OTHER PLAYERS
MIKE MCPHEE — Left wing
BOBBY SMITH — Center
RYAN WALTER — Center/left wing

POWER PLAY

FIRST UNIT:
MATS NASLUND-BOBBY SMITH-CLAUDE LEMIEUX
CHRIS CHELIOS-LARRY ROBINSON

SECOND UNIT:
STEPHANE RICHER-RYAN WALTER-SHAYNE
CORSON
PETR SVOBODA-LARRY ROBINSON

The Montreal power play revolves around NASLUND
at the left boards, ROBINSON and CHELIOS at the
points and SMITH in front. NASLUND controls the
puck at the left boards, dancing up and down the wing
and keeping the passing lanes open with one step
quickness. He plays catch with the points to loosen the
defense to free SMITH for a shot from in front.
Secondary options include point shots, and the forwards
always crash the net for rebounds.

On the second unit, RICHER works the left boards
while WALTER and CORSON work a double-post up in
the slot. RICHER works the puck to the points to
loosen the defense. Point shots are very effective on
this unit with WALTER and CORSON looking for
rebounds, but RICHER will also shoot himself and is the
unit's primary weapon. RICHER will also take a shift or
two at the point to put his excellent slap shot to work.

Last season the Canadiens' power play was POOR,
scoring just 63 times in 397 attempts (15.9 percent,
20th overall).

PENALTY KILLING

FIRST UNIT:
BOB GAINEY-GUY CARBONNEAU
CRAIG LUDWIG-RICK GREEN

SECOND UNIT:
BRIAN SKRUDLAND-SHAYNE CORSON
PETR SVOBODA-LARRY ROBINSON

The Canadiens play a basic box defense, but the forward
nearest the puck will challenge the point. When the puck
moves low the other forward goes to the slot to clog
middle. When possible, LUDWIG and GREEN stay on for
entire two minutes.

Last season Montreal's penalty killing was EXCELLENT,
allowing just 64 goals in 395 shorthanded situations (83.8
percent, third overall).

CRUCIAL FACEOFFS

Montreal is blessed with a lot of good faceoff men.
CARBONNEAU is number one, but CORSON and SMITH
would be 1A and 1B.

GUY CARBONNEAU

Yrs. of NHL service: 6
Born: Sept-Iles, Quebec, Canada; March 18, 1960
Position: Center
Height: 5-10
Weight: 165
Uniform no.: 21
Shoots: right

Career statistics:

GP	G	A	TP	PIM
475	120	178	298	372

1987-88 statistics:

GP	G	A	TP	+/−	PIM	PP	SH	GW	GT	S	PCT
80	17	21	38	14	61	0	3	1	0	109	15.6

LAST SEASON

Guy was the only Canadien to play all 80 games, the second time in his career he's done so. All point totals were career lows. He led the club in shorthanded goals.

THE FINESSE GAME

Carbonneau is an excellent skater, tireless in his pursuit of the puck. He has excellent acceleration skills and balance, quickness and speed. Combined they make him a very powerful, very agile skater.

His other outstanding skill is really three skills rolled into one unit—anticipation, vision and hockey sense. Carbonneau sees all of the ice and he is always aware of where he is in relation to the puck, the net, the opposition and his teammates. He is able to read plays and situations almost perfectly and thus knows where the puck is headed or how the opposition intends to operate.

His skating and mental skills combine to make him an excellent forechecker, penalty killer (in both instances he pressures the puck carrier and creates turnovers, very aggressive as the League's best penalty killer by jumping the puck carrier almost immediately in the Habs' zone) and defensive forward.

Carbonneau can also use his skills to an offensive end. He takes advantage of loose pucks and his hand skills complement his skating skills. He handles the puck well at full speed and in traffic, and his excellent hands can also thread the puck through a crowd onto a teammate's stick. His vision allows him to use his wingers very well.

Carbonneau has a fast wrist shot and he scores from all over the offensive zone because he is always around the puck. He's particularly effective from the edges of the faceoff circles, but has the touch to score from in tight as well.

THE PHYSICAL GAME

Carbonneau doesn't have great size — and he relies more on his open-ice talents than on strength — but he uses his body on the opposition when up against the boards. His balance helps him remain vertical, and his hand skills help him make plays away from the boards. He willingly sacrifices his body, and demonstrates that trait as the NHL's best shot-blocking forward.

Guy is also an excellent faceoff man because of his hand speed, strength and because his balance on his feet gives him an excellent base of support. That hand strength also helps in his battles for the puck along the boards.

THE INTANGIBLES

There are players who are defensive forwards because they can't do anything else, and there are defensive forwards who raise the style to an art form. New York Ranger Jan Erixon is one of the latter. So is Calgary's Joel Otto and Boston's Steve Kasper.

But Guy Carbonneau, following not so coincidentally in the footsteps of teammate Bob Gainey, is the NHL's prototypical defensive forward. He raises checking to an art form.

Make no mistake: Carbonneau has offensive talent he subjugates to his defensive role (and doesn't that say something about his character?), but he's no 50-goal scorer in Frank Selke Trophy-winner's clothing. When the choice is between taking an offensive chance or falling back to defense, Carbonneau falls back; that's where his lost offense is.

But oh how he makes up for it defensively. And finally, after five years as the NHL's best, he was recognized for that skill with the Selke Trophy. It was about time.

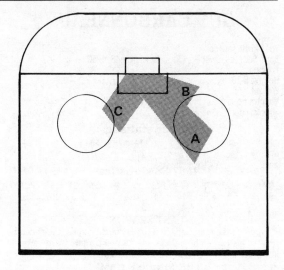

CHRIS CHELIOS

Yrs. of NHL service: 5
Born: Chicago, Ill., USA; January 25, 1962
Position: Defenseman
Height: 6-1
Weight: 187
Uniform no.: 24
Shoots: right

Career statistics:

GP	G	A	TP	PIM
269	48	157	205	462

1987-88 statistics:

GP	G	A	TP	+/−	PIM	PP	SH	GW	GT	S	PCT
71	20	41	61	15	172	10	1	5	3	199	10.1

LAST SEASON

Goal and PIM total were career highs, assist and point totals second highest of Chelios' career. He was Montreal's highest scoring defenseman, fifth overall on the club, and he led the defense in power play goals and shots on goal. He was first on the club in PIM, second on the club in game winners. Finger and back injuries sidelined him throughout the season. He finished ninth in League scoring among defensemen.

THE FINESSE GAME

Chelios boasts a fine package of finesse skills. His outstanding speed, agility, lateral movement and balance make him an excellent skater. He has speed up and down the scale and always finds a reserve burst to use in clearing a defender or heading off an opposing forward. You'll never see him beaten one-on-one because of a lack of speed or skating skill. He has the speed and the skills to go end-to-end to score.

Chelios loves to carry the puck from the Montreal end and does so skillfully. He handles the puck very well when carrying it and can make plays with it at all speeds. He leads his teammates excellently when he passes and he sees the openings because of his excellent ice vision.

That vision and his hockey sense combine to show him all of the ice and the options open to him, and his mental skills work in conjunction with his hand skills to make him a very-good-bordering-on-excellent playmaker. He can either send a teammate into the clear or jump into the hole himself.

Chelios has a strong slap shot from the point and he'll sneak to the top of the circle if he can. He also drifts into the slot for a good wrist shot. Chelios can take those chances because he is fast enough to recover if necessary.

He uses his skills defensively to force the play wide of the net (skating), take the puck from the opposition (hand skills) and immediately start the play up-ice (vision and hands).

THE PHYSICAL GAME

Chris is not a big hitter, but that's not to say he doesn't play physically. Chelios is very strong, certainly strong enough to control the League's big forwards. He takes the body very well and borders on mean with his stick. He can take the puck away from anyone along the boards because of his strength/balance combination.

Chris can hold the opposition out of the play in the corner, and he can clear the front of his net too. He uses his body

very well to shield the puck when he is rushing with it, and he will sacrifice his body by blocking shots.

THE INTANGIBLES

There's no style of game Chelios can't play — and play well. All he has to do is want to do so, and that desire to succeed every night is something that is missing from his game. He turns his talent on and off instead of using it consistently, and his on and off ice work ethics are questionable.

It often takes five seasons for a defenseman to germinate in the NHL, to reach his prime. For Chelios that time is now, and the only thing keeping him from being a consistent Norris Trophy contender are his erratic performances. Cure those and he joins the ranks of the League's superstar defenders.

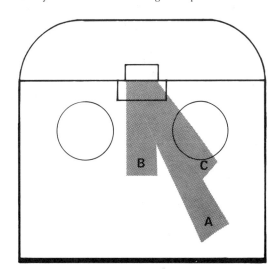

SHAYNE CORSON

Yrs. of NHL service: 2
Born: Barrie, Ontario, Canada; August 13, 1966
Position: Center
Height: 6-0
Weight: 175
Uniform no.: 27
Shoots: left

Career statistics:

GP	G	A	TP	PIM
129	24	38	62	298

1987-88 statistics:

GP	G	A	TP	+/−	PIM	PP	SH	GW	GT	S	PCT
71	12	27	39	22	152	2	0	2	0	90	13.3

LAST SEASON

Corson achieved career highs in assists and points, as well as in PIM. His plus/minus was the team's third highest, best among forwards, and his PIM total was also third highest, second among forwards. He missed two games with a hip injury, three games with a groin injury.

THE FINESSE GAME

Corson is a good skater, bordering on very good at the NHL level. He is a strong skater in terms of balance, and that aids him in his physical game, but he also has good speed and power. He accelerates well and has good foot speed, but is not a very agile player in terms of lateral movement. That's okay, because he is a straight-ahead player, not a fancy one. Corson combines that skating skill with good anticipation and hockey sense to become an effective checker and a good penalty killer.

He is a smart, heady player with a good understanding of the NHL game, and those smarts obviously help him in his play. They tell him when to force a play offensively, and when to fall back defensively. They have also helped him to improve his offensive game.

Corson handles the puck fairly well while carrying it, and he has improved his playmaking ability by staying open to the center of the rink and by keeping his head up. He likes to carry the puck over the blue line — rather than dump it in — whenever possible.

Shayne will succeed as a scorer now by being around the net to force turnovers, and then by pouncing on the loose pucks he forced.

THE PHYSICAL GAME

Corson is a physical player who likes to hit. He checks consistently and in all areas of the ice and he is a hard hitter. His balance helps him in his physical game by keeping him upright after collisions.

He is also a willing fighter, but is not anyone's worst nightmare pugilistically.

THE INTANGIBLES

Corson works hard on the ice, playing with a lot of intensity, and he will continue to improve because he has the determination to succeed. There had been a lot of trade talk surrounding him last season, but because of his tremendous potential Montreal isn't going to move him.

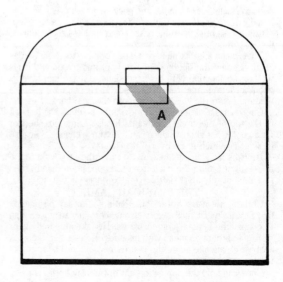

BOB GAINEY

Yrs. of NHL service: 15
Born: Peterborough, Ontario, Canada; December 13, 1953
Position: Left wing
Height: 6-2
Weight: 195
Uniform no.: 23
Shoots: left

Career statistics:

GP	G	A	TP	PIM
1,111	229	255	484	551

1987-88 statistics:

GP	G	A	TP	+/−	PIM	PP	SH	GW	GT	S	PCT
78	11	11	22	8	14	0	0	1	0	101	10.9

LAST SEASON

All point totals were second lowest of his career. His plus/minus was the lowest among the team's fulltime forwards.

THE FINESSE GAME

Skating, anticipation and hockey sense have long been the hallmarks of this future Hall of Famer's game. Gainey remains, even after a decade and a half, a strong and powerful skater. He is a straight-ahead player and his skating style reflects that no-nonsense approach, but that's not to say his skill is limited by that philosophy. He has excellent lateral movement and balance and good acceleration (because of the power of his stride). He's not — and never has been — overwhelmingly fast or quick, but that weakness is diluted by his tireless driving style. That balance aids in his physical game, keeping him upright and in the play after checks.

His anticipation and hockey sense are exceptional and they always keep him around the puck. That way, in turn, he can forecheck or keep the puck away from the man he's guarding. He has tremendous vision of the ice — and his hockey sense correlates what he sees so Gainey always understands a play and its ramifications. Between his mental and physical skills, he can track the opposition all over the rink.

He brings all these skills to bear in his role as one of the game's best defensive forwards. Gainey is an outstanding checker, shadowing his man with dogged persistence all over the ice. Needless to say, he is very strong in his own zone and as a penalty killer. Gainey is very good without the puck at both ends of the ice.

He has never done much offensively, and does even less now. He won't blow you away with his shots from afar (that's why his wing shots are scoring area B) but can convert most of his opportunities around the net (area A).

THE PHYSICAL GAME

Gainey has always been a good, hitting checker, and those insistent checks take a lot out of the opposition. He is very strong along the boards and very hard to muscle off the puck, and Gainey has the strength to hold his man out of the play for as long as necessary.

His physical play is made more meaningful by the fact that he is a clean player. Rarely does his defensive work draw penalties. His conditioning is excellent.

THE INTANGIBLES

There was much off-season talk of Gainey jumping into management roles with different teams across the League, but Bob KOed that talk by re-upping with the Habs. He is the consummate professional, a very dedicated athlete both on and off the ice, and he is a leader for the Canadiens. He is the type of guy who will take the younger players aside to show them the ropes.

The highest compliment a hockey player can earn is that of "an honest player." Gainey is that, along with being a clutch hockey player. He has the heart of a lion and doesn't know when to quit.

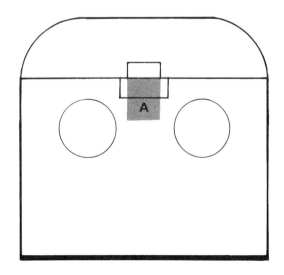

243

RICK GREEN

Yrs. of NHL service: 12
Born: Belleville, Ontario, Canada; February 20, 1956
Position: Defenseman
Height: 6-3
Weight: 200
Uniform no.: 5
Shoots: left

Career statistics:

GP	G	A	TP	PIM
704	40	192	232	619

1987-88 statistics:

GP	G	A	TP	+/−	PIM	PP	SH	GW	GT	S	PCT
59	2	11	13	21	33	1	0	0	0	44	4.5

LAST SEASON

Games played total was third lowest of Green's career, courtesy of groin (one game), ankle and back (10 games each) injuries. Still, his point total was the highest in three years. He finished fourth on the club in plus/minus, third among defensemen.

THE FINESSE GAME

Green's steady but unspectacular defensive play is keyed by his smarts and his ability to play sound positional hockey, because he's no better than good as a skater. He has very little speed to speak of, but his agility and foot speed are good so he'll rarely be beaten by a speedy forward. Rick pivots well and his foot speed helps him effectively close the gap between himself and the puck carrier.

Rick is always aware of where he is on the ice in relation to his net, the opposition and the puck. Because of his vision and play reading skill he can cut off the attack by using his defensive angles to force the opposition to the outside.

When he gets the puck, Rick moves it efficiently. He is not a playmaker, nor is he the kind of defenseman to rush the puck in order to take pressure off the forwards; he just doesn't have the skill.

Though he's shown (over the past two season) a willingness to charge the net for shots, Green is not likely to join the rush as a fourth attacker. His contributions from the offensive blue line will otherwise be minimal and any goals he gets will have to come on shots from the point.

THE PHYSICAL GAME

Green likes to hit and he does so at every opportunity. He is a big man and is difficult for the opposition to get around at the blue line, especially after he wraps his arms around them. He is one of the NHL's best holders.

He is good at steering opponents wide of the net with his size and he can hold them out of the play because of his strength. He uses his reach to poke check effectively or to deflect pucks out of play.

Rick is also very strong in front of the net, and will not be beaten there with any great regularity.

THE INTANGIBLES

After a dozen seasons in the NHL wars durability and the ability to avoid injuries are the questions Green has to answer. The guy has never played a full season; his average of games-played-per-season is under 59 contests a year.

He certainly doesn't have to answer for his performance, because he is a hard worker at all times and is Montreal's best defensive defenseman.

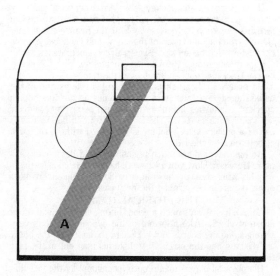

BRIAN HAYWARD

Yrs. of NHL service: 6
Born: Georgetown, Ontario, Canada; June 25, 1960
Position: Goaltender
Height: 5-10
Weight: 175
Uniform no.: 1
Catches: left

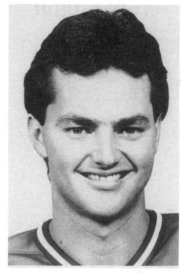

Career statistics:

GP	MINS	G	SO	AVG	A	PIM
241	13,552	859	4	3.80	12	63

1987-88 statisics:

GP	MINS	AVG	W	L	T	SO	GA	SA	SAPCT	PIM
39	2,247	2.86	22	10	4	2	107	1,032	.893	24

LAST SEASON

Hayward and teammate Patrick Roy shared the Jennings Trophy for the League's lowest goals-against-average for the second consecutive season. Games played total was third highest of his career, highest as a Canadien despite missing three games with a thigh injury.

THE PHYSICAL GAME

The difference in style between Brian Hayward and partner Patrick Roy is the difference bewteen night and day. While Roy is what has been called a stylist — acrobatic, flashy and flopping — Hayward is cool, consistent and stand-up. Brian is fairly adept at cutting down the shooters' angles, so you won't often see him flying around the ice. He challenges the shooters in almost all situations and lets the puck do the work of just hitting him.

The only time he doesn't do this is on screen shots. He hangs back in the net instead of coming to the top of the screen, and that's when you'll see him beaten to the extreme ends of the net — beyond his feet and inside the posts on both sides.

He allows those goals because he's not a great skater and is in trouble once he gets his feet moving. Hayward has good foot speed and he moves around the net well, but he has below average balance on his skates and does not recover his stance quickly. That makes him vulnerable in scramble situations, like screens around the net, because he is unable to get into position to stop second and third attempts. For that reason, he is perfect for Montreal, where he makes the first save and the defense sweeps aside the rebound.

Hayward is average at controlling the puck after a save, usually able to direct it out of danger. He does not frequently leave his net to retrieve loose pucks and that's smart because he does not handle it well.

THE MENTAL GAME

Hayward has a fairly good grasp of his concentration, meaning that he applies himself mentally throughout a game. He does have a tendency to fold his tent if he gives up a soft goal, and he can fall into a funk if his bad performances pile up.

Luckily for him, his team provides excellent defensive support, so Hayward can always be confident when he gets in the net.

THE INTANGIBLES

Hayward is the kind of steady, average goaltender that a strong defensive club can make look good. That's no knock on him. A goaltender who plays positionally is always going to be in trouble behind an undisciplined team. For a challenging stand-up goaltender to succeed he has to know that he has only the shooter — and not opposing forwards darting behind defensemen — to worry about.

His steadiness makes him a more dependable goaler than Patrick Roy, but Hayward lacks Roy's ability (albeit Patrick's only shown it once — but it won Montreal a Stanley Cup) to raise his game to the situation, to become a hot and thus unbeatable goaltender. What he does do is give the Canadiens a solid performance every night out.

JOHN KORDIC

Yrs. of NHL service: 2
Born: Edmonton, Alta., Canada; March 22, 1965
Position: Left wing
Height: 6-0
Weight: 200
Uniform no.: 31
Shoots: left

Career statistics:

GP	G	A	TP	PIM
109	7	10	17	322

1987-88 statistics:

GP	G	A	TP	+/−	PIM	PP	SH	GW	GT	S	PCT
60	2	6	8	0	159	0	0	0	0	17	11.8

LAST SEASON

Games played total was a career high, as was PIM total. Kordic finished second on the club in PIM, first among forwards.

THE FINESSE GAME

There ain't much here. Kordic is no better than fair as an NHL skater. He doesn't have the speed and quickness to keep up with the NHL play, and he doesn't have the hockey sense or anticipation skills to compensate for that lack of skating ability.

John has little playmaking ability, both in terms of vision and understanding of the play and in his hand skills. That lack of skill also applies to his shot, which is almost non-existent.

He is a fair defensive player in that he plays positionally. He doesn't understand the intricacies of the game, so a creative winger can do a lot of damage opposite him.

THE PHYSICAL GAME

Kordic is big and strong, but that doesn't make him an effective physical player. He can hit well when he catches somebody, but he's not a real good hitter because he often isn't near enough the puck carrier to make a check.

He is a fighter of some ability, and it's for that ability that Kordic is in the NHL.

THE INTANGIBLES

Kordic is with the Canadiens as a policeman, replacing Chris Nilan in that role. But he is far from Nilan's equal in on-ice smarts and skills and off-ice leadership and character.

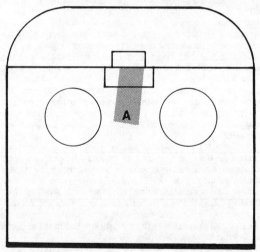

MIKE LALOR

Yrs. of NHL service: 3
Born: Buffalo, New York, USA; March 8, 1963
Position: Defenseman
Height: 6-0
Weight: 193
Uniform no.: 38
Shoots: left

Career statistics:

GP	G	A	TP	PIM
185	4	25	29	216

1987-88 statistics:

GP	G	A	TP	+/−	PIM	PP	SH	GW	GT	S	PCT
66	1	10	11	4	113	0	0	0	0	41	2.4

LAST SEASON

Games played total was a career high. Ditto point and PIM totals. An ankle injury suffered during training camp sidelined him early in the season.

THE FINESSE GAME

Skating is the hallmark of Lalor's game. He skates equally well forward and back and has good agility and lateral movement ability (though he is a little weak on his turns to the left). He also has a good touch of speed and acceleration.

Lalor uses his skating skill defensively and is not inclined to rush the puck. He passes the puck quickly and efficiently to the forwards to get the play started from the Montreal zone. He's also learned to react more quickly to the play at the NHL level and that's made Mike less vulnerable to forechecking pressure. Otherwise Lalor does not frequently handle the puck.

Lalor plays his defensive angles well, better from the right side than the left (his left pivots can be exploited to the outside when he plays the port side). He reads the incoming rush well and he combines that skill with his skating to see some penalty killing time.

Lalor is not a goal scorer, so any goals he does get will come from the points.

THE PHYSICAL GAME

Lalor's physical game is not up to the quality of his finesse game. He has good size but needs to better use it in confrontations in the corners and the front of the net. He can generally handle himself against the big forwards who camp in the crease, and he certainly works at moving them out, but his takeouts could improve.

He has a good reach and can poke check effectively or deflect the puck.

THE INTANGIBLES

Lalor should continue to improve as he gains NHL experience, yet there has been friction in the Canadiens' dressing room because of his presence. A story making the rounds last Christmas had Chris Chelios and former teammate Chris Nilan in a screaming match, with Chelios allegedly pushing for Lalor to sit and for his own ice time to increase. Nilan held a different point of view.

Whether that attitude prevails today, the point is that Lalor is an up and coming player with size, strength, smarts and a good work ethic. That combination may strike a chord with new coach Pat Burns.

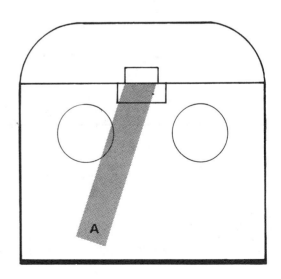

CLAUDE LEMIEUX

Yrs. of NHL service: 3
Born: Buckingham, Quebec, Canada; July 16, 1965
Position: Right wing
Height: 6-1
Weight: 205
Uniform no.: 32
Shoots: right

Career statistics:

GP	G	A	TP	PIM
173	60	60	120	334

1987-88 statistics:

GP	G	A	TP	+/−	PIM	PP	SH	GW	GT	S	PCT
78	31	30	61	16	137	6	0	3	1	241	12.9

LAST SEASON

Games played and all point totals were career highs. He finished fourth on the club in scoring, second in goals and shots on goal. He finished third among forwards in PIM and fourth among them in plus/minus.

THE FINESSE GAME

Lemieux is very much a straight-ahead hockey player and his skating skills demonstrate that. He has good speed and quickness up and down his wing, and because his stride is strong he has good acceleration capabilities.

While his balance is good enough to keep him upright after checking (and that's important because of Claude's penchant for physical play), he is not balanced enough to be agile. He does very little but charge with the puck and he almost completely lacks any lateral movement. The result is, he's easy to predict and theoretically easy to contain.

His hockey sense and skating keep him around the puck and he can be a good forechecker. His good hands carry the puck at top speed and he's talented enough to make plays off his wing while at full speed. Claude's not consistent enough in that skill because he keeps his head down, and right now he thinks like a goal scorer anyway. Lemieux looks to the net first, and his excessive 1-on-1 play against the defenseman also undercuts his playmaking ability.

Lemieux has a terrific shot, strong and accurate, quickly released. That shot is a benefit to the Habs on the power play, when Claude camps in front of the net for garbage goals. He has enough power to blow the puck past the goaltender from the top of the circle.

He has improved the quality of his defensive play, making smoother and quicker transitions to defense and playing his position more attentively in the defensive zone.

THE PHYSICAL GAME

Lemieux is one of the League's power forwards — at least some of the time. He's a big strong winger, an agitator and a chippy/dirty player who can handle most anything his play stirs up. Because he's so strong in his upper body — and because he has excellent balance on his feet to remain vertical after collisions — Lemieux can be a terror up and down the boards.

He bangs around with reckless abandon in the corners and continues around the opposition net.

He operates well in the traffic around the net because of the strength in his arms and hands, one other reason why he succeeds in front of the net when he is on the power play.

There is a great difference between Lemieux and the League's other power forwards, and that is Claude's inconsistent use of his size. There are games that he floats through without touching a soul. Another difference is his unwillingness — note we didn't say inability — to handle the trouble we said his play stirs up.

Part of Lemieux's act is to further goad the opposition by refusing to fight after he's elbowed or highsticked an opponent, and when he does fight he does it behind the protection of his visored helmet. That visor tactic led to the League's adoption of a new rule any player wearing a visor who starts a fight will be assessed a minor penalty.

The rule is jokingly called the Lemieux Rule.

THE INTANGIBLES

Overall consistency is what Claude's game needs. He needs to consistently apply himself in his very strong physical game. Really, players with his size and strength shouldn't be doing as much diving for penalties as Lemieux does.

He also needs to be more consistent in his scoring: 21 of his goals came in the second and third quarters of last season (four goals in the first 20 games, six in his last 19 contests).

Lemieux is a very skilled player, one who could consistently score better than 30 goals a season even though — or because — the strengths of his game are in the physical aspects. In that regard he is no different from Rick Tocchet or Gerard Gallant. But to reach that success Lemieux must want to do well.

He must also adapt to a new coach, who may or may not appreciate Lemieux's style of game.

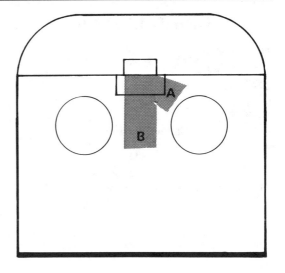

CRAIG LUDWIG

Yrs. of NHL service: 6
Born: Rhinelander, Wisconsin, USA; March 15, 1961
Position: Defenseman
Height: 6-3
Weight: 212
Uniform no.: 17
Shoots: left

Career statistics:

GP	G	A	TP	PIM
450	22	83	105	438

1987-88 statistics:

GP	G	A	TP	+/−	PIM	PP	SH	GW	GT	S	PCT
74	4	10	14	17	69	0	0	0	0	81	4.9

LAST SEASON

Ludwig missed five games with a concussion, but he still played more games than any other Montreal defenseman. He was the team's lowest scoring regular (players with at least 70 games experience).

THE FINESSE GAME

Ludwig is no better than an average skater. He doesn't have great speed, quickness or agility in his movement, but he does pivot well to keep the play on the outside. He plays his position intelligently therefore, not risking things that are clearly beyond his level of play.

He moves the puck quickly to the forwards for a breakout and he backs up the play as the last defenseman back. Craig likes to throw the puck up the middle if he can and he's fairly predictable in that trait, though not to the point where he forces the play. Ludwig won't rush the puck and he won't become a fourth attacker in the offensive zone.

He plays good, positional defense by playing his defensive angles well, not allowing forwards to scoot around him from the outside. He can make a take out and turn the play around quickly because he does have good vision on the ice.

Ludwig is not a goal scorer, so any goals he gets will come on shots from the point.

THE PHYSICAL GAME

Ludwig is a tough guy. He hits hard, usually waiting for forwards smaller than he, but he will take shots as well as give them. He hits consistently along the boards and in the corners, and he keeps the front of his net clean. He has a mean streak and frequently uses his stick, so forwards won't make too many plays with their heads down.

Ludwig is strong and can hold a man out of the play along the boards, tie him up effectively in the crease or steer him wide of the net. He also sacrifices his body by blocking shots.

THE INTANGIBLES

Like teammate Rick Green, Ludwig is quietly effective on defense. Nothing flashy or fancy, just clear the man and move the puck. He can play that style of defense forever, and it perfectly complements the game of more offensive players like Chris Chelios, with whom Ludwig frequently partners.

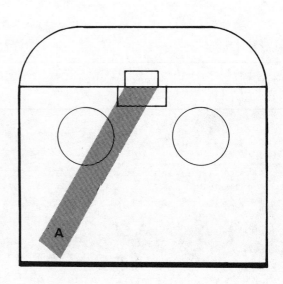

MIKE MCPHEE

Yrs. of NHL service: 5
Born: Sydney, N.S., Canada; February 14, 1960
Position: Left wing
Height: 6-2
Weight: 200
Uniform no.: 35
Shoots: left

Career statistics:

GP	G	A	TP	PIM
310	82	86	168	341

1987-88 statistics:

GP	G	A	TP	+/–	PIM	PP	SH	GW	GT	S	PCT
77	23	20	43	19	53	0	2	4	1	151	15.2

LAST SEASON

Games played total was second highest of career, goal and point totals career highs. Plus/minus rating was second best among full time forwards. He led the club in shorthanded goals.

THE FINESSE GAME

McPhee is a deceptive and unheralded player. For a player labelled a mucker, he has strong skating skills. His strength gives him some speed and acceleration ability, and he also has some quickness that lets him change the pace of his skating to make it more effective. It is his skating skill that makes him a good checker and excellent penalty killer.

As a forechecker, he combines speed with anticipation and forces the play in the offensive zone. That checking forces many loose pucks and McPhee is talented enough to convert on those opportunities around the net. He doesn't have the hands of a Naslund or a Richer, nor their ability to make plays at top NHL speeds, but he can make plays because he sees the ice and because his hands are sensitive enough to make soft passes. He takes a pass well too. He's not a big goal scorer and will get most of his goals from the crease and around the net, not having a good enough shot to consistently score from more than 30 feet out.

His defense is marked by the same traits as his offensive checking. McPhee is a determined back checker and plays good, positional defense, rarely wandering from where he is supposed to be when in his defensive zone.

THE PHYSICAL GAME

The physical game is the strength of McPhee's game, and the reason why he is — not incorrectly — referred to as a mucker. He is big and strong and can be a punishing hitter. He hits relentlessly, and he'll fight too, though most of his physical work is against the boards.

He has good strength, can muscle the opposition off the puck in the corners and will win more than his share of battles along the boards. He plays physically at both ends of the ice and is strong enough to hold his check out of the play when necessary.

THE INTANGIBLES

McPhee is rounding into a complete hockey player, a hard worker who can contribute at both ends of the ice. That de-velopment is good for him personally, because it takes him out of the role player category, as well as good for the team.

Unfortunately, the more obvious of his skills — his toughness and fighting ability — overshadow his skills, but this is a talented hockey player. Because Mike plays a controlled physical game that does not hurt his team, he's a very valuable commodity and frequently asked for in any trade talks involving the Canadiens.

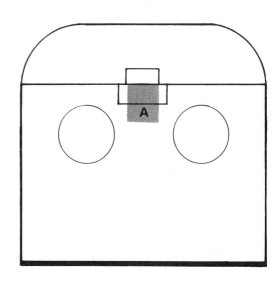

SERGIO MOMESSO

Yrs. of NHL service: 2
Born: Montreal, Quebec, Canada; September 4, 1965
Position: Left wing
Height: 6-3
Weight: 203
Uniform no.: 36
Shoots: left

Career statistics:

GP	G	A	TP	PIM
137	29	38	67	233

1987-88 statistics:

GP	G	A	TP	+/−	PIM	PP	SH	GW	GT	S	PCT
53	7	14	21	9	91	1	0	0	0	72	9.7

LAST SEASON

Momesso's point totals all fell in his second "full" NHL season. He missed five games with a leg injury.

THE FINESSE GAME

Momesso is a swooping kind of skater, the kind that swings wide of the defenseman and then cuts back in. He has some agility and foot speed, but not a lot of speed overall.

He handles the puck well and can use his teammates because of good hockey sense and vision. He has a nice touch around the net and is opportunistic in getting to loose pucks, but he can also score with a wrist shot from a little further out. His slap shot is powerful and delivered low on the ice, but Momesso takes a long time to get it off.

Sergio is not much defensively, mostly through lack of effort. He doesn't pay close attention to his check and he has a tendency to wander out of position in the defensive zone.

THE PHYSICAL GAME

Momesso is strong, the kind of player who succeeds by bulling his way around the corners and the boards, and by using his strength in the front of the net. He does drive to the net and, because of his size, can work effectively there.

He is not a tough guy, but he'll take the rough going to make his plays. Right now though, Momesso is not guaranteed to make plays after taking the hits and that renders his physical play less than effective.

THE INTANGIBLES

We told you last year that, like Stephane Richer, Momesso lacked the intensity necessary to play every night. The difference a year later is that Richer has matured while Momesso has not.

Sergio's biggest problem is his inconsistency of effort from night to night, even shift to shift. He's the kind of guy who could score 30 goals a year but he needs to work at doing so. He seems to be the kind of guy who was a star at the junior level because he was so far above the competition and didn't have to work to succeed. Obviously, that doesn't work in the NHL.

He applies none of his talents consistently. For Momesso, as for many other players, the third season is the most important one. It's time for him to put up or shut up.

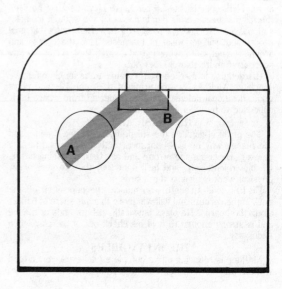

MATS NASLUND

Yrs. of NHL service: 6
Born: Timra, Sweden; October 31, 1959
Position: Left wing
Height: 5-7
Weight: 158
Uniform no.: 26
Shoots: left

Career statistics:

GP	G	A	TP	PIM
468	189	298	487	74

1987-88 statistics:

GP	G	A	TP	+/−	PIM	PP	SH	GW	GT	S	PCT
78	24	59	83	17	14	4	0	2	0	167	14.4

LAST SEASON

Naslund finished second on the club in scoring and assists, third in goals. His PIM total was the lowest for any fulltime Montreal player, and he finished fifth in SOG. His plus/minus rating was third best among forwards.

THE FINESSE GAME

Naslund is an excellent skater in all areas of that skill. He has tremendous speed and acceleration, can change speed and direction within a stride, and moderates his speed to be most effective.

Mats controls the puck at any speed, taking it or dishing it off accurately while in full stride. Because he has great balance on his skates, Naslund can lean away from defenders but still control the puck on the end of his stick and just out of their reach. He is extremely agile — both with and without the puck.

He finds the openings by using his excellent anticipation skills and either takes advantage of them himself with his speed, or leads a teammate into the clear with a soft pass.

Naslund has an excellent wrist shot and can score from anywhere in the offensive zone. He loves to shoot from almost impossible angles but his shot is always on net and keeps the goaltender honest. He likes to go to his forehand on break-aways. Naslund is especially dangerous when he has the puck around the crease, because his excellent hands need just the slightest opening to work with. He doesn't shoot enough for the opportunities he gets, and should be more selfish in that respect.

His foot, hand and mental skills make him the Canadiens' prime man on the power play. He'll set up at the left hashmarks to feed Bobby Smith and Claude Lemieux in the slot.

He is a conscientious defensive player, makes the transition from offense to defense excellently and plays his check well from the red line in.

THE PHYSICAL GAME

His size would seem to mitigate against him, but it is precisely for that reason that Naslund is one of the toughest guys in the NHL. Mats is not very big but he can dish out solid checks, and physical play is the rule with Naslund, not the exception. He is a tough little guy and he can take heavy hitting. He is absolutely fearless and will go to the corner with any player, even though his game is made in the open ice. He backs down from no one.

Tough isn't always beating someone up. Sometimes it's just taking every hit to get the job done. That's the kind of toughness Naslund exemplifies. Obviously, his size is not a factor in his play.

THE INTANGIBLES

A tremendous character player, Mats is also a very hard worker. He willingly applies his skills not only during the game, but in practice too. He is underachieving at 24 goals — he's worth at least 35 and really should score 40 a year — but that unselfish play we talked about demonstrates his team-first philosophy.

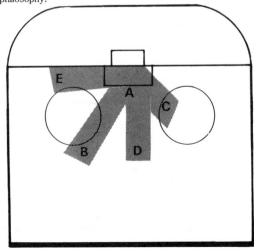

STEPHANE RICHER

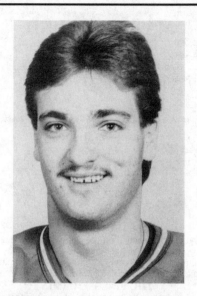

Yrs. of NHL service: 2
Born: Ripon, Quebec, Canada; June 7, 1966
Position: Center
Height: 6-0
Weight: 190
Uniform no.: 44
Shoots: right

Career statistics:

GP	G	A	TP	PIM
195	91	63	154	202

1987-88 statistics:

GP	G	A	TP	+/−	PIM	PP	SH	GW	GT	S	PCT
72	50	28	78	12	72	16	0	11	1	263	19.0

LAST SEASON

All point totals were career highs. Richer led the club in goals, power play goals, shots on goal, shooting percentage and game winners (he led the League in the last category). He missed three games with a twisted knee and five games with a hand injury.

THE FINESSE GAME

Richer is an excellent finesse player. He is an excellent skater with a powerful stride and good quickness, and his agility is suprising for his size. He has explosive acceleration and good foot speed, and he has excellent lateral movement. He's pretty shifty for a big guy.

He carries the puck excellently at whatever speed he's using (and he moderates his speed very well — no predictability in this guy), and he can do that because of his soft and fast hands. Richer can take or give a pass at full speed and he uses his anticipation to lead his teammates into openings with his passes. Because of his ability with the puck and his quick feet, Richer excels on the power play.

Stephane uses his excellent hockey sense in combination with his hand and foot skills to exploit any opening he can. He likes to work 1-on-1 against the defense, and his speed will not only get him to the openings but will create them as well. He is that rare player who could stickhandle through an entire team and score.

His slap shot is one of the two or three best in the League, pretty much unstoppable from the edge of the faceoff circle and in. His soft hands also make him extremely dangerous around the net, as he can finesse the puck through the smallest opening. He is primarily a scoring center, so though he can use his teammates well Richer will look to the net first (hence his relative modest assist total).

While he'll never be confused with teammate Bob Gainey, Richer has made a big (for him) turnaround in his defense by improving his transition game from offense to defense.

THE PHYSICAL GAME

Not previously known as a physical player, Richer has begun to assert himself in that area of the game. He's using his good size to better effect along the boards, bumping the opposition in battle for the puck, and he's also worked at improving his strength and conditioning.

That new strength has greatly aided him in the high traffic area around the net, where it has allowed him to hold the puck longer and withstand checks.

He uses his reach excellently to hold the puck away from the defense (not to mention pokechecking or snaring loose pucks), and he also uses his body well when shielding the puck from the opposition.

THE INTANGIBLES

We told you last year that Stephane had the skills to be an NHL force, that last season would tell us the story of where his career was going. We also told you that he lacked discipline and was immature, lazy and uncoachable.

Richer told you that too, as his year went on. He told the press how he worked out over the summer to be in good shape for the season, and how he discovered he had to play with more intensity. That sounds like much needed maturity and dedication to us.

In fact, so impressive is Richer's turnaround that he's frequently used now as an example to another phenomenally talented yet undisciplined NHL player — Detroit's Petr Klima. If Klima could do the things Richer did to pull his game together, the Wing would be a star too.

But we've gotten off the subject. Richer has just begun to reach his NHL potential; his 50-goal season was no fluke. Now he must demonstrate consistency by approaching that number again, as well as demonstrate he can get along with his new coach. A less selfish game (just 28 assists) would be nice too.

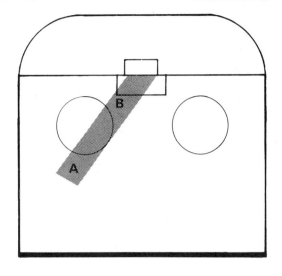

LARRY ROBINSON

Yrs. of NHL service: 16
Born: Winchester, Ontario, Canada; June 2, 1951
Position: Defenseman
Height: 6-3
Weight: 210
Uniform no.: 19
Shoots: left

Career statistics:

GP	G	A	TP	PIM
1,128	193	660	853	684

1987-88 statistics:

GP	G	A	TP	+/–	PIM	PP	SH	GW	GT	S	PCT
53	6	34	40	26	30	2	0	1	1	96	6.3

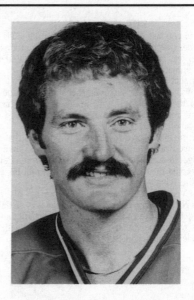

LAST SEASON

Courtesy of a broken leg suffered while playing polo last summer, Robinson's games played total was the lowest of his career, not counting his rookie season when he entered the NHL mid-year. His goal total tied his career low (rookie season excepted) and his point total tied his third lowest total ever and was his lowest in 12 seasons. PIM total was also a career low (again excepting that rookie year). His plus/minus mark was the team's second best.

THE FINESSE GAME

Robinson still skates well, but his once spectacular rushes are now few and far between, a concession to his fading skating legs. Larry still moves the puck for the breakout pass extremely well, and the odd rush to relieve pressure on his forwards isn't out of the question.

He remains a power play staple, using his excellent vision of the offensive zone to quarterback the play from the point. He'll find the open man with ease, though the Habs like to set him up for a shot from the point. He'll do a little cheating, but not much, preferring to control the point and contain the play.

The smarts we are referring to are best evidenced in his defensive play. Larry almost never makes a defensive mistake and plays his position so perfectly that the opposition has almost no chance of creating any kind of threat. Excellent anticipation and play-reading capabilities are the keys. Robinson sees the ice defensively as well as any superstar forward sees it offensively. He understands each play and its ramifications and knows how to counter those plays in the most efficient way possible.

THE PHYSICAL GAME

Robinson still plays a physical game, though he is less aggressive than he was in the past, and less aggressive than a younger defenseman breaking into the NHL feels safe being.

While in the past he always put something extra into his physical play, Robinson is now content to do just whatever he has to. He still hits hard, but he hits hard less often.

He remains immensely strong, and can move anyone from the front of his net or out-muscle anyone against the boards. He can hold the opposition out of the play forever if need be, and he still sacrifices his body to block shots.

THE INTANGIBLES

This will most likely be the final year of Robinson's Hall of Fame career, but that doesn't mean he'll coast to the end. He is still competitive and just because he enjoys playing the game doesn't mean he doesn't want to win. That will to win remains unsurpassed, and is an invaluable example to the team's younger players.

He is personable, and a fun guy in the dressing room, and he deserves every honor his stellar career has accrued.

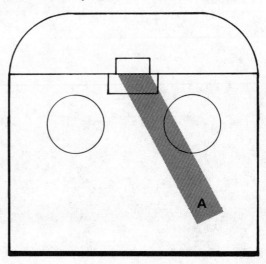

PATRICK ROY

Yrs. of NHL service: 3
Born: Quebec City, Quebec, Canada; October 5, 1965
Position: Goaltender
Height: 6-0
Weight: 165
Uniform no.: 33
Catches: left

Career statistics:

GP	MINS	G	SO	AVG	A	PIM
139	7,943	404	5	3.05	6	26

1987-88 statisics:

GP	MINS	AVG	W	L	T	SO	GA	SA	SAPCT	PIM
45	2,586	2.90	23	12	9	3	125	1,248	.900	14

LAST SEASON

Along with Brian Hayward, Roy won the Jennings Trophy for fewest goals against for the second consecutive season. His goals-against-average was the NHL's third best, as was his shutout total, and Roy led the League in save percentage. Games and minutes played totals were the lowest of his career, as was his goals-allowed figure.

THE PHYSICAL GAME

Roy is a reflex goaltender with good size. He has very long legs and covers almost the entire bottom of the net when he flops, but that's when he gets out of position and is left scrambling for loose pucks around the net.

He is able to make the saves on the low shots because of his fast feet, but Patrick also displays a weakness on his short stick side, and that indicates failure to properly cut down the angle. He does not roam from his net and is no better than average when handling the puck, preferring to leave it behind the net for a teammate.

He has fast hands and feet, but is a little stiff on his glove side with shots that are close to his body and don't allow him to extend his arm.

Though he is very fast up and down and regains his stance easily and with great balance (so that he is always in position to make the second save, something he doesn't have to do courtesy of Montreal's smothering defense), Patrick simply takes himself out of the play by lying on the ice.

He must improve his angle ability and learn to stand up more.

THE MENTAL GAME

Roy has excellent concentration, especially on scrambles around the net. He sees the puck very well and tunnels in on it, and he keeps his concentration intact within games. He is mentally tough and can come right back from giving up a bad goal and he certainly doesn't carry a bad game from one night to the next. He is confident in the net and can make the big save.

He has improved his consistency from night to night.

THE INTANGIBLES

We said last year that it is his defense that has made Roy look good, not the other way around. We'll stand by that for the present. While he has made certain improvements in his game regarding consistency, and some adjustments in his style, Roy has lots of improving yet to do if he wants to be a long term star in the NHL.

He certainly hasn't reapproached his stellar status of 1986's Stanley Cup playoffs, when he was named MVP.

BRIAN SKRUDLAND

Yrs. of NHL service: 3
Born: Peace River, Alta., Canada; July 31, 1963
Position: Center
Height: 6-0
Weight: 180
Uniform no.: 39
Shoots: left

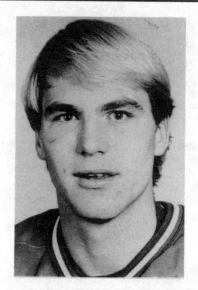

Career statistics:

GP	G	A	TP	PIM
223	32	54	86	276

1987-88 statistics:

GP	G	A	TP	+/−	PIM	PP	SH	GW	GT	S	PCT
79	12	24	36	14	112	0	1	3	0	96	12.5

LAST SEASON

All point totals and PIM total were career highs. He missed a game with a muscle injury. His PIM total was fourth highest among forwards.

THE FINESSE GAME

Quickness and strength make Skrudland a good skater and very effective defensive forward. His skating is strong and almost tireless and, while Skrudland is not a tremendously agile player, his foot speed and quickness help him stay on his man all the time. That extra step helps him close the passing lanes and thus deny puck movement.

Good — and improving — anticipation and sense of the NHL game help Brian in his checking role. That means he can use his skating more efficiently when necessary by closing off areas of the ice through smarts. His offensive skills are growing apace as Skrudland takes greater and greater advantage of the loose pucks his checking creates.

His good vision serves him in those offensive moments as he looks for plays around the net instead of just slamming the puck into the goaltender. Like other on the Canadiens checking staff, his growing ability to contribute offensively makes him more valuable and moves him out of the role player category.

THE PHYSICAL GAME

Skrudland is insistently physical, landing checks whenever possible. He plays a consistently physical style of game (his quickness serves him here by allowing him to close the gaps between himself and the puck carrier. He has good strength and that makes him a hard checker and tough player. He bumps his man at every opportunity, though sometimes to his disadvantage by being too aggressive. Penalties and missed checks are the result, but this aspect of Skrudland's game is also improving.

He plays that physical style home and away and at both ends of the ice. He uses his size well against the boards and can take the puck away from the opposition fairly frequently, if he remembers not to be over-aggressive.

THE INTANGIBLES

Another of many character players on the Canadiens, Skrudland is a very hard worker on the ice. He is a dedicated player and gives 100 percent every night.

He is also vastly underrated because of the presence of Guy Carbonneau, and there are those opposing players and coaches who feel that Skrudland is at the top of his style in the way Wayne Gretzky is at the top of his own game.

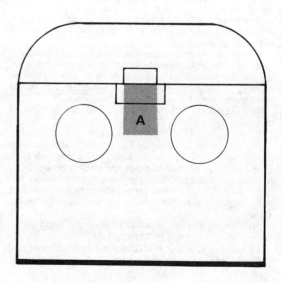

BOBBY SMITH

Yrs. of NHL service: 10
Born: North Sydney, N.S., Canada; February 12, 1958
Position: Center
Height: 6-4
Weight: 210
Uniform no.: 15
Shoots: left

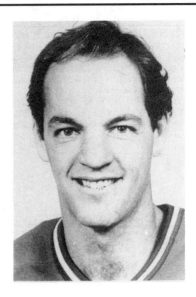

Career statistics:

GP	G	A	TP	PIM
758	284	539	823	634

1987-88 statistics:

GP	G	A	TP	+/−	PIM	PP	SH	GW	GT	S	PCT
78	27	66	93	14	78	8	0	4	0	198	13.6

LAST SEASON

Smith missed two games with the flu, but led the Canadiens in scoring and assists (third in goals). Assist total was the second highest of his career, point total tied for second. He finished third on the team in power play goals, fourth in shots on goal.

THE FINESSE GAME

Smith's skating is reminiscent of other tall centers — Beliveau and Ratelle, perhaps? — in its grace and fluidity. He is very smooth on the skates and doesn't seem to have a lot of speed, but his long stride gets him up-ice and away from the opposition quickly. He also has excellent balance and agility, and those abilities make him very agile. He has excellent lateral movement and combines that mobility with his balance and reach to make plays that would be beyond the capabilities of many NHLers.

Bobby sees the ice very well and combines his vision with anticipation to recognize the openings. He can exploit those openings with his own very good puck control, or he can lead a teammate into the openings wih soft and accurate passes. He is very much a play-making center.

But Smith is also a scorer, and he can put the puck in from almost anywhere in the offensive zone. He has a hard and accurate wrist shot and a very good slap shot, but his sneakiest weapon is a backhand from 10 feet out that hits the upper right corner almost everytime. The Canadiens set Smith up for that shot on the power play, otherwise he's more likely to score from deeper in the slot.

Bobby has improved his positional play defensively, and he is attentive to his defensive responsibilities down ice through an improved transitional game.

THE PHYSICAL GAME

Smith is a finesse player with exceptional size, and his balance makes his size more effective for his finesse game. He plays in traffic though he is not a hitter, and his excellent balance and reach allow him to dislodge opponents from the puck or to take it from them while staying unhindered by the traffic. He is not an overly physical player but he does not shy away from contact and will hit fairly consistently. He takes more physical punishment now than ever before, and also initiates more now than he has in the past.

His reach is exceptional and allows him access to the puck while on the outside of the crowd, and he certainly has the ability to make a play coming away from the boards. His height also gives him a good view of the ice and that meshes well with his anticipation.

Hand and wrist strength help him snare those pucks, and they also make him a good faceoff man.

THE INTANGIBLES

The Bobby Smith that plays for Montreal is very similar to, yet very different from, the Bobby Smith that used to play for Minnesota. Montreal's Smith has developed the maturity and attitude necessary to become a team leader, but the talent he's showing is in the class of the 100-point man who played for the North Stars seven seasons ago.

Now we're not saying that Smith will score 100 points again, but 93 points is certainly not out of character. Bobby's talent no longer runs him wild. He's a disciplined player and his work ethic makes that talent work.

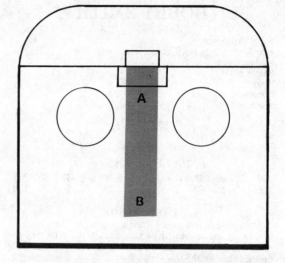

PETR SVOBODA

Yrs. of NHL service: 4
Born: Most, Czechoslovakia; February 14, 1966
Position: Defenseman
Height: 6-1
Weight: 170
Uniform no.: 25
Shoots: left

Career statistics:

GP	G	A	TP	PIM
285	17	84	101	370

1987-88 statistics:

GP	G	A	TP	+/−	PIM	PP	SH	GW	GT	S	PCT
69	7	22	29	46	149	2	0	1	0	138	5.1

LAST SEASON

Games played total was a career low, but goal total was a career high. He led the club in plus/minus and finished with the NHL's second best ranking. His PIM total was second highest among defensemen, as was his SOG total. He missed five games with a late season hip injury.

THE FINESSE GAME

Svoboda's skating is primary among his considerable finesse skills. He is excellent in almost all aspects of that skill—speed, quickness, agility and balance. He has speed in both his forward and backward skating, and his turns and pivots are very smooth. He has good lateral movement and his quickness allows him to efficiently close the gap between himself and the puck carrier. Strength on his skates is the only quality lacking in his skating game.

Svoboda can certainly rush the puck to take pressure off the Canadiens' forwards. Petr handles the puck well and can carry it well in front of him, and he has soft hands that make him a good passer. He also takes the puck off the boards extremely well in the defensive zone and starts the play away almost in one motion.

He has shown an ability to use his teammates in the offensive zone and reads the play there fairly well. Svoboda has an accurate, but un-powerful shot from the point and he will cruise to the top of the faceoff circle if he can.

Because he sees the offensive zone well, he knows when to fall back defensively, and he reads the rush coming at him with good skill before forcing it wide of the net.

THE PHYSICAL GAME

While he is tall, Svoboda is also lanky and hasn't filled out his thin frame. In that respect his lack of bulk hurts him because he has troubles with bigger wingers along the boards and particularly in front of his own net. He is either bounced off the puck or is out-muscled momentarily, forcing him to hook and hold (and thus draw penalties) in order to slow the wingers down.

On top of the forced penalties, Svoboda is a chippy player and will often lose his discipline in favor of a slash or cross check. Petr must bulk up and add upper body strength to be completely effective in his own zone.

THE INTANGIBLES

His superb plus/minus rating forced people to sit up and take notice of him last year, and his consistent play is worthy of attention. He is beginning to fulfill his excellent potential as an above-average NHL defender, and that maturing should continue this season.

His style of play is an aggressive one, and it helps the Canadiens because opposing players hate to play against him because of his chippy (bordering on dirty) play. In that regard he's like teammate Claude Lemieux—an instigator and a pest.

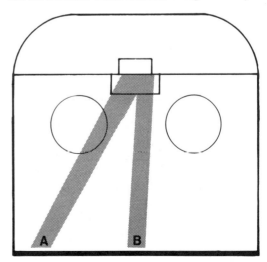

RYAN WALTER

Yrs. of NHL service: 10
Born: New Westminster, B.C., Canada; April 23, 1958
Position: Center/Left wing
Height: 6-0
Weight: 195
Uniform no.: 11
Shoots: left

Career statistics:

GP	G	A	TP	PIM
738	233	337	570	768

1987-88 statistics:

GP	G	A	TP	+/−	PIM	PP	SH	GW	GT	S	PCT
61	13	23	36	12	39	6	0	3	0	93	14.0

LAST SEASON

Games played total was a career low courtesy of bruised ribs and a back injury. Goal total was also a career low.

THE FINESSE GAME

Walter is a very strong skater with good balance and power, and he uses that skating ability to good result as a checking forward. He doesn't have a lot of speed, but is very difficult to dislodge from the puck on offense, and difficult to hide from when he is a checker and in pursuit of the puck on defense. He is a tenacious checker.

Great hockey sense and anticipation are not things Walter was born with, but he has worked to gain a thinking — rather than instinctual — understanding of the game. He positions himself well when checking to be in the right place to break up a pass if he's on defense or to find the opening if he's turning to offense. His strength and tenacity make him valuable in checking the other team's top guns.

Because he has good offensive skills, Ryan can capitalize on the opportunities his checking creates. While not in the class of teammate Naslund, Walter will use his teammates well because he has good hands; more often than not, he'll get a good pass to them. Walter has had a good touch around the net throughout his career and he will score if given the opening.

His scoring strength is in close to the net (as evidenced by his power play success when he just plugs the front of the goal), but Ryan is also good with his wrist shot from the deeper slot.

THE PHYSICAL GAME

Walter, who has a little bit of a mean streak, plays physically up and down the ice. Because of his balance on skates, Walter comes out of most collisions vertical and ready to make a play. He has made better use of his size in front of the net, as his strength and balance allow him his power play success.

Walter is a tough player. He backs down from nothing and he uses his body well, showing good strength along the boards where he out-muscles the opposition. He sometimes concentrates on being a little too aggressive and forgoes the play for an extra shove or elbow.

THE INTANGIBLES

The price of his physical game is injury, and Walter has been sidelined frequently throughout his career because of it. But his determination to maintain that physical style describes him as a player. He is tough and hard-nosed, willing to do whatever necessary to win. He is an honest player, he works hard and he always gives 100 percent of himself.

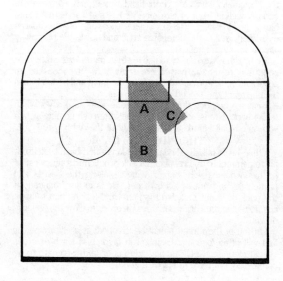

NEW JERSEY
DEVILS

LINE COMBINATIONS
AARON BROTEN-KIRK MULLER-PAT VERBEEK
MARK JOHNSON-PATRIK SUNDSTROM-JOHN
MACLEAN
CLAUDE LOISELLE-DOUG BROWN
PERRY ANDERSON-BRENDAN SHANAHAN

DEFENSE PAIRINGS
RANDY VELISCHEK-JOE CIRELLA
KEN DANEYKO-CRAIG WOLANIN
BRUCE DRIVER-TOM KURVERS

GOALTENDERS
SEAN BURKE
BOB SAUVE

OTHER PLAYERS
ALAIN CHEVRIER — Goaltender
JIM KORN — Left wing
JACK O'CALLAHAN — Defenseman
DOUG SULLIMAN — Left wing

POWER PLAY

FIRST UNIT:
AARON BROTEN-KIRK MULLER-PAT VERBEEK
TOM KURVERS-BRUCE DRIVER

SECOND UNIT:
MARK JOHNSON-PATRIK SUNDSTROM-JOHN
MACLEAN
KEN DANEYKO-CRAIG WOLANIN

On the first unit, VERBEEK will be stationed in front of the net to the goaltender's right, and the Devils want to get the puck to him for a tap-in or on a rebound. KURVERS, at the center of the blue line, and DRIVER play catch along the blue line with each other and with BROTEN at the right wing boards. MULLER is down low, and will cut to the net on a shot for a possible rebound of a point shot.

On the second unit, MACLEAN moves to the front of the net, JOHNSON patrols behind the net and along the left wing boards and SUNDSTROM is in the right circle. JOHNSON and SUNDSTROM feed WOLANIN for a shot, with JOHNSON sometimes working a give and go in the left faceoff circle. DANEYKO is simply a safety valve.

Last season, the Devils power play was GOOD, scoring 98 times in 479 opportunities (20.5 percent, 10th overall).

PENALTY KILLING

FIRST UNIT:
CLAUDE LOISELLE-DOUG BROWN
RANDY VELISCHEK-JOE CIRELLA

SECOND UNIT:
MARK JOHNSON-PATRIK SUNDSTROM
KEN DANEYKO-CRAIG WOLANIN

Both forward duos are extremely aggressive on the puck, forcing the puck handler whenever possible. Both units will send one man deep into the offensive zone if possible, and both units play an aggressive but very disciplined box.

Last season, the Devils penalty killing was FAIR, allowing 101 goals in 467 times shorthanded (78.4 percent, 15th overall).

CRUCIAL FACEOFFS

PATRIK SUNDSTROM is now the man for these draws, and CLAUDE LOISELLE is the backup in the defensive zone.

PERRY ANDERSON

Yrs. of NHL service: 6
Born: Barrie, Ontario, Canada; October 14, 1961
Position: Left wing
Height: 6-0
Weight: 210
Uniform no.: 25
Shoots: left

Career statistics:

GP	G	A	TP	PIM
312	43	45	88	775

1987-88 statistics:

GP	G	A	TP	+/−	PIM	PP	SH	GW	GT	S	PCT
60	4	6	10	-8	222	1	0	0	0	40	10.0

LAST SEASON

Games played mark was second highest of career, but point total was career low. Missed three games with a knee injury, benched the rest. Finished third on the team in PIM, second among forwards, with career high PIM total.

THE FINESSE GAME

If there's one thing Perry Anderson can do in a finesse game, it's skate. He has tremendous speed and from net to net he's one of the fastest guys in the League. However, he has no idea of where he's going, why he's going there and what he's going to do when he gets there.

Anderson is poor positionally. He wanders all over the ice in the hope of belting someone in an opposing uniform, leaving his own wing unguarded. Because of these seek-and-destroy missions, Anderson is frequently caught deep in the opposing zone when the puck turns over and his man is skating up-ice unchecked. This forces him to hook, hold or tackle as he gallops back into the play, and he ends up in the penalty box.

As much speed as Anderson has, that's how little agility and lateral movement. He takes himself out of the play with wide turns, and he also takes himself out of the play by running into the boards (since he is so un-subtle, most players simply sidestep him as he comes in) or falling down behind the net.

Perry can shoot and likes to boom slap shots from long range, shooting from just inside the blue line and from the faceoff circle, but will have to be in tight to score.

THE PHYSICAL GAME

If he can catch anybody, Anderson can be a punishing hitter. He has great upper body strength and can really lay on the muscle along the boards or in the corners, but he'd better have a teammate nearby to make a play with the loose puck because Anderson can't.

What Anderson *can* do, aside from skate fast, is fight. He throws his fists pretty well, and he's more than willing to stand up for his smaller teammates, but he also looks to fight at every instigation.

If he gets decked by a clean check, Anderson takes it as a personal affront. Aside from the finesse abilities, that's the difference between the Tocchets, Neelys and Proberts and Perry Anderson; they accept checks and stay away from taking that retaliatory — and stupid — penalty.

THE INTANGIBLES

Anderson is a role player for New Jersey, bringing toughness and enthusiasm to lineup when he plays. Unfortunately, there's not much else he can deliver. Because of that his role with New Jersey will always be a limited one.

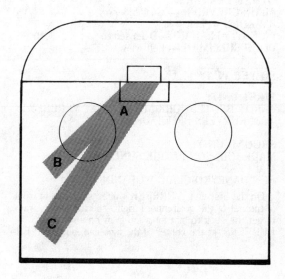

AARON BROTEN

Yrs. of NHL service: 7
Born: Roseau, Minn., USA; November 14, 1960
Position: Left wing
Height: 5-10
Weight: 168
Uniform no.: 10
Shoots: left

Career statistics:

GP	G	A	TP	PIM
519	136	256	392	250

1987-88 statistics:

GP	G	A	TP	+/-	PIM	PP	SH	GW	GT	S	PCT
80	26	57	83	20	80	7	2	4	0	180	14.4

LAST SEASON

Finished second on the club in points with a career high mark in assists and total points. Played 80 games for second consecutive season, and for fourth time in seven NHL seasons, one of just four Devils to do so last year.

THE FINESSE GAME

Skating is the key to Broten's other finesse skills. Though not outstandingly fast, Broten is agile because of his good balance and foot speed. That foot speed gives him one-step quickness that gets him to loose pucks or to hit holes.

He's New Jersey's best puckhandler and though he does not carry the puck well at top speed, Broten can handle it in traffic thanks to his balance. His anticipation helps him find the openings for his teammates and his good hands (he passes well to both sides) generally get them the puck. Those skills make him a power play regular.

Broten's a fair goal scorer and suffers from a bit of unselfishness, as he thinks pass before he thinks shoot. He has a quick wrist shot and likes to go to the upper right corner with it and is pretty dependable from that 15-foot mark. Because his linemates open up the ice for him, Broten is now getting into better scoring positions.

THE PHYSICAL GAME

Perhaps thinking he can't succeed in a physical game, Broten doesn't really play one. He'll accept hits to make his plays, but he rarely initiates contact. He also stays to the outside of traffic and allows his hand skills to work the puck free.

He's tough to catch because of his skating and balance, but if he gets caught along the boards he can be out-muscled.

THE INTANGIBLES

We roasted Broten last year for his admitted intensity problem. He showed no signs of that this year, playing consistently throughout the season. No doubt his upgraded effort helped key the Devils in their run toward the playoffs; 41 of his 83 points came in Patrick Division contests — that's important.

It also indicates just what kind of effort Broten can put forward when he puts his mind to it. Aaron can be a leader on the ice, and you can never have too many of those.

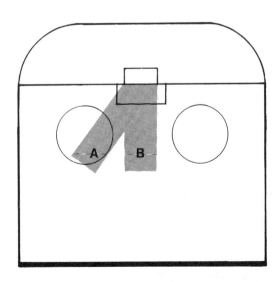

DOUG BROWN

Yrs. of NHL service: 1
Born: Southborough, Mass., USA; June 12, 1964
Position: Right wing
Height: 5-11
Weight: 180
Uniform no.: 24
Shoots: right

Career statistics:

GP	G	A	TP	PIM
74	14	12	26	20

1987-88 statistics:

GP	G	A	TP	+/−	PIM	PP	SH	GW	GT	S	PCT
70	14	11	25	7	20	1	4	2	0	112	12.5

LAST SEASON

Brown's first full NHL season. He led the club in short-handed goals, and his PIM total was the lowest among Devil regulars. A bruised shoulder and the flu sidelined him for a couple of games, while benchings and demotion account for the rest of his absences.

THE FINESSE GAME

Brown is a good skater, possessing more quickness than speed. He moves very well in contained spaces, stopping and starting and changing direction within one step very well. He has less rink length speed, but his good jump will get him ahead of the opposition winger when Doug makes the transition from defense to offense. His skating makes him an excellent, almost tireless, checker, and he's also valuable to New Jersey as a penalty killer.

Though he's shown himself to be a fairly adept scorer at the other levels he's played, Brown hasn't shown that at the NHL level. The most noticeable reason is because of Brown's puckhandling, which is not up to the NHL par.

He doesn't handle the puck well near the opposition *or* at top speed, so when he comes into the offensive zone — and in order to avoid the defenseman — Brown is always moving to the left wing and his back hand side. He takes himself to bad ice and tries to stutter-step past the defender, but the fakes don't work on NHL competition.

And if you think we're kidding about this left wing stuff, just remember where Brown was when he scored the overtime goal that beat the Bruins in Game 2 of the Boston-New Jersey playoff series the top of the left wing faceoff circle.

THE PHYSICAL GAME

Brown deserves all the credit in the world for throwing his body around recklessly, bowling into the opposition, charging the corners. Unfortunately, willing does not always translate into able.

Right now, Brown doesn't have the strength to tie up the NHL's stronger forwards, willing though he may be. Worse, Brown doesn't have the strength to even slow down most NHL left wings. Of course, that makes his checking more special, because he's doing it all with brains and skating.

An improvement in upper body strength (he must be able

to at least serve as a halfway effective roadblock) is mandatory if Brown is to remain in the checking winger role.

THE INTANGIBLES

Brown's a smart player, and he shows that when he plays. He's enthusiastic and hard working, and he's shown that he can rise to the NHL's most special occasions. He brings an enthusiasm and intensity to the club, and he can be a leader in that regard.

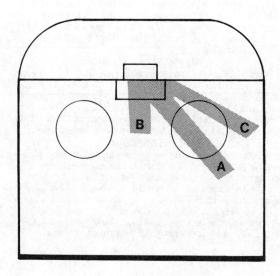

SEAN BURKE

Yrs. of NHL service: 1
Born: Windsor, Ontario, Canada; January 29, 1967
Position: Goaltender
Height: 6-3
Weight: 185
Uniform no.: 1
Catches: left

1987-88 statisics:

GP	MINS	AVG	W	L	T	SO	GA	SA	SAPCT	PIM
13	689	3.05	10	1	0	1	35	300	.883	6

LAST SEASON
Burke premiered with the Devils after the Winter Olympics. He was the Devils' second round selection in the 1985 Entry Draft.

THE PHYSICAL GAME
Burke has great size and he complements it with great reflexes and vision. Burke uses his size to his advantage by playing a standup style that obscures much of the net. He has a well balanced stance and skates very well, so he moves in and out of his net well. He also has good lateral movement, and goes from post to post well.

He has extremely fast feet and legs, so the usual wisdom about shooting to the feet of big men doesn't hold with Burke. That leg quickness also makes itself apparent when Burke butterflies, as he regains his stance with great quickness (his balance helps here). He blocks the lower corners well.

Sean's hand speed is good, but nowhere near as good as his feet. That doesn't mean pucks are going to go sailing over his shoulders. Burke has a good glove hand and a quick stick. He handles the puck well in moving it to his teammates.

Burke moves from his crease well, and he comes to the top of screens to take up as much space as possible and minimize deflections. He also sees the puck extremely well, picking it up on its flight to the net almost 100 percent of the time, and then Burke uses his reflexes to stop the puck.

THE MENTAL GAME
Burke is very tough mentally. He has excellent concentration and is unfazed by bad goals or games. He is always prepared to play and not only has the capability of making the big save, but of winning games by himself.

If there is a weakness, it's Sean's penchant for losing his temper when interfered with around his crease. He can be goaded into penalties by forwards who consistently get in his way around the goal.

THE INTANGIBLES
Burke showed just how good he can be during last spring's playoffs. Some NHL observers believe that there are just three impact goaltenders, goalies capable of winning games by themselves—Grant Fuhr, Ron Hextall and Sean Burke.

We think there may be one or two goalies to add to that list, and we also think that it's too early to canonize Burke. But there's no questioning the talent and potential he's shown to date. What he can mean to the Devils — and what he has already meant — is inestimable.

He must be considered a prohibitive favorite for Rookie of the Year honors.

ALAIN CHEVRIER

Yrs. of NHL service: 2
Born: Cornwall, Ontario, Canada; April 23, 1961
Position: Goaltender
Height: 5-8
Weight: 170
Uniform no.: 30
Catches: left

Career statistics:

GP	MINS	G	SO	AVG	A	PIM
140	7,370	518	1	4.21	4	25

1987-88 statisics:

GP	MINS	AVG	W	L	T	SO	GA	SA	SAPCT	PIM
45	2,354	3.77	19	19	3	1	148	1,117	.867	8

LAST SEASON

Games played was second highest of his career, but his goals-against-average was his career best.

THE PHYSICAL GAME

Chevrier is an angle goaltender, though he doesn't challenge shooters as well as he could. One reason for that is because of his skating. Since he is only an average skater, Alain can't be overly aggressive when challenging because he won't get back into the net in time for rebounds or the second save. He does have good balance on his feet and can regain his stance quickly after sprawling.

His reflexes are good and his glove hand is fairly solid, but he'll have trouble with low shots just inside the posts and high to the stick side (again, because these spaces are open due to his not cutting the angle well enough).

He's not afraid to go behind the net and cut the puck off as it rips around the boards and he can handle the puck fairly well in getting it to his defensemen.

He stays in the net too deep and too long on screen shots, hoping for an extra second of time for the reflex save and to get a better view. He would do better to square himself to the puck.

THE MENTAL GAME

Chevrier suffers concentration lapses that result in successive goals, or goals from bad angles. He can give a good 15-20 minutes and then his concentration starts to slip and his confidence begins to go. Additionally, he's not mentally strong enough to play for long stretches — say, four or more games consecutively. He does not do well when he comes into a game cold.

He anticipates the play well and is especially sharp that way in action around his net. By and large, Alain will come back strongly from a poor outing, but his inability to hold his concentration is bound to affect him again.

THE INTANGIBLES

When Sean Burke arrived on the Devils scene, Chevrier was handed his hat. He dressed for just three of New Jersey's last 10 games (playing two) and dressed for just one playoff contest.

There's no question that he can be a major league goalten-der, though he must improve to be a consistently successful one. However, with Burke the Devils' incumbent — and Bob Sauve fairly well ensconced as the number two — that leaves Chevrier, Craig Billington and Chris Terreri in the background.

Unless New Jersey shows a willingness to axe Sauve (doubtful for two reasons — 1) Lou Lamoriello brought him in and 2) he's shown he can sit for long stretches and then play well), expect Chevrier to be shopped around.

JOE CIRELLA

Yrs. of NHL service: 6
Born: Hamilton, Ontario, Canada; May 9, 1963
Position: Defenseman
Height: 6-2
Weight: 205
Uniform no.: 2
Shoots: right

Career statistics:

GP	G	A	TP	PIM
423	47	140	187	783

1987-88 statistics:

GP	G	A	TP	+/−	PIM	PP	SH	GW	GT	S	PCT
80	8	31	39	15	191	2	0	2	0	135	5.9

LAST SEASON

Cirella played a full season for the first time in his career. His assist and point marks are the second highest of his career. He finished fourth on the club in PIM. He led Devil defensemen in plus/minus.

THE FINESSE GAME

Cirella is a 50/50 skater: he skates well forward, but not well backward, and that's bad for a defenseman. He has some foot speed and can surprise the opposition with some of his quickness on the offensive blue line. His back skating is weaker than his forward skating, particularly in his turns to the boards. His agility and lateral movement when skating backward are not at the same level as when he skates forward, and he'll find himself suffering because of those flaws.

One reason this may be so is Cirella's balance, or lack thereof. He's extremely top heavy, and when he gets hit in the shoulders he'll be knocked off his feet more often than not.

Joe carries the puck well when he skates, and he'll rush it from his zone. His vision and playmaking ability are limited, and he's better off moving the puck from his zone with a breakout pass than he is in becoming part of the attack. Strong forechecking unnerves him, however, and he will hurry his passes and allow turnovers. His mobility makes him a member of both specialty teams.

He takes the pass well in the offensive zone and is smart enough — and talented enough — to get off a good wrist, instead of the more time consuming and easier blocked slap shot. Cirella also can shoot while he's still moving, so that makes his shot more powerful.

Cirella has improved his defensive game by playing more positionally and with less risk. He's tempered his offensive forays, and that caution allows him to set himself for facing the opposing rush. He's forcing the play wide fairly well now, and he can certainly initiate a play up-ice off the transition.

THE PHYSICAL GAME

Cirella uses his strength and size fairly well in front of his own net. He can take the puck from the opposition along the boards or in the corners. He takes the body well and can hit hard, and Cirella is not intimidated by the League's tough guys. He'll fight for himself or a teammate when necessary.

THE INTANGIBLES

Cirella's role as an all-around "I have to do it or it won't get done" defenseman was toned down this season; the addition of Tom Kurvers and the increased second half ice time of Randy Velischek saw to that.

Because of that, Cirella is playing a steadier game, but he still needs to be paired with a smarter player, one who can cover up for Cirella's still-frequent miscues of thought and deed.

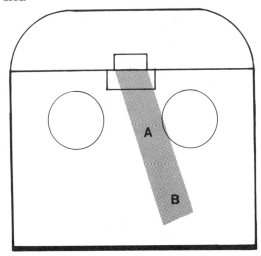

KEN DANEYKO

Yrs. of NHL service: 4
Born: Windsor, Ontario, Canada; April 17, 1964
Position: Defenseman
Height: 6-0
Weight: 200
Uniform no.: 3
Shoots: left

Career statistics:

GP	G	A	TP	PIM
215	8	33	41	549

1987-88 statistics:

GP	G	A	TP	+/−	PIM	PP	SH	GW	GT	S	PCT
80	5	7	12	-3	239	1	0	0	0	82	6.1

LAST SEASON

Daneyko played 80 games for the first time in his career. Though his goal total was a career high, he notched career (full season) lows in assists and points. He led the club in PIM, also a career high.

THE FINESSE GAME

Two full NHL seasons have begun to benefit Daneyko, especially in his skating. While he is far from a speed demon or a Nureyev on his feet, Daneyko has improved his foot speed and his agility.

His stride has lengthened (and thus he has more power and overall speed), and his foot speed has also improved, providing him with more quickness and better lateral movement.

That quickness allows him to better cover the forwards flitting around the Devil net (though he will still lose his concentration on covering the man and instead follow the puck), as well as get to the loose pucks in his zone in order to turn the play around. The improved skating has also helped Daneyko play his defensive angles better, allowing him to force the opposition wide rather than they're going around him.

His improved skating has also made him daring in the offensive zone, where Daneyko will now charge the net for a shot if he sees an opening.

Ken's puckhandling remains average at best, though he is fairly consistent in getting the puck to breaking forwards. He still must adjust completely to the speed of the NHL game, because strong forechecking against him can cause turnovers. While he concentrates on his defensive responsibilities, he could shoot more from the point.

THE PHYSICAL GAME

Daneyko is tough with a capital T. He hits at every opportunity and does so with relish. He is a punishing hitter along the boards and is very strong in front of his net; that's where you'll find him posted on the penalty killing unit.

His low center of gravity makes him difficult to knock down, and so he comes out of most collisions vertical and ready to continue play. As we said last year, Ken needs to use his body more intelligently so that he doesn't cost the Devils via penalty minutes.

He has a habit of adding just one more elbow and that's bad, because he gets caught for it. He also needs to learn to take a hit and not automatically respond, for that retaliation also lands him in the box.

THE INTANGIBLES

Daneyko is a hard worker on the ice and has great potential to improve into a dominant defenseman. Like Craig Wolanin, he too could use an older influence to teach him the rights and wrongs, and that's where coach Jim Schoenfeld might do his best work.

Ken is a good team man and enthusiastic, and he's already shown he's able to learn and to improve.

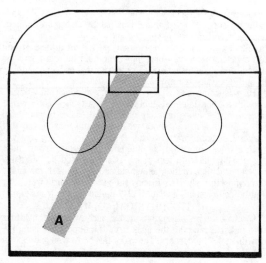

BRUCE DRIVER

Yrs. of NHL service: 4
Born: Toronto, Ontario, Canada; April 29, 1962
Position: Defenseman
Height: 6-0
Weight: 185
Uniform no.: 23
Shoots: left

Career statistics:

GP	G	A	TP	PIM
259	33	108	141	172

1987-88 statistics:

GP	G	A	TP	+/−	PIM	PP	SH	GW	GT	S	PCT
74	15	40	55	7	68	7	0	0	0	190	7.9

LAST SEASON

Driver led the Devils' defensemen in scoring, recording career highs in all point categories en route. He finished fourth on the club in scoring, third in assists and shots on goal. He missed six games with an ankle sprain.

THE FINESSE GAME

As his numbers indicate, Driver is New Jersey's best offensively-oriented defenseman and is definitely a finesse player. Driver is a smooth skater, not overly gifted with speed but quick enough to get a jump on the opposition. Still, he doesn't often rush the puck.

He doesn't have the speed to either force or exploit openings himself, but Driver joins the play as a fourth attacker at the opposing blue line. He sees the play in front of him fairly well and he can get the puck to his teammates in those openings, so he's a power play natural.

He has an average shot from the point, but one reason for his increased offensive success last season was his willingness to shoot more. In 1986-87, Driver had 132 shots on goal; last season 190. That's almost 50 percent more shots, and that's why his offense improved.

He plays positional defense and is adept at forcing the play wide of the net by using his defensive angles; his skating helps him there by allowing him to keep pace with the League's faster forwards.

THE PHYSICAL GAME

Unlike many finesse players, Driver is willing to sacrifice his body for defense. He blocks shots and will play along the boards although he is not outstanding there because he doesn't match up well strength-wise against the opposition. He is a push and shove guy, not a hitter.

THE INTANGIBLES

Driver's durability must be questioned. Though he matched his career high for games played last year, he still suffered that ankle injury and in previous years succumbed to neck, shoulder and knee injuries.

Other than that question, Driver should continue to mature into a dependable player who can make important contributions.

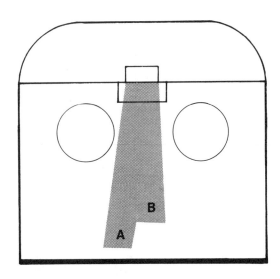

MARK JOHNSON

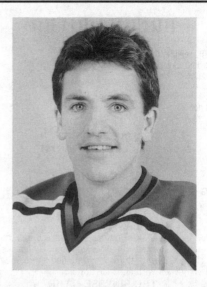

Yrs. of NHL service: 9
Born: Minneapolis, Minn., USA; September 22, 1957
Position: Center/left wing
Height: 5-9
Weight: 160
Uniform no.: 12
Shoots: left

Career statistics:

GP	G	A	TP	PIM
566	174	251	425	224

1987-88 statistics:

GP	G	A	TP	+/−	PIM	PP	SH	GW	GT	S	PCT
54	14	19	33	-10	14	2	3	3	0	121	11.6

LAST SEASON

Knee and foot injuries conspired to limit Johnson to his fewest NHL games last season. He finished second on the team in short-handed goals.

THE FINESSE GAME

Good hands and anticipation are what make Johnson a good finesse player. He handles the puck well at all speeds, and can get it to his teammates with equal ease on the forehand and backhand sides. His hands combine with his anticipation when he leads teammates into openings with quality passes.

Mark's excellent sense and hand skills make him a valuable specialty teams member. In the past he's been used on the point on the power play, but the development of the Devils defense now makes him unnecessary there. Still, don't be surprised if he shows up there every once in a while, because he puts his vision and passing skills to great work on the blue line. That anticipation also serves to make him a good penalty killer.

As a skater, Johnson's hallmark is balance. It gives him good lateral movement and makes him difficult to hit. He is not fast over the long haul but he is quick in any direction. So when he spots the openings, Johnson can either lead a teammate into them or gain them himself with one-step quickness.

Because he concentrates on making plays, Johnson is frequently at a bad angle to the net for shots. Also, a player with his hockey sense should be able to get into better position to score. But because of his positioning, Johnson is weak as a goal scorer. He'll get most of his goals opportunistically, as he breaks for the puck near the crease. He is also very good at deflections because of his excellent eye/hand coordination.

THE PHYSICAL GAME

Johnson is not an aggressive hockey player but, as was demonstrated in the Devils playoff series versus the Bruins, he is unafraid of being hit. He does not initiate contact and will generally stay out of high traffic areas, preferring to dart around the outside of the scrum.

He may feel he can do his best work in the open ice but, as we've seen with players like Pat LaFontaine and Steve Yzerman, a finesse game can be aided by physical play.

THE INTANGIBLES

Durability is the primary question regarding Johnson. He has never played a full NHL season, and is not particularly known for playing with pain. He otherwise has an excellent attitude as a team man, working hard in the games he plays.

He teamed with Patrik Sundstrom and John MacLean late in last season and through the playoffs and that line had tremendous success. In order to keep the Devils progressing, that troika must continue to contribute. Otherwise, the Devils revert to being a one-line team.

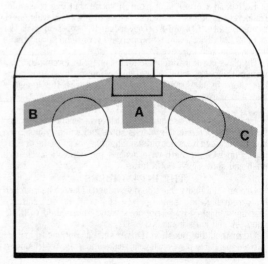

JIM KORN

Yrs. of NHL service: 7
Born: Hopkins, Minn., USA.; July 28, 1957
Position: Left wing
Height: 6-4
Weight: 220
Uniform no.: 14
Shoots: left

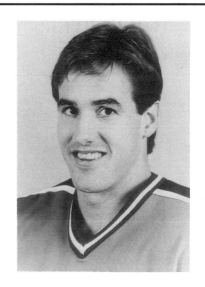

Career statistics:

GP	G	A	TP	PIM
485	49	101	150	1,413

1987-88 statistics:

GP	G	A	TP	+/−	PIM	PP	SH	GW	GT	S	PCT
52	8	13	21	-22	140	3	0	0	0	49	16.3

LAST SEASON

Goal total was second highest of career. Plus/minus was team's worst. Korn missed 24 games because of a shoulder injury and the subsequent surgery.

THE FINESSE GAME

Korn is not as lumbering a skater as his size might dictate, but he is no Nureyev either. He is not overly agile on his feet — one reason he was moved from defense to left wing — and he is not exceptionally skilled with his hands — not for puck work, anyway.

He doesn't handle the puck well when he carries it, and Korn is not gifted in terms of play making skills. He does not see the ice well, does not shoot the puck well and neither gives nor takes a pass well.

Any goal scoring Jim is going to do will have to be accomplished from the front of the net.

THE PHYSICAL GAME

Look at the penalty minute total. What do you think? Korn's obviously playing a very physical type of game and the Devils obviously want that kind of presence.

Korn is big and he can use his size to advantage when he rubs out an opponent along the boards. Of course, he also gets carried away and turns that hitting into fighting.

THE INTANGIBLES

Korn is the team's policeman, plain and simple. The hope was that his presence would allow some of the more physical but talented Devil players — the Verbeeks and Daneykos — to play their games and not have to run up huge PIM totals. Since Daneyko and Verbeek went 1-2 in PIM for the Devils, the plan obviously didn't work.

But perhaps his biggest role was the one of confidant to Lou Lamoriello, for whom Korn played at Providence College. Word is, Korn got the message to Lamoriello about the Devil players' dissatisfaction with former coach Doug Carpenter, and thus Carpenter's firing.

With the threat of rosters being reduced from 18 to 17 skaters for games, there's a chance of Korn riding the bench and playing only against the muscle teams. In his favor is the fact that, except when injured, he was dressed for every game (versus non-physical Minnesota and Los Angeles).

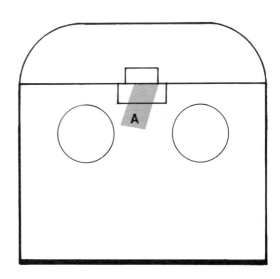

TOM KURVERS

Yrs. of NHL service: 4
Born: Minneapolis, Minn., USA; October 14, 1962
Position: Defenseman
Height: 6-0
Weight: 190
Uniform no.: 5
Shoots: left

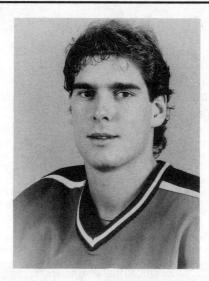

Career statistics:

GP	G	A	TP	PIM
249	28	104	132	136

1987-88 statistics:

GP	G	A	TP	+/−	PIM	PP	SH	GW	GT	S	PCT
56	5	29	34	6	46	2	0	1	0	88	5.7

LAST SEASON

Assist and point totals were second highest of Kurvers' career. He missed 13 games with a broken finger, five with a groin injury and one with the flu.

THE FINESSE GAME

Good finesse skills, particularly in skating and puckhandling make Kurvers a solid offensive defenseman. He has good speed and quickness in his skating, allowing him to move up the ice smoothly to join the offense. His quickness allows him to get into openings, and his balance gives him the agility to stop, start and change direction quickly.

Tom brings those skills to bear as a rushing defenseman, and he's a solid bet to carry the puck from the Devils zone. He does well at that, handling the puck confidently at all speeds.

He likes to run the offense from the offensive blue line, so he won't often carry the puck deeply into the offensive zone. Rather, he'll carry it to center and then get it to a breaking winger before setting up camp at the left point.

Kurvers sees the ice well from there, and that makes him a very valuable member of the Devils power play. He contains the point well with his quickness and anticipation, and he makes good passes to his teammates from there. He has a fine shot from the blue line, low and almost always on net, and Kurvers will almost always move to the center of the line to improve his shooting angle.

His play-reading ability extends to the defensive zone, where Kurvers is competent, if unspectacular. He does have a tendency toward mistakes if rushed, but generally makes the correct outlet pass.

THE PHYSICAL GAME

Despite good size, Kurvers is not much of a physical player. He's strong enough along the boards to not be completely pushed around, but when he's there he'll probably get outmuscled by the opposition.

Ideally, that boards and front of the net job would be taken care of by his partner, allowing Kurvers the freedom to use his finesse skills.

THE INTANGIBLES

The importance of Tom Kurvers became especially apparent when the Bruins played the Devils in last spring's Prince of Wales conference playoff series. Boston's heavy forechecking throttled the Devils in Game 3, which Kurvers missed with an injured thumb, and further emphasized Kurvers' importance to New Jersey.

Though no longer a youngster (he'll be 26 when the season opens) Kurvers can continue to develop and contribute to New Jersey for several seasons to come.

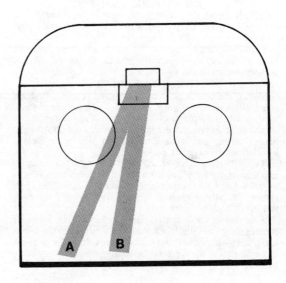

CLAUDE LOISELLE

Yrs. of NHL service: 6
Born: Ottawa, Ont., Canada; May 29, 1963
Position: Left wing
Height: 5-11
Weight: 190
Uniform no.: 19
Shoots: left

Career statistics:

GP	G	A	TP	PIM
271	55	64	119	491

1987-88 statistics:

GP	G	A	TP	+/−	PIM	PP	SH	GW	GT	S	PCT
68	17	18	35	7	118	3	2	2	0	117	14.5

LAST SEASON

A separated shoulder and a concussion limited Loiselle to his second highest games played total and point total, but his goal mark was a career high.

THE FINESSE GAME

Strength and balance are the keys to Loiselle's skating game. He is almost tireless (and that makes him an excellent checker), and his balance helps him immensely in his physical game.

Because he plants his feet so widely, however, he loses agility and some quickness. He doesn't have rink-length speed, but Claude can get something of a jump on the opposition in the first stride or two before he slows down. That jump, because of that wide gait, is going to be strictly straight ahead and won't really help his lateral movement.

Offensively, Loiselle doesn't see the ice well. He can find his teammates if given the space and time but otherwise he's not a playmaker. He does bring good anticipation to bear (which is another reason he's a good checker), and that nets him some scoring opportunities off his checking.

Loiselle's a little tough with the puck and doesn't handle it well at top speed. He also frequently takes himself to the backhand — and bad ice — in the offensive zone. He has neither a goal scorer's hands nor instincts, and will have to collect most of his goals from the front of the net. His 17 goals is about right for him, but remember that he got 10 of those goals in the first 20 games last year.

THE PHYSICAL GAME

Loiselle plays a physical game. He's a digger and a mucker, and his persistent checking will wear down an opponent. He goes to the traffic areas willingly and he takes the body well in all three zones, so we would say he uses his size well. His balance helps him in his physical style, keeping him vertical and ready to move again after collisions.

He also has good hand speed and strength, and that serves to make him a good faceoff man.

THE INTANGIBLES

Loiselle is a role player, but a good one. His checking is very sound and he deserves some recognition League-wide for it. That skill has also served to make him one of the NHL's better penalty killers.

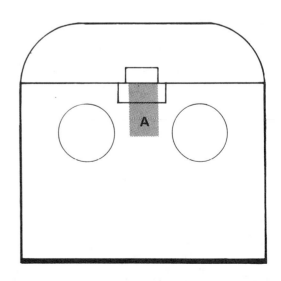

JOHN MACLEAN

Yrs. of NHL service: 5
Born: Oshawa, Ontario, Canada; November 20, 1964
Position: Right wing
Height: 6-0
Weight: 195
Uniform no.: 15
Shoots: right

Career statistics:

GP	G	A	TP	PIM
314	89	108	197	431

1987-88 statistics:

GP	G	A	TP	+/-	PIM	PP	SH	GW	GT	S	PCT
76	23	16	39	-10	145	12	0	4	0	204	11.3

LAST SEASON

Benched for three games, but games played was still second highest of career. Ditto goals. Point total was lowest in three years. Third on the club in power play goals, second in SOG.

THE FINESSE GAME

John's stockiness belies his skating ability. He has fairly good lateral movement and quickness, and his agility is such that he can maneuver in tight spaces. He has a fair burst of speed up ice, but would do well to learn to moderate it. Right now, he does everything at one speed, and that makes him very predictable.

MacLean can carry the puck well in front of him, but he still doesn't handle it well at top speed so he has to slow down to make his plays. He has decent vision on the ice and can make plays to his teammates, but MacLean puts himself at a disadvantage by keeping his head down when he's moving the puck. Therefore he misses openings for himself and his teammates. He is also basically a carry-and-shoot player, as his SOG total indicates. That betrays a goal scorer's mentality.

He has a hard wrist shot in close and a big slap shot off the wing, and MacLean is generally accurate with his shots, forcing the goaltender to make saves. He works particularly well on the power play, when he has room and time to shoot the puck.

His minus offensively is his lack of imagination. He's a straight ahead type of player, and so he's not going to make the creative plays in the offensive zone.

His minus defensively is his defenseit's just woeful. He has yet to learn to stick with his check through all three zones. He must also learn discipline in his defensive zone in order to stay in position and not release too soon in search of a never-to-arrive breakout pass.

THE PHYSICAL GAME

MacLean uses his body effectively, initiating play in the corners and along the boards. He makes the most of his size and strength, but he'll get out-muscled by bigger opponents.

He's a hitter and an aggressive player, and his balance helps him in this respect. He's also effective because he can play out of the corner, but chances are that if he gets the puck he's going to fire it toward the net.

THE INTANGIBLES

MacLean was one of the players who was supposed to take a hint from the Greg Adams trade, that being that the country club attitude fostered by the team's younger foundation players — who could *never* be traded — would no longer be tolerated.

MacLean's consistency from night to night is still questionable, and he must still learn to approach every game with the same consistency of intensity. Evidence? Four times last year he went pointless in three games — an eight game pointless streak. That's a quarter of a season right there. More proof? Twenty three goals, only 11 at even-strength.

MacLean's huge playoff — and the two weeks preceding it — showed just how he can contribute in the NHL. He teams very well with Mark Johnson and Patrik Sundstrom, getting the puck for them while they swirl around, then getting into position to score. That must continue in order for the Devils to continue their improvement.

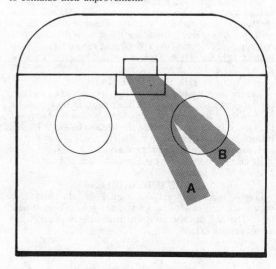

KIRK MULLER

Yrs. of NHL service: 4
Born: Kingston, Ontario, Canada; February 8, 1966
Position: Center
Height: 5-11
Weight: 185
Uniform no.: 9
Shoots: left

Career statistics:

GP	G	A	TP	PIM
316	105	185	290	303

1987-88 statistics:

GP	G	A	TP	+/-	PIM	PP	SH	GW	GT	S	PCT
80	37	57	94	19	114	17	2	1	1	215	17.2

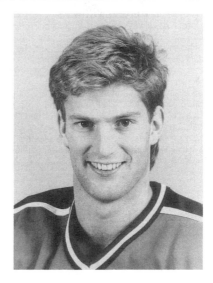

LAST SEASON

Muller played all 80 games for the second time in his four year career, setting personal marks in all three point categories and leading the Devils in scoring (14th overall in the NHL). Muller also led the team in power play goals and SOG, and finished second on the club in goal scoring. He was third in plus/minus.

THE FINESSE GAME

Muller's rise as a finesse player is directly attributable to his improvement as a skater. He's always been a strong skater, but now Kirk has added lateral movement and agility to his repertoire. His balance has improved, along with his foot speed, and both assets serve to make him quicker and more dangerous in the offensive zone.

That improved agility gives Muller the shiftiness necessary so that he doesn't have to go straight at the defense or the net. Muller can also jump into the holes now, and most importantly, his increased quickness translates into more time to make plays.

Keeping his head up has helped Kirk move the puck quicker to his teammates, and to recognize the opportunities as they develop. He's not a Gretzky as passer — in terms of softness and getting the puck through people — but Muller is improving and he's going to make more plays than he misses.

The improved skating has also helped Kirk as a scorer, getting him to those loose pucks a half-step quicker than the opposition. Muller has also moved to the middle of the ice to create plays, rather than looking for loose pucks to squeak through to the perimeter.

All Muller's skills make him a natural for the power play.

None of Kirk's improvement has come at the expense of his defense. He checks well in all zones of the ice and has always taken care of defense before offense.

THE PHYSICAL GAME

Hard as it might be to believe, Muller's physical game suffers because of his size. If he was three inches taller and 20 pounds heavier, we might be talking about him in the same breath as Mark Messier. But as it is, Muller is too small for the very aggressive game he plays.

Kirk backs down from no one in a confrontation, and he effectively uses his strength and body along the boards and in the corners. He willingly sacrifices his body and initiates contact, and his improved balance helps him in these confrontations by keeping him vertical. And, of course, Muller has the hand skills to make a play coming out of the corner.

Unfortunately for him, his lack of size and strength betrays him in confrontations with larger forwards or defensemen.

THE INTANGIBLES

The contrast has always been an obvious one—the artistry of Mario Lemieux versus the digging, mucking play of Kirk Muller. But consider this: Muller scored 94 points for the League's 10th ranked offense. The Devils scored 295 goals. Therefore, Muller was involved in almost 33 percent — one third — of the Devils' scoring.

Not bad for a mucker. And for a guy to score 94 points for a less-than-prolific club . . . well, put Muller on a more explosive club and he gets 115-120 points. Not bad at all.

Kirk was also consistent throughout the season in his scoring, but that's no surprise because he plays all out all the time. He has a tremendous attitude and work ethic, aiming to play his best in every game.

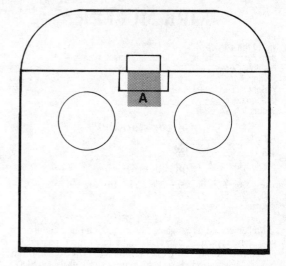

JACK O'CALLAHAN

Yrs. of NHL service: 6
Born: Charlestown, Mass., USA; July 24, 1957
Position: Defenseman
Height: 6-1
Weight: 185
Uniform no.: 7
Shoots: right

Career statistics:

GP	G	A	TP	PIM
353	22	83	105	490

1987-88 statistics:

GP	G	A	TP	+/-	PIM	PP	SH	GW	GT	S	PCT
50	7	19	26	-3	97	4	0	1	0	90	7.8

LAST SEASON

O'Callahan was acquired in 1987's Waiver Draft from Chicago. Goal and point totals were career highs. He missed two games with a fractured eye orbit, four games with strained knee ligaments, one game via suspension and was benched for the rest.

THE FINESSE GAME

Finesse skills are not the high point of O'Callahan's game. He's no better than average as a skater in both directions, but he plays fairly well positionally so he isn't often beaten one-on-one. He doesn't carry the puck, but he'll generally make the right breakout pass. He is vulnerable to turnovers, however, when subjected to heavy forechecking.

He's not a big goal scorer because he doesn't have a good shot from the point. Though he hesitates offensively at the point, the same bit of vision and passing skill that allows him to make the correct breakout pass lets him find the open man — but only if the penalty killers allow him the time and the space.

He doesn't pinch in and doesn't take advantage of opportunities, even when appropriate.

THE PHYSICAL GAME

O'Callahan's strength would have to be his defensive zone play. O'Callahan keeps the zone clean, is willing to hit and can be a punishing hitter. However, he'll need assistance in the play after tying up a forward along the boards.

He will take the man out from in front of his own net, but because his anticipation and concentration are lacking (he tends to get hypnotized by the puck), opposing forwards can sneak in behind him.

THE INTANGIBLES

Age and a fairly large defensive corps mitigate against O'Callahan being a regular contributor. His value is in the depth his presence gives the Devils, allowing them the choice of putting an experienced NHL defenseman into the fray.

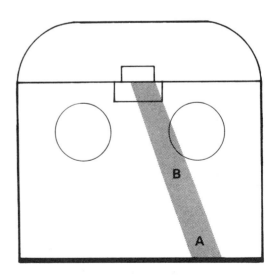

BOB SAUVE

Yrs. of NHL service: 12
Born: Ste. Jenvieve, Quebec Canada; June 17, 1955
Position: Goaltender
Height: 5-8
Weight: 165
Uniform no.: 28
Catches: left

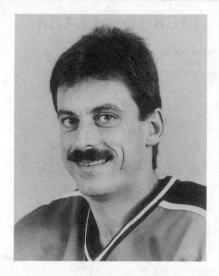

Career statistics:

GP	MINS	G	SO	AVG	A	PIM
405	22,990	1,321	8	3.44	14	57

1987-88 statisics:

GP	MINS	AVG	W	L	T	SO	GA	SA	SAPCT	PIM
34	1,803	3.56	10	16	3	0	107	823	.870	4

LAST SEASON

Sauve was acquired by the Devils as a free agent during the summer of 1987. Games played was lowest in three seasons, while Sauve was under .500 for the first time in six seasons.

THE PHYSICAL GAME

Sauve is a standup goaltender to a fault, always has been and always will be. Efficient is the word that probably describes Sauve's style the best, as he cuts the angles very well and makes almost no excess movement: The puck either hits Sauve or goes in.

Unlike most smaller goaltenders, Sauve is not an acrobat. He knows how to position himself in the net and how to square himself to the puck. He just lets the puck hit him, instead of diving all over the ice.

It's a good thing Sauve doesn't move, because when he does he's in trouble. His lateral movement across the crease is not good, forcing him to open up his stance and become unbalanced and vulnerable. Once he opens up, he's dead.

He's good with his stick and glove, and he's taken to leaving the net to stop the puck for his defense. Because he stands up, Sauve is usually good at controlling rebounds. He'll either direct them from harm or fall on them for a stoppage. He won't overplay it.

THE MENTAL GAME

Sauve's greatest asset, at this point in his career, is his ability to ride the bench for a couple of weeks and then fill in admirably in his spot starts. He's always prepared to play.

He's always been a consistent goaltender, and a bad single performance has never affected his next game. He's upbeat and positive, and those mental traits translate into mental toughness, great concentration and big save capability.

THE INTANGIBLES

If there were questions about Sauve's ability last season — *if* — then they were answered in his late season performances. His play in New Jersey's 2-2 tie against Buffalo — a game the Devils *had* to have to make the playoffs — and then in his playoff appearances proved there's plenty of ability left in his old bones.

He brings to the Devil goaltending corps a tremendous volume of experience and knowledge, things he's more than willing to impart to his younger teammates. That's one big reason why he's always been well-liked by his teammates.

His experience et al, is one big reason he'll probably be backing up Sean Burke this season.

BRENDAN SHANAHAN

Yrs. of NHL service: 1
Born: Mimico, Ontario, Canada; January 23, 1969
Position: Center/right wing
Height: 6-3
Weight: 205
Uniform no.: 11
Shoots: right

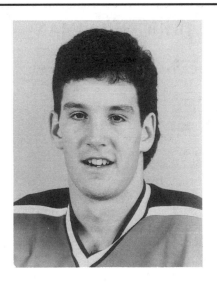

Career statisics:

GP	G	A	TP	+/−	PIM	PP	SH	GW	GT	S	PCT
65	7	19	26	-20	131	2	0	2	0	72	9.7

LAST SEASON

Shanahan was New Jersey's first choice in the 1987 Entry Draft. His plus/minus was the worst among team forwards playing at least 65 games. He missed a handful of games with a broken nose, back spasms and the flu.

THE FINESSE GAME

All of Brendan's skills need to be improved to the NHL level. Currently, he doesn't have great speed, but he does have better lateral movement and agility than a rookie — and a rookie with his size — would be expected to have.

He has shown potential for playmaking at the NHL level, but right now the play is too quick for Shanahan and his passes are into traffic and skates, if they're not intercepted by the opposition. Because he doesn't yet handle the puck at the major league level, Shanahan will lose the puck to opposition checking. He doesn't keep his head up, and even when he does he doesn't move with it well enough to elude the competition.

His shot won't fool many NHL goaltenders, so Brendan will have to be in fairly tight to score. He does, however, have the strength to score from the 30-foot range.

THE PHYSICAL GAME

This is the strength of Shanahan's game right now, and certainly will continue to be as he matures. He already has great size and should only get bigger and stringier as he matures physically.

Shanahan likes to play a hitting game and is fearless about it. He'll go into a corner against anyone, and if that provokes a fight so be it. Brendan isn't intimidated and he'll drop the gloves with anyone.

While unafraid of the League's tough guys, Shanahan showed a tendency to be a bully himself last season. He was much bolder and much more aggressive with European players than he was with North Americans, much more likely to give the Europeans the stick, the punch in the back of the head.

THE INTANGIBLES

There's no question that Brendan Shanahan can and will be *at least* a good NHLer, given time. He has excellent potential in both the finesse and physical games to be an exceptional NHLer. But there is also no question that Shanahan can't contribute consistently at the NHL level right now.

Now he may be too good to send back to junior, but if he is — and if the Devils think doing so would actually *hurt* his development — he should be playing every day.

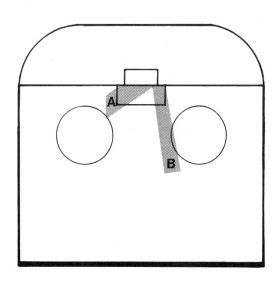

281

DOUG SULLIMAN

Yrs. of NHL service: 9
Born: Glace Bay, Nova Scotia, Canada; August 29, 1959
Position: Left wing
Height: 5-9
Weight: 195
Uniform no.: 22
Shoots: left

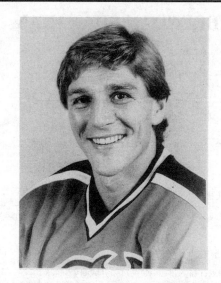

Career statistics:

GP	G	A	TP	PIM
551	151	158	309	170

1987-88 statistics:

GP	G	A	TP	+/−	PIM	PP	SH	GW	GT	S	PCT
59	16	14	30	-8	25	8	1	0	0	89	18.0

LAST SEASON

Games played was lowest in three years due to injury and benchings, and second lowest since Sulliman became an NHL regular. Ditto the above for goal and point totals.

THE FINESSE GAME

Sulliman is a solid two-way player for New Jersey, contributing at both ends of the ice.

Offensively, unlike many of the Devil forwards, Sulliman carries the puck well. He will hold the puck for a few strides and see what plays can be made, rather than getting rid of the puck as soon as it touches his stick.

He sees openings and moves into them well but Sulliman lacks a goal scorer's instincts. He'll throw the puck around the boards and get to the openings, sometimes forcing his way to the front of the net or the base of the right circle. Sulliman would be a better scorer if he had a better feel for the net.

He's a good checker, doing an excellent job of checking without drawing penalties. Because of his checking role, his plus/minus rating is usually deceptive.

THE PHYSICAL GAME

Doug is aggressive at both ends of the ice and his strength makes him an asset on the power play, where he will often be positioned in front of the net to take a pounding.

Sulliman won't back away from anything and he'll tie up the defenseman in front. He is a tough but clean player and will dish it out as well as take it. He plays bigger than his size.

THE INTANGIBLES

Sulliman is a guy who gives whatever he's got. His willingness to play physically continues to haunt him through injury and, great as his character is, his talent is such that he's going to be moved in and out of the lineup as a third/fourth line player.

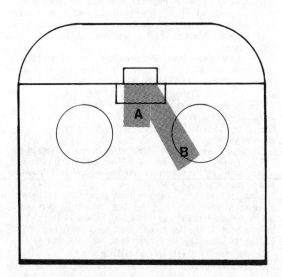

PATRIK SUNDSTROM

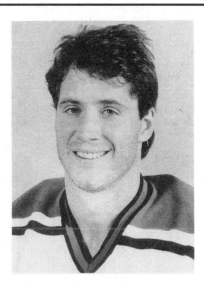

Yrs. of NHL service: 6
Born: Skelleftea, Sweden; December 14, 1961
Position: Center/left wing
Height: 6-0
Weight: 200
Uniform no.: 17
Shoots: left

Career statistics:

GP	G	A	TP	PIM
452	148	245	393	223

1987-88 statistics:

GP	G	A	TP	+/−	PIM	PP	SH	GW	GT	S	PCT
78	15	36	51	-16	42	9	1	0	0	126	11.9

LAST SEASON

Sundstrom was acquired by the Devils in exchange for Greg Adams and Kirk McLean just prior to the opening of 1987-88 training camp. Goal total was the lowest of his career, assist and point totals second lowest. He finished fourth on the club in assists. His plus/minus was the worst among Devil regulars. Bruised foot and abdominal pull sidelined him for two games.

THE FINESSE GAME

Sundstrom is a supremely talented player, blessed with almost unlimited ability. He is an excellent skater, because all components of his skating are excellent. He has superb balance and strength on his skates, and he complements those assets with exceptional foot speed and agility. He stops and starts well, changes direction on a dime and can out-race all but the fastest NHL players to a loose puck.

His skating dovetails excellently with his puckhandling and play making abilities, which are also of superior calibre. Patrik can not only carry the puck well at top speed, but he can also make any play he sees at that speed.

He controls the puck as if it were nailed to his stick and he uses his excellent touch (whether the puck has to be feathered or fired) to pass well to both sides. He handles the puck just as well in traffic as he does in the open ice.

His anticipation and hockey sense are superb, and he reads the ice easily and clearly; that's why he's a power play and penalty killing regular.

The only finesse skill not at the same level as the others is his shot. Sundstrom has a terrific wrist shot, but he doesn't shoot anywhere near enough despite the opportunities he gets. He looks to pass too much, and should become more selfish.

THE PHYSICAL GAME

Sundstrom has good size and strength, so not only can he take the rough going, he can initiate his share as well. That's not to say that he *will* initiate that contact, and his finesse game would certainly expand if he did.

Though he works better in the open ice, Sundstrom is unafraid of skating into traffic to get the puck; that's where his excellent balance and strength combine with his excellent hands to make him a very dangerous player in tight to the net.

He surprises people with his strength in the corners and, again, it's his balance that helps him get the job done. Patrik is also greatly aided by his reach, which puts his hands into places his body can't get to.

Good hand and wrist strength propel his shot and allow him to pull the puck out of traffic, and they also make Sundstrom a good faceoff man. He is also willing to sacrifice his body to block shots (doing so with particularly good effect while penalty killing), and is one of the NHL's better shot-blocking forwards.

THE INTANGIBLES

Patrik's only intangible is himself. For whatever reason, he's been able to bring his tremendous skills to bear only once in his NHL career, for he's much more than the 70 point scorer his numbers indicate. The only conclusion to be drawn is that, when the game matters Sundstrom will turn up the juice — otherwise he's content to coast.

Witness his performance (in conjunction with Mark Johnson and John MacLean) down the stretch and into last season's playoffs. And look at that record-setting eight-point night he had versus the Washington Capitals in the Patrick Division finals. That's not at all out of character for Sundstrom.

The unfortunate thing is that, despite how well he played during April and May, if Sundstrom had played that way all year the Devils never would have had to win on the last night of the season to make the playoffs.

In order for the Devils to continue to progress this year, Sundstrom must play closer to the level of which he's capable.

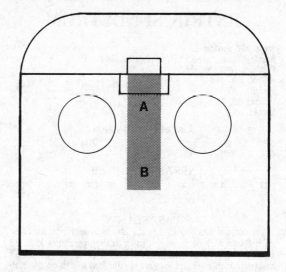

RANDY VELISCHEK

Yrs. of NHL service: 5
Born: Montreal, Quebec, Canada; February 10, 1962
Position: Defenseman
Height: 6-0
Weight: 200
Uniform no.: 27
Shoots: left

Career statistics:

GP	G	A	TP	PIM
250	13	43	56	195

1987-88 statistics:

GP	G	A	TP	+/−	PIM	PP	SH	GW	GT	S	PCT
51	3	9	12	-13	66	0	1	0	0	39	7.7

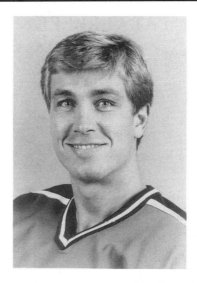

LAST SEASON

Velischek was benched through much of the first, sitting out 22 of the first 40 games and 28 of the first 47. He sat just one game after Jim Schoenfeld was named coach. His plus/minus was the defense's lowest.

THE FINESSE GAME

Finesse and offensive ability shouldn't be confused for if they were, Randy Velischek would be shortchanged in a scouting report. He is not an overpowering offensive player, in fact barely a threat at all in terms of points. What he is, is a smart, consistent defensive force and that's where his finesse abilities come to the fore.

Randy's a good skater, smooth in both directions and with neither outstanding speed and quickness, nor agility and lateral movement. He plays his position, therefore, positionally and understands how to use and exploit his defensive angles to force the opposition wide of the net. He does this by reading the offensive rush well.

Velischek is not offensively gifted, and so will not usually join the attack inside the opposition's blue line. He has an average shot from the point — which he almost never uses because he is falling back on defense — and he adds little else to the attack. He does not pinch in to contain the point.

Randy moves the puck from his end efficiently, though he can be rushed into mistakes (usually because he is covering up for his partner's mistakes to begin with). Occasionally he will carry the puck to center and get rid of it there.

THE PHYSICAL GAME

Though he doesn't have great size, Velischek puts what he does have to work well. He bangs in the corners and ties up men in front of the net, and he'll hold his own with the League's stronger forwards.

He makes his physical game more effective by playing smartly and not taking penalties.

THE INTANGIBLES

It should come as no surprise when a guy who was graduated magna cum laude from college is described as smart. And that's what Randy Velischek is a smart and consistent defensive player. He adds much to the Devils because of his reliability, and it is curious (to say the least) that he was waived by the

Minnesota North Stars, who obviously felt Velischek couldn't compete in the NHL.

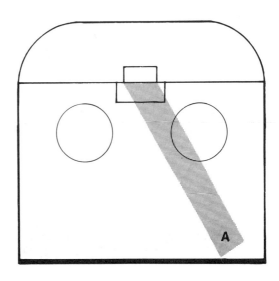

PAT VERBEEK

Yrs. of NHL service: 5
Born: Sarnia, Ontario, Canada; May 24, 1964
Position: Right wing
Height: 5-9
Weight: 195
Uniform no.: 16
Shoots: right

Career statistics:

GP	G	A	TP	PIM
386	144	130	274	754

1987-88 statistics:

GP	G	A	TP	+/−	PIM	PP	SH	GW	GT	S	PCT
73	46	31	77	29	227	13	0	8	0	179	25.7

LAST SEASON

Verbeek set career highs in all point categories, despite missing seven games with a knee injury. He led the team in goals, game winners and shooting percentage, finishing third in the NHL in the last two categories. His PIM total, also a career high, was highest among New Jersey forwards and second highest on the team. He also finished second in power play goals. He led the club in plus/minus.

THE FINESSE GAME

Life is timing. All you have to do is be in the right place at the right time. Just ask Pat Verbeek.

The winger's best finesse asset is his timing, or anticipation if you will (though less charitable observers might call it conditioned response and nothing else). Whatever, Verbeek has learned to be a goal scorer by going to where the puck is going to be. He scores off scrambles in front and is opportunistic, picking up rebounds and other garbage. That skill makes him a premier power play player, and you'll find him posted in front of the net in the man-advantage situation.

But he's more than just a power play specialist. Two seasons back, 17 of his 35 goals came on the power play. Last year, 13 of 46. So it's obvious Verbeek is more than effective at even strength.

He's a strong skater and can plant himself in the crease, but his balance remains a little high because of his barrel-like upper body. He doesn't have great foot speed (so there's not a lot of quickness), but Pat does have some rink length speed he can apply, and he can move pretty quickly once he gets his fireplug body moving.

He handles the puck no better than averagely when he carries it, and don't expect him to make Savard-like moves with it because he can't. Despite what his improved goal totals might indicate, Verbeek's straight ahead style reflects itself in his playmaking ability. He doesn't have great playreading creativity.

THE PHYSICAL GAME

The physical game is Verbeek's game, and he must play that way to be successful. He packs a lot of strength into a small package and is very aggressive, so he can hurt people when he hits them. Certainly he's willing to take hits, and he does so in the slot in order to score.

One disadvantage he suffers is in reach. If he's tied up with a bigger opponent who matches him in strength, Verbeek's lack of reach mitigates against him. But this is a not a major disadvantage, as most of Verbeek's opponents will be knocked on their behinds.

THE INTANGIBLES

We were wrong about Pat Verbeek last year when we said "he will be hard pressed to repeat his goal scoring success." His play the last two seasons shows that maybe he should be mentioned in the same breath as the Rick Tocchets, Bob Proberts and Cam Neelys.

Like Aaron Broten, Verbeek is reaping the benefits of a more consistent work ethic, and he too can be a leader on the ice. His 25 goals against Patrick Division opposition also shows Pat can come through in the bigger games. What he was spurred by this year was the trade of Greg Adams to Vancouver.

The trade by general manager Lou Lamoriello demonstrated to Verbeek, Kirk Muller, John MacLean, Ken Daneyko and Craig Wolanin (in other words, the team's young nucleus) that the country club attitude they had fostered — with the idea that none of them could ever be traded because of their positions as the team's foundation — had come to an end.

Verbeek need not suffer from any job insecurity. He's shown what he can do at the NHL level. Now he and his teammates must work to keep the Devils improving.

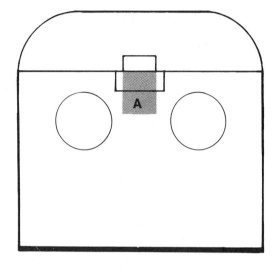

CRAIG WOLANIN

Yrs. of NHL service: 3
Born: Grosse Pointe, Mich., USA; July 27, 1967
Position: Defenseman
Height: 6-3
Weight: 205
Uniform no.: 6
Shoots: left

Career statistics:

GP	G	A	TP	PIM
190	12	47	59	353

1987-88 statistics:

GP	G	A	TP	+/−	PIM	PP	SH	GW	GT	S	PCT
78	6	25	31	0	170	1	1	3	0	113	5.3

LAST SEASON

Games played was a career high, though Craig missed one game due to back spasms and another due to benchings. He set career highs in all point categories, as well as in PIM.

THE FINESSE GAME

Though he is not a finesse player, Wolanin's finesse skills continue to show improvement from year to year. He's become a good skater because of increased foot speed, and his stride has lengthened out to add some more power to his skating. He's got good balance and that aids his foot speed and quickness. He has more agility than would be expected for a big man.

His game has improved defensively because of his improved skating. He plays a positional style and has learned how to force the play wide of the net. He's helped by the fact that he pivots well and is able to keep pace with the opposition, as long as he refrains from wandering all over the defensive zone to belt people.

He reads the rush toward him fairly well, and Wolanin has begun to show signs of understanding the play away from him as well. His puck handling and movement have improved, so that he is now fairly sure-handed in getting the puck from the zone.

Craig has a fairly accurate shot from the blue line, and his improved foot speed has given him the confidence to charge the slot for a shot when he has the chance.

THE PHYSICAL GAME

Wolanin has great size, and when he wants to hit watch out. He's already tremendously strong and a punishing hitter, and he's yet to reach his physical maturity.

The frustrating part is that Craig does not apply his size consistently in front of the net or along the boards. He allows men to slip back into the play (thus forcing him to take penalties) by failing to complete his takeouts, and he pushes and shoves when a solid shoulder would do the trick and free the puck.

Wolanin does sacrifice himself for defense, as in dropping to block shots. All in all, he can be said to play a good — with the potential to be excellent — physical game.

THE INTANGIBLES

We said last year that "Wolanin . . . needs guidance and tutelage from an older defenseman, someone to show him the ropes and to break him of bad habits."

The answer for that may have come in coach Jim Schoenfeld, a former defenseman. Wolanin has the potential to be one of the top defensive defensemen in the league, and Schoenfeld may be the man to bring that out.

That would be good for both Wolanin and the Devils, for while he's become a capable player he's far from proved his worth as a number one draft pick. Still, his potential is worth our patience.

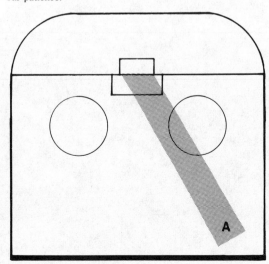

NEW YORK ISLANDERS

LINE COMBINATIONS
DEREK KING-PAT LAFONTAINE-RANDY WOOD
RICH KROMM BOB BASSEN-BRAD LAUER
DALE HENRY-BRENT SUTTER-ALAN KERR
GREG GILBERT-BRYAN TROTTIER-MIKKO MAKELA

DEFENSE PAIRINGS
STEVE KONROYD-TOMAS JONSSON
GERALD DIDUCK-JEFF NORTON
KEN LEITER-KEN MORROW

GOALTENDERS
KELLY HRUDEY
BILL SMITH

OTHER PLAYERS
PAT FLATLEY — Right wing

POWER PLAY

FIRST UNIT:
DEREK KING-BRENT SUTTER-MIKKO MAKELA
-KEN LEITER

SECOND UNIT:
PAT LAFONTAINE-BRYAN TROTTIER-MIKKO MAKELA
-JEFF NORTON

On the first unit, SUTTER works the back of the net with KING and MAKELA in the left and right circles respectively. LEITER and the left point man (DENIS POTVIN before retirement) would play catch with each other and SUTTER to loosen the defense for a shot by MAKELA. KING and SUTTER would crash the net for the rebound. Shots from the points were the second option.

On the second unit, LAFONTAINE and MAKELA assume positions in the faceoff circles, while TROTTIER plugs the front of the net. Shots by LAFONTAINE and MAKELA are the preferred alternatives, with point shots the second option.

Last season the Islander power play was EXCELLENT, scoring 87 goals in 387 power play opportunities (22.5 percent, fifth overall).

PENALTY KILLING

FIRST UNIT:
GREG GILBERT-BRENT SUTTER
JEFF NORTON-KEN MORROW

SECOND UNIT:
RICH KROMM-BRYAN TROTTIER
-GERALD DIDUCK

The Islanders generally play a box defense, but the forwards are very aggressive on the puck. BASSEN, KERR, LAFONTAINE and MAKELA will also see penalty killing time. Now-retired DENIS POTVIN formerly paired with DIDUCK.

Last season the Islanders penalty killing was POOR, allowing 94 goals in 416 shorthanded situations (77.4 percent, 18th overall).

CRUCIAL FACEOFFS:
SUTTER or TROTTIER.

BOB BASSEN

Yrs. of NHL service: 2
Born: Calgary, Alta., Canada; May 6, 1965
Position: Center
Height: 5-10
Weight: 185
Uniform no.: 28
Shoots: left

Career statistics:

GP	G	A	TP	PIM
165	15	27	42	194

1987-88 statistics:

GP	G	A	TP	+/−	PIM	PP	SH	GW	GT	S	PCT
77	6	16	22	8	99	1	0	2	0	65	9.2

LAST SEASON

Games played total equalled career high, and assist and point totals were also career highs. He missed three games with a concussion. His PIM total was third highest among forwards.

THE FINESSE GAME

Bassen is a very good skater with excellent speed and quickness. He gets to the openings and closes them before the opposition can exploit them, and he pursues the puck relentlessly. His checking also forces turnovers by the opposition, and Bob's quickness gets him to those loose pucks. He puts that speed to use as a good checking forward and a penalty killing regular.

Unfortunately his transition game after that turnover is faulty, and that's because Bassen doesn't handle the puck well. His hands are not the greatest, and patience isn't high in his list of assets either. If he took more time and looked for his teammates, he'd be better able to cash in on those loose pucks.

For himself, he'll do his scoring from in close as he pounces on errant pucks.

THE PHYSICAL GAME

Though not a predominantly physical player, Bassen has no distaste for the physical game. He'll take the body when he can and that's usually enough to break up a play, but Bassen is not an overly strong player.

He can be out-matched along the boards, so he's at his best closing the passing lanes rather than trying to physically restrain an opponent.

THE INTANGIBLES

Bob Bassen is another of the plethora of youngsters coach Terry Simpson integrated into the lineup (others include Brad Lauer, Ken Leiter and Alan Kerr). Like the others he plays with enthusiasm and determination, but unlike the aforementioned trio Bassen hasn't shown that he can succeed in anything beyond a role playing situation.

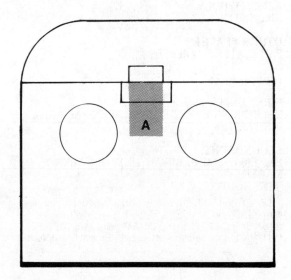

BRAD DALGARNO

Yrs. of NHL service: 1
Born: Vancouver, B.C., Canada; August 11, 1967
Position: Right wing
Height: 6-3
Weight: 215
Uniform no.: 17
Shoots: right

Career statistics:

GP	G	A	TP	PIM
40	3	8	11	58

1987-88 statistics:

GP	G	A	TP	+/−	PIM	PP	SH	GW	GT	S	PCT
38	2	8	10	4	58	0	0	1	0	39	5.1

LAST SEASON

Dalgarno played his games between demotions to the American Hockey League.

THE FINESSE GAME

Dalgarno's skating is just average for the NHL level. He has no outstanding capabilities except balance, and he uses that asset in his physical game. Otherwise there's not much speed, quickness or agility in his foot work. He has a long stride that covers a lot of ground but don't mistake that for speed. Improved foot speed would do him wonders.

He has little concept of the play at the NHL level, either conceptually or in execution. He has below-average hand skills for the NHL level which dovetail perfectly with his below-average vision. He does have a good slap shot when he gets it off, but he barely shoots as it is.

While not contributing offensively, Dalgarno works hard to not be a liability defensively. He plays well positionally, conscientious (maybe too much so) of his check in the defensive zone.

THE PHYSICAL GAME

Dalgarno has great size which he uses inconsistently. It's not that he doesn't want to play physically — because he'll make the attempts — but he doesn't get consistent results. For one thing, he needs better strength because, for all intents and purposes, he's leaning on guys and not muscling them.

Again, his lack of skating skill means he'll have difficulty getting near enough to anyone to use his size. And should he run down an opponent, belt him in the corner and free the puck, Dalgarno can't make a play.

THE INTANGIBLES

When a guy is a number one pick and can't make your team for two years and then runs out of junior eligibility and still can't make your team, he's trying to tell you something. He's trying to tell you he isn't ready for the NHL. That's the situation with Brad Dalgarno.

He can do no more up here than fill space, and it's hard to improve when you can't afford to make a mistake. If he can't play consistently at this level, the Islanders should let him play consistently in the American Hockey League.

Dalgarno had a great deal of difficulty adjusting this year, so much so that he was said to be on the verge of a nervous breakdown over what he felt to be poor treatment from the club. He even let it be known that the club hadn't given him any direction for improvement.

Whatever the case, Dalgarno clearly needs more time before he can contribute regularly in the NHL.

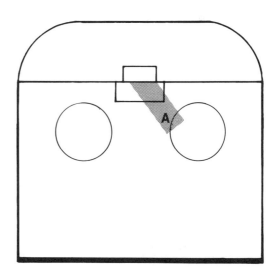

GERALD DIDUCK

Yrs. of NHL service: 3
Born: Edmonton, Alta., Canada; April 6, 1965
Position: Defenseman
Height: 6-2
Weight: 205
Uniform no.: 4
Shoots: right

Career statistics:

GP	G	A	TP	PIM
173	12	25	37	262

1987-88 statistics:

GP	G	A	TP	+/-	PIM	PP	SH	GW	GT	S	PCT
68	7	12	19	22	113	4	0	1	0	128	5.5

LAST SEASON

Games played and all point totals were career highs, despite missing several weeks with a fractured foot. His PIM total was second highest among the club's defensemen and his plus/minus rating was third best on the team.

THE FINESSE GAME

Diduck's career year is not surprising, as he's been growing into his place as one of the team's top defenders. He's a very good skater both forward and back, equipped with good balance and agility. He turns well in both directions and is fairly mobile laterally. He has neither great speed nor outstanding quickness, but he grades out well in both categories. His long stride will pull him away from the opposition and the quickness he does have allows him to pinch in at the offensive blue line to contain the point.

Gerald doesn't use his skating to rush the puck; in fact, he hardly handles it at all. When he does he makes a quick pass to start the play up-ice, and he does have the vision to play the point on the power play. He can find the open man and get the puck to him.

He'll deliver a low and strong slap shot from the point, and he also likes to slide toward the middle of the blue line for a better angle.

He plays his defense positionally, using his angles to force the play outside and then closing the gap on the forward to take away the puck.

THE PHYSICAL GAME

One reason for Diduck's previous bouncing in and out of the Islander lineup was his inconsistent use of his size. Those days are gone. He plays an aggressive physical game now, liberally spiced with elbows, and he plays it effectively.

Gerald puts his excellent size and strength to work along the boards and in front of the net, and he's showing the meanness necessary to be an above average NHL defenseman. He hits whenever possible and makes his hitting more effective by being able to move the puck.

THE INTANGIBLES

Diduck took great strides last year and is finally coming into his own. He's established a presence for himself on the ice and has become a steady and valued commodity. The clue to that is that Diduck partnered Jeff Finley when the latter was making his NHL debut. That move showed the confidence coach Terry Simpson has in Diduck, confidence that Diduck continues to earn with his increasingly impressive performances.

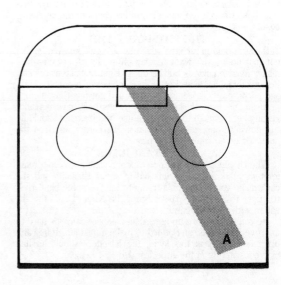

PAT FLATLEY

Yrs. of NHL service: 5
Born: Toronto, Ontario, Canada; October 3, 1963
Position: Right wing
Height: 6-3
Weight: 200
Uniform no.: 26
Shoots: right

Career statistics:

GP	G	A	TP	PIM
270	65	122	187	285

1987-88 statistics:

GP	G	A	TP	+/-	PIM	PP	SH	GW	GT	S	PCT
40	9	15	24	7	28	5	1	0	0	83	10.8

LAST SEASON

Flatley's recurring knee injury finally drove him from the lineup in mid-January. He underwent major knee surgery and didn't play the rest of the season. He was also sidelined last year with a shoulder injury. His games played total was his career low for a full season, the point totals also correspondingly low.

THE FINESSE GAME

Flatley is a strong skater, very sturdy on his feet, and that aids him in his bull-in-china-shop style. He has neither change of pace nor great lateral ability, so he becomes easy to check at the blue line because of his straight-ahead style.

Because of that style, his goal scoring is minimal. However, he's probably just as well off bulling ahead because he doesn't have the hands for the puck work necessary if he were to change that style. Still, he is easily neutralized because he is so predictable, and he could improve if he was willing to work at it.

Pat doesn't have great hands. He tends to hold the puck too long, hoping to make the fancy pass, that spinaround twirl play that looks good on the replays. He doesn't have the skating skill or quickness of foot to do that, to dart between defenders.

Flatley has a quick shot powered by strong wrists. He'll get most of his goals from the corners or side of the net, batting them in off the goaltender because he does his best work in the corners.

THE PHYSICAL GAME

Flatley comes down the ice like a Mack truck and doesn't care if he gets hit and doesn't care if he hits somebody else. Eventually, though, when the youth and strong muscles wear off, those hits are going to become injuries. He should try to avoid some of the hitting, not to the point of being frightened away, but just to be smart. That's where the improved skating skills would help.

He's fearless and willingly goes into the corners. Because he is able to use his size and strength to collect the puck, Flatley is a good choice for goal-mouth duty on the power play, an opportunity where he can — and does — take advantage of his quick shot.

THE INTANGIBLES

We said last year that Flatley had to improve, especially in his skating, but that he wasn't willing to work at that improvement. Now, after major surgery that may sideline him for this entire season (and that's why there's been no change in his report — it's just up in the air pending his return), Flatley may be forced to make those improvements as he attempts his rehabilitation.

His health — and his career — are obviously questionable.

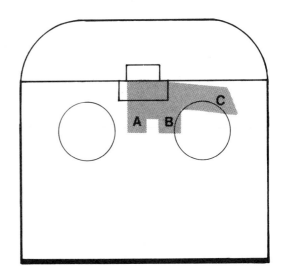

GREG GILBERT

Yrs. of NHL service: 6
Born: Mississauga, Ontario, Canada; January 22, 1962
Position: Left wing
Height: 6-0
Weight: 190
Uniform no.: 7
Shoots: left

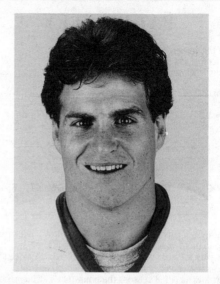

Career statistics:

GP	G	A	TP	PIM
370	85	125	210	276

1987-88 statistics:

GP	G	A	TP	+/−	PIM	PP	SH	GW	GT	S	PCT
76	17	28	45	14	46	1	1	0	0	77	22.1

LAST SEASON

Games played total was the second highest of Greg's career, despite missing a week with the flu. All point totals were also the second highest of his career.

THE FINESSE GAME

Gilbert is an average skater at the NHL level, possessing neither great speed nor agility on his skates. He is strong in his stride and does have good balance, so when he plays his physical style he remains upright and ready to resume play after collisions. Improved foot speed would make him a better skater, as it would combine with his balance to make him more agile — to say nothing of quicker.

He doesn't have a great understanding of the NHL offensive game, and when he overhandles the puck he goes to bad ice. That means he's trapped in a corner at an oblique angle or on his backhand or in need of a fancy pass in order to make an ordinary play. Keeping the game simple — and keeping his head up to see openings — is how Gilbert will succeed offensively. He must move the puck quickly and early.

Greg shoots well and gets the puck away quickly and fairly accurately. He has both the wrist shot and the slap shot and can score from the mid-distances — 25 feet or so.

Gilbert backchecks well, stopping numerous opposing scoring chances through his defensive play.

THE PHYSICAL GAME

Greg is a big, strong man and likes to hit, displaying a mean streak at times that allows him to cross-check opposing forwards into the boards after a play is whistled dead. His size best serves him in the corners, where he digs the puck out well, and in front of the net, where he can and will take the requisite pounding.

His game is the same in the defensive zone, where he will sacrifice his body to block shots or take-out opposing forwards. Gilbert, though not a fighter per se, can more than handle his own because of his upper body strength.

THE INTANGIBLES

Gilbert responded well last year, a season that saw his career at a crossroads. He stayed relatively healthy and was thus able to contribute consistently to the team. He is an enthusiastic and willing player, though he also tends to worry about his own performances, and his work ethic and dedication make him a character player.

He'll be playing under a new contract this season.

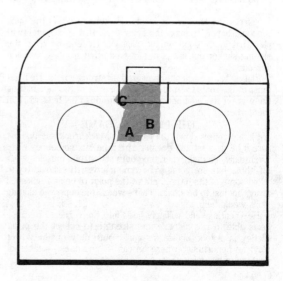

DALE HENRY

Yrs. of NHL service: 2
Born: Prince Albert, Sask., Canada; September 24, 1964
Position: Left wing
Height: 6-0
Weight: 205
Uniform no.: 20
Shoots: left

Career statistics:

GP	G	A	TP	PIM
90	11	22	33	195

1987-88 statistics:

GP	G	A	TP	+/−	PIM	PP	SH	GW	GT	S	PCT
48	5	15	20	8	115	0	0	0	0	53	9.4

LAST SEASON

Henry's longest stay with the Islanders after three previous attempts (16, 7, and 19 games). Point and PIM totals were all career highs, and he finished second on the squad in PIM.

THE FINESSE GAME

Henry's not a bad skater, though no particular aspect of his skating ability leaps out for commendation. Since he's a physical player he could improve his balance; that would keep him on his feet more.

He's used primarily in a checking role and that's good, because Henry has little offensive skill to speak of. He doesn't handle the puck well, doesn't see the ice well and doesn't pass well. How then, if his ice vision is faulty, can he succeed as a checker? Just by staying with the guy he's supposed to guard, like man-to-man defense in basketball.

Any goals he gets will come because of turnovers forced by his line, and Dale will have to be in close proximity of the net to score.

THE PHYSICAL GAME

Henry is a physical player who takes the body when he can. He's not a punishing hitter — and because he won't make a play after jarring loose a puck his physical play is one-dimensional — but he's willing to go to the corner with anyone.

He's also a willing fighter but, despite his good size, isn't a heavyweight in the fisticuffs department.

THE INTANGIBLES

At this point in his career, Henry is a role player. He'll probably be safe in that position for some time because of his physical play — and also because none of the other Islander left wings *curently* play much better than he.

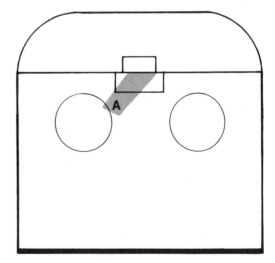

KELLY HRUDEY

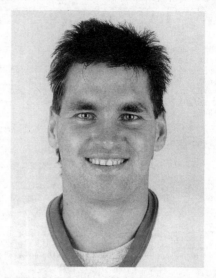

Yrs. of NHL service: 5
Born: Edmonton, Alberta, Canada; January 13, 1961
Position: Goaltender
Height: 5-10
Weight: 183
Uniform no.: 30
Catches: left

Career statistics:

GP	MINS	G	SO	AVG	A	PIM
191	10,802	604	6	3.35	7	88

1987-88 statisics:

GP	MINS	AVG	W	L	T	SO	GA	SA	SAPCT	PIM
47	2,751	3.34	22	17	5	3	153	1,467	.896	20

LAST SEASON

Hrudey established career highs for games and minutes played during a season, as well as most wins and shutouts (he finished fifth in the League in the last category). He finished fourth in the NHL in save percentage.

THE PHYSICAL GAME

Speed and brains are the keys to Kelly Hrudey's game. He is an excellent standup goaltender who backs up superb angle and positioning play with lightning fast reflexes.

Because of his exceptionally fast hands and feet, Hrudey will not let pucks blow past him. He'll make the first save on any shot, so tip-ins or deflections are the keys to beating him. Even so, rare is the puck that Hrudey won't at least get a piece of.

He positions himself very well in the net and sees the puck better than most. He makes the spectacular save, he makes the routine save and he has tremendous ability on the scrambles in front of the net because of his vision and reflexes.

Hrudey has excellent balance on his feet and regains his stance almost instantaneously. He controls the puck well after a save, whether that means holding it for a faceoff or directing it harmlessly to the corner.

Hrudey likes to cheat a bit on the glove side, but will come back and take the opening away. He has good puck handling skills and skates well, but doesn't take many chances outside the net and will not wander astray.

THE MENTAL GAME

Superb concentration is a hallmark of Hrudey's game, as is his ability to bring that concentration to bear night after night. Kelly is mentally tough, able to bounce back from a bad goal and to make yet another game-saving save when necessary.

He rarely makes the mental mistake to beat himself, as in being unprepared to play. He knows the League's shooters and the areas where they are most dangerous and keeps a mental book of that night's opposition in order to prepare for a game.

THE INTANGIBLES

Grossly disappointed in last spring's playoff loss to the Devils, Hrudey is one of the few Islanders who can be proud of his performance. Though not quite the brilliant practitioner of

two seasons back (in the epic Isles-Caps quadruple-overtime win), Hrudey played well enough to win. He remains one of the game's outstanding goaltenders, certainly in the League's top five.

TOMAS JONSSON

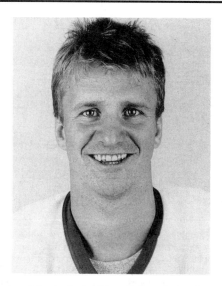

Yrs. of NHL service: 7
Born: Falun, Sweden; April 12, 1960
Position: Defenseman
Height: 5-10
Weight: 176
Uniform no.: 3
Shoots: left

Career statistics:

GP	G	A	TP	PIM
479	75	226	301	426

1987-88 statistics:

GP	G	A	TP	+/−	PIM	PP	SH	GW	GT	S	PCT
72	6	41	47	6	115	1	0	1	0	121	5.0

LAST SEASON

Jonsson finished second in scoring among Islander defensemen, but first in assists for that group. His plus/minus mark was the lowest of any defensive regular. Games played total was the highest in three seasons. Though goal total matched career low, assist total was career high. He was sidelined with a concussion and thigh injury.

THE FINESSE GAME

Jonsson is a very good skater, the best skater among Islander defensemen. He has excellent balance and foot speed, and those two traits combine to make him very agile. Tomas has excellent lateral movement and his outstanding one-step quickness helps him get to loose pucks. He also has good power in his stride, and that gives him good acceleration ability.

That acceleration and quickness are important to Jonsson's game because he is a puck carrying defenseman. Those skating skills gain him the puck and then put him in the clear as he charges up ice. His skating speed also allows him to recover defensively after an offensive foray. Jonsson doesn't forecheck as well or as often as his skating would allow, but he does use his skill to backcheck very effectively.

Tomas handles the puck well when he carries it, and the Islanders' increased dependence on his rushing and play reading ability (because of Denis Potvin's retirement) means that Jonsson should improve in those areas. He is a regular on the power play (28 of his 41 points came on that unit); hence the career-high assist total. His skating and hand skills make him an excellent point man, as he contains the point very well.

His slap shot from the right point is excellent, though Jonsson does have a good wrist shot that he likes to use if he can sneak into the high slot on the power play. He goes for the middle of the net and is usually best high on the glove side. Either way, he is too unselfish and should shoot more; again, note the assists.

THE PHYSICAL GAME

Though his role is that of the breakout (and not takeout) defenseman, Jonsson is still not as strong as he should be. That lack of strength manifests itself when the opposition is able to isolate him in front of the net; Jonsson just can't handle many of the League's forwards because of their greater strength and bulk. This is where you'll see him take penalties, as interference is sometimes his only weapon.

He does take the body fairly well along the boards, and his balance should be credited for that. In the reverse, that balance keeps him from being bumped off the puck.

THE INTANGIBLES

Attitude and intelligence mark Jonsson's play. He's smart enough to know his limits and — generally — not supercede them, and he's also got an excellent attitude and works hard in each game. He is very popular with his teammates and he remains coachable, even after seven NHL seasons.

He'll probably be asked to pick up some of the offensive slack now that Potvin is gone, and Jonsson should use his intelligence to be a more productive even-strength player (27 of his 41 assists came on the power play).

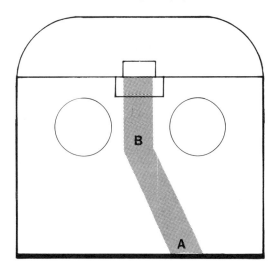

ALAN KERR

Yrs. of NHL service: 2
Born: Hazelton, B.C., Canada; March 28, 1964
Position: Right wing
Height: 5-11
Weight: 195
Uniform no.: 10
Shoots: right

Career statistics:

GP	G	A	TP	PIM
178	34	46	80	413

1987-88 statistics:

GP	G	A	TP	+/-	PIM	PP	SH	GW	GT	S	PCT
80	24	34	58	30	198	4	0	2	1	196	12.2

LAST SEASON

Kerr was the only Islander to play all 80 games. All point totals were career highs. He finished fifth in team scoring, first in plus/minus and PIM total, and second in shots on goal.

THE FINESSE GAME

Kerr's a pretty good skater, with his less than exceptional balance preventing him from being an excellent skater. He has great speed and acceleration ability, and good foot speed and quickness. He does have balance enough to dart in and around defenders and to have good lateral movement. So why are we quibbling about the balance he *doesn't* have? Because Kerr is a physical forward and a physical forward needs balance to be truly effective, that's why.

He does not always come out of collisions in a vertical position, so he must regain his feet and sacrifice valuable seconds of play while doing so. And that's what we mean.

Alan has combined his skating with increased awareness on the ice and that's helped his playmaking. He's keeping his head up and looking at options for his plays and that's important, because his hand skills are nowhere near as good as his foot skills.

With enough space and time, Kerr can get the puck to his teammates, but he's not an outstanding playmaker. He doesn't have great hands — and that means he's a little tough carrying the puck too — so Kerr has to make the most of his speed and quickness. He has begun, however, to improve his handling of the puck at a faster speed.

His non-stop checking and speed create many opportunities offensively, but Kerr is not that gifted an offensive player. He's going to be opportunistic around the net for most of his goals, but he'll catch a goaltender or two napping when he shoots from farther away. His SOG total is obviously one reason for his increased success. Kerr shot just 97 times during the 1986-87 season, compared to 196 times last year.

THE PHYSICAL GAME

Despite his less than intimidating size, Kerr is a buzzsaw on the ice. He hits and plays a general physical game with abandon, often sacrificing his body by charging into the boards — or the opposition — in his single-minded pursuit of the puck. Kerr will fight if need be, regardless of the opponent.

In many ways, most notably his determination, he is very Sutter-like. And that's one reason why Duane Sutter was dispatched to Chicago.

THE INTANGIBLES

Kerr approaches both practices and games with enthusiasm, is coachable and a hard worker. His offensive development wasn't unforeseen (he scored well in both junior and the American Hockey League), and there's room yet for more improvement. Now Kerr has to work on his season-long consistency. He had just five goals and 12 points in his last 20 games — and two of those five goals were on the power play.

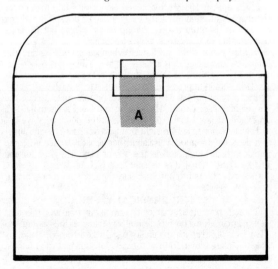

DEREK KING

Yrs. of NHL service: 1
Born: Hamilton, Ontario, Canada; February 11, 1967
Position: Left wing
Height: 6-1
Weight: 205
Uniform no.: 27
Shoots: left

Career statistics:

GP	G	A	TP	PIM
57	12	24	36	30

1987-88 statistics:

GP	G	A	TP	+/−	PIM	PP	SH	GW	GT	S	PCT
55	12	24	36	7	30	1	0	4	0	94	12.8

LAST SEASON

In between demotions and injuries (wrist), King played his first season for the Islanders.

THE FINESSE GAME

King is an average skater at the NHL level, showing neither exceptional speed nor outstanding quickness or agility. He handles the puck fairly well when he skates but, since he doesn't yet possess the skating skills to either drive past the defenseman or cut around him, King often just carries the puck wide of the net and into the corner.

His level of playreading and understanding is also not at the NHL level, or else he'd give himself some options on the play and not keep his back to the center of the ice. He doesn't see the ice well at all, and that also prevents him from getting into position to score himself.

Derek is good around the net and he also has the strength to score from farther out. He must work harder at getting into position to use his shots and to shoot more when he does have the opportunity.

THE PHYSICAL GAME

King is a quiet player physically, despite his good size. He's not very involved in play along the boards and in the corners, and when he does get involved it's more to push and shove than hit. A better physical game would loosen up his finesse game.

THE INTANGIBLES

King is a much-ballyhooed first round draft pick by the Islanders, but he showed nothing last season to justify his selection. To the surprise of practically everyone, King played a tentative, timid game and not the aggressive offensive style his junior numbers indicated.

So let's say King used last season to get his feet wet. This season he must show improvement in many areas in order to avoid classification with the Islanders' other middle-of-the-road left wingers.

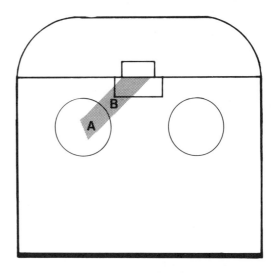

STEVE KONROYD

Yrs. of NHL service: 7
Born: Scarborough, Ontario, Canada; February 10, 1961
Position: Defenseman
Height: 6-1
Weight: 195
Uniform no.: 33
Shoots: left

Career statistics:

GP	G	A	TP	PIM
497	25	119	144	571

1987-88 statistics:

GP	G	A	TP	+/−	PIM	PP	SH	GW	GT	S	PCT
62	2	15	17	16	99	1	0	0	0	105	1.9

LAST SEASON

Konroyd missed one game with a leg injury and nine games with a nose injury to play his fewest ever NHL games (in a full season). His PIM total was the team's sixth highest and a career high.

THE FINESSE GAME

Quietly effective are the words that best describe Konroyd's finesse skills. He's a very mobile skater both forward and back and he pivots excellently. He has a fair degree of agility he can put to use in sliding around a forechecker and some acceleration skill for use when going back for the puck. He uses his skating to play his position in just that way — positionally.

Konroyd excellently and consistently forces the play wide of the net by angling off the incoming forward. Then he takes the forward to the boards, wrests the puck free and sends the play up-ice with a crisp pass. Nothing fancy, just quietly effective.

Steve is very good at moving the puck from his own end. He sees the whole ice surface, finds the open man and gets the puck to him quickly and easily. If a passing option is unavailable, he'll skate the puck from the zone. He handles the puck well, though he does not make himself part of the attack, and Konroyd won't rush the offensive zone.

When play is established in the opposition end, Konroyd will sit back at the point and fire away with a slap shot that is average in power. He can find the open man in the offensive zone (that's why he'll see some power play time) and Steve will more than likely get the puck to him.

THE PHYSICAL GAME

Konroyd is big and strong and he can take players off the puck with his size and strength. He is aggressive in the corners and the front of the net, and knows how to play physically without taking penalties that hurt his team. He uses his reach to contain play at the offensive blue line (especially his reach in getting to loose pucks).

Though strong and aggressive, Konroyd is not a fighter.

THE INTANGIBLES

Konroyd is a smart, confident player with excellent hockey sense. Steve plays a dependable game, and will almost always turn in a 100 percent effort. He's a good team man and is the defensive linchpin of the Islanders' defense.

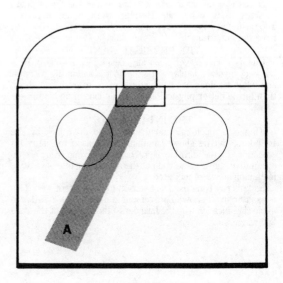

RICH KROMM

Yrs. of NHL service: 5
Born: Trail, B.C., Canada; March 29, 1964
Position: Left wing
Height: 5-11
Weight: 190
Uniform no.: 35
Shoots: left

Career statistics:

GP	G	A	TP	PIM
344	67	95	162	134

1987-88 statistics:

GP	G	A	TP	+/-	PIM	PP	SH	GW	GT	S	PCT
71	5	10	15	2	20	0	1	1	1	84	6.0

LAST SEASON

Kromm missed seven games with a rib injury. All of his point totals were career lows. His plus/minus was second lowest among fulltime Islander forwards.

THE FINESSE GAME

Kromm is an excellent skater, the key to any success he has in the NHL and the reason why he's a good checking forward. He accelerates away from the defense and uses his speed smartly, driving the defensemen off the blue line to create room for his linemates. He uses the same speed and agility to pursue the puck or to close passing lanes. Rich's ability as a checker also allows his more finesse oriented linemates to freelance more in the offensive zone.

He can carry the puck up-ice at full speed, but that's no big deal because he can't make play with it at that speed. He doesn't have a particularly good view of the ice, nor does he possess the hand skills to consistently make the offensive play.

Though he anticipates well and has good speed, Kromm does not leap for the offensive openings. He does not have a goal scorer's sixth sense for the net. He has a good shot from in close because of his strong hands and wrists, but he is not a goal scorer.

He plays well positionally and he pays careful attention to his defensive game.

THE PHYSICAL GAME

Kromm is a wiry forward, muscular and strong. He is effective as a checker because he has a quick recovery rate, so he seems almost tireless. He has excellent balance on his skates and is very difficult to dislodge from the puck. He is not a jarring hitter; rather, he is an insistent one, and Kromm is strong enough to consistently knock the opposition off the puck.

In all, he could be said to use his size most effectively. He just won't make the play after the application of his strength.

THE INTANGIBLES

Kromm is a hard worker, dependable and unspectacular. His failure to put some numbers on the board means he has to be classified as a role player, but his enthusiasm makes him a good team man.

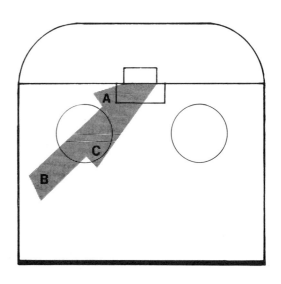

BRAD LAUER

Yrs. of NHL service: 2
Born: Humboldt, Sask., Canada; October 27, 1966
Position: Left wing
Height: 6-0
Weight: 195
Uniform no.: 32
Shoots: left

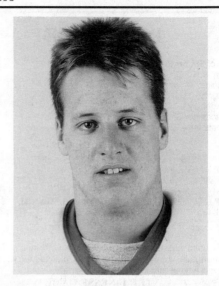

Career statistics:

GP	G	A	TP	PIM
130	24	32	56	132

1987-88 statistics:

GP	G	A	TP	+/−	PIM	PP	SH	GW	GT	S	PCT
69	17	18	35	13	67	3	0	4	0	94	18.1

LAST SEASON

Games played and all point totals were career highs. He missed one game with a knee injury. He finished tied for second in game winners.

THE FINESSE GAME

Brad is an up-and-down winger and his skating reflects that (or causes it, depending on which part of the chicken/egg argument you prefer). He's improved his foot speed and quickness but is not a speed demon. Brad also could do with some improved balance and a lower center of gravity; that would help him add agility to his skating repertoire.

He carries the puck no better than fairly when he skates, and his inability to read the play at the NHL level (both in terms of speed and sophistication) mitigate against his being a good playmaker. He must keep his head up when making plays and try to use the extra time his improved foot speed has gained him to look over the ice before making a play. Thus far he has not demonstrated much flair or creativity in the offensive zone, and broken plays or giveaways are the result.

Lauer has a strong slap shot and could blow the puck past some goaltenders, but he does not yet know how to get into the opening to use it, nor to create openings for himself. Any scoring he will do, consequently, will be from relatively short range; his success on the power play comes from charging the net.

THE PHYSICAL GAME

While he doesn't have great height, Lauer has bulldog-like strength along the boards, Now all he needs is bulldog-like tenacity. He could be much more aggressive in his play along the boards and in the corners, and is far too often content to push and shove instead of using his strength to hit.

When he does apply himself he can hit to great effect in terms of punishment. He does fairly well in taking the opposition out of the play along the boards, but because he does not yet have the ability to make a play off that hit, Lauer's physical work is uni-dimensional, and therefore often ineffective.

He is not very aggressive, and does not fight.

THE INTANGIBLES

Lauer may have come into his own during the Islanders' Patrick Division semifinal playoff series against the Devils, scoring three goals in five games; only Pat LaFontaine had more goals. If he continues to improve, a 25-goal season would be a reasonable projection for this year. But Lauer must learn to take greater advantage — and to *want* to take greater advantage — of his physical game.

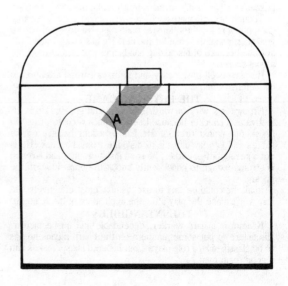

KEN LEITER

Yrs. of NHL service: 2
Born: Detroit, Mich., USA; April 19, 1961
Position: Defenseman
Height: 6-1
Weight: 195
Uniform no.: 29
Shoots: left

Career statistics:

GP	G	A	TP	PIM
139	14	37	51	62

1987-88 statistics:

GP	G	A	TP	+/-	PIM	PP	SH	GW	GT	S	PCT
51	4	13	17	18	24	1	0	1	0	104	3.8

LAST SEASON
Point totals were career lows. He was sidelined by pneumonia during the season's middle stretches. His plus/minus was the team's fourth highest.

THE FINESSE GAME
Leiter skates well both forward and back, so he is not often beaten one-on-one. He has some good speed and has a touch of quickness (which helps him contain the point on the power play), but he is not exceptionally agile.

He has good sense at the offensive blue line, and he finds his teammates when they are open. He has shown glimpses of playmaking skills at a level higher than his current play, and another season's experience may help bring those skills to the fore. He gets the puck to his teammates fairly well, but has yet to recognize the openings — or engineer openings — and use his passing to exploit them. Ken shoots the puck well and often, driving a hard slap shot to the net.

He plays a good positional defensive game and looks to make the correct breakout pass quickly. He exercises good judgement in carrying the puck to the neutral zone, but Leiter won't generally rush the offensive zone. He plays his defensive angles well and his positioning combines with his skating to insure he's not often beaten 1-on-1 defensively.

THE PHYSICAL GAME
Good balance and a strong stride key Leiter's skating and puck handling abilities, as he is difficult to knock off the puck. He otherwise uses his body well against the opposition along the boards and in the corners; again, balance and the ability to remain vertical help here. He doesn't have overwhelming strength in front of the net but will generally hold his own.

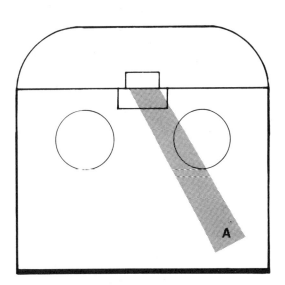

THE INTANGIBLES
His illness slowed Leiter all season long, and he didn't play with the confident aggressiveness — not in terms of fighting but in making plays — that he had in his first year. Considering his age, and considering youngsters Jeff Norton and Jeff Finley behind him, Leiter's continued presence on the Islander roster is questionable.

PAT LAFONTAINE

Yrs. of NHL service: 5
Born: St. Louis, Missouri, USA; February 22, 1965
Position: Center
Height: 5-9
Weight: 170
Uniform no.: 16
Shoots: right

Career statistics:

GP	G	A	TP	PIM
302	147	141	288	203

1987-88 statistics:

GP	G	A	TP	+/−	PIM	PP	SH	GW	GT	S	PCT
75	47	45	92	12	52	15	0	7	2	242	19.4

LAST SEASON

All point totals were career highs. LaFontaine led the team in scoring and goals, and was second in assists. He finished tied for first on the club in power play goals (Bryan Trottier), and led the Islanders in game winners and shots on goal. He finished second in the League in first goals and 17th in overall scoring. Games played total was second highest of his career, missing five games with a knee injury.

THE FINESSE GAME

Lafontaine is an almost complete package of finesse skills. Pat is a phenomenal skater with excellent agility and lateral movement that is matched only by his speed and quickness. He can rev it up, stutter step, breakaway, cut inside — do almost anything with his skating. Excellent balance and foot speed are the keys, as well as an explosive power in his first stride or two for tremendous acceleration capability.

His foot skills are matched by his goal scorer's hands. He likes the deke in tight to the goaltender and he'll be successful at them because1) His balance lets him work in traffic and 2) His hands are super soft for puck work. He carries the puck excellently at all speeds and when he sees a path to the net, he's gone.

Pat's also made some strides in his playmaking, a big step for a scoring center. While he's still going to take the shot if he has it, LaFontaine will now look to make a pass if a teammate is in a better position. He's going 1-on-1 less and letting the puck do some work.

His shot selection is excellent, and Pat can beat a goaltender in many ways. He's not picky; if a backhand shot is all that's available Pat will take it. He's deadly when left alone in front, both because of his quick release and his ability to make the puck dance on his stick. He likes the pretty play that gets the oohs and aahs.

His skills make him a natural for specialty teams duty. His defense continues to be peremptory (really, 92 points and *plus 12*? Forty-seven goals and *plus 12*?). And that's because his transition game from offense to defense hasn't improved as much as his positioning in the defensive zone. Once he gets back, LaFontaine takes his man fairly well.

THE PHYSICAL GAME

For a little guy, LaFontaine's become pretty aggressive. He goes to the corners now and comes out with the puck, though that's more a tribute to his hand skills than his strength. But the point is, LaFontaine has learned that a physical game opens up a finesse game.

He's working closer to the net — and the physical abuse — on the power play to get deflections and rebounds, and the LaFontaine of two seasons back wouldn't have done that. He takes the body well and initiates contact — what more could you ask of a guy called "that — gerbil" by the opposition?

THE INTANGIBLES

The best indication of Pat LaFontaine's progress is that he was the Islanders' best player in their playoff loss to New Jersey. You could feel his intensity on the ice, his desire to perform. His maturity level is high now, and through example LaFontaine is assuming the lead of this club.

What he must work on now is his consistency during the regular season. On some evenings he's unstoppable. On others, invisible — or less of a factor than a player of his talent should be. The comparison again is with Detroit's Steve Yzerman. The Red Wing star plays every game with the same intensity. The maturing LaFontaine must learn that lesson next.

One indication would be his goal scoring. Pat had 28 goals at the season's midway point, so he scored just 19 in the second half. Ten of those 19 came in the season's third quarter, so he had just eight goals in his last 15 games — just seven at even strength.

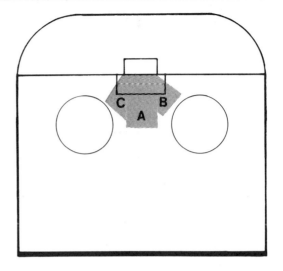

MIKKO MAKELA

Yrs. of NHL service: 3
Born: Tampere, Finland; February 28, 1965
Position: Right wing
Height: 6-2
Weight: 195
Uniform no.: 24
Shoots: left

Career statistics:

GP	G	A	TP	PIM
211	76	93	169	74

1987-88 statistics:

GP	G	A	TP	+/−	PIM	PP	SH	GW	GT	S	PCT
73	36	40	76	14	22	13	2	4	0	142	25.4

LAST SEASON

All point totals were career highs. He missed two games with a back injury. He finished second on the club in goals and power play goals, fourth in assists and first in shooting percentage (fourth overall in the NHL). He also tied with Brent Sutter for the team lead in shorthanded goals. His plus/minus was the team's sixth best, second best among forwards.

THE FINESSE GAME

Mikko is a super-talented finesse player, and that talent begins with his skating. His long, smooth stride disguises his tremendous foot speed and quickness, his agility and his explosive acceleration. He has superb balance, and he combines that balance with his one-step quickness with excellent mobility and lateral movement the result. His stride is very powerful and he can gun past most any defender with breakaway speed.

His hands match the talent of his feet, especially when his feet are in motion. He carries the puck excellently at all speeds, and can shoot or pass off the stickhandle. His passes are soft and accurate, and he's improved his playmaking by looking over the ice surface.

Nowhere are these skills more evident than on the power play, where Makela is a staple. In fact, a reading of his power play stats (13 PPG, 20 power play assists) suggests he's better in that situation than at even strength—only 23 ESG and 20 ESG assists.

He has an excellent shot from the wing, the kind that just blows by goaltenders, yet his hands are soft enough for him to finesse the puck through the slightest opening from nearer the net.

The final attribute that helps him as a scorer is his excellent hockey sense. He knows how to get into position to score. He has excellent peripheral vision and knows where everyone is at all times. Because he looks for his teammates, defenses key on him, thus allowing other Islanders to get free.

THE PHYSICAL GAME

Makela uses his excellent balance and reach in his puckhandling. He can tempt the defensemen with the puck, and that reach and balance allow him to make plays from improbable positions.

He's adapted fairly well to the rigors of the NHL, and his improved conditioning makes him as effective in March as he was in October.

He is willing to play a physical game, but doesn't have the strength to overpower many opponents. He takes his hits to make his plays, and his balance and low center of gravity aid him in working for the puck along the boards and in traffic.

THE INTANGIBLES

Makela is the kind of player that gives coaches ulcers: So much talent and so little drive. If he had the intensity of a Mike Bossy, Makela would be a guaranteed 50-goal scorer. But even Mikko admits that he just can't get up for every game.

That's a shame, because he has almost limitless potential. And that lack of intensity is one reason his even-strength stats are weaker than they should be; Mikko just doesn't consistently exert himself in those situations.

He's just 23 years old, and he could become a higher echelon player, but a major maturity lesson is necessary for that success. He will be playing under a new contract this season, and it will be his responsibility to justify its terms.

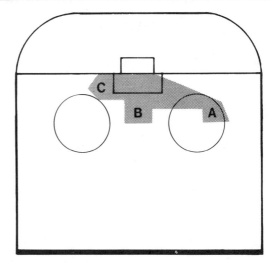

KEN MORROW

Yrs. of NHL service: 9
Born: Flint, Mich., USA; October 17, 1956
Position: Defense
Height: 6-4
Weight: 210
Uniform no.: 4
Shoots: right

Career statistics:

GP	G	A	TP	PIM
516	16	85	101	277

1987-88 statistics:

GP	G	A	TP	+/−	PIM	PP	SH	GW	GT	S	PCT
53	1	4	5	0	40	0	0	0	0	50	2.0

LAST SEASON

Morrow missed one game with a thigh injury and 14 games with a shoulder injury. Games played was lowest in three seasons, second lowest for a full season since he entered the NHL. Point total was career low.

THE FINESSE GAME

You know that sarcastic comment, the one that goes, "If he moved any slower he'd be going backward?" Well Ken Morrow, this is your life. He's never been especially mobile or agile or quick, and after wear and tear and age Morrow is slower than ever.

But he makes up for that with his smarts and anticipation. Because just when it seems that forward is going to cut inside him and have a clear path to the net, Morrow's blocked that path and pokechecked the puck away.

Morrow passes well, and he also passes smartly — if he can get to the puck. Most of the time, a backchecking Islander rightwinger is going to have to pick up that loose puck. Morrow reads the developing play very well, both on the opposition rush and on the Islander break-out, and that reading skill serves him well on the penalty killing unit.

Morrow doesn't have a great shot, so he won't be seen on the power play. His lack of mobility and skating speed prevents him from joining the offense in its attack.

THE PHYSICAL GAME

Morrow's reach and strength are his biggest assets. Simply by moving his legs he covers a lot of ice and his wingspan is enormous, allowing him to pokecheck better than most any defenseman in the League.

Also, his pure size makes him difficult to go around (despite his bad wheels). He has the strength to take the opposing forwards wide of the net and off the puck. However, because of his concern for his knees, he avoids consistent body contact.

THE INTANGIBLES

Quiet in the dressing room, Morrow lets his play do the talking. He has an excellent attitude and brings a strong work ethic and will to succeed to the Islanders. He is on a termination contract with the Islanders.

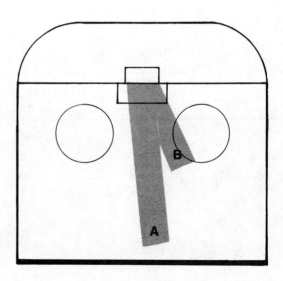

JEFF NORTON

Yrs. of NHL service: 1
Born: Cambridge, Mass., USA; November 25, 1965
Position: Defenseman
Height: 6-2
Weight: 190
Uniform no.: 8
Shoots: left

Career statisics:

GP	G	A	TP	+/–	PIM	PP	SH	GW	GT	S	PCT
15	1	6	7	3	14	1	0	1	0	18	5.6

LAST SEASON

Norton joined the club following the Winter Olympic Games. He was a third round draft coice in the 1984 Entry Draft.

THE FINESSE GAME

Norton is a good skater, with the potential to be very good at the NHL level. He has excellent speed and quickness, as well as balance and agility. He has good acceleration and can pull away from the incoming forward, and he can also snake his way around the opposition because his agility, foot speed and balance give him good mobility and lateral movement.

He complements his foot skills with good hand skills, which also have the potential to improve at the NHL level. He carries the puck when skating with ease, and he makes passes to teammates in better positions. That indicates good hockey sense, vision and judgment. His passes are easy to handle and Jeff leads the man well.

He will rush the puck from the Islander zone, but Jeff will not penetrate to the opposition net. Rather, if he hasn't made a pass to a breaking wing, he'll set up shop at the offensive blue line and control the play from there. His skating, hand and mental skills make him a regular on both specialty team units.

Norton has a good shot from the point, low to the net, hard and quickly released. He should take greater advantage of it by shooting more, and he should shoot to score more and not just hope for deflections and rebounds.

His skating allows him to cheat defensively by challenging in the offensive zone, but Norton is certainly fast enough to get back into the play. In the defensive zone he angles off the man well, and his quickness and agility allow him to effectively close the gap between himself and the opposing forward.

THE PHYSICAL GAME

Norton has good size and isn't afraid to use it. He willingly goes to the corners with anyone, and his balance and strength combine to make him a better than even chance to emerge with the puck. His physical play is amplified by his fine ability to make the play after a hit.

He is an aggressive finesse player, and that aggressiveness makes his finesse game that much more effective. Like his other skills, Norton's physical play — while already good — has the ability to improve.

THE INTANGIBLES

Norton entered the NHL and performed immediately with tremendous poise. He was installed on the power play and penalty killing units very early in his tenure and he responded very well. His improvement should continue this season, and the threat of that improvement — combined with Norton's age — will give the Islanders *at least* six defensemen (maybe more if Jeff Finley sticks with the club). That means that a veteran is going to be sitting.

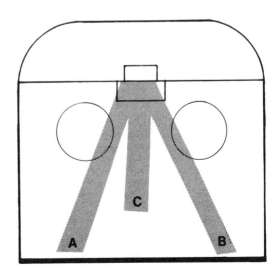

BILL SMITH

Yrs. of NHL service: 16
Born: Perth, Ontario, Canada; December 12, 1950
Position: Goaltender
Height: 5-10
Weight: 185
Uniform no.: 31
Catches: left

Career statistics:

GP	MINS	G	SO	AVG	A	PIM
663	37,684	1,977	22	3.14	12	481

1987-88 statisics:

GP	MINS	AVG	W	L	T	SO	GA	SA	SAPCT	PIM
38	2,107	3.22	17	14	5	2	113	1,062	.893	20

LAST SEASON

Games played total was lowest in three seasons. Goals-against-average was lowest in five seasons. He was sidelined early in the season with an ankle injury.

THE PHYSICAL GAME

Age has taken its toll on Smith in terms of his quickness and foot speed. He has always been a good skater, balanced in his stance, but he moves less and less well in and out of his net and from post to post because of his reduced foot speed. That loss of quickness means that the extreme corners of the net — as well as the space between his legs — are his vulnerable areas.

He counters that by positioning himself well in the net, and last year he raised his consistency in staying on his feet and cutting down the angle. He resurrected a bit of his challenging game. He continues to regain his stance well after going to the ice (balance again), and he'll leave the net to gather loose pucks.

His hand speed is still good — with both glove and stick hands — and that's demonstrated by his ability to make the save close to the net. His good vision of the puck helps here and makes him good in scrambles around the net.

Smith has always handled the puck very well, and he continues to use his teammates well.

THE MENTAL GAME

Smith is mentally tough and comes right back after bad goals, fighting you for the next one. Bad performances don't affect him and he'll bounce right back in his next start.

THE INTANGIBLES

A free agent this past summer, wherever Smith plays it'll be on a new contract. If the pact is a multi-year deal he'll have to justify it, and if it's a one year agreement he'll have to prove he can play beyond this season.

He still wants to contribute (and he remains a fiery competitor), but Smith has come to accept his role as Kelly Hrudey's caddy.

BRENT SUTTER

Yrs. of NHL service: 7
Born: Viking, Alberta, Canada; June 10, 1962
Position: Center
Height: 5-11
Weight: 175
Uniform no.: 21
Shoots: left

Career statistics:

GP	G	A	TP	PIM
467	200	216	416	564

1987-88 statistics:

GP	G	A	TP	+/-	PIM	PP	SH	GW	GT	S	PCT
70	29	31	60	13	55	11	2	2	0	162	17.9

LAST SEASON

Sutter finished fourth in team scoring, tied for first in short-handed goals (Mikko Makela) and was fourth in power play goals. Goal and games played totals were highest in three seasons, PIM total second lowest of career. He missed nine games with a thumb injury.

THE FINESSE GAME

In the case of Brent Sutter, the total is less than the sum of the parts. Sutter, a straight ahead player, is a good skater with balance and power. He isn't a speed demon, but he does have a strong and steady pace that should force defenders to back-pedal far more than it does now. He doesn't have great foot speed (so he won't explode in his acceleration), but Brent is well balanced and fairly agile. Still, he underachieves in using his skating skill.

He continues to underachieve in his playmaking, hesitating and overhandling the puck while looking for the perfect play. His anticipation and hockey sense, and his hand skills, are better than he's showing. He can make passes to lead team-mates into the clear, and he can find the open man.

He is very solid defensively and a fine positional player in all three zones. His anticipation and sense combine with his strong skating to make him an above-average checker.

Brent has a good shot, but he won't score from long distances. He just mucks around the net, coming up with loose pucks because he stays after them. The opposition may be trying to hook him or hold him or tackle him, but his fierce determination gets him those loose pucks.

THE PHYSICAL GAME

Unlike older brothers Darryl and Brian, Brent is not an excessively physical player. Rather, he plays an efficient physical style by taking the body effectively in all areas of the ice. He hits and is unafraid to be checked, as evidenced by his willingness to work in the pits around the net. This is where his balance helps him, as you'll rarely see Brent knocked off his feet.

THE INTANGIBLES

Injuries aside — and that's hard to say considering how he succumbs to something every year — confidence is the problem with Sutter. He plays very tentatively now (and when you play that way, by the way, you get injured), as if he's afraid of making a mistake. Yet he can be an aggressive forward in terms of creating and forcing plays; his shorthanded overtime goal against the Devils in the opening round of last spring's playoffs demonstrated that.

But his inconsistency also forces us to say that Brent seems a lot farther than nearer to the 100-point season he enjoyed four years ago. That season suggested above-average capabilities, but his last three years have not fulfilled that suggestion. We wonder now if he ever will again.

He'll be playing under a new contract this season.

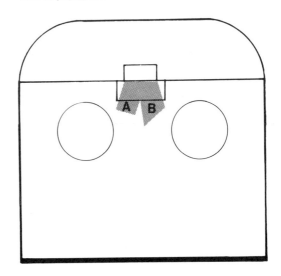

BRYAN TROTTIER

Yrs. of NHL service: 13
Born: Val Marie, Sask., Canada, July 17, 1956
Position: Center
Height: 5-10
Weight: 205
Uniform no.: 19
Shoots: left

Career statistics:

GP	G	A	TP	PIM
991	470	814	1,284	725

1987-88 statistics:

GP	G	A	TP	+/−	PIM	PP	SH	GW	GT	S	PCT
77	30	52	82	10	48	15	0	3	0	176	17.0

LAST SEASON

Games played total was lowest in three seasons. Goal total was three season high. Point total was three season low. Finished second on the team in scoring (third in goals, first in assists). Tied for team lead (Pat LaFontaine) in power play goals. Finished fourth in shots.

THE FINESSE GAME

Trottier is an example of a player whose physical game powers his finesse game. Trottier's skating is keyed by his great balance, and that balance is what has always made him effective as physical forward. He comes out of collisions vertical and ready to make a play. He has never been a speed demon so his decreasing speed and quickness (a result of wear and tear and age) are almost hidden by his steady pace. He was never a fancy skater and didn't moderate the speed he didn't really have. As such, the straight-ahead style he employed suited him perfectly.

Bryan's playmaking ability has been keyed by his excellent hockey sense, anticipation and ice vision. He has tremendous understanding of the play both offensively and defensively, so he almost never makes a mistake. His mental capabilities have always been complemented by fine hands, and Trottier will still get a pass to teammates regardless of the obstructions.

His best scoring opportunities come from the hashmarks in, the traffic area where his great balance allows him to take his knocks but retain control of the puck. He won't beat you with the big slap shot from way out, but instead uses his wrist shot well and will pick up loose pucks around the net for goals. Trottier, too, is a touch unselfish and should shoot more, but is always looking for the better play.

His effectiveness at even strength must be questioned, though, as he scored only 15 even strength goals.

THE PHYSICAL GAME

Balance is just one part of Trottier's physical game. The more obvious — and devastating — aspect has been strength. Because of his relatively (and we mean relatively) small stature, Trottier has never looked as strong as he is. He can be a devastating hitter, willing to sacrifice his body to either take or make a check. His physical ability complements a mean streak, making him dangerous to opposing puck carriers.

His upper body strength, balance and hand and wrist power make him one of the League's premier faceoff men (only now, speed has begun to leave him, making a touchless effective on the draw). Those strong hands will also snare the puck from traffic.

Trottier's balance and strength allow him to charge the net and shake off checkers as he goes. Defensively, you want him on the ice in the last minute because he's like another defenseman in front of the net and in the corners, banging bodies or tying up opposing forwards.

THE INTANGIBLES

Trottier is growing hockey-old gracefully, and he is still an integral part of the Islanders. His on-ice leadership and off-ice work ethic make him an example to the youngsters now populating the Islander lockerroom. He'll need to show recovery from the broken foot that hobbled him during last spring's playoff loss to the Devils, but even that was typical Trottier. No one knew he was injured until weeks after the fact.

But that's Bryan. He lets his actions do the talking. His effort night in and out insures that he will remain a vital piece of any Islander success.

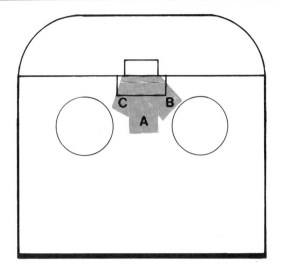

RANDY WOOD

Yrs. of NHL service: 1
Born: Princeton, New Jersey, USA; October 12, 1963
Position: Left wing
Height: 6-0
Weight: 195
Uniform no.: 11
Shoots: left

Career statistics:

GP	G	A	TP	PIM
81	23	16	39	84

1987-88 statistics:

GP	G	A	TP	+/-	PIM	PP	SH	GW	GT	S	PCT
75	22	16	38	-2	80	0	1	2	0	106	20.8

LAST SEASON

Wood played a full season with the Islanders last year after joining them at the tail end of the 1986-87 season. He had the team's lowest plus/minus. He had a short stay in the American Hockey League at mid-year.

THE FINESSE GAME

Wood is an excellent skater in all facets of that skill. He has great speed and balance, quickness and agility, strength and acceleration. As they are in every player, these skills are inter-related and Kerr uses one to amplify another. His strength powers his acceleration, his balance and foot speed contribute to his quickness and agility.

He complements his speed with the ability to handle the puck well as he carries it — at any speed. That doesn't mean, however, that he can make plays at that speed. While Randy can blow by a defender and cut inside him for a shot, he doesn't have the same ability to move the puck to a teammate in a similar position.

Like most NHL newcomers Wood works with his head down. Head down means no vision. No vision means no play-making. No playmaking means blind or ill-conceived passes. Ill-conceived passes mean turnovers and turnovers equal a minus 2 rating. He must learn to moderate his speed in order to give himself more time to make a play, to see the ice.

He needs also to gain greater understanding of positioning when playing defense, and to apply his considerable speed to the transition from offense to defense.

Randy can shoot the puck fairly well and his balance lets him work well in traffic, so most of his goals will come from fairly close to the net.

THE PHYSICAL GAME

Wood is very strong, both in his skates and in his upper body. He plays a physical game and his hitting will create loose pucks. Right now that proficiency is mitigated by his inability to make a play coming out of the corner. He takes the body very well along the boards and his strength can make him a punishing hitter.

THE INTANGIBLES

All in all, not a bad debut for Wood. He worked very hard in the summer preceding last season to be in top shape, and that included exercises to improve his eye/hand coordination (one reason he doesn't pass better — inability to hit a moving target) and overall conditioning.

Still, he fell prey — as most players in his circumstances do — to the grind of the NHL season. Combined with the NHL's growing familiarity with him, it wasn't surprising that his production fell off 10 goals in the first quarter, 13 by half-season.

Wood's work ethic and dedication speak well for his continued development.

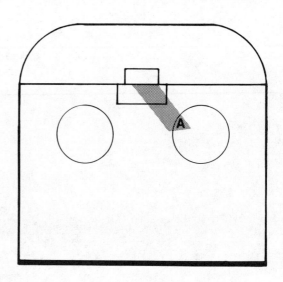

NEW YORK RANGERS

LINE COMBINATIONS
DON MALONEY-LUCIEN DEBLOIS-JAN ERIXON
BRIAN MULLEN-KELLY KISIO-JOHN OGRODNICK
CHRIS NILAN-WALT PODDUBNY-TOMAS
SANDSTROM
PAUL CYR-MARCEL DIONNE-ULF DAHLEN

DEFENSE PAIRINGS
BRIAN LEETCH
DAVID SHAW
JAMES PATRICK
MARK HARDY
JARI GRONSTRAND
MICHEL PETIT
NORM MACIVER

GOALTENDERS
JOHN VANBIESBROUCK
BOB FROESE

OTHER PLAYERS
RON GRESCHNER — Defenseman
PIERRE LAROUCHE — Center

POWER PLAY

FIRST UNIT:
WALT PODDUBNY-MARCEL DIONNE-TOMAS
SANDSTROM
NORM MACIVER-JAMES PATRICK

SECOND UNIT:
JOHN OGRODNICK-KELLY KISIO-ULF DAHLEN
BRIAN LEETCH-MICHEL PETIT

MACIVER and PATRICK play catch at the point and dump it down to PODDUBNY and SANDSTROM to open up the defense and allow SANDSTROM a shot from the faceoff circle. Second choice is a PATRICK blue line shot, and on any shot PODDUBNY and DIONNE get in tight for deflections and rebounds.

The second unit likes DAHLEN to handle the puck in tight, and uses LEETCH and PETIT playing catch to pull the defense forward, or KISIO along the boards to lure a defenseman and open the front of the net for DAHLEN. The other option is setting up OGRODNICK at the left faceoff circle.

Last season, the Ranger power play was EXCELLENT, ranking fourth in the League at 22.6 percent (111 goals in 491 attempts).

PENALTY KILLING

FIRST UNIT:
LUCIEN DEBLOIS-DON MALONEY
MARK HARDY-JAMES PATRICK

SECOND UNIT:
KELLY KISIO-JAN ERIXON
MICHEL PETIT-DAVID SHAW

The Ranger penalty killing units are basically aggressive, with one or both forwards pressuring the points and the defensemen pressuring the puck down deep. When possible, the penalty killers will try to generate an offensive chance. MALONEY pressures slightly less so DEBLOIS and CYR will also see penalty killing time.

Last season, the Ranger penalty killing was GOOD, ranking eighth in the League at 80.6 percent (allowing 82 goals in 423 times shorthanded).

CRUCIAL FACEOFFS

KISIO will see most of the faceoff duty, with DEBLOIS (converted to center) taking many defensive zone draws.

PAUL CYR

Yrs. of NHL service: 6
Born: Port Alberni, B.C., Canada; October 31, 1963
Position: Left wing
Height: 5-10
Weight: 180
Uniform no.: 22
Shoots: left

Career statistics:

GP	G	A	TP	PIM
382	89	124	213	495

1987-88 statistics:

GP	G	A	TP	+/−	PIM	PP	SH	GW	GT	S	PCT
60	5	14	19	-7	79	1	2	1	0	92	5.4

LAST SEASON
Acquired from Buffalo in exchange for Mike Donnelly in December. Games played was fewest of career (for a full season), as were all point totals. He led the Rangers in short-handed goals.

THE FINESSE GAME
Cyr is a good skater with a lot of speed, though not a lot of quickness nor agility. He can motor up and down his wing (and that makes him a good checker), but he lacks a change of a pace and an explosive acceleration. His speed is of a long-haul, rather than short burst, type.

He has good balance and a low center of gravity, and those assets help him in his physical game. He handles the puck fairly well but has the habit of making his plays with his head down so he is unable to take advantage of his modest puck-handling skill. Since he is no better than average in anticipation, he must rely on his speed to make plays and to score. His skating makes him a good penalty killer.

Cyr has a hard, accurate shot and he can blow a few by a goaltender from the top of the faceoff circle, but he prefers to shoot from down lower, mostly from the bottom of the faceoff circle. He's not enough of a goal scorer to take advantage of the opportunities his speed or physical play creates, and so he must be doubly sure to perform well defensively.

Paul is a fair defensive player, playing his check no better than average — mostly because of his lack of anticipation and because his head is down. He also has a tendency to leave his check open by releasing too early in the defensive zone and trying to create a breakout opportunity.

THE PHYSICAL GAME
Though not possessing great size, Cyr willingly plays a physical, grinding game. He goes into the corners and fights for the puck, and he'll win more than his share of confrontations because of his superior upper body strength. His balance helps him here too, but Paul's physical game is limited by the fact that his hand skills coming out of the corner are not great.

He's willing to sacrifice his body to block shots, but for all his diving attempts, Paul rarely gets a piece of himself in the way of the puck.

THE INTANGIBLES
Cyr is a hard-working player on and off the ice, and he's a quiet one as well. He's more a follower than a leader, but his hustle and willingness make him a good example on a team often lacking those assets.

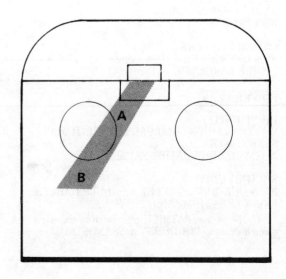

ULF DAHLEN

Yrs. of NHL service: 1
Born: Ostersund, Sweden; January 12, 1967
Position: Center
Height: 6-2
Weight: 195
Uniform no.: 9
Shoots: left

Career statisics:

GP	G	A	TP	+/−	PIM	PP	SH	GW	GT	S	PCT
70	29	23	52	5	26	11	0	4	0	159	18.2

LAST SEASON

Dahlen's first in the NHL. He missed eight games through benchings and had a four-day stay in the minors in November before joining the team for good.

He finished fourth in overall League rookie scoring, and was third on the team in goals and second in shooting percentage.

THE FINESSE GAME

Dahlen is an excellent skater, though not of the usual kind. While he doesn't demonstrate great speed or quickness, he has exceptional balance, probably better than all but the NHL's top — and we mean Gretzky and Lemieux level — players. His balance excellently complements his willingness to play a physical game and go into traffic, allowing him to not just handle but effectively control the puck despite the times when his body is at seemingly impossible angles to the ice.

He is almost impossible to knock down, and once he has the puck he has the hands, the eyes and the brain to do many things with it. He passes well, though Ulf does have a tendency to hold onto the puck longer than necessary simply because he can.

Dahlen handles the puck well at all speeds and he keeps his head up to make plays. That vision and anticipation will combine to make him a good NHL scorer. He has a good shot, released quickly, and he plays a solid, two-way game.

His puckhandling ability, combined with his shooting skill, make him a natural for power play duty.

THE PHYSICAL GAME

Dahlen is not only willing, he's able to play the game at the NHL level of toughness. He has good size, though he is a bit light and could certainly benefit from strength training, and he is unafraid of going into the high traffic areas around the net and in the corners.

We've already discussed his balance, but another thing that makes him successful in confrontations is his reach. When that reach is combined with his hand skills, Dahlen is able to not only gain the puck in the corner and then move out to make a play, but he's often able to create an excellent scoring chance for himself. That makes him a triple threat.

THE INTANGIBLES

If we sound like we're gushing about Dahlen, that's because we are. When he was selected in the 1985 Entry Draft (seventh overall by New York), many at the Draft that day felt that then-general manager Craig Patrick had brought the Rangers the best player in the Draft.

The only negative associated with Dahlen that day was the wait necessary before he could come to North America. He's proven to be worth the wait. Ulf adapted well to the NHL last season and showed few of the signs of slowdown common to Europeans unfamiliar with the rigors of the NHL. Additionally, Dahlen plays a type of game (his willingness to take and initiate contact) that most Europeans don't begin to appreciate (or understand the importance of) for several seasons.

He'll continue to be successful for that reason.

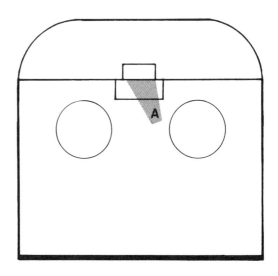

LUCIEN DEBLOIS

Yrs. of NHL service: 11
Born: Joliette, Quebec, Canada; June 21, 1957
Position: Center/right wing
Height: 5-11
Weight: 200
Uniform no.: 23
Shoots: right

Career statistics:

GP	G	A	TP	PIM
733	210	217	427	578

1987-88 statistics:

GP	G	A	TP	+/-	PIM	PP	SH	GW	GT	S	PCT
74	9	21	30	-3	103	2	0	0	0	99	9.1

LAST SEASON

Injuries sidelined Deblois for six games, but GP was still highest in four seasons. His 103 PIM were fourth highest among the team's regulars, second among forwards.

THE FINESSE GAME

Deblois is not a speed demon on skates, but he is strong and balanced. His ability to recognize plays and his willingness to get where he has to be (as opposed to speed) served last year to make him a pretty effective checking center.

Offensively, Deblois' game is almost non-existent. Because he generally mucks up and down, he will almost never beat a defender one-on-one. Lucien can control the puck fairly well, but he's neither exceedingly intelligent nor creative in the offensive zone, and Deblois doesn't know how to continue a play after he's gotten rid of the puck, so he'll make the first play he can see.

He doesn't have a great offensive touch around the net and will need to be in close proximity of the goal to score. He's got a hard shot that he fires from close in, and he'll get most of his goals on second efforts and rebounds.

THE PHYSICAL GAME

Deblois plays hard but clean, and he takes his man out well along the boards. He's also strong enough to hold his man out of the play when necessary, and he complements his physical play with a small degree of ability in making plays off the boards.

He is successful because of good upper body strength and balance on his skates, and Lucien can hit hard enough to hurt.

THE INTANGIBLES

By staying healthy, Lucien made himself a valuable member of the Ranger team, behaving as the strong center they covet. He's not a good enough skater to take on the League's best players (those are assigned to linemate Jan Erixon), but Deblois filled in well last year.

He needs to control his temper more on the ice, as he is apt to respond to the little slashes and trips designed to irritate him.

Most importantly, Deblois may or may not be offered a new contract by the Rangers, depending on what they have been able to turn up at center in terms of a stronger and younger presence. He may not be as effective as he was last season if he is asked to play just part-time this year.

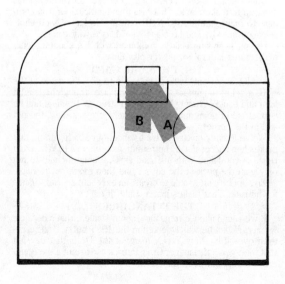

MARCEL DIONNE

Yrs. of NHL service: 17
Born: Drummondville, Quebec, Canada; August 3, 1951
Position: Center
Height: 5-8
Weight: 185
Uniform no.: 16
Shoots: right

Career statistics:

GP	G	A	TP	PIM
1,311	724	1,024	1,748	580

1987-88 statistics:

GP	G	A	TP	+/–	PIM	PP	SH	GW	GT	S	PCT
67	31	34	65	-14	54	22	0	4	1	184	16.8

LAST SEASON

Dionne finished fourth on the team in scoring, second in goals and first in power play goals (third overall in the NHL in that specialty team category). An injury to his left knee sidelined him for 12 games.

THE FINESSE GAME

Once an excellent skater — in all facets of that skill — age and wear and tear have taken a step or two off Dionne's speed. He is still fairly quick on his feet and very agile, so he can maneuver in tight situations around the net.

Marcel has great hands and he knows when to hold the puck and when to pass it, and can certainly handle it at his top speed. He has a good touch around the net and can operate in traffic, whether stickhandling himself or passing to a teammate. That's important, because the Rangers use him tight to the net on the power play.

He retains the vision and anticipation that makes him an effective playmaker, but he is also a goal scorer and is more than willing to shoot the puck (fourth on the team in SOG, despite limited ice time).

Despite his bad plus/minus, Dionne is not a bad defensive player, though his checking is inconsistent. Most of the time, he checks well, but he has a tendency to leave his position in the defensive zone.

THE PHYSICAL GAME

Dionne has good strength for his size and is built like a fireplug. He's willing to mix it up in front of the net and will take the necessary pounding for his plays. However, he won't overpower anyone, so his success in traffic comes from superior hand, arm and wrist strength. That's how he's able to consistently fire the puck while wrapped up.

His low center of gravity and excellent balance have enabled him to withstand — or, more likely, avoid — 17 years of punishment.

THE INTANGIBLES

The NHL's second-leading all-time scorer was used infrequently last season, relegated to the bench for long stretches and released mostly for power-play work. The contributions of rookie Ulf Dahlen, team captain Kelly Kisio and Lucien

Deblois (as a checking center) served to limit Dionne's ice-time, to his chagrin.

While he has said he'd rather be in a supporting role than a leadership one at this stage of his career, his restricted playing time is not what Dionne had in mind. And things are not likely to get better for him this season, what with general manager Phil Esposito looking to add a big, strong center to the roster.

Marcel is 103 points away from becoming the NHL's all-time leading scorer, and any player that scores 31 goals a season is doing more than hanging around and taking up space. But strangely, after 17 NHL seasons, Dionne might find himself a victim of numbers in the Ranger organization.

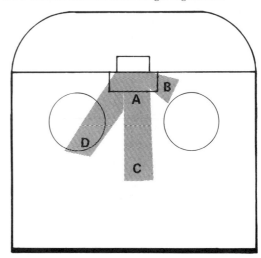

JAN ERIXON

Yrs. of NHL service: 5
Born: Skelleftea, Sweden; July 8, 1962
Position: Right wing
Height: 6-0
Weight: 190
Uniform no.: 20
Shoots: left

Career statistics:

GP	G	A	TP	PIM
310	29	101	130	110

1987-88 statistics:

GP	G	A	TP	+/−	PIM	PP	SH	GW	GT	S	PCT
70	7	19	26	3	33	0	1	0	0	99	7.1

LAST SEASON

Injured ribs and an injured back — along with two early-season benchings — limited Erixon to 70 games, but that total was still the second-highest of his career.

THE FINESE GAME

Superb, but quiet, fundamentals make Erixon a superb, but quiet, player. His ice vision and anticipation are excellent, and Jan combines those qualities with tireless and strong skating to perform as one of the best — if not *the* best — defensive forward in the NHL.

His instincts and foot speed make him a relentless checker and penalty killer, and they also afford him many scoring opportunities. Unfortunately for Erixon and the Rangers, he has almost no scoring touch.

Nonetheless, he will zip in and out of the slot for shots (and he'll have to score from in close if he scores at all) and work the puck tirelessly. Jan handles the puck fairly well, able to get the passes to his teammates, but has little chance to take advantage of that skill because of his checking role.

THE PHYSICAL GAME

Erixon is not the strongest checking forward in the League (that distinction probably falls to either Derrick Smith or Joel Otto), but he may very well be the toughest. He simply cannot be slowed down.

Jan uses his body excellently to deny the puck along the boards or to thwart the attempts of players like Mario Lemieux. Those opposition players become so frustrated by Erixon's shadowing that they slash him, spear him and throw him to the ice. Erixon takes it all, and gets back up to continue his job.

That's tough.

THE INTANGIBLES

Any superlative regarding Erixon's defensive ability is completely applicable. He plays a very intelligent game and performs his checking job without getting penalized, many times forcing the opposition to take penalties in frustration. He is a player any team would like to have.

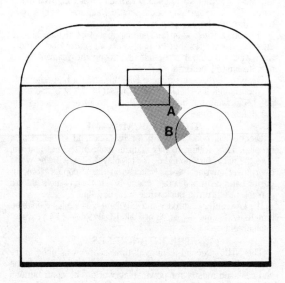

BOB FROESE

Yrs. of NHL service: 6
Born: St. Catherines, Ontario, Canada; June 30, 1958
Position: Goaltender
Height: 5-11
Weight: 178
Uniform no.: 33
Catches: left

Career statistics:

GP	MINS	G	SO	AVG	A	PIM
197	11,018	547	12	2.97	9	84

1987-88 statisics:

GP	MINS	AVG	W	L	T	SO	GA	SA	SAPCT	PIM
25	1,443	3.53	8	11	3	0	85	697	.878	6

LAST SEASON

Games played was fewest in three seasons, partly because of nine games missed with shoulder injury. Last season marked first time Froese posted a losing record.

THE PHYSICAL GAME

Though forced to be more acrobatic with the Rangers than with Philadelphia (because the Ranger defense is more likely to leave rebounds in front of the net than the Flyer teams Froese fronted for), Bob is an excellent angle goaltender and plays a superior standup style.

He has good balance and quick feet, and regains his position fairly speedily. Still, he is much better on his feet than off them. Froese will come out of his net to handle the puck, but will only wrap it around the boards, rather than passing it to a teammate.

However, because of the Ranger defense (only eight teams allowed more shots-on-goal) and their less than strict front of the net coverage, Froese must sit a little deeper in his net than he'd prefer, so an incoming forward can't sneak behind him.

He generally prevents rebounds by directing shots to the corners, and Bob moves well in and out of his net, but his lateral movement is faulty and he is vulnerable to dekes (particularly to his right) on breakaways.

He sees the puck and anticipates well, and Froese will move out to the top of the screen before butterflying his pads on the ice to cover the lower part of the net.

THE MENTAL GAME

Though his concentration will wander at times, Froese is most always in the game. He prepares well for each contest and is capable of making big saves and winning the big game (as he has shown during his playoff appearances).

He is apt to lose his temper if he gets fouled too frequently around the crease, but opponents find it pretty tough to knock Froese off his game.

THE INTANGIBLES

As we said last year, John Vanbiesbrouck needs lots of playing time to be successful. Though he griped about his playing time in Philadelphia, Froese has been the perfect team man for the Rangers. He's loose and funny in the lockerroom, and — though rumors of his imminent trade keep surfacing — he continues along with Vanbiesbrouck to give the Rangers the best 1-2 goalie punch in the business.

Froese's value is best seen in light of Vanbiesbrouck's wrist injury, an injury that will prevent the Vezina Trophy winner from starting the season. With Froese in the fold, the Rangers have no worries.

RON GRESCHNER

Yrs. of NHL service: 14
Born: Goodsoil, Sask., Canada; December 22, 1954
Position: Defenseman/center
Height: 6-2
Weight: 205
Uniform no.: 4
Shoots: left

Career statistics:

GP	G	A	TP	PIM
869	177	412	589	1,079

1987-88 statistics:

GP	G	A	TP	+/−	PIM	PP	SH	GW	GT	S	PCT
51	1	5	6	-9	82	0	0	0	0	67	1.5

LAST SEASON

Games played was fewest in last three seasons, thanks to injured leg and shoulder, the flu and benchings. Career lows for goals and points.

THE FINESSE GAME

There's not a whole lot left here. Never one of the League's fastest skaters to begin with, Greschner keeps going now on balance and stickhandling ability. He remains a super stickhandler, losing none of his talent in that department despite his age. He has the puck on a string.

He still has the lateral movement that made him such a good stickhandler and his reach, his ability to hold a puck tantalizingly close to a defender, is still intact. And, every once in a while, Ron will squeeze enough foot speed out of his battle-scarred body to surprise the opposition.

His puckhandling talent and play reading skill can make him valuable as a power play man.

THE PHYSICAL GAME

Despite age and injury, Greschner can play a smart physical game. He will accomplish something with each check, but he is neither a punishing hitter, nor overly strong. The strength he has, along with his smarts, gets the job done along the boards or in front of the net.

He has a long reach that he puts to good use and Greschner will fight if provoked, and his reach helps him there too, making him a difficult target to hit as he stays away from his opponent's punches.

THE INTANGIBLES

Despite the aches and pains and the long years of service, Greschner puts a lot of himself into each game. He's a quiet leader, both on and off the ice (though he's a definite presence in the locker room) and his presence adds depth and veteran experience to the team.

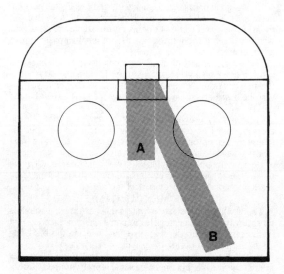

JARI GRONSTRAND

Yrs. of NHL service: 2
Born: Tampere, Finland; November 14, 1962
Position: Defenseman
Height: 6-3
Weight: 197
Uniform no.: 5
Shoots: left

Career statistics:

GP	G	A	TP	PIM
109	4	17	21	90

1987-88 statistics:

GP	G	A	TP	+/–	PIM	PP	SH	GW	GT	S	PCT
62	3	11	14	8	63	1	0	0	0	65	4.6

LAST SEASON

Acquired from Minnesota in the off-season, games played and all point totals were career highs. Gronstrand spent the first two weeks of the season in Colorado of the IHL, and missed 12 late season games with a knee injury. His plus 8 was second highest among full-time Ranger defensemen.

THE FINESSE GAME

Gronstrand's finesse skills are good and improving, but are still not at a consistent NHL level. He skates well forward and has fairly good agility moving toward the offensive zone, but his backskating and turns are weak and need improvement.

Jari moves the puck well from the offensive zone because he has good hands and good vision, but he's not a real threat to rush the puck himself. He can handle the puck well enough when he skates, but Gronstrand is going to get the puck to the open man and then fall back defensively. He won't force an offensive play.

He does, however, follow the play up-ice and will contribute to a small degree at the offensive blue line but — as his shot and point totals indicate — Gronstrand is not a big offensive player.

He understands defensive angles well and usually uses them to his advantage in angling off the opposition. He forces the play wide and can start the play up-ice after gaining a loose puck.

THE PHYSICAL GAME

Gronstrand has height and reach, but he's not a very strong defender. He uses his reach well in pokechecking and in tying up an opponent's stick, but he will be out-muscled in front of the net and along the boards.

That said, Gronstrand isn't afraid to suffer physical abuse. He'll take whatever hits are necessary to make his plays, and he'll certainly initiate contact regardless of the opponent.

THE INTANGIBLES

Gronstrand's persistence has fooled a lot of people, especially his willingness to play physically and to not back down in a confrontation. He can be a solid defenseman for New York, and will continue to improve as his progress in a foreign language — English — and adapting to the NHL increase.

His only problem is that his team has a lot of defensive depth, and many of those defenders play better all-around games than Gronstrand. He could see a lot of bench-time this year.

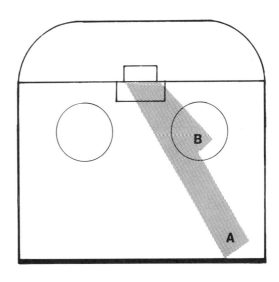

KELLY KISIO

Yrs. of NHL service: 6
Born: Peace River, Alberta, Canada; September 18, 1959
Position: Center
Height: 5-9
Weight: 170
Uniform no.: 11
Shoots: left

Career statistics:

GP	G	A	TP	PIM
383	115	224	339	336

1987-88 statistics:

GP	G	A	TP	+/−	PIM	PP	SH	GW	GT	S	PCT
77	23	55	78	8	88	9	1	1	0	145	15.9

LAST SEASON

Throat, leg and knee injuries limited Kisio to 77 games, which was still a career-high. He finished second on the club in scoring and first in assists.

THE FINESSE GAME

Not a great skater in terms of speed or agility, Kisio has good balance and is difficult to remove from the puck. He is made more effective by the fact that he can handle the puck well at top speed, and is greatly aided by his ice vision and good anticipation skills. Because of those skills, he sees a lot of checking duty and is a staple on both specialty teams.

His puckhandling skills make him a good playmaker (and perhaps he is a little too unselfish — he would score more goals if he shot more) and he uses those skills to get his teammates in position to score. He has a good shot, made better by the fact that Kelly will go into traffic to put it to use.

THE PHYSICAL GAME

His size — or lack thereof — is no limitation to Kisio. He pursues the puck relentlessly, fearlessly banging into bigger and stronger opponents. He plays physically at both ends of the rink, and his grinding ability paves the way for his finesse skills.

He is strong and will win many battles, but he can be over-powered by bigger defensemen or opposing centermen who can put their own strength and reach to work for themselves.

THE INTANGIBLES

He's not blessed with an abundance of natural talent, but Kisio makes what he has valuable through hard work. In that way, Kisio gives the Rangers something they needa consistent game at both ends of the ice from a center, and a hard worker who leads by example.

Low-key in the lockerroom, Kisio succeeds on heart and determination.

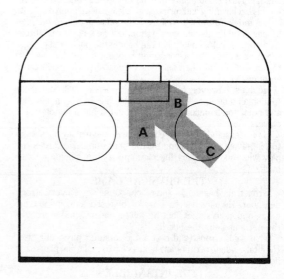

PIERRE LAROUCHE

Yrs. of NHL service: 14
Born: Taschereau, Quebec, Canada; November 16, 1955
Position: Center/right wing
Height: 5-11
Weight: 175
Uniform no.: 10
Shoots: right

Career statistics:

GP	G	A	TP	PIM
812	395	427	822	237

1987-88 statistics:

GP	G	A	TP	+/−	PIM	PP	SH	GW	GT	S	PCT
10	3	9	12	-3	13	2	0	0	0	30	10.0

LAST SEASON

A back injury sidelined Pierre for almost all of the season, forcing him to play the fewest games and score the fewest point of his career.

THE FINESSE GAME

Hands and brains write the story of Larouche as a finesse player.

He has goal scorer's hands, meaning he can bury the puck often and from anywhere. He handles the puck very well and can make it dance, but Larouche also takes himself out of scoring opportunities by being too cute with the puck. His one extra deke should be turned into a shot on goal.

Pierre can pass exceptionally well, but he is a goal scorer first and foremost, not a playmaker.

Larouche can be particularly effective on the power play, when the extra ice gives him room to maneuver. He likes to shoot from between the crease and the left faceoff circle and the Rangers try to set him up there. He can one-time the puck better than almost anyone.

He is absolutely deadly on breakaways, one of the top 10 in the League, all because of his hands.

Larouche is also super at getting into position to score, something that reflects his brains and hockey sense. He has a sense that tells him where the openings will be and he gets there, creating more good scoring opportunities by getting to the open with his brain than any other way.

Larouche's vision of the ice is terrific. He's always standing straight up and looking things over and is always aware of where he is.

By and large, his defense is terrible. He almost refuses to back check, though he will surprise you once in a while by sweeping an almost sure opposition goal off the goal line, leaving you to ask yourself, "What's the big deal about Larouche not playing defense?"

There is no big deal. And that's what Pierre's defense is, no big deal.

THE PHYSICAL GAME

Larouche is not a physical hockey player, but that doesn't mean he won't take his knocks. Though his sense of the game most usually keeps him from getting hit, Pierre will take his punishment when need be.

That doesn't mean he will strain himself to get away from tight checking. Nor will he stand in front of the net and take a pounding for his goals. Rather, he'll materialize in an opening outside of the crowd and wait for the puck to come to him, which it will do much of the time.

THE INTANGIBLES

The above report on Pierre is word-for-word from last season, and the reason for that is simpleThat's the Larouche scouting report *before* his back injury.

There is no way to tell how Pierre will perform if he does return to action this season, and there is great reason to believe that he will not. One reason Larouche may consider sitting out is his pride. An intensely proud man, Pierre is unlikely to return if he is unable to perform at his freewheeling best.

Until we see what Pierre decides, all bets regarding his play are off.

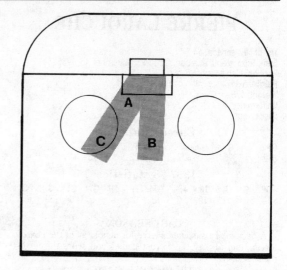

BRIAN LEETCH

Yrs. of NHL service: 1
Born: Corpus Christi, Texas, USA; March 3, 1968
Position: Defenseman
Height: 5-11
Weight: 185
Uniform no.: 2
Shoots: left

Career statisics:

GP	G	A	TP	+/−	PIM	PP	SH	GW	GT	S	PCT
17	2	12	14	5	0	1	0	1	0	40	5.0

LAST SEASON

Leetch made his NHL debut following the Calgary Olympic Games.

THE FINESSE GAME

Leetch is a superb package of finesse skills. He's an excellent skater in all facets of that skillspeed, quickness, agility and lateral movement. He accelerates well with breakaway speed, and his excellent foot speed and balance allow him to turn well in either direction.

He skates as well backward as he does forward, losing nothing in the speed, quickness or agility departments. He combines his excellent skating skills with superb hand and stick skills. He handles the puck very well and can make end-to-end rushes, but Leetch is just as adept at gaining the puck and sending it out of the zone.

Brian is an excellent passer, favoring neither forehand or backhand but passing equally well to both sides. He makes soft passes, but more importantly he makes the right passes. Leetch finds the open man because he has great sense for the game, combined with great anticipation and vision. He is smart with the puck and will make the correct decisions.

Leetch has a good shot (he shoots often) which is almost always on net, so it's an efficient one too. He releases the puck quickly on his wrist shot (he'll sneak to the openings to let it go) and he also has a good slap shot from the point.

He plays his defense positionally, knowing it's the most efficient way to do. He angles the man wide well, and he can certainly make a play coming away from the boards.

THE PHYSICAL GAME

Leetch does not yet have the strength necessary to tackle the NHL's heavy hitters, so he'll have to develop that part of his game. That's not to say he shies away from contact or won't take the body, but Brian realizes that to be successful now, he can't allow himself to get into physical situations where he can be out-muscled. That role is reserved for his defense partner.

THE INTANGIBLES

For a player who's almost guaranteed to be a superstar, the questions can be endless. Can he develop the strength necessary to play a full NHL game? Will he fulfill the expectations of him that portray him as a multi-time Norris Trophy winner? To what heights will he lead the Rangers?

Leetch is a player with tremendous desire and a great attitude toward work and improving his game. He plays at a consistently high level, and he's a team player. He should fulfill all that's expected of him.

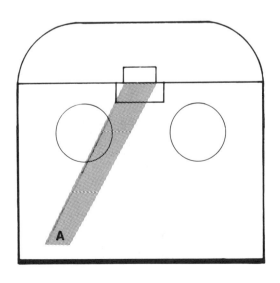

327

NORM MACIVER

Yrs. of NHL service: 1
Born: Thunder Bay, Ontario, Canada; September 1, 1964
Position: Defenseman
Height: 5-11
Weight: 180
Uniform no.: 37
Shoots: left

Career statistics:

GP	G	A	TP	PIM
40	9	16	25	14

1987-88 statistics:

GP	G	A	TP	+/−	PIM	PP	SH	GW	GT	S	PCT
37	9	15	24	10	14	4	0	2	0	65	13.8

LAST SEASON

Began the year with Colorado of the IHL before joining the Rangers in December. His plus/minus was the team's third best overall. He missed 11 games with an injured right shoulder.

THE FINESSE GAME

Maciver is an excellent skater, possessing great quickness, agility and speed. He has excellent change of pace and puts his speed to great use by driving defenders off the opposing blue line. His one-step quickness gets him to loose pucks and, combined with his balance, allows him to change direction within a stride. That gives him great lateral movement.

He is also gifted in puckhandling and will rush the puck when given the opportunity, but he is still guilty of occasionally carrying the puck too deep and getting trapped. His judgement was improving until he got hurt.

Maciver is a good playmaker both in getting the puck from his zone and in feeding his teammates in the offensive zone. He has a good shot from the point and will slide to the high slot if he can, knowing that his skating (and more-defensive-minded defense partner) can rescue him when necessary. Like many of the Ranger blueliners, his skills make him a valuable power play addition.

Norm plays his defense by speed, but he is improving his positional play. That allows him to thwart opponents bigger and stronger than himself.

THE PHYSICAL GAME

Maciver is willing to go into the corners and do the dirty work, but don't confuse willing for able. His lack of size and strength makes him ill-suited for work in traffic, and works against him when he meets a stronger opponent (as in when he suffered his separated shoulder, courtesy of a thunderous Scott Stevens check behind the Washington net).

Added bulk and muscular strength would help prevent such injuries, but shouldn't be added if Maciver's speed will suffer. That added strength would help defensively too, because Norm will be over-matched in many confrontations in front of the net or along the boards.

THE INTANGIBLES

The Rangers recognize the flaws in Maciver's game, and they minimize them by teaming him with a strong, conserv-ative partner — most often David Shaw, who will do the boards and crease work to free Norm for his finesse play.

A rookie last year, Maciver must demonstrate both reha-bilitation from his injury (and an ability to prevent future ones) and continued improvement in judgement. If not, the presence of offensive talents like Michel Petit, James Patrick and Brian Leetch may drive Maciver to the bench.

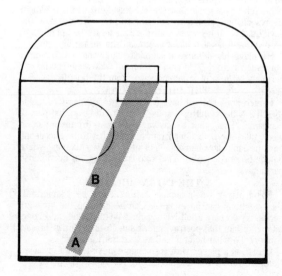

DON MALONEY

Yrs. of NHL service: 10
Born: Lindsay, Ontario, Canada; September 5, 1958
Position: Left wing
Height: 6-1
Weight: 190
Uniform no.: 12
Shoots: left

Career statistics:

GP	G	A	TP	PIM
622	191	298	489	723

1987-88 statistics:

GP	G	A	TP	+/-	PIM	PP	SH	GW	GT	S	PCT
66	12	21	33	12	60	1	0	2	0	88	13.6

LAST SEASON

Injured shoulder, ribs and groin limited Maloney's playing time. His plus/minus was the highest among the team's forwards and second highest overall.

THE FINESSE GAME

Balance and a low center of gravity are the keys to Maloney's skating and to his game. Because of them, he can gain the puck in the corners and that makes him valuable as a forechecker. Otherwise, he has no real speed and is not particularly adept at carrying the puck while moving.

The extent of Maloney's playmaking prowess is throwing the puck in front after gaining it in the corners. His shot is fair and any goals he gets are going to have to come from in tight. He's sound defensively, despite his lack of speed in making the transition from offense to defense.

THE PHYSICAL GAME

Though no longer the dominating corner-man of his youth, Maloney remains a strong, physical hockey player. It is difficult to knock him down and he has a knack of pushing opponents in the direction he wants to go.

Clearly, injuries play a key part in Maloney's career at this point and he'd have to be judged as somewhat brittle. That is the consequence of his physical style.

THE INTANGIBLES

Maloney found a niche last season as a defensive forward alongside Lucien Deblois and Jan Erixon. He can continue to contribute in that role, but he is obviously not an offensive threat. Should Deblois not return to the club (he was a free agent this summer), Maloney will need to re-establish himself as a player of *any* dimension.

His well-established work ethic speaks in his favor.

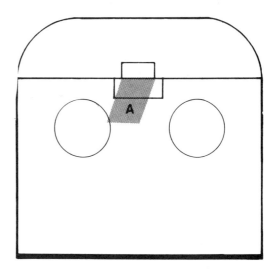

BRIAN MULLEN

Yrs. of NHL service: 6
Born: New York City, NY, USA; March 16, 1962
Position: Left wing
Height: 5-10
Weight: 170
Uniform no.: 19
Shoots: left

Career statistics:

GP	G	A	TP	PIM
446	149	201	350	174

1987-88 statistics:

GP	G	A	TP	+/-	PIM	PP	SH	GW	GT	S	PCT
74	25	29	54	-2	42	10	0	4	0	147	17.0

LAST SEASON

Goal and point totals were third-highest of career, and shooting percentage was third-highest on club. Benchings and an injured knee account for his GP total. He scored 17 of his goals in the first half of the season.

THE FINESSE GAME

Mullen is a finesse player through and through. He's a better than good skater, very quick and elusive on his feet. He has a lot of foot speed and combines that trait with excellent balance to give him good lateral movement and excellent agility. He also has good rink-length speed that will allow him to beat many defenders.

His shot is next among his finesse skills, and it is excellent. He wastes few opportunities (meaning that he almost always forces the goaltender to make saves) and he releases his shot quickly. He can hit whatever openings a goalie leaves.

Mullen handles the puck well, though he has a little difficulty when he's moving at top speed. He uses his teammates fairly well and looks for a play before shooting. He is patient in his puckhandling (sometimes a little too so), but can get the puck to his teammates successfully.

He sees the ice well, and his speed and play recognition allow him to get into openings (one-step quickness is the key here). Importantly, Brian knows how to get into position to score.

THE PHYSICAL GAME

There isn't one. Mullen does his best to avoid the traffic areas, knowing that his best work is done in open ice. He's not afraid of contact, and will throw his weight around on occasion, but don't look for him to win any battles along the boards or in the corners.

In fact, don't look for him in those places at all.

THE INTANGIBLES

Mullen doesn't push himself every night, and that flaw comes home to roost in divisional games. Of his 25 goals, only eight came against Patrick Division foes, and he had only nine points in his last 20 games (and just six points in his last 19 contests).

Those are not good numbers for a guy who's supposed to score goals, especially when combined with a minus 2 plus/minus mark. And for a coach like Michel Bergeron, who prizes toughness, Mullen's contributions may be questionable; the coach didn't even bother putting Mullen in the lineup four times last year.

The winger has to apply himself and play with more intensity, or he will find himself frequently on the bench.

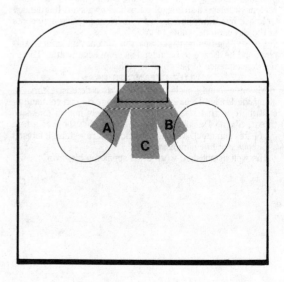

CHRIS NILAN

Yrs. of NHL service: 8
Born: Boston, Mass., USA; February 9, 1958
Position: Left wing/right wing
Height: 6-0
Weight: 200
Uniform no.: 30
Shoots: right

Career statistics:

GP	G	A	TP	PIM
528	90	89	179	2,270

1987-88 statistics:

GP	G	A	TP	+/-	PIM	PP	SH	GW	GT	S	PCT
72	10	10	20	-2	305	0	0	1	0	88	11.4

LAST SEASON

Acquired by the Rangers from the Montreal Canadiens in January 1988, for a swap of 1989 draft picks. He finished first on the Rangers, and fifth in the League, in PIM with the third-highest total of his career. He missed 10 games with New York because of a knee injury.

THE FINESSE GAME

Though physical performance is why Chris Nilan is in the lineup, he keeps himself there because of often-obscured finesse skills. Though he's no better than average as a skater, Nilan is a good forechecker because of persistence and determination. He also has a small dose of speed that he can use effectively, mostly because it surprises the opposition.

He is disciplined in playing his wing, and he has a pretty good view of the ice and ability to anticipate. He stays with his check fairly deeply into the defensive zone, and his presence in an area often forces the opposition to surrender the puck or pursue it with less vigor.

For a fighter, Chris has good hands, and he can make plays to his teammates and even operate in a little bit of traffic. He'll score 17-20 goals a season by lurking around the net and putting home defensive mistakes.

THE PHYSICAL GAME

If it moves in an opposition uniform, Nilan will hit it. He is an exceptionally hard hitter (made so because he has great strength and fairly good balance, so he remains vertical after collisions) and most difficult to dislodge from his skates.

He's one of the NHL's better fighters (certainly unafraid of any opponent) and he uses his stick liberally.

Chris has good upper body strength and can out-muscle many opponents along the boards, but he can often be guilty of being overaggressive and cancelling his good work out with an extra elbow that loses him the puck he could gain.

THE INTANGIBLES

It's the intangibles that make Nilan so valuable to a team. He is an excellent team leader — both through word and deed — both in the room and on the ice. His aggressiveness can turn into a liability in terms of affording the opposition the power play, but chances are any team will willingly kill off any penalty Nilan takes, because his play fires up his team.

He's a tough competitor, a hard worker and a dedicated player. He's also a goon. But he gives the Rangers a presence they have been searching for for years (in the likes of Cam Connor, Frank Beaton, Nick Fotiu, Rick Chartraw and other failed tough guys), and he allows every Ranger to play bigger than his size.

If there's doubt as to his value, consider that after the Canadiens lost to Boston in last spring's playoffs for the first time in 45 years, the absence of Nilan was given as a major — if not the — reason why.

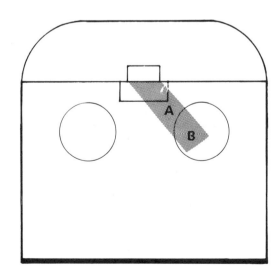

JOHN OGRODNICK

Yrs. of NHL service: 9
Born: Ottawa, Ontario, Canada; June 20, 1959
Position: Left wing
Height: 6-0
Weight: 190
Uniform no.: 25
Shoots: left

Career statistics:

GP	G	A	TP	PIM
635	292	323	615	168

1987-88 statistics:

GP	G	A	TP	+/−	PIM	PP	SH	GW	GT	S	PCT
64	22	32	54	-3	16	7	0	5	1	152	14.5

LAST SEASON

An injured left ankle, injured ribs and a bruised tailbone resulted in Ogrodnick playing the fewest games in a season in his NHL career. His goal and point totals were also the lowest of his career, He had the fewest PIM of any Ranger regular last year.

THE FINESSE GAME

Ogrodnick is a deceptive skater. He doesn't have great agility or one-step quickness, and he doesn't seem to have rink-length speed either. Yet time and again he'll force the defense backward or out-race an opponent to a loose puck.

He accelerates very well and that ability puts him in the clear to use his excellent slap shot. His shot is quickly released (one of the NHL's best) and is very accurate. Ogrodnick also has excellent wrist and snap shots in his arsenal and he can pretty much score from anywhere in the offensive zone. He is a staple on the power play.

He is a scorer first and foremost and will always look to the net before he looks to a teammate, but last year Ogrodnick didn't shoot the puck enough. This could be a direct result of his stepping up his boards-and-corners game.

He reads the play well and certainly knows how to get into position to score, but his style is more of a straight ahead, get-a-step-on-the-defenseman-and-blast-at-the-net mode than a dipsy-doodle one.

THE PHYSICAL GAME

Never before known for his willingness (or ability) to play physically, Ogrodnick stepped up the pace of his physical game last year. He has good size and balance, so he can be successful in battle for loose pucks, and his strength is what propels his shot.

THE INTANGIBLES

Though he made up some ground last year in rounding out his game, Ogrodnick still floats far too frequently in far too many games. His defense remains lackadaisical, so Ogrodnick would have to be called a one-dimensional player.

More damning for him is that in his lack of intensity he was unable to pick up the scoring slack after Pierre Larouche was sidelined with injury and Tomas Sandstrom failed to match his offensive production of 1986-87. Only five of Ogrodnick's goals came against divisional opponents.

Like Brian Mullen, Ogrodnick's continued New York tenure may be directly related to how much coach Michel Bergeron is willing to put up with in the hope of gaining some firepower.

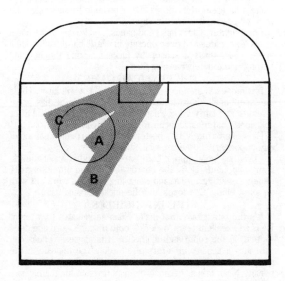

JAMES PATRICK

Yrs. of NHL service: 4
Born: Winnipeg, Man., Canada; June 14, 1963
Position: Defenseman
Height: 6-2
Weight: 185
Uniform no.: 3
Shoots: right

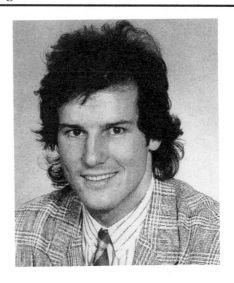

Career statistics:

GP	G	A	TP	PIM
310	50	154	204	275

1987-88 statistics:

GP	G	A	TP	+/−	PIM	PP	SH	GW	GT	S	PCT
70	17	45	62	16	52	9	0	1	0	187	9.1

LAST SEASON

Goal and point totals were career highs, while games played was fewest of NHL career (due to knee injury). He finished eighth among League defensive scorers and he led the club in plus/minus.

THE FINESSE GAME

Patrick is one of the top five defensemen — in terms of skating — in the League. He has speed, quickness and acceleration skills, but it is his lateral movement and agility that boosts his skating from the ranks of the ordinary to the heights of the exceptional.

He carries the puck from his own zone as well as the League's best rushers — Gary Suter, Ray Bourque and maybe even Paul Coffey. Patrick is an excellent puck handler and passer, making him the key to the Rangers' power play success. He sees the open man and gets the puck to him well, but James remains unsure of how to operate in the offensive zone when he's leading a rush.

His shot from the point is good, and while he shoots frequently enough (he was third on the team in shots-on-goal) he does not shoot to score anywhere near enough. James has made himself a double threat by jumping into the slot for an accurate wrist (no small reason his goal total last year was a career high).

But as improved as his offensive play is, Patrick is still lax in his own zone. He continues to have difficulty reading the rush toward him, and he loses his concentration around his own net, thus allowing the opposition to roam free. His plus/minus total is more the result of his offensive proficiency than his defensive efficiency.

THE PHYSICAL GAME

His good size notwithstanding, Patrick is strong neither in the corners nor in front of the net and will either surrender the puck to forwards of superior strength or take penalties to prevent opposition scoring opportunites.

He has increased his willingness to play the body, and he certainly has the skills to make plays out of confrontations. But generally, Patrick is more of a finesse player than a traffic player.

THE INTANGIBLES

Patrick's value to the Rangers lies in his offensive skills, and he has not yet reached his potential in the NHL. However, James seems satisfied with the level his game is at, and he just doesn't seem to have the desire to work on applying his phenomenal talent.

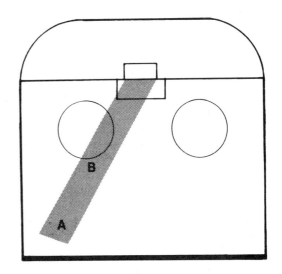

MICHEL PETIT

Yrs. of NHL service: 5
Born: St. Malo, Quebec, Canada; February 12, 1964
Position: Defenseman
Height: 6-1
Weight: 205
Uniform no.: 24
Shoots: right

Career statistics:

GP	G	A	TP	PIM
290	33	81	114	596

1987-88 statistics:

GP	G	A	TP	+/–	PIM	PP	SH	GW	GT	S	PCT
74	9	27	36	-1	258	2	0	3	0	109	8.3

LAST SEASON

Petit was obtained from Vancouver in November in exchange for Larry Melnyk and Willie Huber. He set career marks for assists, points, penalty minutes and games played, and he was second on New York in PIM (first among defensemen).

THE FINESSE GAME

Petit is an excellent skater, equipped with good balance and speed. He's very agile on his skates, especially for a bigger man. He has good lateral movement and change-of-direction skills, all of which could make him an above-average offensive threat.

He is smart enough to keep the play ahead of him, but on the whole his play-reading and vision abilities are not as high as his physical finesse skills, so he is a high risk player prone to get burned on many of the chances he takes.

He has improved his defensive zone coverage and seems to be showing a better ability to angle off the opposition, but he still does choose inopportune times for launching two-on-ones, charging the net or throwing the puck into traffic in order to generate offense. In all, his total play without the puck, though already improved, can be better.

When he has the puck, Michel is dangerous. He handles it very well and will rush if given the chance. He also shoots very well, but nowhere near often enough for a guy that gets so many opportunities.

His skills serve to make him a regular on both the Rangers specialty teams, less so on the power play because the club has a number of offensively proficient blueliners but especially in killing penalties where his mobility and strength are big plusses.

THE PHYSICAL GAME

Petit has good size and strength, and he's developed the willingness to use that strength in the corners and the front of the net, as his PIM indicate. He has shown that he'll drop the gloves when necessary, and he has also become very liberal in his use of his stick on the opposition.

Certainly, he can take the opposing forward off the puck in the corner and make a play up-ice, and that's why he's valuable.

THE INTANGIBLES

Increased playing time is the reason for Petit's improvement. He got a lot of time with the Rangers, probably more than he'd ever gotten in the NHL to date. He's also gotten smarter because of the increased experience and his defense isn't bad: He was a plus player in his 64 Ranger games (plus 30 after his trade).

He's become so willing to be mean in front of the net because of the presence of Chris Nilan, knowing that Nilan will now back his plays.

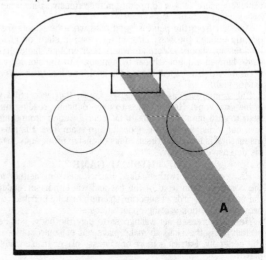

WALT PODDUBNY

Yrs. of NHL service: 6
Born: Thunder Bay, Ontario, Canada; February 14, 1960
Position: Center/left wing
Height: 6-1
Weight: 203
Uniform no. 8:
Shoots: left

Career statistics:

GP	G	A	TP	PIM
342	137	183	320	303

1987-88 statistics:

GP	G	A	TP	+/−	PIM	PP	SH	GW	GT	S	PCT
77	38	50	88	2	76	13	0	4	1	202	18.8

LAST SEASON

Poddubny led the team in games played (a career high), goals, points and shooting percentage. He finished second in shots-on-goal, assists and power play goals. A minor concussion and a finger injury sidelined him for three games.

THE FINESSE GAME

Balance and the attendant agility make Poddubny a good skater, and his skating and scoring skills make him a good player.

He has rink-length speed to out-race the opposition, and his balance and lateral movement make him agile and allow him to absorb checks and still make plays.

Walt combines his foot speed and puckhandling ability with his anticipation skills to get into the open, or to get the puck to his open teammates. Those passing and anticipation skills — along with an excellent wrist/snap shot — make Poddubny a power play stalwart.

Poddubny shoots the puck well and often, using a fast (but not exceptionally hard) wrist shot to beat goaltenders from 30 feet or so. Because he has good hands, Poddubny can also operate well in the traffic around the net, and is very dangerous around the crease.

THE PHYSICAL GAME

Poddubny's balance keys his physical game and allows him to operate with the puck in traffic. He's willing to get involved along the boards, but he's not really a mucker. He'll go into traffic for a loose puck but won't muscle anyone out of the way for it; Walt will let his hand skills pull the puck out for him.

His balance also makes him difficult to dislodge from the puck. Though not an extraordinarily physical player, Poddubny will take his licks and can dish some out as well.

THE INTANGIBLES

Despite being moved from his favored center position to the wing, and despite playing with a variety of linemates all season long, Poddubny showed that he can still be an offensive force.

If coach Michel Bergeron insists on putting Walt on the wing (where, the coach insists, shooters belong), then the Rangers are going to have to find a center (Ulf Dahlen?) to get Poddubny the puck.

And, while last year's success showed that Poddubny was no one-hit wonder, the fact that he had only one goal and four points in the Rangers' last eight games as they strove for the playoffs (and only 13 of his 38 goals in the second half), raises fresh questions about his ability to contribute in the clutch.

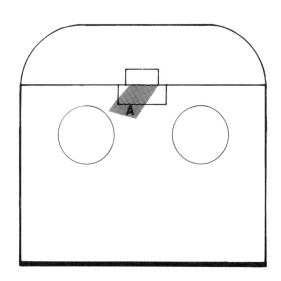

TOMAS SANDSTROM

Yrs. of NHL service: 4
Born: Jakobstad, Finland; September 4, 1964
Position: Right wing
Height: 6-2
Weight: 200
Uniform no.: 28
Shoots: left

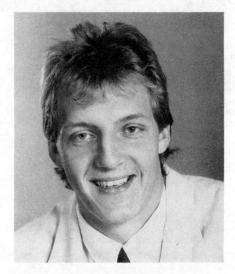

Career statistics:

GP	G	A	TP	PIM
280	122	132	254	315

1987-88 statistics:

GP	G	A	TP	+/-	PIM	PP	SH	GW	GT	S	PCT
69	28	40	68	-6	95	11	0	3	0	204	13.7

LAST SEASON

Assist total was highest, while point total was second-highest of career, despite missing games with finger and back injuries. Finished third in team scoring and first in shots-on-goal.

THE FINESSE GAME

Skating and shooting are the hallmarks of Sandstrom's game. His speed and agility make him an excellent skater, and he can blow by defenders because of that skill. However, he can be easy to defend against because he doesn't moderate his pace approaching the blue line.

His excellent balance makes him difficult to knock off the puck, and allows him to maintain possession in traffic and while being checked. It also gives him his shiftiness, and allows him to shoot accurately and well when he seems to be out of control.

His speed and hockey sense can make him a good checker, and his anticipation allows him to capitalize on the opposition's mistakes.

He is one of the few players in the League who can blow a puck past a goaltender. He likes the long side of the net, low on the ice, and he gets his slap shot away in one touch. For all that, and despite the fact he led the team in SOG, Sandstrom didn't shoot enough last year. In fact, in five more games last season, Tomas had 36 fewer SOG.

Instead, he chose to overhandle the puck and, while his hand skills are excellent (he passes and takes a pass extremely well, and he can execute with all of his skills at top speed), he is not primarily an in-close scorer.

Never a great defensive player, Sandstrom can be downright lazy at times regarding his back-checking. Surprising, considering his skating and anticipation abilities.

THE PHYSICAL GAME

Tomas' aggressiveness — he comes in high with his elbows, butts people with his helmet and puts his stick into almost everyone — is well documented. Because of that, and because he can't be intimidated, he's probably the toughest European in the game. He can also hit cleanly and when he does, he does so well.

His chippy play often gets under the skin of the opposition and when they retaliate he draws penalties.

THE INTANGIBLES

The questions are two.First, will Tomas learn that he needs to put out consistent effort every game, or will he continue to float through many contests because the game is so easy for him?

Second: Just how long will his chippy/dirty play continue, considering the consequences of his actions? His teammates don't back his aggressive plays, although a full season with Chris Nilan alongside may change that. And there can be little doubt that, though his chippiness didn't decrease, Sandstrom's effectiveness was affected by Dave Brown's cross-check (didn't we write this last year?) early in the season.

Sandstrom can be the big gun the Rangers have desperately needed, but only if he is willing to play with considerably more intensity than he showed last season.

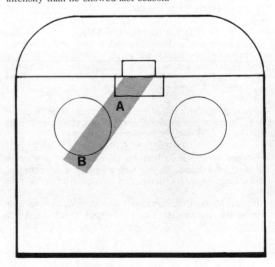

DAVID SHAW

Yrs. of NHL service: 4
Born: St. Thomas, Ontario, Canada; May 25, 1964
Position: Defenseman
Height: 6-2
Weight: 190
Uniform no.: 21
Shoots: right

Career statistics:

GP	G	A	TP	PIM
235	14	63	77	258

1987-88 statistics:

GP	G	A	TP	+/−	PIM	PP	SH	GW	GT	S	PCT
68	7	25	32	-8	100	5	0	1	0	141	5.0

LAST SEASON

Acquired pre-season from Quebec in exchange for Lane Lambert and Terry Carkner. Games played was a career low (courtesy of a separated left shoulder), but point and penalty minute totals were career highs.

THE FINESSE GAME

Shaw is a good skater, not blessed with a lot of speed but sufficiently capable in terms of agility and quickness to get up and down the ice without giving ground to the opposition.

He's a smart player, playing defense positionally and rarely doing things he's incapable of. Shaw sees the rush toward him well and can break up plays by angling off the opposition, and when he gains the puck he generally moves it quickly and correctly.

Since his is a conservative game, Shaw will rarely rush the puck himself and almost never over-commits at the offensive blue line. He does, however, contribute offensively from the blue line and is able to do so because of his vision and good hands. He moves the puck to his teammates fairly well and has a cannon for a shot from the blue line, so he'll get a lot of power play time.

Shaw would be even more effective from the blue line if he could lose the bad habit of putting his head down once he decides to shoot. Many times he tucks his head in for a slapper, only to drive the puck into a shot-blocking forward who made the challenging move after Shaw looked down. The results are far too many odd-man advantages for breaking opponents, an ironic twist for a conservative defender.

THE PHYSICAL GAME

Shaw has both good size and strength and he uses them effectively in the defensive zone. He can force the opposition from the crease, or tie up the incoming forward along the boards, and he'll do it smartly. Though his PIM was a career high, it's a low total for a player that plays a fairly physical game.

He uses the body well and can hit hard, but Shaw is not a punishing hitter. He also puts his reach to work excellently in poking the puck or deflecting from the goal.

THE INTANGIBLES

Willingness to work and improve are the keys for Shaw. Coach Michel Bergeron loves him (and that's why Shaw is in New York), and David is the kind of solid all-around defender a team needs. As for his relatively low plus/minus, bear in mind that he was on the ice against the opposition's top lines almost 100 percent of the time.

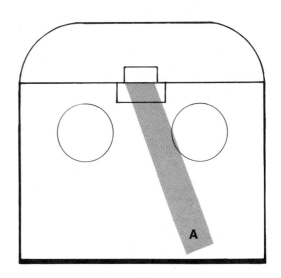

JOHN VANBIESBROUCK

Yrs. of NHL service: 4
Born: Detroit, Mich., USA; September 4, 1963
Position: Goaltender
Height: 5-9
Weight: 165
Uniform no.: 34
Catches: left

Career statistics:

GP	MINS	G	SO	AVG	A	PIM
213	11,899	709	6	3.57	14	99

1987-88 statisics:

GP	MINS	AVG	W	L	T	SO	GA	SA	SAPCT	PIM
56	3,319	3.38	27	22	7	2	187	1,700	.890	46

LAST SEASON

A comeback year for Vanbiesbrouck in a lot of ways. He finished fourth in the League in wins, despite facing more shots-on-goal than all but four other goaltenders (Grant Fuhr, Mike Vernon, Ron Hextall — who finished 1-2-3 in wins above Vanbiesbrouck — and Ken Wregget). He earned 27 of the Rangers' 36 victories, and the win and appearance totals were the second-highest of his career.

Vanbiesbrouck is also one of just three goaltenders (Glen Hanlon and Ron Hextall) to be credited with shots-on-goal last season. He also missed three games with a fractured jaw.

THE PHYSICAL GAME

More so than almost any other goaltender in the League, Vanbiesbrouck excels at squaring himself to the puck, and that is a sure sign of his success. When he plays the puck, the opposition is in for a long night. When he lets the puck play him, he and the Rangers will struggle. Obviously, then, John is an excellent angle goaltender.

He skates well, and his excellent balance almost always puts him in good position for the second save. Vanbiesbrouck is very quick back into his stance and is also very quick to recover from flopping. His skating skill allows him to move from the net to play the puck to his teammates, something he'll do at every opportunity.

His excellent catching hand (probably second only to Edmonton's Grant Fuhr) and left foot speed make him outstanding on the left side of the net. John is merely good on his stick side, but he minimizes that weakness by playing his angles well and standing up to that side. His excellent vision aids him in his angle play.

Vanbiesbrouck protects his crease fairly well, and will jab at opposing forwards who come too close. He can also use his stick well to move the puck, a facet of his game John improved last season.

THE MENTAL GAME

Vanbiesbrouck is pretty tough mentally, readying himself well for each game he plays. He certainly has the ability to make the big save for his team, as best evidenced by his shutout of the Quebec Nordiques last April in a game the Rangers had to win in their unsuccessful playoff bid.

Good though that ability is, Vanbiesbrouck must play a number of games in a row in order to bring his mental focus to its best level.

THE INTANGIBLES

Consistency is the hallmark of Vanbiesbrouck's game, and we told you last year that he must play frequently to be consistent. He was able to achieve that consistency last season because he never went more than two games without a start. As proof of his need to get into a groove, he went 17-10-4 over the last half of the season (16-7-3 in his last 26 starts).

He is a poised and confident individual, and in his own way is the team's hardest worker. As one of the top five goaltenders in the League, his importance to the New York Rangers is inestimable.

Now all he has to do is successfully recover from an off-season severe wrist injury and the subsequent surgery.

PHILADELPHIA FLYERS

LINE COMBINATIONS
BRIAN PROPP-DAVE POULIN TIM KERR
SCOTT MELLANBY-MURRAY CRAVEN-ILKKA
SINISALO
DERRICK SMITH-RON SUTTER-RICK TOCCHET

DEFENSE PAIRINGS
MARK HOWE-KJELL SAMUELSSON
KERRY HUFFMAN-DOUG CROSSMAN
BRAD MARSH-

GOALTENDERS
RON HEXTALL
MARK LAFOREST

OTHER PLAYERS
DAVE BROWN — left wing
J.J. DAIGNEAULT — defenseman
PELLE EKLUND — center
WILLIE HUBER — defenseman
PETER ZEZEL — center

POWER PLAY

FIRST UNIT:
BRIAN PROPP-PELLE EKLUND-TIM KERR
MARK HOWE-KJELL SAMUELSSON

SECOND UNIT:
BRIAN PROPP-PETER ZEZEL-RICK TOCCHET
MARK HOWE-DOUG CROSSMAN

On the first unit, KERR plugs the front of the net, EKLUND operates on the left wing boards and behind the net and PROPP is in the left wing circle. EKLUND will feed PROPP and HOWE in an attempt to open up the defense and free KERR in deep. Otherwise, PROPP and HOWE will shoot and KERR will pick up rebounds.

On the second unit, ZEZEL acts much like EKLUND, except he wants to feed PROPP at the left wing circle or

TOCCHET at the right wing circle for shots. Point shots from HOWE and CROSSMAN are second options, with TOCCHET going to the net on every shot.

CRAVEN, MELLANBY and SINISALO will also see power play duty among the forwards, as will HUFFMAN and HUBER for the defense.

Last season the Flyers power play was POOR, converting 83 times on 461 man-advantage opportunities (18.0 percent, 16th overall).

PENALTY KILLING

FIRST UNIT:
BRIAN PROPP-DAVE POULIN
MARK HOWE-KJELL SAMUELSSON

SECOND UNIT:
MURRAY CRAVEN-PETER ZEZEL
BRAD MARSH-DOUG CROSSMAN

The Flyers' first penalty killing unit is very aggressive. When the puck is in the power play's zone, PROPP and POULIN will go after it, while HOWE is high in the slot and SAMUELSSON is back. In the defensive zone, penalty killers will send two men to the puck and play more of a diamond formation to close down slot. POULIN and PROPP always look to break and will be at the red line for a pass from HEXTALL if he gets the puck with clearing room.

The second unit is also aggressive, but less so than the first. They play a more standard box. Both units will drop the puck back to HEXTALL to waste time when possible. SUTTER and SINISALO will also see penalty killing time.

Last season, the Flyers penalty killing was EXCELLENT, allowing just 90 goals in 475 short-handed situations (81.1 percent, fifth overall).

CRUCIAL FACEOFFS
ZEZEL and SUTTER are the Flyers' top faceoff men. ZEZEL will often take defensive end draws and then return to the bench.

DAVE BROWN

Yrs. of NHL service: 5
Born: Saskatoon, Sask., Canada; October 12, 1962
Position: Right wing
Height: 6-5
Weight: 205
Uniform no.: 21
Shoots: right

Career statistics:

GP	G	A	TP	PIM
263	33	26	59	933

1987-88 statistics:

GP	G	A	TP	+/−	PIM	PP	SH	GW	GT	S	PCT
47	12	5	17	10	114	0	0	4	0	41	29.3

LAST SEASON

Suspensions (for 15 games after cross-checking Tomas Sandstrom), injuries (wrist) and the flu limited Brown to what was effectively his shortest NHL season (forgiving his rookie year and a two-game stint in 1982-83). Still, he posted a career high in goals and matched his career high in points. He was also the Flyers' fifth highest plus-player.

THE FINESSE GAME

Brown remains a below-average finesse player, though he has improved his skills. He still lumbers up and down the ice, though smoother and with better balance than previously. He has little speed and probably less agility.

He can handle the puck when going straight forward in his wing position, but is not really an accomplished puck handler. If given time and space, he can get the puck to his teammates, but he lacks the vision and anticipation (the hockey sense, really) to be a consistent offensive player.

His scoring will have to be done from directly in front of the net. He plays well defensively and is with his man deep into the Flyer zone.

THE PHYSICAL GAME

A physical style of game would seem to benefit Brown, but that's not so. Because he's unable to catch most everyone, and thus can't hit them, a mucking role is currently out of Brown's grasp; opponents just step out of his way and let him thunder by. Additionally, when he is able to connect he's probably going to get the worst of the bargain because his balance is bad.

He is a fighter, and that's what keeps him in the NHL. Brown's fighting clears the way for players like Ron Sutter to be a pest on the ice, for Brown will take care of anyone who disapproves of Sutter's tactics. While he has a big reputation, Brown is not one of the NHL's best fighters, as he has had trouble with smaller opponents who won't be intimidated.

THE INTANGIBLES

It must be said, in fairness, that Dave Brown might very well be the NHL's most improved player. He's shown that he can be put on the ice and not be a liability (if he can keep his temper), but don't lose sight of Brown's purpose in the NHL: to intimidate.

The difference between Brown and a Rick Tocchet is that, while Brown can now be sent onto the ice and not perform negatively, Tocchet performs positively. That's an important difference.

The questions facing Brown this year are several. First, how will his new coach use him, if at all? Second, and probably more important for Brown, how will his injury hold up to the punishment of fighting?

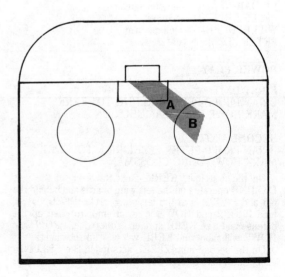

MURRAY CRAVEN

Yrs. of NHL service: 5
Born: Medicine Hat, Alta., Canada; July 20, 1964
Position: Left wing/center
Height: 6-2
Weight: 175
Uniform no.: 32
Shoots: left

Career statistics:

GP	G	A	TP	PIM
353	100	155	255	172

1987-88 statistics:

GP	G	A	TP	+/−	PIM	PP	SH	GW	GT	S	PCT
72	30	46	76	25	58	6	2	2	1	184	16.3

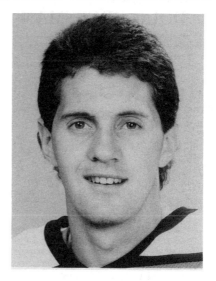

LAST SEASON

Craven led the Flyers in scoring and was second in plus/minus (first among forwards). He finished third in shots on goal. All point totals, as well as PIM, were career highs.

THE FINESSE GAME

Craven is an above-average skater. He's fast and he has good acceleration away from the opposition, and he's begun to learn to moderate his speed as well, no longer going straight at the defense at full steam all the time. He's also fairly shifty on his feet, and his good balance gives him good lateral movement and agility.

Murray is a good puckhandler, putting his reach to work extremely well and handling the puck well at top speed. He can get the puck to his teammates, but Murray is more of a one-on-one player; he shoots first and asks questions later. He has a goal scorer's anticipation and he is able to find the openings in the offensive zone. When he finds a seam, his speed puts him in the open.

He uses a quick wrist shot and will fire from anywhere, but he actually should shoot more for the opportunities his speed and sense create. Murray is also very good on breakaways because of his hands, able to move the puck back and forth at will.

Craven is a good defensive player, conscientious in the neutral and defensive zones.

THE PHYSICAL GAME

Craven is not a physical player per se, but last year he began to demonstrate a willingness to at least use his body in simple ways. He got in front of opponents and also applied himself along the boards. Make no mistake though; Craven is still an open ice player.

Murray is not overly strong, but he is skilled at using his body to shield the puck from the opposition. Combined with his skating, that trait makes it difficult to strip the puck from him.

THE INTANGIBLES

Like all finesse players, Craven must learn that a physical game not only complements a finesse one but improves it. He should increase his strength.

Craven was lucky last year, in that the Flyers had health troubles with all their centers and that allowed him to come to the fore. A new coach this season (one who puts less of a premium on defensive physical play than did Mike Keenan) would allow Craven to continue to expand his offensive game, but depth will again be a problem.

If Ron Sutter and Dave Poulin stay healthy, that makes Craven the number three center already. Add the talented but enigmatic Peter Zezel — and Pelle Eklund — and you can see the odds Craven must overcome to remain *the* cog in the Flyers' wheeel.

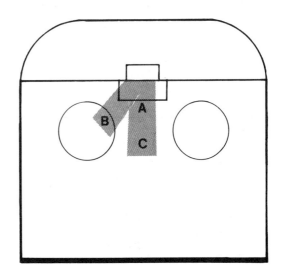

DOUG CROSSMAN

Yrs. of NHL service: 7
Born: Peterborough, Ontario, Canada; June 30, 1960
Position: Defenseman
Height: 6-2
Weight: 190
Uniform no.: 3
Shoots: left

Career statistics:

GP	G	A	TP	PIM
551	60	228	288	327

1987-88 statistics:

GP	G	A	TP	+/−	PIM	PP	SH	GW	GT	S	PCT
76	9	29	38	-1	43	6	0	0	0	153	5.9

LAST SEASON

Crossman (and Derrick Smith) led all Flyers in games played. Point total was his lowest in three seasons, assist total lowest in four. He was the Flyers' second highest scoring defenseman, and the team's least penalized defender.

THE FINESSE GAME

Crossman's defensive style is influenced by his finesse skills. He is a smooth skater but lacks overall speed, so he's best suited for a stay-at-home role.

Since he is not quick he won't jump into openings, but he is able to rush the puck (and contribute smartly from the offensive blue line) because of his hand skills. Crossman handles the puck well in both the offensive and defensive zone, melding his attacking and defending game better than ever previously.

He operates well on the power play, where the ice opens up for him and gives him more time to think and more space to work in, and he also sees time as a penalty killer because of his surehandedness. He is a good passer to both sides.

Doug's improved his positional play defensively, so that opposing forwards who may have been able to take advantage of his slow turns and less-than-good lateral movement now find themselves forced wide of the net.

THE PHYSICAL GAME

Lack of strength remains Crossman's Waterloo, and any of the League's stronger forwards will overpower him in front of the net or in the corners.

He has a good reach and can pokecheck effectively, but Crossman is in trouble when hit because he'll get bounced off the puck. He's lucky that players like Rick Tocchet, Tim Kerr and Derrick Smith are teammates, because Crossman has great difficulty handling their peers around the League.

THE INTANGIBLES

We told you last year that Crossman was quiet, unemotional and uninvolved. In March of last season former Flyers coach Mike Keenan was saying those things to the Philadelphia press.

If Keenan had remained in Philly, there's little doubt that Crossman would be gone. Now Doug gets a reprieve and, like many in the Flyer defense corps, he'll have to prove himself to a new coach.

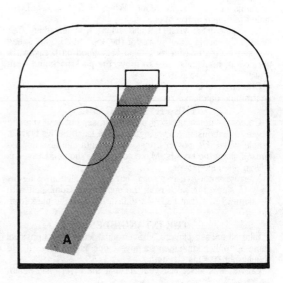

JEAN-JACQUES DAIGNEAULT

Yrs. of NHL service: 4
Born: Montreal, Quebec, Canada; October 12, 1965
Position: Defenseman
Height: 5-11
Weight: 180
Uniform no.: 15
Shoots: left

Career statistics:

GP	G	A	TP	PIM
236	17	64	81	182

1987-88 statistics:

GP	G	A	TP	+/−	PIM	PP	SH	GW	GT	S	PCT
28	2	2	4	-8	12	2	0	0	0	20	10.0

LAST SEASON

Because he shuttled back and forth to the minors, all of Daigneault's totals were career lows.

THE FINESSE GAME

Skating is Daigneault's primary skill. He is an excellent skater in all aspects—smooth, balanced, and fast. J.J. is as good backward as he is forward, turning well and demonstrating good lateral movement and agility.

He likes to carry the puck whenever he can, and handles it well in open ice, but gets in trouble when he gets into traffic. He tries to force plays, carries the puck too deep and turns it over, leaving himself trapped up-ice. His judgement, in short, is not good.

J.J. has good stick skills and he can find teammates from the point, so he can be a serviceable point man. He moves the puck fairly well, but still has difficulty reading the play on the NHL level. He passes well to both sides and is better at feeding his teammates than he is at scoring himself.

His play without the puck in his own zone is bad and needs improving. He doesn't demonstrate a knowledge of how to jump into a hole, nor does he play his position well in checking and marking men.

THE PHYSICAL GAME

Daigneault doesn't play a physical game. He mostly pushes and shoves along the boards, and is not very interested in clearing the front of the net. Additional upper body strength would at least allow him to tie up the opposition, even if he won't out-muscle an opposing player for the puck.

THE INTANGIBLES

We have seen how former Vancouver players, especially the youngsters, can thrive playing for other teams; Cam Neely and Michel Petit are examples of that.

Daigneault has exceptional offensive talents, and it's hard to believe that he went unclaimed when the Flyers waived him and sent him to the minors. He has a chance to start fresh with a new Flyer coach this season, and the fact that the Flyers ran 13 players through their defense corps last season (and not all because of injury) means very little is settled regarding defensemen.

And remember, J.J. is still only 23 years old.

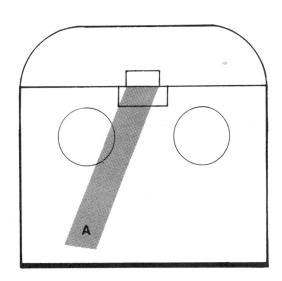

PER-ERIK EKLUND

Yrs. of NHL service: 3
Born: Stockholm, Sweden; March 22, 1963
Position: Center
Height: 5-10
Weight: 170
Uniform no.: 9
Shoots: left

Career statistics:

GP	G	A	TP	PIM
213	39	124	163	26

1987-88 statistics:

GP	G	A	TP	+/−	PIM	PP	SH	GW	GT	S	PCT
71	10	32	42	-6	12	2	0	2	0	101	9.9

LAST SEASON

For the second consecutive season, Eklund had the fewest penalty minutes among the Flyers. A hip injury sidelined him for seven games. He scored 28 of his 42 points in the season's first half.

THE FINESSE GAME

Primary among Eklund's considerable finesse skills are his hands. He can put the puck anywhere he wants to and sticks or bodies don't worry him, because he'll find the openings and ease the puck onto a teammate's stick. He also handles the puck very well when he skates.

Eklund complements those hand skills with excellent ice vision (particularly peripherally) and superb anticipation. He has great hockey sense and understanding of the offensive play, and uses both that sense and those hand/stick skills to great effect on the Flyers' power play.

Skating is — barely — second among Pelle's finesse skills. He's a fine and elegant skater, smooth and fluid and with good lateral movement. Eklund has shown more and more of that ability, but he could still improve at beating the opposition one-on-one and going to the net. He must also shoot the puck more, even when Tim Kerr is perched in the slot for a power play pass.

THE PHYSICAL GAME

Though not afraid of the physical play, by no means is Eklund a physical player. His size mitigates against him, and he is not very strong either. Clearly, his best work is in the open ice and not in the traffic areas.

THE INTANGIBLES

Under former coach Mike Keenan, Eklund rarely saw the ice in close games — especially against physical teams — and even then got minimal time in even-strength situations. Eklund also suffered point-wise last year because of the absence of Tim Kerr, the Swede's power play partner-in-crime.

That, of course, may change with a new coach in Philadelphia, because Eklund is the most talented center on the team — and maybe the Flyers' most talented player overall.

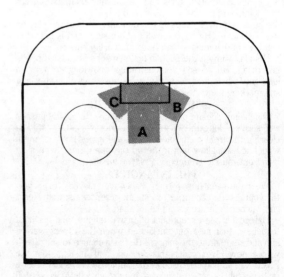

RON HEXTALL

Yrs. of NHL service: 2
Born: Brandon, Manitoba, Canada; May 3, 1964
Position: Goaltender
Height: 6-3
Weight: 174
Uniform no.: 27
Catches: left

Career statistics:

GP	MINS	G	SO	AVG	A	PIM
128	7,359	398	1	3.24	12	208

1987-88 statisics:

GP	MINS	AVG	W	L	T	SO	GA	SA	SAPCT	PIM
62	3,560	3.51	30	22	7	0	208	1,817	.885	104

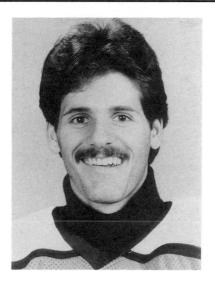

LAST SEASON

Hextall missed the first eight games of last season, serving a suspension levied for his slash of Kent Nilsson in the 1987 Stanley Cup Finals. He still appeared in more games than all but two goalies (Grant Fuhr and Mike Vernon) and Hextall finished third in the League in wins (behind the same pair). He did not, however, lead all goalies in scoring; that credit goes to Fuhr, who had eight points to Hextall's seven.

THE PHYSICAL GAME

The angle, standup style is Hextall's game, and he plays it excellently. He comes out of the net to challenge shooters (and his size masks practically all of the goal), but he also mixes that challenging style with excellent reflexes and extremely fast feet.

In fact, because of his foot speed, the usual tactic of shooting to a big man's feet doesn't work with Hextall. He flashes his pads to both sides with great quickness, and he displays that foot speed again as he moves both from post to post and laterally across the crease. His hands are good, but they don't compare with his feet for speed. He also has great balance and easily regains his stance after going to the ice.

His skating is one part of his great stickhandling game, allowing him to leave the net whenever possible to get to those loose pucks. While there are a number of superior stickhandlers among the NHL's goalies, none demonstrates the ability Hextall shows.

When he retrieves the puck, Hextall will try to bank the puck off the left-hand boards. He is equally adept at using either his forehand or his backhand (though he prefers his forehand) and can also loft the puck over the defenders pinching in at the blue line and right to a teammate at center ice. In fact, Hextall's sending the puck to center is an established part of the Flyers' penalty killing plan. The Flyers also take advantage of Hextall's skills by playing the puck back to him, à la a goalkeeper in soccer.

THE MENTAL GAME

Other than Grant Fuhr, Hextall may be the most mentally tough goalie in the League; his performance in overtime of the Patrick Division Semifinal against the Capitals is proof enough of that. Hextall focusses and concentrates extremely well.

He complements that intensity with great vision and anticipation. He sees the puck on almost every shot, and on the ones he misses usually anticipates correctly. Interference during a game, however, will rattle him. Still, his anger is more likely to motivate him than thwart him.

Bad outings and bad goals don't bother him, and he certainly has big save capability. He can make the big saves and come up with big performances.

345

THE INTANGIBLES

We told you last year that Hextall would have difficulty repeating his rookie success, and in a large part his slump during the playoffs is what killed the Flyers. No doubt too, his slow start after returning from his suspension is another reason for the Flyers' hill-and-valley performance last season. For the Flyers to succeed, Hextall must regain his superlative form.

As a player he has revolutionized the game, all the discussion of World War II scoring goalies and the great Jacques Plante notwithstanding. After all, when before in NHL history did a goalie have to be forechecked?

His influence in hockey has already begun, just as he's brought new meaning to the hockey cliche about a goalie who handles the puck like another defenseman. His character and dedication should carry him to another campaign.

MARK HOWE

Yrs. of NHL service: 9
Born: Detroit, Mich., USA; May 28, 1955
Position: Defenseman
Height: 5-11
Weight: 180
Uniform no.: 2
Shoots: left

Career statistics:

GP	G	A	TP	PIM
654	166	411	577	320

1987-88 statistics:

GP	G	A	TP	+/−	PIM	PP	SH	GW	GT	S	PCT
75	19	43	62	23	62	8	1	4	0	177	10.7

LAST SEASON

Howe finished third on the Flyers in plus/minus, second among defensemen. He led the Flyers' defenders in scoring and finished third on the team in assists and fourth in scoring. Among NHL defenders, Howe was seventh in scoring. A recurring back injury sidelined him for four games.

THE FINESSE GAME

Balance, quickness, speed — all combine to make Howe an excellent skater, one of the best among NHL defensemen. He is not necessarily the most agile skater, but he combines the agility he has with excellent hand skills to become very dangerous with the puck — and the Flyers' key man for developing their offense.

Howe handles the puck excellently when rushing, and he'll take it deep into the enemy zone. He'll stay as another attacker even after he's forced to dish it off, because his speed can get him back into the defensive play.

He uses his hand skills in conjunction with his ice vision and anticipation to pass extremely well. Because of those two skills, he'll lead teammates into the open with his passes, and is especially good at that when he needs to get the puck out of his zone. He's the only Flyer defenseman who does that consistently.

He has a good shot from the left point, low and accurate, perfect for tip-ins or deflections, and he'll sneak into the slot if he can. Mark also likes to tail away to the right wing boards for a shot, because he'll get a better angle at the net. We still maintain that Howe still doesn't shoot to score enough (though his SOG total would seem to contradict that). Too often, he looks for a teammate in front.

All his finesse skills make him a very dangerous specialty teams player.

THE PHYSICAL GAME

Howe is not usually a physical player, but that's not to say he doesn't play a physical game. He takes the body along the boards, but is not a punishing hitter, more of a pusher. He can be worn down with constant physical abuse, and he can be overpowered by stronger forwards because he's just average at clearing the front of the net.

That negative in his game is countered by pairing him with a stronger, more physical defense partner (first Brad Mc-Crimmon and now Kjell Samuelsson), freeing Howe to play the game he knows best — that of starting plays, rather than stopping them.

THE INTANGIBLES

Consistency, willingness to play through pain, character and dedication — these are attributes of Mark Howe. In many ways, he is the Flyers' most valuable player, probably the most irreplaceable. He is a leader on the ice and in the dressing room through his intensity and desire.

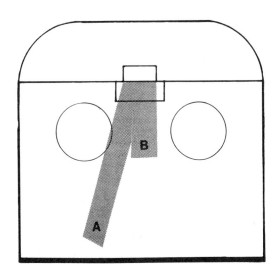

WILLIE HUBER

Yrs. of NHL service: 9
Born: Strasskirchen, Germany; January 15, 1958
Position: Defenseman
Height: 6-5
Weight: 225
Uniform no.: 44
Shoots: right

Career statistics:

GP	G	A	TP	PIM
655	104	217	321	950

1987-88 statistics:

GP	G	A	TP	+/−	PIM	PP	SH	GW	GT	S	PCT
56	9	22	31	-16	70	5	0	0	1	111	8.1

LAST SEASON

Huber was traded twice last year, first by the Rangers (along with Larry Melnyk) to Vancouver in exchange for Michel Petit, and then by Vancouver to Philadelphia for Paul Lawless. A recurring knee injury sidelined him for parts of the season, and his games played mark was the third lowest of his NHL career. Goals scored was his highest in four seasons.

THE FINESSE GAME

Huber skates remarkably well for a man of his size, though his recurring knee problems continue to cut into his effectiveness. He has a long stride because of his size but is not very fast. Still, he's more agile than a guy his size would normally get credit for.

He sees the offensive zone very well, and can contribute from the blue line because of that. Willie has good passing skills, and those hand skills and his vision make him effective on the power play. He has a good slap shot from the point made more effective by a quick release, and Huber also likes to sneak into the high slot if the defense is napping. He challenges at the blue line too frequently, and he'll get trapped because of it.

His ability doesn't extend itself to the defensive zone, and for several reasons. Huber is less mobile going backward than he is forward, so he can be beaten one-on-one by opposing wingers. Also, his anticipation with the play coming toward him is not good. He tends to get out of position, so a more sound knowledge of positional play and defensive angles would help here.

THE PHYSICAL GAME

Never known as a physical player (or perhaps, more accurately, never playing up to his size), Huber nonetheless does play a physical style. He'll take the body along the boards and has become more difficult for the opposition to out-muscle both here and in front of the net.

He is not a fighter and never has been. He has good reach that he puts to use well, especially in the offensive zone where he can keep the puck in at the point.

THE INTANGIBLES

At this point in his career, Huber isn't suddenly going to change. The Flyers know what they have in him: a guy who can contribute offensively but who needs help defensively. What is not in Huber's favor are his physical condition (his rickety knees) and the Flyers' seeming dissatisfaction with their defense corps last year.

Huber's future now is in the hands of the Flyers' next head coach.

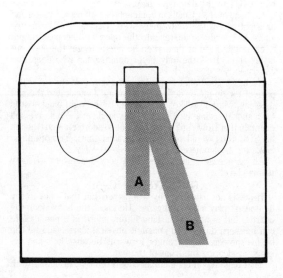

KERRY HUFFMAN

Yrs. of NHL service: 1
Born: Peterborough, Ontario, Canada; January 3, 1968
Position: Defenseman
Height: 6-2
Weight: 180
Uniform no.: 5
Shoots: left

Career statistics:

GP	G	A	TP	PIM
61	6	17	23	36

1987-88 statistics:

GP	G	A	TP	+/−	PIM	PP	SH	GW	GT	S	PCT
52	6	17	23	-11	34	3	0	2	0	84	7.1

LAST SEASON

First full NHL season after nine game stint last season. A leg injury sidelined him through the season's third quarter.

THE FINESSE GAME

Huffman is a good skater with an open stride and good balance and foot speed. That means he's also got good lateral movement and agility, though it could be improved for the NHL level. He also skates well backward, and that bodes well for his defensive play (so he can cover a lot of ground quickly).

He has great offensive instincts and can convert many of them into scoring opportunities. His skating and vision help him to contain the point, and from there he dispenses good passes to open teammates. And Kerry can find those openings and lead his teammates into them.

He reads the play in front of him well, and will open up to the rink to put the play in front of him and judge his options. Huffman is a good puckhandler and carries the puck well from the defensive zone (something he likes to do). He handles the puck well in traffic and looks to make the transition from defense to offense.

Kerry launches a good slap shot from the blue line, hard, accurate and low. That makes it perfect for tip-ins and deflections. He will also charge the slot and has no fear about joining the forwards for a 2-on-1 or 3-on-2.

Huffman uses his good hockey sense on defense too, playing his position smartly and positionally, though he clearly has a lot to learn about the speed of the NHL game.

THE PHYSICAL GAME

Basically, Huffman is a finesse player with excellent size, and he puts it to fairly good use along the boards. He ties up the forwards there and in front of the net fairly well, though increased upper body strength would be to his benefit.

He is not a big hitter and certainly won't knock anyone into the cheap seats. Kerry is more of a push and shove type along the boards, but he also uses his body well to protect the puck and he uses his reach to pokecheck well.

THE INTANGIBLES

For a rookie, Huffman plays a poised and confident game. He has good hockey sense and brings a good attitude to the rink, and he has the desire to learn and improve. His unex-pectedly solid play is one large reason why the Flyers have to make some tough decisions about the veterans on their blue line.

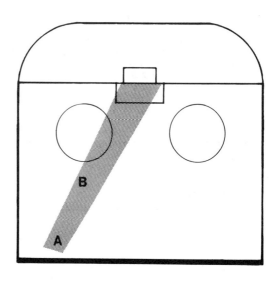

TIM KERR

Yrs. of NHL service: 8
Born: Windsor, Ontario, Canada; January 5, 1960
Position: Right wing/center
Height: 6-3
Weight: 215
Uniform no.: 12
Shoots: right

Career statistics:

GP	G	A	TP	PIM
465	281	209	490	462

1987-88 statistics:

GP	G	A	TP	+/−	PIM	PP	SH	GW	GT	S	PCT
8	3	2	5	0	12	2	0	0	0	34	8.8

LAST SEASON

Off-season shoulder surgery sidelined Kerr through most of the season. He played the fewest games of his NHL career, and his point totals were all career lows.

THE FINESSE GAME

Kerr is, at best, an average NHL skater. He has little speed and almost no lateral movement. What he does have is inertia; you know, an object in motion tends to stay in motion. Well, once Kerr gets himself skating toward the opposition net, nothing is going to stop him. He just steamrolls on.

Kerr stickhandles better than he is given credit for, mostly because he uses his reach and his body to protect the puck well. Still, he is not Denis Savard — or even Brian Propp — and he won't dipsy-doodle through an entire team. He does not use his teammates well, but that's because he thinks goal and because he is often in a better shooting position than they are.

As everyone knows by now, Kerr parks himself in the low slot — sometimes too low — fights off the defenseman and lasers one of the quickest shots in the league toward the net. He'll convert on any defensive miscue around the goal.

He shines on the power play but, strangely, Kerr also does some of his poorer work here. He gets trapped too close to the net to work effectively, and he won't release from the defenseman as often as he could.

Lucky for the rest of the League.

THE PHYSICAL GAME

Kerr is a gentle bear of a player. He is slow to anger, though players who use their sticks on him will get the same in return, and he is impossible to move from the front of the net. Only the strongest of the league's defensemen can even hope to prevent him from moving his arms or curling his wrists to release a shot.

But, despite his size, Kerr is not an overly physical player and does not use his size well in checking.

His strong hands and arms allow the Flyers to use him on faceoffs.

THE INTANGIBLES

If all of this sounds familiar, that's because it is. We've changed nothing from last year's assessment and that's because of the one huge question that colors Kerr's NHL future:

His health. His mangled shoulder was supposed to be good as new. Instead, as we saw during the playoffs, Kerr's shoulder couldn't stand up to NHL punishment. In his favor is a tremendous dedication toward rehabilitation but, until he can prove that his shoulder is 100 percent healthy, all we can do is speculate about Tim Kerr's future.

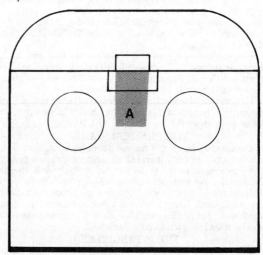

MARK LAFOREST

Yrs. of NHL service: 2
Born: Welland, Ontario, Canada; July 10, 1962
Position: Goaltender
Height: 5-10
Weight: 178
Uniform no.: 33
Catches: left

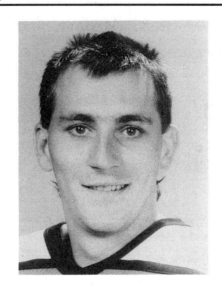

Career statistics:

GP	MINS	G	SO	AVG	A	PIM
54	2,574	186	2	4.33	0	31

1987-88 statisics:

GP	MINS	AVG	W	L	T	SO	GA	SA	SAPCT	PIM
21	972	3.70	5	9	2	1	60	478	.874	8

LAST SEASON

Laforest was traded to the Flyers by the Red Wings for a draft choice at the 1987 Entry Draft. Games played mark was second highest of his NHL career.

THE PHYSICAL GAME

Laforest plays an awkward hybrid style, not quite a standup goalie but not quite a reflex goalie either. He doesn't have great balance, and that makes his movement across the crease and from post to post suspect. He is especially weak moving to his right. Because he's not great with his feet, Laforest is vulnerable after making the first save and has difficulty regaining his stance for a second save.

He comes no further than the top of the crease to challenge the shooter, yet he's not especially strong in any one save area and is particularly vulnerable on shots over his glove hand. He will come out of his crease to cut off the puck, but won't handle it more than that.

Laforest chooses to hang back in the net on screens and rely on his reflexes, but he doesn't see the puck especially well on those screens and so can be beaten by tips and deflections.

He's not especially good at protecting or controlling his rebounds, and always lets out long rebounds after high pad saves. When he goes down in a scramble he falls on his butt, thus limiting his maneuverability as the puck swirls around him.

THE MENTAL GAME

Laforest is not great mentally. He gets distracted on the ice and his concentration wanders, as evidenced by his poor angle play when he loses the net. He's a fighter and wants to do well, and he can rise to an occasion, but has yet to really demonstrate that at the NHL level (former Flyers coach Mike Keenan saw Laforest do just that in the American League when Laforest's Adirondack Red Wings defeated Keenan's Rochester Americans in the playoffs).

THE INTANGIBLES

Laforest is strictly a backup to Ron Hextall, and as such his position is vulnerable. While no one asks him to be another Hextall, he must do better than a 5-9-2 record to be valuable to the Flyers.

BRAD MARSH

Yrs. of NHL service: 10
Born: London, Ontario, Canada; March 31, 1958
Position: Defenseman
Height: 6-2
Weight: 215
Uniform no.: 8
Shoots: left

Career statistics:

GP	G	A	TP	PIM
771	17	137	154	953

1987-88 statistics:

GP	G	A	TP	+/−	PIM	PP	SH	GW	GT	S	PCT
70	3	9	12	-13	57	0	1	1	0	57	5.3

LAST SEASON

A concussion limited Marsh to his fewest games and PIM in five seasons. Goals scored matches his career high, and his minus 13 was the worst among regular Flyer defenders, second worst among all Flyer regulars.

THE FINESSE GAME

Never known as — and never to be mistaken for — a finesse player, Marsh showed a real decline last year. Though still a better skater than he's often credited, Marsh's foot speed is decreasing. The improvement he'd shown in moving up and down the ice over the last few seasons was nowhere to be found last year. He remains a less than agile skater, but makes up for his skating deficiencies with positional play.

He uses his defensive angles very well, reads the rush approaching him excellently. Because he's so determined to help out, Marsh often gets out of position around the net, falling here to block a shot, diving there to stop a pass. Appreciated though this determination may be, it also serves to make Marsh's partner and the goaltender crazy.

Though his role is not that of puckhandling defenseman, Marsh will get it out of his end quickly and well.

THE PHYSICAL GAME

Marsh is a strong, physical player. He clears the front of the net well and probably keeps the opposition out of the play as well as anyone in the League. He's no doubt helped in that last aspect by the fact that he's also the best holder in the League. He willingly sacrifices his body to block shots.

He will muscle the opposition off the puck along the boards and has a good reach that helps him to pokecheck the puck away from incoming forwards.

THE INTANGIBLES

A good case could be made for Marsh's absence affecting the rest of his game, for when he returned from injury he was clearly not at his best. Perhaps his scouting report should be judged in that light.

In any case, what is also clear is that for the first time, then-coach Mike Keenan didn't have the confidence in Marsh he once had, and Brad rode the bench for periods of last season. His play this season will be heavily scrutinized because of that, and Brad (like other Flyers) has some questions to answer on ice.

He remains a leader through his work ethic and dedication.

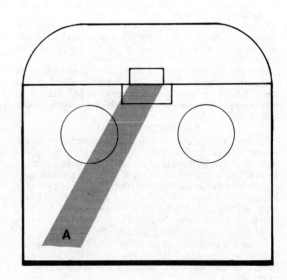

SCOTT MELLANBY

Yrs. of NHL service: 2
Born: Montreal, Quebec, Canada; June 11, 1966
Position: Right wing
Height: 6-1
Weight: 195
Uniform no.: 19
Shoots: right

Career statistics:

GP	G	A	TP	PIM
148	36	47	83	279

1987-88 statistics:

GP	G	A	TP	+/-	PIM	PP	SH	GW	GT	S	PCT
75	25	26	51	-7	185	7	0	2	0	190	13.2

LAST SEASON

Games played and all point totals were career highs, despite missing games with neck and hip injuries. He finished third on the club in PIM and second in shots on goal.

THE FINESSE GAME

Though the strengths of Mellanby's game can be found in the physical aspects of hockey, he is still a good — and improving — finesse player. He's a strong and powerful skater, but he's a little stiff. That means he's not very agile or fluid, and a straight ahead style is to his benefit.

He has good speed, but he is always going at that one speed. So, while he can drive a defender backward, Mellanby is also predictable. Increased foot speed and improved agility and balance would open his game.

Scott has good hockey sense (understanding and reacting to the flow of the game) and he has moved closer to the NHL speed of reading plays and making passes. He uses his teammates fairly well, and can make a play coming out of the corner with the puck.

Mellanby has a good shot, quick and strong, so he can score from the middle distances, but he should learn to shoot quicker — he has the hands to do so. He gets planted in front of the net on the Flyers' power play, and at even strength he has the habit of moving to his off-wing in order to open up to the net more, and that habit affects his defensive game.

His defensive play last season was something less than spectacular, partly because of his habit of wandering from his wing. He also releases too soon in the defensive zone, trying for a non-existent breakout pass while his check is left alone in the Flyer end.

THE PHYSICAL GAME

Mellanby has outstanding size and strength, and he uses both to his advantage. He puts those assets to work in a strong boards and corners game, and he's a good bet to out-muscle the opposition for the puck.

He uses his good upper body strength and strong skating to drive to the net, and he has the strength to get off a quality shot even when being checked; he just muscles the puck away, much like a batter muscling off an inside pitch. He willingly uses his body to check and enjoys the hitting part of the game, but he is not really a fighter.

THE INTANGIBLES

As with Doug Crossman, Scott Mellanby spent a good part of last season as former coach Mike Keenan's whipping boy. Keenan was unhappy with Mellanby's defensive game, and the coach also wanted more in physical play. Mellanby thought that meant more fighting and he refused. His teammates backed him up, several times asking Keenan to lay off Scott. As with many of the other Flyers, Scott must now adapt to a new coach.

He started slowly last season, with just six points in his first 20 games and 22 points in the first half. Keenan also rotated Mellanby onto the left wing late in the season.

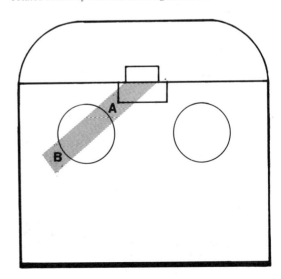

DAVE POULIN

Yrs. of NHL service: 5
Born: Mississauga, Ontario, Canada; December 17, 1958
Position: Center
Height: 5-11
Weight: 175
Uniform no.: 20
Shoots: left

Career statistics:

GP	G	A	TP	PIM
370	134	208	342	242

1987-88 statistics:

GP	G	A	TP	+/−	PIM	PP	SH	GW	GT	S	PCT
68	19	32	51	17	32	1	5	3	0	125	15.2

LAST SEASON

Injuries took their toll on Poulin again (groin injury), limiting him to the fewest games of his NHL career. Consequently, all point totals were career lows. His plus-17 was second-highest among Flyer forwards, and he led the team in short-handed goals.

THE FINESSE GAME

As could be expected from a Selke award winner, skating and intelligence are the hallmarks of Poulin's game.

Poulin is a very strong skater with good speed and excellent acceleration. He teams those assets with great hockey sense to be a fine checker and play maker. He reads plays excellently, whether on offense or defense, and that allows him to use his teammates excellently. Poulin is an excellent checker and defensive player because of his speed and instincts and is also an excellent penalty killer, always a threat for a short-handed goal.

He's unselfish and willing to give up his good shot for a teammate's better one. Dave has excellent hands, soft enough to feather a pass over a defenseman's stick and onto a teammate's, yet strong enough to strip an opposing player of the puck.

He scores most of his goals from within 15 feet or so, but he does have the power to score from a distance. He must become more selfish in this area of the game and learn to shoot more, as his speed and brains afford him plenty of scoring opportunitities.

He prefers to go to his backhand when he is one-on-one with the goalie.

THE PHYSICAL GAME

Poulin makes his skating even more effective because of his strength, both in terms of balance and contact. He drives the net at every opportunity (which is why that's his most effective scoring area), but he's also a very physical forward who uses his body smartly.

Dave hits well and hard, both in the offensive and defensive zones, taking men out of the play intelligently and always positioning his body so that he can make a play after he makes a hit. His great arm, hand and wrist strength makes him an excellent faceoff man.

Poulin will initiate contact and he will take his lumps too, doing whatever is necessary in order to make the play, and this is where his balance comes in. He's very difficult to knock down and comes out of nearly every collision vertical and ready to make plays.

He willingly sacrifices his body to block shots, but the evidence suggests that Poulin's all-around physical play takes its toll in injuries.

THE INTANGIBLES

As captain of the Flyers, Poulin has epitomized the characteristics of the Flyers: grit, heart and determination. He also symbolized the former Flyer hierarchy, arriving in Philadelphia with Ted Sator and thriving under Mike Keenan.

While he gives his all on every shift, and will no doubt remain the heart and soul of the team, he too will have to adapt to a new coach and a possible new role. Regardless, Poulin will continue to be the Flyers' leader both on the ice and in the lockerroom.

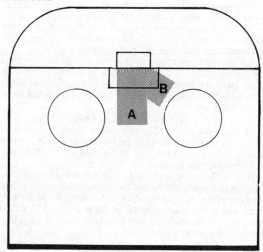

BRIAN PROPP

Yrs. of NHL service: 9
Born: Lanigan, Sask., Canada; February 15, 1959
Position: Left wing
Height: 5-9
Weight: 185
Uniform no.: 26
Shoots: left

Career statistics:

GP	G	A	TP	PIM
673	324	418	742	601

1987-88 statistics:

GP	G	A	TP	+/−	PIM	PP	SH	GW	GT	S	PCT
74	27	49	76	8	76	7	2	6	0	257	10.5

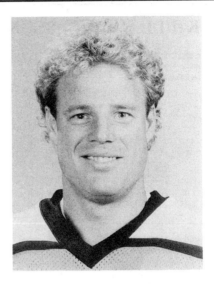

LAST SEASON

Propp missed six games with a knee injury. He led the team in assists, game winning goals and shots on goal. Goal total was second lowest of his career, point total third lowest.

THE FINESSE GAME

Propp remains an excellent finesse player, despite injury and age. He has outstanding speed and good acceleration (though he may be just a hair slower than he used to be), and he makes his speed more effective by moderating it well, shifting up and down the gears to perplex defenders. His balance and lateral movement are excellent, and they make him difficult to hit.

Propp is very good at finding the openings and exploiting them because of excellent anticipation and hockey sense. These skills come to the fore particularly on the penalty killing unit, where all his finesse skills come to bear — look for him at the red line to take a breakaway pass when his PK unit is on.

He's a good stickhandler and takes or gives passes smoothly at all speeds, but Brian is a scorer first (as his SOG total indicates) and will take a bad shot even though a teammate is in better position.

Propp is a sniper with a dangerous assortment of shots. He has a big slap shot from the faceoff circle, but is just as likely to snap a heavy, hard and fast wrist shot from the same spot. His agility and one-step quickness make him a menace around the opposing goal, and he easily converts loose pucks into points. He is a power play regular because of his skills.

For his offensive prowess, Propp is a solid defensive player. He plays his position well, but he rarely comes back any deeper than the top of the faceoff circle, where he'll lurk for a breakout pass.

THE PHYSICAL GAME

Propp is not a physical presence on the ice but, like most smaller players on bigger teams, will dish out some hits because his teammates will back him up.

His balance and agility would make him an ideal traffic player, but he's more of a darter — moving in and out of traffic for loose pucks but not doing the yeoman work there. Otherwise, he avoids physical contact.

THE INTANGIBLES

If Brian Propp has shown anything in nine NHL seasons, it's that he's consistent. He suffered last year as his team stumbled, and he'll have to answer questions about his fall from the 40-goal plateau he's often reached. And, like all of the Flyers, he'll have to respond to a new coach.

He also excels at drawing penalties (a charitable term for diving — for while his finesse skills often force the opposition into penalties, Propp is not above an exaggerated fall to the ice), and then hurts the opposition with a power play goal or assist.

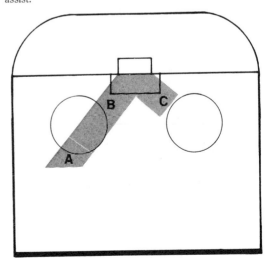

KJELL SAMUELSSON

Yrs. of NHL service: 3
Born: Tingsryd, Sweden; October 18, 1956
Position: Defenseman
Height: 6-6
Weight: 227
Uniform no.: 28
Shoots: right

Career statistics:

GP	G	A	TP	PIM
159	9	36	45	330

1987-88 statistics:

GP	G	A	TP	+/-	PIM	PP	SH	GW	GT	S	PCT
74	6	24	30	28	184	3	0	0	0	118	5.1

LAST SEASON

Point and penalty minute totals were all career highs for Samuelsson, who missed four games with groin injury. He led the team in plus/minus.

THE FINESSE GAME

Samuelsson will never be mistaken for teammate Mark Howe, but his skating is better than he's given credit for. He's gained increased mobility through improved foot speed, and that combines with his long stride to allow him to keep pace with most opposing forwards.

Kjell is not inclined to carry the puck, but he will make the correct pass to an open winger when he has the puck. He can also control the point fairly well, so he'll see time on the power play.

Otherwise, he is not a threat at the offensive blue line, but will score a handful of goals on an average slap shot. He does see the zone well, and can get the puck to a teammate.

THE PHYSICAL GAME

Great size is what Samuelsson puts to use in the physical game. He is almost impossible to get around at the Flyers blue line because of his reach, and he is forever poking pucks away. He's also like an octopus in that he wraps up the opposition as soon as they come close.

He's stepped up the tempo of his own hitting game and is more aggressive, and Samuelsson will take any rough stuff anybody dishes out.

THE INTANGIBLES

Much was made last season of the trade of Brad McCrimmon to Calgary and its effect on the Flyers. One result of that trade was that Samuelsson became the Flyers' steadiest defender. Notice we didn't say best, just steadiest.

He was quietly dependable for a sometimes shaky defense corps, and will continue with more of the same this year.

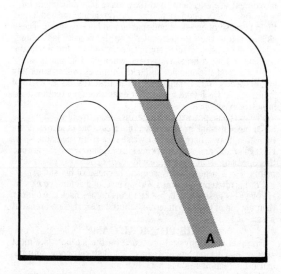

ILKKA SINISALO

Yrs. of NHL service: 7
Born: Helsinki, Finland; July 10, 1958
Position: Left wing
Height: 6-1
Weight: 190
Uniform no.: 23
Shoots: left

Career statistics:

GP	G	A	TP	PIM
454	175	180	355	152

1987-88 statistics:

GP	G	A	TP	+/-	PIM	PP	SH	GW	GT	S	PCT
68	25	17	42	2	30	6	2	4	3	148	16.9

LAST SEASON

Injury sidelined Sinisalo again, this time a back ailment. He finished fourth on the club in goals and led the NHL in game-tying tallies. His shooting percentage was second-highest among regulars.

THE FINESSE GAME

Sinisalo is a finesse player with the typical European skills. He's a superior skater, and is also an effective scorer. He's fast from his first stride and has good acceleration. He also varies his speed to make it more effective. His balance gives him good agility and allows him to make some nice "inside" moves.

He's pretty adept at using his teammates, and that's because he ably combines his stick skills with vision and anticipation. He looks to make the best possible plays in the offensive zone (and Sinisalo passes well to both sides), but he also knows when it's time to stop playing with the puck and shoot.

His shot is very good, quickly released and accurate, as his shooting percentage attests. He's deadly from 15 feet and loves the upper right hand corner of the net. He can also take advanatge of the tight area around the net because of his hands, and is always a threat to convert rebounds into goals.

Because of his shooting ability and ice vision, Sinisalo can be a valuable power play performer. He keeps the passing lanes open with one-step quickness and forces the defense to spread itself thin in attempts to guard both him and Tim Kerr.

THE PHYSICAL GAME

Though originally labelled an aggressive player, Sinisalo is not a physical forward. He much prefers pulling the puck from an opponent's feet to banging the opposition off the puck, so he hits neither hard nor often.

Ilkka is fairly strong on his skates (balance is the key here), making him more than a little difficult to dislodge from the puck, if you can catch him at all.

THE INTANGIBLES

One of the Flyers' most innately talented players, Sinisalo last year pulled himself from coach Mike Keenan's doghouse with an improved work ethic. He worked harder in practice and games than previously, but Keenan still kept him on the bench (as the coach did Pelle Eklund) when the going got rough.

Sinisalo has been extremely consistent in his healthy seasons, and if the Flyers appoint a coach willing to give Ilkka more ice time, he should approach the 40-goal plateau once again.

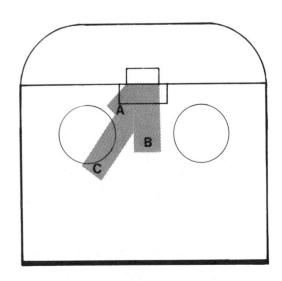

DERRICK SMITH

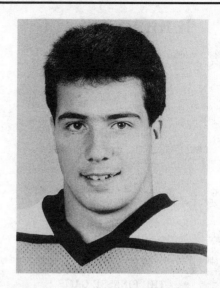

Yrs. of NHL service: 4
Born: Scarborough, Ontario, Canada; January 22, 1965
Position: Left wing
Height: 6-1
Weight: 185
Uniform no.: 24
Shoots: left

Career statistics:

GP	G	A	TP	PIM
293	50	57	107	226

1987-88 statistics:

GP	G	A	TP	+/–	PIM	PP	SH	GW	GT	S	PCT
76	16	8	24	-20	104	0	0	1	0	155	10.3

LAST SEASON

Smith recorded his second-highest goal total. His minus 20 was the Flyers' worst. PIM total was career high. He has yet to play a full season of games.

THE FINESSE GAME

Smith is an excellent skater in terms of strength and balance. He has a strong, steady pace, good balance and good lateral movement. He is also practically tireless. Derrick combines that skating ability with excellent hockey sense, vision and anticipation to be one of the NHL's top checking forwards.

He sees the ice well and forces the play because of his skating and his anticipation, which tells him where to be and when. He enjoys his defensive responsibilities and is also one of the best forecheckers in the League.

For all his skating and hockey sense, Smith should be able to make more of the offensive opportunities he creates, but he's not gifted with the puck. Smith is unsure of what plays to make when he gains the puck, demonstrating a tentativeness and hesitation that indicates a lack of confidence in the offensive part of the game.

Much of that can probably be traced to his shot, and Smith's is awful. If he had any hands at all, he'd score 30 goals a year because his checking creates tremendous opportunities. Instead, he'll collect any goals he gets from in close to the net, though he does possess the strength to score from a distance.

THE PHYSICAL GAME

Smith has become a very strong winger. He takes the body at all times and he hits hard — hard enough to hurt, and certainly hard enough to wear the opposition down by game's end. He has great upper body strength and that makes him very hard to handle in the corners. He puts that strength to work excellently on the boards and against his opponents, whom he routinely out-muscles.

His balance keys his physical game. He's very sturdy on his skates and will come out of most collisions vertical. Derrick is at his best in a physical contest.

THE INTANGIBLES

Smith has great character and determination, and a work ethic to match. He still has improvable skills, notably in the finesse area, and increased confidence would bring them for-ward. But again, as with the other non-borderline Flyers, Smith must show he can adapt to whatever role his new coach envisions for him.

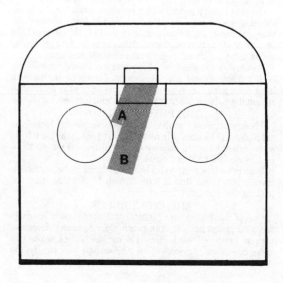

RON SUTTER

Yrs. of NHL service: 5
Born: Viking, Alta., Canada; December 2, 1963
Position: Center
Height: 6-0
Weight: 180
Uniform no.: 14
Shoots: right

Career statistics:

GP	G	A	TP	PIM
345	72	146	218	578

1987-88 statistics:

GP	G	A	TP	+/-	PIM	PP	SH	GW	GT	S	PCT
69	8	25	33	-9	146	1	0	0	0	107	7.5

LAST SEASON

A March rib injury drove Sutter from the lineup. He scored the fewest goals and second fewest point of his NHL career, while his PIM was his second highest. His minus 9 was fourth worst on the club.

THE FINESSE GAME

Though there are many admirable traits Ron Sutter brings to his game, skating is not among them. His short, choppy stride doesn't afford him much balance, and he has neither great speed nor much quickness. Because of his lack of balance, his turns are a little wide and his pivoting could improve.

Middle-of-the-road hand skills (except for faceoffs) can't make up for his skating deficiencies, but his hockey sense can. Sutter succeeds in using his teammates because of that instinct of where to be with the puck and when. Sutter uses that sense well as one of the League's best defensive forwards.

On the offensive side, Sutter will score in the teens. His goals will come from directly in front of the net as he mucks around for whatever he can get. He doesn't shoot enough and must assert himself on offense. When he has the puck near the goal and must beat a defender, Sutter often relies on head fakes so obvious they can be seen in the cheap seats.

THE PHYSICAL GAME

Faceoffs are probably the best of Sutter's "finesse" defensive skills; he's one of the game's best on draws. Sutter's hands are very fast and he gets down almost to the blade on his stick when he positions himself for faceoffs. The wide stance of his skates gives him even more power.

Sutter is extremely physical and hits at every available opportunity. He has no fear about going into the corners with players 40 pounds heavier than himself, and he hits effectively. Quite often, Sutter will fall after belting an opponent because of the aforementioned lack of balance on his skates.

Whether or not his now damaged body can continue to take the pounding will go far toward determining whether or not Sutter returns this year to his position of pre-eminence for the Flyers.

THE INTANGIBLES

He is the kind of player any team would want to have, and not just for his formidable checking ability. Ron is a worker (though he has the tendency to get down on himself if things aren't going well), and he is a dedicated team man.

And because any team would like to have him, rumors ran rampant last year about his being traded to almost everywhere. How he responds under a new coach this season — who may or may not want him around — is one question to be answered. Another is the question of his physical durablity. Ron has yet to play a full NHL season, and his physical game betrays him with injuries that limit his effectiveness.

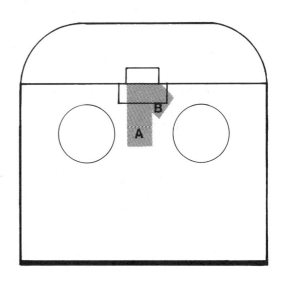

RICK TOCCHET

Yrs. of NHL service: 4
Born: Scarborough, Ontario, Canada; April 9, 1964
Position: Right wing
Height: 6-0
Weight: 195
Uniform no.: 22
Shoots: right

Career statistics:

GP	G	A	TP	PIM
278	80	105	185	1,054

1987-88 statistics:

GP	G	A	TP	+/-	PIM	PP	SH	GW	GT	S	PCT
65	31	33	64	3	301	10	2	3	0	182	17.0

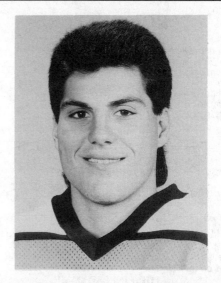

LAST SEASON

While games played (due to recurring shoulder injury) was a career low, Tocchet posted career highs in all point categories, as well as in penalty minutes (he finished eighth in the NHL in PIM). He led the team in goals and shooting percentage, was second in power play tallies and was fifth in SOG. He finished third on the Flyers in scoring.

THE FINESSE GAME

Tocchet is a very strong skater in terms of stride. His strong pushoffs give him a fairly quick start (made more impressive because of his size) and they allow him a fair degree of speed up ice. He is a more agile player now than he was three years ago — or even last year — and a good part of that improvement may come from his growing confidence as an able finesse player. Make no mistake though; Rick is still not Denis Savard in terms of mobility.

His improving offensive ability can be pegged to patience and confidence. Rick keeps his head up now, forsaking his charging bull style when he has the puck, and he looks over the ice to see his options. He's not afraid to hold the puck until a teammate moves into position, and he's learning to hit the holes and get into position to score. He remains, however, a power forward, and is far more likely to go through an opponent than around him.

Tocchet's best finesse asset is his shot, and it's an excellent weapon. He delivers a fast, hard and accurate wrist shot from anywhere, and will get most goals from 30 feet and in.

THE PHYSICAL GAME

In terms of physical play, and what that play does for his total game, Tocchet is in a class few in the NHL can match. He is one of the NHL's most punishing hitters, and we're not talking about fighting (not yet, anyway). He takes the body relentlessly in all areas of the ice and he is absolutely fearless. Rick bangs around like a bull in the corners and because he is so strong in his upper body will jar the puck free more times than not.

Still, Tocchet suffers two disadvantages: First, his center of gravity is a little high, so he's often going to be unbalanced after a collision and not quite prepared to continue the play. Second, his physical play clearly takes a toll on his health, and we've already seen in Tim Kerr (and the retired Barry Beck, for that matter) how fragile once-injured shoulders become.

As for fighting, he's in a small class there too. Few are the players in the League who'll best him in a confrontation. He backs down from nothing and no one.

360

THE INTANGIBLES

Like the Messiers, Proberts and Neelys, Rick Tocchet is one of those players every team would love to have — a rough, physical player with definite finesse skills. Still, Tocchet is at a crossroads.

While he had a brief philosophical disagreement with former coach Mike Keenan last year (with Tocchet balking when — he says — Keenan ordered him to fight), Tocchet must remember that physical play keys his finesse game; that's why he's a power forward.

Chances are Tocchet will remember that. He is a character player, a tremendously dedicated player, and a hard worker. He should continue to improve, and with his shot could easily score 40 goals.

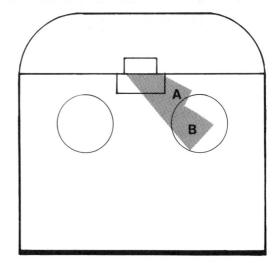

PETER ZEZEL

Yrs. of NHL service: 4
Born: Toronto, Ontario, Canada; April 22, 1965
Position: Center
Height: 5-10
Weight: 195
Uniform no.: 25
Shoots: left

Career statistics:

GP	G	A	TP	PIM
284	87	157	244	215

1987-88 statistics:

GP	G	A	TP	+/-	PIM	PP	SH	GW	GT	S	PCT
69	22	35	57	7	42	14	0	1	0	133	16.5

LAST SEASON

Ankle and shoulder injuries limited Zezel to his second-shortest NHL campaign. Though his goal total was the second highest of his career (and he led the Flyers in power play tallies), only seven of his goals came at even strength. He scored only seven goals in the season's second half, only three in the last quarter. His shooting percentage was third highest among Flyers regulars.

THE FINESSE GAME

The power of Zezel's game is rooted in his feet. He is an excellent skater, fast on his feet, agile and strong. He can stop, start and turn on a dime. He controls the puck with his skates better than anyone in the League (attributable, no doubt, to his soccer-playing ability), and this allows him another dimension of control when he takes the puck off the boards. It also makes him dangerous when the puck seems to have gotten away from him.

Peter's playmaking ability has improved because of patience and confidence. His anticipation and hockey sense are also reasons for that improvement, but Zezel also has good ice vision and stick skills. His increased confidence comes from seeing patience pay off, and knowing that looking the ice over — and not just making the first play he sees — makes for scoring opportunities.

His anticipation, vision and sense (together with his skating ability) also make him a fine defensive center.

Zezel has a good selection of shots. His wrist shot is quickly released and generally accurate, forcing the goaltender to make a save. He also has the power to score from a distance and is good at getting defensemen to set screens.

His finesse talents alone are enough to force the opposition into taking penalties, but Zezel augments that penalty-drawing ability with some of the League's best dives.

THE PHYSICAL GAME

Though gifted in the finesse areas, Zezel is also a good physical player. He carries a lot of muscle on his frame and Zezel hits hard. His size, strength and — above all — balance allow him to plant himself to the side of the opponent's net and stick his butt into the defenseman covering him, thus not allowing the opposing player to get at the puck, or even to hold Zezel's arms.

He plays a very physical game at both ends of the rink, and is not above putting his stick into the opposition. He does not back up that stickwork by fighting.

THE INTANGIBLES

Zezel's lack of concentration — both during practices and games — was a concern of former coach Mike Keenan. Keenan and his staff had difficulty teaching Zezel because of Peter's short attention span, and that flaw makes itself evident in game situations where Zezel more than occasionally is unfocussed — just look at his inconsistent scoring for proof.

It's not that Zezel isn't a hard worker — because he is — or unwilling to correct physical aspects of his game. Even Zezel himself admitted he didn't feel right and sought the services of a sports psychologist last season.

He can continue to mature into a fine NHL player, but he must conquer those funks he gets into where his attitude and drive suffer.

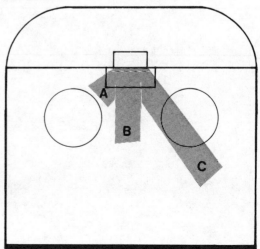

PITTSBURGH PENGUINS

LINE COMBINATIONS
DAVE HUNTER-DAVE MCLLWAIN-PERRY GANCHAR
RANDY CUNNEYWORTH-MARIO LEMIEUX-
BOB ERREY-DAN QUINN-TROY LONEY

DEFENSE PAIRINGS
JIM JOHNSON-ROD BUSKAS
PAUL COFFEY-RANDY HILLIER
DOUG BODGER-
VILLE SIREN-

GOALTENDERS
STEVE GUENETTE
FRANK PIETRANGELO

OTHER PLAYERS
ROB BROWN — Center
BRIAN ERICKSON — Right wing
DAN FRAWLEY — Right wing
GILLES MELOCHE — Goaltender
ZARLEY ZALAPSKI — Defenseman

POWER PLAY

FIRST UNIT:
RANDY CUNNEYWORTH-MARIO LEMIEUX-DAN
QUINN
DOUG BODGER-PAUL COFFEY

LEMIEUX controls the play from the left wing circle.
QUINN is in front, and CUNNEYWORTH works the
back of the net. LEMIEUX distributes the puck to
loosen up the defense for a QUINN shot or COFFEY
shot. CUNNEYWORTH crashes the net for rebounds,
and LEMIEUX will also shoot if defense covers other
options.

BROWN and LONEY will occasionally get power play
time, but the first unit is the main unit.

Last season, the Pittsburgh power play was GOOD,
converting on 110 opportunities in 500 attempts (22.0
percent, sixth overall).

PENALTY KILLING

FIRST UNIT:
DAVE HUNTER-DAN QUINN
JIM JOHNSON-ROD BUSKAS

Penguin penalty killing is now very aggressive, with this
unit playing a diamond to cut off the center. QUINN and
HUNTER force the puck at all times and will also forecheck
one man in offensive zone when possible. BUSKAS will
challenge puck and JOHNSON stays at home.

LEMIEUX and MCLLWAIN also get great amounts of
penalty killing time, and they too are very aggressive.
COFFEY and HILLIER will be the backup defensemen.
Pittsburgh finished fourth in shorthanded goals last year.

Last season, the Pens' penalty killing was POOR, allowing
120 goals in 507 times shorthanded (76.3 percent, 20th
overall).

CRUCIAL FACEOFFS

LEMIEUX and QUINN, but Pittsburgh could use a solid
faceoff man for the defensive zone.

DOUG BODGER

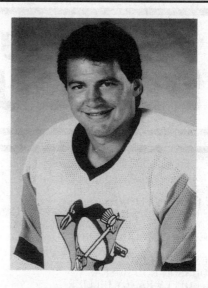

Yrs. of NHL service: 4
Born: Chemainus, B.C., Canada; June 18, 1966
Position: Defenseman
Height: 6-2
Weight: 200
Uniform no.: 3
Shoots: left

Career statistics:

GP	G	A	TP	PIM
289	34	128	162	285

1987-88 statistics:

GP	G	A	TP	+/–	PIM	PP	SH	GW	GT	S	PCT
69	14	31	45	-3	103	13	0	1	0	184	7.6

LAST SEASON

Goal and PIM totals were career highs. Games played was lowest in three seasons, courtesy of a knee injury. He led the Pen defensemen in power play goals, finishing fifth in team scoring.

THE FINESSE GAME

Bodger has good finesse skills, and it is his skating that powers his finesse game. He is a good skater with a strong stride and good agility. He has good lateral movement and one-step quickness (surprisingly so for a man with his size and bulk) and those skills allow him to implement his other finesse skills. He carries the puck confidently from the Penguins zone, and will join the attack from the blue line when he can. Bodger is also smart enough — and poised enough — to know when to fall back to defense.

Doug sees the ice very well from the blue line, so he's able to get the puck to his teammates with good result. He has the hands to make good passes to both sides, and he still has potential left to fill in the playmaking area. Defensively, he consistently makes the safe, smart plays to get the puck out of the zone, and he forces the play wide when it is coming at him.

Bodger brings those vision and puck handling skills to bear on the power play, exploiting those openings for his teammates with his passing skills. He'll lead his teammates into those openings, but Doug's hands are good enough to get a pass to a Penguin in tight quarters.

Bodger's shot is probably the weakest of his finesse skills, in that it is only average in terms of speed and power. He has learned to shoot more frequently, though, and that will help his offense improve. He must also contribute more at even strength, as he scored just once in even strength situations.

THE PHYSICAL GAME

Basically, Bodger is a finesse player with size. Doug uses his body fairly effectively and efficiently around the net and on the boards, but he could use his size and develop his strength so that he becomes a punishing hitter, making opposing forwards think twice before venturing near him. That would also give him some more room for his finesse plays.

THE INTANGIBLES

The knee injury slowed Bodger down for much of this year, and the arrival of Paul Coffey further cut into Bodger's contributions. But Coffey's presence may also serve to take some pressure off of Bodger, as he's no longer forced to command all the offense from the Pens' defense.

He's continuing to improve, and Doug works and takes coaching well. That improvement can make Bodger an All Star defender.

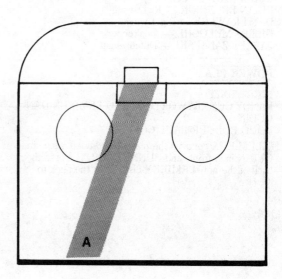

ROB BROWN

Yrs. of NHL service: 1
Born: Kingston, Ontario, Canada; April 10, 1968
Position: Center
Height: 5-11
Weight: 185
Uniform no.: 44
Shoots: left

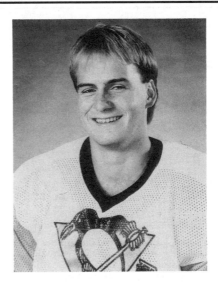

Career statisics:

GP	G	A	TP	+/-	PIM	PP	SH	GW	GT	S	PCT
51	24	20	44	8	56	13	0	1	0	80	30.0

LAST SEASON

Brown's first in the NHL. He split the year with the Penguins and the Canadian National Junior team. He finished second in the League in shooting percentage.

THE FINESSE GAME

As his numbers from junior bear out, Brown is a finesse player with tremendous offensive potential. He is not a fast skater in terms of rink length speed, nor does he have outstanding quickness or agility. But Rob has a deceptive speed, the ability to turn up the juice a notch or two (as well as down when necessary), and good balance.

That balance manifests itself in his puckhandling. Brown has great puck control and he moves well with it up-ice. He can also handle the puck while in awkward position or while he seems to be falling and that's where the balance comes into play.

His hands and brains are his hallmarks, and Brown moves the puck well to both sides. He sees the ice well and can make the quick pass to exploit a sudden opening, and Brown is certainly not afraid to handle the puck under pressure.

Those hand skills also apply to his shot. Brown shoots very well — accurately, quickly and effectively. His hands are also sensitive for work in congested places, so Brown will do well in scoring around the net. He can also drive the puck past the goaltender, so Brown is a scoring threat from in close and afar.

Rob has great hockey sense and a scorer's anticipation. He knows where the holes will be, and if his modest speed won't get him there, he'll lead a teammate to the opening with a good pass. Those brains make him a superb specialty teams player.

He is a fairly conscientious checker, and will stay with his man deep into the defensive zone. Brown also makes the transition from offense to defense well.

THE PHYSICAL GAME

Though he doesn't have great size, Brown willingly takes a hit to make his play (here's where his balance is such a great help). He's not a physical player, but he won't back down from a confrontation.

THE INTANGIBLES

The addition of Brown to the Penguins lineup gives them three tremendously talented offensive centers. It seems obvious Brown was mishandled in the beginning of the year and should have been in Pittsburgh all season. He scored 12g and 12a in his final 19 games.

Rob has great desire and confidence, and he also has the work ethic to insure his continued improvement.

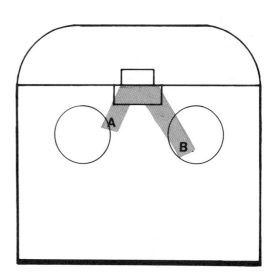

ROD BUSKAS

Yrs. of NHL service: 6
Born: Wetaskiwin, Alberta, Canada; January 7, 1961
Position: Defenseman
Height: 6-2
Weight: 195
Uniform no.: 7
Shoots: right

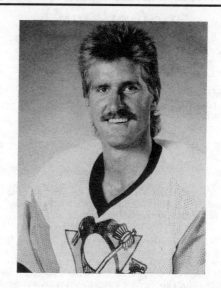

Career statistics:

GP	G	A	TP	PIM
373	15	43	58	841

1987-88 statistics:

GP	G	A	TP	+/-	PIM	PP	SH	GW	GT	S	PCT
76	4	8	12	6	206	0	0	1	0	53	7.5

LAST SEASON
Games played, goals scored and PIM were all career highs, and Buskas led the Pens in the last category. His plus 6 was tops among Pittsburgh defenders.

THE FINESSE GAME
Buskas is not an exceptional finesse player, probably not even good in this category. He's no better than an average skater, and he doesn't possess great agility, quickness or strength on his skates. His passing and puckhandling are also weak, but he has improved his ability to make the right pass under pressure. Buskas is smart enough, though, to not over-extend his game, and he won't attempt the rushes that teammates Paul Coffey, Zarley Zalapski and Doug Bodger successfully complete.

Improved anticipation and understanding of the NHL game have helped Buskas become a solid defenseman. He reads the play coming toward him fairly well, and he uses his defensive angles to force it wide of the net. He also has better understanding of the lateral play around the goal — the cross-ice centering pass, for example — and he dependably covers the front of the net by concentrating in the opposing forward instead of the puck.

His offense will come almost completely from the point, but it is practically non-existent. Once in a very great while he'll sneak into the faceoff circle for a shot.

THE PHYSICAL GAME
Buskas is good along the boards and the corner, but he is more of a pusher and shover than he is a hitter. He doesn't have great strength, but he can generally hold his own against the opposition in the traffic areas. He gets by in front of the net more by holding than by levelling the enemy.

THE INTANGIBLES
His Penguin teammates have respect for Buskas because of his work ethic and willingness to try to improve. He has become a dependable defensive defenseman, though we daresay he's virtually unknown outside of Pittsburgh's Igloo. Unquestionably he's the Pens' best stay-at-home defender and, with the great offensive talent that Pittsburgh's blueliners possess, that's an important trait.

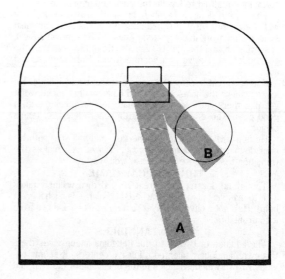

PAUL COFFEY

Yrs. of NHL service: 8
Born: Weston, Ontario, Canada; June 1, 1961
Position: Defenseman
Height: 6-0
Weight: 200
Uniform no.: 77
Shoots: left

Career statistics:

GP	G	A	TP	PIM
578	224	512	736	786

1987-88 statistics:

GP	G	A	TP	+/−	PIM	PP	SH	GW	GT	S	PCT
46	15	52	67	-1	93	6	2	2	0	193	7.8

LAST SEASON

Coffey was traded from the Oilers to the Penguins (along with Dave Hunter and Wayne Van Dorp) in November (in exchange for Craig Simpson, Chris Joseph, Dave Hannan and Moe Mantha). Games played total was the lowest of his career (10 games missed with knee injury, contract holdout accounts for rest). Point total ties for second lowest of his career. He led all Penguin defenders in scoring and SOG, and was second on the team in assists.

THE FINESSE GAME

Without question, Coffey is the best pure skating defenseman in the NHL, maybe the best skater outright. That doesn't mean he always uses his awesome talent to the best effect.

Paul loves to go full throttle, and his play is predictable: When he carries the puck over the offensive blue line, he *always* moves on the right side. But in his skating repertoire are excellent acceleration, lateral movement and change of direction skills, all based on great balance (that's why he also has the tightest turning radius of any NHL player).

After his skating gets him into the clear he will score with a hard, accurate wrist shot or a laser-precise slap shot, and he must shoot the puck to be effective. But Coffey is not selfish in his puckhandling and willingly gets the puck to open teammates.

He has excellent vision and anticipation and he matches those skills with excellent hands and, while he likes to rush the puck and charge the net, Coffey will always look for a breaking forward or a teammate at the offensive blue line.

Paul thrives on specialty team situations, and he is a staple on both units. The open ice created by those situations gives Coffey more room to maneuver and he takes full advantage.

He remains underrated defensively, mostly because of concentration lapses in front of his net (where he forgets to watch an incoming forward and instead looks to the puck). He relies more on his ability to over-power his opponent with speed than he does on the more orthodox method of playing defensive angles to keep the opposition wide of the net.

THE PHYSICAL GAME

Coffey will play a physical style of defense, pushing and shoving along the boards and in the corners. But he is not a hitter and never will be. He is fairly strong in the upper body, but it is the strength in his thighs that powers his fantastic skating or allows him to take the opposition off the puck.

THE INTANGIBLES

Durability and distance from injury. Coffey has a back problem currently under control, but last year he ripped up a knee. There's no questioning his talent, and teamed as he is with Mario Lemieux and a growing Pittsburgh offense, Coffey should begin to re-approach his 100-point seasons.

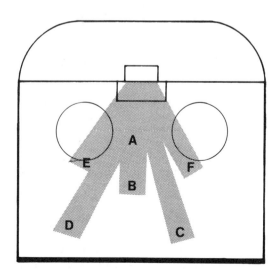

RANDY CUNNEYWORTH

Yrs. of NHL service: 4
Born: Etobicoke, Ontario, Canada; May 10, 1961
Position: Center/left wing
Height: 6-0
Weight: 180
Uniform no.: 15
Shoots: left

Career statistics:

GP	G	A	TP	PIM
246	78	100	178	406

1987-88 statistics:

GP	G	A	TP	+/−	PIM	PP	SH	GW	GT	S	PCT
71	35	39	74	13	141	14	0	6	0	229	15.3

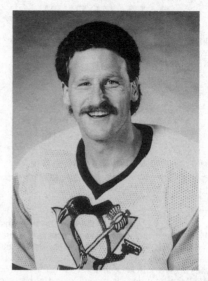

LAST SEASON

All point totals were career highs. He finished third on the club in all three scoring categories, as well as in power play goals and SOG. He was second on the club in game winners and plus/minus. Suspensions accounted for eight games of his nine games missed.

THE FINESSE GAME

Strength on his feet is the key to Cunneyworth's game. Though he has good speed and mobility (and a fair degree of agility), it is balance and strength that allow Cunneyworth to play the physical game necessary to his success. That balance keeps Randy upright through collisions and the strength gets him through the crowds.

All of his hand skills continue to improve—passing, puck handling and shooting. He acts and reacts well at NHL speed, something his growing experience has seen to. Randy anticipates well now, well enough to be a staple on the penalty killing unit, where that mental asset combines well with his skating.

The increased anticipation (or hockey sense) allows Cunneyworth to move the puck well, looking over the ice before making a play. That patience has paid off in higher assist totals. He's not apt to finesse his way around a defender while carrying the puck. Cunneyworth will try to force his way wide of the defense with the puck, but is far more likely to let a teammate carry the puck while Randy charges the net.

His increased point totals can be attributed to his increased shot totals. In 1986-87, Cunneyworth took 169 SOG; last year, 229. That almost 25 percent increase translates into more goals for him and more assists on rebounds.

Randy is still primarily a slot scorer, but his transfer to the left side of Mario Lemieux has moved his primary scoring area just a tad to the left. Cunneyworth gets off those slot shots because his balance and strength render him impervious to the traffic there.

THE PHYSICAL GAME

Scoring statistics aside, the physical game is where Cunneyworth shines (just note the suspensions). He is very tough and aggressive and he uses his body in all three zones. He likes to hit and that tendency is aided by his balance and strength on his skates. Making his physical game more valuable is Randy's ability to make a play with the puck coming out of the corners.

He has good strength for battles with the opposition in traffic, and is unafraid of bigger, stronger players. He plays tough, definitely bigger than his size.

THE INTANGIBLES

With his better than a point per game ratio, Randy showed good scoring balance. He started slowly, with just 8g and 7a in the season's first quarter, but he reached the halfway point with 23g and 17a. He closed the season with 19 points in his last 18 games.

His improved offense didn't cut into Cunneyworth's defensive performance, and that well-rounded — and still improvable — game makes Cunneyworth a valuable member of the Penguins. It also bumps up into the game's higher echelons. He is not out of place among the NHL's power forwards — Probert, Tocchet, Dineen, Claude Lemieux, Gallant.

He has an impeccable work ethic, practicing and playing hard. He's very coachable and a superb team player, the best one on Pittsburgh's roster.

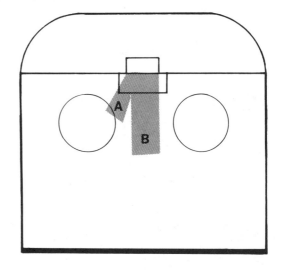

BRIAN ERICKSON

Yrs. of NHL service: 5
Born: Roseau, Minn., USA; March 7, 1960
Position: Right wing
Height: 5-9
Weight: 170
Uniform no.: 14
Shoots: right

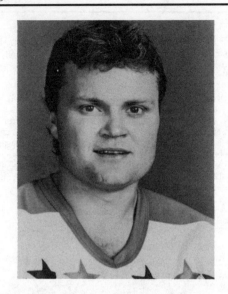

Career statistics:

GP	G	A	TP	PIM
278	74	102	176	173

1987-88 statistics:

GP	G	A	TP	+/−	PIM	PP	SH	GW	GT	S	PCT
53	7	19	26	-12	20	2	0	0	0	81	8.6

LAST SEASON

Acquired at mid-season from Los Angeles in exchange for Chris Kontos. A shoulder injury suffered in March sidelined Erickson for the season. Games played was lowest in four seasons. Though minus 12 on the season, Erickson was plus 2 with Pittsburgh.

THE FINESSE GAME

Erickson is a good skater, improving his skating skill and foot speed to the point that he can be used in even-strength and specialty team situations. His modest speed and acceleration will pull him away from the opposition, and his low center of gravity and balance help his physical game.

He understands the play and its ramifications fairly well, and Brian uses his anticipation and vision on the ice to be an effective checker and penalty killer. He can also use those skills to modest success offensively.

Erickson handles the puck fairly well and can make plays while skating. His poise and patience allow him to hold the puck and look the ice over for the best play.

As a scorer he is most effective close to the net in picking up whatever pucks are lying around. He can surprise the goaltender with a shot from 20 feet or so, and Erickson makes the most of his opportunities by putting the shot on net and forcing the goaltender to make saves.

THE PHYSICAL GAME

Though his size would say otherwise, Erickson is a mucker and a fairly good one at that (of course he would have to be, because his finesse skills are not outstanding at the NHL level). His aforementioned balance keeps him vertical after collisions and able to continue the play.

He has some upper body strength he can apply to his tasks, and Brian also benefits by being skilled enough to make plays after he gains the puck.

THE INTANGIBLES

Erickson succeeds more on desire and hustle than by anything else. He has a tremendous work ethic, staying on the ice after each practice to work on some part of his game. It is his coachability and drive that keep him in the NHL, because his modest skills alone wouldn't do it.

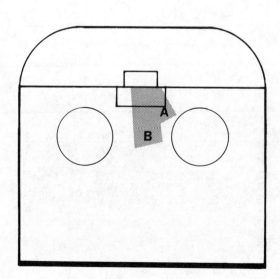

BOB ERREY

Yrs. of NHL service: 5
Born: Montreal, Quebec, Canada; September 21, 1964
Position: Left wing
Height: 5-10
Weight: 185
Uniform no.: 12
Shoots: left

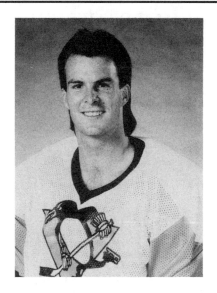

Career statistics:

GP	G	A	TP	PIM
207	39	45	84	108

1987-88 statistics:

GP	G	A	TP	+/−	PIM	PP	SH	GW	GT	S	PCT
17	3	6	9	6	18	0	0	0	0	18	16.7

LAST SEASON

Errey missed 63 games with a broken wrist suffered in the preseason. Games played was, therefore, second lowest of his career.

THE FINESSE GAME

Errey is an exceptional skater: he has speed, agility, balance and quickness, but puts those skills to work haphazardly. He can go places but has no idea of what to do when he gets there, because he lacks NHL-level anticipation or hockey sense.

He sees the ice no better than fairly, and won't make better use of his teammates until he learns to keep his head up while making plays. His shot is fair but won't fool too many goaltenders. He must learn to go to the net more in order to score.

Errey's skating makes him a good checker, and it was in that role that he has had his best success.

THE PHYSICAL GAME

Not originally known as a physical player, Errey has since changed his ways. Where previously he demonstrated a singular unwillingness to hit or use his body, Errey now does so in a pretty smart fashion.

That physical style is a large reason for his long-awaited NHL success, moderate though that success has been.

THE INTANGIBLES

Just as he seemed ready to build on his first fulltime NHL season (1986-87), Errey once again found himself a part time player. This season will present a number of questions for him to answer regarding his health, willingness to continue to work toward improving and — most importantly — just how this former first round draft choice can contribute in the NHL.

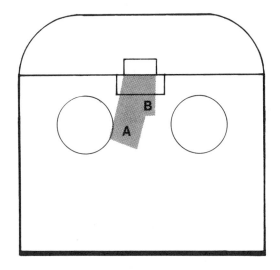

DAN FRAWLEY

Yrs. of NHL service: 3
Born: Sturgeon Falls, Ontario, Canada; June 2, 1962
Position: Right wing
Height: 6-0
Weight: 195
Uniform no.: 28
Shoots: right

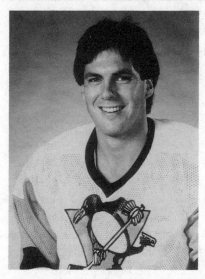

Career statistics:

GP	G	A	TP	PIM
227	34	36	70	608

1987-88 statistics:

GP	G	A	TP	+/−	PIM	PP	SH	GW	GT	S	PCT
47	6	8	14	0	152	1	2	1	0	66	9.1

LAST SEASON

Games played was fewest since joining the Penguins, courtesy of knee injury (29 games) and leg injury. Dan has yet to play a complete NHL season. He finished second on the team in PIM, first among forwards.

THE FINESSE GAME

Dan doesn't really have a finesse game, though his physical play does open up the ice to give him some opportunities. Frawley is an average skater and that's his best finesse skill. His passing is fair because a) his anticipation and ice vision are not particularly strong and b) he does not handle the puck well.

Despite the numbers, his defensive play is average, more from desire than skill, and his shooting is below average. Though Frawley will take a goal from anywhere on the ice, the only time he is any kind of threat is when he is in front of the net.

THE PHYSICAL GAME

Frawley's physical ability is very strong, undoubtedly the strongest tangible aspect of his game. His numbers demonstrate he's more than willing to mix it up and cause commotion in the offensive zone, freeing ice for the team's more talented players.

He hits hard and well, and that hitting serves him as a checker because it discourages his opponents.

THE INTANGIBLES

In the tangible areas, Frawley's continued recovery from last season's serious knee injury must be addressed. But Frawley isn't with Pittsburgh because of tangibles. He's here because of *in*tangibles.

Named captain prior to the season's start, Frawley is a leader for Pittsburgh through effort, dedication and character. Though clearly not counted on for his offensive contributions, Frawley leads by example in other ways. He comes to play every night and works hard in practice — often staying on the ice after practice to work on his liabilities. He is the Penguins' hardest worker.

This is a player who realizes that Pittsburgh may be his one and only shot in the NHL and he's gonna stay here and give it all he has. His attitude is excellent.

Dan Frawley gets by on his hard work and desire to play. He is important to Pittsburgh in filling a role, comparable to any Sutter in desire, if not talent.

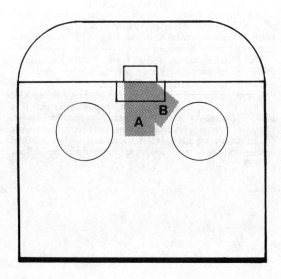

PERRY GANCHAR

Yrs. of NHL service: 2
Born: Saskatoon, Sask., Canada; October 28, 1963
Position: Right wing
Height: 5-9
Weight: 180
Uniform no.: 8
Shoots: right

Career statistics:

GP	G	A	TP	PIM
39	3	7	10	36

1987-88 statistics:

GP	G	A	TP	+/−	PIM	PP	SH	GW	GT	S	PCT
31	3	5	8	-1	36	0	0	0	0	35	8.6

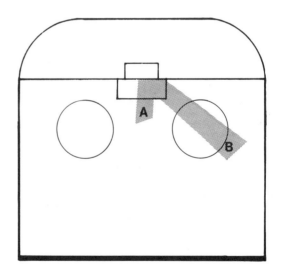

LAST SEASON

Traded to Pittsburgh in mid-season by Montreal. All totals were career highs. He missed 10 games while with Pittsburgh with a knee injury.

THE FINESSE GAME

Ganchar is a strong skater but not a remarkable one. He doesn't have much speed or quickness, nor does he possess great agility or mobility. He is rather tireless in his skating, however, and that aids him as a checking winger.

He is not very talented offensively, but he does have good vision and anticipation and these traits also help him as a checker. He can get the puck to the open man, but he isn't really a playmaker. Any goal he scores will come from the front of the net.

Ganchar is a strong defensive player especially in the Pittsburgh zone, where he sticks with his check at all times. Though finishing as a minus-player, Ganchar was even in his 30 games with Pittsburgh.

THE PHYSICAL GAME

Though he doesn't have great size, Ganchar willingly plays a physical game. His is the kind of checking that will wear the opposition down because of his constant bumping. Notice we didn't say hitting, because Ganchar isn't a big hitter; he doesn't have the strength to be.

THE INTANGIBLES

Perry is a role player, but last season he combined with Dave Hunter and Dave McLlwain to form a solid checking line. But as a role player he's susceptible to the vagaries of the coach, so he may be spotted in and out of the lineup.

STEVE GUENETTE

Yrs. of NHL service: 1
Born: Montreal, Quebec, Canada; November 13, 1965
Position: Goaltender
Height: 5-9
Weight: 165
Uniform no.: 30
Catches: left

Career statistics:

GP	MINS	G	SO	AVG	A	PIM
21	1,205	69	1	3.43	2	2

1987-88 statisics:

GP	MINS	AVG	W	L	T	SO	GA	SA	SAPCT	PIM
19	1,092	3.35	12	7	0	1	61	582	.895	2

LAST SEASON

Bounced between Muskegon of the IHL and Pittsburgh before settling with the Penguins to close the season.

THE PHYSICAL GAME

Guenette is an acrobatic goaltender who makes the most of his reflexes. He is fairly aggressive in challenging the shooters and he has to be because of his size; if he stayed deep in his net, the NHL's better shooters would just pop pucks over his shoulders and past his feet. Even so, those extreme corners are his weakness.

He moves in and out of the net and across the crease well, and that's because of his good balance and foot speed. Guenette also has a good glove. He sees the puck well and his speed helps him on scrambles and screens near the net.

THE MENTAL GAME

Guenette has shown mental toughness and big save capability throughout his hockey career, first backstopping Guelph to the Memorial Cup in 1986 and then last season in the Pens' playoff run when he went 7-1 down the stretch.

He prepares well for each game and holds his concentration through the game and from contest to contest.

THE INTANGIBLES

The Penguins wanted Guenette to lead them last year and, after a few stumbles, he did just that. He'll be leaned on heavily this year, but that's not to say Pittsburgh won't still make an attempt to shore up their goaltending via trade — in which case Guenette is the best goalie bait the Pens have.

RANDY HILLIER

Yrs. of NHL service: 7
Born: Toronto, Ontario, Canada; March 30, 1960
Position: Defenseman
Height: 6-1
Weight: 170
Uniform no.: 23
Shoots: right

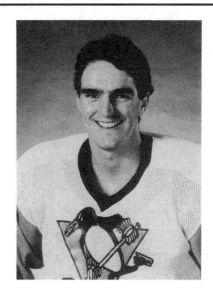

Career statistics:

GP	G	A	TP	PIM
347	10	72	82	603

1987-88 statistics:

GP	G	A	TP	+/−	PIM	PP	SH	GW	GT	S	PCT
55	1	12	13	-6	144	0	0	0	1	44	2.3

LAST SEASON

An ankle injury accounted for three games missed, and games played ties Pittsburgh career high. Minus 6 was worst among defensive regulars.

THE FINESSE GAME

Most of Hillier's finesse play is below average; that fact, along with his propensity toward injury, accounts for his never playing a full NHL season.

He can pass fairly well, but because Randy lacks the anticipation or vision to take advantage of that skill (to say nothing about taking advantage of his teammates), he has to have all kinds of time and room to make an *effective* pass. In other words, he doesn't perform at the NHL level in this department. Still, even if he can't create an attack, Hillier is reasonably dependable getting the puck from his own end.

But again, what especially harms Hillier's play is lack of vision and understanding of the play in front of him. Because he is unsure about what the play should be, Hillier does not carry the puck much — his puckhandling is no more than fair — nor does he shoot the puck frequently. Smartly, then, Hillier doesn't try to force a play he's not capable of.

THE PHYSICAL GAME

Hillier's strength as a defensive defenseman resides in his ability to use his size, which is not outstanding, to good result. He is effective moving people from in and around the net and is a fairly rough customer, as his penalty numbers indicate.

THE INTANGIBLES

Randy's attitude is good. He is a dedicated athlete and a hard worker, and he is coachable, but the truth is, there isn't much to coach. He is a journeyman defenseman, a sixth defenseman, and he survives by playing tough in front of his net.

Real questions must be answered regarding his injuries and inability to remain healthy.

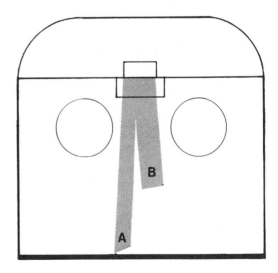

DAVE HUNTER

Yrs. of NHL service: 9
Born: Petrolia, Ontario, Canada; January 1, 1958
Position: Left wing
Height: 5-11
Weight: 200
Uniform no.: 20
Shoots: left

Career statistics:

GP	G	A	TP	PIM
680	127	184	311	831

1987-88 statistics:

GP	G	A	TP	+/−	PIM	PP	SH	GW	GT	S	PCT
80	14	21	35	9	83	0	2	1	0	133	10.5

LAST SEASON

Traded by Edmonton to Pittsburgh in November (along with Paul Coffey and Wayne Van Dorp in exchange for Chris Joseph, Craig Simpson, Dave Hannan and Moe Mantha). Games played was most in three seasons, and Hunter was the only Penguin to appear in all 80 games. He finished third in plus/minus among team regulars.

THE FINESSE GAME

Not a graceful player in the finesse sense, Hunter remains an outstanding defensive forward. He's a good skater with some speed and good balance, but is not really agile on his feet. Hunter is more of a straight-line player than a fancy swirling type forward anyway.

He has good vision on the ice and reads the play well, able to anticipate openings and get to them before his check can. Hunter stays with his check deep into the defensive zone and always plays his position. He doesn't wander, and that's a big reason for his defensive effectiveness.

Dave is not tremendously gifted offensively, so he'll need to be in tight to the net to score. His ability to handle the puck and use his teammates is no better than average.

THE PHYSICAL GAME

Dave is a mean player, extremely physical and effective along the boards, and Dave won't hesitate to put his stick into anyone. He will hit his check in all three zones, and that hitting will wear down the opposition. He has the strength to hold the opposing forward out of the play when necessary.

THE INTANGIBLES

Hunter brings a winning attitude and the knowledge of how to win to Pittsburgh. He is a role player par excellence, an excellent road player because of his toughness and the type of player every club needs to be successful. He won't get a lot of headlines for his hockey playing, but he can be a crucial part of any future Penguin success story.

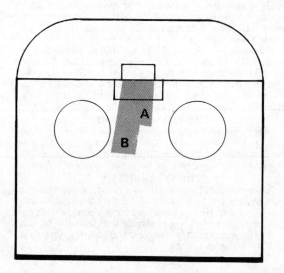

JIM JOHNSON

Yrs. of NHL service: 3
Born: New Hope, Minn., USA; August 9, 1962
Position: Defenseman
Height: 6-0
Weight: 190
Uniform no.: 6
Shoots: left

Career statistics:

GP	G	A	TP	PIM
215	9	63	72	318

1987-88 statistics:

GP	G	A	TP	+/−	PIM	PP	SH	GW	GT	S	PCT
55	1	12	13	-5	87	0	0	0	0	44	2.3

LAST SEASON

Games played, PIM and all point totals were career lows, courtesy in some part of a knee injury (12 games missed).

THE FINESSE GAME

Prior to his injury, Johnson's skating had improved so that it was above average, though not outstanding. He has good mobility in both directions and combines that agility with good playreading ability as Pittsburgh's best defensive defenseman. That defensive ability puts him on the ice frequently, so forget his negative plus/minus.

He remains almost totally defensively oriented, so he won't contribute much from the blue line. His shot is improved — more accurate and more powerful — but he still doesn't shoot enough, so much so that he can actually take away from the Pens' offense and not just not add to it.

His low, powerful shot could be a good weapon for the Pens. While he won't become a goalscorer, he would pick up assists on tip-ins and deflections. He'll also take a few steps into the center for his shot.

Because he will take chances handling the puck, Johnson does have a tendency toward the giveaway. But overall, he is good defensively and plays more intelligently in the defensive zone than any other Penguin defenseman.

THE PHYSICAL GAME

Johnson enjoys a physical style, and he plays it well. He's willing to put his six-foot frame to work effectively and often, sometimes by sacrificing his body while blocking shots, often by taking out opposing forwards in front of the net and on the boards. His strength and reach allow him to move forwards off the puck, or keep the puck to himself to make the play.

He has always been an aggressive player, and he makes his physical play more effective by keeping out of the penalty box.

THE INTANGIBLES

Excellent work habits, excellent attitude, determination and heart. Jim Johnson has all of these things and he brings them to bear in practice and in games. As with others in the Pens' youthful defensive corps, Johnson will improve and play successfully in the NHL for a number of years.

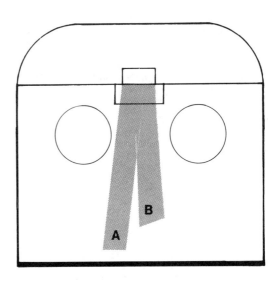

MARIO LEMIEUX

Yrs. of NHL service: 4
Born: Montreal, Quebec, Canada; October 5, 1965
Position: Center
Height: 6-4
Weight: 210
Uniform no.: 66
Shoots: right

Career statistics:

GP	G	A	TP	PIM
292	215	301	516	246

1987-88 statistics:

GP	G	A	TP	+/−	PIM	PP	SH	GW	GT	S	PCT
77	70	98	168	23	92	22	10	7	3	382	18.3

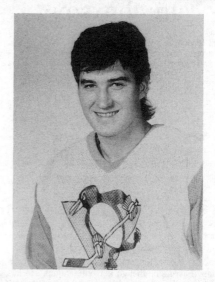

LAST SEASON

Games played was second highest of Lemieux's career, but all point totals were career highs. Lemieux led the NHL in scoring, goals, short handed goals and shots on goal. He was second in assists, and fourth in power play goals and game tying goals. He led Pittsburgh in plus/minus, power play and game winning goals and shooting percentage. His PIM total was a career high. A bruised shoulder and back spasms sidelined him for three games.

THE FINESSE GAME

Where to start for a player whose every finesse ability is excellent?

Lemieux's puck handling ability is first among equals when his finesse abilities are discussed. He just may be the best in the game at manipulating the puck while carrying it, and his size and reach are the reasons for that.

He can show the puck to the defender, and then keep it just a hair's length from danger (because of the NHL's best reach), and he operates with it excellently at every speed and in every circumstance. Lemieux's soft hands just cradle the puck on the end of the stick, and his hand and arm strength are such that he can do anything with the puck regardless of traffic or his own body position.

Naturally, his passing ability relies a great deal on his hand skills, but Mario is aided here by his phenomenal anticipation, vision and superb feel for the game and its opportunities. He can lead players, feather passes to either side, create opportunities with his passes, get the puck anywhere necessary.

Mario is a finisher of the first order, a goal scorer almost without equal. He will shoot and score from anywhere, with any shot. He is excellent around the net because of his reach and hand skills and also likes to take the bad angle shot for the far corner. He's deadly on breakaways.

His long and fluid skating stride makes him an excellent skater and will take him away from 99 percent of the opposition. His stride affords him excellent balance, and that balance allows him to move in and out of traffic and work in awkward positions. The length of his stride will almost always get him to loose pucks before the opposition.

His defensive play is the most underrated part of his game,

as it is with all superior offensive talents. Mario works his end as well as anybody on the team, and his presence on the ice automatically puts the other team on the defensive.

If we had to name a finesse weakness, faceoffs would be it. So they're just good, instead of excellent. Big deal.

THE PHYSICAL GAME

Usually, reach, balance, hand and arm strength would all be included here. Mario has tremendous physical ability and he uses all of the above assets to take and give checks in order to gain the puck. He uses his body extremely well against his opponents, using his hips and long, thin torso to squirt free from the opposition along the boards or to avoid a hit.

Lemieux is not strong in terms of pure muscular strength, but put him on the boards and he'll move people through balance. He is not a fighter, but he won't back away from a confrontation either.

He does not take close checking well, though, and it will put him off his game as he spends more time trying to get even with his checker — through trips and slashes — than he does trying to get free.

THE INTANGIBLES

The complaint against Mario has always been his motivation and lack thereof. But from the Canada Cup Series last summer, through his record setting All-Star game performance to his phenomenal finish last season when he almost singlehandedly dragged the Penguins into the playoffs, Lemieux has answered his accusers.

We said last year that he is Pittsburgh's leader and that he wants to win very badly. In his last 16 games, Lemieux went 16-26-42. Three of those games saw him score four points; two saw him score five. That's the kind of leadership and intensity of performance that's been missing from Lemieux during his first three seasons, the kind that allowed critics to say that when the going gets tough, Mario gets going — in the other direction.

But no more.

His selection as the NHL's most valuable player will undoubtedly be tarnished by some observers who will claim Lemieux won by default over an injured Gretzky. We say Mario's selection is above reproach and entirely justified. We also say that his offensive exploits will continue and — hard as it may be to believe — they'll improve.

And here's a fun thought, just by the way. Has the NHL *ever* had the one-two punch it currently has in Mario Lemieux and Wayne Gretzky?

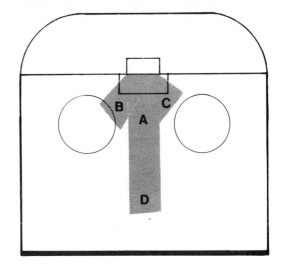

TROY LONEY

Yrs. of NHL service: 3
Born: Bow Island, Alberta, Canada; September 21, 1963
Position: Left wing
Height: 6-3
Weight: 215
Uniform no.: 24
Shoots: left

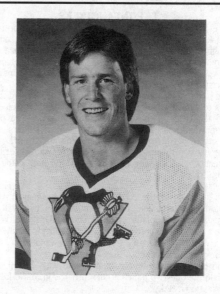

Career statistics:

GP	G	A	TP	PIM
194	26	37	63	338

1987-88 statistics:

GP	G	A	TP	+/−	PIM	PP	SH	GW	GT	S	PCT
65	5	13	18	-3	151	1	0	0	0	87	5.7

LAST SEASON

Games played and PIM totals were career highs; point total tied career best. A preseason knee injury (and the subsequent surgery) sidelined him for the season's first 15 games. PIM total was team's third highest.

THE FINESSE GAME

As a finesse player, Loney isn't much. He's a no better than average skater with little rink speed or one-step quickness, so he's not particularly agile or mobile on his feet. He's no better than just-below-fair as a passer, possessing neither the instincts or hands to make plays in the offensive zone. He keeps his head down and can't see openings, but even if he did his passing skills aren't good enough to lead his teammates into the clear.

He doesn't handle the puck well when skating (head down again), and Troy is simply not a scorer. He doesn't shoot quickly enough, doesn't get into good position to score and doesn't have the hands to finesse the puck in traffic. The goals he does score will come from the faceoff circles, and Loney does launch a lot of shots toward the net, but their accuracy is very bad.

THE PHYSICAL GAME

Troy puts his excellent size to work fairly effectively. He can take opponents out along the boards and has always been more than willing to throw his weight around, although he is not primarily a fighter.

His effectiveness along the boards, however, is tempered by his inability to make a play coming out of the corner. A teammate must help him make those plays, or else the puck will turn over to the opposition.

THE INTANGIBLES

One can't help but get the feeling that the Pens feel Loney could be a Probert or a Neely, if only they could free the goalscorer within that big body. While Troy is a leader both on and off the ice because of his strong character and attitude, his talent dictates that he won't rise above third-line duty in his NHL career. Still, his work ethic and coachability are nearly flawless, and he adds character to a team not usually recognized for heart and dedication.

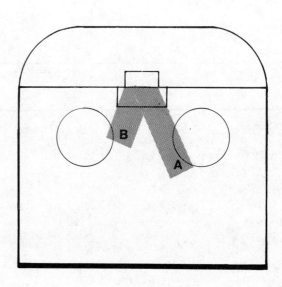

DAVE MCLLWAIN

Yrs. of NHL service: 1
Born: Seaforth, Ontario, Canada; January 9, 1967
Position: Center
Height: 6-0
Weight: 185
Uniform no.: 19
Shoots: right

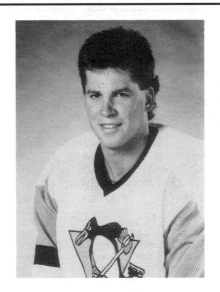

Career statisics:

GP	G	A	TP	+/−	PIM	PP	SH	GW	GT	S	PCT
66	11	8	19	-1	40	1	0	0	0	65	16.9

LAST SEASON

The 1986 draft choice made his NHL debut, though he also spent some time in the International League.

THE FINESSE GAME

McLlwain is a good skater, strong and balanced on his feet but not yet overly agile. He has slightly above average NHL speed, but both his speed and agility could be improved with better foot speed.

Though his junior numbers show that he was a scorer, McLlwain spent last season as a checking forward where he was able to put his scorer's anticipation and vision to good use. He also killed penalties well, combining his skating and hockey sense to good result. As such, his plus/minus number is deceiving.

He has good hands, but last year McLlwain concentrated on his defense so much that he was afraid to handle the puck at the opposition's blue line for fear of turning it over and being caught deep on an opposition rush. He must carry the puck more, and not just dump it in at the bluer line. He can make good passes and works fairly well in traffic, and increased NHL experience should give McLlwain the confidence necessary.

Dave shoots the puck well, but needs a quicker release to consistently beat NHL goaltending. He's opportunistic (which is good, because his forechecking will create loose pucks) and will do most of his scoring from near the crease. He'll succeed there because of his sensitive hands that can operate in traffic.

THE PHYSICAL GAME

McLlwain has good size and balance, but he could benefit from some added weight and muscular strength in his upper body. That would add another dimension to his checking. He is not generally a physical player, and a physical dimension would greatly help his finesse game.

He uses his body now not so much for hitting as he does for getting in the way. He doesn't out-muscle the opposition along the boards, rather he tries to put his balance and hand skills to work in gaining the puck.

THE INTANGIBLES

McLlwain is another of the Penguins' talented youngsters. Like the others, he needs more NHL seasoning in order to determine just how effective he can be at the major league level.

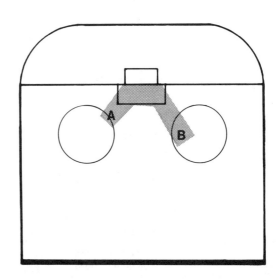

GILLES MELOCHE

Yrs. of NHL service: 17
Born: Montreal, Quebec, Canada; July 12, 1950
Position: Goaltender
Height: 5-9
Weight: 185
Uniform no.: 27
Catches: right

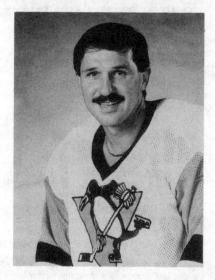

Career statistics:

GP	MINS	G	SO	AVG	A	PIM
788	45,401	2,756	20	3.64	22	111

1987-88 statisics:

GP	MINS	AVG	W	L	T	SO	GA	SA	SAPCT	PIM
27	1,394	4.09	8	9	5	0	95	722	.880	0

LAST SEASON

Games played mark was lowest of NHL career. Goals-against-average was third highest of career, highest in four seasons. Suffered preseason knee injury.

THE PHYSICAL GAME

Seventeen years of NHL experience have paid off in Meloche's approach to the game. No longer the acrobatic stylist he once was, Meloche now combines angle play with what is left of his reflexes.

He plays his angles well, so a shot will have to be a good one to beat him from a distance. Though no longer exceptionally fast with his hands or his feet, does retain some of his former quickness.

He's never had a night in, night out weakness. He has always handled the puck well, and will go behind the net to cut it off or to make a short outlet pass to his defense. He's not like a Vanbiesbrouck, Fuhr or Hextall, in that Gilles won't make the pass to center ice.

Play around the net continues to confound him, and that's for two reasons. One, Meloche isn't seeing the puck well — especially on screens — so he hangs back in his cage for a better look. Two, he can't cover the net as he used to because of his diminished speed. So change of direction plays are very troublesome to Meloche.

That weakness extends itself to shots from 20-feet or so, again because of Meloche's lost speed.

THE MENTAL GAME

Meloche has the ability to come back if he lets in a bad goal and may even get tougher; Gilles has always been fairly tough in the clutch. He certainly won't fold after a poor outing and has fairly good concentration. He communicates very well with the defensemen.

THE INTANGIBLES

Meloche has always been respected by his teammates because of his attitude. He is coachable and is a hard worker, even after 16 NHL seasons. It is Meloche's attitude that makes him so valuable. He sets an example of discipline and good work habits on a Penguin team in need of direction and maturity. His demeanor and the way he plays the game make him a steadying influence for the Penguins and their young goaltenders.

But the writing is more than on the wall for Meloche, as he played only one game after February 1, giving way to Steve Guenette and Frank Pietrangelo. Meloche's return to the Pens this season must therefore be called questionable.

FRANK PIETRANGELO

Yrs. of NHL service: 1
Born: Niagara Falls, Ontario, Canada; December 17, 1964
Position: Goaltender
Height: 5-10
Weight: 184
Uniform no.: 40
Catches: left

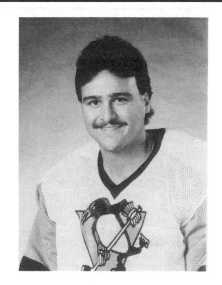

Career statistics:

GP	MINS	G	SO	AVG	A	PIM
21	1,207	80	1	3.98	2	2

1987-88 statisics:

GP	MINS	AVG	W	L	T	SO	GA	SA	SAPCT	PIM
21	1,207	3.98	9	11	0	1	80	600	.866	2

LAST SEASON

Pietrangelo's first in the NHL. He had one of Pittsburgh's two shutouts. He bounced up and down between Muskegon of the IHL and Pittsburgh. He set a club record with five consecutive road wins.

THE PHYSICAL GAME

Pietrangelo is an average skater for a goaltender, but his lateral movement is not good. His foot speed is slow and prohibits him from either moving quickly across the crease or from closing his legs to take away the five-hole.

Though not a challenging goaltender, Pietrangelo stands up fairly well. He has good leg speed, so he'll cover the lower part of the net fairly effectively by reflex. He doesn't play his angles as well as he might, but that could also be indication of Pittsburgh's defense (with Pietrangelo afraid to challenge and allow an opposing skater to slide unchecked to the wide open side).

He has a good glove hand and is just average with his stick. He doesn't show great anticipation skills, and he must improve on his rebound work as he leaves too many pucks in the crease for the opposition.

THE MENTAL GAME

Pietrangelo is generally prepared to play each game. He doesn't seem to be affected by bad games or goals, but neither has he shown big save or big game mentality.

THE INTANGIBLES

Time will tell with Pietrangelo. If the Pens want just one youngster, they'll probably keep Steve Guenette and not Pietrangelo. Frank could be groomed as a backup, but again, time will tell.

DAN QUINN

Yrs. of NHL service: 5
Born: Ottawa, Ontario, Canada; June 1, 1965
Position: Center
Height: 5-10
Weight: 180
Uniform no.: 10
Shoots: left

Career statistics:

GP	G	A	TP	PIM
356	140	201	341	190

1987-88 statistics:

GP	G	A	TP	+/−	PIM	PP	SH	GW	GT	S	PCT
70	40	39	79	-8	50	21	1	4	0	235	17.0

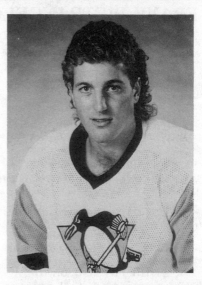

LAST SEASON

Games played total was second lowest of NHL career. Quinn missed 10 games with a broken wrist. He finished second on the club in scoring, with a career high in goals. He was also second in power play goals, shots on goal and shooting percentage.

THE FINESSE GAME

Quinn is an excellent skater, a darter with good speed, excellent acceleration and one-step quickness. He combines those traits with excellent balance so he has great agility and lateral movement, literally able to change direction and stop and start within a step. He has become more selective in how he uses his speed (as in changing gears so as not to be predictable), but when in doubt Quinn will go full throttle.

Dan makes his skating effective by having superior ice vision and anticipation. Those qualities are in best evidence during special team situations, areas where Quinn excels. He is very dangerous on the power play because of the added open ice he has to work with, and is equally at home in short-handed situations, where his speed and vision make him a constant threat for a short-handed goal.

Quinn has excellent hands, and he makes good use of them because he's able to make his plays at full speed. He had been a tad unselfish in previous seasons, but Quinn exploited the openings himself more this year, thus an increase in SOG (from 184 in 1986-87 to 235 last season) and a career high in goals. His hands help him get his shots away quickly, and since he is an opportunist around the net that means rebound and loose puck goals galore (that one-step quickness is a big part of his scoring, as he just beats people to the puck).

When he does use his playmaking skills, Quinn's anticipation and hockey sense, combined with his hands, allow him to lead his teammates into openings.

THE PHYSICAL GAME

Like other smaller finesse players who have found great offensive success, Quinn has learned the value of a physical game. Now this doesn't mean that he's turned into a clone of teammate Randy Cunneyworth (or any of his other more physical Penguin teammates), but it does mean that Quinn has learned to accept hits in order to make plays.

That is, however, a far cry from initiating contact and Quinn will still operate on the periphery of traffic when possible, hoping to be in the clear when the puck squirts free. If he is caught in traffic, the opposition will most likely take the puck from him, because he is not overwhelmingly strong.

THE INTANGIBLES

After a year of solid all-around play, Quinn's defense slipped to its previously low level. He needs to shore up that part of his game in order to be truly valuable to Pittsburgh. He does serve as a good foil to Mario Lemieux, in that Mario will draw the checkers and leave Quinn against — supposedly — less strong defensive players.

Because of his on-ice demeanor, Quinn is not popular among members of his team (he cuts up his teammates while on the ice, in full view and hearing of the opposition). Creating that kind of dissension is never healthy and Quinn could probably get away with it on another club forever.

But Lemieux's presence makes Quinn's offense less necessary than it might be on another club, and management may not put up with Quinn's anti-social behavior for long (and that's another good reason for Quinn to become more than a one-way player).

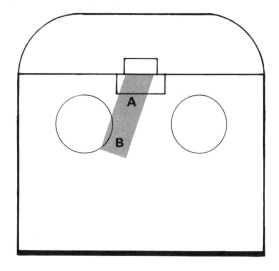

VILLE SIREN

Yrs. of NHL service: 3
Born: Helsinki, Finland; November 2, 1964
Position: Defenseman
Height: 6-2
Weight: 185
Uniform no.: 5
Shoots: right

Career statistics:

GP	G	A	TP	PIM
187	10	46	56	144

1987-88 statistics:

GP	G	A	TP	+/−	PIM	PP	SH	GW	GT	S	PCT
58	1	20	21	14	62	0	0	0	0	53	1.9

LAST SEASON

Siren missed 17 games with a broken ankle (games played was a career low), but still set a career mark in assists. He was second on the team in plus/minus, first for defensemen.

THE FINESSE GAME

Siren continues to improve his finesse skills. His skating is consistently at the NHL level now, and that is the biggest improvement in his game (and has led to his other improvements). He skates well backward and with greater agility and lateral movement, so he's consistently able to angle the opposition to the boards.

His skating has gained him the time to read the play better, and Siren now sees the rush both ways fairly well. He is able to react to the play at the NHL level, and his improved defensive play is attributable to that. He understands the play better and moves better when necessary. He also moves the puck better now than ever before, courtesy of his improved play reading ability. He'll carry the puck to center if he can, but Siren doesn't charge into the offensive zone — not yet, anyway.

Siren reads the offensive play better than before, but he still concentrates on defense. He feels comfortable now in pinching in and containing the point. He still does not shoot frequently enough, and should definitely work on the strength and release of his shot from the blue line.

THE PHYSICAL GAME

While primarily a finesse player, Siren has increased the tempo of his physical play. He is not aggressive, but Siren quietly plays the body and takes a hit.

Additional strength would help him in his corner and crease battles, as he can be outmuscled by the competition. He probably won't ever be a punishing hitter, but Siren now plays an effective physical game, especially since he can make a play after taking the puck away.

THE INTANGIBLES

We told you last year that Siren's durability was questionable. We tell you that again now. We wonder if he'll reach his potential before he falls into pieces completely. We say again, if Siren can remain healthy he'll develop into a dependable NHL defenseman.

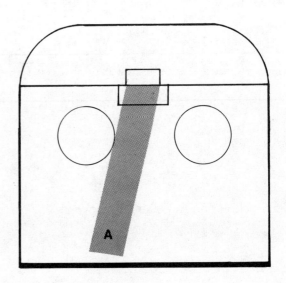

ZARLEY ZALAPSKI

Yrs. of NHL service: 1
Born: Edmonton, Alberta, Canada; April 22, 1968
Position: Defenseman
Height: 6-1
Weight: 195
Uniform no.: 33
Shoots: left

Career statisics:

GP	G	A	TP	+/−	PIM	PP	SH	GW	GT	S	PCT
15	3	8	11	10	7	0	0	0	0	31	9.7

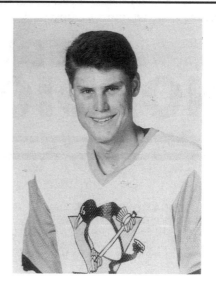

LAST SEASON

Zalapski made his much anticipated NHL debut after the Olympic Games, and turned in the team's fourth best plus/minus rating in that time.

THE FINESSE GAME

Zarley is a good skater, with the potential to be an excellent one at the NHL level. He has excellent rink length speed, and he makes that speed effective by moderating it up and down the ice. Make no mistake though: He can motor and break into the clear if he wants to.

He is also a very mobile skater with great balance and agility. He has good lateral movement and one-step quickness, so he'll get to the loose pucks or into the openings with a high rate of success.

Zalapski complements his speed and agility with good puckhandling skills. He moves well with the puck at all speeds, and he can also control it well in traffic. That ability extends itself to his passing, which is very good. He passes extremely well to both sides, and Zalapski also excels at getting the puck to open teammates. He uses his excellent vision and hockey sense to aid him in his passing.

His shot is probably the lowest rated of his finesse skills. Zalapski keeps it low and on net, so it's good for deflections and rebound goals, but he could also shoot to score more.

His anticipation aids him in his defensive play as well, and he'll cut off or re-direct many opposition passes. His transition game is excellent, and he'll turn the play around very quickly with a rush himself or the appropriate breakout pass.

THE PHYSICAL GAME

Basically, Zalapski is a finesse player with size. He puts that size to use well offensively with his reach and balance, and he's effective at taking out men along the boards and corners. Like many youngsters, he could improve with added upper body strength.

Still, his game is that of the breakout defenseman and not that of the takeout defenseman. So as long as Zalapski holds his own in the trenches, it's not necessary for him to overpower people.

THE INTANGIBLES

Depending on your preference, either Zalapski or Brian Leetch was the best player to come out of the Olympics, and both are game breakers and franchise players.

Zarley has an excellent attitude, and his addition to the

Penguin lineup makes Pittsburgh a much more formidable opponent. He has all the talent to become one of the NHL's top defensemen.

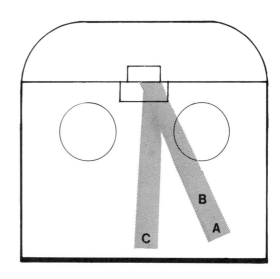

QUEBEC
NORDIQUES

LINE COMBINATIONS
MIKE EAGLES-PAUL GILLIS-ALAIN COTE
GAETAN DUCHESNE-PETER STASTNY-ANTON
STASTNY
MICHEL GOULET-MARC FORTIER-LANE
LAMBERT

DEFENSE PAIRINGS
STEVEN FINN-JEFF BROWN
ROBERT PICARD-RANDY MOLLER
TERRY CARKNER-
TOMMY ALBELIN-

GOALTENDERS
MARIO GOSSELIN
MARIO BRUNETTA

OTHER PLAYERS
GORD DONNELLY — Defenseman
JEFF JACKSON — Left wing
JASON LAFRENIERE — Center
NORM ROCHEFORT — Defenseman

POWER PLAY

FIRST UNIT:
MICHEL GOULET-PETER STASTNY-ANTON
STASTNY
JEFF BROWN-TERRY CARKNER

GOULET is at the base of the left faceoff circle, ANTON STASTNY behind the net on the right wing side and PETER STASTNY at the right circle. P. STASTNY will distribute the puck along the perimeter of the defensive box to free GOULET for a shot. That is the primary focus of the power play, and all forwards will crash the net for rebounds. Shots from the point are a distant second in preference. If the Nords feel the left side of the PK unit is weak, P. STASTNY will work with BROWN and GOULET on a triangular pattern, with GOULET still the focus.

FORTIER will see time secondarily, as will GILLIS posted in front of the net, but the above quintet is the main one and will see at least one minute of time.

Last season the Nordique power play was GOOD, scoring 99 goals in 456 man-advantage opportunities (21.7 percent, eighth overall).

PENALTY KILLING

FIRST UNIT:
MIKE EAGLES-PAUL GILLIS
ROBERT PICARD-RANDY MOLLER

The Nordiques penalty killers all play a straight box defense. The forwards will challenge the puck at the blue line and in the corners leaving the defense stationary in front of the net. DUCHESNE and COTE are other regular forwards, and GOULET will also see a turn.

Last season the Quebec penalty killing was POOR, allowing 96 goals in 410 shorthanded situations (76.6 percent, 19th overall).

CRUCIAL FACEOFFS
GILLIS is the man here.

TOMMY ALBELIN

Yrs. of NHL service: 1
Born: Stockholm. Sweden; May 21, 1964
Position: Defenseman
Height: 6-1
Weight: 185
Uniform no.: 28
Shoots: left

Career statisics:

GP	G	A	TP	+/−	PIM	PP	SH	GW	GT	S	PCT
60	3	23	26	-7	47	0	0	0	0	98	3.1

LAST SEASON

Albelin's first in the NHL. His PIM total was the lowest of any defensive regular.

THE FINESSE GAME

Albelin is a talented finesse player with good potential but with improvement yet to be done. He skates well in both directions and is smooth in his pivots, but he needs to improve the general speed and quickness of his movement. His defense is solid for a rookie and Albelin showed that he understands how to force a play wide of the net by angling off the forward.

He handles the puck well and is unafraid to do so at this level, His movement with it is fairly sure and not at all tentative, which means Albelin isn't worried about making mistakes. He plays with poise and confidence at the point, smoothly pinching in to contain and control the offensive play. He reads the play well in both directions.

Tommy also handles the puck very well, taking it off the boards and shooting it with ease. He'll cheat to the faceoff circle for shots if he can.

THE PHYSICAL GAME

Albelin has good size but could use greater strength in his upper body for confrontations in the defensive zone. Right now he can be overpowered in the traffic areas, and even though he's going to be more of an offensive contributor he'll need strength for the times his defensive partner can't cover the front of the net.

THE INTANGIBLES

Albelin showed well in his rookie NHL season, and his poise speaks very well for his ability to complete the transition from the European to the North American game. His improvement should continue this season.

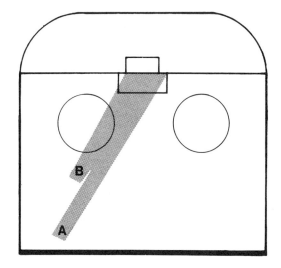

JEFF BROWN

Yrs. of NHL service: 2
Born: Ottawa, Ontario, Canada; April 30, 1966
Position: Defenseman
Height: 6-1
Weight: 185
Uniform no.: 22
Shoots: right

Career statistics:

GP	G	A	TP	PIM
130	26	61	87	86

1987-88 statistics:

GP	G	A	TP	+/−	PIM	PP	SH	GW	GT	S	PCT
78	16	37	53	-25	64	9	0	4	0	208	7.7

LAST SEASON

Games played and all point totals were career highs. Brown led the Nordique defensemen in scoring, finishing fifth on the team. He also led the defense in power play goals (no other defensemen had more than four *total* goals), shots on goal (second on the team) and tied for the team lead in game winners. His plus/minus was the club's third worst, poorest among defensemen.

THE FINESSE GAME

Brown is clearly the quarterback of Quebec's attack, and it is his finesse skills that put him in that position. He is an excellent skater with good speed and acceleration and Jeff also has excellent quickness and foot speed. He can jump into an opening or change direction within a stride, and he adds good balance to that quickness to gain excellent lateral movement. That lateral movement is especially pronounced when he's skating backward and controlling the puck at the offensive blue line.

Jeff loves to carry the puck from the Quebec zone into the offensive end, and then blast a shot from the right faceoff circle. His puck carrying forays are made more effective by his prudence in rushing, and when Brown can't rush the puck intelligently he'll make a quick and accurate breakout pass and then follow the play up-ice. Jeff carries the puck very well when skating, looking over the ice for a developing play.

He is a general at the offensive blue line, using his excellent foot skills and vision to keep the Quebec offense functioning. Brown not only can get the puck to the open man, but he can see a play or two ahead and lead a teammate into an as-yet-unopen opening. Brown has a good shot from the blue line, low and hard, and he also likes to charge the net on give-and-gos.

While the strength of his game is clearly in the offensive zone, Brown's skating allows him to play a good defensive game. He survives more on his speed and hand ability for defense — forcing plays by charging at puck carriers to force turnovers — than he does on the more conservative method of angling the play wide, and Jeff has a concentration flaw in that he gets hypnotized by the puck rather than covering his side of the net.

THE PHYSICAL GAME

We don't usually list hand and foot quickness in the physical game, but they are so critical to Brown's success that they have to be included. They allow him to contain the point very well (at that particular skill he is already one of the League's best). He uses his body to protect the puck from the opposition, and at the offensive blue line Brown is very good at keeping the puck away from defenders.

Jeff will use his body defensively, though he is not a crushing hitter. He just gets in the way of the opposing forward and that play is made more valuable by Brown's ability to make a play after his hit.

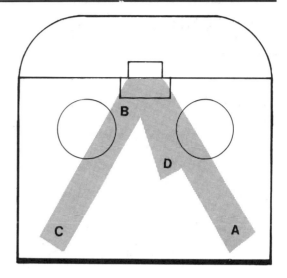

THE INTANGIBLES

We wrote last year that Brown needed an attitude adjustment. Last season he demonstrated good maturity and he is moving into a role of leadership with the now-leaderless (because of Dale Hunter's absence) Nordiques.

He still has great potential to fulfill and in this season (actually his second full season — his NHL experience is spread over three previous seasons) he should continue to improve. His work ethic has improved and that bodes well for his future.

MARIO BRUNETTA

Yrs. of NHL service: 1
Born: Quebec, Canada; January 25, 1967
Position: Goaltender
Height: 6-3
Weight: 180
Uniform no.: 30
Catches: left

1987-88 statisics:

GP	MINS	AVG	W	L	T	SO	GA	SA	SAPCT	PIM
29	1,550	3.72	10	12	1	0	96	778	.876	16

LAST SEASON

Joined the club in January. He was a ninth round pick in the 1985 Entry Draft.

THE PHYSICAL GAME

Brunetta is an anomaly, a goaltender with great size who is not a challenging netminder. He fills the net very well because of his height, yet Brunetta doesn't take full advantage of his size by moving to challenge shooters. Rather, he hangs back in the net and lets the puck play him.

He's also a stylist, a long-legged guy who likes to use his leg speed in the butterfly fashion. That doesn't mean he's always flopping around in the crease; he holds his feet stance fairly well but prefers the butterfly style to cutting the angle.

He is pretty mobile for big guy, so the usual wisdom of shooting for the low corners might not always work (especially given the aforementioned leg speed) as Mario moves well from post to post. Brunetta is very conservative in his puckhandling and won't do more than cut the puck off as it circles the net.

Mario has good hand speed and he uses his stick well to clear rebounds.

THE MENTAL GAME

He has good concentration and anticipates plays well, making his size even more effective. Brunetta holds his concentration fairly well within games and from contest to contest.

THE INTANGIBLES

The Nordiques are looking for another 40-game goalie to complement Mario Gosselin, so they obviously feel that — at this time anyway — Brunetta is incapable of filling that hole (they turned down New York's Bob Froese early in the summer, by the way). Because of that, the youngster will probably have to fight for a job in training camp.

TERRY CARKNER

Yrs. of NHL service: 2
Born: Smith Falls, Ontario, Canada; March 7, 1966
Position: Defenseman
Height: 6-3
Weight: 210
Uniform no.: 4
Shoots: left

Career statistics:

GP	G	A	TP	PIM
115	5	37	42	277

1987-88 statistics:

GP	G	A	TP	+/−	PIM	PP	SH	GW	GT	S	PCT
63	3	24	27	-8	159	2	0	1	0	54	5.6

LAST SEASON

Games played, all point totals and PIM marks were all career highs. He was acquired from the Rangers (along with Jeff Jackson) in the preseason for John Ogrodnick and David Shaw. Terry finished second in scoring among Nordique defenders and he was fifth on the club in PIM. He missed five games with a broken nose.

THE FINESSE GAME

Carkner is not a great skater, though he has improved his foot speed in the four years since he was drafted. He must continue to improve his foot speed in order to become a regular in the NHL. Carkner plays a conservative defensive game to compensate for his skating.

Terry has fairly good offensive skills and because he sees the ice well he can contribute from the blue line. He has improved his transition game in both directions, exhibiting better decision making regarding pinching in and falling back.

He has the skill to move the puck from his zone quickly and efficiently, though he still is not doing so consistently. He rarely rushes the puck from danger, but his puckhandling is improving for major league play.

He is not a real threat to score because 1) he doesn't shoot anywhere near enough and 2) his shot isn't good enough to consistently fool NHL goaltending.

THE PHYSICAL GAME

Carkner is a very physical player, certainly getting the most from his size and strength. He will take the puck away from most players along the boards, just as he will thwart most players in front of the net. When Terry hits you, you know it.

His physical play could be more effective if his ability to make a play following a hit was to grow, and the indications are all his abilities will improve. Carkner is a very tough player who willingly fights the League's toughest players. And holds his own, we might add.

THE INTANGIBLES

Terry has tremendous heart and desire (he's also a great team man, often fighting those tough guys on behalf of a teammate), and those qualities carried him through his earliest NHL games when he had absolutely no confidence in himself.

He has all the talent in the world and Carkner has shown the work ethic necessary to improve. If he continues to improve his skating he can be a dominant NHL defenseman.

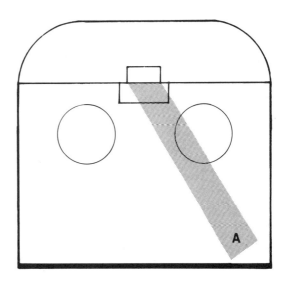

ALAIN COTE

Yrs. of NHL service: 8
Born: Matane, Quebec, Canada; May 3, 1957
Position: Left wing
Height: 5-10
Weight: 203
Uniform no.: 19
Shoots: left

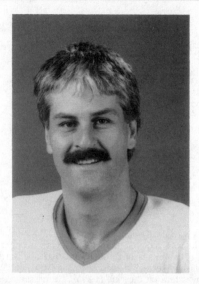

Career statistics:

GP	G	A	TP	PIM
641	101	82	283	369

1987-88 statistics:

GP	G	A	TP	+/−	PIM	PP	SH	GW	GT	S	PCT
76	4	18	22	3	26	0	0	0	0	84	4.8

LAST SEASON

Games played total was lowest in seven years. Goal total was career low and point total was also lowest in seven years. He was one of just four players to finish with a plus rating, and he finished with the team's third best mark.

THE FINESSE GAME

Skating skill and great hockey sense are the keys to Cote's subtle and often unappreciated game. Alain is a good skater with excellent speed and acceleration in his strong stride. Though he has good balance he is not a very agile player, but as a checking wing he more than gets by for keeping up with his man. That balance also helps him in his body checking.

Sense, vision and anticipation are second among equals in Cote's skills. He gets an exceptional read of the opponent's play and combines his mental skills with his speed to become an excellent penalty killer. Though unsuccessful in this area last year, Cote is always a threat for short-handed goals.

At even strength Cote will pull the unenviable assignment of checking the League's best scorers. Given that, and given Quebec's less than sparkling team defense, Cote's plus 3 is even more remarkable.

When he does turn to offense Alain handles the puck fairly well, and he uses his stickhandling ability especially well to rag the puck as a penalty killer. He combines his decent hand skills with his sense to be a good passer, but his role as a checker and mucker minimizes that skill.

He isn't a big goal scorer, so any goals he gets will have to be of the opportunistic, loose-puck-around-the-net variety. He does keep the opposition honest by shooting from farther out.

THE PHYSICAL GAME

Cote is a physical player, a mucker who dumps the puck to the corners and then digs it out. His speed makes him effective in this game, and he makes his finesse skill more effective by playing the body well in the corners.

Though he is not a thunderous hitter his balance is still a factor, allowing him to remain vertical and mobile after collisions in the corners. Additionally, because he is a smart player he can play a physical game without taking penalties. He takes the body regularly — home or away, winning or losing.

He is also one of the few forwards in the League willing to give up his body to block shots.

THE INTANGIBLES

Cote is the League's best unknown defensive forward. That makes no difference to him though, and that lack of caring about attention is a clue to his personality. Cote just does his job game in and out, and his drive and on-ice work ethic make him a very important part of any success the Nordiques accrue.

He is also versatile and can play the right side as well as the left, and can also play defense.

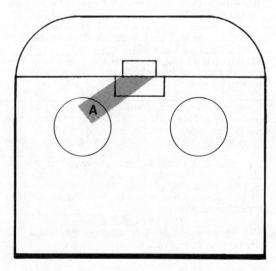

GORD DONNELLY

Yrs. of NHL service: 3
Born: Montreal, Quebec, Canada; April 5, 1962
Position: Defenseman
Height: 6-2
Weight: 211
Uniform no.: 34
Shoots: right

Career statistics:

GP	G	A	TP	PIM
196	6	12	18	622

1987-88 statistics:

GP	G	A	TP	+/−	PIM	PP	SH	GW	GT	S	PCT
63	4	3	7	-16	301	1	0	0	0	46	8.7

LAST SEASON

Games played total was a career high (he missed two games with a rib injury, and then was sidelined by suspension late in the season). All point totals and PIM total were career highs, and he led the Nords in PIM. Donnelly was the NHL's most penalized defenseman last season.

THE FINESSE GAME

Let's just say Gord isn't a finesse player. He needs a big lead to keep up with the opposing forward and isn't real mobile on his feet for turns and pivots in the traffic areas.

Donnelly doesn't handle the puck well and he does the smart thing of not handling it frequently. He won't rush the puck up-ice and rarely joins the play in the offensive zone, but he will get into the action often enough for a shot or two a game. He'll get his goals from the point.

He has a linear understanding of the game in terms of defense, meaning he can see the play in front of him and counter that (or make an attempt to counter it) but he doesn't anticipate secondary options.

THE PHYSICAL GAME

Donnelly is tough, one of the NHL's toughest players as his PIM total bears out. He is in excellent condition and has great strength, and he puts that strength to work as one of the NHL's top enforcers.

THE INTANGIBLES

Gord's role is pretty straightforward. He'll play in the tough intradivisional games to take on the Kordics and the Millers, but he's of little use against the NHL's skating clubs. Still, he'll be in the lineup against those clubs, just in case.

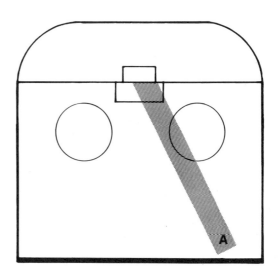

GAETAN DUCHESNE

Yrs. of NHL service: 7
Born: Les Saules, Quebec, Canada; July 11, 1962
Position: Left wing
Height: 5-11
Weight: 195
Uniform no.: 14
Shoots: left

Career statistics:

GP	G	A	TP	PIM
531	111	161	272	334

1987-88 statistics:

GP	G	A	TP	+/−	PIM	PP	SH	GW	GT	S	PCT
80	24	23	47	8	83	4	1	2	0	138	17.4

LAST SEASON

Duchesne played all 80 games for the second time in his career and second time in three seasons. His goal total was a career high, point total second highest. He led the club in plus/minus and was second in shooting percentage.

THE FINESSE GAME

Duchesne is a tireless skater and can stick to any opposing forward because of that, relying heavily on balance and a good change of direction. He doesn't have a lot of speed, but Gaetan has good foot speed and that's what powers his change of direction ability.

His anticipation and vision are excellent, giving him full view of the play and its ramifications so that when the holes open Duchesne is through them almost before his check is. As his modest PIM total indicates, Gaetan gets the job done smartly and doesn't hurt the team with needless penalties.

When Gaetan brings his growing offensive prowess to bear he demonstrates good puckhandling skill and an awareness of teammates that would be expected from a player with his vision and hockey sense.

Though he'll never command the kind of defensive coverage that he himself stars at, Duchesne has a credible offensive touch. He can take advantage of the loose pucks that his checking creates — though he takes way too long to get his shot off — by converting from around the net and from farther out.

THE PHYSICAL GAME

Duchesne is neither a hard-hitting nor dirty player when he checks. Instead he is tough but clean, and persistent in his body checking. That persistence can wear down the opposition, and Duchesne willingly suffers the retaliatory abuse from frustrated opponents.

He does not fight.

THE INTANGIBLES

Gaetan is a dedicated athlete and a tireless worker, the kind of player whose actions make him a leader. He is a character player.

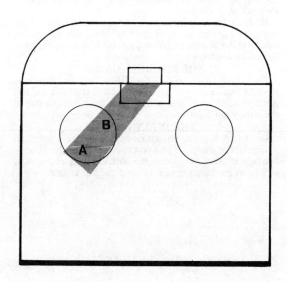

STEVEN FINN

Yrs. of NHL service: 2
Born: Laval, Quebec, Canada; August 20, 1966
Position: Defenseman
Height: 6-0
Weight: 192
Uniform no.: 29
Shoots: left

Career statistics:

GP	G	A	TP	PIM
128	5	13	18	266

1987-88 statistics:

GP	G	A	TP	+/−	PIM	PP	SH	GW	GT	S	PCT
75	3	7	10	-4	198	1	0	0	0	70	4.3

LAST SEASON

Games played, all point totals and PIM mark were career highs. He finished second on the club in PIM, and his plus/minus was third best among defensemen.

THE FINESSE GAME

Finn is an average skater at the NHL level, not showing exceptional — or even above average — talent in any particular area of his skating. Right now, he'd be best described as competent. Still he'll rush the puck when necessary — nothing fast or fancy but he does recognize the openings.

His growing NHL experience has helped him improve his puck movement skills in open ice, and he'll make that correct pass much of the time, but he has difficulty taking the puck off the boards when being checked and will turn over the puck at that time.

He's not an offensive player and won't contribute much at the blue line. His shot is average but Finn takes a long time getting it off because he likes to move to the center of the blue line for the shot.

Defensively, Finn has a good understanding of his position and he doesn't often stray from that position because he knows he may not get back in time to thwart an opposing offensive thrust.

THE PHYSICAL GAME

Finn is an aggressive player with good size but he'd do well to increase his strength or bulk. He takes the body well along the boards and he hits hard, but he seems to lack the upper body strength to hold the opposition out of the play.

He does cover the front of the net well by punishing any forward who happens to wander by, and Steven is also a more than willing fighter who backs down from no one.

THE INTANGIBLES

Finn has progressed well in his two Nordiques season, demonstrating intelligence in his play and determination to improve. He should continue to do so.

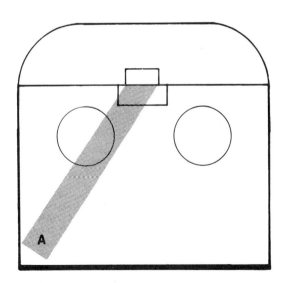

MARC FORTIER

Yrs. of NHL service: 1
Born: Sherbrooke, Quebec, Canada; February 26, 1966
Position: Center
Height: 6-0
Weight: 190
Uniform no.: 9
Shoots: right

Career statisics:

GP	G	A	TP	+/−	PIM	PP	SH	GW	GT	S	PCT
27	4	10	14	-17	12	3	0	1	0	40	10.0

LAST SEASON

Fortier joined Quebec for good in February after spending the earlier part of the season in the American Hockey League. He was signed as a free agent in February of 1987.

THE FINESSE GAME

Fortier is a gifted finesse player, and he already shows the instincts that could make him successful at the NHL level. He has puck smarts and knows to do the simple yet effective offensive things, like keeping the puck and the rest of ice on his forehand so he can give and take passes more easily.

He keeps his head up in the offensive zone and sees the play around him (as well as avoiding hits because he sees the enemy coming), though he does not consistently react to these plays at NHL speed — not yet anyway. The same cannot be said of his defensive play, as Fortier has difficulty playing positionally in his own zone. He releases too quickly for the breakout pass, and that move creates gaps in the Quebec defense.

Marc's vision, instinct and puckhandling ability is good enough for him to see more than limited power play time. His hands are good enough for him to work in the congestion near the opposition net, but he's not at the stage where he'll beat NHL goaltending consistently from farther out.

His skating is no better than good for the NHL level, probably just a touch under that rating. He would benefit greatly from improved foot speed, as that quickness would give him more time to put his sight and hand skills to work.

THE PHYSICAL GAME

Fortier is not a physical player, though physical play doesn't intimidate him. Rather, he doesn't impose himself on the opposition in the traffic areas, preferring to absorb rather than dish out any punishment.

He has good size and further NHL experience and confidence (naturally a guy's going to do what he thinks he does best, so Marc stuck to a finesse game) could open up his physical game.

THE INTANGIBLES

Fortier is one of a number of younger players who might be given a chance to stick with Quebec from the beginning of the year, though he too will feel pressure from the presence of Joe Sakic — Quebec's No. 1 draft choice from 1987. Still, the Nords look at the 201 points Fortier put up in his last year of junior in the Quebec League and — even though he was an average player in that year — 200 points is still 200 points.

The Nordiques would like some of those points for themselves.

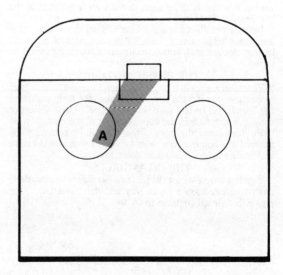

398

PAUL GILLIS

Yrs. of NHL service: 5
Born: Toronto, Ontario, Canada; December 31, 1963
Position: Center/right wing
Height: 5-11
Weight: 190
Uniform no.: 23
Shoots: left

Career statistics:

GP	G	A	TP	PIM
377	61	99	169	863

1987-88 statistics:

GP	G	A	TP	+/−	PIM	PP	SH	GW	GT	S	PCT
80	7	10	17	-29	164	1	0	0	0	82	8.5

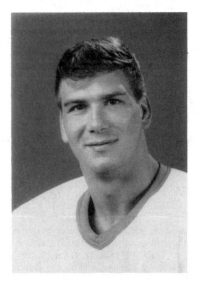

LAST SEASON

Gillis played a full slate for the second time in his NHL career. His goal total was a career low for a full season, assist and point totals lowest in four seasons. His PIM total was also a full-season career low, but was still highest among forwards, fourth highest on the club.

THE FINESSE GAME

Foot speed is the critical component of Gillis' skating game and it is that skill that allows him to succeed as a checking forward. His skating is otherwise unexemplary, lacking overall speed and agility. But his quickness makes him an excellent forechecker and creates many turnovers because of his skating and physical play.

Paul also has good anticipation at his command, and he marshals that ability as a complement to his skating and checking. But Gillis cannot turn that anticipation into goals because of his mediocre hand skills. He can score from around the net if given sufficient time and sufficient opening, but he neither carries nor passes the puck well.

Gillis is another of those players where the plus/minus masks his true ability. While we can't completely dismiss his plus/minus flaw (because he isn't *that* good a defensive forward — like a Carbonneau or Erixon), Paul is good enough as a checker to merit the benefit of the doubt because he plays a conscientious defensive game and plays his position well.

He'll also get the call for any crucial faceoffs.

THE PHYSICAL GAME

Gillis is a rambunctious player, a very physical player who hits everything he can get his body into. His quickness helps him trap opponents and then close the gap to bodycheck them. His willingness also makes him very good in the corners and along the boards. Good upper body strength helps Gillis in his play, as well as excellent balance on his skates so as to remain upright after checks.

He took his lessons well from Dale Hunter, so that Gillis' hits force the opposition to give up the puck, and the loose puck will go to the Nords for a goal.

THE INTANGIBLES

Gillis is a hard worker and an excellent team man with good character, but his play last season was disappointing. Quebec expected him to fill Dale Hunter's shoes, but Gillis — perhaps in an attempt to increase his importance to the team by staying on the ice and out of the penalty box — instead played a tentative and un-Paul Gillis type of game.

His feistiness is a critical part of any success the Nordiques will have, and since he doesn't have Hunter's scoring skill Gillis must be doubly sure to play his effective physical game this season.

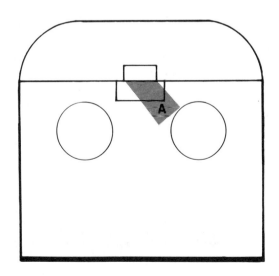

MARIO GOSSELIN

Yrs. of NHL service: 4
Born: Thetford Mines, Quebec, Canada; June 15, 1963
Position: Goaltender
Height: 5-8
Weight: 160
Uniform no.: 33
Catches: left

Career statistics:

GP	MINS	G	SO	AVG	A	PIM
153	8,461	498	6	3.53	6	34

1987-88 statisics:

GP	MINS	AVG	W	L	T	SO	GA	SA	SAPCT	PIM
54	3,002	3.78	20	28	4	2	189	1,422	.867	8

LAST SEASON

Games played and minutes played totals were career highs. He allowed the sixth-greatest total of goals against in the NHL.

THE PHYSICAL GAME

Gosselin is reflex goaltender, and he's an entertaining one to watch because of his acrobatics. He has fast hands and faster feet — his left foot in particular — and he combines his reflexes with excellent vision to get to almost every puck he can see.

His speed makes him very effective in stopping goals off scrambles from in front of the net and he will go down in the butterfly style on shots from in close. The debit in that style is that he leaves the top of the net open for rebounds. However, his foot speed and balance help him to regain his stance very quickly.

Gosselin counters screens and crowds in front of his net by coming out of his net to the top of those screens, where he can use his good vision to pick up the puck. He skates well and will roam for loose pucks, but doesn't really throw the puck around the glass. He'll just leave it for his defensemen.

The downside of Mario's style is the energy expended. Because Mario doesn't play his angles the way he should he's constantly throwing himself in front of pucks instead of letting them just hit him. He gets worn down and suffers from too much work as the season goes by.

THE MENTAL GAME

The Goose is pretty solid in the mental phase of the game. His concentration within a game is good, especially as he tracks the puck near the net, and he also holds that concentration over three and four games to be effective in longer stretches.

He's easy going in that bad goals or games don't stay with him. He has also disciplined himself to be ready to play every night.

THE INTANGIBLES

The talent is here for Gosselin to become an excellent NHL goaltender (though if he's going to make that breakthrough to the higher echelons it's about time for him to make his move), but the Nordiques feel they need further goaltending help to spell Mario: they don't think he can successfully play three or four consecutive games over the course of a season.

MICHEL GOULET

Yrs. of NHL service: 9
Born: Peribonqua, Quebec, Canada; April 21, 1960
Position: Left wing
Height: 6-1
Weight: 195
Uniform no.: 16
Shoots: left

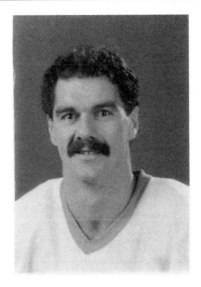

Career statistics:

GP	G	A	TP	PIM
687	414	422	836	504

1987-88 statistics:

GP	G	A	TP	+/-	PIM	PP	SH	GW	GT	S	PCT
80	48	58	106	-31	56	29	1	4	1	284	16.9

LAST SEASON

Goulet played 80 games for third time in his career, first in five seasons. He finished second on the club in scoring (second highest point total of career, 10th overall in the League), but he failed to score 50 goals for the second consecutive season. Still, he led the club in goals, power play goals (second overall in NHL) and shots on goal (fifth in the NHL) and tied for first in game winners. His plus/minus was the team's worst.

THE FINESSE GAME

Goulet is an excellent skater in all aspects of that skill, powerful and balanced on his skates, as well as fast. He has great agility because of his balance and his foot speed, but he is more of a straight-ahead and blast at the net guy than he is a shifty player. When he gets a step on the defender as he rockets up the wing, a blast from the top of the circle is the natural result.

Michel is an excellent shooter, a sniper from anywhere in the offensive zone. Because he can get open (courtesy of his skating) he can get opportunities all over the zone, and that's where his shot comes in. If he has a half-inch of room, he can put the puck in the corner of the net. His wrist shot is as dangerous as his slap shot and he will charge the net for second effort goals. He shoots often and accurately, forcing the goaltender to make saves. Because of the extra room provided, Goulet is especially devastating on the power play.

He controls the puck very well because of his soft hands (along with his hand and wrist strength), but his puckhandling ability is just a tad below that of his other skills. Goulet can pass well, but he obviously looks to the net before he looks anywhere else. He is not selfish however, in terms of one-on-one play; Goulet will make the pass to a free teammate instead of gambling against a defender himself. The anticipation that gets him in position to score helps him make those passes.

As good as his offense is, his defense is often no more than perfunctory, so Michel will never be mistaken for a defensive forward. In fact, one of his linemates is going to have to be a defensively-oriented forward.

THE PHYSICAL GAME

Goulet has great strength in his legs (that's where the acceleration comes from) as well as in his upper body (that's what powers his shot). But though he is strong and hard to contain physically, the tough game is not Goulet's game. He will bump in the corners and drive the net, but Goulet is not a power forward.

He has a temper and can be a little mean with his stick at times, but he can take the abuse that comes his way and dish some out if necessary.

THE INTANGIBLES

There can be little doubt that Goulet is the NHL's best left wing; his consistency over half a dozen seasons proves that. Whether he can regain his status as a 50-goal scorer remains to be seen, but he is still tremendously important to the Nordiques and will continue to see tremendous amounts of ice time.

His goal ratios could stand some improvement. Just 19 of his goals came at even strength, just nine at even strength in the season's second half.

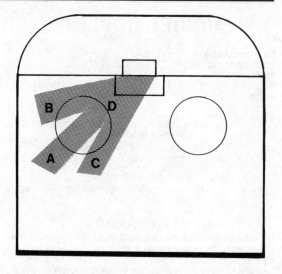

JEFF JACKSON

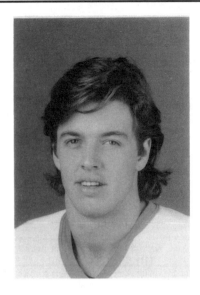

Yrs. of NHL service: 2
Born: Chatham, Ontario, Canada; April 24, 1965
Position: Left wing
Height: 6-1
Weight: 195
Uniform no.: 25
Shoots: left

Career statistics:

GP	G	A	TP	PIM
154	23	29	52	208

1987-88 statistics:

GP	G	A	TP	+/−	PIM	PP	SH	GW	GT	S	PCT
68	9	18	27	5	103	0	2	3	0	98	9.2

LAST SEASON

Jackson was aquired from the Rangers by the Nordiques (along with Terry Carkner) in exchange for John Ogrodnick and David Shaw. Games played total was a career high, as were assist, point and PIM totals. He finished third in PIM among forwards, and his plus/minus was the team's second best. He was sidelined by a late-season knee injury.

THE FINESSE GAME

Jackson is a good skater, fast on his feet and fairly agile. He has a good burst of speed that he puts to use by beating defensemen to the outside, but he doesn't yet have the puck-handling capabilities to complement that speed. For one thing, he doesn't take passes as well as necessary at the NHL level.

He can make plays from the corners to his teammates, and Jackson can pass the puck well, but he's still not acclimatized to the NHL pace. He must learn to move the puck quicker, just as he must learn to examine all his options and show patience instead of making the first play he sees.

Jackson has a good slap shot from the left circle, but needs to shoot it more instead of driving past the defenseman and into the corner with the puck.

THE PHYSICAL GAME

Jackson is a very physical hockey player and he consistently uses his size and strength. He puts that size and strength into action along the boards by constantly bodying the opposition, and because his legs are always moving the opposition has to take penalties to stop him.

Jeff has good strength and can take the puck in those battles and he also has the strength and balance to operate successfully in traffic. Because of that he'll frequently be used to jam the net on the power play.

Jackson has also shown that he can be mean, in that he'll hit opponents from behind with his stick. Shots like that usually force him into fights, where he holds his own but doesn't terrorize anyone.

THE INTANGIBLES

Jackson has the finesse and physical tools necessary to be a good-to-excellent NHLer. Now all that remains to be seen is whether or not — after his first full, untraumatized (as in trades and demotions) season Jackson has the desire and intensity to improve his skills.

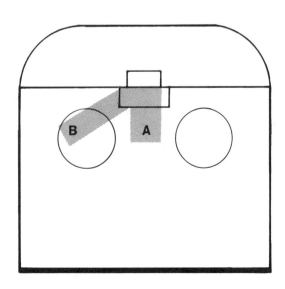

JASON LAFRENIERE

Yrs. of NHL service: 2
Born: St. Catharines, Ontario, Canada; December 6, 1966
Position: Center
Height: 5-11
Weight: 185
Uniform no.: 10
Shoots: right

Career statistics:

GP	G	A	TP	PIM
96	23	34	57	12

1987-88 statistics:

GP	G	A	TP	+/–	PIM	PP	SH	GW	GT	S	PCT
40	10	19	29	-1	4	5	0	1	0	54	18.5

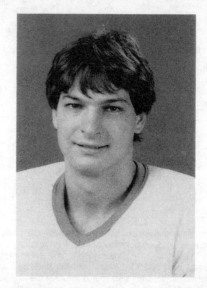

LAST SEASON

Demotions to the American Hockey League covered Lafreniere's NHL absences. He set a career mark for assists.

THE FINESSE GAME

While a good, young skater Lafreniere is not yet at the NHL level in that skill, and that lack of skating ability hampers the rest of his NHL play. He has some quickness in his feet and some agility to complement that foot speed, but he's lacking overall in all skating departments.

Jason is a creative and intelligent playmaker, but he cannot consistently harness that skill because of his failure to move at an NHL speed.

The plays he does make come from his good anticipation and hockey sense and his good hands. Lafreniere can recognize the openings, and he has shown that he can pull his teammates into the clear with accurate and soft passes. Again, Jason's only problem is in consistently using his talent; he sees the openings and they register on his mind, but he cannot yet get his hands or feet to match the speed of the play.

One place he can do that is on the power play, where the extra open ice gives him more room — and more time — to operate. Defensively, Jason is conscientious, but here again he often finds himself overwhelmed by the speed and pace of the play.

THE PHYSICAL GAME

Lafreniere is an artist, not a plumber. He doesn't play an outstanding physical game, nor does he have outstanding size. Jason does make an attempt to get in the opposition's way, but he is not usually found against the boards or in the corners and when he is, he's fairly easy to take off the puck.

As with many young finesse players, Lafreniere would benefit from an increase in strength.

THE INTANGIBLES

We said last year that "Jason gave indications . . . that he can be a better than average NHL player, but how quickly he will reach that level depends on . . . how hard he is willing to work to do so." Lafreniere has since demonstrated that he's unwilling to work on his flaws — notably and most importantly his skating — and would rather complain about not getting the chance to play in the NHL.

He has demanded to be traded and refused to play for the Nords' AHL farm team during last spring's playoffs. The situation doesn't bode well for Lafreniere, who was suspended by the Nordiques last May.

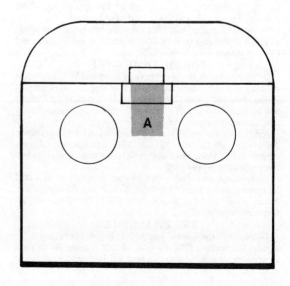

LANE LAMBERT

Yrs. of NHL service: 5
Born: Melfort, Sask., Canada; November 18, 1964
Position: Right wing
Height: 5-11
Weight: 180
Uniform no.: 7
Shoots: right

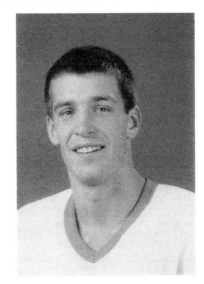

Career statistics:

GP	G	A	TP	PIM
270	56	64	120	498

1987-88 statistics:

GP	G	A	TP	+/−	PIM	PP	SH	GW	GT	S	PCT
61	13	27	40	0	98	0	0	2	0	98	13.3

LAST SEASON

Assist and point totals were career highs, despite missing 13 games with a finger injury. He finished fifth on the club in plus/minus.

THE FINESSE GAME

Lane is a straight-ahead player and his finesse skills are suited for that style of game. He has a strong stride and can get some good acceleration and rink-length speed out of it, but he is neither exceptionally agile nor quick. He does have good balance and that aids his physical game.

Lambert gets a pretty good read of the ice and he checks well in all three zones because of that vision, but that skill doesn't translate into offensive success. He is a little tough with the puck and has a tendency to make his plays with his head down, so he'll need time and space to complete his playmaking.

Also handicapping his offense is his straight-ahead thinking. Lambert isn't a creative player in the offensive zone, and he plays more by reacting than acting upon the opposition. His lack of foot speed also hinders him, preventing him from cashing in on loose pucks.

Lambert has a decent shot from the faceoff circles, but will have to do most of his scoring from in close.

THE PHYSICAL GAME

Lambert not only succeeds when playing a physical game, but he *must* play a physical game to succeed: he isn't good enough otherwise. His problem is that he doesn't take advantage of his excellent upper body strength and physical ability (note we didn't say size) consistently enough. His strength and good balance should add up to an unbeatable physical game; he can be a punishing hitter.

But those parts don't add up to a greater whole. He can play a strong — if not dominating — boards and corners game, but he is just as apt to avoid the corners and the physical play as he is to look for it.

He must initiate more contact.

THE INTANGIBLES

General apathy — for lack of a better word — is what plagues Lambert. He doesn't apply himself well in any partic-ular part of his game and he isn't a good enough player to be waiting around for something to occur when he's on the ice.

What helps Lane is that the Quebec right wing corps could be the NHL's worst, but he might very well find himself a candidate for a benching if Finnish import Iiro Jarvi can crack the lineup.

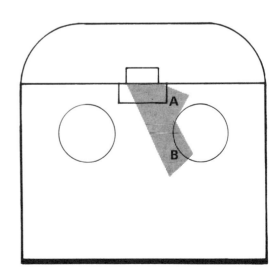

BOB MASON

Yrs. of NHL service: 2
Born: International Falls, Minn., USA; April 22, 1961
Position: Goaltender
Height: 6-1
Weight: 180
Uniform no.: 31
Catches: right

Career statistics:

GP	MINS	G	SO	AVG	A	PIM
101	5,645	331	0	3.51	2	0

1987-88 statisics:

GP	MINS	AVG	W	L	T	SO	GA	SA	SAPCT	PIM
41	2,312	4.15	13	18	8	0	160	1,353	.882	0

LAST SEASON
Games and minutes played totals fell in his second season.

THE PHYSICAL GAME
Mason uses his good size to cover the net as a standup goaltender. He plays his angles well and is at his strongest when he is squared to the shooter; that's a clue to how he'll perform that night. If the puck just hits him, he'll do well. If he has to go fishing, the Hawks are in for a long night. That style lets him stick rebounds away from onrushing forwards and retain his stance and position to make a second save.

Mason is noticeably weaker once his feet are moving. Though he has quick feet, Mason has difficulty regaining his stance once he leaves his feet. What's worse, he also loses his angles once he is on the ice.

He does not handle the breakaway or moving shooter well, because he opens up his entire stance when he moves his feet as he tries to stay square with the puck.

Mason is a sucker for fakes on breakaways. He'll fall for the shoulder dip or the stutter step, make the first move himself and get burned. He is no better or worse than average above his waist, and has demonstrated no great speed in either hand.

Bob also has a tendency to be careless when hugging the post, often leaving an opening between his skates into which the shooter can wrap the puck.

THE MENTAL GAME
Mason anticipates well, and he uses his vision to see the puck well on almost every shot. Because of his style he's susceptible to screen shots at his feet that he doesn't see.

He maintains his concentration well, but his anticipation can sometimes get him into trouble. For instance, on a play from the corner along the goal line — where a pass to the front of the net is almost certainly going to be the play — Mason has been fooled when the forward in the corner shot instead of passed.

He needs to maintain his concentration in those so-called non-shooting situations. Mason has also shown that he can make the big save, as demonstrated by his noble — if vain — performance against the Islanders in last year's playoffs.

THE INTANGIBLES
Confidence is the biggest problem with Mason. He came to Chicago with a lot of pressure on his shoulders and did nothing to ease that pressure. In fact, his own non-stellar performances combined with the success of Darren Pang and the demotion of Murray Bannerman to actually make the pressure worse.

Mason's confidence is so shaken (right now bad goals and games do affect him; he can't get rid of them) that he speaks to his former goalie coach — Washington's Warren Strelow — several times a week.

Bob has the ability. Now what he needs is the maturity to stand on his own — without falling back on Strelow's encouragement — and stop the puck. We said last year that Mason's 1987 playoff success wouldn't necessarily translate to 1988 and that last season was a crossroad in his career.

For Mason, success this season is crucial to his continuing as an NHL goaltender.

RANDY MOLLER

Yrs. of NHL service: 6
Born: Red Deer, Alta., Canada; August 23, 1963
Position: Defenseman
Height: 6-2
Weight: 205
Uniform no.: 21
Shoots: right

Career statistics:

GP	G	A	TP	PIM
430	26	97	123	866

1987-88 statistics:

GP	G	A	TP	+/−	PIM	PP	SH	GW	GT	S	PCT
66	3	22	25	-11	169	0	0	2	0	116	2.6

LAST SEASON

Games played total was the second lowest of his career (he suffered an early season back injury). Goal total was second lowest of his career but assist total tied his career high. He finished third on the club in PIM with a career high total.

THE FINESSE GAME

Moller is a good skater, equipped with speed and agility. He has good balance and quickness for a big man, and that gives him unexpected mobility and lateral movement. His strong stride gives him good acceleration ability and he uses that skill to draw away from the opposition when he rushes the puck.

That's not to say that Moller is a rushing defenseman. His style is a conservative one, but he can avail himself of good puck carrying skills to relieve pressure on the Nordique forwards. Randy also operates well from the point in the offensive zone, pinching in intelligently to sustain Quebec's attack.

He can find the open man and will make good passes to his teammates, but he is not a true offensive threat in the way teammate Jeff Brown is. Moller has a strong slap shot and will score his goals from the point. He could afford to shoot more frequently.

Moller's play reading ability is strong in both zones, and he complements that vision with good defensive anticipation and solid positional play. Randy uses his defensive angles very well to force most any enemy wide and behind the net. Moller's agility also allows him to close the gap on the puck carrier, strip him of the puck and quickly make the transition to offense.

THE PHYSICAL GAME

Mixes a solid finesse game with a solid physical game. Randy has good size and strength and he uses both to keep the front of the Nordique net clean any way necessary. He will hit in the corners and can hold out forwards along the boards, demonstrating good upper body strength.

THE INTANGIBLES

Discipline and hard work are the keys to Moller's work, but he spent much of last season swinging in the trade winds following reports of Quebec's dissatisfaction with his play.

He plays dependable and consistent defense for Quebec, but the fact that he has yet to play a full NHL season, combined with an infusion of young defenders, may mean movement from Quebec for Moller.

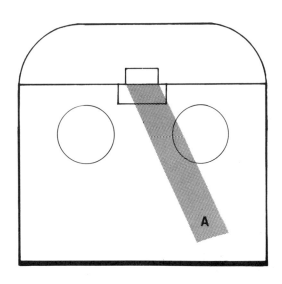

ROBERT PICARD

Yrs. of NHL service: 11
Born: Montreal, Quebec, Canada; May 25, 1957
Position: Defenseman
Height: 6-2
Weight: 203
Uniform no.: 24
Shoots: left

Career statistics:

GP	G	A	TP	PIM
781	97	297	394	916

1987-88 statistics:

GP	G	A	TP	+/−	PIM	PP	SH	GW	GT	S	PCT
65	3	13	16	-1	103	0	1	1	0	110	2.7

LAST SEASON

Games played total was lowest in three seasons. Point total was a career low. His plus/minus led the defensive corps. Knee and back injuries (13 games with the latter) sidelined him throughout the season.

THE FINESSE GAME

Picard is a good skater, both forward and backward, though he needs work on his pivots. Picard has good acceleration up-ice and will carry the puck if the opportunity presents itself. Because of his weakness in turning, however, Picard is a good target for forecheckers. When forced, he throws blind passes around the boards.

Offensively, Picard is a good passer and can spot the open man, though he has no better than average anticipation skills. Still, he sees the ice and can make use of it by jumping into the openings himself or by leading a teammate with a pass.

Picard has a fairly good shot from the point and will see time on the power play because of his passing and shooting skills. He also likes to charge the net when he can.

Defensively, Picard still shows a tendency to gamble too frequently, pinching into the offensive zone too often and too deeply. Though he has the speed to recover, Picard doesn't hustle back and will also wander from his position in the defensive zone, making things difficult for his partners.

THE PHYSICAL GAME

Picard can be a pretty good hitter. He has a mean streak and that makes a good defenseman, but he doesn't hit consistently. He can hurt you when he hits, but sometimes is left checking air because he is so un-subtle.

He has good, not great, strength and can be muscled off the puck by the opposition. Though he hits hard, Picard also does a lot of pushing and shoving and he would be better served by increased upper body strength.

THE INTANGIBLES

What you see here is what you get. Picard is a comfortable player and that's reflected in his intensity level and consistency — which are questionable at best — and his desire and work ethic (which are frequently worse than questionable). He too may fall victim to the young defensemen the Nords are trying to introduce to the NHL.

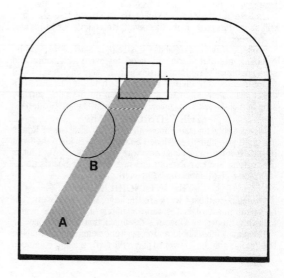

NORMAND ROCHEFORT

Yrs. of NHL service: 8
Born: Trois-Rivieres, Quebec, Canada; January 28, 1961
Position: Defenseman
Height: 6-1
Weight: 200
Uniform no.: 5
Shoots: left

Career statistics:

GP	G	A	TP	PIM
480	32	104	136	452

1987-88 statistics:

GP	G	A	TP	+/–	PIM	PP	SH	GW	GT	S	PCT
46	3	10	13	-2	49	0	1	0	0	70	4.3

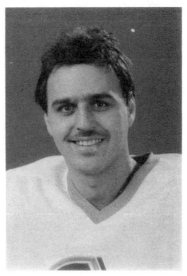

LAST SEASON

Games played total was second lowest of Rochefort's career (he missed 12 games with a back injury, two with a foot injury, and significant time from mid to late season with a knee injury). His minus 2 rating was second best among Nord defenders.

THE FINESSE GAME

Rochefort is an excellent defensive defenseman and his mobility is the reason. He's a good skater, both forward and backward and he is agile on his skates, so he moves well laterally, too. His skating and excellent positional play means that Rochefort is rarely beaten one-on-one.

He steers the play wide excellently and once he takes the opposition off the puck (his good foot speed helps him close the gap on the puckcarrier), Normand has ability to make a quick breakout pass.

Normand sees the ice well, and he plays two-on-ones and three-on-twos well because of his vision and his ability to anticipate the cross-ice pass. He passes well because of that vision and his good hands. Though he doesn't usually rush the puck from his own zone, Rochefort's skills are such that he could do so safely if necessary.

Normand is not a goal scorer, so anything he gets will have to be on shots from the point.

THE PHYSICAL GAME

Rochefort is a good and aggressive player. He hits frequently and well and can rub out a forward along the boards. Rochefort is very strong and very tough in front of his net.

He can out-muscle forwards for the puck along the boards or in the corners, or he can hold them out of the play when necessary. Rochefort is good at shielding the puck with his body in the corners and he will sacrifice his body to block shots.

THE INTANGIBLES

After years of his acknowledged leadership on the blue line, years of being Quebec's best defenseman, Rochefort's time in a Nordique uniform is coming to an end. An influx of younger talent, combined with Rochefort's propensity for injury (he's played just 142 of 240 possible games over the past three seasons — that equals one whole season plus 18 games missed) has put him on the block.

Even so, he performs steadily and well game in and out in a performance that is always under-rated. He is a hard worker and a team leader because of that professional attitude.

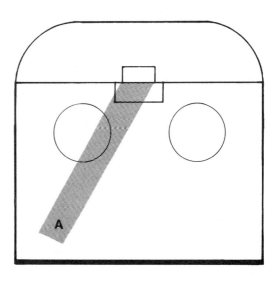

ANTON STASTNY

Yrs. of NHL service: 8
Born: Bratislava, Czechoslovakia; August 5, 1959
Position: Left wing
Height: 6-0
Weight: 185
Uniform no.: 20
Shoots: left

Career statistics:

GP	G	A	TP	PIM
595	245	354	599	138

1987-88 statistics:

GP	G	A	TP	+/-	PIM	PP	SH	GW	GT	S	PCT
69	27	45	72	-9	14	15	0	4	0	177	15.7

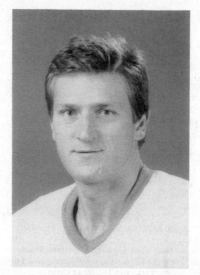

LAST SEASON

Games played total tied second lowest of his career (he missed four games with a sprained knee). He finished third on the club in scoring and power play goals and his PIM total was the lowest among fulltime players.

THE FINESSE GAME

Unlike brother Peter, Anton is not an exceptional skater. He possesses neither great speed nor quickness, and he is not particularly agile.

What makes Anton go is his smarts, his ability to get into scoring position. He is very good without the puck and very creative in the offensive zone, moving to and fro to create holes or getting into the openings because of his vision and anticipation.

He has good puckhandling skills, carrying and passing it well so as to either take advantage of the openings himself or exploit them for a teammate with a good pass. He can lead teammates into the clear, and Anton also has good enough hands to pass successfully in traffic situations.

Stastny likes to work around the net and he sweeps through the crease and circles the cage constantly in hopes of either 1) a loose puck or 2) confusing the defense and getting it to chase him — thus opening holes. He'll get many of his goals because of this, because his hands are good enough to score from in tight. Anton also has a good wrist shot from farther out.

Again unlike his brother, Anton is an average defensive player, attentive to his check along the wing though not very strong positionally in his own end.

THE PHYSICAL GAME

Anton plays an almost 100-percent passive physical game. He will accept being hit to make his plays, but he is not an initiator by any means. When he does bump he is not a punishing hitter and, since he operates mostly in the open ice, has almost no board game.

That's not to say he can't work there when he has to. Stastny has good balance on his skates and that allows him to take hits and keep working without falling to the ice.

He can take the puck off the boards in one motion and make a play with it because of his hands, or he can reach into a crowd and extricate the puck because of hand and wrist strength.

THE INTANGIBLES

Anton is a fine NHLer in terms of skills, though he lacks the innate talent brother Peter has. What Anton brings to the game that Peter does not is a more consistent effort from game to game and at both ends of the ice.

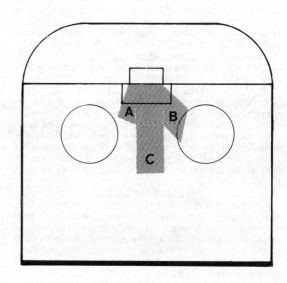

PETER STASTNY

Yrs. of NHL service: 7
Born: Bratislava, Czechoslovakia; September 18, 1956
Position: Center
Height: 6-1
Weight: 200
Uniform no.: 26
Shoots: left

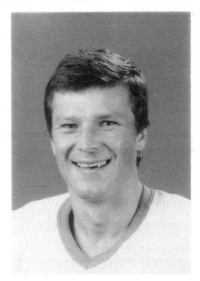

Career statistics:

GP	G	A	TP	PIM
603	321	579	900	546

1987-88 statistics:

GP	G	A	TP	+/−	PIM	PP	SH	GW	GT	S	PCT
76	46	65	111	2	69	20	0	2	1	199	23.1

LAST SEASON

Stastny regained his 100-point plateau after a year's absence from that height, finishing sixth overall in NHL scoring. He led Quebec in scoring, assists and shooting percentage, was second in goals and power play goals and third in SOG total. Goal total was highest in four seasons, PIM total highest in three. He was one of just four regulars to finish with a plus rating, and Stastny was fourth of the quartet.

THE FINESSE GAME

Eight years of top-level NHL play and Peter shows no signs of slowing down. He is a fantastic skater with great balance and exceptional quickness and agility. While he doesn't have rink-length speed, he can turn on the jets to dart past a defender. His one-step quickness is probably the best part of his skating skills, allowing him to swoop into openings and snare loose pucks. Since he works in traffic, Peter's balance allows him make his plays while being checked.

Stastny complements his skating with excellent vision, hockey sense and stickhandling ability to become a superb playmaker. Peter's vision reveals the entire ice surface, and his anticipation and sense show him the soon-to-be-openings. He is excellent at using his teammates because of these skills.

He combines his good hands with his hockey sense to skim passes to those openings and lead his teammates, or to stickhandle his way into the opening for a shot himself; he is one of the NHL's best puckhandlers on the backhand. He and brother Anton run a play of such simplicity — and run it so often — that it should never work, yet after eight years they're still clicking: Peter will fake a shot and slide a pass to Anton cutting behind the defense — and vice versa — whenever the opportunity exists.

Peter uses an accurate wrist shot almost exclusively, and he's going to get as near to the net as he can before shooting. Like Michel Goulet, Stastny is very effective on the power play because of the open ice afforded him.

His high plus/minus figure is more (but not completely) a result of his offensive play. Peter plays perfunctory defense, often being the last man back and the first man out of the Quebec zone.

THE PHYSICAL GAME

Stastny is not a physical player and doesn't often use his body to check — unless hitting someone smaller than he. He doesn't like a hitting game, but will accept hits to make his plays, and he easily fits the European stereotype regarding his stick. He carries it way too high way too often, and will slash and hook with abandon.

THE INTANGIBLES

Offensively he has few peers. Stastny is consistent, a world class player and one of the NHL's top centers. But he is not a leader, and his intensity and dedication to success are questionable at best. His heart and desire don't match up to his offensive talents, and there's little reason to expect a change after eight NHL seasons.

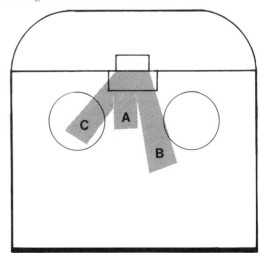

ST. LOUIS BLUES

LINE COMBINATIONS
GINO CAVALLINI-RICK MEAGHER-HERB RAGLAN
TONY MCKEGNEY-BERNIE FEDERKO-MARK HUNTER
-TONY HRKAC-TODD EWEN
-DOUG GILMOUR-BRETT HULL

DEFENSE PAIRINGS
BRIAN BENNING-ROBERT NORDMARK
PAUL CAVALLINI-GASTON GINGRAS
TIM BOTHWELL-

GOALTENDERS
GREG MILLEN

OTHER PLAYERS
STEVE BOZEK — Left wing/right wing
JOCELYN LEMIUEX — Left wing
GREG PASLAWSKI — Right wing
GORDIE ROBERTS — Defenseman

POWER PLAY

FIRST UNIT:
TONY MCKEGNEY-BERNIE FEDERKO-MARK HUNTER
GASTON GINGRAS-BRIAN BENNING

FEDERKO sets up behind net and works the puck around the perimeter with the forwards and point men, all to set up point shots. MCKEGNEY and HUNTER crash net for rebounds. If he can isolate them, FEDERKO will feed one of the forwards inside; that's a spinoff of the perimeter passing. FEDERKO will carry the puck into the zone if he can.

DOUG GILMOUR and TONY HRKAC will see power play time (as will BRETT HULL), with another forward. GILMOUR sets up along the left wing boards and HRKAC gets into the mid-slot between the forward and defense penalty killers. HULL will set up at the right point. ROBERT NORDMARK is generally the other point man.

Last season the Blues power play was FAIR, scoring 82 goals in 413 opportunities (19.9 percent, 12th overall). The Blues allowed the fewest shorthanded goals against last year.

PENALTY KILLING

FIRST UNIT:
RICK MEAGHER-DOUG GILMOUR
TIM BOTHWELL-BRIAN BENNING

SECOND UNIT:
TONY MCKEGNEY-TONY HRKAC
PAUL CAVALLINI-GORDIE ROBERTS

The Blues use a diamond formation on the first unit, with MEAGHER as point man. He and GILMOUR play the first minute and last 30 seconds of the penalty. The second unit uses a box, and both units wait for offensive breakdowns rather than forcing the puck.

Last season the Blues penalty killing was FAIR, allowing 83 goals in 402 shorthanded situations (79.4 percent, 12th overall).

CRUCIAL FACEOFFS
GILMOUR will get the call for these.

BRIAN BENNING

Yrs. of NHL service: 2
Born: Edmonton, Alta., Canada; June 10, 1966
Position: Defenseman
Height: 6-1
Weight: 185
Uniform no.: 2
Shoots: left

Career statistics:

GP	G	A	TP	PIM
159	21	67	88	217

1987-88 statistics:

GP	G	A	TP	+/−	PIM	PP	SH	GW	GT	S	PCT
77	8	29	37	-5	107	5	0	5	0	130	6.2

LAST SEASON

Games played total and all point marks fell in Benning's second full season. He led the Blues defensemen in scoring and power play goals, and led the club in game winners.

THE FINESSE GAME

It might not have been the sophomore jinx, but there's no question that Benning's second year was nowhere near as dynamic as his rookie season. He remains a very talented finesse player and his skating is his best physical talent. He has excellent balance and agility, which makes him very effective laterally, and he also has good speed and acceleration. Brian makes his speed more effective by moderating his pace, and he saves a burst for use in getting around the defender at the offensive blue line.

Brian likes to carry the puck from the Blues' end and up-ice, and he'll pull up to pass when he crosses the offensive blue line. He carries the puck very well at all speeds, and he complements his good stickhandling with good-to-very good (and could be excellent) ice vision.

His skills become even more effective because Benning actively looks to use his teammates; even though he has the talent for it, Benning has avoided the bad habit of becoming a one-on-one player. His vision and anticipation opens up the Blues' offense. And even when he hasn't started the plays, Brian jumps into the offense in the opposing end. He can hit the holes himself, or lead teammates to them with passes.

While he can be a good scorer, he doesn't have exceptional goal scoring ability. Most of his goals will come from the point, but he'll cheat to the faceoff circle if there's an opening.

He plays fairly well positionally in his own zone, but Brian definitely cheats because of his skating (the League's better skater can take advantage of that cheating to force Brian to take penalties in order to stop them). He generally knows his angle steers the opposition wide of the net, and then shows patience in moving the puck to his forwards.

THE PHYSICAL GAME

Brian has good size and strength and he's not afraid to combine a physical game with his finesse one. He gets into the corner and mucks around, but his taking the body is more like pushing and shoving than it is hitting.

Importantly, he'll initiate contact. His balance and hand skills make that contact more effective because they allow him to make plays away from the boards after hitting. The best part of his physical game is that he not only takes his hits to make plays, but he makes the plays after taking hits.

413

THE INTANGIBLES

Benning is unquestionably the Blues' best defenseman. His problem last year had more to do with his work ethic than a jinx. Things went well for him in his freshman season, so Benning assumed he wouldn't have to work hard in sophomore season — that the game would go well once again.

That was not the case, as his five points in his first 17 games (1g-4a) demonstrated.

Benning learned a lot from Rob Ramage when the latter was a Blue. It remains to be seen if he learned from Ramage's work ethic. The Blues would certainly hope he has, because he is a key to any future success they'll have.

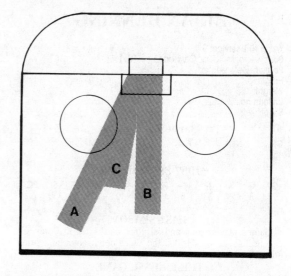

TIM BOTHWELL

Yrs. of NHL service: 8
Born: Vancouver, B.C., Canada; May 6, 1955
Position: Defenseman
Height: 6-1
Weight: 190
Uniform no.: 6
Shoots: left

Career statistics:

GP	G	A	TP	PIM
480	28	93	121	368

1987-88 statistics:

GP	G	A	TP	+/−	PIM	PP	SH	GW	GT	S	PCT
78	6	13	19	6	76	0	0	1	0	88	6.8

LAST SEASON

Games played total was second highest in career. Goal total matched career high and PIM total was career high. Plus/minus rating was second highest among defensemen, fourth highest among club's full time players.

THE FINESSE GAME

Bothwell makes the most of limited talent. He's no better than average as a skater, maybe a cut below that. He has no speed or quickness and little agility — in all directions — and so will not be seen rushing the puck or joining the attack as a fourth defender. He will do little offensively. Once in a very great while he will shoot the puck, and even more rarely he'll slide to the top of the faceoff circle to snare a loose puck.

In a way that's good, because Tom recognizes his shortcomings and avoids them. He doesn't over-extend his game; instead, he just sticks to what he can do best, which is play steady defense.

He has to respect that skating of almost every opponent because almost every opponent skates better than he does. Bothwell counters by playing a strong defensive angle game to force the play wide of the net.

From there he'll move the puck up to the forwards, and he generally makes good decisions.

THE PHYSICAL GAME

As in his finesse game, Bothwell does little to shine in the physical game. He's not afraid of anyone, however, and he does bump and take the body. But none of his actions are spectacular.

Tim uses his reach to poke check the puck effectively. He will also sacrifice his body by blocking shots, if he can get into position to do so.

THE INTANGIBLES

Steady is the word that best describes Bothwell, perhaps the only word to describe his performances. He is an average player and a great worker who always gives everything he has. He never makes the great plays, but he very seldom makes the bad ones. In fact, he deserves a lot of credit for being so steady so long.

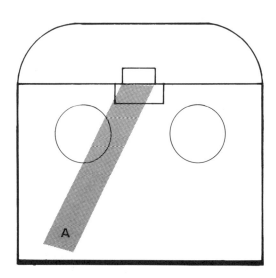

STEVE BOZEK

Yrs. of NHL service: 6
Born: Kelowna, B.C., Canada; November 26, 1960
Position: Left wing
Height: 5-11
Weight: 180
Uniform no.: 26
Shoots: left

Career statistics:

GP	G	A	TP	PIM
392	110	115	225	164

1987-88 statistics:

GP	G	A	TP	+/−	PIM	PP	SH	GW	GT	S	PCT
33	3	7	10	-5	14	0	1	0	0	43	7.0

LAST SEASON

Bozek and Brett Hull were traded by Calgary to St. Louis for Rob Ramage and Rick Wamsley. Recurring knee injuries sidelined him for 20 games and he put up the lowest numbers of his career.

THE FINESSE GAME

Bozek is a very quick skater with exceptional speed. He accelerates well and is also very quick in any direction and has good balance on his skates, allowing him to change direction and move laterally well.

He uses that skill when on the penalty killing unit, where he is a definite threat for the short-handed goal. Additionally, that speed and quickness is a staple of Bozek's role-playing defensive game, a role that he fills very well.

As a goal scorer, Bozek isn't. He plays the game at 100 plies per hour, gets 100 scoring chances and can't score because his hands are terrible. Steve's not very clever around the net and doesn't have the strength to blow the puck past anyone from a distance. He will pick up rebound and junk goals to the tune of 20 goals a year and he'll have to be in close proximity of the net to do so. One reason why Bozek doesn't score more — excepting his defensive role — is that he puts in bad shooting angles.

Bozek can be a good passer, but he doesn't see the ice very well and makes many of his plays with his head down, so he can't be said to use his teammates any better than averagely. Another thing to remember is that Bozek's hands aren't as skilled as his feet, and his hands become less effective the faster he goes.

He does, however, use his smarts as a defensive forward and is able to check not only because of his speed, but also because of his understanding of the action around him.

THE PHYSICAL GAME

Though not predominantly a physical player, Bozek is very strong for his size. This helps him in his checking role when fighting for the puck, but he won't knock anyone into the middle of next week.

Steve is also an exceptionally conditioned athlete, and he works on some phase of conditioning everyday.

THE INTANGIBLES

Bozek has a great attitude, demonstrated by the fact that he doesn't complain when he doesn't play, and he performs well when given the chance. He could score 25 goals, but is not often used in scoring situations because of his checking proficiency. Just ask Detroit's Petr Klima about Bozek. Bozek checked Klima to a standstill in Game 6 of the Norris Division championships.

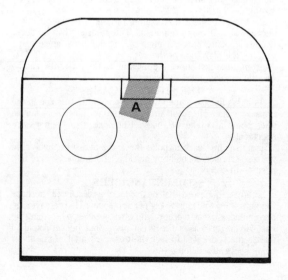

416

GINO CAVALLINI

Yrs. of NHL service: 4
Born: Toronto, Ontario, Canada; November 24, 1962
Position: Left wing
Height: 6-0
Weight: 210
Uniform no.: 17
Shoots: left

Career statistics:

GP	G	A	TP	PIM
228	52	65	117	192

1987-88 statistics:

GP	G	A	TP	+/–	PIM	PP	SH	GW	GT	S	PCT
64	15	17	32	-4	62	2	1	3	0	131	11.5

LAST SEASON

Games played mark and all point totals fell last season. PIM total was a career high. He missed 17 games with a broken hand.

THE FINESSE GAME

Cavallini's finesse skills have improved enough for him to be the Blues' second line left wing. The continuing improvement in his foot speed has made Cavallini quick enough to be a good forechecker, probably the key to the Blues forechecking because of his physical play. He has greater agility, balance and speed than ever before.

He'll use that new-and-improved skating ability in conjunction with his physical play to net 15-20 goals a season by banging loose pucks past the goaltender.

Gino isn't a playmaker, lacking both the hands and the imagination, and he isn't going to stickhandle around the opposition for scores either.

THE PHYSICAL GAME

Cavallini is built like a house and he hits like a wrecking ball. No one on the St. Louis squad hits harder than he does, and Gino keys the Blues forechecking by bashing the enemy defensemen. He really bruises them when forechecking and sets the stage for any further St. Louis incursions.

Cavallini's punishing checks also take the enemy forwards off the puck along the boards, but Gino isn't going to be able to make the play from the boards; a teammate will have to pick up the puck.

He makes his checking more effective by hitting smartly and not taking penalties.

THE INTANGIBLES

Gino is the perfect kind of player to play behind a high scoring wing, the perfect counter punch. He gives everything he has at all times and his contributions are greater than just the numbers he puts up on the scoreboard.

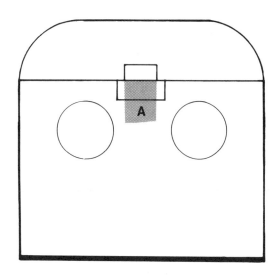

PAUL CAVALLINI

Yrs. of NHL service: 1
Born: Toronto, Ontario, Canada; October 13, 1965
Position: Defenseman
Height: 6-1
Weight: 202
Uniform no.: 14
Shoots: left

Career statistics:

GP	G	A	TP	PIM
78	6	12	18	160

1987-88 statistics:

GP	G	A	TP	+/−	PIM	PP	SH	GW	GT	S	PCT
72	6	10	16	7	152	1	0	1	0	71	8.5

LAST SEASON

Cavallini was traded by Washington to St. Louis in mid-December. He led the defense in PIM (all totals were career highs) and plus/minus, finishing third among the club's regulars in the latter category.

THE FINESSE GAME

What older brother Gino's got in the size department, Paul picked up in the finesse area. Paul has very good acceleration in his skating and, in fact, he uses it a little too well offensively — he's a little more offensive-minded than the Blues would like.

Cavallini shows some good instincts in his puck movement, and his regular ice time in St. Louis has greatly helped him acclimate himself to the speed of the NHL game. Where previously he had trouble moving the puck to the forwards, because he wasn't seeing the game well enough, Paul is now much better in getting the puck up-ice.

He will carry it ocassionally, having tempered some of those offensive urges, and Cavallini can also contrbute from the offensive blue line by pinching in to keep the play in the opposing zone. He also has a good shot from the blue line, and will slide to the faceoff circle if possible.

He uses his skating in his defensive game and has a tendency to be hypnotized by the puck. In general, he plays a steady game in forcing the enemy wide of the St. Louis goal, and he certainly has the ability to turn then play around.

THE PHYSICAL GAME

As we said, the bulk of the physical ability went to Gino, but that doesn't make Paul a lightweight. He takes the body well in the defensive zone and is very willing to get involved in the traffic areas.

Paul just doesn't hit as hard as his brother does.

THE INTANGIBLES

Cavallini is already a steady defenseman (Washington may have given up on him too soon) and has the potential to get better and better; a good indication is his playoff performance, where he tied with Brian Benning for the team's lead in points but had a plus 5 rating (as opposed to Benning's minus 7).

Paul plays with great enthusiasm for the game and is well-liked by his teammates.

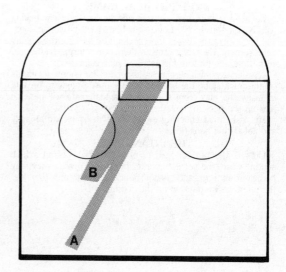

TODD EWEN

Yrs. of NHL service: 1
Born: Saskatoon, Sask., Canada; March 26, 1966
Position: Right wing
Height: 6-2
Weight: 215
Uniform no.: 21
Shoots: right

Career statistics:

GP	G	A	TP	PIM
87	6	2	8	311

1987-88 statistics:

GP	G	A	TP	+/−	PIM	PP	SH	GW	GT	S	PCT
64	4	2	6	-5	227	0	0	0	0	38	10.5

LAST SEASON

Ewen's first full NHL campaign. All numbers were career highs, and he led the club in PIM.

THE FINESSE GAME

There isn't one.

Ewen doesn't have a lot of skating skill, except for strength on his feet. He's tough to move off the puck should he have it, which makes him effective in front of the net. But he's only effective in front of the net if the goaltender's having coffee and the defensemen are discussing the weather.

In other words, Ewen needs plenty of time and plenty of space to make any kind of play, and he certainly won't finesse the puck into a small opening. Anything he gets will have to be because of brute strength.

He wanders from his position, but that's not surprising because he has the turning radius of a battleship. Thus, there are going to be defensive lapses along his wing.

THE PHYSICAL GAME

Ewen is big and tough. How tough? How about he's the only guy in the NHL to beat Bob Probert in a fight?

That's tough. Todd is a big banger, if he can catch anyone. His strength is mitigated by his lack of skating skill. But that's fine, because Ewen isn't in the NHL to skate, he's here to fight.

THE INTANGIBLES

As long as the NHL game stays the way it is presently constituted, there will always be a need for a Todd Ewen. There is little he brings to the Blues but his fists, but in today's game you've got to have him.

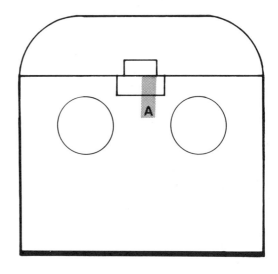

BERNIE FEDERKO

Yrs. of NHL service: 12
Born: Foam Lake, Sask., Canada; May 12, 1956
Position: Center
Height: 6-0
Weight: 185
Uniform no.: 24
Shoots: left

Career statistics:

GP	G	A	TP	PIM
861	379	676	1,006	409

1987-88 statistics:

GP	G	A	TP	+/−	PIM	PP	SH	GW	GT	S	PCT
79	20	69	89	-12	52	9	0	2	1	119	16.8

LAST SEASON

Games played total tied second highest of career, accomplished twice before. Assist total was highest in three seasons. He led the club in scoring and assists. He was fourth in power play goals, third in shooting percentage. PIM total was highest in six seasons, second highest of career. His plus/minus rating was third worst among regulars.

THE FINESSE GAME

The mental aspect of the game has always been the power behind Federko's throne as the Blues' scoring king. He has outstanding hockey sense and anticipation, and those abilities allow him to use his teammates as well as anyone in the league. Federko sees the ice excellently and one simple reason for his success as a playmaker has to do with his setting up behind the net, where he can see the entire offensive picture.

Federko is very dangerous if he gains the blue line because of his ability to immediately set up plays. He'll lead his teammates to the openings with passes that could thread needles, and he's doubly dangerous because he makes his plays quickly and without doubt. The only way to stop that is to cover his linemates. These skills make him a natural for the power play, where the open ice makes Federko's game that much more effective.

Surprisingly, Federko is not a great skater. He is neither exceptionally fast nor agile on his feet, though he obviously has the ability to get where he is going. He has good balance and works well in crowds because of it, able to make plays almost regardless of body position.

His days of 30-35 goals seem to be past, especially since he is so unselfish a player. If he has a choice, Bernie's going to pass the puck. He'll pick up loose pucks around the net for his goals, and his sensitive hands are ideal for slot scoring.

He backchecks well and helps his defense.

THE PHYSICAL GAME

Federko has never been a physical player, but he has always taken hits in order to make his plays. He willingly suffers the abuse necessary in front of the net, and he'll do some bumping in the corners to force loose pucks.

THE INTANGIBLES

Though he was 83 points away — and coming off a 72-point season — we told you Federko would score his 1,000th point this year. Like a fine wine Bernie is aging nicely, and the end of the road is coming for him. Tony Hrkac will probably get some of Federko's ice time, and it'll be interesting to see how Bernie handles both that and new coach Brian Sutter. After all, having a former teammate as your coach isn't always an easy thing to swallow.

Federko is — not "is part of," but *is* — hockey history in St. Louis, keeping tradition in the franchise in much the same way the Plagers have. He'll most likely accept any changes that occur the same way he's played for a dozen years: Like a true professional.

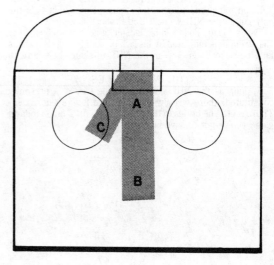

DOUG GILMOUR

Yrs. of NHL service: 5
Born: Kingston, Ontario, Canada; June 25, 1963
Position: Center
Height: 5-11
Weight: 165
Uniform no.: 9
Shoots: left

Career statistics:

GP	G	A	TP	PIM
384	149	205	354	264

1987-88 statistics:

GP	G	A	TP	+/−	PIM	PP	SH	GW	GT	S	PCT
72	36	50	86	-13	59	19	2	4	1	163	22.1

LAST SEASON

Games played total was a career low, but all point totals were second best of his career. He finished second on the club in goals, assists, points and game winners, first in power play goals and shooting percentage. His plus/minus rating was second worst among regulars. He missed seven games with a concussion.

THE FINESSE GAME

There is almost nothing that Gilmour can't do, so talented is he. His anticipation and vision unite to create extraordinary hockey sense that Gilmour uses at both ends of the ice.

In the offensive zone he not only sees openings but uses his sense to create them — he is excellent without the puck — and that's something only the best players can do. In the defensive zone he uses that anticipation and vision to understand the opposition's plays and to break them up. Lest we forget, he spent the first two years of his NHL career bottled up as a checker.

The skill that best allows Doug to take advantage of his smarts is his skating. Gilmour looks unspectacular but he's a very good skater, not overly fast but equipped with a one-step quickness that lets him dart in and out of traffic and change direction quickly. He is very nimble on his feet — even though he won't out-race anyone — and is exceptionally dangerous within 10-feet of any loose puck. Again, he can apply that skill both offensively and defensively.

Doug uses his one-step quickness to get to the openings — he likes to work from the left wing side of the ice (because he shoots lefty) — so he'll attack from there and do damage with opportunistic goals, hence his power play success.

He also uses that skill to get into the clear to make and receive passes. He is a good stick handler and can handle the puck at all speeds. He uses his teammates very well, and shows excellent creativity on the ice.

He uses his skating defensively to close passing lanes, cut off skating lanes and intercept passes.

THE PHYSICAL GAME

Part of the anything Gilmour can do is play aggressively. He is willing to do whatever is needed to make his plays — offensively or defensively — and he'll go to the corner to hit or to the front of the net and get batted around when necessary.

He should learn to avoid some of that traffic because his stature can't handle it, and he'll become fatigued or injured (note last season's concussion as an example). As he gets older it will be more difficult for him to come back from those aches and pains.

His eye/hand coordination and arm and wrist strength make him a good faceoff man.

THE INTANGIBLES

His goal distribution was questionable last year, what with over half his goals coming on the power play (just 17 ESGs). Even worse, in his last 19 games Gilmour scored just 10 goals — and just three of those came at even strength. Doug is too good a player for off-kilter numbers like that.

Gilmour had a tough time with his confidence last year as he struggled to recreate the 100-point season he enjoyed in 1986-87. His confidence flagged badly under the expectations placed on him (especially because he wasn't scoring goals the way he though he should), but he found support in Wayne Cashman, assistant coach of the New York Rangers.

Cashman, a childhood friend of Doug's dad, helped Gilmour regain his confidence and put expectations out of his mind. Gilmour recovered by season's end (he played at a 94-point season pace). For this year Gilmour has to clear his mind and just do what he does best — which is play hockey better than 90 percent of the other NHLers.

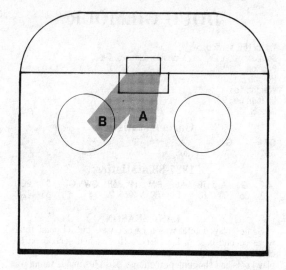

GASTON GINGRAS

Yrs. of NHL service: 10
Born: Temiscaming, Quebec, Canada; February 13, 1959
Position: Defenseman
Height: 6-0
Weight: 191
Uniform no.: 23
Shoots: left

Career statistics:

GP	G	A	TP	PIM
424	58	164	222	153

1987-88 statistics:

GP	G	A	TP	+/−	PIM	PP	SH	GW	GT	S	PCT
70	7	23	30	1	18	3	0	0	0	133	5.3

LAST SEASON

Games played total was a career high, assist total third highest of his career. He was traded from the Canadiens to the Blues in exchange for Larry Trader early in the campaign. He was the team's second leading scorer among defensemen, and he led the blue line corps in shots on goal.

THE FINESSE GAME

Gingras has the quickest feet in hockey. He doesn't necessarily move to the puck or toward his man faster than anyone else (obviously there is more to quickness than just feet), but he moves his feet faster than anyone else in the NHL.

He is a good skater and has some speed heading up-ice. Gingras is a puck carrying defenseman, and he does that well. He won't pass the puck if he can help it, and he'll certainly join the play as a fourth attacker.

Gaston has good vision of the offensive zone, one reason why he plays the power play, and because he handles the puck well in front of him, can pass well to his teammates and has a good sense of anticipation, Gingras is a force at the offensive blue line.

Gingras does try to force many plays, both offensively and defensively, and will turn the puck over by sending it into traffic, or by passing with his head down. While looking for an opening to charge out from, he often holds the puck too long in his own zone, allowing the forecheckers to close in. He must learn to move the puck faster in his own zone.

Gingras has a great shot from the point and he will slide to the middle of the blue line or take a few steps in if the opportunity presents itself.

He is weak defensively, primarily because of lack of effort. He will be caught in the offensive zone, and quick forwards can take advantage of his proclivity to pinch into the zone by scooting around him at the point. When he is back,, Gingras does not play his defensive angles well, and will make most of his plays by getting to the puck instead of forcing the play wide.

THE PHYSICAL GAME

Because he is not strong, Gingras is not a very physical player. He has difficulty holding his man out along the boards or controlling him in front of the net, and is very often out-muscled in the confrontations in the corner.

He needs to gain more upper body strength.

THE INTANGIBLES

Gingras is not a great defenseman, but one who can fill certain areas — as in the power play. He didn't start well in St. Louis but after he moved his family from Montreal he improved rapidly, so much so that by the end of the season he and defensive partner Paul Cavallini were St. Louis' best defensive duo.

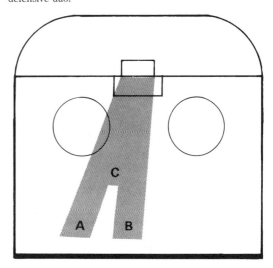

TONY HRKAC

Yrs. of NHL service: 1
Born: Thunder Bay, Ontario, Canada; July 7, 1966
Position: Center
Height: 5-11
Weight: 165
Uniform no.: 18
Shoots: left

Career statisics:

GP	G	A	TP	+/−	PIM	PP	SH	GW	GT	S	PCT
67	11	37	48	5	22	2	1	3	0	86	12.8

LAST SEASON

Hrkac, who played three 1986-87 playoff games, made his Blues regular season debut. He finished fourth on the club in assists and fourth (among regulars) in plus/minus. He finished fifth among the League's rookie scorers and third in assists. He missed five games with a shoulder injury, six games with a lacerated ankle.

THE FINESSE GAME

Hrkac has excellent finesse potential, especially in his skating and playmaking skills. He is very quick because of his excellent foot speed, but he also has the power in his stride to accelerate well and create rink-length speed.

Tony combines his skating with his super anticipation, vision and hockey sense to not only get to the openings but to create them as well. He reads plays and sets up his wingers very well and should only improve with further NHL experience. He likes the drop pass and the give and go, and uses both to A) set up teammates and B) exploit his own quickness for jumping into holes or creating them with his quickness.

He has the hand skills to be an above average NHL playmaker, but he should also learn to balance his selflessness with selfishness and take greater advantage of his speed by going to the net when he can. He shoots from outside the congestion (because he's set up a teammate closer to the net), but will also net a few goals because of his quickness and smarts around the net.

The Blues kept his offensive ability under wraps last season, wanting Hrkac to watch his defensive zone play, and Hrkac showed well defensively. He backchecked consistently and went to the traffic areas to free the puck and move it from the St. Louis zone.

THE PHYSICAL GAME

Size is going to be a concern here. There is a difference between willing and able, and while Tony is willing to do the dirty work along the boards (as demonstrated by his defensive play) he may not be able to accomplish much of anything from there because of his size — or, to be more precise, his lack of it.

Time will tell whether or not Hrkac has the extraordinary finesse skills necessary to play in what has become a huge man's game, for it's skills of that level that are necessary to work 1-on-1 against bigger players.

THE INTANGIBLES

If he can stay healthy, he has the ability to be a tremendous player for a small kid. His offense will gradually be released, maybe as early as this season, for the Blues want to score more goals and play more entertaining (and easier to sell) hockey.

Tony has a good attitude and better poise for a youngster in the NHL, very calm and loose and unaffected by the pressure. He works hard but he doesn't get wound up.

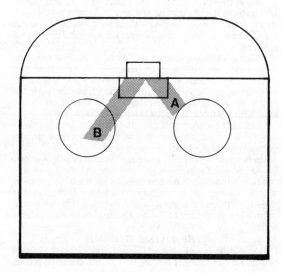

BRETT HULL

Yrs. of NHL service: 1
Born: Bellevile, Ontario, Canada; August 9, 1964
Position: Right wing
Height: 5-11
Weight: 190
Uniform no.: 16
Shoots: right

Career statistics:

GP	G	A	TP	PIM
70	33	32	65	16

1987-88 statistics:

GP	G	A	TP	+/−	PIM	PP	SH	GW	GT	S	PCT
65	32	32	64	14	16	6	0	3	0	211	15.2

LAST SEASON

Hull's first full NHL season. He was traded from the Flames to the Blues along with Steve Bozek for Rob Ramage and Rick Wamsley. He finished third in League-wide rookie scoring, third in goals and fourth in assists. He led rookies in first goals, was second in shots on goal and third in plus/minus. He finished third on the Blues in goals, second in shots on goals and first in plus/minus. He also had the lowest PIM total of any Blues regular.

THE FINESSE GAME

The first thing anyone notices about Brett is his shot, so we may as well lead off with it. To say it duplicates that of his father would be folly, but let's just say it's not far off. Hull loves to glide down the right side (notice we didn't say jet — we'll discuss that later) and blast away.

He's already predictable in where he goes with that shot: from the right wing and against righthanded goaltenders (those who hold the stick in their right hands), Brett is going to go high stickside every time. *EVERY* time. He believes himself to be less accurate to the glove side, but with the velocity he gets on his shot he could shave some off and become more accurate.

Hull also has excellent snap and wrist shots, so he's not just a one-hit wonder. In close, when he can't get the big blast off, he cocks his wrists and delivers a hard and fast shot. The problem is, he's hard even in close.

Skating is the weakest part of Brett's game, so weak that he'll sit up high in the zone and wait for the puck to come to him so he has extra time to shoot. He lacks the exceptional speed that would put him the clear for his shot, and will instead have to work through checking to get his shot off.

Which is the second problem.

Brett has to realize he's no longer facing American Hockey League checkers; this is the NHL and he must keep his feet moving and drive through checks to be effective.

He is primarily a scorer, but he works hard at playing a complete game and using his teammates. He doesn't have exceptional anticipation or play reading ability and he goes to where he knows he can score rather than getting into scoring position.

He works at the defensive game by playing positionally but his slow speed afoot hurts him, especially since he's generally heading to the net in the offensive zone and then has to turn around.

THE PHYSICAL GAME

He's not a very physical player in terms of imposing himself on the opposition. He mucks along the boards but won't knock anyone out with his strength, but it is obviously his strength that keys his shot.

THE INTANGIBLES

Hull must really prove himself this year, because the expectations on him are very high. He showed fairly well in last spring's playoff, leading the Blues in goals, and that bodes well for his performance this season.

His biggest problem is his willingness to get conmfortable when things are going right, where he should be continuing his hard work to keep a streak going. He must demonstrate his willingness to work through checks — that's as much heart as it is body — and he must work to improve his finesse flaws; predictability in his shot and lack of foot speed.

Brett can be a real good player, and his future is in his own hands.

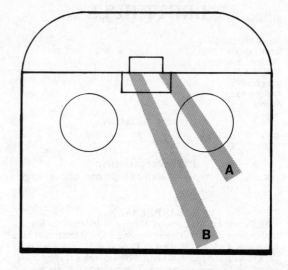

MARK HUNTER

Yrs. of NHL service: 7
Born: Petrolia, Ontario, Canada; November 12, 1962
Position: Right wing
Height: 6-1
Weight: 200
Uniform no.: 20
Shoots: right

Career statistics:

GP	G	A	TP	PIM
414	165	129	294	855

1987-88 statistics:

GP	G	A	TP	+/−	PIM	PP	SH	GW	GT	S	PCT
66	32	31	63	-6	136	14	0	0	1	164	19.5

LAST SEASON

Hunter failed to play 80 games for the seventh consecutive season, and his games played total was the lowest in four seasons. All point totals fell for the second consecutive season. He finished fifth in team scoring, fourth in goals, second in power play goals and shooting percentage. His PIM total was fourth highest among forwards. He missed at least four games with a recurring groin injury.

THE FINESSE GAME

Though he can make an impact in the finesse aspects of the game, Hunter is not a finesse player. He is a strong skater with good acceleration, but last season his skating was affected by his groin injury and it remains to be seen whether that is a chronic problem. He is not every agile and could do better in the area of balance.

He has to have a center get him the puck because Mark isn't going to razzle-dazzle his way to the net from his own zone, nor is he going to make plays coming out the corners. Because of his goal scoring success, Hunter doesn't use his teammates well, often shooting instead of passing to a more open teammate. Since he has neither the hands nor the head for passing (meaning that he neither handles the puck well nor sees the ice well — which is why he needs that unselfish center in the first place), so perhaps it's not a bad thing that Hunter shoots first and asks questions later.

His shot is the best of his finesse skills. Hunter gets great strength behind it and it will get to the net through traffic, but he'll need time to get it off. He'll chase his own rebounds and will get many goals on second effort. The best he'll do is 35 goals — maybe an honest 40, *maybe* — but no more than that. He works best from the faceoff circle for the original shot.

He's improved the level of his defensive game by back-checking more conscientiously, making better transitions from offense to defense.

THE PHYSICAL GAME

The strength of Hunter's game is his strength. He's a hard-nosed player and has to play that way to be successful. He has the strength and the size to play a dominant physical game, but could apply those assets more consistently. Mark can be very good in the corners at creating havoc because of his toughness, yet sometimes he does and sometimes he doesn't.

One area where he has improved his physical play is in the defensive zone, where he is taking the body better than ever.

THE INTANGIBLES

That groin problem is intangible number one, with his questionable durability number two. His work ethic could use some beefing up as well.

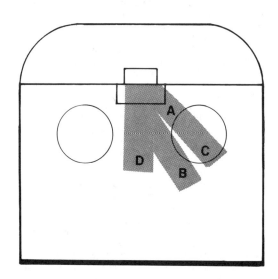

JOCELYN LEMIEUX

Yrs. of NHL service: 2
Born: Mont Laurier, Quebec, Canada; November 18, 1967
Position: Left wing
Height: 5-11
Weight: 215
Uniform no.: 16
Shoots: left

Career statistics:

GP	G	A	TP	PIM
76	11	8	18	136

1987-88 statistics:

GP	G	A	TP	+/−	PIM	PP	SH	GW	GT	S	PCT
23	1	0	1	-5	42	0	0	0	0	19	5.3

LAST SEASON

Lemieux missed most of last season with demotions and then a broken leg. He returned to play five playoff games.

THE FINESSE GAME

For a guy with a reputation as being a physical player, Lemieux demonstrated nice — and improvable — finesse skills. He skates forcefully and is well-balanced, and that helps him in his physical game, but Jocelyn also has some speed to go along with his strength.

He does not yet handle the puck well at the NHL level and, because he is more of a physical than finesse player, that development may take some time. Even so, he will probably top out at the 27-30 goal level, a la John Tonelli, the player Jocelyn admires.

Jocelyn pays attention to his defensive responsibilities and has yet to show a creative bent in the offensive zone. He gets off a strong wrist shot from within 20 feet of the net, but Lemieux hasn't demonstrated that he can create or force openings with his skating.

THE PHYSICAL GAME

This is the area of the game that is Lemieux's forte. He is big and strong and plays a very aggressive style in the offensive and neutral zones (he is too unsure of himself in his own zone to do the same).

Lemieux packs a lot of strength into his 5-11 body, and he hits often and hard. He is unafraid of either the corners or the opposition, and Lemieux isn't above using his elbows or his stick to help him gain an advantage while fighting for the puck.

His balance, as mentioned, helps him here by allowing him to remain vertical after he initiates collisions. Jocelyn's hand skills are good enough that, given time, he'll be able to make plays with the puck after banging bodies along the boards.

THE INTANGIBLES

Maturity is the key here, and it is a quality Lemieux did not demonstrate last season. Following his demotion to the International League he was emotionally wrought, but he felt misunderstood in St. Louis too, where his teammates ragged him about his haircut and his clothes. Jocelyn felt deeply hurt by both circumstances, but he eventually learned a lot from his demotion about effort and self-motivation.

Brian Sutter should work well with Lemieux in coaxing better effort from him, and if Lemieux's head is screwed on right — if he continues along the road toward playing a mature game (and if he can stay healthy) — Lemieux is one of those players who could turn this franchise around.

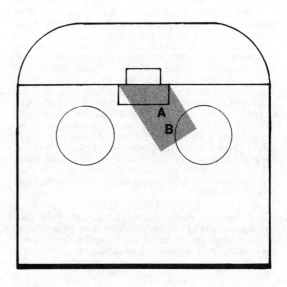

TONY MCKEGNEY

Yrs. of NHL service: 10
Born: Montreal, Quebec, Canada; February 15, 1958
Position: Left wing
Height: 6-1
Weight: 215
Uniform no.: 10
Shoots: left

Career statistics:

GP	G	A	TP	PIM
720	260	273	533	358

1987-88 statistics:

GP	G	A	TP	+/−	PIM	PP	SH	GW	GT	S	PCT
80	40	38	78	10	82	13	3	1	0	241	16.6

LAST SEASON

McKegney played all 80 games for the third time in his career and first time in seven seasons. He was the only Blue to play the entire slate. He led the team in goals with a career high mark and he finished third on the club in scoring with a career high in points and assists. He finished third in power play goals, second in shorthanded scores and first in shots on goal. He finished second on the club in plus/minus rating.

THE FINESSE GAME

Mobility and hockey sense power McKegney's game. He's a good skater with strength on his skates and a good bit of speed and acceleration because of that strong stride. His is a straight ahead speed; he's not much of a darter but he does have some agility he can use for his lateral movement. Still, he won't make anyone forget Denis Savard — or teammate Doug Gilmour for that matter.

He is also a good checker because of his skating skills and that's why he'll see penalty killing time. His breakaway speed makes him a shorthanded goal threat, and it is that speed that puts him in the clear and allows him to use his tremendous shot at even strength.

Tony complements his skating with good anticipation and vision. He has very good hockey sense at both ends of the ice, and he combines that sense with his skating to make very quick transitions in both directions.

His shot is excellent, laser-like and quickly released. It is hard and accurate, and McKegney uses it whenever possible. But even granting his proclivity for scoring, McKegney looks to use his teammates when he can; he just wants the puck when he's in shooting position.

His offensive diligence makes him a solid bet for an annual 25 goals, and that diligence extends to the defensive zone where he plays well positionally.

THE PHYSICAL GAME

Tony is a very strong player, but his physical skills will sometimes take a backseat to his finesse skills. There are times when he could be using his good strength to muscle the puck in the corners or along the boards, but he's found instead outside the scrum and waiting for the loose puck to come to him.

He can be very effective along the boards and especially in front of the net, because — once he plants himself — Tony's balance makes him very difficult to move. He'll take the rough going and return it, but he is not a dirty player.

THE INTANGIBLES

The largest intangible regarding Tony is his reputation of performing well in his first year with a team and less well in the second season, but it's hard to see where this reputation comes from. He had two 30-goal seasons with the Sabres (37 and 36 goal years) that alternated with mid-20 goal years.

When he was traded to Quebec in 1983-84 he scored 24 goals. The next season — with 12 goals in 30 games — he was traded to Minnesota, where he finished with 23 goals. He had 15 goals for the Stars in 1985-86, then in 1986-87 was traded to the Rangers and scored 29 goals for them and 30 on the season. Then last season he had 40.

So none of this supports the second year in the franchise scenario (he never had second years in Quebec and New York, for one thing). If anything, his performance in Buffalo suggests an alternate year theory, but not one rooted in franchise shift. But none of this matters, because in sports perception is reality. And it is perceived that McKegney flops in his second year with a club.

Tony is well aware of the reputation, and he wants to work against it. He's very happy in St. Louis (building a house there, as a matter of fact), and he also knows that end of his career is a lot closer than the beginning. He wants to prove the critics wrong this year.

What McKegney is is a tremendously streaky scorer. It's not that his effort changes during these streaks, but for some reason he can score all his goals within six weeks (last year he was consistent, with nine goals in the first quarter, 19 by the half, 30 at the three-quarter pole and 40 overall).

One other intangible is the health of his knees, which sometimes pain him because he's so bow-legged.

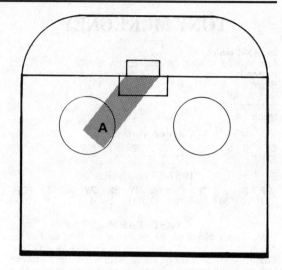

RICK MEAGHER

Yrs. of NHL service: 8
Born: Belleville, Ontario, Canada; November 1, 1953
Position: Center
Height: 5-8
Weight: 170
Uniform no.: 22
Shoots: left

Career statistics:

GP	G	A	TP	PIM
513	118	133	251	277

1987-88 statistics:

GP	G	A	TP	+/−	PIM	PP	SH	GW	GT	S	PCT
76	18	16	34	0	76	0	5	3	0	113	15.9

LAST SEASON

Games played total was lowest in three seasons, goal total tied second highest career total, assist total was lowest in four seasons. He led the club in shorthanded goals.

THE FINESSE GAME

Meagher is an excellent checker and his skating is the reason why. He has excellent one-step quickness and agility, and Rick also has good overall speed in his repertoire.

He uses that speed — and his ability to anticipate and read the plays — as an excellent penalty killer and all-around defensive forward. Meagher is a very aggressive penalty killer and the pressure he applies causes turnovers that he translates into short-handed goals, a category he led the Blues in last year.

His smarts make him an excellent positional player who plays well at both ends of the ice. His plus/minus rating is evidence enough of that. That a defensive center should be even, while his team was minus-16 is testament to his checking ability.

Meagher is the man the Blues send out for the clutch, defensive zone faceoffs. He is not really a goal-scorer, but Meagher has a good touch around the net from the slot area. He doesn't have the power to blow the puck past a goaltender from farther out, but because his speed presents him with opportunities he's going to shoot from the left faceoff circle.

THE PHYSICAL GAME

Meagher's dropped 15 pounds in the last two seasons and he's become stronger because of it. He's one of the team's best conditioned athletes, despite his advanced athletic age — 35 years old.

He uses his body well, willing and able to play a grinding game that will surprise bigger forwards and jar the puck loose. He also likes to irritate the opposition by jabbing them with his stick after the whistle.

THE INTANGIBLES

Meagher is a super-hard worker, a tremendous leader and a great influence on the club. He's also one of the best defensive forwards in hockey and should have been a Selke finalist.

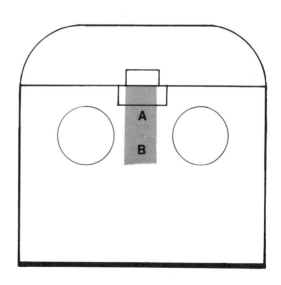

GREG MILLEN

Yrs. of NHL service: 10
Born: Toronto, Ontario, Canada; June 25, 1957
Position: Goaltender
Height: 5-9
Weight: 175
Uniform no.: 29
Catches: right

Career statistics:

GP	MINS	G	SO	AVG	A	PIM
490	28,913	1,897	10	3.93	18	68

1987-88 statisics:

GP	MINS	AVG	W	L	T	SO	GA	SA	SAPCT	PIM
48	2,854	3.51	21	19	7	1	167	1,396	.880	4

LAST SEASON

Games played total was highest in three seasons, while goals-against-average was lowest in same span. Win total tied second best total of career but last season was Millen's first winning season since his rookie year.

THE PHYSICAL GAME

Millen has matured as a goaltender and is much more of a standup goalie than he has ever been. Where he once charged from his net to challenge shooters (leaving himself vulnerable to the cross-ice pass into the empty net) Millen is much more stable in his movement. He's challenging the shooters from farther back in his net (hence the vulnerable areas at the extremes of his feet) and is squaring himself to the puck excellently.

But for all that Millen is still very acrobatic and entertaining in his saves, and frequently that flamboyance will draw a crowd reaction and inspire his teammates.

One reason he's so acrobatic is because his balance isn't as good as it could be. While he pops up and down quickly — and regains his stance fairly well — Greg's balance is flawed in his lateral movement. That means he doesn't move from post to post as well as he once did, and that's another reason for those goals inside the posts.

He is otherwise a good skater, and he'll leave the net to get the puck but he isn't handling it as he once did. Instead of firing it up-ice, Millen is now leaving it for his defense. His glove hand is good when he stands up, but since he goes to the ice on play around the net a lot of pucks elude him up high. He also hangs back on screens, another reason for pucks to fly over his hand and into the net.

Millen doesn't control rebounds off his chest protector well, leaving loose pucks floating around in front of himself.

THE MENTAL GAME

Millen is fairly tough mentally and does come back from bad goals or games. He anticipates the play well and will make many saves per season simply by anticipation, but he lacks the period-in-and-period-out concentration and mental discipline to keep his game at a higher level.

He swings back and forth between good and bad and the fact that he can play excellent games merely underlines the fact that he can keep himself playing at a higher level. Yet, after playing one game by standing on his head, his next game will be as if he has two left feet.

His attitude is good, as he approaches each game minus the nervousness that can infect a team in a domino effect. He is an old-time goalie in that he doesn't practice on game days, which takes coaches a long time to accept.

THE INTANGIBLES

Given his lack of nervousness, Millen didn't play as well as he might have after Rick Wamsley went to Calgary. When he plays at his best Millen is an above-average goaltender, and that's the result the Blues are hoping for this year. This season, in which he assumes the responsibilities of the number one goaltender, will be a good test for Millen.

ROBERT NORDMARK

Yrs. of NHL service: 1
Born: Lulea, Sweden; August 20, 1962
Position: Defenseman
Height: 6-1
Weight: 200
Uniform no.: 27
Shoots: right

Career statisics:

GP	G	A	TP	+/−	PIM	PP	SH	GW	GT	S	PCT
67	3	18	21	-6	60	2	0	0	0	78	3.8

LAST SEASON

Nordmark was St. Louis' third round choice in the 1987 Entry Draft. He missed at least two games with a recurring groin injury.

THE FINESSE GAME

Nordmark is a finesse player who also has physical abilities. He is a an excellent skater, really world class because of his mobility. He has good speed and quickness up and back and he's very agile and balanced in his turns. He has good to very good lateral movement.

His anticipation and play reading abilities are also high, and that goes for both ends of the ice. Nordmark moves the puck extremely well from his own end of the ice because his hand skills mesh with his smarts. He makes good decisions in getting the puck to his wingers. He'll also carry the puck if given the chance, and he does that smartly too. Robert won't force a play that isn't there.

He reads the offensive blue line well and can get the puck to the open man. His shot is good, but like most Europeans Nordmark is going to pass to a player in better position.

His defensive play is fairly solid, as he forces the play wide of the net with regularity.

THE PHYSICAL GAME

Nordmark is big enough, strong enough and willing enough to be a mucker in the corners, but that style is going to take its toll on him because he is not used to the pace of the NHL game. That means he'll tire both within individual contests and over the course of the season.

He sacrifices his body by blocking shots.

THE INTANGIBLES

Nordmark can be a quality NHLer, but his age mitigates against any long term development (he's already 26 years old). That doesn't mean he can't contribute; what it means is that he'll be good for four or five seasons but he doesn't have the long term value of a younger player.

He must improve his conditioning and strength so as to better adjust to the NHL pace and lifestyle.

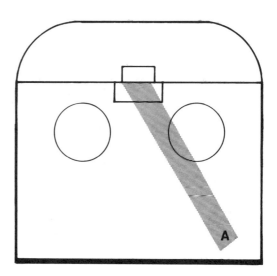

GREG PASLAWSKI

Yrs. of NHL service: 4
Born: Kindersley, Sask., Canada; August 25, 1961
Position: Right wing
Height: 5-11
Weight: 185
Uniform no.: 28
Shoots: right

Career statistics:

GP	G	A	TP	PIM
281	84	77	161	91

1987-88 statistics:

GP	G	A	TP	+/−	PIM	PP	SH	GW	GT	S	PCT
17	2	1	3	-14	4	0	0	1	0	30	6.7

LAST SEASON

Recurring back injury and subsequent surgery sidelined Paslawski until late in the season.

THE FINESSE GAME

Greg's game is based on his ability to get open, and that ability is based in his skating. He's a good skater with a nice burst of speed down the wing. He is also fairly agile, so his lateral movement is good too.

Paslawski has good vision and good anticipation on the ice, and he uses those skills to get to the openings. He exploits those holes with his speed and his shot, preferably from an opening below the faceoff circle, though he has a tendency to get too close to the net and thus tangled with the defensemen.

Greg can be a sniper and definitely has talent that could be further developed. The problem is, Paslawski waits for the holes to open, rather than forcing them open with his speed and better-than-average puck sense.

Paslawski is fairly good with the puck and does look for his teammates, but don't look for him to thread any needles with his passes. Paslawski is fairly conscientious defensively and will come back into his own zone.

THE PHYSICAL GAME

Paslawski will avoid the contact if he can, and that's another area of his game that should be developed. He has decent size but plays smaller, and is definitely not a corner or boards man. His game isn't based on a lot of strength and he likes to stay away from the high traffic areas and operate in the open ice.

THE INTANGIBLES

With his injuries, the key to Paslawski will have been this off season —how much he trains and how he gets ready for the season. The Blues need him on right wing to take some of the pressure off Mark Hunter, and if Greg plays well it will take pressure off him too.

In the past his attitude has been one that's allowed him to coast rather than driving to excel. A good start for him is crucial.

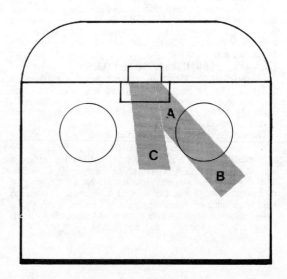

HERB RAGLAN

Yrs. of NHL service: 2
Born: Peterborough, Ontario, Canada; August 5, 1967
Position: Right wing
Height: 6-2
Weight: 200
Uniform no.: 25
Shoots: right

Career statistics:

GP	G	A	TP	PIM
142	16	25	41	354

1987-88 statistics:

GP	G	A	TP	+/−	PIM	PP	SH	GW	GT	S	PCT
73	10	15	25	-10	190	0	0	2	2	95	10.5

LAST SEASON

An early season knee injury sidelined him shortly, but games played and all point totals were career highs, as was PIM total — which was the squad's second highest.

THE FINESSE GAME

There's not a lot of finesse in this body. Raglan is a strong skater and he gets up and down the ice well because of that strength. He doesn't have a lot of speed or agility in his skating (and his turns are awful), but his strength makes him difficult to get away from, which in turn makes him a good checker and a tremendous player without the puck.

His puck skills are no better than average and probably a step down from there. He doesn't carry it well, doesn't pass it especially well and doesn't shoot exceptionally. For Herb, a 25-goal season would be a lot.

Raglan is difficult to dislodge from the puck once he gains it, because of his strength, and as such is a good player for the front of the net and in traffic. He's just going to need a lot of time (which he isn't often going to get) to make his plays.

He'll shoot a lot from the faceoff circle (and from the left wing circle too — remember his bad turns — because he rotates around the net and stays deep on the left wing side, but he'll have to do his scoring from in close.

THE PHYSICAL GAME

Raglan is a bull. And it is because of his strength that he's so good away from the puck; his checks can't get away from him. He hits hard, really punishing the opposition with his checks, and Herb eagerly uses his size and strength in the corners and along the boards.

His physical effectivness is somewhat tempered by the fact that he won't make the play out of the corner, but his points are all going to come via his physical style.

THE INTANGIBLES

Raglan has a great attitude. He's a very hard worker on the ice and does the things he does best at all times. He's a good team guy and stands up for his teammates and consistently uses his best assets.

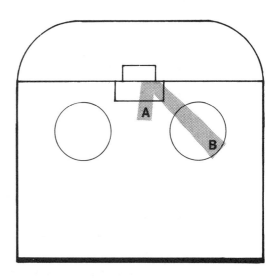

GORDIE ROBERTS

Yrs. of NHL service: 9
Born: Detroit, Mich., USA:
October 2, 1957 Position:
Defenseman Height:
6-0 Weight:
195 Uniform no.:
4 Shoots:
left

Career statistics:

GP	G	A	TP	PIM
684	45	268	313	1,042

1987-88 statistics:

GP	G	A	TP	+/−	PIM	PP	SH	GW	GT	S	PCT
70	3	15	18	-10	143	0	0	0	0	52	5.8

LAST SEASON

Roberts was acquired from Philadephia, which had previously acquired him from Minnesota, in mid-March. Though finishing with a minus rating, Roberts was even in 11 games with the Blues.

THE FINESSE GAME

Roberts is fairly gifted in the finesse areas, with his under-estimated skating ability probably his best asset. He has good speed both forward and backward and he can grab the puck and lug it up-ice, thus taking pressure off the forwards. He is not tremendously agile, and that is evident in his turns. He is especially weak turning to his left, in his case toward the boards.

He has good ability to use his teammates, either by moving the puck quickly to break out of the zone, or to spot the open man in the offensive zone. Roberts throws a good pass to either side because he sees the ice well, and that ability helps him in his defense too.

Gordie reads the rush coming back very well and plays good positional defense, forcing the opposition wide of the net. He has the ability to break up the play and turn it back up-ice quickly, taking the puck of the boards and sending it into the clear in one motion. He had the tendency to rush the puck regardless of circumstance, and he would get in too deep in the offensive zone and be trapped, but Gordie has cut down on that flaw to the improvement of his defense.

He is not much of a goal scorer, but he does have a good slapshot from the point that he gets away quickly and on target, and that makes it good for rebounds or deflections. Roberts will also charge the net for a return pass on a give and go.

THE PHYSICAL GAME

He's not big, but he likes to play strong. He's not strong, but he likes to play tough. Roberts plays a good physical game. He has the strength to keep the front of his net clean and he can also steer the opposition wide of the net and hold them out of the play for as long as necessary.

Roberts can also hit hard and he does, but his game is best when he takes the body and moves the puck. For a guy without the greatest size, Roberts plays an extremely effective physical game. He is very tough.

THE INTANGIBLES

Roberts works very hard and always wants to play, which is kind of startling for a guy with over 1,000 professional games to his credit (WHA and NHL). He was particularly impressive in the playoffs but how long he can keep playing — because his career *is* winding down — is a question needing an answer. He benefits in St. Louis, because the Blues' defensive style meshes nicely with his own style.

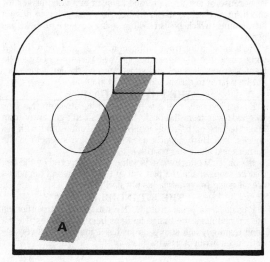

TORONTO MAPLE LEAFS

LINE COMBINATIONS
MARK OSBORNE-PETER IHNACAK-ED OLCZYK
WENDEL CLARK-RUSS COURTNALL-GARY LEEMAN
AL SECORD-TOM FERGUS

DEFENSE PAIRINGS
BORJE SALMING-DALE DEGRAY
LUKE RICHARDSON-AL IAFRATE
TODD GILL-RICK LANZ

GOALTENDERS
KEN WREGGET
ALLAN BESTER

OTHER PLAYERS
VINCENT DAMPHOUSSE — Center/left wing
DAN DAOUST — Center
CHRIS KOTSOPOULOS — Defenseman
SEAN MCKENNA — Right wing
GREG TERRION — Left wing

POWER PLAY

FIRST UNIT:
MARK OSBORNE-PETER IHNACAK-ED OLCZYK
AL IAFRATE-RICK LANZ

SECOND UNIT:
TOM FERGUS-AL SECORD-GARY LEEMAN
BORJE SALMING-DALE DEGRAY

IHNACAK controls the play from the corner on the first unit, distributing to OSBORNE, IAFRATE and LANZ for shots on goal. OLCZYK is in front for rebounds.

On the second unit, FERGUS controls from the left wing circle, with SECORD in front and LEEMAN opposite FERGUS in the right faceoff circle. All four will shoot, with SECORD scooping up rebounds and screening the goaltender, and taking a defenseman with him to open up ice.

RUSS COURTNALL will also get power play time, as will WENDEL CLARK when healthy.

Last season the Leafs' power play was POOR, scoring just 54 times in 347 opportunities (15.6 percent, 21st overall).

PENALTY KILLING

FIRST UNIT:
ED OLCZYK-PETER IHNACAK
BORJE SALMING-AL IAFRATE

SECOND UNIT:
GREG TERRION-GARY LEEMAN
TODD GILL-RICK LANZ

Both penalty killing units use a diamond format. Both are very scrambly and collapse toward the net, leaving the points open. MARK OSBORNE and RUSS COURTNALL will also see penalty killing time.

Last season the Leafs' penalty killing was POOR, allowing 93 goals in 420 shorthanded situations (77.9 percent, 16th overall).

CRUCIAL FACEOFFS

FERGUS is Toronto's best faceoff man, but OLCZYK will take many offensive zone draws.

ALLAN BESTER

Yrs. of NHL service: 4
Born: Hamilton, Ontario, Canada; March 26, 1964
Position: Goaltender
Height: 5-7
Weight: 155
Uniform no.: 30
Catches: left

Career statistics:

GP	MINS	G	SO	AVG	A	PIM
114	6,050	402	5	3.98	424	

1987-88 statisics:

GP	MINS	AVG	W	L	T	SO	GA	SA	SAPCT	PIM
30	1,607	3.81	8	12	5	2	102	879	.884	6

LAST SEASON

Bester missed 13 games with a knee injury. Games played total was second highest of his career.

THE PHYSICAL GAME

Bester plays a standup style. He comes out of his net well to challenge the shooters and that's good, because if he lies back they'll just pop the puck over his shoulders. That's a consequence of being 5-7. But though he stands up, Bester does not always plays his angles well. He doesn't square himself to the puck as well as he could, and he'll frequently react to shots that are nowhere near the net.

He moves out well on screens, and generally forces the opposition to make the first move. He has good balance on his skates and recovers his stance quickly after leaving his feet, so he's in good position to make the second save.

That's important, because Bester will leave rebounds from his pad and glove saves. He has a quick glove hand and will block the puck, but not catch it, frequently juggling it till it falls to the ice. He'll leave rebounds in front from his pad saves too, but is otherwise good about clearing the puck.

He holds the post well and has a quick left foot, but Bester is just average moving across the front of the net. Like goaltending partner Ken Wregget, Bester doesn't handle the puck well and that creates all kinds of defensive confusion.

THE MENTAL GAME

Like Wregget, Bester constantly worries about his performances. Allan is always fidgeting about doing his best, and sometimes that mitigates against him. He tightens up, loses his concentration (because he's worrying about how he's playing instead of stopping the puck) and lets in goals.

One sign that his concentration is good is his vision of the puck. When his concentration is on he sees it well, following the play all through the offensive zone. That allows him to make saves based on anticipation.

THE INTANGIBLES

One of the only things that has saved Toronto from being completely hapless is the fact that when Wregget falters, Bester seems at his own best. Bester's shown flashes across his career, but he must be more consistent in his mental outlook and in his performances to truly help the Leafs.

WENDEL CLARK

Yrs. of NHL service: 3
Born: Kelvington, Sask., Canada; October 25, 1966
Position: Left wing
Height: 5-11
Weight: 194
Uniform no.: 17
Shoots: left

Career statistics:

GP	G	A	TP	PIM
174	83	45	128	578

1987-88 statistics:

GP	G	A	TP	+/-	PIM	PP	SH	GW	GT	S	PCT
28	12	11	23	-13	80	4	0	1	1	93	12.9

LAST SEASON

A recurring back injury sidelined Clark throughout most of the season. Games played, goal and point totals were career lows, with assist total tying his career worst.

THE FINESSE GAME

In terms of "fancy" finesse skills, Clark is merely good. In terms of "strength" finesse skills, Clark is excellent. He is a tremendous skater in terms of explosive acceleration and strength, but he's merely good in balance and agility. He can move fairly well laterally, but his steamrolling style will never be mistaken for something more genteel.

Clark's hockey sense (his ice vision and anticipation) are still at a level no better than average. He does not use his teammates well because he is unsure of what to do with the puck after he gets it. To pass well, Clark needs time and space. He does overhandle the puck and tries to do too much 1-on-1. If he moved the puck better he could get into the open for more shots.

He has a devastating wrist shot, maybe the best in the League in terms of heaviness, release and accuracy. Wendel takes good advantage of that wepaon by shooting frequently, and he does have the hand skills (as well as the strength) to get around a defender for a clear shot on goal.

He does work hard at backchecking, but Clark lacks patience in his defensive end and takes himself out of the play by trying to do too much (like pound an opposing player).

THE PHYSICAL GAME

Clark is very strong, very tough, very aggressive.

And very inconsistent.

He has the ability to smash people, to really hurt them with his checks. He has the ability to work the corners excellently because of his superior upper body strength and foot balance. He has the ability to beat people up. He has the ability to take the body in the corner and come out with the puck.

He does *not* have the ability — yet — to do it consistently within a game and consistently from game to game, so much so that he looks not only uninvolved, but floating.

THE INTANGIBLES

Everything about Clark's career is on hold until his debilitating back injury is cured, or at least made less debilitating.

Wendel is clearly unable to perform in any capacity because of the injury, and certainly unable to perform in his physical game.

He can be a franchise player, and his spirit and enthusiasm fire up the Maple Leafs. He's a hard worker and wants to win very badly, and certainly has great potential ahead of him. But first he must be healthy.

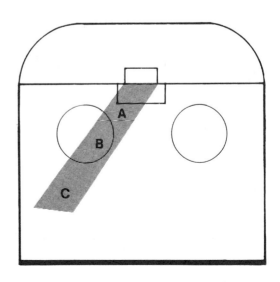

RUSS COURTNALL

Yrs. of NHL service: 4
Born: Duncan, B.C., Canada; June 3, 1965
Position: Center
Height: 5-10
Weight: 175
Uniform no.: 9
Shoots: right

Career statistics:

GP	G	A	TP	PIM
300	89	127	216	239

1987-88 statistics:

GP	G	A	TP	+/-	PIM	PP	SH	GW	GT	S	PCT
65	23	26	49	-16	47	6	3	1	1	212	10.8

LAST SEASON

Games played was fewest since joining NHL fulltime. Goal total was second highest of career, but point total was second lowest (all based on full seasons). He missed five games with a virus and was sidelined late in the season with a back injury. He finished third on the team in shots on goal, tied for third with Mark Osborne for goals and tied for third with linemate Gary Leeman for power play goals.

THE FINESSE GAME

Skating and shooting are the hallmarks of Russ Courtnall's finesse game. He's an excellent skater, possessing breakaway speed, superior balance, excellent quickness and agility. Russ puts that speed to use by driving the defensemen off the blue line, forcing them to backpedal and open up ice for his teammates. He doesn't need to coast to make his plays, and can handle and move the puck at almost full speed. He changes direction and speeds within a step. He's a great forechecker and penalty killer.

Courtnall has good hands and vision, and he combines those abilities with anticipation to become an effective playmaker. However, he undercuts his playmaking ability by overhandling the puck (too much 1-on-1 play versus the opposition). He tries to make a play from a crowd, leading to turnovers (and that horrendous plus/minus rating). If he'd move the puck a little quicker and then jump into the holes he'd be twice as effective.

Russ has an excellent wrist shot, just packed with power. It is a dangerous offensive weapon, and Courtnall uses it to great effect from right in front of the net. The Leafs often have him at a wing position on offensive zone faceoffs in order to take advantage of his shot.

His sense and skating should make him solid defensively, but he loses his check in the Leafs' zone, because he is always looking for the breakout pass.

THE PHYSICAL GAME

For a little guy, Courtnall plays awfully tough. He is not a physically imposing player and he isn't going to knock anyone out with his physical game, but Courtnall hits willingly, frequently and with a good bit of strength.

He plays the body well in open ice (his balance on his skates is the key to that ability), but he won't win many battles along the boards because of his stature. Courtnall is unafraid and — though much more suited to a finesse game — will fight when he has to.

THE INTANGIBLES

Courtnall has a good attitude. He wants to win and he works hard, and if he remedies his 1-on-1 play and his defensive lapses (the Leafs are working with him in that area) he'll be a super player.

But he must also develop some consistency in his performances and play each game at the same level; he had 11 of his 23 goals in the first quarter, 19 of them by game no. 37. Only four goals in his final 28 games? That's what we mean by consistency.

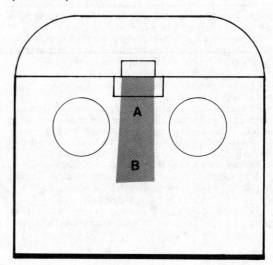

VINCENT DAMPHOUSSE

Yrs. of NHL service: 2
Born: Montreal, Quebec, Canada; December 17, 1967
Position: Center/left wing
Height: 6-1
Weight: 195
Uniform no.: 10
Shoots: left

Career statistics:

GP	G	A	TP	PIM
155	33	61	94	66

1987-88 statistics:

GP	G	A	TP	+/−	PIM	PP	SH	GW	GT	S	PCT
75	12	36	48	2	40	1	0	2	0	111	10.8

LAST SEASON

Assist and point marks were career highs. Damphousse finished second on the club in assists, and was one of just five plus-rated Maple Leafs.

THE FINESSE GAME

Damphousse has shown signs of potential in all his finesse skills, but has yet to bring any to bear in the NHL with great success. He is a good skater with good quickness and nice rink-length speed, but he is short in agility and lateral movement. His balance could be improved, and if it is, an improvement in mobility would follow. Right now, he's a straight-at-the-defender player.

He controls the puck very well and has the skill to carry it at full speed. He can make some moves with it, but because he likes to go one-on-one with the defenseman he can be easily angled off (here's where that agility for inside cuts would help).

Patience makes Damphousse a good playmaker. He looks over his options instead of making the first play he sees, and he does all this with his head up, so he recognizes changes on the ice. He sees the offensive zone very well, and always looks to use his teammates.

His shot is excellent and he could score from anywhere, but Damphousse doesn't move to the net to finish a play. Instead his straight ahead style puts him at bad shooting angles: the goal line, the base of the far side of the faceoff circle. He's got to get into better position to score, better position to exploit his shot. He also doesn't shoot anywhere near often enough.

He's shown good understanding of the defensive game, backchecking conscientiously. His defensive zone positioning is pretty good, but just a little more patience in breaking out (staying with the high opposing player) would help the Leafs.

THE PHYSICAL GAME

One reason Damphousse has had success defensively is his willingness to put his body in the way of the opposition. We're not saying he's a hitter in the class of Wendel Clark, just that Damphousse plays the body fairly well.

He bumps along the boards, and Vincent also uses his good size well to protect the puck. His willingness to play a physical style portends well for him, because that willingess will help him get the room his finesse game requires.

THE INTANGIBLES

After a better-than-average rookie year, Damphousse was Toronto's number one disappointment last season. He's a big talent but he didn't push himself at all last season. He didn't get involved around the net, and the Leafs certainly could have used a greater dose of his scoring and playmaking prowess.

It's often said that the third year of a pro's career is the crucial one. This couldn't be any truer than it is in Vincent Damphousse's case. Since he's already asked for a trade from the Leafs, Damphousse needs to prove he's worth another team's interest.

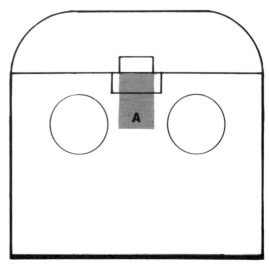

DAN DAOUST

Yrs. of NHL service: 6
Born: Montreal, Quebec, Canada; February 29, 1960
Position: Center
Height: 5-11
Weight: 160
Uniform no.: 24
Shoots: left

Career statistics:

GP	G	A	TP	PIM
389	73	151	224	405

1987-88 statistics:

GP	G	A	TP	+/−	PIM	PP	SH	GW	GT	S	PCT
67	9	8	17	-7	57	0	0	1	0	57	15.8

LAST SEASON

An ankle injury suffered in early March sideline Daoust for several weeks. His goal total was his highest in three seasons.

THE FINESSE GAME

Daoust is a good skater, equipped with speed and balance on his skates, giving him good lateral movement. He changes direction quickly and that is a big help to him as a defensive forward.

He sees the ice very well (another defensive plus), has good anticipation skills and reads the play excellently. Those skills also make him an excellent penalty killer.

Dan has good stick skills and can use his teammates excellently when he has the opportunity. His scoring, what little he does of it now, will come from the slot, as his shot doesn't measure up to his other skills.

THE PHYSICAL GAME

Daoust, despite his small stature, will play a fearless physical game against any team. As a defensive forward Daoust bumps his man up and down the ice, playing tough but clean. He has deceptive strength for his size (though he is still no Samson) and will play with anyone against the boards.

That style, however, takes its toll in terms of injury.

THE INTANGIBLES

Though the numbers game has reduced Daoust to his role-playing status, he's an enthusiastic player on the ice and he dedicates his energy now to a good defensive game. He gives what he has and is always ready to play, even though he's not playing as much as he'd like. His feistiness makes him a good checker against his division's smaller but talented centers: Yzermans, Gilmour, Broten.

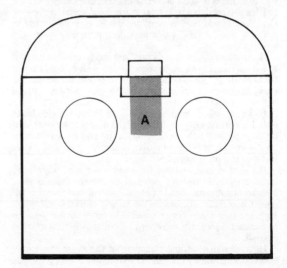

DALE DEGRAY

Yrs. of NHL service: 1
Born: Oshawa, Ontario, Canada; September 1, 1963
Position: Defenseman
Height: 6-0
Weight: 200
Uniform no.: 3
Shoots: right

Career statistics:

GP	G	A	TP	PIM
84	12	25	37	92

1987-88 statistics:

GP	G	A	TP	+/−	PIM	PP	SH	GW	GT	S	PCT
56	6	18	24	4	63	1	0	1	0	122	4.9

LAST SEASON

Degray was traded to Toronto prior to the start of last season. Games played total was a career high, as were assist and point totals. He was one of just two plus-rated defensemen.

THE FINESSE GAME

Degray is a talented skater, fairly mobile on his feet and possessing good speed and quickness. He's able to put that skating skill to work offensively by containing the point well at the blue line and by charging the net for shots.

He has good ice vision and looks to move the puck quickly from the point, and he has good hands for making passes. His quickness allows him to avoid checking at the blue line and all the above skills make him a good point man for the power play.

He has a great slap shot from the point, and Degray should use it more.

He plays a positional defensive game, reading the rush toward him and forcing it wide well. Degray is good in his transitions and rapidly turns the play around.

THE PHYSICAL GAME

Degray has good size and he's not afraid to use it. He takes the body well along the boards to force the opposition out of the play, and he has great strength to tie up the opposition in front of the net or muscle a forward off the puck in the corner.

He is also in great physical condition.

THE INTANGIBLES

Dale is a very upbeat person, and is very good in the lockerroom because of his positive attitude. He plays every night as hard as he can play, and playing regularly brings out his confidence. He's a hard worker and should do nothing but improve.

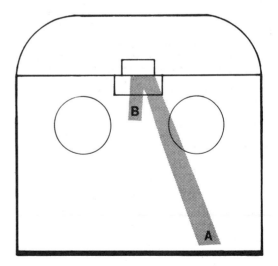

TOM FERGUS

Yrs. of NHL service: 7
Born: Chicago, Ill., USA; June 16, 1962
Position: Center
Height: 6-3
Weight: 210
Uniform no.: 19
Shoots: left

Career statistics:

GP	G	A	TP	PIM
487	169	240	409	340

1987-88 statistics:

GP	G	A	TP	+/-	PIM	PP	SH	GW	GT	S	PCT
63	19	31	50	5	81	5	0	0	0	124	15.3

LAST SEASON

Missed five games with a rib injury. Goal total was second lowest of career, point total tied second lowest of career. Plus/minus was team's third best, second among forwards.

THE FINESSE GAME

For a guy his size, Fergus is a surprisingly good skater. He's gifted with acceleration and a good change of direction, though he doesn't have a lot of foot speed for quickness nor agility for lateral movement. But the amounts he does possess in those categories is above average for a player his size.

He amplifies his skating with good-to-very-good stickhandling. Tom has good hands and carries the puck well in front of him, and he makes good use of his wingers by moving the puck quickly and accurately — when he avails himself of that talent. Unfortunately, Tom has the bad habit of admiring his own work too much and he overhandles the puck. Instead of trying for the perfect play on his own, he would benefit by looking for his teammates. He could especially use his points more.

Fergus has one of the NHL's best wrist shots, but he doesn't use it anywhere near enough. He also should learn to put his good hands to work in tighter to the net for garbage goals and to pick up loose pucks from rebounds and whatnot.

His skating ability makes him a good checker and for the early part of his career Fergus was more concerned with his play in his defensive end than he was in the offensive zone. Though still fairly effective defensively, Fergus now has the tendency to drift through his backchecking duties.

THE PHYSICAL GAME

In what is one of hockey's most left-handed compliments, Fergus is a finesse player with size. He is not at all interested in a physical game, and is more than likely to shy away from contact. He'll wait on the outside of scrambles for the puck, or he'll use his excellent reach and good hands to pull the puck from inside a scrum.

He is not very strong, so he loses battles in traffic, and he does not use his body well to shield the puck from the opposition. When he is against the boards, Fergus pushes and shoves rather than hits. Added strength would help here.

THE INTANGIBLES

Talent drips off Fergus like rain off a flower, but his application of that talent is awful. He is unmotivated and doesn't work anywhere near hard enough on the ice. He doesn't push himself and he certainly doesn't get 6-foot-3, 210-pounds worth of work done. He plays at just one level, and when the level of a game rises he does not.

Greater discipline would make him a better player, but after seven NHL seasons what you see with Tom Fergus is what you get. Or actually, what you see is less than what you get.

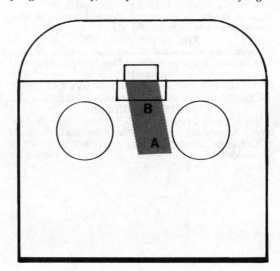

MIROSLAV FRYCER

Yrs. of NHL service: 8
Born: Opava, Czechoslovakia; September 27, 1959
Position: Right wing
Height: 6-0
Weight: 200
Uniform no.: 14
Shoots: left

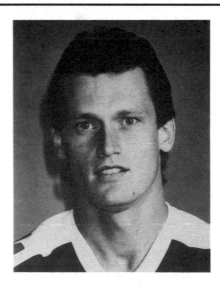

Career statistics:

GP	G	A	TP	PIM
377	134	170	304	421

1987-88 statistics:

GP	G	A	TP	+/−	PIM	PP	SH	GW	GT	S	PCT
38	12	20	32	8	41	1	0	2	1	76	15.8

LAST SEASON

Frycer missed 34 games with a knee injury, four games with a virus. Games played total was second lowest of his career. His plus/minus was the team's overall best.

THE FINESSE GAME

Once upon a time, several major injuries ago, Frycer was a good skater. He had good balance (which helped him play in traffic), and he had a nice change of pace and good speed. Miro was both fast and strong enough on his skates to go barrelling right at the defense, but smart enough to know when to moderate his speed. He also had good agility and one-step quickness and changed direction well, making him good laterally as well as up and back. We use the past tense because of his injuries; time will tell if he still has those abilities.

He has excellent hands and was often used to control the power play, and that hand skill also made him a successful player in tight quarters close to the net. He carried or moved it equally well, but he did have a tendency to move to his backhand once across the opposing blue line. While moving that way is usually the kiss of death in terms of playmaking, Frycer was talented enough to make plays off his backhand.

He uses his teammates well because he has good vision on the ice, coupled with good anticipation. Miro is able to spot the openings and will cut to them himself or lead a teammate into the hole. He has good touch around the net and a good wrist shot, and will score from farther out as well, releasing the puck quickly, frequently and (generally) accurately.

He used those skills to particular success on the power play, where his quickness kept him in the clear as well as kept the passing lanes open.

THE PHYSICAL GAME

Frycer played a physical up and down his wing and was quite willing to get in front of the net and take the requisite abuse. He wasn't a devastatingly hard hitter, but he took the body well and muscled the opposition off the puck.

Frycer also had the talent to make the plays after hitting and the fact that he has good balance and remains vertical most of the time after a collision is a big help here.

THE INTANGIBLES

New settings in Detroit, playing for a coach dramatically different from John Brophy (Frycer's avowed enemy, so to speak) may do wonders for the right wing. His acquisition also helps the Wings, who have been looking to improve their starboard side.

In any case, Frycer has to prove that he's not the injury prone player he's been for the last two seasons (we told you his durability is questionable) and he must prove that his actions can back up his mouthing off.

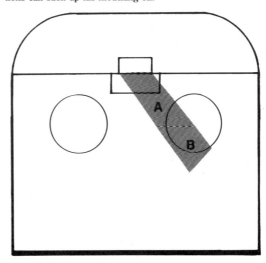

TODD GILL

Yrs. of NHL service: 2
Born: Brockville, Ontario, Canada; November 9, 1965
Position: Defenseman
Height: 6-1
Weight: 185
Uniform no.: 23
Shoots: left

Career statistics:

GP	G	A	TP	PIM
151	14	46	60	264

1987-88 statistics:

GP	G	A	TP	+/−	PIM	PP	SH	GW	GT	S	PCT
65	8	17	25	-20	131	1	0	3	0	109	7.3

LAST SEASON

Games played total was a career high, though Gill was sidelined for some time with an ankle injury. Goal total (second highest among defensemen) was also a career high, as was PIM total. His plus/minus rating was the team's sixth worst, third worst among the defense.

THE FINESSE GAME

Todd Gill has made much of his mark on the NHL through a physical game, but he is also a talented finesse player with good potential to improve.

He skates well and can carry the puck well doing so, but a lack of foot speed and balance makes him a straight ahead skater instead of a shifty one. He has good speed but is mostly unable to moderate it, and that makes him easily defended against. His lack of agility also evidences itself in his backskating, where opponents can beat him to his left (bad pivots).

Todd does have good vision, so he reads the ice fairly well when the play moves in front of him. Because his head is up, he will generally make good breakout passes (and he joins the play as a fourth attacker better than any other Leaf defender), but like most of Toronto's defense he has a tendency to overhandle the puck. That's when he gets in trouble. Gill also has the tendency to charge into the offensive corner, make a blind pass and then be caught deep while the opposition breaks out.

As an offensive threat, he'll score from the blue line, but will cheat to the faceoff circle when he can. He'll also crash the net after one of his forays into the corner, and his hands are good enough for him to score in tight.

THE PHYSICAL GAME

Aggressiveness is the highlight of Gill's game, but it is also his Waterloo. He loves to hit and can do so effectively against the boards or in front of the net, as well as banging in the offensive zone. He'll out-muscle many of the League's forwards, and he does have the talent to make the play after taking the puck.

His less-than-great balance, however, means that he'll often land on his butt after a check, and that means he's out of the play. He'll also go out of his way to chase people to hit them, and that leaves him out of position and an enemy uncovered.

Gill is also a good fighter, and willingly mixes it up.

THE INTANGIBLES

Concentration is a big question mark for Todd, and that makes him a streaky player. When he's concentrating and thinking about his tasks, he contributes well. When he fails to concentrate he gets out of position and hurts the club. He must bring a more consistent attitude to the rink.

On the other hand, Gill is a fine kid and eminently coachable. He's very competitive and wants to win. That attitude should stand him in good stead as he tries to improve.

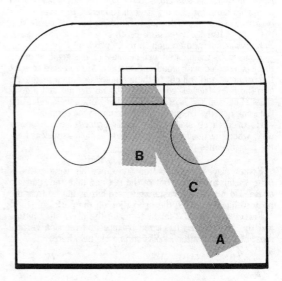

CHRIS KOTSOPOULOS

Yrs. of NHL service: 8
Born: Toronto, Ontario, Canada; November 27, 1958
Position: Defenseman
Height: 6-3
Weight: 215
Uniform no.: 26
Shoots: right

Career statistics:

GP	G	A	TP	PIM
420	43	95	138	773

1987-88 statistics:

GP	G	A	TP	+/–	PIM	PP	SH	GW	GT	S	PCT
21	2	2	4	-3	19	0	0	0	0	22	9.1

LAST SEASON

Games played total was lowest of Kotsopoulos' career, courtesy of a recurring groin injury. Point totals were all career lows.

THE FINESSE GAME

Kotsopoulos is a no better than average finesse player. He is not a good skater, and he lumbers around the rink with neither speed nor agility. He won't rush the puck except on the rarest of occasions, though he can handle the puck fairly well and will move it from the defensive zone well if unpressured. Otherwise, Kotsopoulos will make hurried, blind passes that result in turnovers.

He has a very hard slap shot from the point and it can be a good offensive weapon, but Kotsopoulos doesn't shoot enough for it to be effective.

What Chris does to make himself effective — and this is a new development in his career — is play smartly. He's found the limits of his play and he stays within them, so that he rarely over-extends himself.

THE PHYSICAL GAME

Chris' previous problem in the physical game was his inconsistent use of his size. Like playing smartly, Kotsopoulos has learned to use his body more effectively by using it more consistently.

He's very strong and plays that way in front of the net and along the boards. Chris hits hard and has a mean streak within him that allows for an extra elbow here or there. His strength powers his slap shot and also allows him to clear the front of the net or outmuscle the opposition in the corners, though he is not very good with the puck after gaining control of it.

He's also gotten his weight under control.

THE INTANGIBLES

The groin injury that has hobbled Kotsopoulos for two seasons is the main question regarding the defenseman. Ironically, he'd begun to keep himself in better shape before succumbing to the injury. He'd also improved his attitude toward work and was applying himself game in and game out.

He likes to chirp and talk and that annoys the opposition, and he was also Toronto's most effective physical defenseman. But we also told you that he frequently falls into disfavor with management, and his mouth got him in trouble with Coach John Brophy last season. Again the injury was to blame, as Chris and the coach had public disagreements over the defenseman's ability to play.

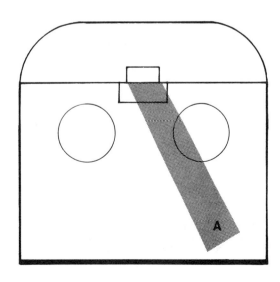

AL IAFRATE

Yrs. of NHL service: 4
Born: Dearborn, Mich., USA; March 21, 1966
Position: Defenseman
Height: 6-3
Weight: 215
Uniform no.: 33
Shoots: left

Career statistics:

GP	G	A	TP	PIM
290	44	92	136	226

1987-88 statistics:

GP	G	A	TP	+/-	PIM	PP	SH	GW	GT	S	PCT
77	22	30	52	-21	80	4	3	4	1	169	13.0

LAST SEASON

Iafrate set career marks in all three point categories and in PIM, though he recorded only his second best games played mark. He finished fourth on the club in scoring, first among defensemen, and he led the club in game winners. His plus/minus rating was the club's third worst.

THE FINESSE GAME

Iafrate's strongest skill is his skating. Though still not outstandingly mobile because of his size, Al does have rink-length speed, and he gets to that speed within two or three strides. Because he is fairly well balanced he has some agility, and he has improved his pivots and changes of direction.

He's combined his improved mobility with better playreading ability (particularly defensively), so that he now plays defense more positionally and less haphazardly. He may still get hypnotized by the puck, but in general his defense is the best it's ever been. He plays his defensive angles better and is more able to steer the opposition wide of the net.

Obviously, though, it is in the offensive game that Iafrate best contributes. He rushes the puck extremely well, and it is on those rushes that most of his goals will come. He reads the play in front of him well and moves the puck to the forwards for outlet passes very well. He also joins the play as a fourth attacker and follows it to the net.

He handles the puck very well when he carries it, but like many of the Leafs defensemen can be guilty of overhandling the puck and forcing a play. That extra half-step he takes means he can get trapped in the offensive zone after a turnover, and that contributes to Iafrate's bad plus/minus in more than a little way. He has a super shot — excellent for deflections — but he needs to shoot more from the point, and to shoot more to score instead of just getting the puck on net.

THE PHYSICAL GAME

Basically, Iafrate is a finesse player with size. He's primarily a clutch-and grab physical player and doesn't like to be hit, though he will initiate some contact on his own. His strength for one-on-one battles in front of the net or along the boards is no better than average. While his skills clearly indicate that he should be the breakout and not takeout defenseman, his lack of above average physical play makes it imperative he be paired with a more physical partner.

In previous seasons Iafrate's weight was a concern, but he seems to have stabilized at about 215 pounds and plays well at that size.

THE INTANGIBLES

Iafrate was a revelation for the first 30 games of last season, the League's best defenseman in that time. His usually erratic concentration was 100 percent and his play showed that — 15g, 17a and 32 points in his first 41 games.

But his concentration plummeted after that, in both games and practices (7g, 13a and 20 points in the season's second half). Part of his problem is that the game comes so easily to him, that he is so innately talented, that full dedication is often unnecessary; Iafrate can get by by coasting. That allows him to become lackadaisical.

He's a good kid, and he's attempting to be a leader. He's clearly Toronto's best defenseman, but he has a long way to go to become the premier defenseman he showed glimpses of last year.

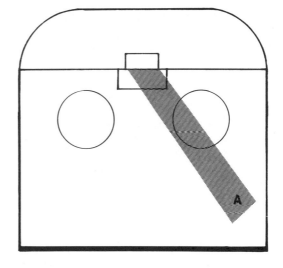

PETER IHNACAK

Yrs. of NHL service: 6
Born: Poprad, Czechoslovakia; May 5, 1957
Position: Center
Height: 6-0
Weight: 180
Uniform no.: 18
Shoots: right

Career statistics:

GP	G	A	TP	PIM
386	100	147	247	165

1987-88 statistics:

GP	G	A	TP	+/−	PIM	PP	SH	GW	GT	S	PCT
68	10	20	30	-6	41	0	0	0	0	75	13.3

LAST SEASON
Goal total tied career low.

THE FINESSE GAME
Ihnacak is a good skater in terms of strength and balance, and those qualities helps him in his physical game. He also has some speed that he can apply to his game, but Ihnacak is best served by his sense and anticipation.

He sees the ice and can read the plays and thus knows where the holes will open. Peter is a good playmaker and can lead his teammates into those openings with soft, easy to handle passes and he passes well from both sides. He is very patient and will look over all his options before making a play. He has very good hockey sense.

Ihnacak carries the puck well too, and can stickhandle past opposing defensemen. He prefers to carry the puck over the blue line. He has a good shot but he doesn't shoot enough, preferring to pass to a teammate with a better opportunity. He is fairly attentive to his defensive play and plays his position well back into the Leafs' zone.

THE PHYSICAL GAME
Ihnacak, unlike many Europeans, is a boards and corners player. This is where his strength on his skates and his great balance help him, allowing him to bang bodies and remain vertical and able to make a play. Ihnacak cannot be intimidated.

He handles the puck very well with his skates, probably as well as anyone else in the League. His physical game makes him one of those "last minute to play with the puck in his own zone and you have to get it out" guys.

THE INTANGIBLES
He has yet to play a full NHL season, and what you see with Ihnacak is pretty much what you get. He works hard and, though he might take a night or two off, Ihnacak usually gives all he has to give.

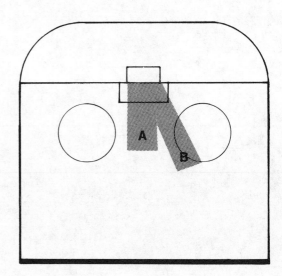

RICK LANZ

Yrs. of NHL service: 8
Born: Karlouyvary, Czechoslovakia; September 16, 1961
Position: Defenseman
Height: 6-1
Weight: 195
Uniform no.: 4
Shoots: right

Career statistics:

GP	G	A	TP	PIM
536	64	212	276	428

1987-88 statistics:

GP	G	A	TP	+/−	PIM	PP	SH	GW	GT	S	PCT
75	6	22	28	-12	65	3	0	0	0	145	4.1

LAST SEASON

Lanz was second in defensive scoring for the Leafs. His SOG total was second highest for defenders.

THE FINESSE GAME

Lanz is a very talented finesse player, and it's in that role that he contributes to the Leafs. He's an excellent skater, good at skating forward and backward and he can go both ways with speed, making him very difficult to get around. His lateral movement and change of direction are also very good and Lanz is a threat to rush the puck from his zone.

He has exceptional vision and anticipation, making him very difficult to fool. He reads the offensive and defensive plays well, but makes his mark on the power play.

Lanz is a power play specialist. He combines excellent puck control skills with his hockey sense and manipulates the power play very well from the point, passing to the open man, keeping the lanes open with one-step quickness or blasting his excellent slap shot at the goaltender.

Lanz does not allow the opposition to stop him and he does that by performing all his tasks quickly. He moves the puck quickly and releases his shot just as fast.

Defensively, his speed gets him back into position after a rush and he has the talent to break up a play (anticipation again) and start it up ice. His only flaw comes when he overhandles the puck, trying to do too much instead of passing the puck and letting it do all the work.

THE PHYSICAL GAME

Lanz's NHL weakness has long been his lack of physical play. While he doesn't have great size or strength, he also doesn't get the most from what he does have. He doesn't consistently take out the opposition as well as he should in front of the net or along the boards, but for a month or so last year he did do that, so he is capable of playing that way.

At best he can take the body effectively, but he best uses his strength when he reaches into traffic and pulls out the puck. He uses his strength to propel his slap shot, a bullet-like blast from the blue line.

THE INTANGIBLES

Lanz is another of the type of players for whom the game comes easily. His problem is that he also plays the game easily instead of working at it; his inconsistent physical play is evidence of that.

His talents have begun to age, but part of that decline is attributable to the team's misfortunes: A bad team brings out the worst (or in Lanz's case doesn't bring out the best) in its players. Lanz would be a better player with a better team.

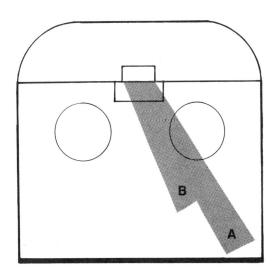

GARY LEEMAN

Yrs. of NHL service: 5
Born: Toronto, Ontario, Canada; February 19, 1964
Position: Right wing/defense
Height: 5-11
Weight: 175
Uniform no.: 11
Shoots: right

Career statistics:

GP	G	A	TP	PIM
318	69	119	188	251

1987-88 statistics:

GP	G	A	TP	+/−	PIM	PP	SH	GW	GT	S	PCT
80	30	31	61	-6	62	6	0	0	0	234	12.8

LAST SEASON

Leeman played the full slate for the second consecutive year (one of just two Leafs to do so last year). Goal and point totals were career highs, and Leeman finished second on the club in both of those categories, as well as in power play goals and shots on goal. Among forwards, his plus/minus was fourth best.

THE FINESSE GAME

Gary Leeman is probably the Leafs' most talented player. His skating and puckhandling skills are primary among his talents. He is an excellent skater, equipped with tremendous speed and quickness complemented by agility. Gary is very mobile, able to change directions and speeds literally within a step. He has explosive quickness and can drive around a defender, or he can stutter step around the opposition toward the goal. His skating forces the opposition into penalties, and Leeman helps the referees along by performing some of the League's prettiest dives.

His great skating skill is amplified by his equally superior hand skills. He handles the puck well at all speeds, particularly his fastest speed, and he's smart with it as well. He can lay a pass over sticks, lead a teammate into an opening or stickhandle around the opposition on his own, but he also constantly overhandles the puck, trying to do too much because of his abundant natural talent in his hands and feet — that's why he has a modest assist total. He must make better use of his teammates and his own good ice vision, instead of exploiting all the openings himself.

His great hands extend to his shotaccurate, quickly released. Leeman can score from anywhere because of his shot, and is especially adept at holding the puck and forcing the goaltender and defense to commit themselves. He also one-times the puck extremely well. He'll be moved to a defensive position on offensive zone faceoffs so that the Leafs can take advantage of that shot.

His defense has improved tremendously, so that Gary is no longer waving at opposing forwards as they race by him toward the Toronto net. He can still show more patience in leaving his defensive zone (and more positional discipline), and he could make better transitions from offense to defense when the puck turns over.

THE PHYSICAL GAME

Gary doesn't have great size, so most any physical game he plays will be a benefit. He showed greater strength last year (or greater determination) in working through checks and getting shots off while wrapped up.

A deceiving quality about him is his fighting ability, which is fairly high. He just doesn't like to fight and generally won't. Still, he's not a thumping player and should learn the lesson finesse players like Steve Yzerman and Pat Lafontaine learnedA physical game can and does open up a finesse one.

THE INTANGIBLES

Leeman's natural puckhandling talent leads to a creative, open ice style. He's another player to whom the game comes easily, and sometimes he needs a boot in the pants to perform. His ability to play both forward and defense makes him the team's biggest plus, and he should continue to improve.

He scored on a fairly consistent basis last year (17g and 17a in the season's first 40 games), and his continued high performance is crucial to any Leaf hopes of success.

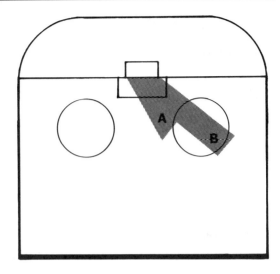

SEAN MCKENNA

Yrs. of NHL service: 6
Born: Asbestos, Quebec, Canada; March 7, 1962
Position: Right wing
Height: 6-0
Weight: 185
Uniform no.: 8
Shoots: right

Career statistics:

GP	G	A	TP	PIM
406	82	79	161	161

1987-88 statistics:

GP	G	A	TP	+/-	PIM	PP	SH	GW	GT	S	PCT
70	8	7	15	-25	24	0	0	1	0	80	10.0

LAST SEASON

McKenna was acquired by the Leafs in exchange for Mike Allison near the season's midway point. Games played total was highest in four seasons, point total was career low. Plus/minus rating tied for team's worst.

THE FINESSE GAME

McKenna is a good skater, and he's got a lot of speed at his disposal. He's also fairly agile, and he has the ability to cut past a defender or snare a loose puck because of his agility and quickness.

His hands skills are nowhere near as good as his foot skills. He handles the puck no better than fairly, and looks better than he is because he's going faster than most of the other players on the ice. But McKenna doesn't handle the puck well at that speed. For that reason he's not a very good playmaker, and for that reason he fails to convert on the many opportunities his speed provides for him.

He has no real anticipation skills, and very little sense of the game at the NHL level. His checking can be good because of his speed and ability to close holes, but McKenna doesn't think well on the ice.

Whatever scoring he's going to do will have to come from in close. His shots are not great, and most certainly won't consistently fool NHL goaltending. He also comes to the net too quickly for his hands to work and literally runs out of room to get a shot off.

THE PHYSICAL GAME

McKenna has good size but fails to use it consistently. He pushes and shoves in the corners instead of hitting, and generally prefers to wait outside the scrum for the puck to emerge instead of forcing the issue himself.

He has good strength and could hold his own in some of those battles, but McKenna frequently bails out and just moves his legs for show.

THE INTANGIBLES

A fourth line player on a bad team. That's what McKenna is. He remains a marginal hockey player.

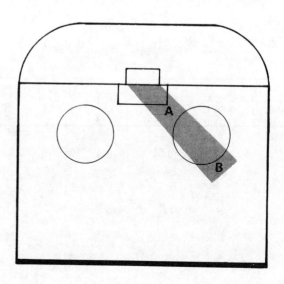

ED OLCZYK

Yrs. of NHL service: 4
Born: Chicago, Illinois, USA; August 16, 1966
Position: Right wing
Height: 6-1
Weight: 200
Uniform no.: 16
Shoots: left

Career statistics:

GP	G	A	TP	PIM
308	107	148	255	288

1987-88 statistics:

GP	G	A	TP	+/−	PIM	PP	SH	GW	GT	S	PCT
80	42	33	75	-22	55	14	4	3	1	243	17.3

LAST SEASON

Games played total was career high. Olczyk led the club in scoring, goals, power play goals, shorthanded goals and shots on goal. Goal total was a career high, point total was second highest of career. His plus/minus was the team's third worst, second among forwards. He was one of only two players to play all 80 games.

THE FINESSE GAME

Of Olczyk's formidable finesse skills, his primary ability is his hockey sense. Olczyk has tremendous sense for the game, using anticipation and instinct to make the right play almost 100 percent of the time. He has great patience and poise, and seldom makes a bad play regardless of how much pressure he's under. That sense makes him a good penalty killer.

Olczyk is also a good skater, blessed with speed and quickness not usually found in bigger men. He can out-race an opponent in the long haul, but his quickness will also get him to a lot of loose pucks. That quickness gives him agility, and also allows him to force offense from a broken play.

He is somewhat selfish, as his SOG total indicates, but he can make good passes to his teammates. Just don't expect him to make those passes at the expense of a shot on goal. His shot is excellent, a strong and accurate snap shot that is quickly released. Olczyk also loves to pick the top corners for his goals, and his ability to get into position to score makes him a natural for the power play.

Though his plus/minus total doesn't indicate it, Olczyk is a fairly good defensive player. He'll never be mistaken for Bob Gainey, and Olczyk still makes positional mistakes through the neutral and defensive zones, but his minus 22 is more an indication of tremendous ice time than defensive ineptitude.

THE PHYSICAL GAME

Olczyk is a ballerina in a linebacker's body. He has great size but has done almost nothing to develop his strength, and he does very little with the strength he does have. He stays away from contact and prefers the open ice to traffic.

That's suprising, because his skills should combine with his size to make him a fine physical player. If he were to incorporate a physical game into his repertoire he would be a very dangerous player, not unlike Cam Neely.

Part of Olczyk's problem is his lack of stamina. He comes off the ice after 30 seconds as if he were half-dead. Better conditioning would make him a better and more valuable player.

THE INTANGIBLES

The key to Ed Olczyk is going to be desire. Right now, he doesn't work at becoming a better player and is satisfied where he is. That doesn't mean he doesn't work on the ice during games, or that he doesn't honestly care. What it means is that he isn't motivated enough to work at improving.

Still, it's important to remember that Olczyk is only 22 years old. He has a lot of hockey ahead of him.

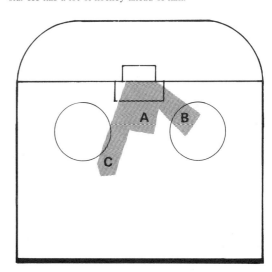

MARK OSBORNE

Yrs. of NHL service: 7
Born: Toronto, Ontario, Canada; August 13, 1961
Position: Left wing
Height: 6-2
Weight: 200
Uniform no.: 12
Shoots: left

Career statistics:

GP	G	A	TP	PIM
471	133	183	316	560

1987-88 statistics:

GP	G	A	TP	+/–	PIM	PP	SH	GW	GT	S	PCT
79	23	37	60	-3	102	4	2	0	0	155	14.8

LAST SEASON

Games played total was highest in five seasons, with point total second highest of Osborne's career. Goal total was highest in six years and tied second highest of his career. Assist total was also second highest of career. He finished third on the team in scoring, first in assists.

THE FINESSE GAME

For a guy with his size and bulk, Osborne is a surprisingly good skater. He has some rink-length speed and great strength in his strides and on his feet, but Mark lacks great foot speed. His balance is also a little high, and that affects his physical game, sometimes leaving him on the ice after hits and unable to rejoin the play immediately.

His other great finesse ability is his shot, which is very powerful. It looks good, but doesn't live up to its billing. He's not a very accurate shooter, nor does Osborne have the quick release and touch a goal scorer has to have to be successful. He is, therefore, not a gifted scorer.

He doesn't handle the puck very well, especially when he carries it at full speed, nor (assist total aside) does Osborne see the ice very well. As such, he really has no idea what to do with the puck when he gets possession of it in the corner. He doesn't think ahead to what he wants to accomplish, and so will just toss the puck around the boards rather than looking for a play out front.

THE PHYSICAL GAME

Osborne was a much more successful physical force last year than he has ever been before. Where previously he had been inconsistent in the use of his size and strength, he last year threw more checks than anyone on the team. And he did so game in and game out, which goes a long way to repealing his reputation for selective body checking (as in playing a tough physical game at home against Vancouver, but disappearing on the road in Detroit).

He is also the best conditioned guy on the team, and he finishes his checks all over the ice.

THE INTANGIBLES

We told you a change of scenery would do Osborne good, and he certainly fulfilled that prophecy. He was Toronto's hardest worker in both practices and games, and that's important because Mark can't succeed on just talent alone. He has to work hard to be successful. Now let's see if he can continue that success.

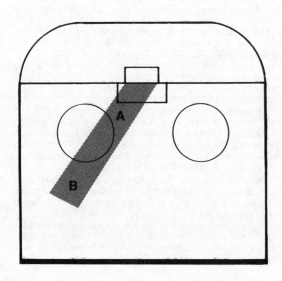

456

LUKE RICHARDSON

Yrs. of NHL service: 1
Born: Ottawa, Ontario, Canada; March 26, 1969
Position: Defenseman
Height: 6-3
Weight: 210
Uniform no.: 2
Shoots: left

Career statisics:

GP	G	A	TP	+/−	PIM	PP	SH	GW	GT	S	PCT
78	4	6	10	-25	90	0	0	0	0	49	8.2

LAST SEASON

Richardson was Toronto's first round pick in the 1987 Entry Draft. His minus 25 was tied for the team's worst mark.

THE FINESSE GAME

Richardson is an outstanding skater, made even more so by virtue of the bulk he carries around the rink. He skates excellently both back and forth, and he also has good mobility and lateral movement to close the gaps and force the play. Good acceleration skills help him here, and right now Richardson uses his skating skill defensively. He won't challenge at the blue line, preferring to fall back and defend.

He plays defense smartly by not putting himself in bad situations. Luke protects his area of the ice as well as any player on the Leafs, but he also possesses the ability to recover if he becomes trapped. He closes the skating lane down and takes the man out of the play.

When he does play offensively, Richardson moves the puck from his end well. He has a good slap shot from the blue line, though it's not as strong as it could be.

THE PHYSICAL GAME

Luke is the team's best 1-on-1 defensive bodychecker, and he's very good at checking in the open ice. He patrols the front of the net and the corners well and with good strength, and he won't often be out-muscled in those areas.

He hits willingly, but he could apply his strength to those hits better to make them more punishing.

THE INTANGIBLES

Luke has an excellent attitude and will work on anything the coach asks. He played well last year for an 18-year-old, and would certainly have shown better if the team could have levelled out. He wants to succeed and be a leader and he will, making him a legitimate number one draft choice.

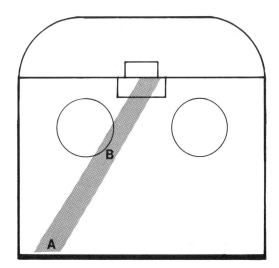

BORJE SALMING

Yrs. of NHL service: 15
Born: Kiruna, Sweden; April 17, 1951
Position: Defenseman
Height: 6-1
Weight: 185
Uniform no.: 21
Shoots: left

Career statistics:

GP	G	A	TP	PIM
1,036	145	603	748	1,206

1987-88 statistics:

GP	G	A	TP	+/−	PIM	PP	SH	GW	GT	S	PCT
66	2	24	26	7	82	1	0	0	0	92	2.2

LAST SEASON

Games played total was highest in three seasons, though Salming was hobbled by a back injury for five games. Goal total was a career low, with assists and points highest in three years. His plus/minus total was the team's highest among regulars.

THE FINESSE GAME

The venerable remains a tremendous player, despite his 15-year NHL career. He's still a tremendous skater, fluid in his stride and still speedy and quick though obviously not as outstanding as earlier in his career. He's lost a little of his balance though (evident in his less-than-perfect cuts to his left), so that he'll go to the ice after hits, even ones he initiates. Still, he recovers to make a play somehow, someway.

He rarely rushs up-ice now, hanging back and reading the defensive play and freeing his more offensive minded partners. He just moves the puck out of the defensive zone with consistent excellence, handling the puck exceptionally well. He can carry it around most any opposing player.

Borje sees the ice very well and can always find the open man in the offensive zone, or the forward for the breakout in the defensive zone. Defensively, Salming plays his angles very well, steering the opposition wide of the net. He can anticipate the play well and will break it up and turn it up-ice quickly.

THE PHYSICAL GAME

Salming is very well conditioned and, though he has had his bouts of injury throughout his career, has been fairly durable. He has good strength and can tie the opposition up in front of the net — again, smartly — or along the boards.

He is not much of a hitter now, more of a pusher and shover, but Salming can be effective in muscling opposing forwards off the puck.

THE INTANGIBLES

Salming is one of the most complete defensemen the NHL has ever seen. He skates, takes the man out, moves the puck — all of it. And, as a historical note, he's probably the first player in NHL history to have consistently one-timed the puck for a shot. He was ridiculed at first, but now everyone does it — or tries to.

He's a super team guy, giving his all in practices and games.

Unfortunately, this future Hall-of-Famer has fallen into disfavor with coach John Brophy, and Salming's public criticisms of the coach probably mean he'll be playing elsewhere this season. Bear in mind though, he's always been one of owner Harold Ballard's favorites. That may mitigate in Salming's favor in his conflicts with the coach.

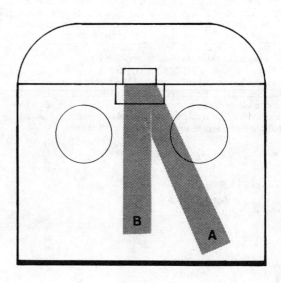

AL SECORD

Yrs. of NHL service: 10
Born: Sudbury, Ontario, Canada; March 3, 1958
Position: Left wing
Height: 6-1
Weight: 210
Uniform no.: 20
Shoots: left

Career statistics:

GP	G	A	TP	PIM
663	253	205	458	1,853

1987-88 statistics:

GP	G	A	TP	+/−	PIM	PP	SH	GW	GT	S	PCT
74	15	27	42	-21	221	2	0	0	0	149	10.1

LAST SEASON

Games played mark was lowest in three years. Goal total matches full season low. PIM total was team high, and second highest of career. Plus/minus rating was tied for fourth worst. He was sidelined early in the season with a rib injury.

THE FINESSE GAME

Secord is a strong skater, but not a fancy one. He goes in and out of the corners and charges the net, all with a straight-ahead bull in a china shop style. There's not a lot of dipsy-doodling in his play, and Secord is smart enough to not play outside his limits.

He's a bull around the net, and it's from there that Secord will get his goals. He won't stickhandle past an entire team, and he won't blow the puck past a goaltender. He'll just knock in the rebounds and the garbage, and occasionally pot the odd 20-foot shot.

His assists will come from pucks he's knocked loose and his teammates have converted.

His problem last season was that he attempted to do too much, handling the puck when he should be passing it and so on. He was also not being patient around the net, not taking that extra half-second to secure the puck and score.

THE PHYSICAL GAME

Secord remains one of the NHL's strongest men, courtesy of his fanatical approach toward working out. His upper body strength makes him difficult to dislodge from the puck, and it also adds to his power as a hitter.

Secord goes to the front of the net to take his beating there, knowing that in traffic his strength serves him best by allowing him to shrug off the opposition and shovel in the puck.

He has always been mean and tough, and he remains a vindictive player, determined to pay back every check. That tends to get him in trouble vis à vis penalties. When he was scoring 40 and 50 goals a club could withstand Secord's penalties. But 15 goals makes his play a little excessive (less kind critics might call his play stupid).

THE INTANGIBLES

Last year Secord worked as hard as he ever has — and he is one tremendous worker on and off the ice in practice and in games. But he got almost nothing accomplished offensively.

Age is a big question here, and last year Secord looked like he got old in a hurry.

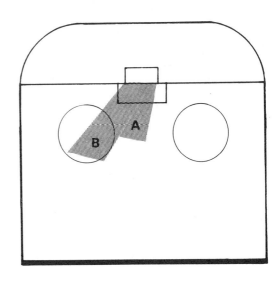

GREG TERRION

Yrs. of NHL service: 8
Born: Marmora, Ontario, Canada; May 2, 1960
Position: Left wing
Height: 6-0
Weight: 190
Uniform no.: 7
Shoots: left

Career statistics:

GP	G	A	TP	PIM
561	93	150	243	339

1987-88 statistics:

GP	G	A	TP	+/−	PIM	PP	SH	GW	GT	S	PCT
59	4	16	20	-6	65	1	0	1	0	57	7.0

LAST SEASON

Games played was a career low, with goal mark correspondingly low (a five-game groin injury was partly accountable, as was a stint in the minors).

THE FINESSE GAME

Terrion is a great skater, equipped with good speed and lateral movement. He has above average foot speed so he's fairly agile, and that skating combines with his good vision and hockey sense to make him a good checking or defensive forward.

He sees the ice well and can read the play and Greg is especially proficient in doing so during penalty killing situations. Because of his speed and ability to anticipate, Terrion is a threat for a short-handed goal; last year, 25 percent of his goals came during that specialty team situation.

Terrion has been largely unable to translate that ability to his offensive game. Though he sees the openings, Terrion is a little tough with the puck and has difficulty getting it to his teammates. He gets excited when handling it, or when he's in traffic and he has neither the patience nor the hands to make the plays. Also, he doesn't shoot enough. That's bad, because he has a great shot. Therefore, any scoring is going to have to be from in close.

He is extremely conscientious about his defense, as any good checking forward would be, and backchecks very deeply into his own zone.

THE PHYSICAL GAME

Terrion takes the body fairly well, though he is neither overwhelmingly big nor strong. He's strong enough to slow down his check or tie him up, and will smartly hold his own against the opposition without taking penalties.

Terrion also has great stamina and is in tremendous condition. This makes him an almost tireless skater and allows him to drive the opposition crazy with his relentless checking.

THE INTANGIBLES

Terrion is a role player, but an important one if unspectacular. He's an extremely hard worker, a great team player and has a super attitude.

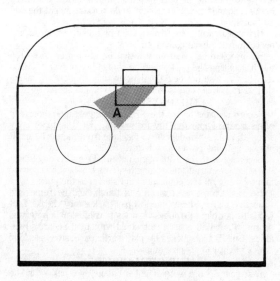

KEN WREGGET

Yrs. of NHL service: 4
Born: Brandon, Man., Canada; March 25, 1964
Position: Goaltender
Height: 6-1
Weight: 180
Uniform no.: 31
Catches: left

Career statistics:

GP	MINS	G	SO	AVG	A	PIM
168	9,035	652	2	4.32	10	86

1987-88 statisics:

GP	MINS	AVG	W	L	T	SO	GA	SA	SAPCT	PIM
56	3,000	4.44	12	35	4	2	222	1,712	.870	40

LAST SEASON

Wregget finished ninth among the League's goaltenders in minutes played, third in shots faced. His 35 losses led the League. Games played matched his career high, with minutes played just 26 minutes away from his career high.

THE PHYSICAL GAME

Wregget's style of goaltending is a challenging, standup one. He is at his best when he squares himself to the puck and allows it to hit him. He follows that same pattern on screen shots, coming out to the top of the screen to prevent deflections. It's important for Wregget to play this style because he's not a great skater and he tends to become scrambly when forced to move his feet. When he starts flopping around on the ice (or when he has to move his feet to make a skate save), you know he's in trouble.

When he doesn't go to the ice Wregget has fairly good balance, meaning he'll generally regain his stance for a second shot. He has good peripheral vision and sees the play at the side of the net or moving across his body well. That helps him cover the posts and move across the net well.

He has good hands in terms of reflex speed, but he doesn't control the puck well with his glove. He'll get his hand in the way of a shot but won't catch it, so when the puck falls to the ice he has to make another save on the rebound. Wregget also doesn't handle the puck well, and that leads to a lot of defensive confusion. As such, he can be said to be a poor communicator with his defensemen.

THE MENTAL GAME

Wregget uses great anticipation to complement his positional play, and when he's on, the combination makes him tough to beat. He has big save capability, but he can be his own worst enemy in terms of his mental outlook.

He goes beyond concentration to worry and puts too much pressure on himself. He'll burn up energy in one game that another goalie needs three or four games to disperse. Sometimes he'll burn up so much energy in pregame fidgeting and worrying that he'll be completely out of gas within the game's opening minutes and has to get pulled because he has nothing left.

THE INTANGIBLES

He's shown in the past that he can and should be Toronto's number one goaltender, but until he can consistently control his worrying and learn to pace himself, Wregget is going to have a very up-and-down NHL career.

VANCOUVER CANUCKS

LINE COMBINATIONS
PAUL LAWLESS-BARRY PEDERSON-TONY TANTI
PETRI SKRIKO-GREG ADAMS-RICH SUTTER
-DOUG WICKENHEISER-DAVID BRUCE
-DAN HODGSON-JIM SANDLAK

DEFENSE PAIRINGS
JIM BENNING-GARTH BUTCHER
DOUG LIDSTER-DAVE RICHTER
-LARRY MELNYK
-DARYL STANLEY

GOALTENDERS
KIRK MCLEAN
STEVE WEEKS

OTHER PLAYERS
STAN SMYL — Right wing

POWER PLAY

FIRST UNIT:
PETRI SKRIKO-BARRY PEDERSON-TONY TANTI
JIM BENNING-DOUG LIDSTER

PEDERSON controls behind the net and distributes to the point men. SKRIKO is in the left circle, and TANTI at the right. Puck moves along the perimeter until one of the forwards can get free for a shot off a return pass. Point shots are the second option, with all forwards crashing the net.

SANDLAK and ADAMS will also see power play time, with SANDLAK posting up in front and ADAMS working from his opposite side.

Last season the Vancouver power play was FAIR, scoring 81 goals in 435 attempts (18.6 percent, 14th overall). The Canucks, however, allowed the second most shorthanded goals in the League last year.

PENALTY KILLING

FIRST UNIT:
BARRY PEDERSON-DOUG WICKENHEISER
DOUG LIDSTER-DAVE RICHTER

Vancouver's penalty killing is conservative, with the four men playing a basic box. They force the play outside and along the perimeter, and will occasionally pressure the puck, but not on a consistent basis. SKRIKO, when he works this unit, is the only player to really jump the puck carrier. BENNING and BUTCHER will also see time, with SUTTER and SMYL other forwards.

Last season the Canuck penalty killing was FAIR, allowing 83 goals in 404 shorthanded situations (79.5 percent, 11th overall).

CRUCIAL FACEOFFS

PEDERSON will get most of these, with WICKENHEISER seeing some time.

GREG ADAMS

Yrs. of NHL service: 3
Born: Nelson, B.C., Canada; August 1, 1963
Position: Center
Height: 6-2
Weight: 185
Uniform no.: 8
Shoots: left

Career statistics:

GP	G	A	TP	PIM
266	103	118	221	93

1987-88 statistics:

GP	G	A	TP	+/−	PIM	PP	SH	GW	GT	S	PCT
80	36	40	76	-24	30	12	0	3	0	227	15.9

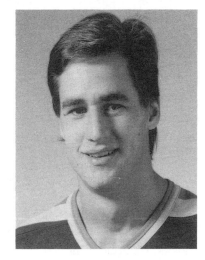

LAST SEASON

Adams (along with Kirk McLean) was traded to the Canucks in a preseason deal that sent Patrik Sundstrom to New Jersey. Games played and goal total were career highs, assists and point totals second highest of his career. He finished second on the team in all point totals, power play goals and game winners, and he led the Canucks in shots on goal. His minus 24 was the team's worst.

THE FINESSE GAME

The thing that powers Adams as a scorer is his anticipation. He gets into position to score very well and that sense makes his other finesse skills better.

He is a good but not outstanding skater in terms of speed and agility, but his long stride can carry him past the opposition. Once in the clear his good balance lets him lean and swoop inside and around the opposition, but he is not a very agile player in terms of quick turns or stops and starts.

He could improve his skating by improving his foot speed; that way he'd snare more loose pucks around the goal by going for them, instead of reaching for them as he does now. He has almost no lateral game, preferring to go up and down instead of side to side, and that's tied in to his lack of agility.

His straight-at-the-goal style is complemented by his puck-handling and reach. Greg carries the puck well when he moves up-ice and he uses his reach and balance to lean away from the defense and head to the net.

Adams' shot is good, a hard wrist shot released fairly quickly. He has the strength to blow a few past the goaltender from farther out, but he's going to move in closer for his goals. That shot and ability to get open makes him a power play regular.

THE PHYSICAL GAME

Greg doesn't play a physical game and his lack of strength is one good reason why. He has great size in terms of height and reach, but he lacks the bulk to make a physical game work. Because of that he can be taken off the puck by smaller and/or stronger forwards. Improved strength would be of great benefit to his game.

He uses his reach excellently to snare loose pucks, and Adams is very good at shielding the puck with his body.

THE INTANGIBLES

When he works to free himself from his checks Adams will be successful. His movement creates openings in the offensive zone and the defense has to respect his scoring ability. But Greg's problem is one of inconsistent effort (especially defensively).

For example, 15 of his 36 goals came in the first quarter of last season, 23 of 36 by Game 43. So he scored only 13 goals in his last 37 games (just seven in his last 18 games), contests where Vancouver was still in the race for a playoff berth. And of those last seven goals in his final 18 games, just three came at even strength.

So consistency over the course of the year, as well as greater even-strength play efficiency (just 24 ESG) are the things Adams must aim for.

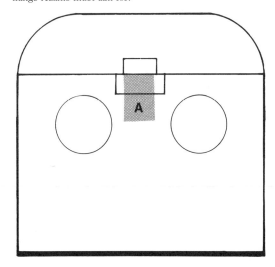

JIM BENNING

Yrs. of NHL service: 7
Born: Edmonton, Alta., Canada; April 29, 1963
Position: Defenseman
Height: 6-0
Weight: 185
Uniform no.: 4
Shoots: left

Career statistics:

GP	G	A	TP	PIM
495	46	173	219	387

1987-88 statistics:

GP	G	A	TP	+/-	PIM	PP	SH	GW	GT	S	PCT
77	7	26	33	0	58	1	1	1	0	102	6.9

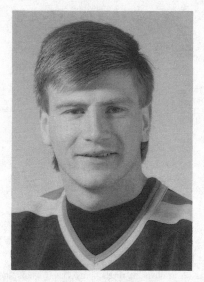

LAST SEASON

Games played total was highest in three seasons and point total was third highest of his career. He finished second on the club in defensive scoring and his plus/minus rating was the team's second best (best among defensemen).

THE FINESSE GAME

Skating is clearly the best of Benning's finesse skills. He's a very agile, very mobile defender with excellent acceleration and lateral movement abilities. He combines those skills with good puckhandling talent to become an effective rushing defenseman.

Jim is generally poised and intelligent in his defensive zone play in terms of turning the play up-ice, but he can be forced to make blind passes around the boards by strong forechecking. But when he has the play ahead of him, Jim is efficient at getting the puck from his zone by either passing or carrying it.

He's demonstrated good vision and anticipation, but Benning has been unable to consistently get his mental skills in harness with his physical ones, so he is definitely under-achieving as an offensive player.

There is a benefit to Benning's hamstrung offense and that's his solid defensive play. Still, he will follow the play up-ice and can control the point well. His skills make him valuable on the power play, and he has a good shot from the point.

Defensively, Benning plays a positional game, though he will sometimes get caught wandering in search of the puck. He generally keeps the play wide of the net by using his skating ability to force the opposition rather than by playing his defensive angles, so part of Benning's defensive problem is that he is focussed on the puck and not the man. But even with that weakness his plus/minus throughout his career has always been good.

THE PHYSICAL GAME

Jim is a finesse player with size. He'll tie men up along the boards or in front of the net, but he won't knock anyone into the nickel seats. And since he always has his attention on the puck and not the man, it's no surprise he could play the body better than he does.

THE INTANGIBLES

Benning is a good offensive complement to Doug Lidster, except Lidster didn't hold up his end of the bargain last season. But Jim gives the Canucks another solid offensive presence from the blue line and he should continue to do so for quite some time. In fact, if he could ever play with a team that wasn't struggling Benning would no doubt improve tremendously.

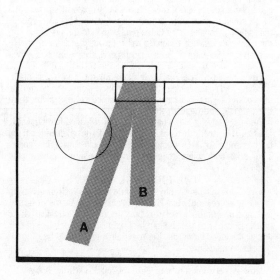

DAVID BRUCE

Yrs. of NHL service: 2
Born: Thunder Bay, Ontario, Canada; October 7, 1964
Position: Right wing
Height: 5-11
Weight: 177
Uniform no.: 25
Shoots: right

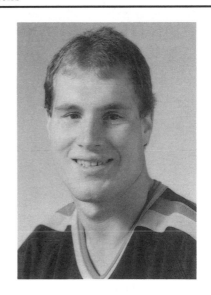

Career statistics:

GP	G	A	TP	PIM
90	16	11	27	180

1987-88 statistics:

GP	G	A	TP	+/−	PIM	PP	SH	GW	GT	S	PCT
25	7	3	10	-6	57	1	0	0	0	46	15.2

LAST SEASON

Bruce was sidelined by mononucleosis early in the season and was sent to the American Hockey League before finishing the season with Vancouver.

THE FINESSE GAME

He's never going to be known as a super-talented finesse player, but Bruce has some developable finesse skills. He's become a good skater at the NHL level through hard work, improving his stride and foot speed so as to become quicker and more mobile; he stops, starts and changes direction well.

David has a fair dose of hockey smarts, possessing a good idea of how a play will develop and how he can either help it or prevent it. He is not tremendously creative in open ice, but his vision is good enough that he will recognize openings and get to them. Bruce concentrates now — when he plays that is — on using those skills defensively, but his history shows he can contribute offensively.

Bruce has a hard wrist shot but doesn't shoot enough (again, the defensive role taking priority), but he'll have to be within 30 feet of the net to score. At this point, he's not going to blow slap shots past anyone.

THE PHYSICAL GAME

The physical game is okay by David Bruce, despite his less-than-intimidating size. He has good balance on his skates and that helps him remain vertical after hitting so he can continue his plays, and he combines that balance with good upper body strength to continue handling the puck when being checked himself.

He is also strong in the hands and wrists, and that strength powers his shot and makes him effective when going after the puck in traffic, because he can pull it out from a tangle.

THE INTANGIBLES

Bruce is determined to make the Canucks, but the thing he must do more than that is stay healthy. If he can stay off the disabled list he might finally get a full season's chance to show the results of his hard work toward improvement.

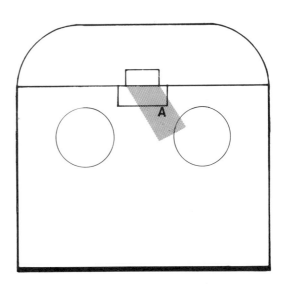

GARTH BUTCHER

Yrs. of NHL service: 6
Born: Regina, Sask., Canada; January 8, 1963
Position: Defenseman
Height: 6-0
Weight: 200
Uniform no.: 5
Shoots: right

Career statistics:

GP	G	A	TP	PIM
383	21	61	82	979

1987-88 statistics:

GP	G	A	TP	+/−	PIM	PP	SH	GW	GT	S	PCT
80	6	17	23	-14	285	1	0	0	0	77	7.8

LAST SEASON

Butcher played a full season for the first time in his career. He led the club in PIM, which was also a career high. His plus/minus total was the second worst among Vancouver defensemen. All point totals were career highs.

THE FINESSE GAME

Increased finesse skills have a lot to do with Butcher's playing a full season without demotion. His skating skills continue to improve and he is more mobile now than ever before. He has increased his balance and foot speed and that has helped him improve his turns and agility, all to the point of keeping up with the opposing forward and closing the gap on the puck carrier when possible. He's now a solid level NHL skater.

Garth's improved skating ability has also improved his puckhandling. He has the ability to rush the puck, and can make good plays for offensive chances at the opposition's blue line because of the extra time his skating has gained him. Butcher also moves the puck well to the forwards for breakout passes. He is fairly poised and will look for the right play, and that patience/concentration is also used when he chooses to rush the puck.

He forces the play wide of the net consistently, and because of his improved skating his positioning has improved. He is now stronger without the puck.

His improvement has not made him into Gary Suter — or even Doug Lidster — but Butcher can generate some offense from the opposing blue line with his good, low slap shot from the point. His offense will also be limited because he's the defensive safety valve (the first player to fall back), but he can spot the open man and get the pass to him. Even with his improved skating, Butcher is not likely to pinch in or challenge toward the net.

THE PHYSICAL GAME

We'll resist the temptation to say that Butcher lives up to his name, but he certainly is a tough and aggressive player. He led the club in PIM for the fourth straight year, though more as a policeman than anything else. He willingly takes on the League's heavyweights to protect his teammates, and Garth has increased his upper body strength so as to be better prepared for the wrestling/fighting.

Butcher is a good hitter, especially since he's now catching people more often than he's missing them. He can take a forward off the puck with a check, though he's no guarantee to make a subsequent play, and Butcher is very physical in front of the net.

THE INTANGIBLES

Butcher is a dedicated player and a good team man, and his maturation as a player corresponds to the unwritten rule that defensemen take five years to come into their own. He is never going to be a super player (and certainly Vancouver could have done better with a number one draft choice — both Al MacInnis and Chris Chelios were taken after Butcher in 1981), but he is an earnest and honest one.

He is Vancouver's most consistent defensive force.

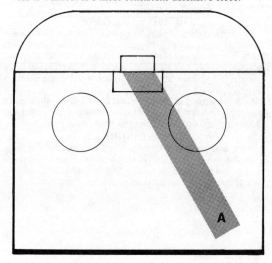

DAN HODGSON

Yrs. of NHL service: 2
Born: Fort McMurray, Alta., Canada; August 29, 1965
Position: Center
Height: 5-11
Weight: 173
Uniform no.: 16
Shoots: right

Career statistics:

GP	G	A	TP	PIM
91	25	32	57	39

1987-88 statistics:

GP	G	A	TP	+/−	PIM	PP	SH	GW	GT	S	PCT
8	3	7	10	1	2	1	0	1	0	7	42.9

85 Junior Player of the Year: If he's healthy, don't bet against him.

LAST SEASON

Games played total was a career low, courtesy first of starting in the minors and then a broken leg.

THE FINESSE GAME

Hodgson has exceptional skills. He is an excellent skater, quick, fast and agile, and he complements that skating with good hands, because he has a lot of puck ability.

Dan can carry the puck and handle it well as he skates, and he is also a good passer to both sides. He anticipates the play well and has good hockey sense, though he is a touch predictable in his play-making. Because he is a right-handed shot, for example, he likes to drive the net on the right hand side, pull up at the goal line and then pass to an incoming winger.

Because of his ability to use his teammates and to get to the openings (good foot speed), Hodgson is a good power play man. He has a good shot, accurate and well-released, but right now he'll have to be in close proximity of the net to score. Besides, his quickness makes him an ideally opportunistic player.

He is less than proficient defensively because of his offensive bent, and so is likely to be caught deep when the puck is turned over. Better positional play in his own zone would help too.

THE PHYSICAL GAME

Hodgson is small, and his game is one of finesse over size. While he is unafraid of the traffic areas, his size mitigates his working well from there, and that's something Hodgson knows. However, because he has such superlative hand skills, Dan can perform well when caught in a tangle along the boards or in the corners.

Just don't ask him to take anyone off the puck, and don't ask him to check Mark Messier.

THE INTANGIBLES

Hodgson showed well in his short stint with the Canucks last season, but we've left his report alone because that short stint wasn't long enough for another look at him. Vancouver needs offense and they need excitement, so Hodgson should get another chance this year — if he has sufficiently recovered from his broken leg.

His credentials are excellent — despite his lack of size — and we'll repeat what we said last year about Canada's 1984-

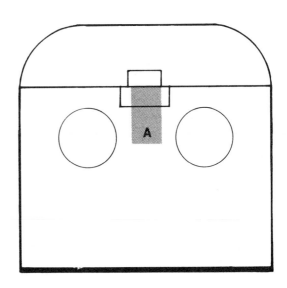

PAUL LAWLESS

Yrs. of NHL service: 4
Born: Scarborough, Ontario, Canada; July 2, 1964
Position: Left wing
Height: 5-11
Weight: 185
Uniform no.: 17
Shoots: left

Career statistics:

GP	G	A	TP	PIM
225	49	76	125	54

1987-88 statistics:

GP	G	A	TP	+/−	PIM	PP	SH	GW	GT	S	PCT
48	4	11	15	-11	16	0	0	1	0	91	4.4

LAST SEASON

Lawless was acquired late in the season from Philadelphia in exchange for defenseman Willie Huber. He had been traded from Hartford to Philadelphia in exchange for Lindsay Carson. Games played total was the second lowest of his career and lowest in the last three years. Goal total was a career low.

THE FINESSE GAME

Lawless has excellent speed on his skates, and he complements that with excellent foot speed for good agility and lateral movement. The downside is that he is reckless in his approach because he does everything at full throttle. He is a good checker because of his skating and Paul checks by watching his man and sticking with him, rather than by examining the play and seeing what will happen next.

His speed creates many opportunities and it is his speed, rather than his hands, that gets him his goals. His hands are a little tough and are certainly not as well developed as his feet, and Paul has difficulty successfully carrying or passing the puck. He doesn't have the touch necessary for soft passes, and his feet are often moving too fast for Lawless' hands to catch up.

Though he's begun to demonstrate a playmaking ability Lawless has limited vision and anticipation, mostly because he makes his plays with his head down (and that's why his shot isn't on net as often as it should be). As such, he's going to have to be in fairly close proximity of the net to score.

THE PHYSICAL GAME

Lawless likes to hit and he'll hit hard. Because he is strong along the boards Paul will jar the puck free, but his aforementioned difficulties handling the puck make it hard for him to make a play coming away from the boards. Though a hard hitter Lawless is a clean player, and his upper body and leg strength push you where he wants to go.

THE INTANGIBLES

He's a hard worker, willing to learn and coachable, but Lawless must learn to moderate his speed if he is ever going to be successful. His speed says 30 goals, but his hands say 20. The third season is generally when a player makes his move, and Lawless' third season was twice interrupted by

trades. This year in Vancouver should gives us a clue as to where he is going with his career.

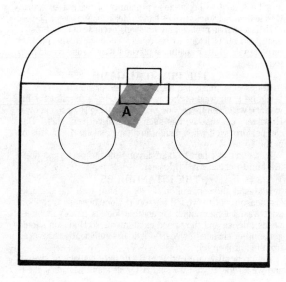

DOUG LIDSTER

Yrs. of NHL service: 4
Born: Kamloops, B.C., Canada; October 18, 1960
Position: Defenseman
Height: 6-1
Weight: 195
Uniform no.: 3
Shoots: right

Career statistics:

GP	G	A	TP	PIM
308	34	123	157	260

1987-88 statistics:

GP	G	A	TP	+/−	PIM	PP	SH	GW	GT	S	PCT
64	4	32	36	-19	105	2	1	0	0	133	3.0

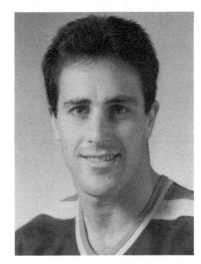

LAST SEASON

Games played total was lowest (for full season) of Lidster's career; he missed 16 games with a knee injury. He led the Canuck defensemen in scoring but goal total was a career low (assist and point totals second highest of career). He finished fifth on the club in shots on goal, but his plus/minus was tied for second worst (with Larry Melnyk).

THE FINESSE GAME

Lidster is a very good skater, and his foot speed and balance are the keys to his skating skill. He has excellent mobility and agility — especially laterally — and the ability to move in any direction within a step. The only thing he doesn't have is explosive acceleration ability, but he'll get to loose pucks before many other players because of his quickness.

He uses his skating ability to carry the puck from the zone, but Lidster tempers his offensive bent with good judgement. If a breakout pass is the more efficient way of moving the Canucks from their own end, then Lidster will make that pass. But when the forwards are bogged down Doug will rush the puck with authority.

Lidster joins the play as a fourth attacker whenever prudent, and he amplifies his skating ability to handling the puck well in motion. He has big, strong and soft hands and he manipulates the puck excellently. He passes well off the stickhandle and his vision and hockey sense make him a power play regular.

Doug doesn't have a great shot (and he doesn't use the one he has enough anyway) from the point, but his wrist shot from the faceoff circle is a good weapon.

Lidster is a good player defensively, and his plus/minus rating is more an indication of his large ice-time and team's woes than it is Lidster's defensive mistakes. He plays well positionally, forcing the play wide and then closing the gap on the puck carrier.

THE PHYSICAL GAME

Strength and physical play aren't the highlights of Lidster's game, as he is basically a finesse player with size. He does take the body well when he can, but he can be out-muscled along the boards and in front of the net by stronger forwards. The result of those mismatches is interference penalties that put Lidster in the box and Vancouver in a hole. An improvement in strength would make him more effective defensively.

THE INTANGIBLES

Lidster's game took a step backward last year for several reasons. The injury was one, but Doug is no longer an unknown property around the League and teams know that he has to be keyed on.

So he saw much more checking last year than before and that checking restricted his productivity. That checking also served to affect Lidster's judgement and he was not as aggressive in his offensive play as he had been; he played much more tentatively.

He is a hard worker and an enthusiastic player, and he's also the Canuck's most important defenseman. For that reason — and for any conceivable Vancouver success — Lidster must force himself through the checking and raise his game.

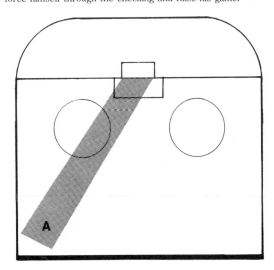

KIRK MCLEAN

Yrs. of NHL service: 1
Born: Willowdale, Ontario, Canada; June 26, 1966
Position: Goaltender
Height: 6-0
Weight: 195
Uniform no.: 1
Catches: left

Career statistics:

GP	MINS	G	SO	AVG	A	PIM
47	2,651	168	1	3.80	2	8

1987-88 statisics:

GP	MINS	AVG	W	L	T	SO	GA	SA	SAPCT	PIM
41	2,380	3.71	11	27	3	1	147	1,178	.875	8

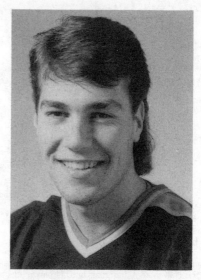

LAST SEASON

McLean was acquired from New Jersey (along with Greg Adams) in exchange for Patrik Sundstrom in a preseason deal. He finished second in games and minutes played by a rookie goaltender, and he had Vancouver's only shutout of the season.

THE PHYSICAL GAME

McLean has excellent size and he uses it well in playing his position. He challenges the shooters by playing his angles, and Kirk's size and pure bulk fills a lot of net. McLean generally squares himself to the puck well and moves in and out of his net well when challenging the shooters.

He has fairly good balance but could improve it for play at the NHL level, just as he could improve his foot speed. Right now McLean is susceptible to the shots every tall goalie is supposed to be susceptible tolow and on the ice to the outsides of the feet. While he is less likely to automatically give up this goal than other goalies (Pete Peeters, notably), McLean is not yet as fast in the feet as Ron Hextall. That lack of foot speed also prevents him from closing the gap between his legs (the five-hole) as quickly as he should.

The other thing improved foot speed and balance would do is help Kirk regain his stance after he goes to the ice. He is much better on his feet than off them, and once he gets his feet moving he can be in trouble. He can redeem himself by getting one or another of his long limbs in the way of the second shot, but he can't last in the NHL that way.

Kirk has good hand skills and reflexes and generally handles his rebounds well, though miscommunications with the defense will leave rebounds in the crease for opposing forwards to feast on. McLean will come out of his net to flag down the puck and will wrap it around the boards, but his miscommunication with the defense and his failure to adequately see the play means a lot of turnovers.

THE MENTAL GAME

McLean has shown that he can be mentally tough, but right now he has difficulty carrying his concentration from period to period within games. He is apt to not be concentrating at the starts of periods and will be vulnerable then, and Kirk also loses his concentration if he's kept idle for long stretches.

THE INTANGIBLES

Though he didn't play a game in March, giving way to Frank Caprice and later Steve Weeks, McLean is still the Canucks' goalie of the future. Vancouver management is very high on him, saying that he played as well as Ron Hextall at the American League level and that it's only a matter of time until McLean plays that well in the NHL. Proof? McLean was named one of the game's three stars more often last season than any other Canuck.

One major difference between the two, though, was that Hextall broke in with a much stronger team and didn't have to constantly revive his confidence. The key with McLean is going to be time, and whether the Canucks can surround him with enough quality personnel to prevent the youngster from falling into the bad habits that are inevitable with a bad team.

LARRY MELNYK

Yrs. of NHL service: 6
Born: Saskatoon, Sask., Canada; February 21, 1960
Position: Defenseman
Height: 6-0
Weight: 190
Uniform no.: 24
Shoots: left

Career statistics:

GP	G	A	TP	PIM
291	8	50	58	513

1987-88 statistics:

GP	G	A	TP	+/−	PIM	PP	SH	GW	GT	S	PCT
63	2	4	6	-19	107	0	0	0	0	40	5.0

LAST SEASON

Melnyk and Willie Huber were traded to the Canucks early in the year for Michel Petit. Games played total was second highest in his career, as was PIM mark. His plus/minus tied for the team's second worst, and he was sidelined for several weeks after the trade because of an eye injury.

THE FINESSE GAME

Intelligence is the key to Melnyk's NHL success, the intelligence to play within himself and not get fancy.

Melnyk skates on his heels and doesn't have a lot of mobility or speed because of that. He makes up for that by playing his defensive angles well, and that makes him tough to get around. He forces the opposition wide of the net extremely well, not allowing enemy forwards to get good shots at the goaltender.

He is not at all offensive minded and will pinch into the offensive zone only on the rarest of occasions. He does not have an exceptional shot and he hardly shoots at all for that matter. Melnyk reads the opposing rush very well and then blunts it through smarts.

THE PHYSICAL GAME

Melnyk uses his size well in front of the net and along the boards, where he has good strength. He is willing to sacrifice his body to block shots and is aggressive in a non-fighting way, doing whatever he can to help the team.

THE INTANGIBLES

Melnyk is prey to inconsistency in his own performance and he must concentrate for the game's full 60 minutes to be effective. He must work hard every night to get the best from his modest talent, and he can and should be a steadying influence on the Vancouver blue line.

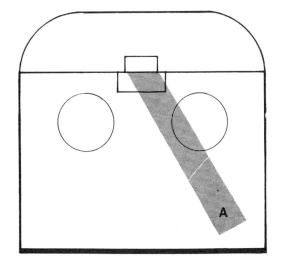

BARRY PEDERSON

Yrs. of NHL service: 8
Born: Big River, Sask., Canada; March 13, 1961
Position: Center
Height: 5-11
Weight: 185
Uniform no.: 7
Shoots: right

Career statistics:

GP	G	A	TP	PIM
502	206	349	555	382

1987-88 statistics:

GP	G	A	TP	+/−	PIM	PP	SH	GW	GT	S	PCT
76	19	52	71	2	92	4	1	1	1	163	11.7

LAST SEASON

Games played total was lowest in three seasons. Goal total was lowest of any full season, ditto point total. He finished third on the club in scoring, first in assists and plus/minus. He missed one game with a concussion.

THE FINESSE GAME

Pederson is a very good skater in all facets of that skill. He has strength and balance on his feet, as well as quickness. The result is an agile player with good lateral movement, foot speed and the ability to remain vertical after taking hits.

Barry complements his skating by handling the puck very well and forcing the opposition to respect both his ability to take the puck into the openings himself or to lead his teammates into those openings with excellent passes. He's aided in his puckhandling by his excellent anticipation, vision and instinct. He reads the entire ice surface.

Pederson is a dangerous shooter, most particularly from the slot with a hard wrist shot. He does have the ability to blow the puck past the goaltender from farther out, but he doesn't shoot anywhere near enough. A touch of selfishness would help.

While a dangerous offensive player (especially on the power play where all his skills can be brought to bear with even greater result), some of Barry's offense was sacrificed to defense — that plus/minus rating on a team that was itself minus 48 is incredible. The anticipation and smarts noted above aid Pederson in his defensive game.

THE PHYSICAL GAME

Though not gifted with great size, Pederson plays a physical game. He is strong for his size and his hand and foot skills (most notably his balance) make him very effective along the boards. He'll always initiate contact to knock an opponent off the puck and will take a hit to make his own plays.

Strong forearms and wrists power his shots, just as they power his hands for faceoffs, an area where he does well.

THE INTANGIBLES

Heart, character, dedication, these all mark Barry Pederson as a player and they serve to make him a leader for Vancouver.

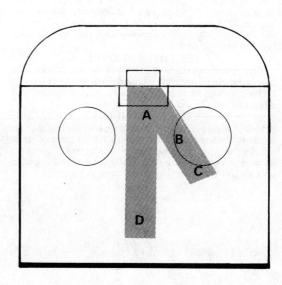

DAVE RICHTER

Yrs. of NHL service: 4
Born: Winnipeg, Man., Canada; April 8, 1960
Position: Defenseman
Height: 6-5
Weight: 217
Uniform no.: 6
Shoots: right

Career statistics:

GP	G	A	TP	PIM
297	8	35	43	931

1987-88 statistics:

GP	G	A	TP	+/−	PIM	PP	SH	GW	GT	S	PCT
49	2	4	6	-5	224	0	0	0	0	18	11.1

LAST SEASON

Games played total was lowest in four seasons (he missed 11 games with a knee injury, five with an eye injury). His PIM total was a career high, second highest on the club.

THE FINESSE GAME

Richter is not talented in the finesse areas of the game. He sees the play poorly at both ends of the ice, meaning he cannot help sustain an attack in the offensive zone, nor help thwart one in the defensive zone.

He has little foot speed or agility, so he can't close the gap between himself and a forward, and he can't turn well enough to go after them as they pass him. He is easily confused in his own end, wandering from position and leaving openings.

He will give the puck away if forechecked, and is not likely to make good passes if left alone because he doesn't understand a play and his hands aren't good enough to move the puck quickly and efficiently. He will score only rarely, and then on shots from the point.

THE PHYSICAL GAME

Richter has been obtained by Minnesota, Philadelphia and Vancouver for one thingPhysical play. He has been traded by Minnesota and Philadelphia because of a lack of one thing: Physical play.

Richter will coast if the game is not mean, and he doesn't like to be pushed to be aggressive. He'll use his size to knock people off the puck (though he can't do much of anything after that) but he could certainly be more aggressive in normal game situations.

He would have to be judged as playing smaller than he is.

THE INTANGIBLES

What can you say about a guy like this? To call him a role player demeans role players who can play the game. An enforcer, a policeman, a goon: call him what you want. And doesn't every team need a guy who averages 116.375 penalty minutes for every goal he scores?

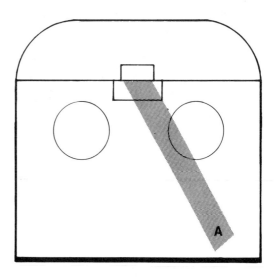

JIM SANDLAK

Yrs. of NHL service: 3
Born: Kitchener, Ontario, Canada; December 12, 1966
Position: Right wing
Height: 6-3
Weight: 205
Uniform no.: 19
Shoots: right

Career statistics:

GP	G	A	TP	PIM
150	32	39	71	157

1987-88 statistics:

GP	G	A	TP	+/–	PIM	PP	SH	GW	GT	S	PCT
49	16	15	31	-9	81	6	0	2	1	96	16.7

LAST SEASON

Games played total courtesy of early season demotion to the American Hockey League. He also missed one game with a jaw injury. Goal total was a career high, as was PIM total.

THE FINESSE GAME

Sandlak is a strong skater and that works well for him in his straight-ahead style: It allows him to work through checks along the boards. His game will never develop beyond average, however, if he doesn't develop better foot speed and balance for added quickness and agility. He is not a very mobile player in the open ice, so he's not much of a threat away from the boards, and his lack of quickness makes him easy to avoid.

Jim is balanced enough to be effective at plugging the net, but he can't take advantage of that position because he isn't quick enough — or agile enough — to take advantage of many of the loose pucks that come his way.

Greater mobility would also improve Sandlak's best finesse qualityhis shot. Jim's shot is excellentheavy, fast and powerful. His wrist shot and slap shot are both fairly accurate and, again, if he could deliver them from different areas of the ice — and if he could get into the clear to shoot them — he'd be much more difficult to thwart.

Playmaking is not high on Sandlak's finesse list, for a number of reasons. First, he can't get away from the opposition when he has the puck. Second, his vision and anticipation skills are not yet accustomed to NHL speed. Third, his entire style is an un-creative one. Sandlak will have one play in mind and won't look at options. Sorry to keep beating a dead horse, but added mobility would give him added time and space to make his plays.

He's no better than average defensively, and he has difficulty keeping up with speedy opposition forwards during the transition from offense to defense. He maintains his position fairly well.

THE PHYSICAL GAME

Right now, Sandlak is a ballerina in a linebacker's body. To be a finesse player with his kind of size is to be wasting 50 percent of his talent. He was drafted for his strength and size — both of which are excellent — and Jim can be effective in a hitting game, but he doesn't apply his immense physical talent consistently.

He *can* use his size and strength effectively along the boards or in front of the opposition net, he can play an aggressive style of game and refuse to be intimidated and has the talent to be a physical force, but that doesn't mean Sandlak *will* use those talents.

He doesn't fight through checks and traffic as well as he could, and he certainly doesn't have anyone running from him in fear.

THE INTANGIBLES

Everything necessary for Sandlak to join the ranks of the League's best power forwards — the Neelys and the Proberts — is either already in Jim's possession or is easily attainable. But Jim hasn't shown the attitude necessary to take advantage of his gifts, neither the willingness to improve the finesse skills that have to be improved nor the meanness to make his physical size most effective.

He's a good kid (still only 22 years old this season), but is comfortable with where he is right now. As with many other players this, his third season, will be a put-up-or-shut-up year. It's all up to Sandlak.

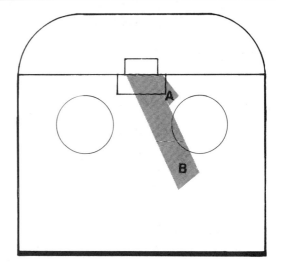

PETRI SKRIKO

Yrs. of NHL service: 4
Born: Laapeenranta, Finland; March 12, 1962
Position: Right wing
Height: 5-10
Weight: 172
Uniform no.: 26
Shoots: right

Career statistics:

GP	G	A	TP	PIM
301	122	129	251	120

1987-88 statistics:

GP	G	A	TP	+/-	PIM	PP	SH	GW	GT	S	PCT
73	30	34	64	-12	32	10	2	2	1	172	17,4

LAST SEASON

Skriko finished fourth on the team in scoring, third in goals. Games played total was lowest in three seasons, second lowest of career (he missed five games with a knee injury). He finished third on the squad in power play goals, tied for first in shorthanded tallies and third in shots on goal.

THE FINESSE GAME

For the talent Skriko shows in the finesse game, he should be one of the NHL's top players. He's an excellent skater, blessed with good speed, acceleration and tremendous balance. He is superbly agile and has excellent quickness and lateral movement. He uses his agility and speed to drive right at defensemen and create scoring opportunities. Petri uses his speed to great advantage on the specialty teams, where his one-step quickness keeps the passing lanes open on the power play and gets him to the loose pucks while killing penalties.

His great intelligence and hockey sense combines with his skating to allow him to exploit the openings in two ways. Skriko will either charge the hole himself, or he'll lead a teammate with a soft, pin-point pass. He handles the puck very well at all speeds and likes to carry it from the Vancouver zone. He is, however, guilty of keeping his head down when rushing the puck, so he is susceptible to losing it on a pokecheck. When passing his head is up, so he won't often turn the puck over.

Skriko likes to shoot the puck, something he does well. He has a quick and accurate wrist shot, so Petri makes the most of his opportunities by putting the puck on the net and forcing the goaltender to make saves. He didn't shoot as often as he should have last year (172 SOG compared to 224 in 1986-87), and that cut down on his offense. Because he is a right-handed shot playing his off-wing, Skriko will circle to his forehand for most of his scoring opportunities.

THE PHYSICAL GAME

Skriko is neither strong nor aggressive by nature, but he plays the body efficiently in all three zones and accepts hits to make his plays. Still, he lacks the size and strength necessary to check and restrain some of the League's bigger forwards, so if he can't make a defensive play by finesse, he's going to be in trouble. He will, though, use his stick to offset some of that imbalance he suffers in strength.

His conditioning and strength are not great enough to sustain him throughout the year and he goes through periods of fatigue that limit his effectiveness.

THE INTANGIBLES

Petri is just one of those players who is a streaky commodity. He has excellent on-ice work habits, so his swings aren't the results of non-application of talent. But Vancouver needs every bit of talent it can get at all times. And despite the signals his talents give out, it seems Skriko is right at home at the 30-goal mark.

What doesn't help him is the fact that Vancouver has only one center (Barry Pederson) who can effectively move the puck to his wingersGreg Adams wants to shoot and Rich Sutter doesn't have the talent. Also, very few of his teammates can keep up with his talents. That's one reason why Skriko has to do so much himself. He'd be better with a better team.

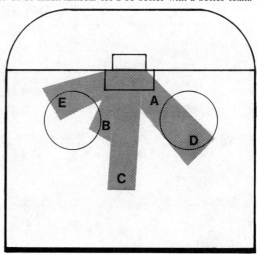

STAN SMYL

Yrs. of NHL service: 10
Born: Glendon, Alta., Canada; January 28, 1958
Position: Right wing
Height: 5-8
Weight: 195
Uniform no.: 12
Shoots: right

Career statistics:

GP	G	A	TP	PIM
729	252	366	618	1,296

1987-88 statistics:

GP	G	A	TP	+/−	PIM	PP	SH	GW	GT	S	PCT
57	12	25	37	-5	110	5	1	0	0	96	12.5

LAST SEASON

Games played total was the lowest of his career (a February groin injury KOed him for the season). Goal and point totals were career lows.

THE FINESSE GAME

Smyl is strong in his stride, but time and injury have slowed him to a crawl. He retains his balance and that helps him in his physical game, but he has never been an agile or fancy player.

Hockey sense and smarts are the skills most used by Smyl now, and they are best showcased on the penalty killing unit. Once an above-average threat for shorthanded goals, Smyl is still smart enough to get into position for that breakaway chance. The chances of his getting that breakaway, however, are small.

His anticipation — as well as the good vision and understanding he used when he was an offensive threat — continues to serve him in his defensive game, where he has been reduced to the role of a checking forward.

Stan can still dig the puck out of the corner and make a play with it, but the chances of his getting to the net in time to complete the move and go are now remote. He will need to be opportunistic for his goals from now on.

THE PHYSICAL GAME

Smyl has always been a very aggressive player who got the most from his size and strength, but his now-persistent injury problem has been the payback for that style. Once an excellent open ice body checker, often bouncing opponents much bigger than he, Smyl no longer has the skating skill to consistently deliver those hits.

He has always played his best when mucking around the corners or fighting through a scramble in front of the net. He remains very strong and very difficult to knock down, making him extremely effective in those high traffic areas.

THE INTANGIBLES

With all due respect, isn't this career over yet? Can the Canucks' pantry be so bare that no youngster can step in and do what Stan Smyl is doing? There can be no questioning Smyl's tremendous heart and dedication, and his hate-to-lose attitude makes him a good leader for the Canucks, but intangibles can only go so far.

For this season Smyl must recover from the groin injury that shortened his season last year. There's no question that he has the heart to come back; he always has. The question is, what's left to give, and what will Smyl have left in terms of skating ability?

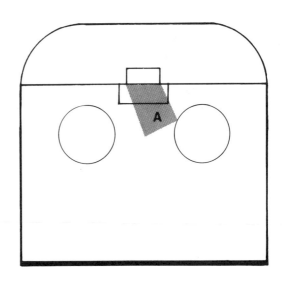

DARYL STANLEY

Yrs. of NHL service: 2
Born: Winnipeg, Man., Canada; December 2, 1962
Position: Defenseman
Height: 6-2
Weight: 200
Uniform no.: 29
Shoots: right

Career statistics:

GP	G	A	TP	PIM
146	4	15	19	367

1987-88 statistics:

GP	G	A	TP	+/−	PIM	PP	SH	GW	GT	S	PCT
57	2	7	9	-12	151	0	0	0	0	27	7.4

LAST SEASON

Stanley was traded to Vancouver from Philadelphia (along with Darren Jensen) in exchange for Wendell Young and a draft choice in August 1987. Games played, all point totals and PIM mark were career highs. He finished fourth on the club in PIM. Shoulder, groin and back injuries sidelined him throughout the season.

THE FINESSE GAME

Stanley is not a phenomenal finesse player, but he does have developable skills. He's not a bad skater up and down, though he could use some help in his agility. Better foot speed and balance would improve his turns and pivots, and they'd also allow him to better close the gap between himself and the puck carriers.

He doesn't have a great read of the ice defensively and he can get hypnotized by the puck. Stanley also has a tendency to think defensively rather than to think defense, and that means that he reacts to the opposition rather than acting on his own initiative and forcing the forward to react to him. Greater mobility would help Daryl initiate his plays.

Stanley can make a good breakout pass, though he'll usually take the first play he sees, rather than looking for the best one. He can be forced into turnovers but minimizes that by not handling the puck — leaving it for his partner — whenever possible.

His shot is nothing to write home about, so his goals will come on whatever dribbles through from the point.

THE PHYSICAL GAME

Stanley is a very tough player, a very physical defenseman. He's going to punish any forward he can lay his hands on by using his good strength to hit hard. He's also liberal in the use of his stick in front of the net, and he's probably the team's best fighter.

THE INTANGIBLES

Daryl has a spirit to win, and his fire and heart are worth having for the Canucks. He's a limited player but works very hard at improving his skills, and that effort too serves as an example to the team.

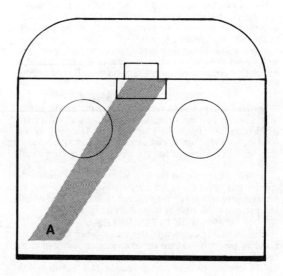

RICH SUTTER

Yrs. of NHL service: 5
Born: Viking, Alta., Canada; December 2, 1963
Position: Right wing
Height: 5-11
Weight: 170
Uniform no.: 15
Shoots: right

Career statistics:

GP	G	A	TP	PIM
367	71	84	155	639

1987-88 statistics:

GP	G	A	TP	+/−	PIM	PP	SH	GW	GT	S	PCT
80	15	15	30	-4	165	2	1	2	1	132	11.4

LAST SEASON

Sutter played all 80 games for the first time (a career high), yet his all point totals are lows as a Canuck. PIM total was second highest of his career, and he was Vancouver's most penalized forward.

THE FINESSE GAME

Finesse has never been big in any of the Sutters and Rich is no exception. He is just average as an NHL skater in terms of his balance and agility, but he has power in his stride and can accelerate well. For a straight-ahead guy, that's about par for the course.

Sutter has difficulty handling the puck especially as he skates up-ice and cutting to his right. He has a sense of the game and can read its ebbs and flows (and that's why he succeeds as a checking forward) but he can't do much offensively.

He'll never score more than 25 goals a year and many times won't even come near that mark. His shot is undistinguished and won't often fool NHL goaltending, so he'll have to be opportunistic and score off scrambles and loose pucks created by his checking.

THE PHYSICAL GAME

As with every Sutter, Rich is a physical player. His own style begins at chippy and moves swiftly to dirty, as he hits anyone in an enemy uniform and finishes the check with his stick. Naturally he refuses to fight after stirring up all kinds of troubles, and that just frustrates the opposition more.

Rich is good on the boards and will run at anyone, but is no good after hitting because he's unlikely — for two reasons — to make a play: First, he lacks the requisite hand skills. Second, his balance isn't good enough for him to stay vertical after all those collisions. Those flaws make his physical play one-dimensional.

THE INTANGIBLES

Like him or hate him, you have to admit that Sutter's work ethic is unassailable. He's an honest hockey player, but he'll never approach the heights hit by any of his five brothers.

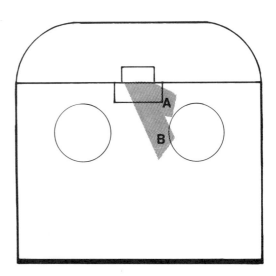

TONY TANTI

Yrs. of NHL service: 6
Born: Toronto, Ontario, Canada; September 7, 1963
Position: Right wing
Height: 5-9
Weight: 185
Uniform no.: 9
Shoots: left

Career statistics:

GP	G	A	TP	PIM
416	213	177	390	370

1987-88 statistics:

GP	G	A	TP	+/−	PIM	PP	SH	GW	GT	S	PCT
73	40	37	77	-1	90	20	0	4	0	202	19.8

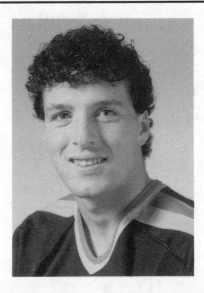

LAST SEASON

Games played total was second lowest of career (for full seasons; he was sidelined with a foot injury). He led the team in scoring, goals, power play goals, game winners and shooting percentage; was second in shots on goal and plus/minus among forwards (third among all regulars) and fourth in PIM among forwards.

THE FINESSE GAME

Tanti is an excellent skater, equipped with great balance, speed and agility. He also has a one-step quickness that allows him to dart in and out of openings, as well as to change direction immediately. He is very dangerous without the puck because of his smarts, and his tremendous anticipation combines with his skating ability to get him into scoring position.

He has a tremendous shot because of his exceptional release (maybe the best in the League) and that is the reason he is so successful. He gets rid of the puck as soon as it's on his stick and he generally forces the goaltender to make a save, even if the shot is not overpowering. He is a good one-touch shooter and his wrist shot is better than his slap shot. Tony needs very little open net to score and loves to go upstairs on goaltenders. He is also very good on tip-ins because of his eye/hand coordination, and he augments that skill by using a big blade on his stick.

Tony is a shooter first and a passer second (as his assist total attests), so he needs a center that will feed him the puck. He can use his teammates well because he's a fairly good passer, but Tanti's talent is in his ability to get himself in position to score. His efficiency at scoring is so great that, despite taking 40 fewer shots last year than in 1986-87 (202 to 242 in 86-87) he scored just one fewer goal.

THE PHYSICAL GAME

Tanti's skating ability is keyed by his strong thighs, and it is his skating that makes his game go. Otherwise, Tony isn't a physical player, but he is fairly willing to get involved. That is, he'll take a hit to make his plays (he must because of his scoring from the high traffic area in front of the net). Though he looks small, Tanti is sturdy on his feet and Tony's not afraid to go back at a bigger player whom he feels has been over-zealous in the physical department.

Don't expect to see him banging around along the boards, though. That's not his game and he wouldn't be effective there, despite the degree of strength he has. He is an open-ice player who can bump the opposition off the puck and quickly take advantage of the situation, but he's not a grinder.

THE INTANGIBLES

To score 40 goals for the Vancouver Canucks (the NHL's 19th ranked offense last season) is to score at least 50 goals on a better team; if the Canucks had another scoring threat that required checking Tanti might get those 50 goals.

But until they get such a player Tanti is their most important player in a number of ways, entertainment not the least of those ways.

The only complaint about his play would be his power play goal/goal total ratio. Fully 50 percent of his goals last season came on the power play, which makes Tanti less than awe-inspiring at even strength. One reason for that proportion might be some of those SOG he didn't take, but for whatever reason his even-strength play should be better than just 20 goals a year.

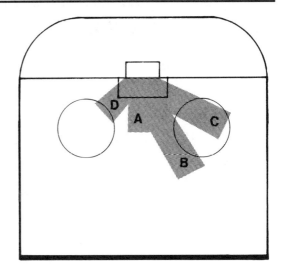

STEVE WEEKS

Yrs. of NHL service: 7
Born: Scarborough, Ontario, Canada; June 30, 1958
Position: Goaltender
Height: 5-11
Weight: 165
Uniform no.: 31
Catches: left

Career statistics:

GP	MINS	G	SO	AVG	A	PIM
197	11,148	694	5	3.73	2	10

1987-88 statisics:

GP	MINS	AVG	W	L	T	SO	GA	SA	SAPCT	PIM
27	1,468	3.51	10	10	4	0	86	674	.875	2

LAST SEASON

Weeks was traded to Vancouver in exchange for Richard Brodeur on the trading deadline. Games played total ties second highest of his career.

THE PHYSICAL GAME

Steve is a good skater and has learned to rein-in his forays around the ice and that has made him a better goaltender. In previous seasons he roamed all over the ice to pick up loose pucks and, because his puckhandling isn't good, would turn the puck over and have to scramble back to the net.

Steve is a good angle goaltender and he is particularly good at shots at his feet because he keeps his entire skate blade on the ice as he kicks his foot out, rather than raising the toe as he moves, so he'll get that shot headed for the far post.

He is good on screen shots because he moves to the top of the screen. Weeks has a good glove hand above his waist, but it is suspect below his waist. He directs pucks to the corners well but fails to control rebounds from high off his chest protector.

Steve is also weak on the short side and that indicates a failure to cut the angle completely and a failure to be completely squared to the puck. He is not very quick to regain his feet after going down and that's because he usually winds up on his butt rather than his knees, and there's no way to be mobile in that position.

THE MENTAL GAME

Weeks starts a game with tremendous concentration and he can maintain it for the full 60 minutes unless — and this is a big unless — he gives up a bad goal.

Bad goals devastate him, and he won't recover if he allows one. He doesn't have the mental toughness to put that goal out of his mind, and that's a big flaw for a goalie.

He is otherwise consistent from night to night, and that concentration gives him something of a big save capability.

THE INTANGIBLES

Steve is a solid team player. His game is to make the first save and have the defense clear the rebounds, which should make his stay in Vancouver quite interesting. His performance for the Canucks after arriving last March (he went 4-3-2) shows that he can play well on a consistent basis, and he will

probably split the goaltending fairly evenly with Kirk McLean this season.

DOUG WICKENHEISER

Yrs. of NHL service: 8
Born: Regina, Sask., Canada; March 30, 1961
Position: Center
Height: 6-1
Weight: 195
Uniform no.: 14
Shoots: left

Career statistics:

GP	G	A	TP	PIM
512	107	152	259	262

1987-88 statistics:

GP	G	A	TP	+/−	PIM	PP	SH	GW	GT	S	PCT
80	7	19	26	-15	36	0	2	2	0	123	5.7

LAST SEASON

Wickenheiser was acquired by the Canucks in the 1987 Waiver Draft. He played 80 games for the second consecutive season, and the second time in his career. Goal total was a career low for full seasons, but his assist total was the highest in three seasons. He tied for the team lead (Petri Skriko) in shorthanded goals.

THE FINESSE GAME

Wickenheiser is a perfect example of slow and steady. He is a good skater in terms of balance and energy, but is slow of foot and not particularly agile. He goes up and back strongly and is a good defensive player, regardless of the plus/minus figures.

He is a good checker and a staple of the penalty killing unit. He sees the ice well and has good enough control skills to use his reach and size to keep the puck from the opposition.

Doug is not a creative hockey player, never has been and never will be. Even with his slight puck moving ability he remains almost hopeless offensively, and his lack of speed and quickness has to take the blame for that. He doesn't think ahead in his offensive plays, seeing only what is in front of him at the moment, and that lack of anticipation hurts him offensively too.

Any goals he gets will have to come from opportunistic play around the net, with plenty of time to make the scoring play.

THE PHYSICAL GAME

Wickenheiser uses his strength and size to play the body, and he does so fairly well — when he can catch anybody. He plays the same way at both ends of the ice, and Doug is good at working the boards to gain the puck and clear the zone. He positions himself well along the boards and obviously takes hits to make his plays.

He is good on faceoffs because of his good eye/hand coordination and the good strength in his wrists and hands.

THE INTANGIBLES

His entire performance is an intangible, given that he has a role to play. If he doesn't play it, Wickenheiser has no value. He's a hard worker and no one can fault that, but he adds little to the team other than a defensive presence. On the team with the 17th best defense, how important can a checking forward be? Wickenheiser is a part. Depending on what's available in the 1988 Waiver Draft, he might be moving again.

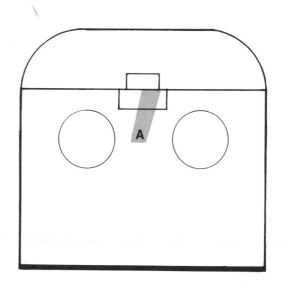

WASHINGTON CAPITALS

LINE COMBINATIONS
MICHAL PIVONKA-BENGT GUSTAFSSON-DAVE CHRISTIAN
KELLY MILLER-MIKE RIDLEY-MIKE GARTNER
GREG ADAMS-BOB GOULD-LOU FRANCESCHETTI
YVON CORRIVEAU-DALE HUNTER-

DEFENSE PAIRINGS
SCOTT STEVENS-LARRY MURPHY
ROD LANGWAY-KEVIN HATCHER
GREG SMITH-
GRANT LEDYARD

GOALTENDERS
CLINT MALARCHUK
PETE PEETERS

OTHER PLAYERS
GARRY GALLEY — Defenseman
PETER SUNDSTROM — Left wing

POWER PLAY

FIRST UNIT:
DAVE CHRISTIAN-BENGT GUSTAFSSON-DALE HUNTER
SCOTT STEVENS-LARRY MURPHY

SECOND UNIT:
GREG ADAMS-MIKE RIDLEY-MIKE GARTNER
SCOTT STEVENS-KEVIN HATCHER

On the first unit, HUNTER plants himself in front of the net to screen the goalie and get rebounds. GUSTAFSSON and CHRISTIAN circle around the perimeter and feed STEVENS and MUPRHY to get the defense moving. If the defense commits to the Capital pointmen, they'll feed CHRISTIAN for a faceoff circle shot. Otherwise, STEVENS and MURPHY will bombs away at the net, hoping for rebounds.

ADAMS fills HUNTER's role on the second unit, while RIDLEY controls the puck behind the net and tries to set up GARTNER in the left wing circle. RIDLEY will play catch with HATCHER to loosen the defense, and will also work a give-and-go for himself at the base of the right wing circle.

Last year the Capitals' power play was FAIR, scoring 94 goals in 469 attempts (20.0 percent, 11th overall).

PENALTY KILLING

FIRST UNIT:
BENGT GUSTAFSSON-DALE HUNTER
ROD LANGWAY-SCOTT STEVENS

First unit very aggressive, with GUSTAFSSON and HUNTER pressing puck and forechecking when possible. GUSTAFSSON will play almost entire two minutes. STEVENS will also force puck, and LANGWAY covers net.

Other forwards who get time are BOB GOULD-KELLY MILLER (both aggressive), MIKE GARTNER, MIKE RIDLEY and DAVE CHRISTIAN. On defense, KEVIN HATCHER will split time with STEVENS and LANGWAY.

Last season the Capitals' penalty killing was GOOD, allowing just 75 goals in 394 times shorthanded (81.0 percent, sixth overall).

CRUCIAL FACEOFFS
HUNTER, with GUSTAFSSON a close second.

GREG ADAMS

Yrs. of NHL service: 6
Born: Duncan, B.C., Canada; May 31, 1960
Position: Left wing
Height: 6-2
Weight: 200
Uniform no.: 22
Shoots: left

Career statistics:

GP	G	A	TP	PIM
448	72	126	198	1,023

1987-88 statistics:

GP	G	A	TP	+/−	PIM	PP	SH	GW	GT	S	PCT
78	15	12	27	-3	153	3	0	0	0	109	13.8

LAST SEASON

Adams finished third on the team in PIM, second for forwards. His minus 3 was the second worst among the team's regulars.

THE FINESSE GAME

Though not a great skater, Adams has fairly good mobility for a bigger man. He does need some room for his turns and is wanting in the foot speed department, but Adams is a strong skater with fairly good balance and a little acceleration because of that leg strength. He uses his skating in his defensive play, going deep into his zone.

Greg is not a playmaker of any great note, but he does make the attempt to keep his head up and use his teammates when he can. He doesn't have NHL level hands in terms of sensitivity for making or receiving passes, and the play has to be slowed down for Adams to be successful at moving the puck. It is his checking (and particularly his hitting) that frees up pucks and creates scoring opportunities.

His shot is average, a slapper blasted from just inside the blue line or the top of the circle that catches the goaltender by surprise. If he shot more, and gave himself some tighter angles, Adams could score more goals, but that argument comes back to smarts and understanding of the game — combined with ice vision — and those are not the strengths of Greg's game.

THE PHYSICAL GAME

Adams enjoys a physical game and that's good, because that's where he's most effective. He hits anything in an opposing jersey with abandon, and that forces the opposition to worry about his hitting and takes their minds off making their own plays.

He'll also plug the front of the net on the power play every once in a while, and he can succeed there because he pesters goaltenders beyond belief with little pokes and shoves and elbows.

Adams uses his size to tie up the opposition as he backchecks and is effective at taking his check out of the play. He can duke it out too.

THE INTANGIBLES

Greg Adams is the kind of guy that would probably be called an honest player. He sticks to what he does best and doesn't try to do what is beyond his abilities. He works to succeed within the framework of his game, and is a tough, hard-nosed player who will sacrifice himself for the good of the team.

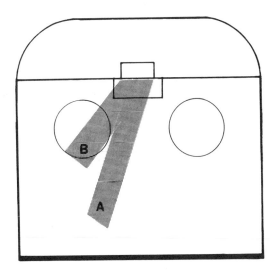

DAVE CHRISTIAN

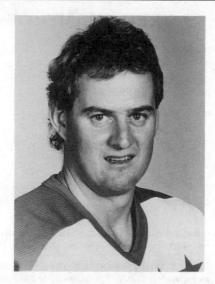

Yrs. of NHL service: 8
Born: Warroad, Minn., USA; May 12, 1959
Position: Right wing/center
Height: 5-11
Weight: 180
Uniform no.: 27
Shoots: right

Career statistics:

GP	G	A	TP	PIM
626	235	315	550	166

1987-88 statistics:

GP	G	A	TP	+/−	PIM	PP	SH	GW	GT	S	PCT
80	37	21	58	-14	26	14	0	5	0	187	19.8

LAST SEASON

Christian was one of only four Capitals with a perfect attendance mark (the sixth time in eight seasons he's played every game). Goal total was the second highest of his career, but assist total was the lowest of his career and point total was lowest for a full season. He finished second on the club in goals, power play goals, fourth in SOG (second among forwards) and his plus/minus was the team's worst.

THE FINESSE GAME

Sense and hand skills are what make Christian a good — with potential to be very good — offensive player. Though he doesn't have eye-opening speed or quickness, Christian knows how to get into position to score.

He has excellent anticipation for the openings, and he gets to those breaches in the defense for the puck. Dave combines that asset with great hand and stick skills, moving very well with the puck when he carries it or laying good passes to open teammates. He is also very patient, and will wait as long as is necessary for the defense or goaltender to commit before making his own play. Patience and poise are the signs of a scorer.

His best asset is his shooting. He is an excellent shooter, deadly accurate from around the net and able to one-time a shot with the NHL's best. He likes to work between the crease and the lower edge of the right faceoff circle and on two-on-one breaks wants the puck at the crease's edge for a shot upstairs.

His sensitive hands and excellent release — as well as his ability to get open — make him especially valuable on the power play. All in all, Christian is the kind of player who is better when shooting first and asking questions later, and he must shoot to be successful.

The proof? In 1985-86 Christian shot 218 times and scored 41 goals. In 1986-87, he had 152 SOG and just 23 goals, a career low. Last season, 187 SOG and 37 goals.

THE PHYSICAL GAME

Christian is a finesse player, and his physical game reflects that. Because of the balance he has on his skates, Christian avoids most hits, and he doesn't really go out of his way to instigate contact either. Most of the time he'll be on the outside of the scrum looking in.

THE INTANGIBLES

The reappearance of Bengt Gustafsson energized Christian, as it was Gustafsson who centered for Christian when the latter scored 41 goals three seasons back.

Christian showed that he can contribute as a character player, scoring 16 of his 37 goals (almost 50 percent) against Patrick Division foes and having a respectable playoff. But harder work on the ice — especially on the defensive end of the game — would make Christian a more successful player. The question is whether or not this eight-year veteran will suddenly change his spots.

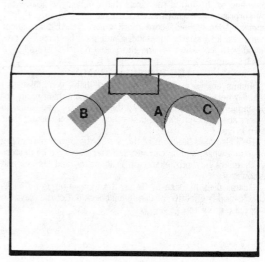

YVON CORRIVEAU

Yrs. of NHL service: 1
Born: Welland, Ontario, Canada; January 8, 1967
Position: Left wing
Height: 6-2
Weight: 205
Uniform no.: 26
Shoots: left

Career statistics:

GP	G	A	TP	PIM
63	11	10	21	108

1987-88 statistics:

GP	G	A	TP	+/−	PIM	PP	SH	GW	GT	S	PCT
44	10	9	19	17	84	0	0	1	0	52	19.2

LAST SEASON

Shuffled back and forth between the American Hockey League and the NHL before arriving in Washington for good on Dec. 28, 1987. Finished second overall in the club in plus/minus.

THE FINESSE GAME

Though the physical game is where Corriveau will excel (if he is to succeed at the NHL level), he does have finesse skills that can be brought to bear.

He is a strong skater, not particularly agile or fluid, but with good balance and a strong stride. That portends some speed in his future, and the balance means he can become more agile (greater foot speed is necessary there).

Corriveau has good hands for a big man, but as yet he's not shown the ability to consistently contribute offensively at the NHL level. He'll move the puck to the open man and lead a teammate into an opening, and he also has the ability to handle the puck in traffic (balance helps here), but right now the NHL game moves too quickly for him.

He has a good wrist shot, heavy and generally accurate, and Corriveau will score from the faceoff circle and in.

He is a conscientious defensive player and will contain his check well, but he also has a tendency to get hypnotized by the puck and wander from his position. Otherwise, he's a good positional player.

THE PHYSICAL GAME

Corriveau has good size and strength, thick in the upper body and willing to put that strength to use at all times. He can be a punishing hitter because of his size and strength, and he uses his body well along the boards. He'll overpower people along the boards because of his strength and balance.

THE INTANGIBLES

Yvon has great desire and a very good attitude. He works extremely hard and wants to succeed, and he is very coachable. Time is needed to see whether that desire can be translated into NHL-level ability.

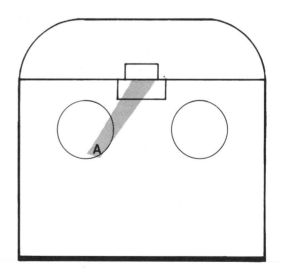

LOU FRANCESCHETTI

Yrs. of NHL service: 4
Born: Toronto, Ontario, Canada; March 28, 1958
Position: Left wing
Height: 6-0
Weight: 190
Uniform no.: 32
Shoots: left

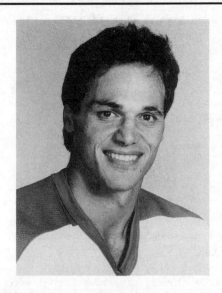

Career statistics:

GP	G	A	TP	PIM
264	29	48	77	439

1987-88 statistics:

GP	G	A	TP	+/−	PIM	PP	SH	GW	GT	S	PCT
59	4	8	12	2	113	1	0	1	1	53	7.5

LAST SEASON

Games played was lowest in three seasons, courtesy of demotion to American Hockey League and a late-season leg injury (five games). Finished fifth on the club in PIM despite reduced playing time.

THE FINESSE GAME

Franceschetti is a below average finesse player. He gets up and down his wing without a great deal of speed, doesn't handle the puck particularly well, won't terrorize enemy goaltenders with his shot and probably won't score when he shoots anyway.

He's never been and never will be a scorer, because his hockey sense and anticipation are poor at the NHL level. He stays to the outside of any offensive play and shows no ability to think on the ice.

THE PHYSICAL GAME

Clearly, this is the heart of Lou's game. If it moves, Franceschetti will hit it. Contact is his game at both ends of the ice and Franceschetti, well muscled, makes anyone he hits pay a price.

Franceschetti is a fairly disciplined player — in terms of using his body — and he hits purposefully rather than recklessly. He will also back up his actions with his fists, if need be, something he is not frequently called upon to do because he does fight well and no one wants a piece of him.

THE INTANGIBLES

Franceschetti exists as a threat to the opposition, someone the Caps can send out to battle the other team's tough guys so that a Scott Stevens need not be sacrificed.

We told you that Lou's limited abilities could be his downfall, and his stint in the minors shows that the Caps agree with us. He's a 30-year-old role player, and his role will probably diminish as this season progresses.

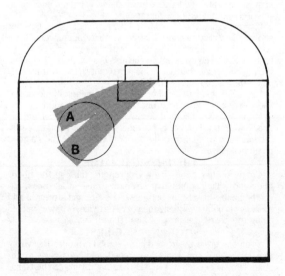

GARRY GALLEY

Yrs. of NHL service: 4
Born: Montreal, Quebec, Canada; April 16, 1963
Position: Defenseman
Height: 5-11
Weight: 190
Uniform no.: 2
Shoots: left

Career statistics:

GP	G	A	TP	PIM
233	30	87	117	239

1987-88 statistics:

GP	G	A	TP	+/−	PIM	PP	SH	GW	GT	S	PCT
58	7	23	30	11	44	3	0	0	1	100	7.0

LAST SEASON

Point total was second highest of his career, as was games played, despite being shuffled in and out of the lineup all season. Plus/minus was fourth best among all Capitals.

THE FINESSE GAME

Galley is a good skater and he adds some mobility to the Caps backline corps, in the form of backup to Larry Murphy, the man to whom Galley's skills are most similar.

He has good speed forward and back and is also agile. He handles the puck well and likes to rush it from the defensive zone, and under Bryan and Terry Murray's coaching has toned down his defensive gambles. He does gamble by carrying the puck when he is the last man back, or going too far into the offensive zone, but his thought process and positional play have improved.

Garry plays his position fairly well, and has learned to concentrate on the man rather than the puck. That has helped him to improve his angle play at forcing the opposition wide of the net. He does think well on the ice and has good anticipation skills, making him valuable on the power play. He can find the open man and get the puck to him.

THE PHYSICAL GAME

Galley has good size and takes the body fairly well, but because he's often looking to start the play up ice the opposition will sneak back into the play. He is effective if not spectacular along the boards and in front of the net, but he will never really be a hitter.

His conditioning has improved since he entered the League, and he will also sacrifice his body to block shots (as he did in the Patrick Division playoffs against New Jersey where he dove head first to make a block).

THE INTANGIBLES

Garry is willing to learn and brings a good attitude and work ethic to the rink. His playoff heroics (vis à vis that blocked shot) won't go unnoticed either. Though Bryan Murray prefers to work with four defensemen, Galley is developing into a solid defensive player and that will make his offense more valuable and could result in more playing time.

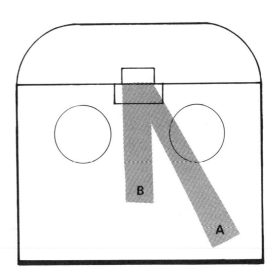

MIKE GARTNER

Yrs. of NHL service: 9
Born: Ottawa, Ontario, Canada; October 29, 1959
Position: Right wing
Height: 6-0
Weight: 180
Uniform no.: 11
Shoots: right

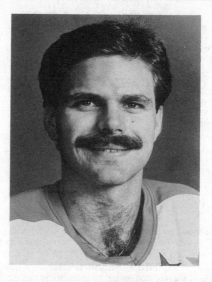

Career statistics:

GP	G	A	TP	PIM
702	371	360	734	699

1987-88 statistics:

GP	G	A	TP	+/–	PIM	PP	SH	GW	GT	S	PCT
80	48	33	81	20	73	19	0	7	1	316	15.2

LAST SEASON

Gartner led the team in points, goals, plus/minus, power play goals, game winners and shots on goal (he finished third in the League in the last category). He played an entire season for the fifth time in his career and first time in three seasons, tying his second highest goal total.

THE FINESSE GAME

As a successful finesse player, Gartner has two main skills he brings to bear against the opposition his skating and his shot. He has explosive skating speed coming down the wing, speed that he puts to use by blowing past his check and breaking wide on a defender before cutting behind him for a swoop in on goal.

Mike's acceleration is outstanding and he commands an almost instantaneous burst of speed from a stationary position. He is tremendously agile, has terrific lateral movement for his inside cuts and an outstanding change of pace to turn his speed up another notch.

Gartner's slap shot is just as lethal. It is a rocket from the edge of the right faceoff circle that drives goaltenders backward because of its speed and heavyness. If a goaltender isn't fully in front of that shot, it's going in the net, and obviously, the NHL's goaltenders see a lot of shots from Gartner.

He gets into position to score on the power play (where he is a natural), but he is a shooter first and a playmaker second. He can handle the puck at top speed and his vision shows him the entire ice surface. He'll look for a play (and is a good passer), but Gartner expects the puck.

Gartner is also a good defensive player, making a concerted effort to play a solid defensive game.

THE PHYSICAL GAME

Gartner has long known the value of adding a physical element to a finesse game. Though not a thunderous hitter, he willingly hits and takes the body well along the boards and in all three zones. He excellently protects the puck with his body, shielding it from the opposition when he swoops around the defenseman and leans away from checks.

He's also very strong on his skates and almost impossible to dislodge from the puck.

THE INTANGIBLES

The general thought regarding Mike Gartner is that he's an excellent character player, a hard worker who aims to contribute at all times. Though he slowed down in the season's final quarter (just nine goals after quarters of 13, 11 and 15) and had a poor playoff, we still concur with the conventional wisdom.

He scored almost 33 percent of his goals against the Patrick Division (though almost 40 percent of his goals came on the power play — greater goal distribution is needed), and that says Gartner is a leader by example. He is a first rate player in nearly every aspect of the game.

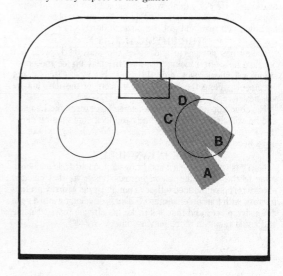

BOB GOULD

Yrs. of NHL service: 7
Born: Petrolia, Ontario, Canada; September 2, 1957
Position: Right wing
Height: 5-11
Weight: 195
Uniform no.: 23
Shoots: right

Career statistics:

GP	G	A	TP	PIM
545	132	129	261	419

1987-88 statistics:

GP	G	A	TP	+/−	PIM	PP	SH	GW	GT	S	PCT
72	12	14	26	-1	56	0	0	2	0	119	10.1

LAST SEASON

Games played total was lowest since Gould became an NHL regular; he missed the season's first eight games with a broken bone in his foot. Goal and point totals were career lows, and assist total was second lowest of his career.

THE FINESSE GAME

Gould's a good skater with a strong, steady pace. He uses that pace well in his role as a defensive forward, enabling him to stay with his check up and down the ice. He does not have a lot of speed.

He combines that pace with good anticipation and vision — and superior hockey sense — to excel in his defensive work. He reads the offensive plan and counters it either by shadowing his check or by protecting a certain zone of the ice and cutting off passing lanes.

His checking affords him many scoring opportunities, but Gould is a straight ahead type of player who sticks to his wing. Though he doesn't show great offensive creativity, he can handle the puck fairly well, sometimes working a little give and go from the right corner. His goals will come from in close to the net, and he is a threat for the short-handed goal, using his anticipation to read the power play and find an opening.

THE PHYSICAL GAME

Bob is not an overly physical player, certainly not the kind of player that throws his weight around. He uses his body intelligently, holding his man out of the play for the extra second necessary to make a good defensive play.

Gould does not run from contact and is not a thumper, but will certainly hit or be hit if the play dictates. He can't be intimidated.

THE INTANGIBLES

Gould is easy to coach because he has a terrific attitude, placing the team's success before his own. He works hard all the time, playing for the team first and himself second. He's a fine defensive forward, so ignore the bad plus/minus.

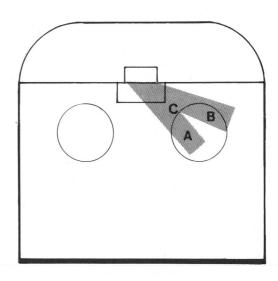

BENGT GUSTAFSSON

Yrs. of NHL service: 8
Born: Kariskoga, Sweden; March 23, 1958
Position: Left wing
Height: 6-0
Weight: 185
Uniform no.: 16
Shoots: left

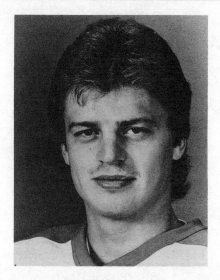

Career statistics:

GP	G	A	TP	PIM
557	178	308	486	178

1987-88 statistics:

GP	G	A	TP	+/−	PIM	PP	SH	GW	GT	S	PCT
78	18	36	54	2	29	7	5	3	0	136	23.2

LAST SEASON

Gustafsson returned from a year's sabbatical in Sweden to post his second highest games played total. His point total, however, was a career low for a "full" season (43 points in 51 1984-85 NHL games). He led the club in shorthanded goals.

THE FINESSE GAME

Gustafsson is a superb skater and puck handler. He has excellent speed (a long, fluid stride with great balance) and great hands, and he has the ability to do everything at high speed. He has outstanding acceleration and one-step quickness, using that ability when he is penalty killing to "jump" the power play unit and soar in for a short-handed score.

Gustafsson uses the same abilities on the power play, where his vision and anticipation also come into play. He can get the puck to his teammates on sheer quickness and keeps the passing lanes open because he moves so quickly, even within his first stride. Because he is such a good skater, he is also a good checker and a solid defensive player.

He has a good snapshot that he releases quickly and he should score more goals but is a touch unselfish. He is deadly from 10-feet and in and loves to stand at the base of the faceoff circles, especially on the power play, and hammer home the pass from behind the net. Because of his package of playmaking abilities, Bengt will also see some time on the point of the power play.

THE PHYSICAL GAME

Gustafsson is not afraid of the tough going and is more physically tough than most Swedes. He can dish out his share of punishment too, and will bump in the offensive zone though he is not especially strong. He makes the most of what he has physically.

THE INTANGIBLES

Depending on your outlook, Gustafsson's return was either part success or part failure. If Gustafsson didn't float through the regular season, he did a pretty good imitation of a disinterested bystander. But his value was evident throughout the playoffs, when he led the club in scoring.

We questioned last year whether, after a year's absence, Gustafsson could return to the form he showed two years ago in his best NHL performance to date. Bluntly, he didn't. But his return certainly benefited Dave Christian, who regained some of his goal scoring glory.

Gustafsson remains excellent in all categories. He still comes through in the clutch with great mental toughness, as his playoff run shows. He has the potential to be a great player, but he must want to perform to that potential. His intensity and desire, therefore, must be questioned.

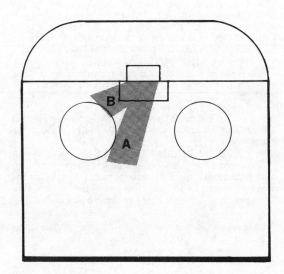

KEVIN HATCHER

Yrs. of NHL service: 3
Born: Detroit, Mich., USA; September 9, 1966
Position: Defenseman
Height: 6-3
Weight: 205
Uniform no.: 4
Shoots: right

Career statistics:

GP	G	A	TP	PIM
230	32	53	85	402

1987-88 statistics:

GP	G	A	TP	+/−	PIM	PP	SH	GW	GT	S	PCT
71	14	27	41	1	137	5	0	3	0	181	7.7

LAST SEASON

Though he played the fewest games of his NHL career, Hatcher set personal marks in all point categories. He led all Cap defensemen in goals and game winners, and minor knee surgery sidelined him for the year's first nine games.

THE FINESSE GAME

Hatcher is greatly improved in the finesse department, now showing NHL level talents in all finesse areas. Strange as this will sound for a player of his size, Kevin's stride is lengthening. That means he has greater agility and balance than previously, and that agility manifests itself in his foot speed and turns. He has a tight turning radius for a big man, and can make direction changes fairly quickly. His longer stride also moves him past the opposition, but don't confuse that with rink-length speed.

Additionally, NHL experience has deepened Hatcher's already good playreading ability. He thinks well and understands the play at the NHL level, and he no longer creates openings for the enemy by leaving his position unnecessarily.

Kevin's hand skills remain the weakest in his finesse arsenal. He doesn't receive passes well, nor is he outstanding in moving the puck to his teammates; he needs some time and space to do so. Additionally, he's not outstanding at carrying the puck (though he may become reliable in this department as his skating continues to improve).

He has a good shot from the blue line, and Hatcher is smart enough to just wrist a quick shot on net when he's pressured. He'll also sneak to the slot if there's an opening, but he doesn't create openings by cutting to the slot. He upped his SOG total by 81 percent last year (100 SOG in 86-87, 181 SOG last season), and that no doubt accounts for his improved offensive totals.

THE PHYSICAL GAME

Hatcher has excellent size, and he uses it very well. He hits hard and can punish the opposition, and he also is playing a smarter physical game now. He's less interested in evening the score with an opposing forward than he used to be, and takes fewer stupid intimidation or retaliatory penalties.

He won't be out-muscled along the boards or in front of the net, and his improved balance means he's still involved in the play after a check instead of picking himself up off the ice after a collision.

THE INTANGIBLES

We told you Hatcher would develop into a well-rounded defenseman, and his performance in last season's playoffs (when he led all Cap defensemen in scoring) has shown that he can indeed play the offensive game to complement his defensive game. He is still an NHL youngster, and his willingness to work and learn means that he'll continue to improve.

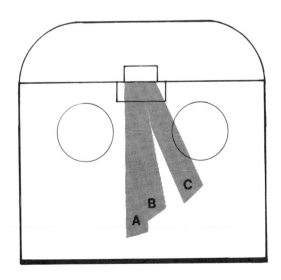

DALE HUNTER

Yrs. of NHL service: 8
Born: Petrolia, Ontario, Canada; July 31, 1960
Position: Center
Height: 5-10
Weight: 190
Uniform no.: 32
Shoots: left

Career statistics:

GP	G	A	TP	PIM
602	162	355	517	1,785

1987-88 statistics:

GP	G	A	TP	+/–	PIM	PP	SH	GW	GT	S	PCT
79	22	37	59	7	238	11	0	1	2	126	17.5

LAST SEASON

Hunter led the club in PIM. He finished third in assists and fourth in power play goals.

THE FINESSE GAME

Hunter is generally under-rated in an assessment of his finesse skills.

He has good speed and is very strong on his skates, so he serves as an excellent forechecker and backchecker. He has good vision and anticipation skills, and he can bring those skills to bear as an offensive player.

Hunter is a good playmaker, though his hands are a little tough, and he puts the open ice his physical game earns him to good use by getting the puck to his teammates. Those vision and anticipation skills help here.

As for scoring, most of his goals will come from in close on rebounds or tip-ins.

THE PHYSICAL GAME

Hunter is a very physical player, and that opens up the ice for himself and his teammates. He loves to throw his elbows along the boards and he hits a lot. Hunter has excellent upper body strength.

His strength and willingness to take abuse are evident in the goals Hunter scores. He can work around the net because of his upper body and arm strength, as well as his strength on his skates to stay upright after collisions.

Dale is a good fighter, but he's usually content to let his abrasive style goad the opposing player drop his gloves first. Hunter is also willing to sacrifice his body and does so by frequently blocking shots.

THE INTANGIBLES

Hunter is one of the League's premier disturbers, an instigator of the first order. But he is also a gutsy, determined leader. He plays with tons of heart and character and is an excellent team man, willing to do whatever is necessary to win.

He justified any doubts observers had regarding his trade to Washington by scoring in overtime to carry the Capitals past the Flyers in game seven of last spring's Patrick Division semifinals. The goal may only be the biggest in Caps' history.

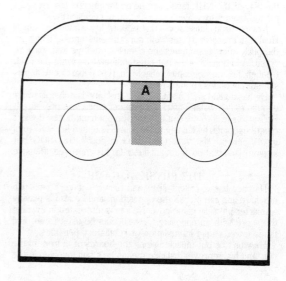

ROD LANGWAY

Yrs. of NHL service: 10
Born: Formosa, Taiwan; May 3, 1957
Position: Defenseman
Height: 6-3
Weight: 215
Uniform no.: 5
Shoots: left

Career statistics:

GP	G	A	TP	PIM
719	48	231	279	679

1987-88 statistics:

GP	G	A	TP	+/−	PIM	PP	SH	GW	GT	S	PCT
63	3	13	16	1	28	0	0	1	1	49	6.1

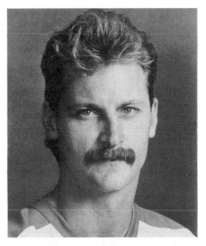

LAST SEASON

A back injury sidelined Langway for 14 games, keeping him from the 80 game mark for the fourth consecutive season. Games played total was career low, as were point, assist and PIM totals.

THE FINESSE GAME

Though he has really never been a finesse player, skating and brains — finesse skills — have always been the key to Langway's success. After 10 years he's no longer the excellent skater he once was (credit the injuries for that), but Langway still has outstanding mobility and lateral movement for his size. Combined with his size, that agility contributes to the image of Langway being everywhere at once. He moves just as well backward as he does forward.

Rod's playreading and hockey sense — his brains — are just as good, as is his anticipation. He sees the defensive play with superb clarity, and sees the break up-ice equally well. His concentration on-ice is excellent, and he is always prepared for the offensive rush because of his mental catalogue of the League's forwards and their preferred moves. He almost always makes the correct pass to get Washington started and, though it's not his game, Langway will carry the puck when forced to.

At his very worst he is not a goal scorer (but he does have a good shot from the left point), though the Capitals will give him a turn on the power play because of his vision and smarts. Naturally, he kills penalties exceedingly well and will occasionally take a defensive zone faceoff because of his upper body strength.

THE PHYSICAL GAME

Very tough, very strong, very mean. They all add up to make Langway a punishing hitter who makes opponents pay the price for progress in his zone. He uses his body excellently and intelligently, not taking penalties that hurt the team. He ties up men in front of the net or along the boards, and cuts off any offensive shooting or passing angle.

He excels at gaining position along the boards and turning the play back up-ice. The best bet is to try beating him inside (good luck), but that's just choosing your poison.

THE INTANGIBLES

Clearly, the toll of Rod's physical game is telling on his body and ability to perform without injury. And just as clearly, though he is still a superb defensive player, Langway is not the defensive force he once was. At his best, Langway was to defense what Wayne Gretzky is to offense.

The effect of that "decline" on the Caps has been a positive rather than a negative one, because it has forced Scott Stevens to step forward as the team's leader. Make no mistake; Langway still has the heart of a lion and is a fierce competitor, commanding respect from his teammates and the opposition. But he is no longer the heart and soul of the Capitals. That mantle has been passed to Stevens. Still, as he ages nicely, Langway remains one of the NHL's top players.

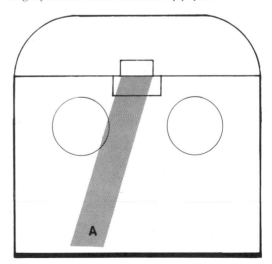

GRANT LEDYARD

Yrs. of NHL service: 4
Born: Winnipeg, Manitoba, Canada; November 19, 1961
Position: Defenseman
Height: 6-2
Weight: 190
Uniform no.: 28
Shoots: left

Career statistics:

GP	G	A	TP	PIM
232	36	72	108	310

1987-88 statistics:

GP	G	A	TP	+/-	PIM	PP	SH	GW	GT	S	PCT
44	5	10	15	-11	66	2	0	1	0	81	6.2

LAST SEASON

Ledyard was acquired from Los Angeles on Feb. 9 in exchange for Craig Laughlin. Games played total was the second lowest of his career, and point totals were all career lows. His plus/minus was second worst overall for Washington; he was minus 4 in 21 games for the Caps.

THE FINESSE GAME

Grant is a very skilled finesse player. He's a very good skater vertically as well as horizontally (up and down the ice and laterally, that is) and he has good quickness and agility for a big man.

He reads the play offensively very well, but fails to do the same thing defensively. He still gets hypnotized by the puck as he backskates, and because of that he begins his turns to angle off the opposition too late. That means passes that shouldn't even get released get completed, and it also means that Ledyard can be left grabbing at air despite his skating skill. He also has a tendency to wander, thus leaving openings.

He handles the puck well and can rush it from his zone, and he has learned to be less predictable with it once he crosses the opposing blue line. He no longer boxes himself into bad ice by carrying the puck too deeply, and he looks for his teammates to make a play. He knows how to move the puck quickly on both offense and defense, and thus does a fair job of getting it to the open man.

His best talent is unquestionably his shot, which is one of the League's better ones. Grant shoots a hard, accurate and fast slap shot from the blue line; the shot is one of the League's hardest.

THE PHYSICAL GAME

Ledyard is a very strong player (as his shot indicates), but he doesn't use his strength in front of his net or along the boards, where he could combine it with his hand skills to great advantage (making a play out of the corner after taking the puck from the opposition). Because he just pushes and shoves, the enemy will occasionally get away from him and re-enter the play, so Ledyard must improve his takeouts.

In short, he's a finesse player with size — and he doesn't play up to that size.

He has a long reach and uses it well to contain the offensive point and to pokecheck the puck.

THE INTANGIBLES

Ledyard will be 27 in November, no youngster despite his relatively short NHL tenure. He's a hard worker and an enthusiastic player, but at 27 what we see is pretty much what the Caps will get. His presence lends an offensive talent, and some more depth, to the Washington blue line corps.

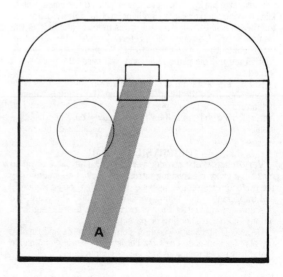

CLINT MALARCHUK

Yrs. of NHL service: 5
Born: Grand Prairie, Alta., Canada; May 1, 1961
Position: Goaltender
Height: 5-10
Weight: 170
Uniform no.: 30
Catches: left

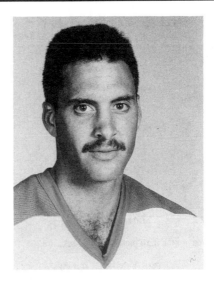

Career statistics:

GP	MINS	G	SO	AVG	A	PIM
194	10,910	636	9	3.49	7	77

1987-88 statisics:

GP	MINS	AVG	W	L	T	SO	GA	SA	SAPCT	PIM
54	2,926	3.16	24	20	4	4	154	1,340	.885	10

LAST SEASON

Games played total matched career high, while goals-against-average was career low. Shutout total tied career mark, and he finished second in the League in that category.

THE PHYSICAL GAME

Malarchuk is a good angle goaltender, but he is strong on the reflex side as well. He has very fast hands and feet and his improved angle play has helped him to subdue his stickside weakness, though he is still weak there.

Top of the net glove shots will elude him, and he generally does not control pucks he stops with his glove. He'll get a piece of a shot but he fails to hold the puck much of the time, so a shot to his glove will often result in rebounds.

On the whole he does not control any rebounds well, and that is where his reflexes serve him best, allowing him to quickly get into position to get a piece of the second shot. When he is playing his best he is square to the puck and doesn't need to scramble after a rebound.

Clint is a good skater and he likes to leave the net to handle the puck, but is not a great puck handler. He has good foot speed and so he regains his stance quickly, and Malarchuk also moves well from post to post.

His fast hands and feet make him very effective in scrambles near the net, but he does not always see the puck well, so he'll stay deep in the net on screens to get a longer look.

THE MENTAL GAME

Malarchuk is mentally tough and will fight you for the next goal after giving up a bad one — most of the time. He does have a tendency to give up goals in bunches, but he is able to pull himself together and forget a bad outing.

Clint has good anticipation and concentration, another reason why he is so effective around the net.

THE INTANGIBLES

We told you Malarchuk was going to carry the burden of work as he replaced Bob Mason, the free agent gone to Chicago. But the problem with Clint — as the Nordiques don't hesitate to point out — is that he has yet to win a playoff game. Ever.

Considering that Pete Peeters can't win the big game, and that Malarchuk can't win in the playoffs, one would have to think that neither goaltender should consider himself indispensable in Washington.

KELLY MILLER

Yrs. of NHL service: 3
Born: Lansing, Mich., USA; March 3, 1963
Position: Left wing
Height: 5-11
Weight: 185
Uniform no.: 10
Shoots: left

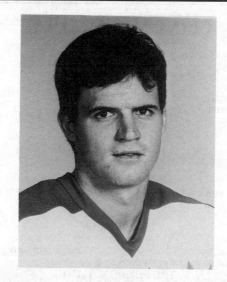

Career statistics:

GP	G	A	TP	PIM
236	38	71	109	137

1987-88 statistics:

GP	G	A	TP	+/−	PIM	PP	SH	GW	GT	S	PCT
80	9	23	32	9	35	0	1	3	0	96	9.4

LAST SEASON

Miller was one of just four Capitals to play all 80 games. His plus/minus was third highest among regulars, second among forwards.

THE FINESSE GAME

Speed is the basis for Miller's game, and it affects all of his finesse skills. Kelly is an excellent skater with tremendous speed down the wing, and he can blow by a defenseman from outside. However, he doesn't moderate his speed, and so — even if the defender can't catch him — Miller remains utterly predictable.

Kelly carries the puck fairly well, but his hands aren't good enough to keep up with his feet. His feet also out-race his brain, so he does not use his teammates well on those rushes. He almost never passes the puck after cutting behind the defenseman — he's just going right to the net with no doubt about it. Miller doesn't have exceptional vision of the ice, mostly because he still keeps his head down when making plays.

The good news regarding his speed is that it makes MIller an excellent checker. And, because he keeps his head up when he doesn't have the puck, Miller augments his speed in checking with vision and brains. He anticipates the play fairly well and is a natural penalty killer.

If his hand skills were better, he'd be an overwhelming threat for short-handed goals. As it is, Miller will do most of his scoring from 25-feet and in on a fair-to-good wrist shot.

THE PHYSICAL GAME

Miller plays larger than his size, which is not substantial. He's dramatically increased his upper body strength to compensate for his lack of natural bulk and to put him on more even footing with the League's bigger players. That strength makes his willing board work more effective.

He'll always pursue the puck, regardless of the physical price, and his added strength has put a greater oomph into his body checking.

THE INTANGIBLES

If one could succeed on hard work alone, then Miller would be an All-Star. His increased upper body strength is a fine indication of his willingness to improve and his dedication to that willingness. A lot of players *want* to be better, but Miller has taken the steps to become better.

Unfortunately, desire doesn't make a star — though it will prolong a career. His lack of hand skills will keep Kelly a role player, but his excellent character and work habits make him more valuable than just his skills would allow.

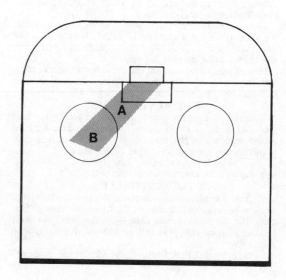

LARRY MURPHY

Yrs. of NHL service: 8
Born: Scarborough, Ontario, Canada; March 8, 1961
Position: Defenseman
Height: 6-1
Weight: 210
Uniform no.: 8
Shoots: right

Career statistics:

GP	G	A	TP	PIM
630	130	385	515	517

1987-88 statistics:

GP	G	A	TP	+/–	PIM	PP	SH	GW	GT	S	PCT
79	8	53	61	2	72	7	0	1	0	201	4.0

LAST SEASON

Murphy finished second on the club in assists, third in shots on goal, and he led all Cap defenders in power play goals.

THE FINESSE GAME

Murphy is an excellent skater, and that ability is the key to his success as an offensive force. He has a strong stride and good acceleration — so he'll pull away from the opposition — and he's also learned to moderate that speed to make it more effective. His gear shifts are tough to defend against, and he'll use that skating skill to rush the puck.

His defensive play slipped a notch last year, but Murphy has generally learned to rush at the right times so as not to hurt the Caps defensively. He does a good job of containing the point offensively and of forcing the play wide defensively. He can, however, be beaten to his left, and Murphy needs to maintain his concentration in the defensive zone by focussing more on the man and less on the puck.

The Caps rely on Murphy's puckhandling and playmaking abilities. Those skills are good-to-excellent and Larry uses his teammates well because of them. He is, of course, a natural on the power play and can carry the puck up-ice at full speed.

Primarily a playmaker from the point, Murphy's shot is low and accurate to the net, allowing for deflections, rebounds and tip-ins. Murphy likes to let his shot go from the edge of the left faceoff circle, but he'll walk into the slot for a wrist shot if he can.

THE PHYSICAL GAME

Murphy is a finesse player with some size, but he's not a big physical player. He'll take the body along the boards more by getting in the way than by rubbing the man out, and Murphy's checks won't knock anyone into the cheap seats — if he hits at all.

He is adequate in front of the net, but his is the job of the breakout and not take out defenseman. Whatever physical play he contributes is made more effective by his ability to make a play after a hit.

THE INTANGIBLES

Murphy struggled last year and the Caps did too. That's not a coincidence. He is for Washington what Ray Bourque and Gary Suter are to their teams in terms of moving the play from the Caps' zone (most important) and generating offense (next most important).

In one sense, Murphy's struggling was good because it forced Scott Stevens to extend his own game and truly take charge for the first time in Stevens' career. Lack of confidence last year was Murphy's problem (14 games before he got his first goal, then subsequent goal-less stretches of eight, 10, 11 and an unbelievable *18* games without a score), and a confident Murphy is necessary to any success the Caps will have.

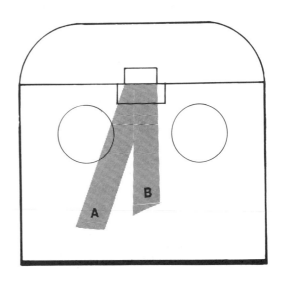

PETE PEETERS

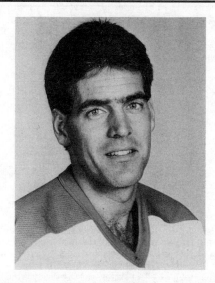

Yrs. of NHL service: 9
Born: Edmonton, Alta., Canada; August 1, 1957
Position: Goaltender
Height: 6-0
Weight: 180
Uniform no.: 1
Catches: left

Career statistics:

GP	MINS	G	SO	AVG	A	PIM
406	23,435	1,203	15	3.08	11	180

1987-88 statisics:

GP	MINS	AVG	W	L	T	SO	GA	SA	SAPCT	PIM
35	1,896	2.78	14	12	5	2	88	866	.898	10

LAST SEASON

Knee, thigh and ankle injuries limited Peeters to a career low for games played (he missed 13 games with injury). He led the League in goals-against-average and was second in save percentage.

THE PHYSICAL GAME

Peeters is a standup goaltender to a fault. He is rigid in that style and almost never leaves his feet. He can get away with his 99 and 44/100ths percent angle game because of the defensive orientation of the Caps. All he has to do is make the first save and let his defense take care of the rebounds.

Peeters uses good hand quickness and is solid with saves from the waist up, but is far too suspect from the waist down. He gives away the shot between his legs far too frequently, and he does not handle the puck well when shot at his feet, allowing rebounds and failing to clear the puck to the corner. He is tall and covers most of the net, but his lack of foot speed and lateral movement doom him on low shots to the corners of the net and on criss-cross plays in front of him on scrambles in the crease.

He plays his angles well and handles the puck well, though far too frequently. He strays from his net for loose pucks but fails to show consistently good judgment in doing so. He'll make a pass up the boards with his head down, and that results in turnovers and sometimes uncontested empty net shots.

THE MENTAL GAME

Concentration and consistency have long been Peeters' problems. He has difficulty maintaining his concentration both within games and from contest to contest. That difficulty in maintaining his concentration is the key to his consistency problems.

His ability to make the big save and to pull out a crucial game is questionable.

THE INTANGIBLES

For some reason, the Capitals love Pete Peeters. Yes, he had the League's best goals-against last year. Yes, he has at least a .500 record against every team in the League but two (Philadelphia and the Islanders). Yes, he even went a step toward hero status with his seventh-game OT win versus Philly in the Patrick Division semis.

But he was revealed again against the Devils in the Division Finals. No, Peeters didn't lose the series, but he didn't win it either. Again Peeters failed to deliver in the clutch, yet for some reason he continues to hang on.

His style meshes well with the Caps and Peeters is lucky for that, because if he played for a poor defensive team the rebounds he leaves around and his lack of mobility would haunt him — and his team — nightly. Peeters plays well enough to lose, and until the Capitals find stronger goaltending they'll play well enough to lose too.

MICHAL PIVONKA

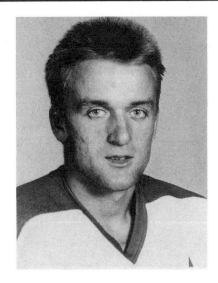

Yrs. of NHL service: 2
Born: Kladno, Czechoslovakia; January 28, 1966
Position: Center
Height: 6-2
Weight: 192
Uniform no.: 20
Shoots: left

Career statistics:

GP	G	A	TP	PIM
144	29	48	77	69

1987-88 statistics:

GP	G	A	TP	+/−	PIM	PP	SH	GW	GT	S	PCT
71	11	23	34	1	28	3	0	0	0	96	11.5

LAST SEASON

Games played was a career low (a late season ankle injury absented him from four games). All point totals were career lows.

THE FINESSE GAME

Skating and puckhandling are the strengths of Pivonka's game. He has excellent balance on his skates and combines his inborn agility with nice quickness and acceleration for great mobility.

He handles the puck well, especially when carrying it, but even after two years remains unable to consistently make plays at NHL speed. Part of his problems remains his not-yet-at-NHL-caliber understanding of the game. As he stands around trying to analyze the play, Pivonka finds himself a second behind. Though he has excellent hands, his passes and general playmaking are also affected by this current inability. Thus, his passes often skitter past teammates or into their skates instead of finding their sticks.

Michal shoots the puck quickly with a wrist shot and, like most Europeans, uses the slap shot only rarely. He knows how to get into position to score, and his skating helps him to get to those scoring positions. He remains weak (almost uninterested) defensively and must consciously integrate himself more into the total NHL game, rather than just operating from above the red line.

THE PHYSICAL GAME

Just as Pivonka must integrate defense into his play, so must he incorporate physical play into his repertoire. Currently a finesse player with size, Michal is not a very physical player in terms of initiating contact to gain the puck. He will willingly go to the high traffic areas to score, but his great balance could be put to good use in tussles along the boards. He doesn't have to become a Dale Hunter or a Scott Stevens, but an element of physical play would open up Pivonka's finesse game.

He has very strong hands and wrists (which is why his shot is good), but needs more strength in the upper body so that he is not so easily pushed off the puck.

THE INTANGIBLES

Looking at just the regular season numbers, Pivonka seems to have gone backward in his sophomore year instead of for-ward. But Pivonka seemed to come into his own in the Patrick Division playoffs and had a fine post-season, indicating that he is ready to make the move toward his potential this season.

As his third NHL season, this will be his most critical, his put-up-or-shut-up year. The Caps, who expected big things from him last year, eagerly await his response.

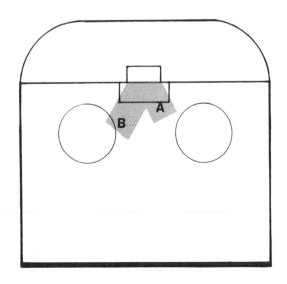

MIKE RIDLEY

Yrs. of NHL service: 3
Born: Winnipeg, Man., Canada; July 8, 1963
Position: Center/left wing
Height: 6-1
Weight: 190
Uniform no.: 17
Shoots: right

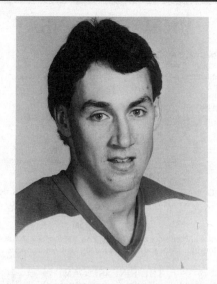

Career statistics:

GP	G	A	TP	PIM
228	81	113	194	131

1987-88 statistics:

GP	G	A	TP	+/−	PIM	PP	SH	GW	GT	S	PCT
70	28	31	59	1	22	12	0	3	0	134	20.9

LAST SEASON

Games played total was career low, due in part to seven games missed with a knee injury. Point total was lowest of career, goals second highest. He finished fourth on the team in scoring, third in goals and power play goals and first in shooting percentage. His PIM total was lowest among Cap regulars.

THE FINESSE GAME

Balance is the key to Ridley's skating ability. He doesn't have blazing speed, but his excellent balance gives him superb agility and lateral movement. He won't beat anyone to a loose puck with foot speed but will instead gain the puck through that balance, using it to extend himself beyond a normal range of motion. His balance also makes him a fine player in traffic, and it powers his physical game.

He passes very well and complements his good hands with good anticipation, hockey sense and peripheral vision. He knows where the net is at all times (and where he and his teammates are in relation to it), and he'll either lead a teammate into an opening with a good pass or get to the opening himself.

His soft hands get the passes to those openings, and his passes are easy to handle because of his touch. He carries the puck well and can fire a good wrist shot from anywhere, forcing the goaltender to make good saves.

The low plus/minus rating is completely deceptive, because Mike is a fine defensive player. He will often find himself opposing the other team's top center, thus the low plus/minus. Ridley comes back deeply into his own zone and gets the puck out quickly and well.

THE PHYSICAL GAME

Ridley's low center of gravity makes him very difficult to knock down, so he can play a physical game and not suffer for it because he comes out of most collisions in a vertical stance and ready to go. He amplifies his physical ability with his playmaking ability out of the corner.

He is not overwhelmingly strong along the boards but is aggressive and stays involved in the action at all times. Ridley will bump anyone he has to in order to make his plays and he is impossible to brutalize, ignoring the abuse to concentrate on his assigned task.

THE INTANGIBLES

An interesting note: Though nearly 50 percent of Ridley's goals came on the power play (12 of 28), 10 of his first 12 goals last year came on the power play. In other words, he had only two power play goals in his final 44 games.

Heart, character, dedication. Those words describe Ridley's attitude toward the game. He is eminently coachable and is a very hard worker in practice and during games, making him a quality individual and hockey player. He will always turn in a solid performance, and he still has the potential to improve his game.

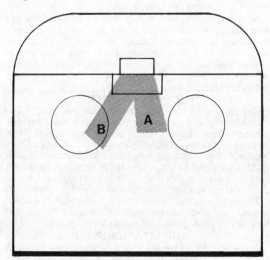

NEIL SHEEHY

Yrs. of NHL service: 4
Born: International Falls, Minn., USA; February 9, 1960
Position: Defenseman
Height: 6-2
Weight: 215
Uniform no.: 0
Shoots: right

Career statistics:

GP	G	A	TP	PIM
213	13	36	49	722

1987-88 statistics:

GP	G	A	TP	+/−	PIM	PP	SH	GW	GT	S	PCT
62	3	10	13	13	189	0	0	0	0	40	7.5

LAST SEASON

Sheehy was traded to Hartford by Calgary (along with Carey Wilson and Lane MacDonald) for Dana Murzyn and Shane Churla. Games played total was the second highest of his career and he led the Whalers in plus/minus. He missed 10 games with a groin injury and three games with a hip injury.

THE FINESSE GAME

Sheehy is a far better finesse player than he is given credit for. He is a good skater though not especially fast or agile, but he is strong on his skates and improving in the areas of balance (he took ballet lessons for that) and foot speed. He moves fairly well forward and backward and maintains his position well when checking in his own zone.

In puck handling, Sheehy again is more than adequate and improving. He sees the open man and makes the smart plays, and Neil can also handle the puck and rush it when necessary, though he prefers to move the puck rather than skate it.

He will not frequently become a fourth attacker in the offensive zone, but Sheehy can move into the play and control the point — which is where his goals will come from — though he will rarely pinch in. He is smart enough to know his limitations and not force his offensive game beyond its boundaries.

THE PHYSICAL GAME

Sheehy is as tough as they come and he hits hard and often. He is a very strong presence in front of his own net (though not as strong as he could be when killing penalties) and he is also mean with his stick.

He will outmuscle almost anyone along the boards and is a very good fighter — as would be expected of a guy who was on his university's boxing team.

THE INTANGIBLES

Sheehy is a very intelligent player (as demonstrated by his staying within his limits as a player) and he is also a prime disturber on the ice.

He is a good player and may make some small improvements in his play over the next few seasons, but at 28 years old what you see is basically what you get.

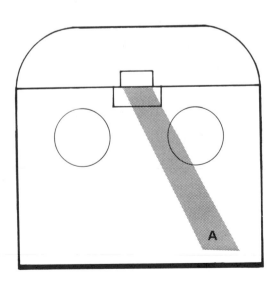

GREG SMITH

Yrs. of NHL service: 12
Born: Ponoka, Alta., Canada; July 8, 1955
Position: Defenseman
Height: 6-0
Weight: 195
Uniform no.: 19
Shoots: left

Career statistics:

GP	G	A	TP	PIM
829	56	232	288	1,110

1987-88 statistics:

GP	G	A	TP	+/−	PIM	PP	SH	GW	GT	S	PCT
54	1	6	7	5	67	0	0	0	0	31	3.2

LAST SEASON

Games played was second lowest of his career, as Smith shuffled in and out of the lineup. He also missed four games with a throat injury.

THE FINESSE GAME

Smarts are the key to Smith's game now, rather than physical finesse skills. He's never been an exceptional skater, getting by instead of standing out, but he can still perform at the NHL level by applying his knowledge and experience to a situation. He does have a little snap in his moves up-ice despite his age and length of league tenure.

Greg has always been smart in his defensive zone and had a fairly good grasp of the play around him. He concentrates now on using his defensive angles to force the play wide of the net, and he remains a fairly sure-handed passer from his zone, looking over the ice and making the right breakout play. He doesn't over-extend himself in either the offensive or defensive zone, staying smartly within his limits.

Any scoring Smith will do will be from the point on a less-than-extraordinary slap shot. Smith does almost no cheating in from the blue line, and will fall back rather than pinch in at the point.

THE PHYSICAL GAME

Smith is not a tremendous hitter, playing more of a smart game in front of his goaltender, but that's not to say he won't hit at all. He keeps the front of his net clean and is tough along the boards as well, using his size and good strength to out-muscle his opponents when necessary.

THE INTANGIBLES

Smith's best value to the Capitals is to add depth and experience to the lineup, and at 33 years old he'll be in a backup role henceforth. He's a valuable — though quiet — component of the Capitals.

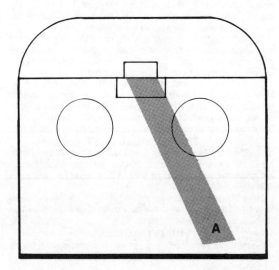

SCOTT STEVENS

Yrs. of NHL service: 6
Born: Kitchener, Ontario, Canada; April 1, 1964
Position: Defenseman
Height: 6-1
Weight: 210
Uniform no.: 3
Shoots: left

Career statistics:

GP	G	A	TP	PIM
465	80	241	321	1,251

1987-88 statistics:

GP	G	A	TP	+/-	PIM	PP	SH	GW	GT	S	PCT
80	12	60	72	14	184	5	1	2	0	231	5.2

LAST SEASON

Stevens played all 80 games (one of just four Caps to do so) for the second time in his career. His assist and point totals were career highs, and he finished second on the team in scoring, PIM (last season was the first time in his career he *didn't* lead the Caps in PIM) and shots on goal. He led the team in assists, and finished fourth in scoring among the League's defenders.

THE FINESSE GAME

Stevens is a very good skater, and he combines excellent balance and strength with suprising acceleration for a player his size. He can pull away from the opposition within a couple of strides, and he also has excellent foot speed. The combination of balance and foot speed gives him excellent agility and lateral movement, and he can maneuver in tight circles and with one-step quickness.

He handles the puck very well in all situations but especially so in traffic because of his strength and balance. He carries it well and makes his plays with his head up, using his good vision and hockey sense to best effect. That vision extends from defensive to offensive play, as Scott reads the rush toward him excellently. He is patient in his play selection, taking the time to make the right play. He generally cannot be forechecked into a mistake.

Scott will charge the net when the opportunity arises, but his offensive forays don't harm his defense because he is fast enough to get back into position. His slap shot is hard and accurate from the point, but because he doesn't have a quick release many of his shots get blocked. He increased his SOG total by more than 33 percent last year, with his offensive success the end result.

THE PHYSICAL GAME

Stevens is an incredible physical specimen. He has amazing strength, both in his upper body and in his legs. His upper body power makes him almost invincible along the boards or in front of the net, and he'll have trouble physically with only a handful of players in the League.

His leg strength and balance power his great skating and make his physical game that much more effective, because he is always on the vertical side of his collisions. He's a good

open ice hitter and an excellent fighter, one very few players are willing to engage.

THE INTANGIBLES

We told you last year that Scott Stevens was "still a step away from the plateau he could attain." Scott must have been reading this book, because he took his game to its furthest limits yet. Finally, instead of all the years of "he'll be a Norris contender one day," Stevens became that Norris contender.

He has matured tremendously, and he now dominates games the way few players can. He is a tremendous competitor who hates to lose, and he has supplanted Rod Langway as the heart and soul of the Washington Capitals. The mantle sits well on him.

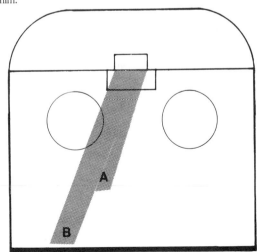

PETER SUNDSTROM

Yrs. of NHL service: 4
Born: Skelleftea, Sweden; December 14, 1961
Position: Left wing
Height: 6-0
Weight: 180
Uniform no.: 12
Shoots: left

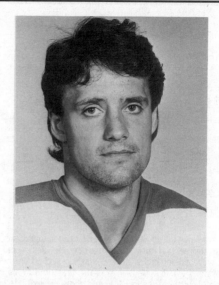

Career statistics:

GP	G	A	TP	PIM
282	56	79	135	104

1987-88 statistics:

GP	G	A	TP	+/−	PIM	PP	SH	GW	GT	S	PCT
76	8	17	25	-2	34	0	1	1	0	89	9.0

LAST SEASON

Sundstrom returned to the NHL after a year's absence. Of the Capital regulars, Sundstrom was the lowest scoring forward and he had the fewest SOG of any Capital fulltimer.

THE FINESSE GAME

Sundstrom has the fundamentals of good hands, good speed and acceleration and the ability to think on the ice. None of these things help him with goal scoring, at which he is poor.

He is a well-trained player, a smooth skater who can take off into the openings and carry the puck with him; a player that knows how to use his teammates and can pass well, and a player that sees the ice and can anticipate the play.

But for some reason these qualities don't combine to allow him to score goals. His shot is very weak and not at all difficult for NHL goaltenders to handle. If he's going to score at all it will be by converting the loose pucks sprung free by his checking.

Sundstrom gets scoring opportunities because he's a good checker, using his skating and anticipation to good effect as a defensive player and a forechecker.

THE PHYSICAL GAME

Sundstrom is weak physically and doesn't usually use his body for hitting, preferring his speed and stick checking to do the work. He's not very strong and is therefore much better in open ice than along the boards.

THE INTANGIBLES

Peter can be an effective role player for Washington, but it is doubtful he'll ever rise above that role.

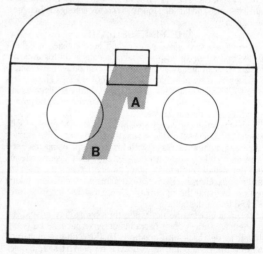

WINNIPEG JETS

LINE COMBINATIONS
IAIN DUNCAN-DALE HAWERCHUK-ANDREW
MCBAIN
GILLES HAMEL-LAURIE BOSCHMAN-
STEVE ROONEY-DOUG SMAIL-RAY NEUFELD

DEFENSE PAIRINGS
DAVE ELLETT-FREDRICK OLAUSSON
RANDY CARLYLE-PETER TAGLIANETTI
JIM KYTE-MARIO MAROIS

GOALTENDERS
DANIEL BERTHIAUME
ELDON REDDICK

OTHER PLAYERS
BRENT ASHTON — Left wing
HANNU JARVENPAA — Right wing
THOMAS STEEN — Center

POWER PLAY

FIRST UNIT:
ANDY MCBAIN-DALE HAWERCHUK-PAUL MACLEAN
RANDY CARLYLE-DAVE ELLETT

SECOND UNIT:
IAIN DUNCAN-LAURIE BOSCHMAN-FREDRICK
OLAUSSON

On the first unit HAWERCHUK plants in the mid-slot, with MCBAIN working the left wing boards and MACLEAN the right wing side. The two wings played catch with CARLYLE and ELLETT at the points, trying for give and go's that would free the wingers.

Otherwise, all forwards would converge on the net for rebounds of point shots.

On the second unit, BOSCHMAN would feed the points from the left circle and OLAUSSON would prowl behind the net. DUNCAN plugged the net. TAGLIANETTI and MAROIS would see power play time, but the first defense pair got the majority of action.

Last season Winnipeg's power play was EXCELLENT, scoring 110 goals in 432 opportunities (25.5 percent, second overall). The Jets did, however, allow the third most shorthanded goals in the NHL.

PENALTY KILLING

FIRST UNIT:
LAURIE BOSCHMAN-DOUG SMAIL
RANDY CARLYLE-PETER TAGLIANETTI

SECOND UNIT:
ANDY MCBAIN-THOMAS STEEN
MARIO MAROIS-DAVE ELLETT

All members of the unit pressure the puck, including the defense. SMAIL and BOSCHMAN will look to create some kind of offense and forecheck aggressively. All the forwards also collapse toward the net and free the points. HAWERCHUK is also a staple on the PK units.

Last season the Winnipeg penalty killing was FAIR, allowing 94 goals in 444 shorthanded situations (78.8 percent, 13th overall).

CRUCIAL FACEOFFS

BOSCHMAN in the defenseive zone and when penalty killing, HAWERCHUK offensively.

BRENT ASHTON

Yrs. of NHL service: 9
Born: Saskatoon, Sask., Canada; May 18, 1960
Position: Left wing
Height: 6-1
Weight: 200
Uniform no.:
Shoots: left

Career statistics:

GP	G	A	TP	PIM
657	191	215	406	401

1987-88 statistics:

GP	G	A	TP	+/−	PIM	PP	SH	GW	GT	S	PCT
73	26	27	53	10	50	7	2	3	0	161	16.1

LAST SEASON

Ashton was traded to Winnipeg by Detroit during June 1988, in exchange for Paul MacLean. Ashton finished fifth on the Wings in goals; on Winnipeg he'd have been fourth in that category. He would also have led the Jets in plus/minus.

THE FINESSE GAME

Ashton is a good bordering on great skater. He has a great deal of speed and he has learned to moderate it, controlling it up and down the scale. When he does that, when he shows the defensemen more than one speed, Brent will score his goals.

He also has quickness and the agility to change speeds immediately. He'll go from a standstill to top speed within six feet and he complements that speed and quickness with good agility. Brent moves his feet quickly and he can change direction as well as he changes speed.

Brent has fairly good hands and a decent view of the ice, and he has learned to keep his head up when he makes his plays. That allows him to look over his options and choose the correct play, rather than just the first play he sees.

He can carry the puck well, better now that he's moderated his speed and his feet aren't out-racing his hands, and Ashton passes well and looks for his teammates. He handles the puck well and can get around defensemen with some inside moves. Brent's shot is exemplary. Though not hard, it is quick and very accurate.

He plays his position defensively and is not a liability.

THE PHYSICAL GAME

Ashton's success is directly related to his willingness to play physically. Whereas earlier in his career he went out of his way to avoid contact, Ashton has grown to accept the physical and to use his good size to knock the opposition off the puck. His physical play is made doubly effective because of his ability to make plays after hits.

He's also able to get goals from in tight (his excellent balance helps here), and he gets those goals now because of his willingness to play in traffic.

THE INTANGIBLES

Ashton is very bitter about his trade to Winnipeg, as he had grown comfortable in Detroit. The move may affect his confidence, which would certainly affect his game, but Ashton's good attitude and team concept should get him over any rough spots.

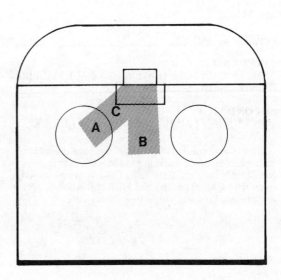

DANIEL BERTHIAUME

Yrs. of NHL service: 2
Born: Longeuil, Quebec, Canada; January 26, 1966
Position: Goaltender
Height: 5-9
Weight: 150
Uniform no.: 30
Catches: left

Career statistics:

GP	MINS	G	SO	AVG	A	PIM
87	4,768	269	4	3.38	2	14

1987-88 statisics:

GP	MINS	AVG	W	L	T	SO	GA	SA	SAPCT	PIM
56	3,010	3.51	22	19	7	2	176	1,489	.882	12

LAST SEASON

Games and minutes played totals were career highs. He finished tied for fifth in games played among League goalies, seventh in minutes played.

THE PHYSICAL GAME

Berthiaume is a hybrid goaltender, one who succeeds via reflexes and a standup style. He handles shots off the ice as a standup, challenging goaltender, but butterflies to cover the lower part of the net. Berthiaume has very quick legs and feet and is very balanced in his stance, so he's able to regain his position in the net quickly after making a save.

Daniel is a good skater, moving in and out of his net well. He has fairly good lateral movement post to post, but is better going to his left than his right. He uses his skating to play a challenging game, but Daniel doesn't skate from his net to flag down loose pucks, nor is he the type to even cut the puck off around the net; he rarely handles the puck at all.

Berthiaume covers or deflects his rebounds well, particularly off pad saves. He does less well (but only marginally so) above his waist. His quickness extends to his hands and he'll intercept passes across the crease or poke check the puck when it's in reach.

He stands up well on bad angle shots and doesn't often allow the bad short side goal. He plays the first bounce on high, bouncing shots and that prevents him from handling the puck safely after the save.

THE MENTAL GAME

Daniel plays a solid game mentally. He makes his reflexes work better by applying his good anticipation skills. He also sees the puck well at all times. He maintains his concentration and intensity throughout the game, and also keeps his concentration high from game to game.

He's also a tough kid. He'll make the big save to keep the Jets in the game, and his flashy saves pump up the team. He shakes off bad goals and maintains his confidence.

THE INTANGIBLES

Berthiaume showed last year that his rookie success was no fluke. He is a confident player who wants to excel, and he has the dedication and willingness necessary for his improvement.

LAURIE BOSCHMAN

Yrs. of NHL service: 9
Born: Major, Sask., Canada; June 4, 1960
Position: Center
Height: 6-0
Weight: 185
Uniform no.: 16
Shoots: left

Career statistics:

GP	G	A	TP	PIM
650	181	269	450	1,696

1987-88 statistics:

GP	G	A	TP	+/−	PIM	PP	SH	GW	GT	S	PCT
80	25	23	48	-24	227	10	1	3	0	166	15.1

LAST SEASON

Boschman played 80 games for the fourth time in his career and second consecutive season. He finished fourth on the club in goals and first in PIM; the latter total was the third highest of his career. His plus/minus rating was the team's second worst.

THE FINESSE GAME

The finesse game is not the strength of Boschman's success, but he does have certain finesse talents. He's a good skater with average-to-slightly-above-average quickness and agility. He puts that quickness to work as a solid two-way center.

Laurie combines his strong, tireless skating with his on-ice smarts to be a very heady player, able to anticipate and read the ice very well. That makes him an excellent defensive forward (so forget that plus/minus; it's an unfair indication of Boschman's skills).

Good as he is without the puck, Boschman is also good with it. He can take good advantage of his teammates when he gets an offensive opportunity, passing well to both sides, and that ability to make offensive contributions from his defensive work makes him a valuable player.

For his own goals Boschman will be most effective in front of the net, where he is more than willing to take his lumps and where he can cash in on the turnovers his checking has forced. He has a good wrist shot and is fairly accurate with it, making the goaltender make saves. He can occasionally score from farther out if the goaltender is napping.

THE PHYSICAL GAME

The physical game is Boschman's game, and he thrives on the emotion his hitting game creates. He is very strong, especially in the hands and wrists (which is why he's such a good faceoff man) and he'll run into anything that's wearing a non-Jet sweater, regardless of who and how big. Laurie can't be intimidated.

Boschman will win many of the battles along the boards or in the corners because of his leg strength. He uses his hips and legs to drive through a check in pursuit of the puck, and his balance helps him remain vertical and able to make a play.

He stands up for himself and his teammates without prompting, and Boschman also wields a nasty stick.

Because of his shoulder injury, Boschman avoided many of the fights he would otherwise have engaged in.

THE INTANGIBLES

Boschman is a tireless and dedicated worker with an excellent attitude. He's a complete team man and gives 100 percent of himself at all times. That makes him a good leader for the Jets.

He must now rehabilitate from late-season shoulder surgery.

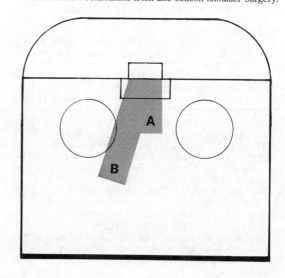

RANDY CARLYLE

Yrs. of NHL service: 12
Born: Sudbury, Ontario, Canada; April 19, 1956
Position: Defenseman
Height: 5-10
Weight: 198
Uniform no.: 8
Shoots: left

Career statistics:

GP	G	A	TP	PIM
784	128	417	545	1,160

1987-88 statistics:

GP	G	A	TP	+/−	PIM	PP	SH	GW	GT	S	PCT
78	15	44	59	-20	210	8	0	1	0	165	9.1

LAST SEASON

Games played total was a career high, assist and point totals highest in six seasons (and highest as a Jet). He was Winnipeg's leading scorer among defensemen, but was third among defenders in shots on goal. His PIM total (a career high) was the club's third highest, first among defensemen. His plus/minus total was the team's third worst, worst among defensemen. He finished fourth on the club in scoring, third in assists.

THE FINESSE GAME

Carlyle is a good skater, down from the rank of excellent he enjoyed earlier in his career. He's still very good forward and backward, as well as smooth in his turns, but he has lost some of the foot speed (and hence agility) that made him very mobile for his size. He still rushes the puck proficiently, and this combination of quickness and agility plus his puckhandling makes him difficult to contain.

Carlyle complements those physical skills with good vision, especially peripherally. He sees his teammates and his anticipation shows him the openings. He leads his teammates with a good pass and is excellent at controlling the point once he has established play in the offensive zone. He can always find the open man and get him the puck.

These skills serve to make him almost the prototypical power play defenseman. He is not primarily a goal scorer, but will get some goals from the point on a low accurate slap shot. Randy will sneak to the tops of the faceoff circles if the opening exists, but he doesn't charge the slot.

As his offensive skills diminished (with the exception of last season), Carlyle's defensive skills improved. He won't ever be mistaken for Rod Langway, but Randy is fairly solid positionally. He cuts off the rush through his defensive angles, steering the opposition wide of the net. Carlyle is susceptible to strong forechecking, in that he has a tendency to make blind, panicky passes around the boards. Those lead to giveaways.

THE PHYSICAL GAME

Never known as a physical player, Carlyle showed last year that you can teach an old dog new tricks. He can rough it up along the boards, and Randy is rather free in the application of his stick. Otherwise, he pushes around in the corners instead of hitting. He can hold the opposition's forwards out of the play along the boards and is pretty dependable clearing the front of the net.

THE INTANGIBLES

Randy is the Jets' on-ice general, stewarding much of their play on the offensive zone. That makes him their most important defenseman. He's also realized he's not as young as he used to be, and so he works hard at staying in condition. That maturity of outlook melds well with his on-ice generalship to make him an overall leader by example for the Jets.

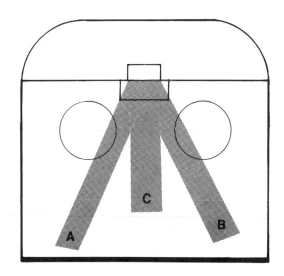

IAIN DUNCAN

Yrs. of NHL service: 1
Born: Toronto, Ontario, Canada; October 6, 1964
Position: Left wing
Height: 6-1
Weight: 205
Uniform no.: 36
Shoots: left

Career statistics:

GP	G	A	TP	PIM
68	20	25	45	73

1987-88 statistics:

GP	G	A	TP	+/−	PIM	PP	SH	GW	GT	S	PCT
62	19	23	42	-2	73	4	0	4	0	104	18.3

LAST SEASON

Duncan's first full NHL season after a six-game stint in 1986-87. Among players with at least 62 games played, his plus/minus was the team's third best. He finished third on the club in shooting percentage. He missed five games with a groin injury.

THE FINESSE GAME

Duncan is a very strong skater with good acceleration and speed, and the balance necessary for a successful physical game. He has good power in his stride that pushes him through checks along the boards and also keys his acceleration and speed down the wing. He is not a very agile player, and does not have outstanding quickness, but he can out-race the opposition over a longer distance.

Duncan has fairly good hands and a good view of the ice, so he can use his teammates well. He is not yet completely fluent in playmaking at the NHL speed, and is no doubt aided in his passing by having Dale Hawerchuk as a linemate (because Hawerchuk opens up a lot of ice), but Iain showed last year that he has a good undersatnding of offensive zone play.

His speed and hockey sense give him good scoring potential, and he has a strong shot that will net him some goals. If he is to constantly beat NHL goaltending,, however, Duncan must get his shot off quicker.

He is a conscientious defensive player, and in fact a good positional player in all three zones.

THE PHYSICAL GAME

Iain is a physical player, stronger and well balanced on his skates. He uses his body and his strength very well along the boards to gain the puck, and that style perfectly complements the open ice style of Duncan's center, Dale Hawerchuk.

Iain is also talented enough to make a play coming out of the corner, so his physical play is doubly effective. He also uses his strength by going to the front of the net and outwrestling the defense there.

THE INTANGIBLES

Willingness and desire perfectly complement Duncan's game. He's not afraid to get messy by doing the dirty work, and that's a big difference between his play and that of Hawerchuk's former linemate and teammate Brian Mullen. Duncan gets involved where Mullen was absent.

Playing that physical style right off the bat makes the eventual adjustment to the NHL easier, but Duncan must also work on his conditioning and be prepared for an 80-game season with its attendant rigors. He has a good work ethic and a willingness to improve, and he should do so this season.

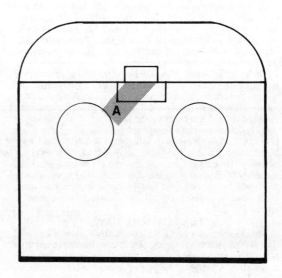

DAVE ELLETT

Yrs. of NHL service: 4
Born: Cleveland, Ohio, USA; March 30, 1964
Position: Defenseman
Height: 6-1
Weight: 200
Uniform no.: 2
Shoots: left

Career statistics:

GP	G	A	TP	PIM
306	52	134	186	340

1987-88 statistics:

GP	G	A	TP	+/−	PIM	PP	SH	GW	GT	S	PCT
68	13	45	58	-8	106	5	0	1	0	198	6.6

LAST SEASON

Games played total was career low, courtesy of a late-season thigh injury, but assist, point and PIM totals were career highs. He finished second in defensive scoring for Winnipeg but led all defensemen in assists (second overall on the club) and shots on goal (again, the club's second best total).

THE FINESSE GAME

Ellett is a very good skater and the best thing about his skating is his agility and mobility. He moves with a lot of grace and fluidity for a big guy, and that's because he has good to very-good foot speed and balance. Because of that, his turns and pivots are smooth and sure-footed. He also has good speed and power in his stride, and he skates well both forward and back.

Dave carries the puck from his end well, and he does so because of his hand skills. Those skills combine with his skating in helping him contain the point when — not if — he joins the offense. His good ice vision and anticipation allow him to see both openings and teammates, and Ellett will exploit both. He can find the open man, but he can also lead the man to the hole with a good pass. Or, he'll jump into that opening himself courtesy of his foot speed.

Ellett's shot is the best of any of Winnipeg's defensemen. His shot is low and hard (backed up by his strength) and creates all kinds of opportunities for rebounds and deflections, but Dave must also shoot to score more. He'll cheat toward the net a few steps if he can (because his speed allows him to take chances) and he flips to the opposite side on the power play.

Dave plays a basic positional game defensively. His foot speed allows him to close the gap between himself and the puck carrier quickly. He forces the play wide and has good patience when he gains the puck in his own zone, able to hold the puck until he can make a play rather than just flinging it blindly around the boards.

THE PHYSICAL GAME

Ellett has made the transition from the college game to the NHL game by adding the requisite bulk and strength needed to succeed at the major league level. His upper body strength powers his shot (as does his balance), but Dave also uses that size and strength defensively. He clears the front of the net with authority and is also effective along the boards and in the corners, holding the opposition out of the play and out-muscling opposing wingers off the puck in traffic situations.

Because he has good size, Ellett is also difficult to get around at the blue line, but he also takes the body well in all three zones. He's made his strength more effective by not sacrificing his speed while getting stronger.

THE INTANGIBLES

Ellett is a fine two-way defenseman and, at 24 years old, is only going to get better. If he can regain his health (he's been injured in consecutive seasons) he could become Winnipeg's most important defender, a role he's already close to assuming from Randy Carlyle.

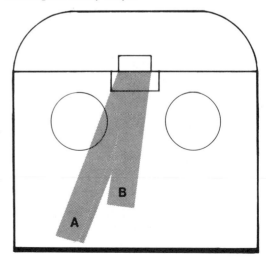

GILLES HAMEL

Yrs. of NHL service: 8
Born: Asbestos, Quebec, Canada; March 18,1960
Position: Left wing
Height: 6-0
Weight: 185
Uniform no.: 11
Shoots: left

Career statistics:

GP	G	A	TP	PIM
507	127	146	317	274

1987-88 statistics:

GP	G	A	TP	+/−	PIM	PP	SH	GW	GT	S	PCT
63	8	11	19	-16	35	1	0	0	0	106	7.5

LAST SEASON

Hamel followed his career best season with his career worst. Goal total was a career low for full seasons, ditto assists and points. Games played total was lowest in six seasons.

THE FINESSE GAME

Speed is the principal asset of Hamel's game, and he generally uses that speed well in his checking and defensive games. But all the things he learned in his career year in 1986-87 went out the window last year. While he had learned to moderate that speed and be less predictable — and to keep the play in front of him — Hamel went back to his bad habits last year of full throttle all the time.

First of all, his hands don't come anywhere near his feet for ability to perform at high speed. So when he blazes down the wing it's about all Gilles can do to hold onto the puck. Secondly, when he blazes down the wing he out-races all of his teammates; the play ends up behind him.

When he moderated his speed, Hamel had the play in front of him and the chance to use his hands. Last year he put himself at a disadvantage offensively because of his relapse. His moderated speed also made him more effective as a penalty killer, able to react better to what the opposition presented. That changed too.

Hamel has a decent shot, but will score more from opportunties created through his checking (and collecting loose pucks near the net because of his quickness) than he will by bursting down the wing, rearing back and firing.

Defensively he checks with his speed, but the vision and anticipation he can bring to bear while killing penalties helps him here too.

THE PHYSICAL GAME

Hamel has good strength, so he won't often be muscled off the puck in a one-on-one situation. He's willing to play a physical game, and will use his size to advantage when checking along the boards.

THE INTANGIBLES

While his offense wanders up and down the scale, Hamel and the Jets can at least take refuge in his sound defensive ability (forget the plus/minus). If he could play neither physically nor defensively, coach Dan Maloney wouldn't keep him around. Hamel has shown that he can produce offensively, but it's hard to do so on a team as schizophrenic as the Jets. If they were more dependable, he'd be too.

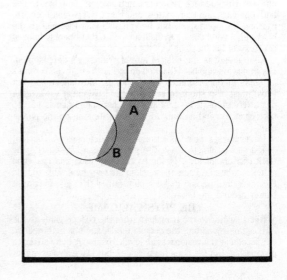

DALE HAWERCHUK

Yrs. of NHL service: 7
Born: Toronto, Ontario, Canada; April 4, 1963
Position: Center
Height: 5-11
Weight: 185
Uniform no.: 10
Shoots: left

Career statistics:

GP	G	A	TP	PIM
559	312	440	752	382

1987-88 statistics:

GP	G	A	TP	+/−	PIM	PP	SH	GW	GT	S	PCT
80	44	77	121	-9	59	20	3	4	1	292	15.1

LAST SEASON

Hawerchuk played 80 games for the sixth of his seven years in the NHL, one of just two Jets to do so. He led the club in scoring and scored 100 points for the fifth straight year (six out of seven). He led Winnipeg in goals and assists, shots on goal and shorthanded goals. He was second on the club in power play goals and finished fourth in the League in scoring, shots and assists. Point total was the second highest of his career (but goal total was lowest in four years, assist total lowest in three seasons).

THE FINESSE GAME

Primary among Dale's tremendous talents is his skating. His long stride gives him speed and quickness, balance and power. He has great acceleration ability and rink-length speed to stay ahead of the pursuing defenders, and Hawerchuk also has terrific one-step quickness (courtesy of his foot speed). His balance combines with that foot speed to make him extremely agile. In fact, next to Wayne Gretzky, Hawerchuk has the best lateral movement of any skater in the League. He can move within a step in any direction — at any speed.

His anticipation and hockey sense are superb, and they are the keys to his playmaking skills. He's always around the puck because of his sense, and his anticipation and play reading ability put him in position to make those offensive plays.

Hawerchuk has excellent hands. He passes extremely well to both wings and will lead his teammates into the clear with some of the best passes in the League. Dale also handles the puck extremely well and can bedevil an entire opposition team with his stickhandling. That is also a shortcoming, for he has a tendency to over-handle the puck and work himself into predicaments that lead to turnovers. He often leaves his teammates standing around by going one-on-one with a defenseman, the result of which are three-on-twos when Hawerchuk eventually turns the puck over and his wingers are trapped deep.

In that sense, Hawerchuk fails to take advantage of his superior vision — and excellent peripheral vision. However, his vision and passing skills make him a power play natural.

He has a good selection of shots, and will shoot and score from anywhere in the offensive zone. He's deadly around the net because of his great hands, able to work with the puck regardless of the lack of space, proximity to the goal or angle. Dale also has excellent eye/hand coordination and that makes him expert at deflecting or tipping the puck.

Hawerchuk is no better than average defensively, though a large part of his plus/minus is attributable to his tremendous amounts of ice time. But minus 9? Just to get a plus/minus rating of zero Hawerchuk would need nine more points. And to be a 130-point scorer and just even? That's ridiculous.

THE PHYSICAL GAME

Though he has never been known for his physical play, Hawerchuk has increased his physical involvement in the game. He will initiate contact in the offensive zone and he will take the body — albeit inconsistently — on defense.

He has always played in traffic and that's something he does better than Gretzky, probably because Wayne can get away from hits whereas Dale can't completely avoid them. Though Hawerchuk can take the pounding make no mistake; he is definitely an open-ice player.

But just because he's accepting hits doesn't mean he likes them. Hawrchuk has a short fuse and he'll lose his temper over close checking, frequently taking stupid retaliatory penalties in the offensive zone.

He remains a durable player, having missed only one game in his entire career.

THE INTANGIBLES

There's only one thing to quibble about here, and that would be Dale's goal scoring consistency. He finished the season less strongly than might be expected, with just seven goals in his last 20 games, but that fact shouldn't disguise Hawerchuk's consistency of attendance and effort over his career. That consistency shows just how much of a character player he is. He is certainly a superstar center, almost certainly one of the top five players in the NHL. Unfortunately he has never had great support in Winnipeg, and this year he will have to break in a new rightwinger (longtime teammate Paul MacLean is gone to Detroit).

He wants to win badly — and he hates to lose, which is even better. It's just his misfortune to be thwarted constantly by Wayne Gretzky and the Edmonton Oilers, or else more people — especially in the East — would be familiar with Dale's achievements and be more willing to recognize them.

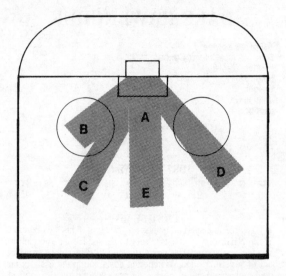

HANNU JARVENPAA

Yrs. of NHL service: 1
Born: Ilves, Finland; May 19, 1963
Position: Right wing
Height: 6-0
Weight: 193
Uniform no.: 23
Shoots: left

Career statistics:

GP	G	A	TP	PIM
61	7	19	26	42

1987-88 statistics:

GP	G	A	TP	+/−	PIM	PP	SH	GW	GT	S	PCT
41	6	11	17	0	34	1	0	0	0	52	11.5

LAST SEASON
Games played total was a career high.

THE FINESSE GAME
Jarvenpaa is a gifted finesse player in the typical European skills of skating and puckhandling. He has good speed and quickness up and down his wing and handles the puck well when he carries it, but he does have some trouble operating with it when he gets into traffic.

Hannu has good hockey sense and that sense gets him into position to score. His hands are very soft and he can fire a wrist shot quickly to the net off a pass, and the Jets used that talent on the power play last year.

He has a fairly good understanding of the play at the NHL level, both offensively and defensively, and Jarvenpaa plays fairly well in all three zones. He plays defense positionally, so he is always ready to make a play coming from his own zone.

THE PHYSICAL GAME
Jarvenpaa accepts the phsyical part of the game, even if he doesn't initiate any part of it himself. He has good balance on his skates and that helps him retain the puck and his position along the boards or in the corners.

He's also willing to take his hits for his goals, and he goes to the front of the net without complaint.

THE INTANGIBLES
Jarvenpaa has missed parts of the last two seasons with injury and personal problems. If he is to play in the NHL he must prove more durable. The Jets are obviously confident in him, because they signed him to a new contract post-season.

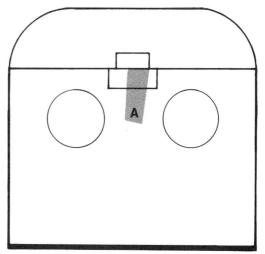

JIM KYTE

Yrs. of NHL service: 5
Born: Ottawa, Ontario, Canada; March 21, 1964
Position: Defenseman
Height: 6-5
Weight: 200
Uniform no.: 6
Shoots: left

Career statistics:

GP	G	A	TP	PIM
323	8	16	24	582

1987-88 statistics:

GP	G	A	TP	+/–	PIM	PP	SH	GW	GT	S	PCT
51	1	3	4	1	128	0	0	0	0	59	1.7

LAST SEASON

Games played total was a career low, as Kyte was sidelined throughout the year by a recurring back injury.

THE FINESSE GAME

Improved overall skills have brought Kyte to his highest level in the NHL. His skating has improved tremendously, and that's because he's improved his foot speed and balance. He turns fairly well now and his added foot speed not only lets him force the play wide but also close the gap between himself and the opposing puck carrier. He has become more mobile in general because of improved foot speed, and can keep up with his own teammates and the opposition both forward and backward.

Jim reads the rush toward him well and plays a solid positional game (no doubt his size helps here) in his own end. While he still isn't an All-Star (and probably never will be) in his puckhandling, Kyte has improved in his ability to read the play heading away from him and will make the right breakout pass.

He is little of a factor offensively, rarely becoming an attacker and rarely even following the play in an offensive mode, though he does have a good slap shot from the point. He'll be the first defenseman to fall back.

THE PHYSICAL GAME

The physical game is where Kyte's talents are in abundance, and he makes very good use of them especially in front of his own net. Kyte is the kind of player who leads with his elbows and, while he likes to hit and use his strength in all parts of the defensive zone, he's at his meanest defending his crease, especially while penalty killing.

While his physical play isn't the product of anger, Kyte plays mean just the same. Needless to say this provokes many fights. Kyte doesn't like to fight, but he doesn't often lose.

As for checking, he hits anything he can catch and he hits hard. He can jar the puck loose with a check, and that hit is now doubly effective because he can now make a play with the puck. His size makes him very difficult to get around at the blue line, and he will sacrifice his body to block shots.

THE INTANGIBLES

Kyte is a quality player, and his desire to not only make the NHL but to play a complete game (and shed some of the goon label his low talent/high physical game have gained him) make him a character player as well. He's already aggressive without being overly stupid, and continued play should help him improve even more.

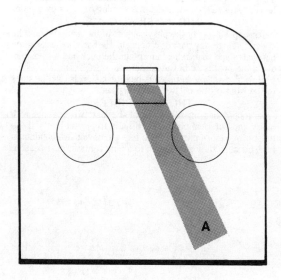

MARIO MAROIS

Yrs. of NHL service: 10
Born: Ancienne Lorette, Quebec, Canada; December 15, 1957
Position: Defenseman
Height: 5-11
Weight: 190
Uniform no.: 22
Shoots: right

Career statistics:

GP	G	A	TP	PIM
724	67	312	379	1,376

1987-88 statistics:

GP	G	A	TP	+/−	PIM	PP	SH	GW	GT	S	PCT
79	7	44	51	5	111	3	0	1	0	170	4.1

LAST SEASON

Games played total tied for second highest of NHL career. Assist and point totals were career highs. His plus/minus total was the team's best. He finished fourth on the squad in shots on goal.

THE FINESSE GAME

Marois is a good skater, fairly agile and with a good burst of speed up-ice. Even after a decade in the NHL, he can still rush the puck from the defensive zone when he chooses to. He's also a good skater backward, but his turns are a touch slow and make him a little weak in one-on-one situations.

He's played smartly and patiently since coming to Winnipeg, creating plays only if an opportunity exists and not forcing situations. Though he handles the puck well while skating (always has) and will follow the play up-ice to become an offensive force at the opposition blue line, Mario's success over the last two seasons has come because of his improved judgement in choosing *not* to rush the puck.

Marois moves the puck well at both ends of the ice because he sees the zone well and can certainly find the open man; that's why he plays the point on the power play. Defensively he makes the smart and easy play.

His improvement in judgement has also imporved his defense. He's playing better positionally now than at any point in his careerplaying the man well, forcing the play wide, taking the puck and beginning the play up-ice.

THE PHYSICAL GAME

Marois is a very physical player who will hit whenever possible. He hits the opposition, rather than just pushing and shoving in the corners, and the hitting jars the puck free. Marois has the ability to take advantage of those loose pucks, making his hits more effective.

He also isn't afraid of putting something extra into his checks. He'll slash or elbow in front of the net and will do the same while fighting for the puck in the corners or along the boards. His extra-curricular stickwork is some of the NHL's worst.

THE INTANGIBLES

Marois has always been an emotional player, and that emotionalism used to make him run amok. He was the NHL's easiest mark for being goaded into penalties, and his concentration could be ruined for shifts at a time.

But the confidence expressed in him by management has matured him, and he's rewarded the Jets with the best performances of his career. Though he has the shorter (rather than the longer) part of his career ahead of him, he remains dedicated and committed to the game.

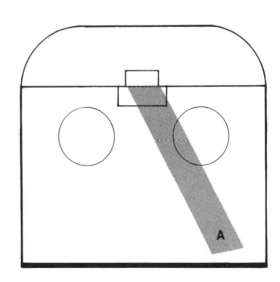

ANDREW MCBAIN

Yrs. of NHL service: 5
Born: Toronto, Ontario, Canada; February 18, 1965
Position: Right wing
Height: 6-1
Weight: 190
Uniform no.: 20
Shoots: right

Career statistics:

GP	G	A	TP	PIM
328	65	89	154	350

1987-88 statistics:

GP	G	A	TP	+/−	PIM	PP	SH	GW	GT	S	PCT
74	32	31	63	-10	145	20	0	5	1	146	21.9

LAST SEASON

Games played total was highest in three seasons, but all point totals were career highs (ditto PIM total). He finished third on the club in scoring, second in power play goals and shooting percentage. He was tied for first in game winners.

THE FINESSE GAME

McBain has improved sufficiently to be a good skater at the NHL level, but he is still closer to "plodder" than "artist." Improved foot speed is the key to his improvement, but added strength in his stride has given him some speed. He is not a very agile player, in large part because he doesn't have great balance, so he's not going to do a lot of swirling and circling.

His stick skills have improved along with his skating skills because quicker feet equal more time to operate with the puck. Andy carries the puck fairly well up-ice but isn't a wizard at making plays with it. He does take advantage of his teammates by picking up his head and examining the ice, but McBain isn't going to do more than make the simplest play available.

He doesn't take a pass exceptionally well, nor does he read the ice or understand the play well on the Jets' breakout plays.

He remains weak offensively, almost overwhelmingly so; just 12 of his 32 goals came at even strength, and of those 12 just two were scored in his last 20 games. He's got a decent shot but he needs a lot of time to get it off; one reason he's so successful on the power play is that he'll get that extra time. He'll get most of his scores from near the net on the power play.

THE PHYSICAL GAME

McBain is a straight-ahead player with good size, and he uses that size fairly consistently, but he doesn't have the finesse talent to make an aggressive game work. He is a one-play player, making a hit if he can but having very little idea what to do afterward.

THE INTANGIBLES

If we count last year as just his third season, and ignore his injury-plagued 1986-87 season, then McBain is developing fairly well. That does not mean he's begun to approximate a first round draft choice, especially not when players like Cam Neely, Claude Lemieux and Dan Quinn were taken after McBain

was selected (McBain was eight overall, while Neely was ninth, Quinn 13th and Lemieux 26th).

He must improve his even-strength play to remain successful. This year would be a good place to start that improvement.

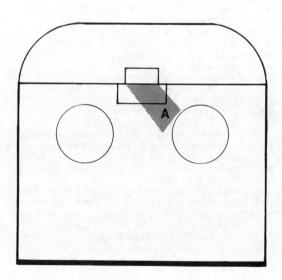

RAY NEUFELD

Yrs. of NHL service: 8
Born: St. Boniface, Man., Canada; April 15, 1959
Position: Right wing
Height: 6-2
Weight: 215
Uniform no.: 28
Shoots: right

Career statistics:

GP	G	A	TP	PIM
549	151	195	346	734

1987-88 statistics:

GP	G	A	TP	+/−	PIM	PP	SH	GW	GT	S	PCT
78	18	18	36	-29	167	9	0	2	0	115	15.7

LAST SEASON

Neufeld's point totals exactly duplicated his 1986-87 performance. All of his point totals, therefore, tied career lows. His PIM total was the team's fourth highest, third highest among forwards and second highest among forwards with more than 56 games played. His plus/minus was the team's worst.

THE FINESSE GAME

Strength is the key to Neufeld's game, so it's only fitting that strength would be the highlight of his skating. Ray has a lot of power in his stride and that power gives him good speed and acceleration ability. He won't rocket past every NHL defender, but Neufeld will draw away from many NHL opponents. He also has good balance on his skates and that serves him well in his physical game, keeping him upright after collisions so he can make his plays.

He is poised and confident enough to handle the puck while skating, or to move it patiently to a teammate, but Neufeld will not turn anyone inside out with his puckhandling. His big move is going to be the swoop behind the defenseman after using his outside speed — and that's if he makes a move at all.

He does use his teammates fairly well and will get the puck to them after he grinds around in the corners. He sees the ice well in terms of finding open teammates and he can get the puck to them in front of the net. He just needs time and space to do so, but not so much that he can't functions in the NHL.

Neufeld is an opportunistic scorer, banging in goals from around the crease, where he takes advantage of his size and strength. If he had anything other than cement hands he could get 30 goals a year because of his other skills. He's just not a finisher.

That plus/minus largely reflects his checking status. He generally plays well defensively, though he's not above a positional — and costly — lapse or two.

THE PHYSICAL GAME

Neufeld is a very physical player, very tough but generally clean. His skating strength allows him to drive through his checks along the boards, as well as to hit hard when he checks. When his feet stop moving he uses his good upper-body strength and balance to out-muscle the opposition along the boards.

Ray can also take the abuse, demonstrated most notably on the power play when he positions himself in front of the enemy net. He is difficult to control in front of the net because of his strength and he is also fairly strong on his skates, making him difficult to knock down.

Neufeld plays his style consistently — home or away, winning or losing — and does so in all three zones.

THE INTANGIBLES

Missing from Ray's repertoire are the finer — as in less coarse or powerful — skills of agility and quickness. He is not a fancy player in any of his skills, so Neufeld smartly sticks with what he can do. He was acquired to offset some of the size Winnipeg faced in its Smythe Division opponents in Calgary and Edmonton, and has largely succeeded in that capacity.

He is a smart and capable player, and he knows who to hit how and when, and his are the kind of hits that pick up a team. He's an honest hockey player, consistent and dependable.

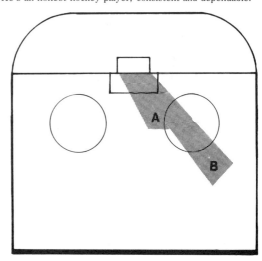

FREDRICK OLAUSSON

Yrs. of NHL service: 2
Born: Vaxsjo, Sweden; October 5, 1966
Position: Defenseman
Height: 6-2
Weight: 200
Uniform no.: 4
Shoots: right

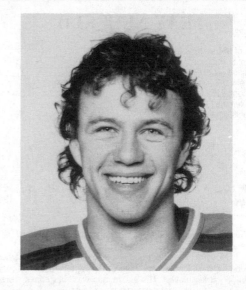

Career statistics:

GP	G	A	TP	PIM
110	12	46	58	42

1987-88 statistics:

GP	G	A	TP	+/−	PIM	PP	SH	GW	GT	S	PCT
38	5	10	15	3	18	2	0	2	0	65	7.7

LAST SEASON

Preseason shoulder surgery sidelined Olausson until after the New Year.

THE FINESSE GAME

Olausson has great potential in the finesse game. Despite his relatively short NHL stay, he already moves up-ice with a long stride and acceleration at the majorleague level. Though not overwhelmingly fast, Olausson gets where he has to because of his stride. He is also fairly agile for his size, though he needs help turning to his right. His foot speed is good and he uses it to step into the play and take the body.

His other NHL-level skill is his puckhandling. Fredrick carries the puck well and he'll follow the play up-ice after making a pass. He sees the ice well and makes good passes to the open man in both zones. His passing and playreading ability have already made him a valuable member of the Jets' power play. He also has a good shot from the point which he should use more frequently.

His defensive poise and confidence is suprising for a youngster and doubly surprising for a European. Olausson makes good defensive decisions in most situations, but could still use some fine tuning in his positioning and breakout pass selection — not that he's making bad plays, but he could make better ones.

THE PHYSICAL GAME

Fredrick is basically a finesse player with size, but he has shown that he's willing to use his size physically. He'll take the body in all three zones and is already a pretty good open ice hitter. His size also makes him successful in front of his own net, but he's not going to knock anyone into the cheap seats.

THE INTANGIBLES

His improvement was naturally slowed by last season's injury and subsequent rehabilitation, but Olausson is already well along the way to an above average NHL career.

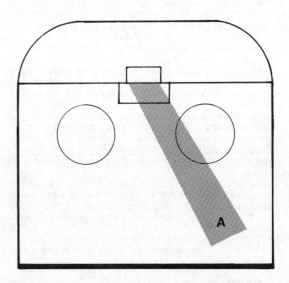

ELDON "POKEY" REDDICK

Yrs. of NHL service: 1
Born: Halifax, N.S., Canada; October 6, 1964
Position: Goaltender
Height: 5-8
Weight: 170
Uniform no.: 33
Catches: left

Career statistics:

GP	MINS	G	SO	AVG	A	PIM
76	4,249	251	1	3.54	0	14

1987-88 statisics:

GP	MINS	AVG	W	L	T	SO	GA	SA	SAPCT	PIM
28	1,487	4.12	9	13	3	0	102	712	.857	6

LAST SEASON

Reddick's second NHL season. Games played total was NHL low, and he was demoted to the minors during the season.

THE PHYSICAL GAME

Reddick is by and large a standup goaltender, though he does not challenge the shooter as often as one might expect from a standup goalie. He plays his angles fairly well but is rarely further out of the net than the top of his crease.

He works from a deep crouch, in order to see around players rather than over them, and he picks up the flight of the puck fairly well. He complements his standup play with very quick feet, and he is also quick to regain his feet after going to the ice, though he is not always balanced and back in his stance as quickly.

Reddick has had some trouble with his style because smart shooters go right over his shoulders and past his feet due to his depth in the net. He is also weak at controlling rebounds from his blocker saves.

He leaves the net to retrieve the puck now, something he didn't do in his rookie season. He stops the puck and hands it off to the defensemen, but he doesn't handle or move it especially well. Reddick does, however, communicate well with his defensemen, so they aren't flying blind.

THE MENTAL GAME

Reddick is a very cool customer, akin to — but not in the same class as — Edmonton's Grant Fuhr. He just stands in the net and does his job, regardless of circumstance or goals previously allowed — good or bad.

He can perhaps be too nonchalant, but generally he seems to be poised and confident, concentration intact.

THE INTANGIBLES

Reddick has done whatever the Jets have asked during his tenure with the organization, but his lackluster play last season forced Winnipeg to call upon the previously-banished-to-the-minors Steve Penney for some kind of support.

If Reddick is to play in the NHL beyond this year (or even through this season), he must rebound from last year's performance. He just might not be talented enough to do so.

STEVE ROONEY

Yrs. of NHL service: 2
Born: Canton, Mass., USA; June 28, 1962
Position: Left wing
Height: 6-2
Weight: 200
Uniform no.: 18
Shoots: left

Career statistics:

GP	G	A	TP	PIM
129	12	12	24	417

1987-88 statistics:

GP	G	A	TP	+/-	PIM	PP	SH	GW	GT	S	PCT
56	7	6	13	2	217	0	0	0	0	62	11.3

LAST SEASON

Games played total was a career high, as were all point and PIM totals. Ankle, back and rib injuries sidelined him throughout the season. He finished second on the club in PIM.

THE FINESSE GAME

Rooney is a strong skater with some speed but not a lot of agility. He motors up and down the wing fairly well, but his skating is strictly suited to his straight-ahead style. There isn't going to be a lot of swirling or cute manuevers in Rooney's work as a checking forward, but his strength and power help him stay with the opposition and win the battles along the boards.

He has little other finesse skills to speak of in terms of offensive productivity. Rooney's shot is not an NHL-level weapon, nor is his passing. Any points he accumulates will come on broken plays and opportunistic goals.

Steve isn't overly gifted in the anticipation department either, but he does have a good enough understanding of the NHL play to function as a checking forward.

THE PHYSICAL GAME

This is the strength of Rooney's game and he uses it well. He has good size and takes the body well in his checking to slow down the opposition. He is strong along the boards because of his upper body strength and his strength on his feet, and he uses that strength to wrestle the puck free and cause turnovers.

He is a very tough player and he also uses his muscle to stand up for his teammates.

THE INTANGIBLES

Rooney is one of those players who will do whatever is necessary to win, as demonstrated by his run-in with Edmonton Oiler Glenn Anderson during last season's playoffs.

Rooney is a John Ferguson/Dan Maloney type of player, one with the character and toughness they feel is necessary for any winning team to have. As long as those two guys are running the show in Winnipeg, and as long as Steve keeps answering the bell, Rooney will play for the Jets.

DOUG SMAIL

Yrs. of NHL service: 8
Born: Moose Jaw, Sask., Canada; September 2, 1957
Position: Left wing
Height: 5-10
Weight: 175
Uniform no.: 9
Shoots: left

Career statistics:

GP	G	A	TP	PIM
549	149	167	316	341

1987-88 statistics:

GP	G	A	TP	+/-	PIM	PP	SH	GW	GT	S	PCT
71	15	16	31	5	34	0	3	5	0	110	13.6

LAST SEASON

Games played total was lowest in four seasons (preseason knee surgery and subsequent injury). Goal total was lowest in five seasons, assist and point totals lowest for full seasons. He finished second in plus/minus (best among forwards), tied for first in shorthanded goals and game winners.

THE FINESSE GAME

The key to Smail's skating — and thus his game — is his incredible quickness. Within six feet, there may not be anyone quicker in the game. Doug adds to his speed and overall good skating by being very agile in his direction changes and starts and stops. He also makes his speed and quickness more effective by always showing speeds other than "Full." That makes him unpredictable, a particular advantage when killing penalties.

Smail also has good anticipation skills and sees the ice well, and those skills combine with his skating to make him an excellent penalty killer, a role he's filled well his entire NHL career.

The big "But," is that his hand skills aren't at the levl of his foot skills. Doug isn't a great puckhandler but he can control the puck while he is in motion and can get the puck to his teammates if given ample opportunity. Just don't expect to see him thread any needles with his passes. He likes to stutter-step just over the blue line to get the defense committed, and then jump in another direction, when he carries the puck.

He has an average shot but will get to pucks because of his quickness, making him an opportunistic scorer. That's good, because he lacks the hands of a natural scorer.

THE PHYSICAL GAME

Smail offsets his diminutive size with superb — and surprising — strength. He is very strong and very well conditioned, so he's very effective along the boards. Hit-and-run missions work well with him, because he'll knock the opposition off the puck and be gone in an instant.

Like many of the other Winnipeg players, Doug shows a proficiency in using his stick to punish the opposition.

THE INTANGIBLES

Desire is the key with Smail, and he makes the most of everything his skill has to offer. He is a character individual with a solid work ethic, and that allows him to contribute offensively and defensively.

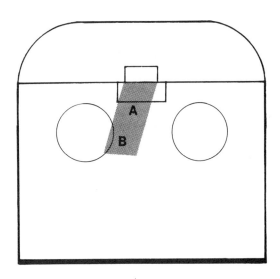

THOMAS STEEN

Yrs. of NHL service: 7
Born: Tocksmark, Sweden; June 8, 1960
Position: Center
Height: 5-10
Weight: 195
Uniform no.: 25
Shoots: left

Career statistics:

GP	G	A	TP	PIM
533	141	279	420	439

1987-88 statistics:

GP	G	A	TP	+/−	PIM	PP	SH	GW	GT	S	PCT
76	16	38	54	-12	53	3	1	1	0	167	9.6

LAST SEASON

Goal total was second lowest of his career. Finished sixth on the club in scoring.

THE FINESSE GAME

Steen is an excellent skater, equipped with speed and good lateral movement. He also has good acceleration and his balance makes him a very agile forward with excellent quickness.

He combines his skating skill with good anticipation to be a better-than-average defensive forward. He can read the play very well, seeing the openings and cutting for them defensively to close them, or he can lead a teammate to them with good passes after the transition to offense.

Thomas plays that way throughout all three zones and is especially dangerous in specialty team situations. He'll see power play time on the point because he can contain that area through his foot speed and can exploit the openings with his hand skills. Likewise, he's superlative as a penalty killer because of his quickness and anticipation. He is able to aggressively pressure the opposition's puck handlers at the point, and will often break up passes because of his one-step quickness.

Steen also handles the puck well and is very effective when carrying it — a typical European skill. He is patient with the puck and that allows him to use his abilities to see the ice.

THE PHYSICAL GAME

Steen excels in the physical part of the game, more through desire and determination than through sheer size and strength. He does have good strength and can wear down an opponent with his persistent hitting. Though breaking down one European stereotype through his willing physicality, Steen reinforces another by being very mean with his stick.

THE INTANGIBLES

Steen's emotionalism and on-ice work ethic, his determination to succeed, is a key to any success Winnipeg enjoys. Through playing a complete game at all times, and by playing hard at all times, Steen is a quiet leader for the Jets.

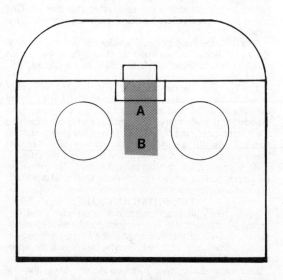

PETER TAGLIANETTI

Yrs. of NHL service: 1
Born: Framingham, Mass., USA; August 15, 1963
Position: Defenseman
Height: 6-2
Weight: 200
Uniform no.: 32
Shoots: left

Career statistics:

GP	G	A	TP	PIM
92	6	17	23	242

1987-88 statistics:

GP	G	A	TP	+/−	PIM	PP	SH	GW	GT	S	PCT
70	6	17	23	-13	182	2	0	1	0	92	6.5

LAST SEASON

Taglianetti's first full NHL season after 22 games over the 1985-86 and 86-87 seasons. He finished fourth on the club in PIM total, second among defenseman. His plus/minus was the defense's second worst. He missed three games with muscle spasms and one with a foot injury.

THE FINESSE GAME

Taglianetti is an average skater at the NHL level. He moves well enough both forward and back, but because his pivots are a little weak a speedy forward can get him turned and out-race him to the net. Better balance and foot speed would be helpful.

Peter reads the defensive play fairly well but his lack of foot speed often forces him out of position as he chases the puck-carrier. In order to keep the play in front of him he backs in on the goaltender and thus creates openings near the blue line.

He can make a breakout pass but his job in the defensive zone is to be the take-out and not breakout defenseman, so he'll generally let his more mobile partner handle the offensive chores.

Taglianetti will step up into the play in the offensive zone and he'll score some goals from the point with a good low slapshot. That slapshot also gets him power play time. He carries the puck fairly well, but he won't stickhandle around an entire team. He tends to hold the puck too long when he does carry it and misses the opportunity to take advantage of open teammates.

THE PHYSICAL GAME

Taglianetti is a physical player and enjoys playing that style of game. He generally uses his body well to support his stay-at-home style and he is a difficult opponent in front of the net. He hits hard along the boards but can sometimes be knocked off the puck because of his high center of gravity.

He's not afraid to back up his physical play with his fists if need be.

THE INTANGIBLES

Taglianetti spent a lot of time in the minors before getting his chance last season, and while he has improvable skills time is not on his side. He'll begin this season as a 25-year-old, and that's old for a second year player.

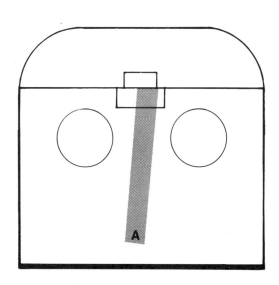